THE
EMPTY
GARDEN

EMPTY GARDEN

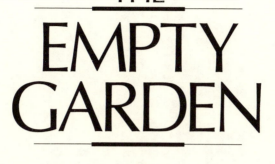

The Subject of Late Milton

ASHRAF H. A. RUSHDY

UNIVERSITY OF PITTSBURGH PRESS

Pittsburgh and London

Published by the University of Pittsburgh Press, Pittsburgh, Pa.
15260
Copyright © 1992, University of Pittsburgh Press
All rights reserved
Manufactured in the United States of America
Printed on acid-free paper

Library of Congress Cataloging-in-Publication Data

Rushdy, Ashraf H. A., 1961–
   The empty garden : the subject of late Milton / Ashraf H. A. Rushdy.
      p.   cm. — (A Milton studies monograph)
   Includes bibliographical references (p.   ) and index.
   ISBN 0-8229-3719-0 (cl)
   1. Milton, John, 1608–1674 — Criticism and interpretation.
   I. Title. II. Series
PR3588.R86 1992
821'.4 — dc20   92-9975
                                                                                    CIP

A CIP catalogue record for this book is available from the British Library
Eurospan, London

I dedicate this to My Family:
my Grandmother, my Mother, my Father, and my Brother

a grateful mind
By owing owes not, but still pays, at once
Indebted and discharg'd.

CONTENTS

Preface   ix

Acknowledgments   xv

PART ONE
THE SUBJECT

1. Confronting the Subject:
The Art of Self-Knowledge   3

PART TWO
PARADISE REGAINED

2. Confronting the Self:
The Art of Meditation   117
3. Confronting the Other:
The Art of Hermeneutics   191

PART THREE
MILTON

4. Confronting the Book:
The Art of Liberty   277
5. Confronting the Author:
The Art of Politics   345

Notes   441

Index   507

PREFACE

The most any preface to a study of Milton may hope to accomplish is to declare outright what sort of Milton the book is going to construct. Will Milton resemble Christopher Hill's proto-democrat with a lingering devotion to the aristocracy and whose major works are retrospective political explanations of what Hill calls "the experience of defeat?" Or will he be C. A. Patrides's neo-orthodox Anglican, a poet whose major works are slightly ambiguous articulations of a genuine belief in the Church of England's theology, or, and this is my favorite, A. L. Rowse's puritan with a highly problematized sexual identity and a poet whose major work is the articulation of an unconscious desire to be God and a woman.[1]

The Milton I present is a religious-cultural critic whose primary tension exists between a faint desire for a community of faith and an unrelenting inability to accept the institutions forming such a community. The most useful method of tracing Milton's agonistic crisis of affiliation is found in the Delphic oracle's call to self-knowledge. From this, we may discern the two processes most often used by Milton to mediate the world he inhabited: culture and religion.

"Know thyself," proclaimed the Delphic oracle, producing, with that declaration, the foundations for both Socratic theology and anthropology. Knowing a self means, in the case of theology, understanding what the constituent spiritual features of that self may be in light of a transcendent divinity or, in the case of anthropology, understanding what the social qualities of that entity may be, given its modes of interaction within the economy of a culture. For either discipline, the concept of self-knowledge would be impossible to comprehend without accepting that the self is constituted in the act of discernment under the auspices of whatever discipline is studying it. For the anthropologist, Clifford Geertz maintains, "there is no such thing as human nature independent of culture." For the religious person, according to Mircea Eliade, the "sacred reveals absolute reality and at the same time makes orientation possible." The concept of self, then, along with the possibility of self-knowledge, belongs to the mode of its study—culture or religion.[2]

The Delphic oracle, then, is perhaps responsible for the original crisis of epistemology in Western thought. By posing the concept of selfhood in relation to the concept of knowledge, the oracle made problematic the ways that selfhood and knowledge constitute each other. The Delphic dilemma can be defined as follows: a self is made up of what it knows, but there must be a self in order for it to know. If the self is constituted by its knowledge, and yet knowledge requires a previously constituted self in which to enter, then we have a dilemma of priority. The answer to the problem of recursion has two forms: the possibility of understanding the self by referring to an ontic state when it did not suffer carnal limitations (the theological approach) or the possibility of understanding the self in reference to the social symbols which create it (the anthropological approach).

For Socrates, the problem that the object of inquiry and the inquiring subject happened to be one and the same entity—both being the self—could be solved only with reference to a preexistent state of a pure *episteme*—a state akin to divinity. Socratic philosophy proposes a concept of selfhood that relies on the self's perpetually recollecting discrete and ever untethered opinion, which it transforms into knowledge and thereby recollects what that self might have been before the sleep and the forgetting—what it might have been when the self had been a "friend of god." For the anthropologist who maintains, with Geertz, that the concept of self cannot exist outside of culture, culture becomes, as Mary Douglas writes, a "series of related structures which comprise social forms, values, cosmology, the whole of knowledge and through which all experience is mediated." Because the self is constructed through its interaction with human rituals, signs, and forms, the self can best be understood by reference to those modes of construction.[3]

In essence, we may say that the Delphic oracle proposed the first hermeneutic circle. Although his Jesus described the silencing of the Delphic oracle with some degree of relish in *Paradise Re-*

gained, Milton did not escape that crisis of epistemology established with the oracle's most famous dictum, nor did he wish to. Milton's characters never achieve an unproblematized self-knowledge, nor do they ever escape that oracular hermeneutic circle. Their recognition of agency, body, and soul as the things that make them what they are is always accompanied by the recollection that their knowledge is both the product and the process of their constituted selves.

Theology and ethnography best serve our examination of Milton's attempts to deal with the problem of self-knowledge because they encompass the two grounds of representation on which Milton established his politics and his psychology. Jesus, in *Paradise Regained,* is doing nothing less than founding a religious culture. It is, to use one of Kenneth Burke's favorite methods of explication, both a *religious* culture and a religious *culture.* Jesus espouses a new way of knowing and a new way of being, and he does so by reconfiguring the relationship between self and knowledge. In the end, Jesus' doctrine in *Paradise Regained* is culture-forming because it proposes anew how to deal with the Delphic dilemma.

I am interested in considering how Milton represents the idea of selfhood and the forms by which a self can come to any reflective knowledge. My primary object of inquiry is Milton's own act of establishing a constituted selfhood by employing a representative form of self-knowledge.

At the heart of the issue in both Milton's late political prose tracts and in his last published poems is the question of what constitutes a political life. From his earliest public appearance in 1641, Milton insisted on conflating the social fabric and the individual citizen. In 1641, he did so through the trope of synecdoche, employing, in fact, what Burke calls the "'noblest synecdoche' . . . proclaiming the identity of 'microcosm' and 'macrocosm.'"[4] In *Of Reformation,* Milton writes, "a Commonwealth ought to be but as one huge Christian personage, one mighty growth, and stature of an honest man, as big, and compact in vertue as in body." The paradigm of that virtue, and indeed of that body, is "a savory obedience to *Christs* example." Thirty years later, Milton undertook a far more searching analysis of how the body politic relates to the body of Christ, and he does so by casting and recasting, through a series of tropological modes, the lives of Jesus, Samson, and John Milton in his 1671 binary. It is Jesus' "life" that is the object of contention in the temptation scenes of *Paradise Regained,* just as it is Samson's "life" in the accompanying drama, and, I will suggest, Milton's "political life" in between the two works (*Of Reformation,* CM III, p. 38).

In the end, late Milton is the main subject of this study—not *Paradise Regained,* not *Paradise Lost,* and not *Samson Agonistes,* although, in order to get at late Milton, I write at length about each of these works. The second half of chapter 1 is a reading of *Paradise Lost;* chapters 2 and 3 take a look at *Paradise Regained;* most of chapter 4 is a reading of *Samson Agonistes,* and chapters 4 and 5 study the 1671 volume as an integral unit.

Because my interest is Milton's self-knowledge as it is performed in 1671, in between the two poetic works on which he concluded his career, this book is constructed in a way that leads most comfortably toward a discussion of that subject. In its basic structures, the book falls into three interrelated parts. The first part discerns what Milton means by self-knowledge; the second discusses how the hero of *Paradise Regained* comes to self-knowledge; and the third suggests how Milton does the same.

In the first part I consider the issue of the subject. Before turning to how Milton's brief epic deals with self-knowledge, I delineate and discuss two models of culture formation. I define the models individually and then suggest how each establishes premises allowing or disallowing self-knowledge. On the whole, this first part notes the conditions for subjectivity in either of the two models I am defining, establishing the foundation for the rest of the study.

The second part falls into two chapters, both dealing with *Paradise Regained.* Chapter 2 discusses the act of reading as a way of coming to self-knowledge. By *reading* I mean the act of being moved or directed to accepting certain tenets about oneself, that is, reading as the theorists of meditation articulated it in seventeenth-century England. I am interested in the way the reader is situated in *Paradise Regained* and how Jesus reads his life in the opening soliloquy. Chapter 3 encompasses what happens when Jesus reads Satan's offers in the temptation to the kingdoms. This chapter deals with three epistemic constructs—doubt, enigma, and transcendence, and I discuss the ways that Jesus' act of coming to self-knowledge is also a feat of cultural construction.

The overall concern of the third part is Milton and how he came to self-knowledge in his 1671 volume. In chapter 4, I discuss *Samson Agonistes* under the same terms I had used to study *Paradise Regained*—the ways that the hero can come to self-knowledge. In order to understand how the two books in the 1671 volume are related one to the other, I read *Samson Agonistes* as a study in the failure of Samson (and the tribe of Dan) to achieve self-knowledge in the same measure and under the same general conditions by which Jesus succeeded. In the chapter 5 I suggest in what ways Milton came to self-knowledge between 1651 to 1671, especially how he came to political self-knowledge. Here I will be contesting the regnant trend in Milton studies which dismisses Milton's "politics" as retrograde after *Paradise Lost*. I discuss more fully how Milton comes to self-knowledge in his 1671 book by discerning Milton's evolving political self-representation from *A Defence of the People of England* (1651) to the interrelationship of *Paradise Regained* and *Samson Agonistes* (1671). I also discuss Milton's late politics by comparing them with those of the foremost political theorist of seventeenth-century England—Thomas Hobbes.

My study begins and ends with Hobbes. There seems to be a dearth of studies concerned with the relationship between Hobbes and Milton. This book, I hope, will suggest some new ways of considering the potential for further study in that relationship. There are few dialogues in the seventeenth-century more entertaining or more suggestive. The other dialogue in which I situate Milton might be a little more difficult to justify—and that is the dialogue between Milton and contemporary political and psychoanalytical theory.

By placing Milton in a dialogue with modern and postmodern literary and cultural theories, I am able to elucidate the sophistication of Milton's thinking on the issue of representation and the concept of the subject. By placing Milton in a dialogue with his contemporaries, especially Hobbes, but also Descartes and Spinoza, as well as a host of theological writers from the beginning of the fourth to the end of the seventeenth century, I demonstrate, with some historical detail, Milton's contribution to the political, theological, and philosophical trends of early modern Europe.

The purpose of the first engagement—Milton and modern literary and cultural theories—is to dispel the notion that Milton's late works constitute what Walter Raleigh called a "monument to dead ideas." In examining Milton and his contemporaries, I attempt to dispel the notion that late Milton is apolitical or, in Fredric Jameson phrase, "post-political." In either case, Milton is treated here as a political and philosophical thinker of the first order, not, which is too often the case, as a poet who dabbled in politics and philosophy.[5]

ACKNOWLEDGMENTS

I wish to acknowledge granting agencies for their generous funding of my education, research, travel, and the incidental expenses incurred in the completion of this book. I would like to thank the Social Sciences and Humanities Research Council of Canada for granting me a doctoral fellowship; the Committee of Vice-Chancellors and Principals of the Universities of the United Kingdom for an Overseas Research Studentship Award; Christ's College, Cambridge, for two timely travel grants and a dissertation bursary; and the University Research Grants Committee and the Trustees of the Endowment Fund at the University of Calgary for awarding me a publication subvention. I would also like to thank Mrs. Barbara McLeod, Mrs. Joyce Kee, Mrs. Myrna Sentes, and to remember the late Mrs. Barbara McQuaid of the Department of English for their efficient and generous services in the course of writing this book.

Books are the basic tools of a scholar, and so she or he judges a library by its wealth of material. I was fortunate enough to be able to make use of several libraries, all justly renowned for their splendid collections. But it is the human resources in these libraries that I find memorable and worthy of memorial. I would like to thank the librarians and support staff of the Cambridge University Library, the English Faculty Library, the Wren Library at Trinity, and the Old Library at Christ's. I wish especially to thank the staff of the Rare Books Room at Cambridge University Library for their efficiency and friendliness, and Mrs. Courtney, the librarian of the Old Library at Christ's College. Mrs. Courtney allowed me special reading privileges and offered me aid in bibliographical searches; however, I should like to thank her most for her enthusiasm and her warm spirit, both of which were invaluable in sustaining me in what is climatically the coldest library I had to work in.

xv

This book is the product of a long and ongoing education, in which I was taught, supervised, and allowed to converse with a series of wonderful people. I would like to thank Bob Mallett for teaching me to love literature in my days at secondary school; I would like to thank the professors who taught me undergraduate English at the University of Alberta, especially Rowland McMaster, Juliet McMaster, Ronald Ayling, Richard Hoffpauir, and Linda Woodbridge. I would also like to thank Pat Clements and Shirley Neuman, professors from whom I did not have the good fortune to take courses, but who have subsequently taught me more than they know. My master's thesis was written under the kind and supportive supervision of James Forrest at the University of Alberta, and my doctoral dissertation under the generous and patient supervision of Howard Erskine-Hill at Cambridge University. I would also like to thank Alastair Fowler and Mindele Triep for the encouragement and kindness they showed in examining the dissertation.

Throughout the years, I have had the good fortune to have friends whose intelligent conversation helped me maintain a desire for scholarship and whose magnanimity facilitated my retaining a zeal for the scholarly life. I would like to thank Maria Vargas, Molly Andrews, Edwin Abel, and Annie Abel for making my stay at Cambridge as pleasurable as it could be. I would especially like to thank the two people who became my immediate family at Cambridge, Shirin Rai and Patricia Jackson, without whom I should have been lost in every way. I would like to thank all my colleagues in the Department of English at the University of Calgary, who have shown me a warmth well beyond the call of professional courtesy. I would especially like to thank Ron Bond, Pamela McCallum, Roderick McGillis, Victor Ramraj, and Susan Rudy-Dorscht. Jeanne Perreault and Eric Savoy have exemplified for me the essence of collegiality. Over dozens of meals and through hundreds of conversations, they have been selfless in sharing their ideas with me. Because our talks rarely strayed into the area of Milton, their ideas will not be reflected here; but, because of those talks, I know how better to reflect on ideas.

Once a student, now a teacher, I would like to thank my own students who have taught me definitively what I always suspected — that the teacher learns as much as she or he professes. I would like to thank all the students who have taken my English 316 course for helping me in my thinking about Milton.

While I was writing this book, I was fortunate enough to be

able to supervise two graduate students, Bernadette Andrea and Anne Cumming. From their dissertations I learned a great deal about Milton's sexual politics and about Eve's subjectivity, and from them I learned an enormous amount about integrity, intelligence, and excellence.

Richard Lanham once wrote that, as scholars, we do not know what we think until we see what we have written; I think few will disagree with this. When we also add the infinite capacity humans have for deluding themselves, we can conclude furthermore that we often believe that what we have written is what we thought. I was fortunate enough to have had two very kind readers at the University of Pittsburgh Press who saw what I wrote and knew that I did not write quite what I thought. By employing the insightful and generous suggestions of Jeff Morris and Joseph Wittreich, I was able to save myself from writing a bad book, and instead I was able to write this one. Kathy McLaughlin, the assistant editor at the University of Pittsburgh Press, was invaluable throughout the process of getting this book completed. I would like to thank her very much for her unstinting support and for her superlative editorial skills. I would also like to thank James Simmonds, who was enthusiastic about the first proposals for this book, and who has kindly countenanced my work over the years in his role as editor of *Milton Studies*. I would also like to thank Kathy Bennett for preparing the index.

Two of my closest friends volunteered (well, almost) to read the penultimate draft of the book in order to purge it of inconsistencies, inaccuracies, and imbecilities. I would like to thank Shannon Murray and Gerald Wandio for taking time off from their own work to read and correct mine. Those mistakes which still remain are not only wholly mine, obviously, but are adamantly mine; they have had to survive many readers more sapient than I to get here.

Let me conclude by thanking those to whom this work is dedicated—those, in fact, without whom this work would not have been possible. My family has supported me in every possible way at every possible time. It is simple biological fact that without my family I would not be in this world; it is elemental emotional reality that without my family I should not wish to be in this world. This study is the product of an education in the ascendant value of linguistic systems. But a single reflection on the amount of love I have for my family teaches me beyond persuasion that words are simply incapable of expressing that which is truest.

PART ONE

The Subject

"For human knowledge which concerns the mind, it hath two parts; the one that inquireth of the substance or nature of the soul or mind, the other that inquireth of the faculties or functions thereof."
—*Francis Bacon (1605)*

1

Confronting the Subject: The Art of Self-Knowledge

𝕰

C ULTURE," as Raymond Williams has pointed out, is one of the two or three most complicated words in our language. Until the fifteenth century, the word was used as a "noun of process," signifying the "tending" of crops or animals. From the sixteenth to the nineteenth century, it assumed a metaphorical significance whereby the "tending of natural growth was extended to a process of human development." Just as one could cultivate land, so too could one cultivate one's mind. In the last third of the seventeenth century, however, the word underwent an important transmutation whereby it assumed what Frank Lentricchia has called its "politically active senses." Williams traces one sign of this new valency in "culture" to a passage in the second edition of Milton's *The Readie and Easie Way to Establish a Free Commonwealth* (April 1660). Milton suggests there that the "schools and academies" of the English commonwealth ought to

> spread much more knowledge and civilitie, yea religion through all parts of the land, by communicating the natural heat of government and culture more distributively to all extreme parts, which now lie numm and neglected, [and this] would soon make the whole nation more industrious, more ingenious at home, more potent, more honorable abroad.

Milton, as Williams notes, "is writing about a general social pro-

3

cess, and this is a definite stage of development" in the significance of "culture." For Lentricchia, this "leap in Milton" is the beginning of the dissemination of the "politically active senses" of the word.[1]

In these senses, culture becomes "a validation of the state, a process whose goal is saturation of the social." Indeed, as Lentricchia continues, "'culture' is knowledge precisely at the point at which knowledge becomes power, or is on the way to power." In this tract, Milton is indeed using the term *culture* as a validation of the state (witness the conjunction of "government and culture"). Likewise, Milton is also aligning knowledge with power (the fact that the "schools and academies" are the forces of dissemination and control). But this tract of April 1660, it must be noted, represents a unique moment of crisis for Milton. In fact, Milton was validating the state in a way that he had not done before and was never to do again. Feeling the pressure of the imminent Restoration, Milton made political concessions in April 1660 that he would not have made even two months earlier. Milton's changing attitudes toward the decentralization of government might be traced to determine the degree of his political concessions. In February 1660, when he published the first edition of *The Readie and Easie Way*, Milton confidently proposed a decentralized political structure: "civil rights . . . may be best and soonest obtain, if every county in the land were made a little commonwealth." By April 1660, Milton significantly altered this proposal in beating a hasty retreat to the defense of a centralized government: "civil rights . . . may be best and soonest obtain, if every countie in the land were made a kinde of subordinate Commonaltie or Commonwealth."[2] The threat of a renewed English monarchy was enough to persuade Milton to palliate his political radicalism to the extent of theorizing a partially centralized government in order to prevent the reestablishment of a wholly centralized one. Milton uses "culture" in this period of stress in the sense Williams and Lentricchia note.

An examination of Milton's only other relevant use of the term *culture* reveals a different political sense—one more in line with his usual antiauthoritarian sentiments. In the prologue to his *Second Defence* (1654), Milton describes the effect of his *Defence of the People of England* (1651): "I am bringing back, bringing home to every nation, liberty, so long driven out, so long an exile. . . . I am he, who laid low that redoubted satellite of tyrants, hitherto deemed invincible in the general opinion" (CM VIII, pp. 14–15). He represents himself as both the restorer of liberty and the destroyer of Salmasius. And the term he uses in 1654 to describe the dissemination of liberty—in a tract that delineates Milton's period of ambivalence between euphoria and doubt—is *culture:* "I am spreading abroad among the cities, the kingdoms, the nations, the restored culture of citizenship and freedom of life."[3] This sense of culture is more in line with Milton's usual politics as they are expressed in times of less compelling stress. With this usage, culture does not validate the state apparatus or align knowledge with power (at least not in the strictly Foucauldian sense of that alignment as it operates in social agencies). Rather, culture here is the operation of theorizing about the destruction of centralized governments.

By 1671, in his last volume of poetry, which is also his most mature political statement, Milton returned to this 1654 sense of culture and articulated a different attitude toward that alignment of "government and culture." Although *culture* is not the term Milton used in 1671, it is nonetheless the most apt term for describing the entity and process he is theorizing about. In accord with his usage in 1660, he is still concerned with the best way to spread knowledge, civility, and religion; corresponding to his usage in 1654, he remains attentive to the destruction of centralized governments. In fact, he would have one of his heroes theorize the destruction of centralized governments and the other literally destroy one. In *Paradise Regained,* Jesus founds a culture which "shall be like a tree / Spreading and over-shadowing all the Earth, / Or as a stone that shall to pieces dash / All Monarchies besides throughout the world" (IV, 147–50). In *Samson Agonistes,* Samson destroys a centralized state apparatus and liberates the tribe of Dan who then have the opportunity, as Manoa points out, to form their own political structure if they but "lay hold on this occasion" (1717).

Given Milton's full statements about culture in 1654 and 1660, it appears that *culture* is the most useful term to give to the structure and process Jesus founds in *Paradise Regained.* For Jesus, in a series of encounters with himself and with Satan, produces nothing less than a structure for gaining knowledge and a process for understanding experience. And that, in terms of a broadly defined modernism, is what culture, in one sense anyway, has come to mean. A culture, Mary Douglas writes, "is a series of related structures which comprise social forms, values, cosmology, the whole of knowledge and through which all experience is mediated." Culture, according to Matthew Arnold's definition, is "a pursuit of our total perfection by means of getting to know . . . and through this knowledge, turning a fresh stream of fresh and free thought upon our stock notions and habits, which we now follow staunchly but mechanically. . . . And the culture we recommend is, above all, an inward operation." Culture, as Douglas defines its basic structures or as Arnold defines its major operations, is substantially concerned with two primary aspects of human existence: knowledge and experience. Or, as Williams states the case, culture is a "mode of interpreting all our common experience, and, in this new interpretation, changing it." In other words, culture may be defined by the structures and operations which involve the ways of knowing and the ways of being.[4]

Since culture is comprised of operations concerning ways of knowing and ways of being, it may therefore be studied by the methods of epistemology and ontology. However, because culture as a system also determines the ratio between knowledge and experience, the field of psychology must also be added to these methods of study. Finally, because culture as a model also determines the relationship between experience and knowledge it must be treated under the rubric of politics. Thus, epistemology is concerned with discerning how one experiences knowledge, ontology with how knowledge forms experience, psychology with how experience transforms knowledge, and politics with how knowledge transforms experience. Knowledge and experience are the *aspects* of culture, and the four ways of discerning the relationships between the aspect are its *methods*. Within this general framework of culture exist distinct ways of being—the *principles* of culture—and distinct ways of knowing—the *forms* of culture.

In order to distinguish between two principles, then, I will use the oldest Western distinction between the two ways of being: freedom and necessity. These terms will serve us well not just because they exist as the polarities of a problem at the heart of Milton's theology and his politics, but because they also represent the broadest framework of Western thought. The interplay between freedom and necessity can be traced from the philosophical dialogue between Hellenic materialism and realism to the dialogue between the two regnant theories of modern subatomic physics. Our concern, for the most part, will be the two sixteenth- and seventeenth-century forms of that debate, which includes the renewed theological debate of the Reformation between the Calvinists and the Arminians on free will and determinism and the renewed philosophical debate between English materialists and realists of the seventeenth century. Before defining the contours of those early modern dialogues, I will examine some of the late modern forms of establishing the principles within that debate.

Recently, Fredric Jameson has restated the Marxist critical position clearly and with a great deal of vigor. Part of Jameson's strategy in arguing that Marxism ought to be considered the "untranscendable horizon" of all critical operations rests on Marxism's unique ability, he states, to give "an adequate account of the essential *mystery* of the cultural past." Materialist historiography can give us "a single great collective story" whose theme, however symbolically represented, is "for Marxism, the collective struggle to wrest a realm of Freedom from a realm of Necessity." In a slightly different way, Freud also argued that culture includes two aspects—human knowledge, which allows for the control of nature, and human regulations, which ensure a stable, social system of distributing the wealth of nature. In his further discussion of civilization's discontents, Freud develops this dialectic into one between the freedom of Eros (love) and the control of Ananke (necessity). Kenneth Burke, in his study of the basic forms of human motivation, its "grammar" as he calls it, found the same basic distinction much to his purpose: "there are two primary generalizations that characterize the quality of motives: freedom and necessity."[5]

There are, then, two ways of being, two principles, in any given culture. Either the individuals of that culture are free or they are determined by necessity. But, of course, ways of being are inseparable from ways of knowing, so one must distinguish between the two *forms* of knowledge in relation to the two principles. *Narrative* can be defined as the form of knowing oneself to be free; *science* is the form of recognizing oneself as being determined. This distinction follows upon one made by William James in his arguments about the two forms of human knowledge: "All human thinking is essentially of two kinds—reasoning on the one hand, and narrative, descriptive, contemplative thinking on the other." Jerome Bruner has recently restated the same distinction between what he calls the "two modes of cognitive functioning," the first being "the paradig-

matic or logico-scientific one" and the second "the narrative mode."
Each way, as both James and Bruner contend, provides a distinctive
mode of "ordering experience" and of "constructing reality"; that
is, each is a mode of cultural formation.[6]

It might be helpful now to situate these distinctions within a
seventeenth-century framework. The two principles would still be
necessity and freedom. Their representative forms in a European
theological framework would be Calvinism and Arminianism; their
representative forms in an English political framework would be
the models of Hobbesian science and Miltonic narrative. Their two
ends, in either setting, would still be the ones defined by Bruner—
the ordering of experience and the construction of reality. The
culture each model would construct is, in the theological framework, either a world determined by a supralapsarian decree (Calvin) or a world dynamically engaged in its own evolution (Arminius). The culture each model would construct is, in the political
framework, either the necessary state of Leviathan or the potential
state of the regained Eden. Schematically, then, each model presents a way of knowing that determines the individual subject's way
of being. To give us an idea of the distinction, let me define what I
will call the Miltonic narrative model, based primarily, although
not exclusively, on *Paradise Regained,* and the Hobbesian scientific
model, based substantially, but not solely, on the *Leviathan.*

The Miltonic narrative model represents the vocation of individuals choosing to become subjects of a certain culture. It is both
a mimetic enactment and an invitation to mimesis. Not only is it a
historical narrative demonstrating the original constitution of that
culture in a unique performance by a special individual undergoing
the rites required to transform oneself from an individual into a
subject, it is also a maieutic representation of the conditions required of any individual becoming a subject of that same culture.
In its own way, *Paradise Regained* is a narrative *Imitatio Christi.*
Calling it a "narrative" means that it represents a sequential order
of events and that it reconstitutes its own world. Since it is about
vocation and choice, it represents a world in which human will has
free agency. It posits the preconditions of subjectivity because it is
about how an individual becomes a subject. Its theoretical foundation is based on the premise that all individuals have a choice about
becoming subjects, and that there is, therefore, a difference between an individual self and a subject and a way for the former to

"become" the latter. Since it is about the formation of a culture, it deals with the ways in which an individual self becomes a subject — the most significant way being knowledge. The most significant form of knowledge required of the individual concerns the conditions by which choice, will, and subjectivity are possible. In other words, this narrative model about choosing to be a subject of a culture depends on the potential any individual has for self-knowledge and the ways that an individual self can become a subject of a given culture.

The Hobbesian scientific model represents the interpellation of subjects into an ideology. Neither educative nor representational, this model is radically theoretical. As a science it does not deal with narrative sequence but, rather, denies the possibility of diachronic development and the liberty of choice that diachronic representation allows. Since it is concerned with interpellation, it denies the possibility of choice and therefore denies any agency to the human will. That it is about subjects *qua* subjects means that it deals with the idea of subjection. The model has as its theoretical foundation the fact that there is no such thing as an individual who is not already subject to ideology and that there is no process involved in subjection — it just is. That it is about ideology means that it deals with the ways subjects are "always already" subjected. Its main interest is not knowledge, but rather misrecognition or *méconnaissance*. On this basis, the object of study for this science is the synchronic situation in which, under the illusion of a culture allowing for choice, will, and subjectivity, there exists an ideology that fosters a *méconnaissance* of the actual impossibility of anything other than submission, interpellation, and subjection. Because it has already elided the concept of an individual self and has cast under a shadowy light the notion of knowledge with its insistence on misrecognition, it disallows the very idea of self-knowledge.

The Hobbesian scientific model, obviously, is taken primarily from Hobbes's *Leviathan,* although it is clear that I have borrowed the vocabulary for describing it from two contemporary French theorists — Louis Althusser and Jacques Lacan. In fact, not only the vocabulary but also the models of subjection Althusser and Lacan develop will prove to be fundamental to my elaboration of the Hobbesian scientific model in its final form. The Hobbesian model has its own psychology (including its own epistemology and ontology) and its own politics (involving exploration of state apparatus, ideological and repressive). Given the general sufficiency of his model, what purpose do Althusser and Lacan serve to this study of two distinct seventeenth-century models of the workings of the subject?

First of all, I employ Lacan and Althusser's theories to establish a relevant context of the problems surrounding our contemporary discussions of the category of the subject. Althusser's theory of how individuals are subject to the state and Lacan's theory of how individuals are subject to their unconscious desires both reflect Hobbesian concerns as well as establish the contemporary relevance of those concerns. Secondly, by having each theorist develop his concept of subjection strictly in his chosen realm of exploration (at the level of the state and at the level of the psyche), I may more carefully distinguish between the first and second parts of the *Leviathan,* between Hobbes's psychology and his politics. Once I have done that in relation to Althusserian politics and Lacanian psychoanalysis, I will be better able to resolve some of the more salient relationships between the various elements of the complete Hobbesian model. Third, there are meaningful points of convergence (and not just contradiction) between these contemporary theorists and Milton. In the first chapter, especially, I will detail some interesting relationships between Milton's sense of self-knowledge and the Lacanian model of cognition. This is important because in the end I am not simply juxtaposing the two models. Like both Lacan and Althusser, Milton did not believe in the idea of an autonomous subject. Like Lacan, Milton asserted that language reconstitutes a sense of selfhood, and, like Althusser, Milton thought that there are forms of temporality which coexist and interconnect but never achieve a mutual integration.

At the basis of this study is the question of self-knowledge, which involves its own series of problems, some of which are transparently paradoxical. According to most epistemologists and anthropologists, knowledge can occur only in a cultural setting, however broadly defined. There is no possibility of knowing outside the structures, modes, or languages of a given culture. According to these same theorists, following with varying degrees of skepticism or faith the famous Cartesian formula, there is no such thing as a sense of selfhood divorced from the activity of being a cognitive entity; there is no possibility of possessing a self apart from possessing the capacity for knowing. According to anthropologists intent on demystifying the object of their study, the basic habits and available modes of experiencing "being" or experiencing "knowing" make up culture. In other words, there is either a state of paradox or irreducible recursion between the three terms *self, knowledge,* and *culture.* Each makes the existence of the next possible, and each likewise requires the possibility of the next for itself to exist. The relationship between self and knowledge involves the recursion by which the activity (knowing) constitutes the actor (self), and the actor (self) is comprised of the activity (knowing). The relationship between these two terms and the third term involves a further level of recursion in which the actor-activity ratio (self-knowledge) depends on a setting (culture), and likewise the setting (culture) is constituted by the actor-activity ratio (self-knowledge).[7]

The relationship between a knowing subject and the field of knowledge has been at the basis of various crises in Western epistemological debates. Its origin can be traced back to the most famous pronouncement involving both terms, knowing subject and known object: the Delphic oracle's "Know thyself." In fact, according to Ernst Cassirer, in "all higher forms of religious life the maxim 'Know thyself' is regarded as a categorical imperative, as an ultimate moral and religious law." As the categorical imperative of religious activity, one would think, it ought to have been taken to be as clear as any other law. But, as Cassirer shows in his brief history of the Delphic oracle's influence from Heraclitus to Pascal, the statement was never clear. In fact, the ambiguity was quite often ascribed to the very Father of Lies. As Sir John Davies ruefully notes in his *Nosce Teipsum* (1599),

> For how may we to others' things attain
> When none of us his own soul understands?
> For which the Devil mocks our curious brain
> When "Know thyself" his oracle commands.[8]

A thorough history of attitudes toward the possibility of self-knowledge would probably demonstrate that there was never a time when ambiguity and paradox did not reign. A brief history would probably demonstrate that the most discernible break came with a renewed Christian humanism in the European Renaissance.

Fortunately, there has never been a thorough study. Equally fortunate is the fact that Cassirer has offered us a viable brief study.

Cassirer traces the oracle's influence in four distinct stages based on the crises located in the thinking of four prominent theorists. The first stage, the pre-Socratic form of self-knowledge, begins with Heraclitus's enigmatic statement, "I searched out myself." At its basis is the Heraclitian logos, a structural element of arrangements common to all entities; to search out one's self the self had to discover the basic physical fact of the universe, the logos. The second stage, the Socratic form of self-knowledge, begins with Socrates's declaration in the *Phaedrus*, "[I] direct my inquiries . . . to myself." At its basis is the Platonic logos, the process of transcendent dialectic; self-knowledge in its Socratic form was possible only by the self's employing the form of all knowledge, the logos. The third stage, the Stoic-Christian form of self-knowledge, begins with Marcus Aurelius and Christianity. Fundamentally disagreeing on the question of the absolute dependence or independence of human beings, Stoicism and Christianity parted ways on the topic of the logos, which for Stoicism retained its Platonic form and for Christianity assumed the place of God. Whereas the Stoic would gain self-knowledge primarily by a linguistic dialectic, the Christian would gain it by persistent reference to the transcendent Logos who created the self and on whom the Christian believed the self to be still depending. The fourth stage, the early modern form of self-knowledge, begins with Pascal, whose work, according to Cassirer, is the "last and perhaps most impressive expression" of anthropological self-knowledge. Pascal makes the fundamental distinction between the "geometrical spirit" and the "acute or subtle spirit." Presupposing a Christian fall and redemption and therefore positing the theory of a "double man" (prelapsarian and postlapsarian), Pascal alters the Delphic saying radically by situating God as the only way to self-knowledge. He may stand as the culmination of the career of the Delphic oracle's pronouncement.[9]

In tracing a Miltonic model of self-knowledge we will find that it does not fall easily into any of the four basic stages Cassirer posits. Nonetheless, the distinction Pascal makes is essential to understanding the premises and the major actors in Milton's model of self-knowledge. In effect, Milton establishes what I am calling a *narrative model,* which I will define at length in the second part of this chapter. For now, it is important to use that Pascalian insight into the "double man" and express the basic forms of self-knowledge we will discover in Milton's narrative model.

FROM DELPHI TO EDEN:
THREE FORMS OF SELF-KNOWLEDGE

The first and most consistently held distinction most human beings make is a perceptual one between being a self and perceiving an other. This happens, according to child psychologists following Freud, when the suckling baby is weaned from his or her mother's breast and recognizes that there is a spatial distinction between the baby who is self and the mother who is other.[10] In the early modern period, this primary recognition finds its happiest expression in the way Don Quixote bases the distinction between himself and the enchanted Dulcinea on the fact that he is a perceiving subject: "Now, since I am not enchanted and cannot be, according to sound judgment, it is she who is enchanted, injured, changed, altered and transformed."[11] Assuming a self incapable of being contaminated by the world's systems of enchantment, the Don simply divides the universe into two entities—the pure, perceiving self and the impure, perceived other. I will call this original division of the manifold world into a self and an other the primary, perceptual distinction, or the prelapsarian form of self-knowledge.

In a more complex psychology and at a maturer understanding, the self begins to perceive its own stages and to acknowledge that in its fluidity the self is made up of a series of different selves. The previous selves that the present self perceives begin to take on the qualities the self had previously ascribed to others. "I am not now what I once was" translates into "I am another self; my former self was other." This happens for most of us on a daily basis. When we have bad days, we claim that we were not ourselves; when we perceive other people to be having an equally bad day, we claim that they are not themselves.

This happens in more drastic proportions to someone who, more fundamentally, loses a previous self. Few more pertinent, and more humbling, examples serve us than the case of the Russian soldier known as Zasetsky, one of Alexander Luria's patients and the hero of one of his case studies. Zasetsky received a severe wound in 1943 to the left parieto-occipital area of his cranium. The scar tissue from the wound caused an incipient atrophy of the medulla. The result was that Zasetsky lost his memory, half his field of vision, his language skills, and, most significantly, his ability to organize whatever he perceived into a synthesized whole; his world, Luria concludes, became fragmented. For the next thirty years, Zasetsky worked patiently at recovering his verbal skills and his memory. To aid in the exercise of both, he wrote down his life story. Because he had lost half his field of vision, he could not see the right half of any given object. Even when he wrote, he could not perceive what he was writing when it fell on the right half of the page. In fact, for all intents and purposes, Zasetsky could not read what he was writing about his own life. Zasetsky claimed that the reason he undertook this huge effort was to regain his previous sense of selfhood—"to become the person I was before the war."[12] His sense of self was fragile because he had no past from which he could accumulate a sense of presence, no language in which to articulate a selfhood, and no sense of coherence in anything he perceived. Given the loss of his memory of what he was, his language of what he may be, and his ability to synthesize what he perceives, Zasetsky conceives of a self that is absolutely present, inarticulate about its being, and fragmented. Zasetsky's case is drastic, but it is nonetheless a pertinent study of what each person does in assessing a present, perceiving self and a past, perceived self. This ability to discern previous selves and recognize their otherness may be termed the secondary, cognitive distinction, or the lapsarian form of self-knowledge.

In a yet more complex psychology and at an even maturer understanding, the self begins to perceive that it is never stable in any given tract of time. This understanding leads to the conclusion that the self operates in representation or, what amounts to the same thing, the self is constituted in its representation. The self is what it represents itself to be in any given situation; there is no other self than the one in representation. The basis of the primary and secondary distinctions had been that there were two categories of being—self and other. The discovery of the power of representation involves adding a third category, the category of the social experience. The self represents itself in order to effect the other, usually to persuade the other that the self really is this way (and not that way). Part of the overall effect, however, is that the self also is attempting to persuade itself of its being this way (and not that). In the words of George Herbert Mead, there "are all sorts of different selves answering to all sorts of different social reactions. It is a social process itself that is responsible for the appearance of the self; it is not there as a self apart from this type of experience."[13] The social process is responsible not only for the appearance of the self, but also for structuring the modes of representing desire: "so organizing the reaction towards the object [of desire], thus perceived, that one indicates the reaction to himself as he might to another" (p. 357). The process of representation is stated in a more extreme way by William James: "We need only in cold blood ACT as if the thing in question were real, and keep acting as if it were real, and it will infallibly end by growing into such a connection with our life that it will become real."[14] In other words, as he states later, "the emotion both begins and ends with what we call its effects or manifestations" (p. 458). I will, following Werner Jaeger and Richard Lanham's usage, call this ability to discern a variety of selves existing only in representation the tertiary, rhetorical distinction, or the postlapsarian form of self-knowledge.[15]

None of these three forms of selfhood, however, is established on an essential distinction, and none, therefore, is meant to be the basis of an ethics. In other words, the self's ability to represent itself as being a different self does not, in a social situation, allow the self to escape its history.[16] In other words, not only the first distinction is perceptual; in a way they all are. These three distinctions and the commensurate forms of self-knowledge they signify will serve as the foundation of my study of the two cultural models.

I have suggested that the primary distinction of the self is perceptual. Its form of self-knowledge is based on an ability to see that there are others and to see that there is a self capable of seeing. This is the primary act of experiencing a self; in other words, the primary form of self-knowledge establishes the *field of being*. The second distinction of the self is cognitive. The cognitive form of self-knowledge is based on an ability to know what a previous self did not know. Its evolving sense of selfhood is based on the economy of knowledge, either accumulation or loss. Cognition is the primary act of recognizing a self, and it properly establishes the *field of knowledge*. The third distinction of the self is rhetorical. The rhetorical form of self-knowledge is based on an ability to persuade either its own self or others of the constituent features of the self—

that is, rhetoric is the way the self personates its being and cognition. It is the primary act of depicting or personating a self, or what Lanham calls the ability of "enselfment"; and, therefore, it constitutes the *field of will*. To give these three forms of self-knowledge a seventeenth-century accent, I have described them in terms of the fall from Eden.

This Pascalian distinction between prelapsarian and postlapsarian humanity (actually it is Pauline, but we can accept Cassirer's historicizing of it) does not just refer to Milton; it applies equally well to Hobbes. For instance, the state Hobbes calls "meer Nature" possesses the same properties as the prelapsarian form of self-knowledge. What Hobbes proposes to escape the state of "meer Nature" is the "Covenant," which possesses the same qualities as the lapsarian form of self-knowledge. Finally, the "Covenant" leads to the "Common-wealth," which is substantially based on the form of postlapsarian self-knowledge. I realize how odd it might seem to speak of what Hobbes describes as "meer Nature" (which, after all, is the state of "warre . . . of every man, against every man") as being Edenic; but I will explain the appropriateness of this in the following pages. Even though the terms of what we may call "lapsarian historiography" are capable of describing Hobbes's model—even if in a seemingly perverse way—we have to admit nonetheless that Hobbes's model, and the scientific model generally, attempts to dismiss diachrony altogether. In other words, the scientific model bases its reading of human necessity in synchronic terms. As we shall shortly see, for Althusser, ideology becomes an infralapsarian decree of subjection, for Lacan the unconscious becomes an anarchic chaos always surrounding a partially organized psyche, and for Hobbes the covenant is dehistoricized in a variety of ways to suggest that it always was. We should, then, adapt our terms to accommodate the scientific model's premise of synchrony. Respectively, the field of being becomes the *category of spirit,* the field of knowledge the *category of authority,* and the field of will the *category of representation.*

The concept of self-knowledge, in whatever fields or under whatever categories it has been studied, has been based on the primary distinction I posited earlier—that between self and other. In order to gain anything that can accurately be called self-knowledge, there first had to be a distinguishable self. There has never been a time in the history of Western philosophy when that distinction between self and other could be made confidently and without qualification; and if there was such a time, there really shouldn't have been. In our own day, this primary distinction is undergoing yet another, and useful, skeptical examination. Those modern thinkers who are predicting or representing a revolution in this basic distinction tend to do so by revising the Delphic oracle's statement in ways that can accommodate the new categories of enselfment. Those categories are numerous and subtle, but for our purposes we may locate two pertinent ones that play a large role in our analysis — language and desire.

According to some modern theorists, that primary distinction between self and other eventually will not have the force it has had and seems yet to have. In some circles, this eschatology takes on the form of Foucault's proclamation that the category of a "knowing human being" has been only recently developed and that it is, furthermore, a category moving toward obsolescence: "It is comforting, however, and a source of profound relief to think that man is only a recent invention, a figure not yet two centuries old, a new wrinkle in our knowledge, and that he will disappear again as soon as that knowledge has discovered a new form." In others, it takes on the mode of Jameson's prophesy that the category of the "bourgeois subject" will soon be dissolved with the "emergence of a post-individualistic social world."[17]

In either case, Jameson's or Foucault's, the category of the individual self or subject has itself undergone one more "division." For Foucault, the human individual had "been a figure occurring between two modes of language"; more precisely, the concept of individuality is premised on fragmentation: "Man composed his own figure in the interstices of that fragmented language" (p. 386). For Jameson, on the other hand, the Lacanian category of the "subject in its division" lends itself nicely to a description of the perpetually desiring "bourgeois subject." His model, like Foucault's, is premised on the potential relationship between a knowing subject and the processes of knowing. In fact, Jameson translates what he calls "a specifically Lacanian version of 'know thyself'" into the following oracular pronouncement: "Where do you stand with respect to your desire?" Both Foucault and Jameson are working within a basic dichotomy originally traceable to the first recorded crisis in Western thought — the Delphic oracle's pronouncement, "Know thyself."[18]

PART ONE: HOBBES AND
THE SCIENCE OF SUBJECTION

Subject to Ideology: Althusser and Mosaic Interpellation

In proposing his model of Marxist praxis, Althusser focused at the outset on establishing that Marx founded nothing less than a science. Historical materialism, Althusser contends, is the third scientific "continent"—the first being mathematics and the second physics. The knowledge available in the explorations opened up by the discovery of this new continent is "*scientific* knowledge," which Althusser set up "against all the mystifications of *ideological* 'knowledge.'" Althusser places philosophy, religion, and ethics under the rubric of ideological knowledge, and is especially interested in demoting philosophy: "Science is then the real itself, known by the action which reveals it by destroying the ideologies that veil it: foremost among these ideologies is philosophy." Or, as Marx himself stated it in a more prosaic way, "Philosophy and the study of the actual world have the same relation to one another as masturbation and sexual love."[19] Marx's achievement is not to have proposed another philosophy, but to have placed philosophy as a continuation of politics—and politics, of course, is the object of Marxist science. As Althusser phrases it, "Marxism is not a (new) philosophy of praxis, but a (new) practice of philosophy" (p. 68). What distinguishes Marx's science from philosophy, from ethics, and from religion is that it is based on a critique of the category of the subject.

The Marxist-Leninist critique takes up two essential theses of Kantian subjectivism and contests their validity. According to Althusser's reading of Lenin's reading of Hegel, the Kantian "thing-in-itself" is eliminated and converted into the "dialectical action of the identity of essence and phenomenon" (pp. 118-19). Also, the "category of the Subject" is eliminated (p. 121). With these two critical actions—this "double elimination"—philosophy and critique merge to become a science. What Lenin rediscovers in employing a Hegelian critique of Kant in his *Philosophical Notebooks* (1915) is what he had underlined in his earlier *Materialism and Empirio-criticism* (1908)—that is, the conditions of Marxist science: "*the liberation of scientific practice,* finally freed from every dogma that would make it an ossified thing, thus restoring to it its rightful living existence—this life of science merely reflecting the life of reality itself" (p. 119). Lenin's elimination of the category of the subject is the basis of Althusser's reading of Marx.

Marx, according to Althusser, upheld the thesis that history is the process of the alienation of the subject in such early texts as the *Economic and Philosophical Manuscripts* (1844) and *The Holy Family* (1844). The so-called "rupture" in Marx's thought began when he first reconsidered this "untenable thesis" in what Althusser has called "the Works of the Break," especially the two volumes of 1845, the *Theses on Feuerbach* (1845) and *The German Ideology* (1845–46). The works that came after what Althusser calls the "epistemological break" fall into two categories. First, the works in which Marx is still involved in the project of "separating the scientific from the ideological"—those written between 1845 and 1857—belong to what Althusser calls the "Works of Marx's Theoretical Transition." Second, those works written after 1857—the *Grundrisse* (1857), the *Contribution to the Critique of Political Economy* (1859) and, especially, the first volume of *Capital* (1867)—in which Marx thoroughly rejected his earlier "radical anthropology," fall into the category Althusser has designated as the "Works of Marx's Maturity." The final formulation of Marx and the foundational basis of a Marxist science, then, is that history is "a process without a subject."[20] Quite simply, Althusser's insistence about the defining characteristic of scientificity rests on the elimination of the notion of the subject.

Althusser argues that Marx's rediscovery of Hegel in 1858 allowed him to appreciate that, whatever Hegel's failings, Hegel was the first to conceive of history as a process without a subject. In accepting the Hegelian notion of history, then, Marx eliminated the subject in two distinct senses. First, he denied that the subject was an organizing principle and/or driving force of history: "The dialectic at work in history is not the work of any Subject whatsoever, whether Absolute (God) or merely human."[21] Second, Marx freed the subject of history from its previously philosophical moorings: "The origin of history is always already thrust back before history, and therefore there is neither a philosophical origin nor a philosophical subject to History" (p. 122). Individuals do not, therefore, make history in either sense. Their actions are not the principle agents of historical events and their writings are not grounded in a defensible historiographical tradition. The first tenet allows Althusser to emphasize that history has no subject—it is, as he claims at the end of his final essay in *Reading Capital*, "an authorless theatre" (p. 193). The second tenet allows him to emphasize that history has no time. As he says, "the origin of history is always already thrust back before history." A single sentence from his early book, *For Marx*, alerts us to Althusser's concern about temporality and about the subject-structure debate in Marxism: "What makes *such and such* an event *historical* is not the fact that it is an *event,* but precisely its *insertion into forms which are themselves historical*" (p. 126).

The first form which Althusser attends to is temporality. The phrase at the heart of his operation is that often-heard, less often-understood, *always-already*. Part of the difficulty with the phrase is that its own history is misconstrued (but, then again, it is a phrase that hardly lends itself to historicization). For instance, Arthur Danto calls *always-already* a "locution from Derrida," while Jameson has recently suggested that Althusser is the one who "seems to have coined" the expression "always-already."[22] Most people probably first encountered the phrase *"toujours déjà"* in Derrida's 1967 publication, *De la grammatologie,* but it is actually a false origin.[23]

George Herbert Mead, possibly as early as 1900, but certainly by 1927, had used a similar phrase to describe the worldview of ancient Greek civilization: "A world-view according to which nothing of which the final cause was not given (and eternally given) in reality could come into existence; i.e., nothing could come into being except as or by the individual realization of a fixed universal type that was *always there and always had been there*" (p. 294).

Marx had perhaps anticipated all modern uses in his 1857 *Grundrisse:* "In this first section, where exchange values, money, [and] prices are looked at, commodities *always appear as already present.*" Should one wish to embark on such a project, the history of this key phrase could probably be traced back to an Augustinian *nunc stans.* It is enough for us here to note that its currency in Marxist thought is at least traceable to Marx (although Althusser nowhere, to my knowledge, cites this passage from the *Grundrisse*). It is important to recognize, also, that Marx is differentiating appearance from existence.

Although Jameson might not be correct in assuming that Althusser is the one who coined the phrase, he is absolutely right in crediting Althusser with giving it the most currency. And it is a term, as Jameson notes, that represents a temporality that "is at once rectified and booby-trapped by a dialectical operation now most commonly associated with poststructural synchronics."[24] Not only is the phrase either ambiguous or redundant, it also acquires quite different meanings when it is taken from phenomenology and applied to grammatology. When applied to political explication, it acquires what I consider a nonsensical meaning, and it certainly belies at least one form of Marxist understanding of historical evolution and ideological formations. But that form of Marxist understanding (mildly humanist and radically historicist) is precisely what Althusser seems intent on controverting. Part of his strategy in attempting to disrupt those humanist and historicist readings of the classical Marxist texts rests on his strategical use of the term *always-already*.

In discussing the theater of Bertolazzi and Brecht, Althusser contends that there are "forms of temporality that do not achieve any mutual integration, which have no relation to one another, which coexist and interconnect, but never meet each other, so to speak" (*For Marx*, p. 142). In his later *Reading Capital*, Althusser develops this insight by contesting what he calls the two "essential characteristics of Hegelian historical time." He claims, first of all, that the "homogenous continuity of time is the reflection in existence of the continuity of the dialectical development of the Idea." He then claims that the Hegelian notion of the "contemporaneity of time, or the category of the historical *present*," is, in fact, the "condition of possibility" for the idea of the continuity of time. The "present," he concludes, "is never anything but the phenomenon of the presence of the concept with itself in all its concrete determinations" (pp. 94–95). What makes the Hegelian idea of time so noxious for Althusser is that it is "borrowed from the most vulgar empiricism, the empiricism of the false obviousness of everyday practice" (p. 96). Althusser begins his reformulation of classical Hegelian temporality by arguing for what he calls the "Marxist totality" of the "structure in dominance" (*For Marx*, pp. 203–06).

According to Althusser, Hegel proposed a totality that was premised on the idea of a simple unity devoid of any meaningful contradiction: "Every concrete difference featured in the Hegelian totality . . . [is] negated as soon as [it is] affirmed." These "differ-ences," he notes, "are all equally 'indifferent.'" Its second flaw was that the totality did not correspond to any recognizable social structure: "The totality of Hegelian society is such that its princi-ple is simultaneously immanent to it and transcendent of it, but it never coincides in itself with any determinate reality of society itself." Against this model, Marx proposed a totality in which the basic principle was the "structure in dominance" (*structure à domi-nante*), which is, Althusser asserts, "the absolute precondition for a real complexity to be a unity and really the object of a *practice* that proposes to transform this structure: political practice." The Marx-ist totality is rife with meaningful contradictions precisely because of its architectonics, namely the model of the "structure in domi-nance": "The structure of the whole and therefore the 'difference' of the essential contradictions and their structure in dominance is the very existence of the whole." Only within the model of the Marxist totality of the "structure in dominance" can one find the reflection of the "conditions of existence of the contradiction with-in itself." And that, Althusser contends, "is the most profound characteristic of the Marxist dialectic" (*For Marx*, pp. 203–06). Thus, Althusser uses the model of the "structure in dominance" to controvert the two essential characteristics of the "Hegelian idea of time" (*Reading Capital*, p. 96).

Once the Marxist totality is posited, it becomes impossible to maintain the "Hegelian category of the contemporaneity of the *pres-ent*." The "co-existence of the different structured levels" of this totality, Althusser maintains, cannot be thought of in terms of "the ideological present in which temporal presence coincides with the presence of the essence with its phenomena." In other words, the classical concept of continuous time is inadequate to represent the multifaceted temporality of the different levels of the Marxist to-tality. So far, Althusser is simply maintaining what Marx had inti-mated in his comment in the *Grundrisse*—that the presence of a phenomenon (of the commodity, for instance) is only an appear-ance. Althusser, however, goes on to conclude that "in consequence" of this appearance, the whole "model of a *continuous and homoge-neous time* which takes the place of immediate existence, which is the place of the immediate existence of this continuing presence, can no longer be regarded as the time of history." The different levels of the Marxist totality—the economic infrastructure and the ideological superstructures—operate in different times and are in different stages of historical evolution. As Althusser argues, because each level does not have "the same type of historical existence," we cannot therefore "think the process of the development of the different levels of the whole *in the same historical time*." Each level, he maintains, has its own "peculiar time" (*Reading Capital,* p. 99). He argues, then, that "we must, of absolute necessity, pose the question of the mode of existence of *invisible* times, of the invisible rhythms and punctuations concealed beneath the surface of each visible time." Finally, he concludes that this "time, as a complex 'intersection' of the different times, rhythms, turnovers . . . is only accessible in *its concept,* which like every concept is never immediately 'given,' never *legible* in visible reality: like every concept this concept must be *produced, constructed*" (p. 101). In the end, if such a phrase still has any meaning now, time or, more accurately (as Althusser argues), "this concept of differential temporality" is only an epistemological category in a basic theory of the structural intricacy of the Marxist totality. Having elucidated the necessity of rethinking the Hegelian concept of time in the wake of Marx's "Copernican revolution," Althusser turns to what is the final object of his interrogation—the relationship of a "differential temporality" to the concepts of synchrony and diachrony.[25]

Given Marx's intervention in the ideological conception of time, it becomes clear, Althusser writes, that "the synchrony/diachrony opposition is the site of a misconception." Once stripped of this misconception, the opposition can be rearticulated accurately. The "synchronic is then nothing but *the conception* of the specific relations that exist between the different elements and the different structures of the structure of the whole, it is the *knowledge* of the relations of dependence and articulation which make it an organic whole, a system" (*Reading Capital,* p. 107). Like synchrony, diachrony also operates only in the realm of theory: "Diachrony is then merely the false name for the *process,* or for what Marx called the *development of forms*." But here, too, Althusser affirms, "we are *within knowledge,* in the process of knowledge, not in the development of the real-concrete" (p. 108). To conclude his explication of Marx's philosophy, Althusser sums up the meaning of *synchrony.* "When I say that 'synchrony' thus understood is primary and governs everything, I mean two things." First of all, "that the system of the hierarchy of concepts in their combination determines the definition of each concept, as a function of its place and function in the system." Secondly, "that the system of the hierarchy of concepts determines the 'diachronic' order of their appearance in the discourse of the proof." But these concepts, he again emphasizes, are operational only in theory—"existing purely inside knowledge" (pp. 67–68). Based on the distinction between what is outside knowledge and what is inside, and on the distinction between the "knowledge effect" and the "concrete-real," the "synchrony," writes Althusser, is "eternity" (p. 108).

To demonstrate that Marx himself distinguished between the "concrete real" and the "process of knowledge," and that the synchrony is then indeed "eternity," Althusser quotes a passage from *The Poverty of Philosophy:* "How, indeed, could the single logical formula of movement, of sequence, of time, explain the body of society, in which all economic relations co-exist simultaneously and support one another?" Althusser concludes that "this is really what synchrony is."[26] This passage from Marx's early work (1847) seems hardly capable of sustaining the significance Althusser gives it. In fact, only a few paragraphs earlier, Marx had disputed the preconditions of a synchronic analysis. Having expressed a preliminary theory of historical materialism in his first observation on Proudhon's work—"the movement of history produces social relations" (*Poverty of Philosophy,* p. 106)—Marx concludes his second observation by noting that the "only immutable thing is the abstraction of movement" (p. 110). Otherwise, as he writes, "these ideas, these categories, are as little eternal as the relations they express. They are *historical and transitory products*" (p. 110). In this he is repeating what he had written a year earlier in a letter to P. V. Annenkov: "The economic forms in which men produce, consume, and exchange, are *transitory and historical*" (p. 182). In other words, if, as Althusser contends, the "synchronic is eternity," then Marx will have nothing to do with the "synchronic"—even in analyzing "economic forms." Rather than denying the premises of a Hegelian conception of time, Marx simply inverts their idealism into his materialism. Because economic forms, along with all ideas and all categories, are historical and transitory, they can be understood only in terms of their movement (in terms, that is, of the concept of diachrony). As Marx says in the *Grundrisse* about another category of his science, "Since labour is motion, time is its natural measure" (p. 205). When in *The Poverty of Philosophy* he writes that "all history is nothing but a continuous transformation of human nature," he presupposes, I would argue, that time is also its natural measure.[27]

The problem with Althusser's synchronics, as Jameson has noted about poststructural synchronics in general, is that it is a "booby-trapped" model. In the case of Althusser, this occurs in the shift from theory to the concrete-real. After he notes the first of the two things he means in his use of synchrony, Althusser concludes that it "is this definition of the place and function of the concept in the totality of the system which is reflected in the immanent *meaning* of this concept, when we put it in one-to-one correspondence with its real category" (*Reading Capital*, p. 68). In other words, after emphatically asserting that the categories of synchrony and diachrony are radically theoretical, and not correspondent to the concrete-real, Althusser reverses his direction and argues that their reality is immanent in the structural model that he has been arguing is only within thought. It is a form of thinking that can rightly be called "Hegelian." When we come to Althusser's most mature exploration of the workings of the ideological state apparatus, we will find in what ways he has refined the term *always-already* into a system of synchronics necessary for representing his model of ideological interpellation. First, though, we have to examine his other presupposition—namely, that history has no subject.

I began my examination of Althusser's theory of temporality by noting a sentence in *For Marx*: "What makes *such and such* an event *historical* is not the fact that it is an *event,* but precisely its *insertion into forms which are themselves historical.*" The first form, as I noted, was temporality. The second form is subjectivity. Étienne Balibar spells out the relationship between the two forms: "Just as, in Althusser's words, there are different *times* in the social structure, none of which is the reflection of a common fundamental time, so for the same reason, i.e., what has been called the *complexity* of the Marxist totality, there are different forms of political, economic, and ideological individuality in the social structure, too" (*Reading Capital*, p. 252). In other words, the Marxist totality not only causes a revolution in the conception of time, but also in the conception of the potential relationship between the economic infrastructure and the subject in history. As Althusser writes in *Reading Capital*, "the *historical* fact, as opposed to all other phenomena that occur in historical existence, can be defined as *a fact* which causes a mutation in the existing structural relations" (p. 102). And, as he implies, because no individual can do that, no individual can be a historical fact. Hence, history sans subject.[28]

In a less abbreviated form, Althusser's argument goes as follows. The economic is, of course, the base in Marxist thought. In Althusser's model of the Marxist totality of the "structure in dominance," the economic assumes the place of "a structured region occupying its peculiar place in the global structure of the whole." Because it "functions as a regional *structure*," the economic "determines its effects." In other words, it is the structure in dominance. Althusser spells out the significance of that structural alignment in terms of the basic structure/subject Marxist debate:

> The structure of the relations of production determines the *places* and *functions* occupied and adopted by the agents of production, who are never anything more than the occupants of these places, insofar as they are the "supports" (*Träger*) of these functions. The true "subjects" (in the sense of constitutive subjects of the process) are therefore not these occupants or functionaries, are not, despite all appearances, the "obviousnesses" of the "given" of naïve anthropology, "concrete individuals," "real men"—but *the definition and distribution of these places and functions. The true 'subjects' are these definers and distributors: the relations of production* (and political and ideological social relations). But since these are "relations," they cannot be thought within the category *subject*. (*Reading Capital,* p. 180)

Because the Marxist totality of the structure in dominance has hitherto been misunderstood, Althusser dismisses the conventional form of interrogating the relationship between individuality and history. Instead of asking about "the role of the individual in history," he asks rather about the *"historical forms of existence of individuality"* (p. 112). The answer to that problem, according to Althusser, is that the capitalist mode of production constructs the "different forms of individuality required . . . according to functions, of which the individuals are 'supports' (*Träger*)." Again, Althusser is adamant about maintaining that the subject is never anything more than the dependent effect of the structure.

Once the subject is elided from the Marxist model, there remains a single problem for those theorists who come down on the structure side of the debate, as Althusser so resonantly does—how to explain historical change. We can return to Althusser's original tenet and discover there the implicit answer: how does one define a historical fact, which he defines as "a fact which causes a mutation in the existing structural relations"? The answer, implicit obviously in the form of the question, is that one defines a historical fact as "a fact which causes a mutation in the existing structural relations." And this answer, he proclaims, is "entirely summed up in the concept of '*Darstellung*,' the key epistemological concept of the whole Marxist theory of value, the concept whose object is precisely to designate the mode of *presence* of the structure in its *effect,* and therefore to designate structural causality itself" (*Reading Capital,* p. 188).[29] In other words, the subject is merely an effect of the structure, especially of the structure in dominance, and causality operates only within the structure—even when it appears that the effects are the causes.

There are numerous ways of raising objections to Althusser's solution. Hayden White, for instance, notes that Marx's conception of history is "dialectical-materialistic" precisely because it conceived of "the processes of the Base of society mechanistically and the processes of the Superstructure Organicistically." In accordance with the basic difference between the two processes, Marx "emplotted" all "historical progress on two levels." On the level of the base, there is indeed a "succession of distinctive means of production and of the modes of their relationships, a succession that is governed by strict causal laws." On the level of the superstructure, however, there is a "genuine *progressus,*" which consists of a "deepening of human consciousness' perception of man's alienation from himself and from his fellow man and a corresponding development of the social conditions within which that alienation can be transcended."[30] In other words, because the Marxist totality is comprised of different levels operating in various stages of historical evolution (a point Althusser can hardly contest, since it is his), there would concomitantly be different histories with assorted forms of relations between causality and subjectivity.

Moreover, White's reading finds its first exponent in Engels, whose letter to J. Bloch has long been regarded as the standard piece of evidence for the exponents of the subject side in the subject/structure debate. As Engels writes,

According to the materialist conception of history, the *ultimately* determining element in history is the production and reproduction of real life. More than this neither Marx nor I have ever asserted. Hence if somebody twists this into saying that the economic element is the *only* determining one, he transforms that proposition into a meaningless, abstract, senseless phrase. The economic situation is the basis, but the various elements of the superstructure . . . also exercise their influence upon the course of the historical struggles and in many cases preponderate in determining their *form*.[31]

Althusser spends many pages of his early work attempting to demonstrate why Engels is here dealing with a "false" problem, concluding that Engels began at the *wrong level*. In other words, because Engels did not begin at the level of the base ("precisely that level at which *its concepts find a content*"), he was doomed to come to a philosophical rather than a scientific conclusion. As Althusser anathematizes him, "Engels is merely a *philosopher*" (*For Marx*, pp. 111-13, 117-28). Keeping in mind the conjunction Marx (and Engels) had made between philosophy and onanism in *The German Ideology*, this is two-handed criticism indeed. Nonetheless, Althusser's dismissal of Engels, and his explication of the reasons Engels reached the conclusion he did, is hardly criticism sufficient to its purpose. It does not account for the conclusion White reaches—that the presuppositions about the role of human volition and agency in historical movement are different at different levels—which seems eminently sensible, given Althusser's resolute distinction between the two levels. It is also the conclusion warranted by what Marx said.

In *The German Ideology*, Marx noted that the "first premise of all human history is, of course, the existence of living human individuals. . . . The writing of history must always set out from these natural bases and their modification in the course of history through the action of men" (p. 42). But this, it will be claimed by those who read Marx after Althusser, is an early work of Marx's and therefore has no place in the full expression of the model of Marx's theoretical maturity. One can, of course, with the support of Lentricchia, discount Althusser's formulaic breakdown of Marx's career—"I am insisting, against Louis Althusser, that we read with no break inserted between *Capital* and the work prior to 1845" (*Criticism and Social Change*, p. 95). And one may do so, indeed, by finding those articulations in Marx's late work (as defined by Althusser's calendar) which support the reading provided by Engels and White.

In the *Grundrisse*, for instance, Marx makes individual subjectivity (as opposed to subjection to capital) possible in both a precapitalist economic formation—"the individual relates to himself as proprietor, as master of the conditions of his reality"—and a postcapitalist economic formation—when the possession of "free time" has "naturally transformed its possessor into a different subject, and he then enters into the direct production process as this different subject" (pp. 471, 712; cf. pp. 272, 296, 298, 323, 463, 515, 708). The process between these two historical moments is, as Marx noted in *Capital*, "accomplished through the action of the immanent laws of capitalist production itself, through the centralization of capitals" (p. 929). And an examination of Marx's comments on the "original accumulation of capital" in the *Grundrisse* demonstrates that he has located this site of accumulation and centralization as the place where the subject emerges into consciousness (pp. 463–65). Marx concludes his consideration of the original accumulation of capital by demonstrating the process by which labor's alienation from its "own life's expression" (*Lebensäusserung*) subtly becomes labor's "recognition" (*Erkennung*), its "realization" (*Verwertung*), and its "awareness" (*Bewusstsein*) of the process by which the "objective conditions of labour attain a subjective existence *vis-á-vis* living labour capacity" (pp. 462–63). The base, then, is the ultimate determinant, but not the only one. The consciousness of resistant labor, an impossibility according to Althusser, an element of the superstructure able to exercise influence on "historical struggles," according to Engels and White, is another form of historical movement. In the preface to the first edition of *Capital*, Marx claims that his examination in this volume will be limited to the "economic" and that, therefore, "individuals are dealt with here only in so far as they are the personifications of economic categories." He concludes that paragraph, however, by noting that in his system the individual is not responsible for "relations whose creature he remains, socially speaking, however much he may subjectively raise himself above them" (*Capital*, p. 92). In sum, then, Marx, as Engels acutely pointed out, does not make the claim for the economic as the unique and only determinant, but as the ultimate one. There is presupposed throughout his late work, as Marx explicitly states here, the possibility for any individual to rise "subjectively" above the basic constraints of those relations. This is a point, however, which Althusser spends much energy attempting to subordinate to his model of the Marxist totality, especially in his most famous essay, "Ideology and Ideological State Apparatus."

When Althusser presents his model of how history exists without a subject, he makes two gestures. First of all, in presenting how a capitalist state maintains its operation, Althusser notes that the state must reproduce the means of production as well as reproducing the conditions of production. The means of production signifies the material reproduction of labor power through wages and children. The conditions of production suggest the ideological apparatus necessary for keeping labor power submissive to the rules of the established order. That operation falls properly into the category of ideological subjection, and works through what Althusser calls the "ideological state apparatus." The role of ideology, then, is primarily to deceive laborers into submission. In two notable equations, Althusser writes that "ideology = an imaginary relation to real relations," and that "ideology = misrecognition/ ignorance." Between these two equations, he presents a model and an example of how subjection works.[32]

The model is presented in the form of a staggered Aristotelian syllogism, but its functioning depends on a subtle process of rhetorical accretion. For that reason, it is worth exploring the stages Althusser establishes in his categorical attempt to deny subjectivity. To begin, Althusser offers us the formulation of a "subject with a consciousness which contains the ideas of his belief." This subject may have beliefs about God, duty, justice, or whatever. What matters is that, in this instance, the subject possesses "a consciousness in which he freely forms or freely recognizes ideas in which he believes." This subject is granted the power of willing, of choosing, and of cognition. Moreover, the subject acts in accord with his or her beliefs. The subject believing in God attends church, believing in duty fulfills responsibilities, and believing in justice obeys laws. The basic premise underlying everything so far stated is that beliefs without action are either hypocritical or wicked and to be hypocritical or wicked is less worthy than being sincere or good, and being worthy is important for the subject. The "ideology of ideology," Althusser notes, speaks about "actions inserted into *practices*," which in turn are governed by "*rituals* in which these practices are inscribed, within the *material existence of an ideological apparatus*." At the end of this first stage of explora-

tion, Althusser concludes that actions are the determinants of belief—that is, the "ideology of ideology" (*Lenin and Philosophy*, pp.
167–69).

In his second stage, Althusser reflects on the original subject. If
all the subject's ideas lead to actions, what may be said about the
subject's freedom to choose and to think? Althusser reformulates
the subject's position in this second instance: "His ideas are his
material actions inserted into material practices governed by material rituals which are themselves defined by the material ideological
apparatus from which derive the ideas of that subject." Those ideas
that had been the product of the subject's free thinking are now
seen to be the derivative effects of an ideological apparatus. That
is, the subject believes in God, for instance, because it is effective
for the state's attempt to keep that subject submissive. When Althusser reformulates the subject and elides the subject's "ideas," he
sets out a wholly new concept of the subject. Without ideas, the
subjects no longer have liberty of agency or cognitive freedom,
but, rather, they become "effects" of a larger order: "It therefore
appears that the subject acts insofar as he is acted by the following
system" (*Lenin and Philosophy*, p. 170). At the end of his second
stage, Althusser develops two theses and makes one final reformulation in his thinking on the subject. The first thesis is that
"there is no practice except by and in an ideology." His second
thesis is that "there is no ideology except by the subject and for
subjects." The reformulated subject, within the standards of subjection established by these two premises, loses what had been the
hallmark of subjectivity (ideas and agency), and now becomes nothing other than an operational category. At the end of this second
stage, then, one no longer speaks about a subject since Althusser
subtly transforms the entity into a categorical function: "This destination for ideology is only made possible by the subject: meaning, *by the category of the subject* and its functioning" (p. 171).

From these two theses and with the reformulated "category of
the subject," Althusser then presents his theory of interpellation.
Even so, at this level and at this point in his argument (the third
stage), Althusser does not deny that subjects might *become* subjects. What ideology does, he offers as a tentative premise, is constitute "concrete individuals as subjects" (*Lenin and Philosophy*, p.
171). So far, then, the model does not deny that there are two
possible states for any self—the individual and the subject. Given

the possibility of having two separate states, the model still allows for a free choice of whether or not an individual chooses to become a subject. However, Althusser quickly forecloses that possibility. All individual selves, he offers as an answer to his earlier premise, are *"always already* subjects" (p. 172). To prove this final formulation of the category of the subject, he embarks on an explanation of his model of interpellation: *"all ideology hails or interpellates concrete individuals as concrete subjects,* by the functioning of the category of the subject" (p. 173). Having granted that there are two possible states — individuality and subjection — he goes on to define interpellation as the method by which individuals are "recruited" or "transformed" into subjects. And his intent is to show that they were "always already subjects." To that end he presents a pedestrian model and a Christian example of interpellation (p. 174).

The first model of interpellation involves the explanation of what Althusser means by "hailing." As an example of how interpellation functions, Althusser describes how a police officer hails the individual walking down the street: "Hey, you there." The hailed individual turns around to hear who is calling and in this "mere one-hundred-and-eighty-degree physical conversion, he becomes a *subject*" (p. 174). He becomes a subject simply because he has "recognized" that the hailing was really addressed to him. What is left unclear by Althusser is why hearkening to an ambiguous call should mean an irrevocable submission to subjection. After all, this scenario does provide many alternatives. The person hailed does not have to turn around; or, after turning around, the individual may renounce the subjection and simply keep on walking. These alternatives are based on another premise — that there is a choice involved in whether an individual will or will not become a subject. That is, these alternatives are available only in a narrative model. And, despite the appearance of having narrative form, this pedestrian model, Althusser insists, eschews its narrative elements: "in reality these things happen without any succession. The existence of ideology and the hailing or interpellation of individuals as subjects are one and the same thing" (p. 175).

Even though the only example Althusser could find to represent his model of interpellation has a narrative form, he denies it the essential quality of narrative liberty. In the narrative of the police officer and the pedestrian, the individual pedestrian has a choice about whether or not to turn around. In any representation of a temporal sequence, there must reside an essential moment of choice (which usually carries with it the premise of a freedom to choose). But against the preconditions of the narrative model, Althusser's scientific model simply presents an eternal moment in which all actions occur on the basis of the stated fact that "ideology is eternal," or nontemporal. What is immediately striking is that Althusser chooses to represent a synchronic phenomenon in a diachronic narrative form; in fact, even the acts of recruitment and transformation involve narrative form (that is, they operate in time). Of course, it is not so curious a choice since there is simply no synchronic form analogous to his theory of how ideology interpellates its subjects. That is, Althusser's model has no model. Or, if we grant that the model works to explain its theory, then we must insist that the model undermines the theory since the pedestrian does have options precisely because he or she is operating in time.

Let us grant that Althusser might have a theory, even though he does not yet have an analogy. His argument is that because ideology is eternal and operates in a nontemporal fashion, it has "always already" constituted its subjects. In his concluding syllogism, Althusser presents his final formulation of the subject in ideology:

> Ideology has always-already interpellated individuals as subjects, which amounts to making it clear that individuals are always-already interpellated by ideology as subjects, which necessarily leads us to one last proposition: *individuals are always-already subjects*. Hence individuals are "abstract" with respect to the subjects which they always-already are. (Pp. 175–76)

In effect, then, Althusser concludes by noting that there is only one possible role for any citizen of a state—as subject. The subject never was anything but a subject, and there was no choice and no moment of transformation in the assumption of that subjection. To prove the sheer eternity of ideology in his argument, Althusser goes so far as to argue that individuals are always-already subjects before they are born. On the evidence that every child is born into a name (the "Father's Name"), into a form of "familial ideological configuration," and into a system of gender identification, Althusser concludes that even before "its birth, the child is therefore always-already a subject" (p. 176).

Aside from an inability to find an analogy or even a nonsubversive form for demonstrating its theory, Althusser's pedestrian model of interpellation has other problems. First of all, Althusser maintains that because all individuals are always- already subjects they are "acted by" ideology. In this system, it is impossible to say that an individual acts against his or her subjection to the state because the agency of acting has already been elided. So, taking Althusser's model to its logical conclusion, ideology encompasses even the forms of resistance exercised by its subjects against its own workings. An act of rebellion is but another form of a subject's being "acted by" the ideological apparatus. In effect, ideology becomes a system which possesses its own undermining agency. While it is probably true that most systems do possess the qualities that will lead to their own undoing, and this is a lesson Marx, more than anyone else, has taught us, there is nonetheless a problem in asserting that each system can be undone *only* by its own set of its own rules.

In the first instance, part of the problem is Althusser's use of the all-encompassing term *ideology* to refer to any practice — whether or not it is beneficial to the state's reproduction of its labor force. This usage might well be liable to Adorno's critique of the "indiscriminately total concept of ideology," which "terminates in nothingness."[33] Moreover, one suspects that in Althusser's model there is an unstated premise that the state has its own subjectivity and understands its own best interests; that, of course, is something Marx criticized Hegel for proposing and something history book after history book makes patently ridiculous. At the basis of this first problem, though, is a much more important problem: What status does a revolutionary have when he or she is being revolutionary? According to Althusser, the revolutionary is always-already a subject. So a revolutionary acting against the reproduction of a state's mode of production is still acting within ideology and is still subject to the state. What Althusser has failed to provide is a model whereby subjects may deny their subjection in acts of resistance to the state apparatus. That would entail providing two roles, the role of individual and the role of subject, and assuming the possibility that an individual has a choice in maintaining or rejecting the role of subject.

Using Althusser's pedestrian example, we could present an imaginary case in which individuals would not turn around when they are hailed, thereby refusing the state's subjection. To account for such resistance, we propose that an individual who does not turn around, who chooses not to accept the state's invitation to work within its explicit ideological functioning, remains an individual. That individual is not subject to the state—at least not in terms of the state's ideological apparatus. That person obviously is still subject to the state's repressive apparatus—its police and military force, and its power over the bodies of its citizens. To carry the model further, if the pedestrian refuses to hearken to the hailing and refuses thereby to be "recruited" or "transformed" from an individual into a subject, he or she might be carried off to jail. In this example, the state would be using its repressive apparatus because of the failure of its ideological apparatus. There must be another name and another state of being for the pedestrian who refuses subjection. I propose to employ the name Althusser has already given him or her—the "individual self."

Althusser's second attempt involves what he calls the "example" of the "Christian Religious Ideology," although it should be more precisely described as a model of Mosaic interpellation. First of all, Althusser maintains that the category of the *individual* is nonexistent, although the term does prove to be "convenient because of the contrasting effect it produces" (*Lenin and Philosophy,* p. 178). From there he goes on to argue a point he had not made during his earlier exploration—namely, the function of the state in the interpellation of subjects. The model he uses is the relationship between God and a religious subject: "There can only be such a multitude of possible religious subjects on the absolute condition that there is a Unique, Absolute, *Other Subject,* i.e. God" (p. 178). The way that the Absolute Subject interpellates subjects is still by hailing (calling). The example Althusser uses is the Old Testament scene in which God calls the "individual named Moses." Moses responds by recognizing that God has called him, and he therefore "recognizes that he is a subject, a subject *of* God, a subject subjected to God, *a subject through the Subject and subjected to the Subject*" (p. 179). It is important to notice the rhetorical accretion here. From being a "subject," Moses eventually suffers "subjection." The "proof" that Moses has been interpellated, according to Althusser, is that "he obeys" God.

The structure of this interpellation, as of all ideological interpellations, involves what Althusser calls "a mirror structure." It is a "speculary" structure—in fact, doubly so because the Absolute

Subject "interpellates around it the infinity of individuals into subjects in a double mirror-connexion such that it *subjects* the subjects to the Subject, while giving them in the Subject in which each subject can contemplate his own image (present and future) the *guarantee* that this really concerns them and Him" (p. 180). This mirror structure ensures, therefore, that ideology is self-perpetuating. Althusser finishes his analysis of the Christian example by schematizing the "quadruple system of interpellation":

> 1. the interpellation of "individuals" as subjects;
> 2. their subjection to the Subject;
> 3. the mutual recognition of subjects and Subject, the subjects' recognition of each other, and finally the subject's recognition of himself;
> 4. the absolute guarantee that everything really is so, and that on condition that the subjects recognize what they are and behave accordingly, everything will be all right: Amen—"*So be it.*" (P. 181)

Having elaborated this scheme, Althusser returns to distinguish what he had earlier conflated—the difference between subjectivity (being a *subject of* something) and subjection (being *subject to* something).

The "mystery" of interpellation, he writes, resides in the first two moments of the quadruple system, and it rightly resides in the ambiguity of the term *subject*. As he notes, the term refers to two quite different qualities: "(1) a free subjectivity, a centre of initiatives, author of and responsible for its actions; (2) a subjected being, who submits to a higher authority, and is therefore stripped of all freedom except that of freely accepting his submission." In the final argument, however, Althusser says there is no "ambiguity" but merely "a reflection of the effect which produces it." The subject is always-already subject still; freedom is merely an illusion in parentheses: "The individual *is interpellated as a (free) subject in order that he shall submit freely to the commandments of the Subject, i.e. in order that he shall (freely) accept his subjection,* i.e. in order that he shall make the gestures and actions of his subjection 'all by himself.' *There are no subjects except by and for their subjection.* That is why they 'work all by themselves'" (*Lenin and Philosophy,* p. 182). This is Althusser's concluding statement on how interpellation works. What seemed a radical difference between two forms of being a subject turns out to be merely an effect of the ideological order's workings. There is no substantial freedom, only an apparent one.

Some of the basic foundational problems in Althusser's argument can be found in his denial of the difference between subjectivity and subjection. First of all, it is important to have distinct phrases for describing subjectivity and subjection; to do so we might adopt Althusser's usage, which can be traced back to at least Hobbes. Subjectivity involves the precondition of the individual's having a choice to become a *subject of* something, while subjection involves the precondition of the subject's being already *subject to* something. In the end, in Althusser's model, there is no possibility available to any individual to be a subject of ideology; all are subject to ideology.

Second, the Christian analogy of how ideology interpellates its subjects simply does not work because a state cannot be compared to the traditional idea of the Judeo-Christian divine being. The state does not promise an eternal rest, and it has no way of scrutinizing the individual resolve of any subject. The state can govern only the body; it educates the mind so that it promotes submission to its order. But such education cannot wholly regulate the thinking of any individual who goes through the system. For example, despite undergoing the most thoroughly ideological of educations, a given citizen of the state may still think that some act the state forbids is not so heinous as the state makes it out to be. The state does nothing about that thought as long as the citizen does not commit the forbidden act. Once belief is inscribed in practice, the state will employ its repressive apparatus. In other words, while it is true that an individual's ideas are determined by material practices—or, as Marx more precisely puts it, "social existence" determines "consciousness"—it is also true that the state can govern *only* material practices. This is a fairly important difference because it means that Althusser's original elision of the individual's ability "freely" to think an "idea" was based on what Marx would call a subject-predicate inversion, a concept I will discuss in relation to *Samson Agonistes* in chapter 4.

Moreover, in the Christian example, belief is the most important element of an individual's being. It is expected that a Christian will not perform practices that are contrary to a Christian life, but what is more important, in either a Protestant or a Catholic setting, is that the individual believes. In a Protestant case, faith is more important than works, and therefore salvation is based on a scheme in which inner promptings weigh more heavily than failures to perform appropriate material actions. In a Catholic case, bad works may be remedied by applying or performing appropriate good works; but, nonetheless, the premise is that the sinner must have faith in order to admit that the first work was bad and to pursue ways of remedying it by good works. Whether or not it may be representative of contemporary Christian communities, Pascal's model of acting as if one believed is not the Christian norm. In the end, then, Althusser's model fails because the state is not omniscient; it can scrutinize only material actions. The traditional Judeo-Christian God is omniscient and can scrutinize beliefs as well as actions.

Thus, Althusser's analogy of a state's having godlike powers is both unconvincing as well as dangerous, because it proposes a model of the state that prevents individual skepticism about the state's human basis. Althusser is doing just what the early Marx criticized Hegel for doing and the late Marx criticized Ricardo for suggesting. As Marx writes in his 1843 critique of Hegel, "The affairs of state are nothing but the modes of action and existence of the social qualities of men." Once one assumes that the "political state" is something "existing apart from civil society," which means assuming that an ideological apparatus may work abstractly from the economic transfer of the citizens of the state, one enters into what Marx tellingly calls "the *theological* conception of the political state." Or, as Marx writes more generally in his 1857 *Grundrisse,* whoever takes "as the *natural properties* of things what are social relations of production among people" and thereby "imputes social relations to things as inherent characteristics, and thus mystifies them" is falling into a crude idealism, even, as Marx here first calls it, into a "fetishism." That, in every sense, is what Althusser does in his theory of interpellation.[34]

Third, I wish to note that, once again, Althusser could find only a narrative form to demonstrate his non-narrative, nontemporal, nonsequential model of interpellation. The moment between God's calling and Moses' replying is, after all, a moment in which Moses exercises his choice to respond. In fact, Moses was a subject of another ideology before God called him. Only after God called Moses did Moses establish certain ritual practices, such as circumcision. Before that moment of vocation, Moses had inscribed his beliefs in material practices of another ideology. So what this model allows is that one may change ideologies; one has a choice. Given that this is a model allowing freedom of choice, both because it is a temporal narrative and because it demonstrates how an individual was recruited from being subject to one ideology to becoming a subject of another, we can only conclude that Althusser has himself made a rather unfortunate choice. What Althusser gives us here, for the second time, is not what Kenneth Burke would call a "representative anecdote" — to be truly representative it must "be synecdochic rather than metonymic; or, in other words, it must be a *part for the whole* rather than a *reduction of the mental to the physical*." Moreover, an *example* — with due respect to Habermas's argument that "evolution-theoretic explanations" need not be brought into narrative form — must, if it is going to explain a synchronic structure, be capable of representing that structure within its own synchronic form. In every way, then, Althusser's example fails its purpose of demonstrating or representing the workings of ideology as a synchronic structure.[35]

The problem might have begun at the second stage of his elaboration, when Althusser first transformed the subject from an entity into a categorical function. As Burke has reminded us in *The Philosophy of Literary Form*, when "one talks of 'functions,' one necessarily brings in nonhistoric assumptions of structure." Not only does Althusser do precisely that; he goes so far as to essentialize nonhistoricity. For example, Burke noted that one way of explaining *essence* narratively is to represent it in terms of "*temporal* priority." This discursive strategy, which he most fully explained in *A Grammar of Motives*, he calls the "temporizing of essence." In *Language as Symbolic Action*, he elaborates:

> What I am aiming at is to show how the "essence" of motivation ties in with terms of one sort or another for the *temporally* prior, even the temporally primal. I mean: Instead of saying that something "essentially *is*" such-and-such," the narrative style says that "it has been this way from away back," or "it was so from the very beginning."

Although the "temporizing of essence" is clearly a strategy available to both conservative discourses (witness the Edmund Burke of *Reflections on the Revolution in France*) and revolutionary discourses

(Marx in those sections of the *Grundrisse* and *Capital* where he explains the history and prehistory of capital), it is, one would suppose, an especially useful tool for dismantling conservative ideas of immanent structures. In other words, it is a strategy especially useful for a materialist historiography. A materialist dialectician, like Marx, employs precisely this strategy when, for instance, he demonstrates that "the economic structure of capitalist society" is not simply the "one thing fit for all age-groups and all stages of development" (which is what the ideological state apparatus would teach), but rather that it has a history, "the history of . . . expropriation [which] is written in the annals of mankind in letters of blood and fire."[36] What Marx does is dismantle supposedly immanent structures by historicizing them, by temporalizing essence. Althusser, on the other hand, does not temporalize essence, but rather essentializes temporality, most emphatically in his explanation of the atemporal structure of ideological interpellation and most revealingly in his excessive and ill-considered use of the phrase *always-already*. In that way, he essentializes nonhistoricity.

Fourth, that Moses may make a choice about leaving one ideological formation and entering another suggests something about Althusser's earlier comment about how all subjects are always-already subjects from birth. Just as Moses changes his subjection from idolatry to monotheism, so too can any individual be re-educated to recognize his or her subjection. Althusser's model simply ignores the question of educability. Any individual may change names, if she or he comes to recognize that the "Father's Name" is prohibitive. Furthermore, while it is true that the "familial ideological configuration" does "structure" a child's identity, and especially a child's sexual identity, these constructions are not final. An understanding of how identity is constructed and why this particular identity was constructed—in its historical moment— can lead an individual to an examination that alters that identity or at least recognizes the terms of its construction. What is allowed by entertaining the notion of educability is that subjection is not durative and irrevocable, but that it is possible for any subject to learn and to resist.

Finally, the model I am proposing in juxtaposition to Althusser's involves an ability to choose between various options based on the possibility for re-education. The primary act of such re-education in this narrative model is the potential for self-knowledge. And the possibility for self-knowledge rests on the premise that there is a self which can recognize its subjection and make gestures toward subjectivity. In order for the self to recognize its subjection, it must either imagine or remember another possible state of being. In the case of subjects who have been subjected all their lives, the process has to be imaginative. As in the last century, where an exploited class came to a general consciousness of its exploitation, so each subjected subject must come to a conscious realization of his or her subjection. In the case of a person who has not been subjected his or her entire life—that is, in the case of the pedestrian who was hailed or Moses who was called—the process can be one of anamnesis. The subject may replay in her or his mind the events that led to subjection and remember the time before subjection. In either case, it is self-knowledge. What is worth noticing is the way that Althusser forecloses the place of the self and the process of knowledge.

Althusser notes that there is "recognition" in three instances. First of all, there is the mutual recognition of the subject and Subject. God created the Son because the "Subject needs to become a subject, as if to show empirically, visibly to the eye, tangibly to the hands . . . of the subjects, that, if they are subjects, subjected to the Subject, that is solely in order that finally . . . they will . . . re-enter the Subject" (*Lenin and Philosophy,* p. 180). Christ's coming was an emblem of a final salvation and an eternal rest, but one is hard-pressed to think of an analogous situation in the state. Second, there is the subjects' recognition of each other. Althusser does not explain this, but one assumes that it follows on the heels of the former recognition; that is, this recognition has the effect of promoting individual submission on the evidence that others have already submitted. The third recognition is the most important one for our study—"the subject's recognition of himself." By placing it at the end of the train of knowledge, Althusser suggests that self-knowledge is based on a submissive knowledge of a social situation which is in turn based on a submissive knowledge of an absolute power. In other words, this subject's recognition of himself or herself is not knowledge at all; rather, it is knowledge of only the fact that one is a subject and that there is no way to escape subjection. The term cannot be *self-knowledge* because there is no individual self; nor can it be called *knowledge* so much as it is, in the end, what Althusser rightly calls "*méconnaissance.*" *Méconnaissance*

is also a term Lacan uses avidly in his descriptions of the unconscious.

Althusser insisted that historical materialism was the discovery
that opened up the third continent. He was willing to allow, however, that Freud's discovery of the unconscious may have opened up
"a new continent" (*Lenin and Philosophy,* p. 39). In fact, later he
found it very much to his purpose to propose a continental drift
between Marx and Freud: "*Ideology is eternal,* exactly like the unconscious. And I may add that I find this comparison theoretically
justified by the fact that the eternity of the unconscious is not
unrelated to the eternity of ideology in general" (*Lenin and Philosophy,* p. 161; cf. pp. 195–219). Neither Althusser nor Lacan makes
the relationship between ideology and the unconscious explicit,
but Foucault does. Discussing the way power works on individuals, Foucault writes:

> This form of power applies itself to immediate everyday life which
> categorizes the individual, marks him by his own individuality, at-
> taches him to his own identity, imposes a law of truth on him which
> he must recognize and which others have to recognize in him. It is a
> form of power which makes individuals subjects. There are two mean-
> ings of the word *subject:* subject to someone else by control and
> dependence, and tied to his own identity by a conscience or self-
> knowledge. Both meanings suggest a form of power which subjugates
> and makes subject to.[37]

Before conflating the concepts of subjection and subjectivity by
arguing that their alleged ambiguity is merely an effect of ideology's functioning to give the illusion of liberty, Althusser had at
least conceived of a substantial difference between the two meanings of *subject.* One could be a subject with a consciousness who
initiates and is responsible for one's actions; that is, one could be a
subject of one's Self instead of being subject to an Other. Foucault,
on the other hand, sees that a subject is always subject to something, whether that something be an Other or a Self. That, precisely, is Lacan's discovery.

Subject to Nescience: Lacan and the Cartesian Departure

Like Althusser, Lacan establishes his claims about the significance of psychoanalysis by first establishing its scientificity. What

"specifies a science," he writes, "is having an object." And the object must be available at the "level of operation known as *experiment*." Nonetheless, "experience" in the "sense of a field of praxis" does not in itself "define a science." In Cartesian fashion, Lacan makes *expérience* mean both lived relations and scientific observation. Experience begins to form its own continent when Freud coordinates "experience, *qua* deceiving, with a real that will henceforth be situated in the field of science, situated as that which the subject is condemned to miss." At the basis of its scientificity, Lacanian psychoanalysis poses an individual who is subject to *méconnaissance* concerning his or her lived experience. Lacan goes so far as to insist that no "praxis is more oriented towards that which, at the heart of experience, is the kernel of the real than psycho-analysis." In fact, psychoanalysis exists in a more refined state than science, as it had been defined from Plato to Freud. Psychoanalysis exists, he writes, as a "beyond of science" — as something he calls "Science *itself*."[38]

The unconscious makes psychoanalysis a science. Lacan first defines the function of the unconscious and its relationship to the other features of the analysand: "What the unconscious does is to show us the gap through which neurosis recreates a harmony with a real — a real that may well not be determined." The subject of this sentence is *neurosis;* the psyche has been displaced by its illness. In fact, when Lacan discusses the role of the analysand in psychoanalysis, he defines the object of the analysis with this interesting equation: "psych = fiction of." Lacan then situates the primary function of the unconscious within a historical framework: this "gap of the unconscious may be said to be *pre-ontological*." Like Althusser's ideology, the unconscious in Lacanian science exists in the realm of the "eternal." That, of course, is indeed one of Freud's original and revolutionary tenets. As early as 1915 and as late as 1920, Freud had argued that the "processes of the system *Ucs.* are *timeless;* i.e. they are not ordered temporally, are not altered by the passage of time; they have no reference to time at all." This theory of the unconscious is a refinement of his preliminary formulations in *The Interpretation of Dreams* (1900). Not only is the unconscious atemporal, but it is, as Lacan posits, "pre-ontological." As Freud writes in 1919, "Man's archaic heritage forms the nucleus of the unconscious mind."[39]

The unconscious is also, according to Lacan (but again these are Freud's ideas), "ethical," "inaccessible to contradiction," and wholly freed from "spatio-temporal location." Like Althusser's *ideology,* the unconscious in the end is situated in "the dimension of a synchrony." In fact, according to Lacan, the "very originality of psycho-analysis lies in the fact that it does not centre psychological ontogenesis on the supposed *stages*" of psychical development. Even though Freud apparently did discern stages in an individual's development—from oral to anal to genital to phallic—Lacan argues that, in fact, these stages operate in the synchronic unconscious and therefore are in no way sequential or have any relation to "natural metamorphosis." The basis of that abstraction is what Lacan does beyond Freud—and that is (1) to categorically deny the subject; and (2) to disestablish the possibility for a diachronic exploration of the psyche. As Lacan writes in his famous Rome report, "Psychoanalysis will provide scientific bases for its theory or for its technique only by formalizing in an adequate fashion the essential dimensions of its experience which, together with the historical theory of the symbol, are: intersubjective logic and the temporality of the subject." He sums up his conclusion about why the stages cannot be understood to refer to natural development in children by again remarking on the qualities of the unconscious: "I have been able to articulate the unconscious for you as being situated in the gaps that the distribution of the signifying investments sets up in the subject." Not only is the subject hardly a subject in this sentence, but this sentence follows the one in which Lacan calls the subject a "headless subject." All drives, all supposed stages and tensions—in a word, "everything . . . has no relation to the subject other than one of topological community." That is, the subject is rightly considered under erasure and merely the map onto which a series of significations are inscribed. "It is always a question of the subject *qua* indeterminate."[40] How that subject comes to be indeterminate is, finally, the question on which Lacan most eagerly embarks. With the same sort of logical format Althusser had followed, Lacan also works by formulating four evolving concepts of the subject and, as was the case in the Althusserian model, the subject in the Lacanian model has only a limited relationship to any given individual.

Lacan goes about constituting this subject by first of all appropriating an Aristotelian concept—that of the *tuché*—and redefining it to signify the "encounter with the real" (*Four Fundamental*

Concepts, p. 53). The *real* is that which is beyond the *automaton,* which is another Aristotelian concept Lacan borrows. Aristotle distinguished the *tuché* as having the power of intellect (and therefore choice), whereas the automaton is merely an appetitive being. What Lacan does in borrowing these differentiated categories is elide the basic quality of their difference. He controverts Aristotle's distinction and eliminates the primary quality of the *tuché,* which is *proairesis* — the ability to choose (p. 69). In the end, then, there is no difference between the *tuché* and the *automaton* on the question of being able to exercise will or choice. Ultimately, individuals can be said to be subjects only when they are *automata,* or what amounts to the same thing, annihilated of their subjectivity: "The mode of my presence in the world is the subject in so far as by reducing itself solely to this certainty of being a subject, it becomes active annihilation." This, Lacan insists, is the philosophical culmination — from the emergence of the subject in the work of Descartes to its final annihilation in the works of Martin Heidegger and Maurice Merleau-Ponty (p. 81). The first step to subjection, then, is the operative loss of choice (entailing, obviously, the premise of a free will to choose).

The importance of Lacan's mentioning Merleau-Ponty is that the second formulation of the subject's subjection involves its relationship to perception. The subject, having now lost the will to choose, is indeterminate in a second sense because its appetite is governed only by its sense of perception. And perception gains its "virulent, aggressive function" only insofar as "all human desire is based on castration" (*Four Fundamental Concepts,* p. 118). That is, in this phallic model, what the subject wishes to see is "the object as absence" (p. 182). This gaze aimed at an absent object is a form of "*méconnaissance,* as — using a term that takes on new value by being referred to a visible domain — *scotoma.*" Lacan names the absent object "*objet a,*" which signifies the small "other" whose relation to the large "Other" is of the greatest importance.

In looking at the object, the subject finds itself constituted by its gaze: "In the scopic relation, the object on which depends the phantasy from which the subject is suspended in an essential vacillation is the gaze" (p. 83). The relationship between the perceiving subject, the perceived object, and the agency of perception may be mapped out as follows. The "phantasy" plays the most prominent structural role; from the "phantasy" depends the object, which has as its dependent the subject. But what is the object—that middle piece in this chain? It proves to be the gaze itself: "The object . . . is the gaze." But the gaze is also what constitutes the subject. As Lacan elsewhere notes, "The object, here is the gaze— the gaze that is the subject" (p. 182). We may conclude that the chain really isn't a chain at all, but rather a complex (or tri-level palimpsest) made up of a subject constituted by a gaze looking at itself. In the final analysis, both subject and object lose their status as the gaze becomes, in essence, the drive between them.

In summarizing Lacan's argument so far, we discover that the subject *is* the object; that is, the subject is gazing at itself, wishing it were other. Moreover, the object is absent. "What the voyeur is looking for and finds is merely a shadow, a shadow behind the curtain." Because the object is absence itself, and the subject is the object, then the subject must also be absence itself. The subject, as Lacan concludes, exists in the dimension of "a headless subjec-tification, a subjectification without a subject." The *objet a* had been that at which the subject was gazing, and we noted that the object is eventually discovered to be the subject itself. Now, Lacan tells us, we can understand that the "*objet a* in the field of the visible is the gaze." There has been only one thing in all the chain of the subject, the object, the gaze—all have been only the *objet a*. What, finally, is this *objet a* that plays so prominent a role in this system? Lacan was never explicit about defining this term. In fact, he directed his translators not to translate it so that it would take on the status of what he called an "algebraic sign." At the end of the third formulation of the subject, we discover that the subject has lost the will to choose and has gained the ability to perceive, but in doing so has become the gaze and the object of that gaze.[41]

As his third formulation, Lacan entertains the place of desire in the subject. In fact, Lacan makes desire precisely that drive which replaces *proairesis* in the Aristotelian *tuché*. The "subject in ques-tion is not that of the reflexive consciousness, but that of desire" (*Four Fundamental Concepts*, p. 89). And the *objet a*, as Lacan writes, has the function of symbolizing the "central lack of desire" (p. 105). In the Althusserian model, the subject is incapable of choice because all its ideas had to be inscribed in material prac-tices. This prohibited the concept of self-knowledge by posing a situation in which the self is no self and knowledge is only a problematized misrecognition. Lacan offers a scenario that has some analogous points of agreement with Althusser's. First of all, the subject is incapable of choice because it is subject to desire. Second, desire is not just a lack, but a misrecognition of that lack: "an element necessarily lacking, unsatisfied, impossible, misconstrued (*méconnu*), an element that is called desire" (p. 154). Like ideology, desire in the Althusserian model is based on a subjective *méconnaissance*. The reason desire is misrecognized in the Lacanian model, however, is because of language—and here the Lacanian model begins to differ somewhat from the Althusserian.

In his fourth and final formulation of the subject, Lacan notes that the function of desire "is a last residuum of the effect of the signifier in the subject. *Desidero* is the Freudian *cogito*" (p. 154). Having now defined the cognitive system of desire—signification—Lacan's model of the unconscious takes on its final, complete shape. In an essay of 1958, Lacan had suggested that "language . . . structures everything concerning relations between human beings." By 1964, following tenets he had first elaborated in his 1953 Rome report, Lacan undertakes a full articulation of the ramifications of that thesis. He begins by analyzing the structure of that entity which is the object of his science. "The unconscious is the sum of the effects of speech on a subject, at the level at which the subject constitutes himself out of the effects of the signifier." But, even so, the subject is still not a subject in, say, the Cartesian sense of subjectivity, because signification is a system based on differences and gaps. A subject whose attempts at self-knowledge rest on signifying desire will ultimately be involved in a subjectification without subjectivity. As Lacan boldly puts it, "a subject, through his relations with the signifier, is a subject-with-holes (*sujet troué*)."[42] Lacan presents, thus, a "subjectless subject" working within a system of signification. Finally, having defined the factors of subjection, Lacan establishes the original synchrony of the unconscious in order to argue that the subject has always-already been subject to desire in signification.

The subject is indeterminate, Lacan argues, because it is "split," "alienated," and, finally, subject to misrecognition. First of all, the subject is split when it enters the realm of language because any entity entering the field of language must deal with the way language disperses *being* at two distinct levels. Using the Cretan paradox as his example, Lacan notes that it is logically impossible to say "I am lying." With de Saussure, then, Lacan distinguishes between

the "I" of the "enunciation" (*énonciation*) and the "I" of the "statement" (*énoncé*) (*Four Fundamental Concepts,* p. 139). This entire
communication operates in the analysis, and so the analysand (the
"I") is addressing the analyst (whom Lacan had called "that other
who is the analyst" [p. 124]) and, indeed, is trying to keep the
analyst from recognizing what the analysand cannot understand.
This whole operation is for the analysand a game of attempting to
misrecognize misrecognition. Of course, the analyst does have
some eminent talents, and so the analyst is able to understand the
"I." The process of that understanding is worth noting in detail:

> The division between the statement and the enunciation means that,
> in effect, from the *I am lying* which is at the level of the chain of the
> statement—the *am lying* is a signifier, forming part, in the Other, of
> the treasury of vocabulary in which the *I,* determined retroactively,
> becomes a signification, engendered at the level of the statement, of
> what it produces at the level of the enunciation—what results is an *I
> am deceiving you*. (P. 139)

What happens, then, to try to simplify this complex transference,
is that both the signifier (the act of lying) and the signification (the
liar) exist at the level of statement only in the Other. It is, returning
to our primary, perceptual distinction, only the Other who finally
constitutes the self: "Thus is marked the first split that makes the
subject as such distinguish himself from the sign in relation to which,
at first, he has been able to constitute himself as subject" (p. 141).

Second, this relationship between the self and the Other acts,
as it does in Althusserian ideology, in the form of a specular structure. It is "in the Other that the subject is constituted as ideal
. . . that is to say, to constitute himself in his imaginary reality" (p.
144). The Other, then, acts as a flattering mirror in which the self
may constitute itself in a better form than it really is. However,
unlike more conventional mirrors, this one assumes a rather distur-
bingly prominent place in the self's analysis of itself:

> It is in the space of the Other that he sees himself and the point from
> which he looks at himself is also in that space. Now, this is also the
> point from which he speaks, since in so far as he speaks, it is in the
> locus of the Other that he begins to constitute that truthful lie by
> which is initiated that which participates in desire at the level of the
> unconscious. (P. 144)

In other words (and this is a phrase that is now taking on a different meaning), the self gazes at itself and speaks for itself from the place of the Other. The analysand on the couch begins to conceive of how he or she looks from the chair. Also, the analysand addresses the analyst in order to hear what the *analysand* has to say. The gaze had been the place of desire, and now, although he had earlier made a clear demarcation between the "scopic register" and the "vocational field" (p. 118), Lacan makes speaking and hearing also the place of desire. Moreover, this scenario of being a self in the Other by hearing what the self says in the Other is basically the obverse of what Heidegger had written about "hearing." In Heidegger's model, "Hearing constitutes the primary and authentic way in which Dasein is open for its ownmost potentiality-for-Being — as in hearing the voice of the friend whom every Dasein carries with it." In other words, Heidegger assumes that instead of the self's hearing itself in the Other, the Other is always implicit in the self; Lacan argues the opposite.[43]

All the factors that Lacan had up to this point developed discretely come into play in this scene — the unconscious, desire, the gaze, and the subject/object in signification. The Other, though, is ambiguously both a system and another subject. As a system, "the Other is the locus in which is situated the chain of the signifier that governs whatever may be present of the subject" (*Four Fundamental Concepts,* p. 203). In this definition, the Other operates identically to the unconscious, which Lacan had earlier defined: the "unconscious is the sum of the effects of speech on a subject, at the level at which the subject constitutes himself out of the effects of the signifier" (p. 126). So, when the statement "the subject as such is uncertain because he is divided by the effects of language" becomes "the subject is subject only from being subjected to the field of the Other, the subject proceeds from his synchronic subjection in the field of the Other," the "field of the Other" has taken on the properties of being a language. The Other, though, is also the analyst. By a curious shift, Lacan makes the *other* into the *Other*. Lacan first considers "that other who is the analyst" (p. 124). But by the time he comes to examine the situation in practice of an analysand who "begins to constitute that truthful lie by which is initiated that which participates in desire at the level of the unconscious," which occurs, he tells us, in "the locus of the Other," that Other has indeed become the analyst (p. 144). As he concludes, "the presence of the pyscho-analyst . . . must be included in the concept of the unconscious" (p. 127).

Moreover, in this scene the subject is moving from an epistemic state (uncertainty) to an ontic one (subjection). We may conclude our analysis of Lacan's model of the subject, in theory, by saying that the *objet a* signifies the desire for the unknowable Other in the self as the self can only know the Other, through language and the analyst. All this operates at the level of the desiring unconscious, which is eternal and which is structured as a language. As a concluding comment on subjection, then, Lacan returns to two Hegelian-Marxist notions — alienation and dialectic. There is no subject in the Cartesian sense, he concludes, because the "split" in the subject (a split that results from language) requires a form of resolution that is processual: "There is no subject without, somewhere, *aphanisis* of the subject, and it is in this alienation, in this fundamental division, that the dialectic of the subject is established" (p. 221). With this final formulation of the role signification plays in subjection, Lacan concludes his study of the category of the subject. The problem arises, as it does in Althusser's attempt at explaining the workings of interpellation, when Lacan attempts to demonstrate the way that the subject is subject to signification.

We must remember that this subject is always-already subject because the unconscious, where everything occurs, is eternal and operates in a synchrony. But, like Althusser, Lacan cannot find an analogy for his model. He too must resort to a model of diachronic dialectic in order to demonstrate how synchrony works, and he meets with the same specious success as Althusser. Lacan begins by defining the "signifier [as] that which represents a subject." A signifier, however, represents a subject not for another subject, but rather "for another signifier." The concept of the *subject* is merely an "effect" of language. Signifiers are the genuine agents in this case; a signifier employs a human subject as a point of transition or mediation with another signifier. Language works at expressing itself *through* human subjects. Signification here is very much like Althusser's ideology. And so, too, is the subject in the Lacanian model always-already subject to signification. Lacan illustrates how this subject is always-already subject with this brief analogy:

Suppose that in the desert you find a stone covered with hieroglyphics. You do not doubt for a moment that, behind them, there was a

subject who wrote them. But it is an error to believe that each signifier is addressed to you—this is proved by the fact that you cannot
understand any of it. On the other hand you define them as signifiers,
by the fact that you are sure that each of these signifiers is related to
each of the others. And it is this that is at issue with the relation
between the subject and the field of the Other. . . . The subject is born
in so far as the signifier emerges in the field of the Other. But, by this
very fact, this subject—which was previously nothing if not a subject
coming into being—solidifies into a signifier.[44]

Lacan's analogy, like Althusser's, gives the lie to what he is attempting to argue.

The first problem with Lacan's analogy is it posits two distinct
cultures and then conflates the distinctions between them. The
reason the individual who finds the stone does not understand the
signs written on it is because they are foreign. Rather than "prov-
ing" that the stone is not addressed to the individual who finds it,
this analogy merely proves the stone's foreignness. Had the stone
been found by a native of the culture of the desert who understood
the signs, that also would not have proven that the communication
was addressed to this second, native discoverer. It would only have
proven that the native could understand the signs, while the for-
eigner could not, because the one is native to the culture and the
other not—or, more precisely, one understands the language of
that culture while the other does not. The more plausible scenario
is that even the native of the culture of the desert would not have
been able to understand the hieroglyphics because they belong to
an older, probably dead version of that culture. But this also does
not prove that the communication is not addressed to that individual; it only proves that there are three cultures, one of which is
dead because no one understands its language anymore. But that
leads us to assume diachrony because we now recognize that cultures decline and fall while others rise and flourish. But diachrony
is precisely what Lacan has already asserted does not exist in his
model of the unconscious.

The discoverer cannot be sure that the signifiers are related to
each other, at least not so long as he or she cannot understand the
language. At best, it is a supposition that the language has some
degree of coherence because this is the case with any known language. In the end, then, this analogy does not demonstrate with

any degree of competence that the relationship between the subject and the field of the Other turns out to be one in which the subject becomes a signifier. What is truly demonstrated is that communications can get lost, that cultures and languages can perish, and that time is irrevocable.

Nonetheless, misrecognizing the limitations of his analogy, Lacan goes on to draw his conclusions. The headless subject has undergone a change and become first an "apparatus" and then a mediator for signifiers (*Four Fundamental Concepts,* p. 185). "What must be stressed at the outset is that a signifier is that which represents a subject for another signifier" (p. 207). In this act of mediation, "at the level of the other signifier, the subject fades away" (p. 236). In other words, this is all about "the division of the subject" — an initial act in which because "the subject appears somewhere as meaning, he is manifested elsewhere as 'fading,' as disappearance" (p. 218). What this split, this alienation, this division, this fading, and finally this disappearance signify is "the function of the subject defined as the effect of the signifier" p. 207). The subject is made a functional category (an apparatus) and operates as an effect of some larger system — whether ideology or signification. These are the preconditions of subjection.

Finally, I wish to discuss Lacan's elaboration of the possibility for self-knowledge. Because he has proposed a situation in which the subject is merely a mediating effect between two signifiers, he effectively negates a concept of subjectivity in which an individual might signify a relationship with language that allows some form of self-expression. That is, by working within a synchronic model, he denies the possibility of a self's *coming* to knowledge; the very process becomes impossible by his denial of diachronic development.

However, there are some, like Jacques-Alain Miller and Paul Smith, who see a way out of this dilemma. Manipulating the concept of the *suture,* Miller argues that it is possible for the Lacanian subject to "figure" between itself and the chain of discourse an "element which is lacking, in the form of a stand-in."[45] According to Smith, "Lacan speaks of that stand-in as the *objet petit a,*" which he speaks of as an image that acts for the subject to fill "the gaps in the discourse of the Other." Smith suggests that Lacan allows the subject subjectivity. It can come to self-knowledge because the *objet petit a,* "as stand-in . . . allows the 'subject' to construe itself as coherent in language." The suture, in effect, is the "mechanism by which the 'subject' is closed off from the unconscious," which then allows the subject to assume the status of a "speaking subject" (p. 76).

Lacan's brief comments on the suture do not seem to argue quite the liberation that Miller and Smith are suggesting. For one thing, Lacan begins his comments by emphasizing the "total distinction between the scopic register and the invocatory, vocatory, vocational field." The suture, he notes, is only a "pseudo-identification" that operates only during "the moment of seeing." Not only is the suture merely another form of misrecognition, it is also a form that might be effective in allowing the subject to figure itself only during the "moment of seeing." As Lacan comments, in "the scopic field, the subject is not essentially indeterminate." One must conclude that in the "vocational field," in language, the subject is not so fortunate (*Four Fundamental Concepts*, pp. 117–18). There, the subject is still only the mediating effect between two signifiers; this is the subject of subjection, constantly indeterminate, fading, disappearing, and without subjectivity.

Lacan, I have suggested, works within a structure in which the subject misrecognizes what is essential to know—the real. Despite the implications that this *méconnaissance* has for a concept of knowledge, Fredric Jameson asserts that there is such a thing as a "Lacanian version of the 'know thyself,'" which takes on the form of a question: *"Où en es-tu par rapport à ton désir?"* ("Where do you stand with respect to your desire?") This Delphic question, moreover, requires a coordination between "two kinds of 'self-knowledge.'" The first is the answer to the question, which means locating desire and assuming a pose for dealing with it: "what my desire—my 'object' *a*—is right now; and how—also right now—I mean to handle it, what I am in the process of doing with it, what position on it I can see myself adopting (resignation, active appropriation, contemplation, repression, and so forth)." The second is a slightly more complex form of self-knowledge:

As for the second kind of self-consciousness measured by the Lacanian question, it should be understood that it does not call for action, but it seeks to reveal or deconceal the practical distance that we already entertain to our object of desire, which is somehow already implicit in the desire itself. Indeed, no "practical" recommendations at all are implied by this ethics, which is an "existential" one in the sense that it deliberately abandons the subject before the void of the choice itself.

Jameson's assumption that the desired *objet a* is knowable does not take into account that the *objet a* is also the misrecognizing desire itself; what he proposes, then, is that the subject may be free enough from the desire to recognize the desire. Lacan spends much energy arguing against this possibility.

In both the first and second forms of self-knowledge, Jameson suggests that there is an element of "choice" allowable in the Lacanian model. We have already seen how Lacan elides choice from the Aristotelian *tuché*. Moreover, revelation is not an act the unconscious can entertain toward its desire. Desire is precisely that absence that is "misconstrued (*méconnu*)," as Lacan insists. In the final analysis, as Lacan notes, "the subject in question is not that of the reflexive consciousness, but that of desire." And that distinction speaks volumes about their incompatibility.[46]

In the end, what we may say about Lacan concerning the question of self-knowledge is simply that he doesn't allow its possibility. Most of his work since 1953 has attempted to disrupt the possibility of what he, in an essay of 1957, called "the empty adage 'Know thyself'" (*Écrits*, p. 174). The problem may be traced back to the diachronic/synchronic dilemma. For self-knowledge to be an available option, there must be a temporal, narrative framework allowing the individual the capacity to will, think, and choose. There must also be the possibility of two positions—the individual self and the subject. Those are the rules governing the narrative model of self-knowledge and subjectivity. These two twentieth-century proponents of the scientific model have shown the rules governing the obverse case of subjection. The model character in Althusser's Christian example had been Moses, and the model situation his calling. For Lacan, the model character is Descartes, and the model situation is his act of knowing, his proclamation of "*Cogito*."

No historical figure plays as prominent a role in *The Four Fundamental Concepts of Psycho-Analysis* as Descartes. Not only has Lacan modeled the Freudian discovery of the place of desire on the Cartesian discovery of the role of cognition—"*Desidero* is the Freudian *cogito*"—but he has, in fact, established the very premises of psychoanalysis' right to scientificity by its relation to the Cartesian narrative model. As a matter of course, Descartes becomes an object for Lacan to work through. First of all, Lacan describes what he calls the "Cartesian approach, which, in its origin and in its end, is directed essentially not towards science, but towards its own certainty" (p. 231). If psychoanalysis were premised on a cogito, it would be a religion but (as Lacan insists), "psychoanalysis is not a religion" (p. 265). This concluding remark is an answer to his earlier speculation about the possible parameters of the "corridor of communication between psycho-analysis and the religious register" (p. 8). In fact, the subject Lacan has constructed at the end of his seminar is precisely an answer to the emergent subject of the Cartesian cogito.

Descartes's mistake, he argues, is to think that the annihilation of skepticism *is* knowledge: "To say that he knows something of this certainty. Not to make of the *I think* a mere point of fading." Attempting to find a site for situating knowledge—a place "in which all this knowledge wanders about"—Descartes, according to Lacan, constructs his God. "He puts the field of this knowledge at the level of this vaster subject, the subject who is supposed to know, God" (*Écrits*, p. 224). Lacan too incorporates this concept of a "subject who is supposed to know" into his model, and in tracing the process of this incorporation we find the parallel to the sliding of the other into the Other that I noted earlier. In order to "decipher the diachrony of unconscious repetitions," writes Lacan in his 1958 essay, "The Direction of the Treatment and the Principles of Its Power," "interpretation must introduce into the synchrony of the signifiers that compose it something that suddenly makes translation possible—precisely what is made possible by the function of the Other in the concealment of the code, it being in relation to that Other that the missing element appears" (p. 233). This Other is, as usual in Lacan, ambiguously situated between the system of signification and the analyst. In *The Four Fundamental Concepts,* Lacan notes that a "lack is encountered by the subject in the Other, in the very intimation that the Other makes to him by his discourse" (p. 214). Indeed, as Lacan elaborates in his conclusion, the "plane constituted by the locus of the Other, from the place where the subject, realizing himself in his speech, is instituted at the level of the subject who is supposed to know" (p. 271). According to Lacan, then, this Other operates as the "subject who is supposed to know, [which] in analysis, is the analyst" (p. 225).

Having then given the analyst this attribute of the Cartesian God, Lacan goes on to suggest that what the analyst knows in the end is not knowledge. The transference, he writes, is "unthinkable unless one sets out from the subject who is supposed to know." What the analyst is supposed to know turns out to be the unescapable knowledge of the effects of signification—"that from which no one can escape, as soon as he formulates it." Having then realized the complete subjection language requires of anyone who comes to it, Lacan's analyst determines in the end that there is an "absolute point with no knowledge." In fact, this point "is absolute precisely by virtue of being in no way knowledge" (p. 253). Because thinking is not a path to knowledge, but rather to subjection—subjection to language which operates here as the Other—Lacan is able to conclude that "in so far as we are the subject who thinks, we are implicated in a quite different way, in as much as we depend on the field of the Other, which was there long before we came into the world, and whose circulating structures determine us as subjects." Given this relationship between the self and knowledge in Lacan, it might be reasonable to translate the Delphic "Know thyself" into the Lacanian "Misrecognize the Other."[47]

Science, in Lacan's model, does not strive for certainty because it recognizes that the inquiring subject is liable to its own limiting rules. That is, the analyst who had been given God-like attributes becomes subject to signification as much as the analysand. In the end, Descartes ought not to have claimed certainty because even the very Absolute Subject he used as his evidence for being certain could not be certain. There is no such thing as certainty, which Lacan calls knowledge. Having worked through what he called the "Cartesian approach," to what he now calls the "Cartesian departure," Lacan proclaims in the concluding lecture of the seminar series in 1964, "analysis implies, in effect, a beyond of science—in the modern sense of Science *itself*."[48]

The problem with Lacan's reading of Descartes, however, is that he is intent on eradicating most of the complexity of the Cartesian subject. In one notable instance, he simply declares that the basic property of that subject is in attaining certainty by transforming doubt: "The Cartesian subject . . . appears at the moment when doubt is recognized as certainty" (*Four Fundamental Concepts*, p. 126). But the Cartesian subject is not a simple entity moving from one epistemic state to another, or changing one epistemic state into another. That subject, when we return to Descartes to see what he himself said, turns out to have much more flexible cognitive relations to itself and to its God. Just to offer an example, we might turn to the third meditation in the *Meditations on the First Philosophy,* which plays the same prominent role in this tract of 1641 as the fourth discourse played in the *Discourse on the Method* of 1637.

First of all, Descartes makes the distinction between *understanding* or *knowing* and *apprehending* or what he calls *grasping*. He explicitly makes this distinction in his letter to Marin Mersenne, dated May 27, 1630: "To grasp something is to embrace it in one's thought; to know something, it suffices to touch it with one's thought" ("*Car comprendre, c'est embrasser de la pensée; mais pour sçauoir vne chose, il suffit de la toucher de la pensée*"). In the Latin *Meditations,* he makes this distinction between *comprehendere* (to grasp) and *attingere cogitatione* (to touch with one's thought). Secondly, he declares that his interest is not to discover his origin, but to determine what sustains him. His object of inquiry is not the original fiat of creation, but the durative power of preservation. He then suggests that the proof for the existence of God involves recognizing the innate idea of God in himself. That, in the end, is the answer to his inquiry into the power of preservation, and it is a product of intimate self-knowledge:

> That is, when I turn my mind's eye upon myself, I understand that I am a thing which is incomplete and dependent on another and which aspires without limit to ever greater and better things; but I also understand at the same time that he on whom I depend has within him all those greater things, not just indefinitely and potentially but actually and infinitely, and hence that he is God.

Having then reached this level of apprehension, he returns to that original distinction between knowing and grasping: "By 'God' I mean the very being the idea of whom is within me, that is, the possessor of all the perfections which I cannot grasp [*ego non comprehendere*], but can somehow reach in my thought [*modo attingere cogitatione possum*], who is subject to no defects whatsoever." Lacan's caricature of the Cartesian subject who had allegedly appeared certain at the moment of greatest doubt, and who supposedly claimed that "he knows something of this certainty," is misrepresentative. Only by failing to negotiate the significance of Descartes's distinction between knowledge and apprehension may Lacan represent the Cartesian subject as somehow a naive version of the Lacanian subject.[49]

The distinction Descartes makes between knowing and grasping is based on the principle that cognition is a process. One moves from a state of doubt to one of knowledge to one of apprehension. There is room for growth in knowledge; nor, for that matter, is apprehension the last act of certainty. There is one other division Descartes makes that Lacan ignores, the division between what he considers the two modes of thinking: "perception, or the operation of the intellect, and volition, or the operation of the will." Apprehension allows the subject to act, but it is by no means the end of the process of intellection. Lacan, like Spinoza, makes perception and volition one and the same thing, and thereby, like Althusser, negates the difference between having an idea and acting on that idea. Descartes's distinction between thinking and willing, and his distinction between knowing and grasping, involves the premise that God is at a "distance" from the human subject.[50] What is distant can only be "known," what is close "grasped."

Discussing how human volition may coexist with divine preordination, Descartes posits once again the difference between knowledge and apprehension: "We may attain sufficient knowledge of this power [to preordain] to perceive clearly and distinctly that God possesses it; but we cannot get a sufficient grasp of it to see how it leaves the free actions of men undetermined." Because there is a distance between God and the individual subject, the subject may know that God is able to preordain anything without yet grasping how the subject still retains its freedom of will. The distance is premised on Descartes's distinction between knowing and grasping—between touching what is distant and embracing what is close. In the end, what Descartes establishes is what John Hicks has helpfully called "epistemic distance"—the "kind of distance between God and man that would make room for a degree of human autonomy." The purpose of that autonomy is to establish the difference between having certain apprehension of the grounds for material action and having ever uncertain knowledge of God. As Descartes concludes the third meditation, "just as we believe through faith that the supreme happiness of the next life consists solely in the contemplation of the divine majesty, so experience tells us that this same contemplation, albeit much less perfect, enables us to know the greatest joy of which we are capable in this life."[51]

In other words, the Cartesian subject finds its grounds for volitional, material action by "knowing" God, but even so it still retains its desire for apprehending an infinite amount of knowledge intellectually. Knowledge, then, for the Cartesian subject, is never certain, never wholly determined, but always on an epistemic horizon. With those presuppositions, he articulates the seventeenth-century rhetorical ideal of enselfment and constructs the narrative model of subjectivity. Its counterpart is the Hobbesian scientific model with its philosophical ideal of the determined self. Like the Cartesian model, and in fact like the Lacanian and the Althusserian models, Hobbes's model is ultimately concerned with the question of the status of what each of these thinkers calls "God."

"Very Like a Whale": Hobbes's Science of Subjection

The God of the Althusserian model was the Absolute Subject and played the role of the ideological state apparatus. The God of the Lacanian model was the "subject supposed to know" and played the role of the analyst in transference. The God of the Cartesian model exists at an epistemic distance from the individual subject who has a choice about whether or not to pursue knowledge about that God. The God of the Hobbesian model is an interesting construct whose existence is also at an epistemic distance from the individual subject; but, in this Hobbesian model, the subject does not have the choice to pursue knowledge of that God. In the final assessment, all the attributes of God *as they affect material human conditions* are assumed by Hobbes's absolute sovereign.

Hobbes also asserted that what he was doing was "scientific." As he declares at the end of the twentieth chapter of the *Leviathan*, "The skill of making, and maintaining Common-wealths, consisteth in certain Rules, as doth Arithmetique and Geometry; not (as Tennis-play) on Practise onely: which Rules, neither poor men have the leisure, nor men that have had the leisure, have hitherto had curiosity, or the method to find out." Hitherto, as he says, politics was not governed by a scientific method. At the conclusion of his chapter on the reasons every citizen of the commonwealth is always-already subject to the absolute sovereign, he proclaims that his document is scientific. It is, pointedly, what he had written about the earlier version of the *Leviathan:* "Civil Philosophy [is] no older . . . than my own book *De Cive.*" And in *De Cive,* he notes that "philosophy" comprehends "all manner of Sciences." Later, in the 1642 tract, he argues that what differentiates the field of faith from the field of knowledge is precisely that the latter can be called science, whereas the former cannot, because to suggest that it can be determined by human reasoning would be "prejudicall to *Faith.*" This gesture is part of Hobbes's persistent strategy to place the mysteries of faith either subordinate to the policies of state or beyond the realm of material action. In the 1651 *Leviathan,* he condemns all philosophy that is not based on geometrical princi- ples — such as a materialist philosophy of motions — as being "rath- er a Dream than [a] Science."[52]

Having pronounced his study to fall into the field of science, Hobbes determines the object of his science. Quite simply, the object of Hobbes's science is subjection. In concluding his treatise, he defines the process of its working in a tone and rhetoric re- markably similar to Althusser's: "The point of time, wherein a man becomes subject to a Conquerour, is that point, wherein having liberty to submit to him, he consenteth, either by expresse words, or by other sufficient sign, to be his Subject." Defining the strate- gies at work in Hobbes's proclamation, we find a temporal aspect (when subjection occurs) and a contractual basis (how subjection occurs). Moreover, that contract is either explicit or implicit in Hobbes's scheme. Hobbes establishes the basis and workings of his commonwealth on the fertile ground of the implicit contract. No citizen receives the opportunity to declare explicitly his or her consent to subjection. The reason for that is that Hobbes's model, like the other scientific models, is based on a synchronic represen- tation of an originary covenant. In the end, Hobbes allows free- dom only in theory and never in material practice, and he makes the distinction between subjectivity and subjection by employing the common prepositions Althusser would later use.

According to Hobbes, everyone who is subject to an absolute power must follow that power's commands: "There is simple obe- dience in those that are subject to Paternall or Despoticall Domin- ion." But not everyone is subject to an absolute power. The sover- eign, for instance, "is not Subject to the Civill Lawes. For having power to make, and repeale Lawes, he may when he pleaseth, free himselfe from that subjection." An absolute sovereign, that is, enjoys subjectivity in the sphere of civil law and is therefore not subject to the laws of that society. *Subject to* signifies only subjection. On the other hand, even the absolute sovereign is a "Subject of God, and bound thereby to observe the laws of Nature." Being a subject of God allows certain liberties beyond civil law, but within natural law. For that reason, Hobbes gives the liberties accruing to whoever is a "subject of God" only to the absolute sovereign. *Subject of* signifies only subjectivity, which in this scenario means liberty from all constraints except divine commandments. Hobbes makes the distinction elsewhere between slaves and servants, and he likewise bases that analogy on this same distinction between being a *subject of* or being *subject to* an absolute power. So, too, as we shall see, Milton makes the distinction between being a subject of God or being subject to God in terms of having a relationship with God that is either filial (subjectivity) or servile (subjection).[53]

Part of Milton's strategy in distinguishing between the status of the filial and the servile involves a conception of the place of the "Spirit" in human affairs. Part of Hobbes's strategy of denying the opportunity for someone who is subject to the monarch to assume the possibility of becoming a subject of God involves the evisceration of the Spirit's significance. In order either to valorize or to dispute the existence of Spirit, both Hobbes and Milton make a primary distinction between earthly politics and heavenly politics. As Hobbes states in the *Leviathan*, "Humane Politiques . . . teacheth part of the duty which Earthly Kings require of their Subjects," and "Divine Politiques . . . containeth Precepts to those that have yeelded themselves subjects in the Kingdome of God." He later defines the two realms of these two politics as the "Temporall" and the "Ghostly." Once this division is made between two "kingdoms," there necessarily develops a situation of strife because each kingdom will attempt to conscript its subjects from the same population. "When these two Powers oppose one another, the Common-wealth cannot but be in great danger of Civill warre, and Dissolution" because "every Subject is subject to two Masters." In such a state of conflict between secular and divine powers, the secular commonwealth is invariably disrupted. Milton's strategy is to invoke the power of the Spirit and to make secular power subordinate to divine.

Hobbes, on the other hand, attempts to make secular power superordinate to divine by denying the existence of the Spirit. He manages to do so in his unique form of rhetorical appeal. Almost invariably, Hobbes will assert the existence of something before he carefully plots out the logical formation in which the existence of that thing is proved to be impossible, or the thing takes on such a radically different form as not to be the same thing. In our present case, for instance, he begins by assuming that there is such a thing as spirit: "The Scriptures by the Spirit of God in man, mean a mans spirit, enclined to Godlinesse." It is not quite as confident an expression of the Spirit's existence as we would find in, say, Henry More, who expresses the Spirit's attributes as "self-unity, self-activity, self-penetrability," but it is nonetheless an allowable degree of spirituality in Hobbes's materialist philosophy. Hobbes then turns his attention to an important representation of the Spirit in the Scriptures, the case of the Spirit's inspiring the Old Testament judges. He determines, in a nominalistic fashion, that the "Spirit of God" that excited the judges to acts of heroic courage is nothing else but "an extraordinary Zeal, and Courage." He continues to take every expression of the Spirit's activity and rename it as an attribute of human functioning. The Holy Spirit leading to righteous living is called a "sign"; the angels are shown to be corporeal; spirit is meant to signify "life," "the gift of predicting," "the gift of understanding," and, simply, "wind." In the end, Hobbes will allow that there is such a thing as "spirit," but only with the proviso that it has the attributes of corporeality: "Nor does it follow from hence, that Spirits are *nothing:* for they have dimensions, and therefore really *Bodies.*" Having refined spirit into matter, Hobbes clinches his case by suggesting that the greatest function of the Spirit is to promote submission: "The Spirit of unfained Christianity" means "*submission* to that main Article of Christian faith, that Jesus is the Christ." And, finally, he defines Spirit as "Mind."[54]

It would be hard to understate the role Hobbes's materialist philosophy plays in his politics.[55] Only by denying the Spirit does he make gestures toward denying the power that the "Ghostly kingdom" might wield over subjects who ought to be subject to only the temporal kingdom. And only by denying every individual's spiritual right to belong to the kingdom of God may Hobbes establish the absolute sovereign's right to subject every citizen to his power. Instead of allowing the Spirit the power to lead every potential Christian to a heavenly kingdom, Hobbes places the absolute sovereign as the mediator of the only way of gaining knowledge about the Spirit, God's Word: "The interpretation of the Bible [is] authorized by the Common-wealth." In fact, Hobbes even defines heresy by reference to this same authority: "*Hæresie is nothing else, but a private opinion, obstinately maintained, contrary to the opinion which the Publique Person* (that is to say, the Representant of the Common-wealth) *hath commanded to bee taught*." By removing the Spirit from Scripture, Hobbes is able to argue that the absolute sovereign is the only mediator between any believer and that believer's God. While it is true that "Christian Kings are no more but Christs Subjects," they are nonetheless the "Supreme Pastors of their own Subjects." I would place this doctrine next to Milton's extremely anti-Erastian position and Milton's own definition of heresy. In his last polemical prose tract, Milton defined heresy as "a Religion taken up and believ'd from the traditions of men and additions to the word of God." And the Word of God is to be understood, Milton continues, "by reading, by learning, by study, [and] by prayer for illumination of the holy Spirit."[56] It is just this Spirit and just this Word of God that Hobbes would respectively deny and place under the absolute sovereign's rule.

What Hobbes proposes is the possibility for subjectivity, that is being a "subject of God," but it is a possibility available to only one "person." His political theory insists that any wider range of subjectivity would cause havoc and conflict in the commonwealth. Because there can be only one person who enjoys subjectivity, the rest must suffer subjection. "And he that carryeth this Person, is called soveraigne, and said to have *Soveraigne Power;* and every one besides, his subject." The absolute sovereign, in Althusser's model, had been the ideological state apparatus; in Hobbes's model, the state apparatus is embodied in one individual given absolute sanction by an original covenant.

Hobbes's description of subjection has both a temporal and a contractual aspect. Like Althusser, Hobbes represents the covenant by which any individual becomes subject to the absolute sovereign as a narrative moment, and it appears to occur diachronically. Like Althusser also, Hobbes's apparent diachrony is belied by his insistence on a synchronic politic. Hobbes describes the covenant solemnly:

> The only way to erect such a Common Power . . . is, to conferre all their power and strength upon one Man, or upon one Assembly of men, that may reduce all their Wills, by plurality of voices, unto one Will: which is as much as to say, to appoint one man, or Assembly of men, to beare their Person; and every one to owne, and acknowledge himselfe to be Author of whatsoever he that so beareth their Person, shall Act, or cause to be Acted, in those things which concerne the Common Peace and Safetie; and therein to submit their Wills, every one to his Will, and their Judgements to his Judgment. This is more than Consent, or Concord; it is a reall Unitie of them all, in one and the same Person, made by Covenant of every man with every man. . . . This done, the Multitude so united in one Person, is called a common-wealth, in latine civitas. This is the Generation of that great leviathan, or rather (to speake more reverently) of that *Mortall God,* to which wee owe under the *Immortall God,* our peace and defence.[57]

The concluding comment about the relationship of the Leviathan to God is not just an interesting aside. The commonwealth Hobbes describes owes its very structure to what he will later describe as the kingdom of God. Hobbes later states that the most important lesson the Spirit teaches is "submission," and the founding of the commonwealth begins with an act of mutual submission, primarily of each individual's will.

Earlier I had noted that the terms of lapsarian historiography — to wit, prelapsarian, lapsarian, and postlapsarian — could be translated adequately as being either the fields of being, knowledge, and will, or the categories of Spirit, Authority, and Representation. Hobbes argues the first category of Spirit into a state of nonexistence, allowing for the possibility of a covenant in which an individual must renounce his or her individual property of being. In other words, we can now see why Spirit and Being are intimately related; and we can recognize why Hobbes had to promote a materialist philosophy in order to remove the field of being. He is left, then, with the fields of knowledge and will — the categories of authority and representation. For all intents and purposes, Hobbes will soon argue *will* and *knowledge* out of existence, and then manipulate *authority* and *representation* so that they become attributes solely of the absolute sovereign and traceable to no historical covenant. For the interim, let us grant that there is a covenant in place in order to see how Hobbes deals with will and knowledge.

The covenant Hobbes describes is based on certain preconditions that involve three concepts concerning the possibility of subjectivity. The first concerns the place of *will,* its powers and limitations in a materialist philosophy. The second concerns the site of *authority,* the questions of responsibility, and the role of the *subject* in relation to a power containing all the qualities of individual governance in the form of a "person." The third concerns the power and uses of *representation,* in the sense of being both a political model and a rhetorical form.

As in the scientific models we described above, Hobbes's model effectively eradicates the volitional power of the individual by having him or her become an automaton within the commonwealth. The primary covenant requires a submission of the individual's will to the will of the absolute sovereign. In the first part of the *Leviathan,* Hobbes had described *will* as the "last Appetite in Deliberating." Not only has volition become merely an appetitive action, but *deliberation* itself becomes not so much a cognitive function as loss of freedom. Hobbes establishes this tenet by punning on the term *deliberation:* "And it is called *Deliberation;* because it is a putting an end to the *Liberty* we had of doing, or omitting, according to our own Appetite, or Aversion." As Lacan had done, Hobbes makes appetite the condition of "being," and does so in order to elide *will* from the category of the subject. In fact, he goes so far as to say that enduring desire is the basis of all human life: "to have no Desire, is to be Dead."

Moreover, in this conflation of volitional ability and material actions, Hobbes follows the paradigm Althusser and Lacan followed in the twentieth century, and the paradigm Spinoza follows at the end of the seventeenth century. Given this conflation, one cannot accept as wholeheartedly religious Hobbes's remarks that salvation is available to anyone who has the "will to obey." For Hobbes, faith and works are not even distinct. In fact, the will to obey is not an act of will because, as Hobbes stated earlier, whether "men will or not, they must be subject always to the Divine Power." In other words, being "subject to" involves the operative loss of the power of willing. There is, however, one will in Hobbes's *Leviathan,* and that is the will of the absolute sovereign, who has the accumulated will of all the citizens of the commonwealth. Given this absolute will, that sovereign becomes the embodiment

of law: "the will of the Law-maker is a Law."[58] This tenet that the
will resides in the sovereign leads us to the second concept of
Hobbesian science—the site of authority.

Descartes had noted seven years before the *Leviathan* was published that will and authority were intimately linked. As he writes
in the *Principles of Philosophy,* "it is a supreme perfection in man
that he acts voluntarily, that is, freely; this makes him in a special
way the author of his actions and deserving of praise for what he
does." What Hobbes would have, on the other hand, is for all
authority to repose in the absolute sovereign's power, and for every
citizen to consider himself or herself the "author" of the sovereign's actions. That is to say that loss of will entails the loss of
individual liberty and the assumption of collective obligation. The
individual self would not be responsible for just its own actions,
but it would also be responsible for an other's actions. This, we
must remember, becomes operative only when the primary distinction (being/spirit) is eviscerated. Hobbes does achieve a philosophy in which the primary distinction between self and other is
erased; whereas responsibility for one's own actions is a characteristic of subjectivity, responsibility for another's actions is a characteristic of subjection. As Hobbes argues, "seeing every Subject is
Author of the actions of his Soveraigne; he punisheth another, for
the actions committed by himselfe." Hobbes does nothing less
than controvert the primary, perceptual distinction of selfhood. In
effect, Hobbes has already established one possible form of the
"post-individualistic" state by reducing the individual to a bundle
of responsibility for actions he or she does not commit, except by
implicit covenant with the actor of those actions.[59]

That primary, perceptual distinction is what I called the prelapsarian form of self-knowledge. When we turn to a prelapsarian
moment in *Paradise Lost,* we see how Milton controverts the Hobbesian model of postindividualistic authority by having his God
assert that each individual can be responsible for only her or his
own actions. For instance, Adam and Eve are, as God says, "Authors to themselves in all" (*PL* III, 122). Not only is this an assertion of God's generally Arminian principles—he did not will their
fall—but it is also an assertion of the limits of responsibility. A self
can be the author only of her or his own act. Thus, Milton has Eve
and Adam fall separately. The reason Hobbes wishes to have each
individual author the absolute sovereign's actions is so that no

individual may claim to disapprove of those actions. As Hobbes says, no subject may disapprove actions which he or she has authored, whoever may have acted them. It would be an act of self-contradiction, and although Hobbes makes selfhood a specious category he is not unwilling to exploit it for his own purposes. Logically speaking, whatever the sovereign does is done by the authority of the people, and the people cannot undermine their own authority; therefore, the people cannot undermine the power of the sovereign. At the foundation of this logic is what is also the basis of Hobbes's science, and at the heart of his synchronic model of the covenant—the concept of representation.

The people cannot question the sovereign's will or his authority because it is the collective will and their own authority. In other words, the absolute sovereign is the representation of the people's wills, desires, and judgments. Hobbes had already defined the conditions by which representation must entail the loss of individuality: "For it is the *Unity* of the Representer, not the *Unity* of the Represented, that maketh the Person *One*" (*Leviathan*, p. 220). The representative in the Hobbesian model is the embodiment of a unanimity that cannot be revoked. Once the sovereign has assumed absolute will and authority, his power cannot be usurped. The only way for the people to undermine the sovereign is to try him; the events of 1649 demonstrated this adequately. Hobbes had already foreclosed the possibility of the sovereign's breaking the law by having him wholly represent the law. Just as each citizen cannot claim to disagree with any of the sovereign's actions because they are done by that citizen's authority, so too the sovereign cannot break the law because all actions become legal or illegal only at his will. By this logic, the sovereign cannot break the law, and therefore he cannot be tried by any state apparatus. In fact, the only power above the sovereign is the power he mediates for the believing multitude: "he is obliged by the Law of Nature . . . to render an account thereof to God, the Author of that Law, and to none but him" (p. 376).

Because the sovereign represents a unified collective will, he can never be misrepresentative. In most Western democracies we say ministers of parliament have broken the covenant to represent their constituency when they do not represent the will of the majority of the constituents. We can ignore for the moment that most parliamentarians abide by guidelines established by their parties rather than principles willed by their constituents, and say that a covenant between the parliamentarian and the constituents carries with it the parliamentarian's responsibility to represent those constituents. Likewise, in theory, the covenant can be revoked either at an election or by an extraordinary impeachment if the majority feels its will has been misrepresented. But Hobbes does not deal with majorities. Once the covenant is established it is irrevocable and unanimous — unanimous because whoever does not abide by it breaks the covenant and becomes, therefore, no part of the civil state. In other words, whoever does not abide by the covenant is excluded from the state; therefore, that dissenting individual does not compromise the unanimity of the collective will. The will remains unanimous because whoever does not agree is, by dint of that disagreement, no longer a part of the collective. More important, however, is how Hobbes makes this scenario of entering a covenant synchronous. Representation, after all, is both a political model and a rhetorical gesture.

Hobbes first establishes the rhetorical gesture's viability: "There are few things, that are uncapable of being represented by Fiction" (p. 219). He then says that the covenant which establishes the commonwealth is merely "Artificiall"; it, in fact, is a fiction of agreement. To bolster that covenant, he suggests, "there be somewhat else required." That "somewhat else" turns out to be the "Common Power." And the only way for the "Common Power" to be established is with a covenant (pp. 226–27). In other words, Hobbes uses a fictional device (the "Artificiall" covenant) to argue for the establishment of a substantial political model (which becomes "that *Mortall God*"). Hobbes then uses representation (in its rhetorical sense) to argue that this covenant has always already been established. He represents the sovereign by the term *Artificiall Man* and the right of that sovereign to appoint heirs to the throne as an "Artificiall Eternity of life" (p. 247). Of course, it would be to little avail to be able to appoint heirs if they did not have subjects to rule. Here, Hobbes begins to collapse the possibility for a covenant to be either implicit or explicit into a scenario in which the covenant is always already implicit.

Hobbes, as Althusser would do after him, uses a metaphorical family to suggest how each individual is always already subject to the monarch. He defines the terms of subjection: "Preservation of life . . . [is] the end, for which one man becomes subject to another" (p. 254). Because a father feeds his child, that child is subject to the father. (Chapter 5 will analyze what Hobbes makes of the scenario in which a mother feeds her child). Hobbes then goes on to consider that if a child is subject to its father because the father has the power either to nourish or to destroy it, then the child owes *everything* ("all that is his") to the father who nourishes it. That concept of *everything* includes a variety of essentially personal qualities—including will, judgment, and liberty—but here Hobbes also includes the power of reproduction. "He that hath the Dominion over the Child, hath Dominion also over the Children of the Child; and over their Childrens Children. For he that hath Dominion over the person of a man, hath Dominion over all that is his; without which, Dominion were but a Title, without the effect" (p. 255). This solves the problem of the absolute sovereign having heirs, or an "Artificiall Eternity," without having subjects for those heirs. The present generation of subjects will reproduce an "Artificiall Eternity" of individuals who are already subject to the future absolute sovereign. So, in these terms which Hobbes manipulates—an artificial man, artificial covenants, and artificial eternities—we conclude with the possibility of an artificial subjection.

In its artificiality—and Hobbes, remember, had proposed that anything could be represented by fiction—subjection seems to be just one more element in a grand science. What is lost, however, once the artificiality is removed, is the possibility of an *explicit* contract; and what the explicit contract had was the potential for a willful decision to subject oneself. Now, one is simply subject by birth. Thus, Hobbes does not have difficulty arguing that, inasmuch as future subjects would be produced by virtue of the present subjects being subjects, the present subjects are subject because their parents were previously subjects. What was "artificiall," what was first offered as a fictional representation, loses its fiction once the power is in place. What Hobbes is saying at the end of this passage is that, without power over future subjects, the present sovereign's title is but a fiction.

Representation is the postlapsarian form of self-knowledge, which falls into the field of will. This is indeed the role it assumes in Hobbes's model. In Hobbes, representation begins as a rhetorical method but becomes a political model. By exploiting a fictional representation of an implicit contract, Hobbes concludes by making the absolute sovereign the representative "Person" of the collective will and the collective judgment. Hobbes first denies the prelapsarian form of self-knowledge by denying the Spirit, and then denies the lapsarian form of self-knowledge by divorcing authority from action. What he is left with is the postlapsarian form of self-knowledge in which the subject is subject to the absolute sovereign because that is the way things are represented. Does it have to be this way? According to Hobbes, the answer would be a resounding "yes." It is the only answer he can give, because his is a scientific model.

Ironically, Hobbes answers that question in the chapter entitled "The Liberty of Subjects." Hobbes first establishes a dialectic between *freedom* and *necessity* in order to determine victory for the latter:

> *Liberty* and *Necessity* are Consistent: As in the water, that hath not only *liberty*, but a *necessity* of descending by the Channel: so likewise in the Actions which men voluntarily doe; which (because they proceed from their will) proceed from *liberty*; and yet because every act of mans will, and every desire, and inclination proceedeth from some cause, and that from another cause, which causes in a continuall chaine (whose first link in the hand of God the first of all causes) proceeds from *necessity*. (P. 263)

Hobbes exploits the idea of epistemic distance as much as Descartes does. Hobbes, however, does so not to establish that humans can be said to have freedom because they cannot grasp any other verity, but rather to grasp the fact that humans *are* determined: "To him that could see the connexion of those causes, the *necessity* of all mens voluntary actions, would appear manifest" (p. 263). In other words, Hobbes is working not from the limitations of human cognition, but rather from the assuredness of divine insight.

Having established the manifest necessity in all human actions in terms of a divine perspective, Hobbes transfers his attention to the Leviathan. The "continuall chain" which links human action to God becomes, in a secular model, the "Artificiall Chains, called *Civill Lawes*" (*Leviathan,* p. 263). Only once these chains or "Bonds" are in place can Hobbes properly discuss the liberty of the subject. Since the absolute sovereign *is* the law, the liberty any individual who is subject to the sovereign may possess depends entirely on what the sovereign allows: "The Liberty of a Subject, lyeth therefore only in those things, which in regulating their actions, the

Sovereign hath prætermitted" (p. 264). In cases where the sovereign has not absolutely stated one way or the other whether the subject is free to act, the liberty of the subject depends on "the silence of the Law" (p. 271). That is the liberty of the individual "subject to" the sovereign. The absolute sovereign, on the other hand, "never wanted Right to any thing, otherwise, than as he himself is the Subject of God, and bound thereby to observe the Laws of Nature" (p. 265). The absolute sovereign, in other words, is the only person who is a "subject of God," the only individual in the commonwealth who enjoys subjectivity. There will be a time, Hobbes insists, when all shall enjoy subjectivity, but that time in this materialistic philosophy is no time at all. Only on the day of judgment, Hobbes states, will every individual "rise again, with glorious, and spirituall Bodies, and bee his Subjects in that his Kingdome, which shall be Eternall" (p. 646).

Given what Hobbes has already said about the spirit, the promise of that "spirituall" body is not much. What is important for Hobbes, though, is that he has utterly distinguished the spiritual world from the earthly, has completely ascribed God's powers to the absolute sovereign, and has founded a model of political subjection that is, all in all, logically coherent. The only recourse any seventeenth-century polemicist had left was the often-invoked "law of nature." Hobbes attempted to proscribe that law and even to incorporate it into the sovereign's power base.

Initially, Hobbes suggested that part of the liberty of the subject is gained in the act of submission: "In the act of our *Submission,* consisteth both our *Obligation,* and our *Liberty*" (p. 268). But later, he perverts that construction: "For *Right* is *Liberty,* namely that Liberty which the Civil Law leaves us: But *Civill Law* is an *Obligation;* and takes from us the Liberty which the Law of Nature gave us" (pp. 334–35). By conflating *right* and *liberty,* and then translating the realm by which either is allowable into "Civil Law," Hobbes does what he did earlier with authority—translates it into responsibility for another's actions. Here he leaves the subject with no will, no liberty, no rights, and only enduring responsibility for the sovereign's actions. Even the only realm by which one could claim some degree of liberty—the "Law of Nature"—is lost, according to Hobbes.

The lesson—that one was determined, without volition, always already subject to an absolute sovereign—in a word, the lesson of subjection, Hobbes maintained, was the essence of self-knowledge. He prefaced the *Leviathan* by stating his own version of the Delphic oracle's pronouncement: *"Nosce teipsum, Read thyself."* And whoever does read is supposed to confirm what Hobbes claims to have read in himself: "When I shall have set down my own reading orderly, and perspicuously, the pains left another, will be onely to consider, if he also find not the same in himself. For this kind of Doctrine, admitteth no other Demonstration" (*Leviathan,* pp. 82–83). In the end, this representation had no other court of appeal. In effect, the *Leviathan* itself, Hobbes's text of his own act of coming to self-knowledge, assumes the place of that representation. The *Leviathan* constitutes its own reality and establishes its own culture.

PART TWO: MILTON AND
THE NARRATIVE OF SUBJECTIVITY

The scientific model's basic assumption is that subjects are always already subject to something, whether to the unconscious or the ideological state apparatus or the absolute sovereign. Each of the models I've examined begins by proposing a situation in which there is an illusion of choice and volition, but each then goes on to produce a scenario in which those factors are shown to be illusory. Each model produces a situation in which there are available roles, but then goes on to develop its case that these roles are merely effects of the way the system determines the single role any person is doomed to play — the role of subjection. However, also as I noted earlier, the two models — narrative and scientific — are not simple opposites, and it is important to note their points of concordance.

For instance, the narrative model shares with the Althusserian model the belief in the concept of interpellation, although the narrative model's vocation is premised on the called person's choice for responding or not. Likewise, the narrative model shares with the Lacanian model an appreciation for the role language plays in the formation of subject positions, although the narrative model does not posit submission to systems of signification but suggests, rather, a potentially dynamic interaction between subject and discursive systems. Finally, the narrative model shares with the Hobbesian model an understanding of limited choice between positions of responsibility on the continuum of subjectivity, of how subjects are always "subjects of" or "subject to" something, although, once again, the narrative model poses a different realm for figuring that difference.

The basic difference between the scientific and the narrative models and the one difference with which we ought to begin our discussion of the narrative model's theoretical presuppositions concerns volitional liberty, and on this basis we can make the distinction between subjectivity and subjection. Like Descartes, Milton presents God as his narrative model's Absolute Subject. The terms Hobbes develops—*subject of* and *subject to*—are translated in Milton's narrative model to *son* and *servant,* respectively, and the Absolute Sovereign is translated to *God.* Unlike the Hobbesian model, however, the narrative model proposes that the process of assuming filiality or servitude in relation to God involves the ability or inability to gain self-knowledge. It is, therefore, premised on the narrative principle of agency.

Sons and Servants: Milton's Politics of Agency

Liberty is the key word in Milton's vocabulary, whether he is establishing a lexicon for politics or for religion. As Mary Ann Radzinowicz has recently argued, the word occupies a place of mediation between Milton's religion and his politics, "between the spheres of spirit and state." Likewise, the contradictory term at the same locus between his Christianity and his politics is *idolatry.*[60] I believe, with Radzinowicz, that an understanding of Milton's politics requires an appreciation of how they cohere in his theological program. We might say, to employ C. S. Lewis's famous metaphor, that if studying Milton without reference to his theology is akin to studying a centipede freed of its irrelevant legs, then studying Milton without seeing the relationship between his politics and his theology is akin to studying that same unfortunate centipede without seeing the relationship between its left and its right legs.

If we look briefly at the general form of Milton's career, we may see how persistently in the relationship between his politics and his religion he tended to place the priority more heavily on his religion, and indeed derived his politics from that realm. From 1641 to 1645, he undertook the defense of ecclesiastical and domestic liberty—the period of the antiprelatical and divorce tracts.

From 1649 to 1660, he undertook the defense of civil liberty—the period of his republican writing. But, even so, he never turned his attention very far from the question of religious liberty. In both *A Defence* (1651) and the *Second Defence* (1654), he makes explicit mention of the necessity of freeing the Church from the powers of civil magistrates. His anti-Erastian politics are expressed with notable eagerness in the *Second Defence,* which was written after Parliament initially voted on April 29, 1652, to continue with the tithe system until another was formulated, and after the Rump later voted in March 1653 to use civil power to support the church. Likewise, in his prose tracts of 1659 Milton was at least as concerned about removing civil restraints from the realm of ecclesiastical matters as he was about the imminent return of monarchy, judging by not only his two tracts explicitly devoted to arguing the anti-Erastian point—*A Treatise of Civil Power* (February 1659) and *Considerations* (August 1659)—but also to his underlying arguments in the six short tracts from October 1659 to April 1660 which dealt overtly with the ready and easy way to establish the commonwealth. In his final piece of political prose, *Of True Religion* (1673), he did not so much return again to defend what seemed to be uppermost in his mind, but he resumed what had always been his persistent concern—ecclesiastical liberty.

Moreover, not only can we trace Milton's concern with ecclesiastical liberty in both his overtly political tracts of 1651 and 1654, as well as his explicitly anti-Erastian tracts of 1659, but we can also trace how Milton's republican years were spent writing his thorough tractate of theology. As Maurice Kelley has definitively demonstrated, Milton composed the *Christian Doctrine* during the years 1655 to 1660.[61] So, even during the years in which he was most wholly immersed in state politics, he still found time to develop his spiritual politics. Moreover, even in those prose tracts of the mid-1650s putatively concerned with the politics of state, Milton is inscribing a theological base. That is to say, then, that Milton's politics are always a product of his theology—and his theology, likewise, is always attuned to his political thought. When in *A Defence* he turns to an examination of Christ's person and its relationship to the question of liberty, he addresses Salmasius: "I do not speak of inward freedom only and omit political freedom."[62] Political liberty, he goes on to intimate in this tract and to make explicit in his next, is so involved with religious that it would take incessant labor to cull one from the other. The place to begin an examination of the politics of the 1671 volume, especially if our interest is in the modes of expressing subjectivity in that volume (both by characters and by author), is Milton's defense of agency.

Joseph Hall begins his contemplations on the Temptation with a prayer in which he desires to be transformed into a Son of God, to hear the announcement of the Baptism from the Father: "Make thou me as strong as he [Satan] is malicious; Say to my soule also (*Thou art my Sonne*) and let Satan doe his worst." Elsewhere he asks, "What is it then, oh what is it, to be the true adopted sonne of the King of glory?" He is answered by Henry Lawrence: "You have the print and Character of a sonne upon you, aswell as the relation of a sonne, which is nothing els but a certaine image and likenesse of his holinesse," and again by John Preston: as the Son was so shall you be; he "shall make thee a Priest, as himselfe," "a King, as he is a King," and "a Prophet, as he is a Prophet."[63]

Although sonship was comprised of these mystical attributes for Milton, liberty was primarily the defining principle of a filial nature. Milton comments on the distinction Paul made in his letter to the Galatians, "Thou art no more a servant, but a son" (iv, 7), in order to base that dichotomy in the matrix of "Christian liberty." Where "Christian liberty" exists, Milton argued, there also exists the possibility of "being made sons instead of servants." If, however, that liberty is not accepted, and if "we be not free," then "we are not sons, but still servants unadopted." As Milton writes in *A Defence,* "Peter was a son, and therefore free."[64] The logic of that "therefore" ("*proinde*") suggests that sonship rests precisely on that essentially Miltonic theme, liberty. Sons of God are free—that is their defining nature—while servants of God are not, for they serve idols. As the Chorus notes to Samson in the tragedy, "Yet *Israel* still serves with all his Sons" (241). The sons of Israel serve, Jesus answers in the companion poem, because they have "wrought their own captivity" (III, 413). "All men," Satan counters, "are Sons of God" (IV, 517). But the poem and the tragedy with which it is bound are contrasting studies demonstrating the falsity of Satan's remark. In 1671, Milton offered us two poems, one an epic that portrays the Son of God, the other a tragedy that portrays a servant of God.[65]

How did Milton define the conditions concerning the possibility of being free or being bound in servitude, being a Son or a

Servant? Milton's theology, as it is expressed in the all-important years from 1655 to 1660, insists that religious liberty presupposes free will and, what is more important, underwrites the very possibility of political liberty. For Milton, religious liberty was the most important possession of a culture. Political liberty was always but an effect of that prior spiritual freedom. Moreover, under the topic of religious liberty, Milton developed the enabling conditions of agency. In order to see how Milton treats the question of agency, we might best compare him to the foremost English Calvinist of the time—William Perkins.

In his epistle dedicatory to *A Golden Chaine,* Perkins defined what he felt were the four possible opinions concerning predestination. The first idea, whose followers he called "the old and new Pelagians," was that humanity possessed the free will either to "reject or receive grace offered." The second idea, whose followers "(of some) are called Lutherans," was that God, knowing in his foresight who would or would not accept grace, did "choose some to salvation of his meere mercie, without any respect of their faith or good workes," rejecting the rest because he knew they would reject him. The third idea, whose adherents he scoffingly called "Semi-Pelagian Papists," was that God predestines "partly to mercie, and partly to mans fore-seene preparation and meritorious workes." Finally, the fourth idea, whose followers needed and received no name other than "Christian," was that "the cause of the execution of Gods predestination, is his mercie in Christ, in them which are saved; and in them which perish, the fall and corruption of man: yet so, as that the decree and eternall counsell of God, concerning them both, hath not any cause beside his will and pleasure." Perkins thus developed his Calvinistic view of predestination, fully upholding Calvin's view that "reprobation" is the predestined rejection of "certaine men unto eternall destruction."[66] And this, Perkins wishes to make clear, makes his system of soteriology a supralapsarian one; that is, he upholds the "position that the decrees of election and reprobation have logical priority over the decree of both Creation and the Fall." Therefore, predestination "refers to the destinies of men not yet created, much less fallen."[67] Milton, as is well known, abjured the concept of reprobation, especially when it was expressed in a supralapsarian or infralapsarian soteriology.

But before this discussion should lead us too far into the hellish mazes of "Providence, Foreknowledge, Will, and Fate, / Fixt Fate, Free Will, Foreknowledge absolute" (*PL* II, 559–60), I must promptly state that it is not my purpose here to determine the purity of Milton's logic on this point or that of his adversaries. Rather, it is my purpose to explore how Milton comes to resolve what might be seen as the crux of Protestant thought: the relationship of divine omniscience to human liberty. Milton states, as clearly as the case allows, that God did not decree the Fall.[68] Moreover, he believed that the Fall, whatever it did to damage the rectitude of human nature, did not effectually remove free will. Perkins, on the other hand, held quite the opposite.

Let us offer Perkins's formulation first. When we turn to his fullest expression of this theme, *A Treatise of Gods free Grace, and Mans Free-Will,* we find Perkins maintaining that, since the Fall, the "liberty of the will" is "joyned with a necessity of sinning." He argues that, whereas humanity in the original state of innocence had the power both to "will that which is good" and "to will that which is evill," humanity in the state of corruption loses the first power: "Though liberty of nature remaines, yet liberty of grace, that is, to will well, is lost, extinguished, abolished by the fall of Adam." Therefore, in the state of "weaknesse and imbecility," though "the will can will, it cannot doe, unlesse God will." Stated more strongly, though "the will can will, it cannot doe without the helpe of God." Given this premise, Perkins redefines liberty in a most interesting way. It is, he writes, the "greater perfection of liberty freely and onely to will that which is good, then to be able to will both good and evill. Hee is at more libertie, that cannot be a servaunt, then he which may be either a freeman or a servant" (Perkins, *A Treatise,* in *Workes* I, pp. 722, 729, 735). This passage contains the premise to Perkins's definitions of the kinds of graces necessary for any human being to do good work. Milton would disagree with this premise, for Milton held strongly to the idea that it was necessary to have choice—son or servant—for liberty to be said to exist. Without choice, without the possibility of an agency allowing for a lapse, sonship meant very little, if anything. Before the Fall, God notes that the type of obedience Perkins has in mind would be repugnant to him:

> What pleasure I from such obedience paid,
> When Will and Reason (Reason also is choice)

Useless and vain, of freedom both despoil'd,
Made passive both, had serv'd necessity,
Not mee.   (*PL* III, 107–11)

Here is Milton's disagreement with Perkins, which is only one of degree, but nonetheless an important degree.

Whereas Perkins, following Calvin, held that the Fall "extinguished" and "abolished" the liberty to will well, Milton believed the death of the will was only partial.[69] Milton notes in the *Christian Doctrine* that the second degree of mortality is spiritual death, which took place at the very moment of the Fall ("in evil hour"). "This death consists, first, in the loss, or at least in the obscuration to a great extent of that right reason which enabled man to discern the chief good, and in which consisted as it were the life of the understanding." It consists, secondly, in "that deprivation of righteousness and liberty to do good, and in that slavish subjection to sin and the devil, which constitutes, as it were, the death of the will."[70] Milton then moderates, however, his already palliated vision of the effects of spiritual death. It cannot be denied, he argues, that "some remnants of the divine image still exist in us, not wholly extinguished by this spiritual death."

The first of these "vestiges of original excellence" is to be found "in the understanding." Nor, he continues, "is the liberty of the will entirely destroyed." Not only is it free in regard to things indifferent; it is also able to will well, however weakly. "Secondly, the will is clearly not altogether inefficient in respect of good works, or at any rate of good endeavours; at least after the grace of God has called us: but its power is so small and insignificant, as merely to deprive us of all excuse for inaction, without affording any subject for boasting."[71] Whereas Perkins, following Calvin, however confusedly, determines that the will is abolished in terms of its agency toward good deeds, Milton, following Arminius, believes the will still to have the potency to act toward "good endeavours"—to have, however feebly, an agential liberty.

In concluding the chapter on "The Punishment of Sin," Milton proposes a prose theodicy that is worth quoting at some length:

There can be no doubt that for the purpose of vindicating the justice of God, especially in his calling of mankind, it is much better to allow to man (whether as a remnant of his primitive state, or as restored through the operation of the grace whereby he is called) some portion of free will in respect of good works, or at least of good endeavours, rather than in respect of things which are indifferent. For if God be conceived to rule with absolute disposal all the actions of men, *natural as well as civil,* he appears to do nothing which is not his right, neither will any one murmur against such a procedure. But if he inclines the will of man to moral good or evil, according to his own pleasure, and then rewards the good, and punishes the wicked, the course of equity seems to be disturbed; and it is entirely on this supposition that the outcry against divine justice is founded. (My italics)

Milton is here answering attitudes expressed cogently enough in Perkins. For Perkins, too, had found three kinds of liberty: "naturall, humane, ecclesiastical." The natural refers to the sensual aspect of humanity, and so has no real place in this context. Under "humane," though, Perkins lists three heads: (1) the study and practice of arts, trades, and professions, which humans have full freedom to do; (2) the government of societies; and (3) the practice of civil virtue, justice, and temperance. Humans have the liberty to perform the second and third by two gifts of the Holy Ghost— the gift of restraint, which reins in the corruption of nature, and the gift of renovation, which mortifies corruption at its root. According to Perkins, restraint is available to the natural person, and renovation to the person in Christ. Ecclesiastical liberty, Perkins maintains, refers only to the outward duties of worshipping God, and for which humans have only a limited liberty.[72]

Milton responds almost directly to Perkins's distinctions in the liberty allowed human beings in their worship:

It would appear, therefore, that God's general government of the universe, to which such frequent allusion is made, should be understood as relating to natural and civil concerns, to things indifferent and fortuitous, in a word, to anything rather than to matters of morality and religion. . . . For if our personal religion were not in some degree dependent on ourselves, and in our own power, God could not properly enter into a covenant with us; neither could we perform, much less swear to perform, the conditions of that covenant.[73]

Here we find Milton's fullest examination of the very vexed question of agency. Given the premise of a being whose will has been dissipated by an act of historical disobedience, what sort of subjectivity might be accorded that being? The Calvinistic scheme would propose a subject who has no will, which is synonymous, Milton would have maintained, to a subject without subjectivity. The question is historically the crux of the Protestant dilemma, as well as being (still) the heart of the question of the difference between subjection and subjectivity.

What is at stake is the essential tension between the doctrine of God's omniscience and the appearance of human freedom: "Wee must relie our selves upon God onely," John Downame states, "but yet with the Lords assistance wee must joyne our endevour."[74] What was the relationship of divine knowledge to human volition? Calvin had solved it by abolishing the latter and thereby asserting the potency of the former in governing the course of history. This led to a supralapsarian system in which God was, by virtue of his omnipotence and omniscience, responsible for the Fall. It also led to a soteriology that was frankly painful for its adherents—a system that asserted an inscrutability in its workings that Calvinists quite simply could not abide. History has traced the outcome of this unequal balance—from the parody of the justified sinner to the frightening continuance of the justified capitalist. Calvinists (not Calvin) replaced the pardons and indulgences of Catholicism with either a sickly introversion or a more dangerous extroversion. Whether the result was the Puritan diary, tracing in printed and published forms the motions and life of the pained and sorrowful soul, or the Protestant work ethic, tracking the soul's advancement toward God through capital gain, Calvinists found some sort of register to define quantitatively the weight and worth of the human heart.

Milton asserted that God was not the author of sin. But, for all his noble sentiments about the power of human volition, he did not diminish the strength of his assertions on the omnipotence and omniscience of God. Indeed, his Arianism is based precisely on a will to assert the singularity and uniqueness of God's powers. God is, according to Milton, the "efficient, material, formal, and final" cause of everything—"the primary, and absolute, and sole cause of all things" (CM XV, pp. 20–21). As "efficient" cause of everything, then, we might expect God to be held causally responsible for the Fall. But Milton attempted to circumvent such an objection. The "efficiency of God," he wrote, "is either internal or external." The internal efficiency is independent of all extraneous agency—these are his decrees, of which only two are named (the "creation" and the "removal of the curse from the ground"). Milton's tone is difficult to assess when he deals with the issue of divine omnipotence and human will. In the first place, Milton believed God's original decree gave liberty to humans: "It is wholly impossible, that God should have fixed by a necessary decree what we know at the same time to be in the power of man; or that that should be immutable which it remains for subsequent contingent circumstances either to fulfill or frustrate." That first decree, therefore, precludes any future decree which might override it. Should God proclaim anything contrary to that original decree, he would be considered mutable. Therefore, Milton argues, God does not issue any decree contradictory to that first, and therefore he cannot have abolished free will: "God is not mutable, so long as he decrees nothing absolutely which could happen otherwise through the liberty assigned to man; he would indeed be mutable, neither would his counsel stand, if he were to obstruct by another decree that liberty which he had already decreed, or were to darken it with the least shadow of necessity."[75]

Milton manages to satisfy his own mind about the cooperative existence of divine omniscience and human liberty:

> Nothing happens of necessity because God has foreseen it; but he foresees the event of every action, because he is acquainted with their natural causes, which, in pursuance of his own decree, are left at liberty to exert their legitimate influence. Consequently the issue does not depend on God who foresees it, but on him alone who is the object of his foresight.

Under these conditions, *knowledge*, as we'll see in greater detail in chapter 3, is at the basis of Milton's soteriology. Without the opportunity to know the truth and salvation, there can be nothing resembling justice — and without justice, there can be no theodicy. Not only is knowledge the basis of his doctrine of salvation, but Milton insists that the very agency for gaining knowledge — reason — argues that the will is still animated, and that thereby human beings still hold the power of agency. As he states it in its logical form: "God of his wisdom determined to create men and angels reasonable beings, and therefore free agents."

Rational choice: in Milton's thought no argument was a more

suitable opponent to the arguments for predestination. He writes in *Areopagitica,* "Reason is but choosing," and again in *Paradise Lost,* "Reason also is choice."[76] The "therefore" [*ideo,* which the amanuensis writes *adeo*] between "reasonable beings" and "free agents" might alert us to the relationship Milton is establishing between reason and agency—the same sort of logic we noted earlier between sonship and liberty. The logic of the phrase would be that only in the exercise of reason does agency accrue to the reasonable being. Likewise, in the phrases from *Areopagitica* and *Paradise Lost,* choice is the operation of agency that occurs only when reason is said to be exercised; under those conditions, and only under those conditions, can reason be said to have become synonymous with choice. Because choice is the exercise of agency, reason becomes to that extent the register for agency in any human subject. Put into the contradistinction I have been tracing, the reasonable being is an agent who is a Son of God, and the unreasonable being loses that agency upon demonstrating recalcitrant unreasonableness and becomes, therefore, the servant of God. Reason, moreover, in the mature poetry is expressed most of all when any given character attempts to aspire to self-knowledge by reading his or her life.

I will examine this development in detail in a moment, but it is worth noting here that reason, choice, and agency, as they belong to and support knowledge, are neither static nor autonomous properties. They together, and knowledge as a whole, are in perpetual movement. Knowledge in Milton's works, to employ a sort of Heideggerian shorthand, is most accurately described as an always coming-to-knowledge. It is emphatically an ongoing process. This is especially true of self-knowledge in Milton's works. First of all, Milton argues that the self is not a simple entity with a contained ability to recognize its qualities. Secondly, he argues that knowledge is not a simple activity which the self is able to employ in a reflexive act. Thirdly, he maintains that neither self nor knowledge is static, and that the act of self-knowledge involves an enduring meditation in which God is the mediating object of desire. That is, for Milton, self-knowledge is premised on what both Descartes and Spinoza equally held to be the basis of knowledge: the ability to know God. We have seen above how Descartes expresses this assumption. Spinoza, much as he might be in disagreement with Milton's Arminianism, also posits that knowledge of self is possible only with an attempt at knowing God, what Spinoza calls the "third kind of knowledge" which "proceeds from an adequate idea of certain attributes of God." Moreover, it is this third kind of knowledge — the intuitive knowledge of God — that gives meaning and substance to, and indeed is the precondition of, any attempt at self-knowledge.[77] As Milton puts it in *Paradise Regained,* the way to self-knowledge is "To know . . . God aright" (II, 475). So the act of coming to self-knowledge is not static because it is a process of perpetually striving for a higher knowledge, and the knowing self is not autonomous because it is able to know itself only by way of knowing God. I will be employing a Heideggerian phrase to describe the relation the self has to God, and that is *being-toward.* Adam, for example, is a being-toward God until he becomes a being-toward Eve. For knowledge, like desire, has direction.

The dichotomy we have been noting in Milton's theology — sons and servants — has as its Hobbesian political counterpart the distinction between being a "subject of" or being "subject to" something. The something in Milton is God; as in the Cartesian model, his existence is the necessary and first premise of subjectivity. In translating Milton's dichotomy from the field of theology to the field of state politics, one finds that Milton begins to make alterations in his concept of subjectivity. The major alterations in Milton's political discourse will be discussed in chapter 5, but it is important to note just a few points here.

First of all, Milton still retains the concepts of filiality and servitude in his political thinking, although the appellations are somewhat changed. In *A Defence of the People of England,* for instance, having insisted that "law is right reason above all else," Milton adopts Henry de Bracton's distinction of "servant of God" and "servant of the Devil" to designate the attitudes of filiality or servility in terms of a political representative of God. Second, implicitly by the late 1650s and explicitly by 1671, Milton will make a firmer distinction between subjectivity and subjection, and the former will be available only in relation to God, the latter *in potentia* in relation to the state. Third, when discussing the conditions concerning subjection to the state, Milton makes the distinction between individuals and subjects — a distinction the scientific model attempted to deny. Again employing Bracton's political distinctions, Milton argues that, although "everyone is subject to the king" ("*Omnis sub rege est*"), that subjection does not argue for an absolute monarchy, nor does it elide the concept of the individual (*singuli*).

For Milton, subjection in the political sphere does not entail the same sort of limitless abject submission required of the citizen in the Hobbesian model. Toward the end of the 1651 tract, he answers Salmasius's Hobbesian arguments by proclaiming, "as for our being 'subjects,' all such subjection, as our own laws declare, is limited to what is 'honorable and beneficial.'"[78] The way of defining "honorable and beneficial," as Milton makes clear, depends on an understanding of the "Law of Nature," that same law Hobbes had tried to proscribe.

In the final analysis, then, Milton makes a firm distinction between subjectivity and subjection on the basis of which realm the individual is seeking in order to discern a subject status, the realm of the state or the realm of the cosmos, in relation to a monarch or in relation to God. Milton will argue for a unique relationship between the two realms, between potential subjectivity and potential subjection. The basis of his argument rests on what he does with the Delphic oracle's pronouncement. Throughout his career, Milton was suspicious of the oracle. Like the persona in Sir John Davies's *Nosce Teipsum*, Milton associated the Delphic oracle with Satan and he held that the oracle had been silenced at the coming of Christ. Prior to that silencing, the oracle, Milton maintained, made pronouncements that were ambiguous and dangerous. As early as the Nativity ode (1629), Milton described how the "Oracles are dumb" and were thereby unable anymore to utter their "words deceiving" (*Nat.*, 173–75). And as late as *Paradise Regained* (1671), he described how the "Oracles are ceast" and were therefore unable to declare their answers "dark / Ambiguous and with double sense deluding" (*PR* I, 456, 434–35). What Milton does in each case is establish a different form of and medium for gaining self-knowledge. In the Nativity ode, the birth of Christ joins the "darksome House of mortal Clay" to the divine "glorious Form, that Light unsufferable" (14, 8). In *Paradise Regained*, the Delphic oracle is replaced by God's "living Oracle," an "inward Oracle" manifesting God's "Spirit of Truth" (I, 460–64). That "Spirit" is the medium for the individual's gaining of self-knowledge because it acts as the link between the human and the divine realms. The "Spirit" gives the acquisition of self-knowledge a novel basis because it presupposes that the self exists only insofar as the resident spirit, which is the gift of God, is acknowledged. The Spirit, it hardly needs to be said, is precisely the point where Milton is answering Hobbesian materialism.

It would be hard to overstate the importance of the "Spirit" in Milton's entire theology, but in order to appreciate its importance, I must note the differences in Milton's theological and narrative strategies in order to interpret the Spirit's significance. An examination of the *Christian Doctrine* demonstrates fairly conclusively that the Spirit, as part of the orthodox Trinity, is depotentiated in Milton's theology to the extent that it seems to have no function other than symbolizing the synergistic energy of the Father and the Son. When we turn to the narratives, we find Milton's insistence on the role of the Spirit. The plot of *Paradise Lost* turns on how Adam misconceives the Spirit's role in self-knowledge. Moreover, the whole of Milton's rhetorical strategy in the induction to *Paradise Regained* rests on the place of the Spirit in human reading skills. Milton's entire epistemology, in fact, rests on the individual's capacity for discerning the Spirit in a phenomenal world, and one may understand Samson's misconstrued sense of selfhood precisely on the question of the Spirit. With an appreciation of the role the Spirit plays in Milton's narratives, we might return to his unorthodox Trinity and assess anew its constituent components.

So far, I have argued that Milton's theology proposes "liberty" or the function of "willing" to be the essence of the filial nature; to be able to will is to be a "Son" in Milton's narrative model. The act of willing is always directed toward the Father, who is the Absolute Subject or, as Milton says in *Paradise Lost,* who is "one first matter all." In other words, inasmuch as the Son is willing, God the Father *is* Being. The Spirit performs the function of allowing the Son (and any who aspire to be filial) to direct his attempts at self-knowledge toward the Father. Thus, just as the Father is Being, and the Son is willing, the Spirit becomes the way of knowing. It would not be inaccurate to say that the Spirit is basic to all acts of self-knowledge in Milton's narratives.

Willing and knowing (liberty and reason) are almost inseparable in Milton's cosmos. So, whereas Milton's epistemology represents precisely the three functions of the traditional Augustinian Trinity, the functions do not sit exactly as they do with the persons in that Trinity. As Augustine writes in his *Confessions,* the Trinity consists of "*esse, nosse, velle*" ("to be, to know, and to will"). Milton alters the final two functions, but they are inseparable. He also makes individual being an effect of the role of God the Father, who is Being. In other words, when Milton represents the Trinity of functions in his narratives, he conflates all three functions into those three forms of self-knowledge I described earlier—the fields of being, knowledge, and will.

Of course, Milton's ascribing the functions to the persons of the Trinity is in no way compromising his Arian ideals. The Spirit is still only an effect of the intersection of the Father and the Son, but it is an effect crucial to humanity's strivings; that is the most we may say Milton is willing to concede.[79]

Toward Paradise Lost: *The Failure of Self-Knowledge*

Milton's reformulation of the Delphic oracle's pronouncement involves placing the Spirit prominently within the individual self. In effect, the act of knowing a self becomes the act of discerning the Spirit within. This reformulation carries with it several important ramifications for the concept of self-knowledge. For one thing, Milton resolves what I earlier called the Delphic dilemma—the idea that there is an irreducible recursion between the self and knowledge—and he does so in much the same way as Plato did. In the Platonic model of self-knowledge, the self aspires to recognize in earthly forms the heavenly ideals it once intuited; by this process the self acquires its knowledge and thereby constitutes itself. Plato conflated the more famous Delphic pronouncement ("Know thyself") with the less famous ("Be temperate"), promoting in that conflation a philosophy of understanding based on the Dorian harmony of word (*logos*) and deed (*ergon*), as Socrates says in *Laches*.[80] Nonetheless, this philosophy is not entirely without its problems. In fact, in the *Charmides,* Socrates makes this harmonic form of self-knowledge the object of his skepticism.

Debating on the question of *sophrosyne,* Socrates utterly confuses Charmides who thought he had successfully defined the meaning of self-knowledge. Charmides maintains that temperance *is* self-knowledge:

> For I would almost say that self-knowledge is the very essence of temperance, and in this I agree with him who dedicated the inscription "Know thyself!" at Delphi. . . . If I rightly understand the mean-

ing of the inscription, the god speaks to those who enter his temple, not as men speak, but whenever a worshiper enters, the first word which he hears is "Be temperate!" This, however, like a prophet he expresses in a sort of riddle, for "Know thyself!" and "Be temperate!" are the same, as I maintain.

Socrates here is in an even more quibbling mood than usual, and he tests the reader's patience as much as Charmides's when he begins to discuss whether or not temperance and self-knowledge fall under the same rubric.

> Tell me, then, I [Socrates] said, what you mean to affirm about wisdom.
> I mean to say that wisdom is the only science which is the science of itself as well as of the other sciences.
> But the science of science, I said, will also be the science of the absence of science.
> Very true, he said.
> Then the wise or temperate man, and he only, will know himself, and be able to examine what he knows or does not know, and to see what others know and think that they know and do really know, and what they do not know and fancy that they know when they do not. No other person will be able to do this. And this is wisdom and temperance and self-knowledge — for a man to know what he knows, and what he does not know. That is your meaning?[81]

Charmides is baffled, and perhaps with some justice. The main point we ought to take from Socrates here is that self-knowledge is always problematic to the extent that the self is always a construction of what it knows, and what it knows is always limited by its cognitive capacities. An Athenian Descartes of the fifth century might have established a *via media* by proposing that what the self was striving to attain was a *knowledge* and not a *grasp* of the divine ideals. That is, the self would recognize its limitations and yet strive for knowledge. The complete *grasp* of things knowable and unknowable, which Socrates is proposing as a definition of *knowledge*, requires some refinement. That refinement involves suggesting that the self can know its nescience although it cannot apprehend it; self-knowledge, in other words, is always the partial knowledge of a dependent self. *Self-apprehension* might be the term to employ in describing the complete knowledge of an autonomous self—and this self-apprehension would belong solely to God, Platonic or Christian.

As much as he maintained temperance as the subsuming quality of a person's life—"How great a vertue is temperance, how much of moment through the whole life of man?" (*Areopagitica*, CM IV, p. 309)—Milton would also have disagreed with Charmides, although not on the same grounds as Socrates. The basis of Milton's disagreement concerns the question of the place God has in self-knowledge; that is, it properly concerns the Christian idea of the logos. The logos, which was the structural design of the world in Heraclitus and the dialogical way of knowledge in Plato, becomes God in Christianity. As John says at the beginning of his gospel, "In the beginning was the Word [Logos], and the Word was with God, and the Word was God" (John i, 10). Accordingly, as Paul states, it is in God (Logos) that "we live, and move, and have our being" (Acts xxviii, 17).[82] For Milton, the effect of God in every individual self is the Spirit. For that reason, self-knowledge is an act any individual is capable of undertaking only under the auspices of God and only through the exercise of the spirit.

In the end, self-knowledge for all of Milton's characters, whether successfully undertaken or not, is a matter of comprehending the ways they are situated within a cosmology in which, as Raphael tells Adam, "one Almighty is, from whom / All things proceed, and up to him return" (*PL* V, 469–70). To know oneself, then, in a cosmos where God is "the *efficient, material, formal,* and *final*" cause of all being would require the sort of patent impossibility that Socrates pointed out to Charmides—to know both what one knows and to know what one does not know (CM XV, pp. 20–21). Self-knowledge, then, in Milton, as for Socrates, is a problematic issue which does not consist of any easy program of ethical behavior. In each of Milton's late major works, from *Paradise Lost* to *Samson Agonistes,* the major characters undergo various "confrontations," which lead to a limited form of self-knowledge.

Each of Milton's major characters (for example, Adam, Jesus, and Samson) expresses a long autobiographical soliloquy in which he examines his previous life and determines to what cause he must claim allegiance.[83] That autobiographical moment leads each character "within" in order to determine what innate ideas exist there. In going within, each undergoes a profound act of meditation. Having undergone an autobiographical examination and a moment of meditative interiority, the character formulates a concept of subjectivity that will determine the rest of his career. At the end of his moment of crisis, Adam represents himself to himself as a votary of desire and a fallen subject. At the end of Jesus' meditation, he represents himself as an agent of God and a transforming subject. Samson represents himself as a vessel of God and a subject of retribution. How each represents himself to himself determines how each is incorporated within a divine plan. In the end, self-knowledge constitutes the self, performing in effect what Richard Lanham calls rhetoric's capacity for "enselfment."[84] That, as we said earlier, is the postlapsarian form of self-knowledge.

What is within is, of course, the Spirit, and the Spirit is both the means and the end of self-knowledge—the means because it is the light that allows the self to examine itself, the end because it is the representative of God's fiat of creation in every individual. The Spirit is at the heart of what Jesus grants humanity in the first book of *Paradise Regained*—the "inner Oracle." The Spirit is what God is praising Adam for expressing in his second act of self-knowledge:

> Thus far to try thee, *Adam,* I was pleas'd,
> And find thee knowing not of Beasts alone,
> Which thou hast rightly nam'd, but of thyself,
> Expressing well the spirit within thee free,
> My Image, not imparted to the Brute.
>
> (*PL* VIII, 437–41)

This trial is a test of self-knowledge: "knowing . . . of thyself." Moreover, self-knowledge is an act of expressing what comprises the self, which is, as God makes pointedly clear, "the spirit within." This spirit is both the agency of discovery and the true self within awaiting discovery, precisely because this spirit is what expresses God's "Image." Self-knowledge, under these conditions, becomes a Platonic anamnesis of the original logos expressed through the spirit and discovered under the stress of trial.

Adam had been created for just this purpose—to know himself and therefore know something of God. The narrator's prefatory remarks to Adam's creation indicate all the factors involved in the Miltonic scheme of self-knowledge:

> There wanted yet the Master work, the end
> Of all yet done; a Creature who not prone

> And Brute as other Creatures, but endu'd
> With Sanctity of Reason, might erect
> His Stature, and upright with Front serene
> Govern the rest, self-knowing, and from thence
> Magnanimous to correspond with Heav'n,
> But grateful to acknowledge whence his good
> Descends, thither with heart and voice and eyes
> Directed in Devotion, to adore
> And worship God Supreme who made him chief
> Of all his works.   (VII, 505–16)

Humanity's uniqueness is premised on the fact that humans are reasonable beings and therefore "self-knowing." By being self-knowing they are capable of being grateful to the cause of their being. The cause is God, but the way of expressing gratitude involves the spirit (that is why self-knowledge is premised on, and rewarded by, "magnanimity"). As Raphael tells Adam, "in thy nostrils breath'd / The breath of Life; in his own Image hee / Created thee, in the Image of God / Express, and thou becam'st a living Soul" (VII, 525–28). That, in the end, constitutes the premise of the Miltonic narrative model of self-knowledge.

Like the Althusserian model of interpellation, the narrative model involves a "calling." But whereas the Althusserian model is based on a premise that the calling must be heeded—that ideology cannot be resisted—the narrative model is based on the premise of free choice. In the Miltonic model, prelapsarian and postlapsarian interpellation follow exactly the same pattern. In a postlapsarian world, every individual will be called to become a subject of God. He or she has a choice about whether to respond to the call or not. As God says, humanity "shall hear me call . . . for I will clear thir senses dark, . . . And I will place within them as a guide / My Umpire *Conscience*" (III, 185–95). In a prelapsarian world, Adam and Eve are created subjects of God. They have the choice to remain subjects *of* God or to break the commandment and become therefore subject *to* God. As God says, Adam and Eve are "free to fall" (III, 99). At the basis of either a prelapsarian or a postlapsarian world, then, is the agency of reasonable choice. And that agency differs as it belongs to different selves in the same individual. Unlike the scientific model, the narrative model allows for diachronic development between different concepts of selfhood and different forms of self-knowledge. Keeping in mind the three salient forms of self-knowledge, we may turn to *Paradise Lost* and see the ways Adam gains, loses, and potentially regains subjectivity. When Adam describes his first conscious thoughts, we discover that he has been created to the specifications God and the Son had decided appropriate. His immediate response upon awakening as a conscious being is to look up to heaven and attempt to discover his original cause:

> Straight toward Heav'n my wondering Eyes I turn'd,
> And gaz'd a while the ample Sky, till rais'd
> By quick instinctive motion up I sprung,
> As thitherward endeavouring, and upright
> Stood on my feet.
> . . . .
> Myself I then perus'd, and Limb by Limb
> Survey'd, and sometimes went, and sometimes ran
> With supple joints, as lively vigor led:
> But who I was, or where, or from what cause,
> Knew not.   (VIII, 257–71)

His first impulse is to know himself—first physically and then, more profoundly, to know his identity, his being, and his origin. He reaches the conclusion that he could not have been self-created and decides that he must have been the creature of "some great Maker." He is rewarded for this insight by being allowed to converse with God. As in the Althusserian scientific model, interpellation in the Miltonic narrative model occurs prior to the subject's becoming conscious. Althusser had proposed that the subject was a subject before he or she was born; Milton simply replaces "born" with "created." Adam is created as a subject of God; he is, following Milton's own terminology, created a "Son of God."

The difference, of course, is that whereas the Althusserian model is based on an interpellation that makes the individual "subject to" the ideological state apparatus, the Miltonic model is based on an interpellation that allows the individual to be a "subject of" God; the latter enjoys liberty of choice based on the agency of reason. There is, therefore, a spirit within Adam letting him understand that he is indebted to another order of being, his God. His concept of selfhood, from his first conscious thoughts, does not entertain the possibility of autonomy: "Not of myself." Adam makes an original distinction that is basically perceptual. He recognizes that he is on one plane, but that his creator is on another. Adam's "instinctive motion" directs him, in a Platonic way, to heaven. He recognizes heaven as the plane on which his sense of selfhood depends. He also recognizes that there is an "epistemic distance" between himself and his creator, which is why he is "thitherward endeavouring." Adam's first act is to understand that he is a creature with perceptive skills and that he is indebted to a creator he wishes to perceive. In effect, Adam's initial act of knowing himself follows the first form of self-knowledge we noted above—knowing the distinction between a self and the Other. In this case, however, it is not merely perceptual because it is a distinction between a created self and a creating Other. In the original state of being, for Adam the Other is heaven and only heaven.

It is only in conversation with that Other that Adam begins to recognize that he has a lack in his life. In a colloquy with God, Adam recognizes that he is "defective" alone because he requires "conversation with his like" both for love and population. It is important to realize that Adam has two distinct desires—one for earthly company by which he can "solace his defects" and another for divine conversation by which he can maintain his selfhood. In fact, we can accurately call only the first *desire*. The second is more rightly called *love* because God's spirit is within Adam. The distinction, of course, is based on Hobbes's insight. He had written, "by Desire, we alwayes signifie the Absence of the Object" and "by Love, most commonly the Presence of the same" (*Leviathan*, p. 119). What Adam feels a longing to have is what is absent in his life. The spirit functions as God's presence in Adam.

Only in terms of answering the first desire does God grant Adam Eve, whom he calls Adam's "other self" (*PL* VIII, 450). Eve is not "part" of Adam's self, not the missing Aristophanic other half making him complete; she is, quite simply, an other self. This concept, however, is one Adam has a very difficult time understanding (and neither God nor Raphael helps him with this problem). His problems begin when he conceives of Eve as complete in herself. He knows that his sense of selfhood depends on heaven, but he fails to understand that Eve's does also: "so absolute she seems / And in herself complete." Moreover, it is only at that moment that he begins to consider the relationship such "completeness" may have to self-knowledge. She seems, he continues, "so well to know / Her own" (*PL* VIII, 547–49). In response to this, Raphael tells Adam to return to his prior form of gaining self-knowledge:

> weigh with her thyself;
> Then value: Oft-times nothing profits more
> Than self-esteem, grounded on just and right
> Well-manag'd; of that skill the more thou know'st,
> The more she will acknowledge thee her Head.   (570–74)

I cannot argue that Raphael's, or Milton's, is not a hierarchical system that is unabashedly sexist; it unhappily is. What I would like to note here, though, is that Raphael's directions do suggest to Adam the process by which he might recognize that Eve is, as God said at her creation, an "other self," and that she was therefore liable to the same degree and forms of dependent selfhood as is Adam.

But Adam does not attend to Raphael's directions for understanding how others are selves. Instead, Adam, as his sons will lamentably do and keep doing, uses this misprision of female autonomy as a justification for subordinating Eve.[85] What Adam missed perceiving, then, is what a more astute anthropologist would have considered basic—that self-knowledge and community are intimately related—or what a keen theologian would have considered primary—that self-knowledge is always dependent on God and there is no such thing as human completeness. In other words, Adam mistakes both his desire and his love. He does not appreciate that Eve is also liable to her own "instinctive motion" or that part of Eve's self-knowledge, like his, is a product of their conversations.

Like his mistake, Adam's failure is also twofold. First, by subjecting Eve to a state of infantile dependence, he fails to understand how Eve as "partner" would have allowed both of them a fuller self-knowledge. Second, by choosing to fall with Eve instead of attempting to glean God's will by comprehending the terms of his interdiction of eating the fruit, he fails to choose to follow the love that would have allowed him to maintain his status as a subject of God. By choosing instead to fall with Eve, Adam makes the choice to become subject to his earthly desire and thereby subject to God. He loses the potential for self-knowledge in two interrelated ways. In truth, Adam begins to fail to attain self-knowledge once he fails to bring to consciousness the "idea" of his "passion." And that failure is the beginning of his fall.

His fall, as has long been noted, begins in the eighth book. In his defensive response to Raphael's advice about the need to garner self-

evaluative skills, he states that he has generated a stock of self-knowledge answerable to any crisis:

> Yet these subject not; I to thee disclose
> What inward thence I feel, not therefore foil'd,
> Who meet with various objects, from the sense
> Variously representing; yet still free
> Approve the best, and follow what I approve. (VIII, 607–11)

The key word in Adam's reply is *subject*. What he says to Raphael,
in effect, is that the spirit within him is capable of dealing with any
trauma, should he ever confront a situation in which he would be
subject to passion. The reason he brings the word and concept of
the *subject* so prominently in place here is that he is answering
Raphael's suggestion that Eve deserves Adam's love, not his "subjection" (569–70). Adam states that he has the liberty of a subject
of God because he knows what is really "inward thence." Possessing the spirit within, he feels he may confidently deal with any
situation from without.

Of course, as Raphael seems to know too well, Adam's problem
is already within. When Adam confronts the original crisis of
humanity in the next book and does indeed delve "inward" in order
to determine what is "best," he finds himself inadequate to the
moment. When Eve comes to him fallen, he enters a meditative
state — "to himself he inward silence broke" — only to return a fall-
en being: "Certain my resolution is to Die" (IX, 895, 907). Adam's
fall is a complex issue in itself and requires a more extended study,
but the choice he makes here — Eve over God — alerts us to the
conditions by which he governs his life. He has not approved the
best, as he thought he would be able to do, because he has not
internalized a state of obedient love to God. His meditation, which
should have allowed him to see how a wisely governed internal
state can provide a model for dealing with any external crisis, fails
him because he is able to see only an internal state in turmoil. His
inner state is in turmoil because, according to the conventional
Renaissance scheme of internal government, passion has usurped
rule from reason, and, according to the conventional Christian
scheme of mediation, Adam has chosen to love Eve for herself
instead of loving her for God's sake (IX, 1119–31).

What Adam does when he falls is conform to a Hobbesian

concept of an appetitive subject. Hobbes, as we will see more clearly in chapter 5, makes desire the constituent and enduring fact of human existence. Even more than Hobbes, Spinoza develops a scientific model of how desire governs action. In the second part of *The Ethics,* Spinoza suggests, as a prelude to the gesture Althusser would make three centuries later, that "Will and understanding are one and the same." This is clearly a departure from the Cartesian model, in which will and intellection are strictly distinct. What Spinoza's model offers is the necessity of deducing acts of understanding from acts of will; it might stand in the realm of philosophy as the anti-Lutheran idea of the importance of works over faith stands in the realm of Reformation theology. That, however, is not the end of Spinoza's agenda. In the following section, he likewise conflates the category of thinking with the category of desiring: "The dictates of the mind are but another name for the appetites." And, following his earlier proposition, he also conflates the category of willing with the category of desiring. "This endeavour, when referred solely to the mind, is called *will,* when referred to the mind and body in conjunction it is called *appetite*." Furthermore, in bringing his system to a scientific close, he proclaims, "Desire is appetite with consciousness thereof."[86]

Nonetheless, Spinoza does propose a way for the mind to overcome its appetitive desires. In the fifth section, he discusses how the mind can free itself by bringing its own passions to consciousness. His third proposition states, "An emotion, which is a passion, ceases to be a passion, as soon as we form a clear and distinct idea thereof" (*Ethics,* p. 248). The way to reform a passion into an idea is to employ what Spinoza calls the "second kind of knowledge" — reason. By doing so, the individual may then go on to use the "third kind of knowledge" — intuition or "knowledge of God" (p. 113). As Spinoza notes, "Who clearly and distinctly understands himself and his emotions loves God, and so much the more in proportion as he more understands himself and his emotions" (p. 255). Spinoza offers a program to follow in moving from self-knowledge to the love of God. The first thing one must do is gain knowledge of the emotion, then separate the emotion from the thought of an external cause. After knowing what the emotion is and determining its external cause, one must define the relationship of that "external cause" with the "eternal cause" of all things —

God. It is only after all three axes of the traditional triangle of desire have been defined — the desiring subject, God, and the desired object — that the subject may understand how desire can be translated into true love. Spinoza calls this final understanding true apprehension, "a love towards a thing immutable and eternal, whereof we may really enter into possession." He concludes that we "may thus readily conceive the power which clear and distinct knowledge, and especially that third kind of knowledge, founded on the actual knowledge of God, possesses over the emotions." In effect, Adam falls because he does not fully understand his desire at the end of his conversation with Raphael. He has not brought his emotion to consciousness and made it a clear and distinct idea in his mind. Instead, he attempts to convince Raphael (and probably himself) that he is not confusing the external objects of his desire with the Spirit within him directing him to love God. He claims that he would be able to approve what is best and to understand that Eve must be desired only through a love of God. But he has not clarified the issues for himself. Adam fails to achieve the self-knowledge that he ought to have achieved. He falls, as we are told, against "his better knowledge" (IX, 998).

Adam acts against his best self-knowledge and against the dictate of temperance. The only way for him to act out this fall against both Delphic pronouncements is to conceive of a wholly new self, which is precisely what he does in his last words before the fall. He concludes his speech to Eve:

> So forcible within my heart I feel
> The Bond of Nature draw me to my own,
> My own in thee, for what thou art is mine;
> Our State cannot be sever'd, we are one,
> One Flesh; to lose thee were to lose myself.
>
> (IX, 955–59)

Adam's final sentiment is, of course, a parody of Christ's words: "He that loseth his life for my sake shall find it" (Matt. x, 39). Adam has only omitted the "for my sake." In fact, Adam has simply reconceived of the ways that selfhood is preserved. The "instinctive motions" directing him toward heaven are transformed into egocentric motions directing him into himself: "Draw me to my own." It is precisely because he has conceived a new sense of selfhood that he may fall. Conversely, and this is the liberty of the narrative model, he may fall because he can conceive a new sense of selfhood.

Adam chooses his desire for Eve over his love of God. Throughout his discussion with Raphael, it becomes apparent that Adam's yearning is to transcend the limitations which flesh is heir to. Having accepted the first distinction between his earthly self and his creator Other, Adam seems unable to accept otherness in his earthly partner. God introduces Eve very carefully as being Adam's "other self." Adam accepts her carelessly as being "my Self / Before me" (VIII, 495–96). Adam does not accept Eve as an other self; he would have her be himself. Like Lacan, Milton saw in what ways the desiring subject attempts to displace itself in order to make room for the absolute interpenetration of the desired object. The sort of desire Adam expresses here is precisely that form of desire Sir Thomas Browne felt had to be experienced and then transcended: "United souls are not satisfied with embraces, but *desire each to be truly the other;* which being impossible, their desires are infinite and must proceed without a possibility of satisfaction."[87] This desire is what makes misery of so long a life. But it is not impossible for Adam to achieve that state of sublime desire.

In fact, just after Adam expresses most powerfully his "vehement desire" for precisely this sort of "Union of Mind," Raphael tells him about how angels communicate (VIII, 526, 604). Raphael's answer to Adam's query about the sexual engagements of angels is supposed to suggest to Adam a future time when desire does truly allow the self to become the other, and the other the self:

> Whatever pure thou in the body enjoy'st
> (And pure thou wert created) we enjoy
> In eminence, and obstacle find none
> Of membrane, joint, or limb, exclusive bars:
> Easier than Air with Air, if Spirits embrace,
> Total they mix, Union of Pure with Pure
> Desiring; nor restrain'd conveyance need
> As Flesh to mix with Flesh, or Soul with Soul.
>
> (VIII, 622–29)

Had Raphael not already promised Adam the possibility of enjoying the same sort of unmediated love and sexual bliss, this moment in his discourse might strike us as unnecessarily titilating, if not

downright cruel. After all, it does come immediately after Adam
has expressed the most intense longing for just this sort of communion with Eve. Raphael might well seem to be taunting Adam by
describing his own sexual prowess, a prowess simply unavailable to
Adam.

It is, however, not *yet* available to Adam—and that is the point
Raphael is trying to make. His concluding remarks about the perfection of spiritual sexuality, a union of desire answered perfectly
with desire, is not meant to titillate or to depress Adam but to
remind him of his ultimate end. That end, as Raphael had earlier
told Adam, is to enjoy exactly the same sort of immediacy as do the
angels:

> time may come when men
> With Angels may participate.
> . . . .
> Your bodies may at last turn all to spirit,
> Improv'd by tract of time, and wing'd ascend
> Ethereal, as wee, or may at choice
> Here or in Heav'nly Paradise dwell;
> If ye be found obedient, and retain
> Unalterably firm his love entire
> Whose progeny you are.   (V, 493–503)

Essentially, Raphael tells Adam and Eve that they may eventually
become wholly spiritual by maintaining their sense of a prelapsarian selfhood. As they gain self-knowledge—and here is why it is
important that the agency for gaining self-knowledge (Spirit) is
also the end of gaining self-knowledge—they will fulfill what is
innate in them. They will become spirits by exercising their spiritual capacity for knowing themselves.

Desire in this scheme, as Raphael and Sir Thomas Browne
make pointedly clear, is best mediated through loving God. Raphael begins his discourse in Book V by promising Adam and Eve the
potential to become spiritual and he closes in Book VIII by offering Adam both a description of and a diet for a more satisfying sex
life: "Be strong, live happy, and love, but first of all / Him whom to
love is to obey" (VIII, 633–34).

Because the narrative model allows the self to conceive another
form of selfhood—for the subject of God to become subject to

God—it can be said that its model of interpellation is based on choice. The narrative model's interpellation allows the subject the liberty of falling out of subjectivity. Adam had hitherto been a subject of God; he had been a Son of God. His "instinctive motion" had been toward heaven. Now, though, at the moment of the Fall, he does not feel that "instinctive motion," but rather he feels the "Link of Nature draw" him (IX, 914). This is the same "Nature" he had used to explain to Raphael why he felt incomplete in Eve's presence: "Or Nature fail'd in mee, and left some part / Not proof enough such Object to sustain" (VIII, 534–35). Raphael sternly replies, "Accuse not Nature, she hath done her part" (561). This particular scene is significant because it marks the moment when Adam starts to renege on his responsibility, the instant when he begins to credit anything but the spirit for his actions and his thinking, when, in Hobbesian terms, he accedes to another (Nature) the authorship of his own deficiencies. It is the moment, therefore, when he starts to move from a prelapsarian self-knowledge to a lapsarian self-knowledge.

Adam's failure to exercise his reason and to choose freely to maintain his status as a subject of God is a failure of self-knowledge. He did not attend to the spirit within when he was subject to passion. By subjecting himself to passion, he has lost the sense of being a subject of God. His choice issues from that loss. When the Son comes to judge Adam, he makes it quite clear that this lapse is in fact the failure of self-knowledge. "Was shee thy God, that her thou didst obey / Before his voice," asks the Son. This mistaken loyalty would not have occurred, he tells Adam, "hadst thou known thyself aright" (X, 145–46, 156). The fall, then, is an externally articulated effect of what has already happened internally in Adam and Eve. Before they lose Eden, they lose the "paradise within"; and the loss of an internal paradise is premised on the prior loss of an internal government based on temperance and the acknowledgment of God as its head. The eating of the fruit is only what Milton would call a breaking of a "pledge" to what has already been transgressed (CM XV, pp. 114–15).

This completes the paradigm I noted earlier. Adam meets his original moment of consciousness by turning to a brief autobiographical exposition in which he discovers within himself the idea of a greater being. At the moment of crisis, he turns within himself again only to find that he is another self, based on a different concept of selfhood. He is no longer a being-toward God but rather a being-toward himself. This is specifically characteristic of the act of foregoing subjectivity. He finally represents himself as a votary of passion, a desiring being whose devotion to nature is stronger than his devotion to God. Having done so, he can be no other than as he represents himself. In this narrative, saying "Myself am Hell" is as much a way of ensuring that fact as of describing it. Precisely because of the way self-representation constitutes self in the narrative model of self-knowledge, Adam and Eve conclude their career by being granted the possibility of representing themselves anew.

We have seen, then, the first and second forms of self-knowledge. In the first instance, Adam perceived a self and an Other. The first act of knowing himself is knowing the boundaries of his self. In the second instance, Adam and Eve had to acknowledge that their lapsed selves were different from their prelapsarian selves. At the end of Book IX, they have not yet reached the stage of maturity to do that. Each accuses the other of being guilty, and neither attempts to assume personal responsibility; they are, as the narrator says, "neither self-condemning" (IX, 1186). But by the end of Book X, they have come to that maturity—Eve first—and they realize that it is fruitless to "blame / Each other" (X, 958–59). At this point, they are able to send their contrite prayers to heaven. And these contrite prayers begin the process of propitiation, which will end in a completely new sense of collective selfhood. As the Son says to God, in presenting him with Adam and Eve's first prayers, "Accept me, and . . . with mee / All my redeem'd . . . Made one with me as I with thee am one" (XI, 37–44). The end result of Adam's failure to achieve absolute communion with Eve is the absolute communion humanity will enjoy with God.

From Paradise Lost: *Postlapsarian Self-Knowledge*

Postlapsarian self-knowledge involves the transmutation of desire into faith or, more correctly, into love. This transmutation is established on the grounds of language and involves an act of rhetorical self-representation. The rhetorical ideal, then, rests on the same grounds Burke uses to argue for the points of convergence between *dialectic* and *dramatistic*. Using his definition of dialectic, the rhetorical ideal of life, or postlapsarian self-knowledge, means the "employment of the possibilities of linguistic transformation" (*Grammar of Motives*, p. 402). In fact, Adam's final lesson is to manipulate language to represent to himself a state he strongly desires, to articulate his being as if this state were *actually* so, and then to live his life in accord with that imagined, represented state. By imagining himself to be saved, and acting as if he were indeed saved, Adam will find himself, in the fullness of time, to be saved. The obvious argument against this thesis is that Adam cannot be saved without the mediation of Christ. Given that this mediator is absolutely necessary, the narrative model finds itself unmoored from its tenets of will, liberty, and agency. That, though, is not quite the case. I would like to argue that Milton's conception of salvation did not imply necessity, even the necessity of Christ's crucifixion. In other words, Milton believed that Christ's life was more efficacious for the promotion of a Christian culture than Christ's death was for its basis.

In order to accept such a contentious representation of Milton's christology, we have to gain a finer understanding of Milton's soteriology. While I will be examining this element of Milton's thought in fuller detail later, I would here note one significant point in Milton's thought on the question of salvation. Milton, in his consistent effort to promote the power of God the Father over the Son, claimed that there are two sorts of justification, either by the Father and Son conjointly, or by the Father alone. Milton called this second form of salvation "justification and adoption" (CM XVI, pp. 24–25). Here, then, Milton suggests that there is a greater mediating power than Christ's in his cosmos; and by doing so, he implicitly suggests that Christ's crucifixion is not the only means of salvation. Moreover, it is difficult to find any explicit statement in the whole of the *Christian Doctrine* signifying that Milton believed the Crucifixion to be any more effective in the salvation of humanity than the life and ministry of Christ. Let me emphasize that I am not denying he might have thought so; I am only pointing out that Milton never explicitly emphasized the point. Even in the third book of *Paradise Lost,* God does not so much emphasize the efficacy of Christ's death as the event crucial to salvation, as he emphasizes Christ's "merit" and "love" as the motivating and enduring qualities underlying the Crucifixion. In Milton, we will not find an explicit statement such as Henry More's, that it is on the literal cross that we may discover the "Inchoation of the Kingdome of God so much spoken of in the Gospel." Milton seems more to be in the spirit of the school of covenant theology or federal theology on the question of the Atonement as local event or eternal quality. In this, he seems more in line with William Ames: "This Mediation was equally necessary in all ages: Also it was sufficient, and effectuall from the beginning, by vertue of Gods decree, promise, and acceptation."[88]

Milton sees an intricate relationship between representation, which falls into the field of the possible and the present, and actuality, which falls into the field of the necessary and the future. Before exploring the significance of that relationship, I must note the foundation upon which Milton makes this distinction. In order to argue that humanity had free will after the Fall, Milton made an Arminian distinction between a *present assurance of present salvation* and a *present assurance of final salvation*. Jacob Arminius makes this distinction by exploiting William Perkins's error in confusing the Heidelberg school's doctrine of "temporary faith" with Calvin's doctrines generally. The crucial verse, as R. T. Kendall has demonstrated, is 2 Peter i, 10: "Wherefore the rather, brethren, give diligence to make your calling and election sure: for if ye do these things, ye shall never fall." Whereas Theodore Beza cited this passage to argue a protovoluntaristic doctrine of faith, Calvin never cites this verse in connection with the question of salvation.

In that difference, made most clearly by the Heidelberg school, we may trace the origin of the European version of covenant or federal theology. Calvin eradicates will and desire from his soteriology; for that reason he chose not to cite a passage in which diligence and desire are implied. Perkins, thinking he was being faithful to Calvin, nonetheless suggested that desire could play a part in salvation. As he writes, "the desire to believe is faith indeed; and the desire to repent is repentance itself." When Arminius noted this disparity, he proposed his model of salvation based on the power of representation. As he writes in response, "It is possible for him who believes in Jesus Christ to be certain and persuaded, and, *if his heart condemns him not,* he is now in reality assured, *that he is a son of God, and stands in the grace of Jesus Christ.*"[89] According to Arminius, then, desire translates itself into representation. Wishing to be saved, the individual acts as if he or she were saved. The power of representation, according to Arminius, helped compensate for the despair engendered by Calvinistic determinism. Milton also believed that representation could offset possible despair. I call this form of representation the rhetorical ideal of life, or the postlapsarian form of self-knowledge.

If we were to trace Arminius's distinction back to a patristic debate, we would discover its basis in the dialogue between Irenaeus (ca. 130–ca. 202), the church's first systematic theologian, and Augustine (354–430), the church's most famous theologian. Augustinian theodicy was established on the principle that humanity was created finitely perfect; its Fall, therefore, was incomprehensible and unredeemable except by divine intervention. Irenaeus, on the other hand, maintained that humanity was created as an imperfect entity. The entelechy of humanity was to achieve perfection, and the Fall, while an unfortunate step, did not deter humanity's development and growth toward a final, perfect state on its own terms.[90] Milton fell somewhere between these two theodicies. Like Augustine he believed Adam and Eve were created perfect but, like Irenaeus, he believed that they could strive toward perfection after the Fall. Milton's theodicy, then, accounts for desire and the power of representation.

To gain an appreciation of how important representation is to Milton's doctrine of salvation, we must look at God's distinction between representation and actuality. True to the symmetry of *Paradise Lost,* just as God makes prelapsarian self-knowledge possible by giving the command not to eat of the Tree of the Knowledge of Good and Evil, so does God make postlapsarian self-knowledge possible in reference to the Tree of Life. He says he must send Adam and Eve out of the garden because they might eat of the Tree of Life. Keeping in mind that Adam and Eve's eating of the Tree of the Knowledge of Good and Evil was merely a formality signifying their internal decision, let us consider the way God phrases his fear of what may happen should they eat of this Tree of Life:

> His heart I know, how variable and vain
> Self-left. Lest therefore his now bolder hand
> Reach also of the Tree of Life, and eat,
> And live for ever, dream at least to live
> For ever, to remove him I decree,
> And send him from the Garden forth to Till
> The Ground whence he was taken, fitter soil.   (XI, 92–98)

God then goes on to instruct Michael to "guard all passage to the Tree of Life: / Lest Paradise a receptácle prove / To Spirits foul" (122–24). What relationship does God see between actuality and representation? He first states that if Adam should eat of the Tree of Life, he would "live for ever"; this is the reflection of actuality or necessity. But then God continues by stating that Adam would only "dream" that he could live forever; this is the power of representation or desire. What relationship does God see between these two powers?

First, God commands certain things that are unnecessary to him but prove to be necessary to his agents. The instance of God's sending Raphael to guard hell during the Creation in order to "enure" the angels to prompt obedience is but one notable example (VIII, 229–46). Sending the angels to guard the Tree of Life might fall into the category of commands meant to "enure" his subjects. Second, God has stated that death is now a boon to humanity because humanity has lost the other quality that would have made immortality bearable, which is happiness (XI, 57–66). Thirdly, the whole exercise of banishing Adam and Eve from Eden, and of guarding the Tree of Life, seems to be done for the benefit of the angels:

> from them I will not hide
> My judgments, how with Mankind I proceed,
> As how with peccant Angels late they saw;
> And in thir state, though firm, stood more confirm'd. (68–71)

In effect, it would appear that Adam and Eve's fall and banishment is another spectacle, like Satan's fall, meant to confirm the good angels even more in their faith in God. Granting all this, and even granting that the distinction between living forever and dreaming to live forever is addressed to the angels, we still have before us, unanswered, the question concerning the relationship between actuality and representation. Could Adam and Eve have lived forever if they had eaten from the Tree of Life? Or would they only have dreamed of immortality? And what precisely is the difference between living forever and dreaming of living forever in the Miltonic cosmos? There are no easy answers to these questions in Milton's poetry or his theology. What answers I tentatively offer are based on a reading of the postlapsarian form of self-knowledge as Milton describes it in the close of the narrative.

In the Miltonic cosmos, human desire is, in tract of time, transmuted into heavenly love; that, we may say, is redemption in Milton's theology. But the way Adam and Eve learn to love God requires them to undertake an exercise in training and regulating their desires. The final psychological result of the fall, we might say, is that desire usurps the place of love; it is the fitting conclusion to what initiated the fall—Adam's confusion between his earthly desire and his heavenly love. In order to learn to love God anew, which is the presupposition of their regaining the communion they have lost, Adam and Eve must learn to transmute their earthly desires into heavenly love. But this will require a new self and a new form of self-knowledge. They cannot love God as they did in their prelapsarian way because they have now gained the knowledge of distinctions other than the simple one between self and Other. Likewise, they cannot love God as they did in their lapsarian way because they have to deal with the fact that desire is a governing function of their present selves. They are now able to distinguish between their previous selves and their present selves on the basis of the fact that they are desiring entities. They have to learn to love God by assuming a postlapsarian form of self-knowledge, which requires the ability to represent desire in a certain way. They must learn to direct themselves toward God by representing themselves as being-toward God.

One querulous way of saying this is to maintain that Adam and Eve fall into rhetoric, and that they will be redeemed because they represent themselves as being worthy of redemption. That, to a large extent, is true. In order to make it less contentious, one must recognize, as Richard Lanham, Kenneth Burke, and Stanley Fish have so admirably taught us, that rhetoric is not a dishonest way of representing oneself; nor is representation somehow an act or a product that is not true. These implicit judgments of the rhetorical ideal are based on incorrect assumptions about the place of rhetoric in all acts of self-knowledge and the sincerity of representation in all acts of being. An examination of what Adam and Eve do learn after they fall might help us appreciate better the rhetorical ideal of life, or the postlapsarian way of self-knowledge.

Summarily put, in the final two books of the epic Adam and Eve have to learn to represent themselves in the best possible way. After they leave Eden they will never possess as unified a sense of selfhood as they do living there. Eve's way of accommodating the loss of selfhood following the loss of the garden is to make Adam her Eden: "with thee to go, / Is to stay here / . . . thou to mee / Art all things under Heav'n, all places thou" (XII, 615–16, 617–18). In the end, she finds a way of answering her earlier lament about losing Eden: "Must I leave thee Paradise? thus leave / Thee Native Soil, these happy Walks and Shades, / Fit haunt of Gods?" (XI, 269–71). She has to feign that she will find in Adam the "Gods" she might have had an opportunity to converse with in Eden. Adam is obviously not "all things under Heav'n," but by pretending he is Eve is able to represent to herself a different sort of world — apparently a world she can face.

Adam too learns to represent himself in a certain way; in fact, it seems to be what Michael's whole educational curriculum is designed to teach him. Like Eve, Adam must learn to pretend to discover in something else what he had most lamented losing at the Son's judgment. As he tells the Son when he hears at the news of having to leave Eden,

> This most afflicts me, that departing hence,
> As from his face I shall be hid, depriv'd
> His blessed count'nance here I could frequent,
> With worship, place by place where he voutsaf'd
> Presence Divine, and to my Sons relate;
> On this Mount he appear'd, under this Tree
> Stood visible, among these Pines his voice
> I heard, here with him at this Fountain talk'd:
> . . . .
> In yonder nether World where shall I seek
> His bright appearances, or footsteps trace?
> (XI, 315–22, 328–29)

What Adam most laments losing is God's "Presence Divine." It is another form of "epistemic distance" — the feeling that God is far from one's thinking. Eve feels this as soon as she eats the fruit: "Heav'n is high, / High and remote" (IX, 811–12). Whereas Eve is here hoping that this alienation will mean that God did not see her eat of the forbidden fruit, Adam is expressing the fear of being alienated from God. Like Eve, Adam associates Eden with being-toward God, with being in God's presence.

At the end of his education, Adam learns how to answer this
fear of alienation. As he tells Michael in summary:

> Greatly instructed I shall hence depart,
> Greatly in peace of thought, and have my fill
> Of knowledge, what this Vessel can contain;
> Beyond which was my folly to aspire.
> Henceforth I learn, that to obey is best,
> And love with fear the only God, to walk
> As in his presence, ever to observe
> His providence, and on him sole depend.   (XII, 557–64)

In effect, Adam is going to represent himself as being in God's
presence. It is a representation: "*As* in his presence." By imagining
himself to be in the presence of God, Adam is able to transmute
desire (which is premised on absence) into love (which is premised
on presence). Both Adam and Eve learn the third way of self-
knowledge, the postlapsarian rhetorical ideal of life. Only by assuming this form of self-knowledge can Adam and Eve face the
future and accept the past.

By representing Eden as present in Adam, Eve is able to leave
Eden (her past) and to fulfill her role as mother of the Redeemer
(her future). By accepting the rhetorical ideal of self-representation as she does, Eve translates her desire into love. In fact, her
earlier inability to find a way to overcome desire led her to propose
suicide to Adam. Fearing that their offspring will only be food for
Death, she proposes to Adam that they forego sex. True to her
lapsarian self, she argues that if this prove impossible, they should
kill themselves. Simple, unrelenting desire is at the basis of her way
of perceiving the world:

> But if thou judge it hard and difficult,
> Conversing, looking, loving, to abstain
> From Love's due Rites, Nuptial embraces sweet,
> And with desire to languish without hope,
> Before the present object languishing
> With like desire, which would be misery
> And torment less than none of what we dread,
> Then both ourselves and Seed at once to free
> From what we fear for both, let us make short,
> Let us seek Death.   (X, 992–1001)

By considering generation, not death, as the solution to their problems, Eve also learns to change desire into love. By representing herself in a certain way, she learns to be that way, and only because she has been repentant. That act, in the end, is the first step toward a postlapsarian form of self-knowledge. It is, in effect, the recognition that there was a previous sinful self and the hope that there will be another future self who is more obedient. Only on the grounds of that recognition and that hope is the third way of self-knowledge possible.

To give a counterpart to Eve's recognition, we might examine Satan's soliloquy on Mount Niphates. His first recognition is that he is not now what he once was. As he says, God was ill paid by the ingratitude Satan has shown: "He deserv'd no such return / From me, whom he created what I was / In that bright eminence" (IV, 42–44). Satan recognizes that he once enjoyed "bright eminence" — what he "was" — but that now he "is Hell; myself am Hell" (75). Just after that moment, Satan meditates on the one possible way of repairing his loss — "Repentance" (80). But for Satan repentance can only mean "submission"; in other words, he does not understand what repentance is. He cannot imagine true contrition for a previous self's action and true hope for a future self's salvation. And so he concludes without "hope" and accepts that he is going to represent himself as "Hell" even when he is not in hell. This helps us understand the partial truth in his earlier pronouncement that the "mind is its own place."

Adam also learns to represent himself in the way he wishes to be. His wish to have God's presence is answerable by imagining himself ever in God's presence. By representing himself in that way, Adam is able to leave Eden and fulfill his role. His lesson, then, is to represent himself as if he were a being-toward God. After Adam has articulated this lesson, Michael elaborates a set of general guidelines to help Adam and Eve regain the paradise they have lost:

> only add
> Deeds to thy knowledge answerable, add Faith,
> Add Virtue, Patience, Temperance, add Love,
> By name to come call'd Charity, the soul
> Of all the rest: then wilt thou not be loath
> To leave this Paradise, but shalt possess
> A paradise within thee, happier far.   (XII, 581–87)

The "paradise within" — the internalizing of the state of perfection based on the external place they are about to leave — is both the process and the product of Adam and Eve's final form of self-knowledge. They will possess the paradise within once they have learned to be faithful, virtuous, patient, temperate, and charitable. All these qualities, according to Michael, constitute the parameters of self-knowledge: "This having learnt, thou hast attain'd the sum / Of wisdom" (575–76). In the end, both Adam and Eve internalize that quality of Eden that had made paradise desirable. They internalize it by representing themselves in the state of internalizing it. Just as Satan internalizes hell because he represents himself as being hell, so will Adam and Eve regain paradise because they represent themselves as possessing it within.

What is worth noting, moreover, is that the virtues of patience, temperance, charity, and faith fall into the realm of deeds to be added to knowledge. We are made aware, first of all, of the Platonic character of Michael's educational scheme — what Socrates calls the "Dorian mode, which is a harmony of words [*logos*] and deeds [*ergon*]" — and, second, of the division I noted in those anthropologists and cultural critics who define culture as ways of knowing and ways of being. This final scene also demonstrates Milton's federal theology belief in the Atonement's eternal efficacy. After all, Adam, who can hardly have the historical benefit of Christ's crucifixion, is nonetheless a beneficiary of Christ's life, his example. As Adam says, what makes Christ his redeemer is the knowledge he gains from the narrative of his life, not the effective redemption of his death: "Taught this by his example whom I now / Acknowledge my Redeemer ever blest" (572–73). Finally, the way Adam and Eve demonstrate the intricate relationship between self-representation and selfhood helps us accept the value of some of the questions which God's words about the Tree of Life raise, even if the answers to those questions appear insufficient. That relationship between representation and selfhood is the basis of the final form of self-knowledge — and it is the form of self-knowledge Jesus will demonstrate and exemplify in *Paradise Regained*.

But in the brief epic Jesus is more than an exemplary figure; he is also the founder of a novel religious culture. By demonstrating how to represent oneself as a being-toward God, and by teaching how to know oneself by regulating desire and transforming it into love, Jesus both articulates and exemplifies the enabling conditions toward founding a new political state of being—in other words, he constitutes a new culture. Such self-regulation of desire is, according to Milton, the basis of entering into any political sphere. Jesus will fulfill that mandate, moreover, by performing what Adam failed to do. He will employ the Spirit to gain self-knowledge, and from self-knowledge he will be able to maintain self-government. In the end, Milton does not contest the terms or the basis of the relationship within the knowledge-power ratio; he only suggests a way to internalize that ratio by making self-knowledge a way of gaining self-empowerment. Thus, any individual so constituted would be able to avoid subjection—the state in which the Other's knowledge leads to his or her empowerment over the self.

Toward Paradise Regained

The idea of presence is crucial to *Paradise Regained* because the narrative model's entire epistemology and its revolutionary politics are based on the premise that self-representation is the only way to self-knowledge. Like Adam, Jesus will also transcend desire by representing himself to be in the presence of God. The first act of Jesus' self-knowledge is meditation, which is premised on the assumption of what William James calls the "sudden realization of the immediate presence of God," or what Kenneth Burke more generally calls "the very substance of the present."[91] Such self-representation, however, does not lead to a situation of atomic individuals in Milton's cosmos precisely because of this "presence." What is at the heart of the act of self-representation in this narrative model is the involvement of *direction*. Adam represents himself as being in the presence of God in order to direct himself toward God. In other words, representation involves self-transformation— and that properly, in the seventeenth century, is the definition of meditation. To determine what narrative qualities accrue to the art of meditation, we might return to the two scientific models delineated earlier and try to see how the narrative model transforms psychoanalysis and historical materialism to its own ends.

In one aspect, meditation is akin to psychoanalysis because it proposes a way for an individual to represent a self in order to reformulate that self. Hayden White notes the narrative properties of this form of psychoanalysis. According to White, what the therapist attempts to do is convince the patient that she or he has "overemplotted" certain events in her or his life. One way of convincing patients of this is to get them to "reemplot" their life history so as "to change the *meaning* of those events" for the patients and to alter "their *significance* for the economy of the whole set of events that make up" that life. By showing the narrative flexibility of the patient's life, and its vulnerability to retelling, the therapist allows the patient to narrate another form of that story and to act out another type of life. The "talking cure," in other words, promotes a sense of flexibility concerning the ways overdetermined events (which then become pathogens) can be renarrated into a subordinate functionality, which leads to the equilibrium of mental health.

At the levels of nations, classes, and cultures, such narratives are called revisionist histories. In either case, these narratives— personal or political—reconstitute the world by telling another version of it. If narrative, according to Edward Said, expresses a "kind of appetite for wanting personally to modify reality" and, according to White, expresses the forms by which the imagination "both constitutes and colonizes the world it seeks to inhabit comfortably," then we must insist that such an act of constituting or modifying a narrative world is always revisionist. That is, what each act of narration attempts to do is reconstitute the conventional perception of the world. In this way, the constitution of cultures that narrative theory proposes is situated about halfway between what David Lewis calls the "plurality of worlds" available to the counterfactualist and what Nelson Goodman calls the "ways of worldmaking" available to the "irrealist."[92] Meditation posits a world that it wishes to inhabit in order to direct the mind into a set of behaviors that will promote the construction of that particular world. In other words, meditation does not contently contemplate possible worlds (Lewis) or assert that every subjective perception is another world (Goodman); it directs the mind toward establishing the world it represents itself as inhabiting.

In another way, meditation is akin to one form of materialist historiography. This history would involve the sort of transformative activity Walter Benjamin proposes: "History is the subject of a structure whose site is not homogeneous, empty time, but time filled by the presence of the now [*Jetztzeit*]." This history is cogni-

zant of the importance of an imagined present and also takes on
the form of a cultural critique in which the "past [is] charged with
the time of the now." Moreover, as Benjamin states, such history
serves each individual who "takes cognizance of it in order to blast
a specific era out of the homogeneous course of history—blasting a
specific life out of the era or a specific work out of the lifework." It
is a history that transforms the individuals who participate in its
meditation. Like this form of materialist history, which, as Perry
Anderson has noted, is cast into a language that would have been
"virtually incomprehensible" to Marx or Engels, meditative theory
requires an enduring sense of presence with the subject the individual is meditating on, and it likewise suggests that the act of
meditation is transformative. In this, Milton is at one with Benjamin.[93]

The objects of the two contemporary scientific models—Althusserian Marxism's history and Lacanian psychoanalysis' unconscious—are available for reworking within any given narrative
model. Psychoanalysis can take on a narrative form in which there
is a possible freedom from the systems of signification and over-
determination. History can take on a narrative form in which the
subjects find themselves once more actors and not merely effects
of historical shifts. In the implicit dialogue between Milton and
Thomas Hobbes, we will discover how Milton assumes both history and psychology into his narrative model. Hobbes's scientific
model proposes a specific psychology (with desire as the defining
characteristic of humanity) and a unique political history (with
subjection as its primary object and aim). In *Paradise Regained*
Milton will confront and controvert both Hobbesian psychology
and Hobbesian political history within his narrative model. My
own assumption is that Milton's dialogical counterpart is always
Hobbes. In the ensuing four chapters, while I will not explicitly be
concerned with the scientific model's premises, I will be implicitly
assuming them as the counterpoints to Milton's narrative model.

In the end, we can say that *Paradise Regained* is a narrative
about history and a narrative about how to use history to transform a self into a subject of God. In the brief epic, Milton criticizes
radically the groundings of his cultural context in order both to
question historically the establishment of the ecclesiastical institutions Milton felt were a compromise of Christ's spiritual mission
and to restructure psychologically the relationship between the

contemporary individual reader as a political agent and the founder of the political movement Milton knew as his unique brand of
Christianity. Simply put, what Milton was revising in his brief epic
was the origin of his faith—as institution and inheritance. And,
like Hobbes, he was doing it so that the reader may also "*Nosce
teipsum*, Read thyself."

PART TWO

Paradise Regained

"Assuredly there is no poem of epick form, where the sublimest moral instruction is so forcibly and abundantly united to poetical delight: the splendour of the poet does not blaze indeed so intensely as in his larger production; here he resembles the Apollo of Ovid, softening his glory in speaking to his son, and avoiding to dazzle the fancy, that he may descend into the heart. His dignity is not impaired by his tenderness. The Paradise Regain'd is a poem, that deserves to be particularly recommended to ardent and ingenious youth, as it is admirably calculated to inspire that spirit of self-command, which is, as Milton esteemed it, the truest heroism, and the triumph of Christianity."

—*William Hayley (1794)*

2

Confronting the Self:
The Art of Meditation

OBBES'S GESTURE of translating "*Nosce teipsum*" as if it were "*Lege teipsum*" is interesting not only because it confirms our own postmodern belief that our way of knowing the world is to read it, but also because it suggests how a text, such as the *Leviathan,* is a model of cultural formation. Baldly stated, Hobbes wrote the *Leviathan* so that whoever read it would gain the sort of self-knowledge Hobbes wished the reader to gain; and he wished that reader to gain this form of self-knowledge so that the commonwealth he represented would indeed come to actuality. I am not interested in knowing whether Hobbes wished to erect the state of Leviathan or even whether he believed it possible. In 1651, the year in which he published the *Leviathan,* two years after the execution of Charles I, and with the now clear emergence of a new power in Cromwell, it would have appeared highly unlikely that a return to monarchy was imminent. Even though Charles II had been crowned king on the first of the year, Hobbes, I imagine, was aware of the improbability of Charles II's assuming the English throne, let alone of his assuming the absolute forms of power that Hobbes delineated in the *Leviathan.*

Paradise Regained is a text of cultural formation in precisely the same way it recruited its readers to a specific form of self-knowledge. The circumstances of its publication are curiously similar to those surrounding the *Leviathan.* The brief epic was published

eleven years after the Restoration at a time when there was no hint
of the possibility of the events of 1688. What, we may ask, are
Hobbes and Milton striving to achieve, the first in an unflinchingly
severe antiparliamentarian tract written at the onset of the new
English republic and the other in a stridently antimonarchist tract
written at the height of a renewed English kingdom?

The answer I suggest in my introduction is that each writer
promotes the postlapsarian form of self-knowledge as a means of
cultural formation. Hobbes represents the ways of being and ways
of knowing necessary for the erection and maintenance of the
Leviathan. By representing it he constitutes that culture. He does
not employ the strategies of the writer of utopias; he represents
the commonwealth to suggest that it is necessarily the only way to
promote peaceful and commercially advantageous existence. Milton, like Hobbes, also represents a culture in order to constitute it.
He too eschews the strategy of the utopia writer. He represents the
regained garden both as an internal state consisting of a set of
virtues and as a potential collective state possible only in the widespread activity of those virtues. In other words, Milton represented self-government, the art of temperance and of self-knowledge (two different arts), as the way to exist in the "paradise
within." The radical difference between Hobbes and Milton concerns their attitudes toward history. Whereas Hobbes would hide
the explicit history of England's political evolution, Milton would
expose and relish the history of the one significant moment of
cosmic revolution. In other words, Milton, like Marx, teaches his
readers how to read history in a certain way so that it becomes
meaningful for their lives. Like Marx, Milton represents both a
paradigm for reading historical confrontations and a telos for understanding the significance of those clashes. Of course, Milton's
historiography is not concerned with the paradigm of the clash of
economic classes or with the telos of the development of a market
system from feudalism to capitalism to socialism. Milton's paradigm, quite simply, is the life of Christ. In its unfolding, in its
manifold confrontations with various antagonistic forces, in its
ethical example, he found the paradigm for both understanding
history and for transforming it. His telos, likewise, is the historical
evolution of a regained paradise.

Hobbes, as exemplar of the scientific model, proposed neither
paradigm nor telos. He proposed a static, synchronic politic in

which no citizen should query the history of the political form under which he or she served. The structure of the *Leviathan* is ostensibly logical. Hobbes moves through the four realms—human, civil, heavenly, chthonic—in order to demonstrate how anyone who properly does "Read thy self" will submit to the political establishment of the commonwealth. Hobbes's two key terms are *doctrine* and *demonstration*. What he teaches can only be shown because it is true; his rhetorical gesture is to submit to the apparent truth he found in himself and proposes to his readers. The two key terms for Milton, on the other hand, are *doctrine* and *discipline*. He presents his theological treatise, he writes, as a "methodical tractate of Christian doctrine" (CM XIV, pp. 6–7). Inasmuch as the *Christian Doctrine* is just that—doctrine—so must we insist that *Paradise Regained* is a model of Christian discipline. Not only is it disciplinary in its general theme, that of self-knowledge tending toward self-regulation, but it is also a discipline in Milton's favorite sense of the word—its being a tractate of education (*discere*). The two work toward the same end. As Milton wrote early in his career, "Discipline . . . is the *execution* and *applying* of Doctrine home" (CM III, p. 6). Home, I will argue, is the reader, the site of a complex of ethical behaviors to be transformed.

Hobbes invoked his readers in order to establish a certain set of behaviors for them based on a certain necessity in their ways of gaining self-knowledge. Whoever know themselves to be determined by motions and desires and fears—of the sort Hobbes represented—will conform to the pattern of the commonwealth. And, by having a certain number of readers conform to that pattern and act toward that conformity—a critical mass, as it were—that pattern will become a culture. In other words, texts are cultural formations because they form their readers into their culture's subjects.

Before I turn to what Milton had to say about this subject, let me anticipate the possible criticism that the sort of reader I am imagining here is either mad, like Don Quixote, or fanciful, like Emma Bovary, or simply an ahistorical construct based on a crossbreeding of Barthian reader and Derridian world. A potential critic might argue that I am assuming a world something like the one Derrida describes in *Of Grammatology* in which he proclaims, to the confusion of all his critics and followers, that *"Il n'y a pas hors-texte"* ("There is nothing outside of the text"); that I am assuming a citizen of this textual world who is himself or herself a textualized reader, the persona Barthes described as the "space on which all the quotations that make up a writing are inscribed without any of them being lost."[1] To this charge the first answer must be that the idea of the world's textuality not only is part of the philosophical baggage of, but may even be said to originate with, the early modern period.

To substantiate the significance I assume Hobbes's "Read thy self" carries, we might add a less famous example of the textualized world. We may turn to M. R.'s maternal advice book of 1630, *The Mothers Counsell or, Live within Compasse*. In telling her daughter to avoid lewd company, M. R. casts her declaration in terms that might seem to be right out of a postmodernist belief system that there is no world outside of textuality: "Corrupt company is more infectious than corrupt aire; therefore let women be advised in their choise; for that *text of thy selfe* that could never bee expounded; thy companion shall as thy commentarie, lay open to the world." In a deliciously suggestive and generally subversive declaration, M. R. links up being ("selfe") with text and makes textuality and sexuality generally synonymous. Keeping a text inviolate requires keeping it free from critical commentary. Moreover, M. R. deploys what may be perhaps the single most damaging critique of commentary books. After all, it is hard to imagine any good coming out of a commentary that uses its primary text so loosely. True to her Puritan tenor throughout, then, M. R.'s biblicism does not countenance traditional commentary. In fact, commentary books prove to be the best analogy she can find to declare just how pernicious lewd company may be to her daughter. More to our purpose, however, is the importance of the general synonymity of knowing and reading, and, especially, the importance of the metaphor of the "text."[2]

To return to the problem of the political activity of reading in the early modern period and to help support our interpretation of reading's political significance, we need only examine the famous Baconian idea of reading as incorporation: "Some books are to be tasted, others to be swallowed, and some few to be chewed and digested." In this metaphor, Bacon is suggesting something like a physical transformation in the act of reading; whoever reads does so not cursorily or without ideological identification, but with an interested and impressionable attitude. A book can change one's being; it can, to exploit the metaphor to its fullest, alter the constitution of whoever reads. In both senses, then, Bacon's concluding comment about reading is true: "Reading maketh a full man."

An equally famous instance regarding the politics of reading is based on a different metaphor. In the letter meant to "give great light to the Reader" of *The Faerie Queene,* Spenser tells Raleigh that he intends to "*fashion* a gentleman or noble person in vertuous and gentle *discipline*." Is he not declaring that his intent is to implicate an actual reader whose sense of aristocratic behavior will be translated into action by reading this text, which allegorically represents all the necessary virtues? In other words, Spenser sets out to write a text that both implicates and, in doing so, constructs the perfect gentleman. And, like Milton's, Spenser's discipline will become, as Spenser puts it, "doctrine by ensample."[3]

Modern theorists of reading—those who are beginning now to discern ways of reading that radically depart from New Critical paradigms—are generating theories of affective readers similar to Spenser's or Bacon's. "Reading," Robert Scholes has pointed out, "is not just a matter of standing safely outside texts, where their power cannot reach us. It is a matter of entering, of passing through the looking glass and seeing ourselves on the other side." Scholes develops what Barthes said a decade earlier, "And no doubt that is what reading is: rewriting the text of the work within the text of our lives." These are theories not simply interested in the effect of what Wolfgang Iser called the "entanglement of the reader"; rather, these are theories of readers whose ethics are at stake in the act of reading. In effect, Wayne Booth's partially facetious term—"behavioro-biblio-modification"—is an apt description of these readers who indeed have a personal, subjective investment in reading.[4] Their "modification" concerns the ways ideologies are transmitted and the ways that transmission forms our sense of selfhood. Scholars during the Renaissance knew this idea thoroughly, and it is one we would do well to learn anew.

Spenser's "fashioned" reader is Milton's "fit audience." Not only does Milton invoke that "fit" reader in *Paradise Lost,* but he likewise entreats the "candid and judicious readers" of his *Christian Doctrine.* The modern term for the affective invocation and construction of the reader within a narrative model is *narrativity.* Teresa de Lauretis has defined this engagement and solicitation between text and reader as consisting of "the effective functioning of narrative on and with the reader/spectator to produce a subject of reading or a subject of vision." In de Lauretis's definition, *narrativity* is not merely another term used to describe the reader who may be the rhetorical auditor of any given text; it is rather used to describe the ways that texts are deployments of ideology and how these deployments operate in and through readers. In other words, *narrativity* refers to actual readers who become *implicated* and *constructed* in the text. This definition is in line with the Renaissance definition of how texts "fashion" their readers both by actually soliciting and by artificially constructing them. When Milton describes how a text effectively functions, he turns to the metaphor of the pulpit. The poet, he argues, has the "power beside the office of pulpit, to imbreed and cherish in a great people the seeds of vertu, and public civility" (CM III, pp. 238–39). That metaphor of the pulpit is useful and telling. Milton's idea in 1641—that the poet may be a preacher—is transformed by the later stages of his career when he determines that the "pulpit" itself is not worthy the comparison. In other words, if in 1641 Milton felt he was "church-outed" by the prelates, by 1655 he himself "outed" the church (p. 243). In the end he believed only in his Petrine Church of One—John Milton, Englishman.[5]

The reason this insistence on individuality is significant is because it forces us to alter the metaphor of the pulpit into the more traditionally accepted form of individual faith—the discipline of meditation. Here narrativity assumes its importance. The meditative theory of the Renaissance—beyond the sectarian division of Reformation or counter-Reformation—posited that meditation was indeed a way of implicating oneself into another culture. The kingdom of God could be reached by a meditative reader because meditation was transformative; it allowed persons to assume the status of heavenly beings so that they could act as if they should be heavenly beings. Meditation takes on the properties of the postlapsarian form of self-knowledge, allowing an individual to represent himself or herself as if he or she were in the presence of God. This representation ought to lead to ethical behavior proper to one in the presence of God, ensuring that, in time, that individual's representation would become actuality. Meditative theorists would have called this form of narrativity *meditative motion*.

Returning to our two authors, Hobbes and Milton, we can now discern the basic structural design of each of their models. Each author had to propose first of all a *method* of reading and then a *doctrine* to read, having to show how to read before showing what to read. Hobbes does this in the first part of the *Leviathan* when he proposes his model of materialist philosophy premised on the motions governing the automatons of the human world. Having proven that there are chains of necessity from the divine to the human realm, Hobbes subtly shifts to the realm of civil politics in order to install the chains of civil law. Hobbes constructs a materialist reader once he has implicated him or her. Milton, on the other hand, constructs a spiritual reader.

Like Hobbes, Milton constructs and implicates his reader in the early part of the narrative. Critics of *Paradise Regained* have discerned that the poem falls into two general parts. As Barbara Lewalski initially demonstrated, and Earl Miner since corroborated, the poem may be divided into its beginning, a hundred-and-ninety-three-line "induction," and into its substance, the rest of the poem. The induction is meant to establish the perspective which will govern the rest of our reading. That is, the induction is the method, the rest the doctrine.[6]

There is also a highly significant relationship between the method of reading and the content of reading, or what Milton might have called the discipline and the doctrine. For learning to read a certain way means learning to read the world in a certain way. A materialist reader will perceive a materialist world, and a spiritual reader will perceive a spiritual world; or, the materialist reader will perceive a scientific determinism while a spiritual reader will discover a narrative freedom. Milton explicitly described the reader of *Paradise Regained* only once, and only in potentially confusing terms. In his rejection of Athenian learning, Jesus remarks,

> However many books
> Wise men have said are wearisom; who reads
> Incessantly, and to his reading brings not
> A spirit and judgment equal or superior,
> (And what he brings, what needs he elsewhere seek)
> Uncertain and unsettl'd still remains
> Deep verst in books and shallow in himself,
> Crude or intoxicate, collecting toys,
> And trifles for choice matters, worth a spunge;
> As Children gathering pibles on the shore.   (4, 318–27)

William Cain argues that this statement is "radically subversive" in the judgment it makes on the act of reading. In effect, Cain contends, the "poet's critique of his own text's claims to authority leaves only the inner authority of readers — an authority that is not required to exercise itself on texts like *Paradise Regained*."[7] What Milton is saying, then, is that the reader who understands this sentiment does not need to read it.

There are certain grounds on which we may question Cain's extrapolation from what Jesus is saying about the classics to what Milton might be saying about his own poem. This is not so self-referential a moment as Cain might be suggesting. But Cain, I think, has hit on the right note. Why does Milton put these words into his Jesus' mouth? Perhaps the reference to the innate qualities of the good reader will help us out. First of all, the reader ought to have spirit and judgment. It hardly needs to be mentioned that these are two properties Hobbes explicitly denies. We saw how he transformed spirit into matter, and we likewise saw how judgment is one of the qualities the subject must renounce in accepting the covenant of the commonwealth. So, at least on one level, Milton is subverting a text other than *Paradise Regained*. Second, the question Jesus is asking is not directed just at Satan nor, for that matter, is it answered: "And what he brings, what needs he elsewhere seek?" The key to that answer is the relationship between a method of reading and the doctrine to be read. The basis of that relationship concerns the structure of the induction itself.

HAVING DESIGNS ON THE READER

Toward the end of the first part of John Barth's metafictional novel, *Sabbatical,* one of the two narrators, Fenwick Turner, states to the other narrator, Susan Seckler, that what "the reader doesn't know yet would fill a book." What we don't know yet about the reader not only would fill volumes, but has done so. Confronted with proliferating concepts of the "text," Terry Eagleton, echoing Barthes, suggests that in the poststructuralist scheme of things the "reader" is the only "place where this seething multiplicity of the text is momentarily focused." But the reader, it seems to me, is just as much a place of "seething multiplicity" as the text itself. This is the case, first of all, in the sheer number of the types of readers, ranging from Wayne C. Booth's "postulated reader," Gerald Prince's "narratee," Christine Brooke-Rose's "encoded reader," Stanley Fish's "informed reader," Wolfgang Iser's "implied reader," or to a member of Walter J. Ong's "fictionalized audience."[8] Diverse as these readers are, they nonetheless share the property of being formulated abstract entities which, we are told, writers construct as dialogic sites within their texts, and whose purpose is to act as the auditors complementing the writers' rhetorical stances. For the critic working within the paradigms of New Criticism, their significance resides in their demonstrating that narrative worlds are self-sufficient (and that the critic is then only occupying a ready-made place). For what we may call the postformalist critic, these reading sites are places by which to measure the degree of intervention any given text is making into its culture. The site of the reader is also a register for what sort of ideological submission or resistance the author is making. In either case, these are theorized entities whose competence as readers resides in the competence of their theorists. There is no escape yet from the fact that the postulated reader shares the actual theorist's deficiencies and ingenuities as a reader. This, of course, is not necessarily a bad thing; I would even go so far as to say it is a good thing. Only those who view pluralism of any sort as inherently troubling will be dismayed at the idea of another heterogeneous entity in the already complex act of reading. Those who are honestly self-conscious will, with Stanley Fish, feel that it is better to have "an acknowledged and controlled subjectivity than an objectivity which is finally an illusion" (*Is There a Text in This Class?*, p. 49).

The second area of heated debate is concerned with the amount of subjectivity any reader might be able to employ in his or her reading. The question, then, is how much creativity is the responsibility or privilege of the reader. Invariably this debate attempts to circumscribe, and inevitably finds itself caught in, a hermeneutical circle. This is the case whether the debate is theoretical or practical. As an example of the debate in its theoretical form, we might turn to a confrontation between Wolfgang Iser and Karlheinz Stierle. For a phenomenologist such as the early Iser, although the convergence of text and reader is required to bring the "literary work into existence," the exact configuration of that relationship "can never be precisely pinpointed, but must always remain virtual." The reader is as responsible for creating the text's meaning as is the text, but how responsible is not for anyone to say exactly. Stierle responds to this by arguing that the "reader of fiction experiences a preestablished relationship of theme and horizon that is set up by the text itself." The text, then, according to Stierle, establishes the disposition of the reader; it is ontologically prior to the reader and therefore governs the reader's creative input in its unfolding. As Tzvetan Todorov puts it, the "text always contains within itself directions for its own consumption."[9] One might contest this by stating that those directions are also liable to readers' interpretations, in fact liable to the very readers they are supposedly directing. The problem of establishing anything like an exact relationship between actual reader (critic), implied reader (critical mask), implied text (reading), and actual text (the bound volume in all its inviolate glory) is insoluble—if it is a problem, that is. Believing in the pluralistic basis of critical inquiry, but equally assuming that any critical act not articulating its own theory of reading is to that extent less pluralistic than it thought itself to be, I will be working with something like Todorov's insight by suggesting that *Paradise Regained* proposes its own directions for situating the reader within its workings. That reader, I will argue presently, is moved to a cosmic situation as something akin to an angel.

In Milton criticism, it is no novel thing to propose a reader who is cast into a cosmic role, especially given the predilection of Milton critics to suggest that they belong to the "fit audience" of Christian readers and that their detractors are of the "devil's party." All "superficial readers of Milton," writes Northrop Frye, are in the "position of minor devils," implying, one assumes, that more profound readers would be in the position of minor angels. In a more daring gesture, Christopher Grose has recently suggested that the reader of *Paradise Regained* should assume a place in what he calls the "Satanic corporateness"; in other words, the fit reader of the brief epic is the satanic reader. Robert Crosman suggests that there are three types of readers in *Paradise Lost:* the "truly saintly reader," the "Satanic reader," and the "middling reader." Whereas the usual gambit of critics is to divide the types of readers according to the cosmic planes of action in the poem, as Crosman has done, when we turn our attention to the fullest and most suggestive exploration of the "reader in *Paradise Lost,*" we find Stanley Fish constructing a plethora of readers existing on different planes of action, within alternate schemes of perception, and in simply other worlds.[10]

A brief survey of Fish's reader(s) might prove enlightening. First of all and primarily, Fish suggests throughout his book that the reader is a fallen being whose own lapsed tendencies are the subject of the poem (pp. 1, 11, 39, 107, 162, 208, 239, 256, 259, 303). Postlapsarian being that he or she is, this reader is "split" in a variety of ways—torn between "the experience of individual poetic moments and the ever present pressure of the Christian doctrine" (p. 42); divided between wishing creatively to "read into the passage" some desirable interpretation and knowing "from unimpeachable sources" what "is really there" (p. 214); having to choose between experience and revelation (pp. 225–26); experiencing the tension between a "responsible reading" and a careless inference (p. 228), between the letter and the spirit (p. 234), or finally between horizontal verbal units and totalizing vertical myth (p. 315). Not only is this reader split, but also sometimes forgetful (pp. 14, 46), often indiscriminate (pp. 183–84, 188) or outright careless (p. 220), prone to be neurotic (p. 207), ambiguous (p. 272), and occupies the roles of both spectator (p. 286) and hero (pp. 206–07). Given the variety of functions this reader plays in Fish's scheme, one hardly wonders that the reader is "physically and psychologically" exhausted at the end of the poem (p. 143). Perhaps it is this weariness that forces the reader to have to read some verses twice to understand them (pp. 17–18, 25) and others thrice to get the meaning straight (p. 137).

Fish also casts the reader into a cosmic frame, only this time it is a Calvinistic one. As the reader moves through the poem toward an "illuminative height," each episode, each marker "indicating subordination and emphasis," must recede into the background and reveal itself to be artificial. There is only one truth in *Paradise Lost*, which is, Fish tells us, "self-evident to the purged eye" (p. 354). The reader, then, is finally "elect," although he or she will have to return to the poem because the fallen mind is incapable of maintaining the "moment of vision to which dialectical self-examination can occasionally bring it" (p. 355). What is most worth contesting about Fish's abstract reader is not so much that reader's inconsistencies or often implausible ineptitude, but rather the questionable relationship that reader has to the form and structure of the poem. For here we find the theoretical debate about the status of the text in relation to the status of a reader writ large in practical terms. Quite simply, Fish believes that the text has no form: "It is the experience of works, not works, that have beginnings, middles, and ends."[11]

The reader may be discussed, in the engagement with form or design, not as an abstract potential but as a constructed and implicated political agent. Following de Lauretis's insight about the political implication of any such reader, I suggest that readers are fashioned not only to act out a role of auditor, but to *become* the agents of the culture the narrative is establishing. To gain an insight into any text's narrativity we might approach the text through an examination of what Fredric Jameson calls the "ideology of form"—a mode of revealing "the active presence within the text of a number of discontinuous and heterogeneous formal processes." Moreover, that form, which for Jameson is to be apprehended as "content," must be discovered through its functionality. As Jonathan Culler has pointed out, "The discovery of formal structures is an infinite process and must, if it is to be fruitful, be grounded on a theory of how the literary text functions." Ideally, this appreciation of the functionality of structures should be grounded, Culler maintains, "on a theory of reading." Barbara Herrnstein Smith goes as far as to say that "any theory of narrative structure that did not account for, or take into account, the ways that readers experience narratives would be to that extent incomplete."[12]

De Lauretis uses the concept of narrativity to demonstrate the ways that any given spectatorship in any given text is gendered; for Milton, this has to a large extent been done, and done admirably.[13] The concept of narrativity may be used to discover the ways that the spectatorship is acculturated, the ways in which the subject is implicated and constructed within the parameters Milton and his hero herald as the boundaries of a new religious culture. By stressing the idea of *becoming* in this reader's undergoing acculturation, we can recognize the cost of cultural implication for a Renaissance reader—the reader Spenser undertakes to "fashion." Writers intent on fostering or radically reorienting a culture's ideology work upon readers whose own cultural affiliation is at stake. We may never be able to appreciate the outlook of such a reader, but this was the reader Spenser and Milton were addressing, and moving.

I have already called the Renaissance form of narrativity "meditative motion." Movement in Milton's poetic does not only mean an affective allure to virtue, which is where Sidney believed the poet's strength existed—"being the most familiar to teach it, and most princely to move towards it." Movement is crucial to Sidney's apology because poetry more than philosophy allows us "to be moved to do that which we know, or to be moved with desire to know." Indeed, according to Agricola, the pre-Ramist logician to whom Sidney may owe this insight, there is "no difference between moving and teaching, for to move someone is to teach him as far as this is possible."[14] Milton would have agreed with this formulation, but, over and above the affective denotation, he connoted a scheme and rhetoric of perspectival shifts involving something like kinetic energy.[15] Milton moves us perceptually as well as affectively. I mean by shifts in perspective those abrupt transitions from one form of focalization to another—the focalizer being the prism that mediates perception within the narrative. As many readers have noted, Milton's poetry gives the effect of insistent motion; that effect is partly caused by the shifts in perspective.

Not only is this the case in the general outline of *Paradise Lost* which, after all, begins in hell, takes us to heaven, and then places us firmly on earth (in Book VII, when the "fit audience" is invoked), but also in the microstructural movements of the poem. Those movements involve spatio-temporal transitions in focalization within the world of the poem. By understanding the underlying motive behind those transitions, we may appreciate the "narrativity" of the narrative—the way the reader is moved to occupy a subject position.

In suggesting any relationship between the reader's experience and the text's formal properties (its movements and alterations of perspective, its design), we are treading within a hermeneutical circle, which was theoretically shown in the debate between Iser and Stierle on whether the reader's horizons determine the text's or whether the text's govern the reader's. In Milton criticism, the circle finds its articulation in an implicit debate between E.M.W. Tillyard, who argues that "the location of the reader is of the highest moment for understanding the construction of the poem," and Fish, who maintains that "if the meaning of the poem is to be located in the reader's experience of it, [then] the form of the poem is the form of that experience."[16] Whereas Tillyard would argue that the reader's experience depends on his or her location within the poem, and that location in turn depends on the form in which the poem unfolds, Fish would argue that the poem has no formal features outside of the reader's experience. The poem itself, he

argues, is static; it is "the reader who moves, or advances, until his
cleansed eye can see what has always been there" (p. 345). My
feeling is that Tillyard has developed here a more useful way of
approaching Milton's text. With Todorov, I believe that the text
directs its readers to consume it in a particular way (however liable
those directions are to the reader's experiencing of them). We can
use Book X of *Paradise Lost* as our text for discerning in what ways
the formal designs of a narrative implicate the reader kinetically
and affectively.

Microstructural movements within the narrative, I have suggested, involve spatio-temporal transitions which in turn govern
the reader's affective responses to the narrative. Book X is comprised of eight distinct tableaux, and in the perspectival shifts
between these tableaux one might properly find the rhetorical design of the poem.[17] The book begins in heaven, with the angels
depressed by the recent fall of Adam and Eve: "dim sadness did not
spare / That time Celestial visages" (X, 23–24). We, as readers, are
both situated in heaven and made to comprehend the affective
response the fall should have on any perceptive member of its
heavenly audience. We are transported both literally and emotionally to earth when the Son descends to judge the fallen pair (90–
97). After the judgment, the reader is cast backwards in time and
location to a prelapsarian perspective:

> *Meanwhile ere thus was sinn'd and judg'd on Earth,*
> Within the Gates of Hell sat Sin and Death,
> In counterview within the Gates, that now
> Stood open wide, belching outrageous flame
> Far into *Chaos.*   (229–33, my italics)

Here is a transition not only in space, but also in time. And in that
transition the reader is made privy to another side of the fall, not
that involving the actors who profess love as their motivation, but
to the results in their allegorical forms. We see Sin, not as acted
out, but as effect; and likewise Death. Milton makes an interesting
move by presenting us with the fall twice in the poem, and this
second time it is horrific. At about the same time Eve and Adam
might be eating of the fruit, and "fancy that they feel / Divinity
within them breeding wings," Sin feels "new strength within me
rise, / Wings growing, and Dominion giv'n me large / Beyond this

Deep" (IX, 109–10; X, 243–45). Whatever we might have felt about Adam and Eve's fall as it was presented in the previous book, our second perspective on it allows us to reread it as the exaltation of Sin; in this way, this perspectival shift establishes somewhat of a palimpsest on the original sin.

The first three tableaux establish heaven, earth, and hell as the three loci of action, with earth acting as the fulcrum for a cosmic struggle between good and evil. The fourth tableau parodies the first in the same way that Book III parodies Book II by placing the Holy Trinity of the Father, Son, and the Spirit in counterpoint to the infernal trinity of Satan, Sin, and Death (X, 325–409). Moreover, the parody extends to the emotive response to the fall. Whereas the heavenly audience had been saddened, the infernal audience find "rejoice" (396). The fifth tableau parodies the second in having Satan descend to hell in the same way the Son had descended to earth (410–584). Ironically, though, whereas the Son went to judge, Satan finds himself the recipient of judgment (510–20). Meanwhile, in the sixth tableau, Sin and Death begin to rule their dominion (585–613).

Milton makes the transition from the sixth to the seventh tableau in what becomes arguably his unique narrative gesture — that of a perspectival shift that displaces one actor into the vision of another. As Sin and Death set out to devour the world, God views them: "which th' Almighty seeing / From his transcendent Seat the Saints among" (613–14). Once the focalizers of the narrative, Sin and Death are suddenly transformed instead into the objects of God's focus. There are few more significant gestures in Milton's narratives than these shifts, this employing a gap between event and perspective that alerts us to the hierarchy of viewpoints in the Miltonic cosmos. The same sort of perspectival shift occurs when God sees Satan flying between Chaos and earth: "Him God beholding from his prospect high, / Wherein past, present, and future he beholds" (III, 77–78). Just as Satan is translated into God's beneficence in the third book, so too are Sin and Death literally displaced here in the tenth and made to operate in a gap whose tragedy is resoundingly renounced in the assumption of God's vision.

But do we assume that vision? According to Iser, the reader who is somewhat lacking in motility assumes the displaced vision rather than the displacing one. Whenever a "segment becomes a theme," Iser tells us, "the previous one must lose its thematic relevance and be turned into a marginal, thematically vacant position, which can be and usually is occupied by the reader so that he may focus on the new thematic segment."[18] That is, if we apply Iser's insight to our case, we as readers should lag behind God's vision and occupy that vacant position opened up by the displacement of Sin and Death. Rather, I would suggest that, because Milton's readers are constructed as mobile entities, they are able to occupy the novel perspective in order to look on that one just preceding. In other words, when Sin and Death are displaced, we as readers no longer look out at the world ripe for mortality through their eyes, but instead look on their act of destruction through God's eyes, in which that act becomes a futile and self-consuming gesture within the total telos of the universe. The final tableau of the book, to conclude our summary, creates a suspension between the optimism aroused by our assuming God's perspective (momentarily) and the tragic element of the beginning of Sin and Death's reign. For the final tableau has the angels rearranging the cosmos in accord with God's new order, thus emphasizing the total disruption that the fall has wrought (707–1104).

Book X of *Paradise Lost* serves to do two things. First, it acts as the hinge for the rest of the poem as a whole in its function of tying up the loose ends of hell, heaven, and earth. Second, there is a subtle and complex movement in this poem which is both affective and spatio-temporal. Spatially and temporally, we see the fall from the perspective of its allegorical effects; Sin and Death are not only subsumed into God's encompassing perspective, but are also made to serve his ultimate purpose. The pessimism of their entry into the now mortal earth is recast as the optimism of the *felix culpa* tradition: "Then Heav'n and Earth renew'd shall be made pure" (638). Affectively, then, the Book X shows how a temporal perspective must give way to an eternal—how *chronos* gives way to *kairos*.[19] That shift is both a shift in space and time, and a shift in the affects of the reader's response to the poem. Moved both ways, the reader takes his or her place in the "fit audience."

Keeping in mind the division between the induction and the rest of *Paradise Regained,* we might now turn to the puzzle William Cain located in Jesus' reference to the reader in the rejection of Athens. Cain, we recall, noted that the reader is self-sufficient to the degree that the poem comes close to being made redundant. If the reader brings judgment and spirit to the reading, the text itself becomes unnecessary inasmuch as it purports to provide judgment and spirit. *Paradise Regained* comes very close to being what Fish might call a self-consuming artifact, then. Indeed, Fish founds his argument that Milton's poems have no formal plot to speak of on the same theoretical basis of readerly activity as does Jesus in *Paradise Regained*. According to Fish, the "temporal-spatial structure of the poem" is a "temptation, since the reader may fall into the error of looking to *it* as a revealer of meaning: that is, to the limited and distorting, though organized, picture of reality it presents, rather than to the inner light developing within him [the reader]." Fish seems to be echoing Milton's own reading theory: that humans are able "by the Spirit" to discern that "which is good" (CM III, p. 33).[20] The more carnal husks of that Spirit, things like plot and form, are only to be threshed in order to find the spiritual meaning, which is after all inherent in the individual. Reading is, then, the way to reach a state within. Early in his career, Milton would have disputed Fish's reading with a simple assertion of authority: "How can they bring satisfaction from such an Author, to whose very essence the Reader must be fain to contribute his own understanding?" Authors, in Milton's world, are not passive beings (CM III, p. 90). But that is what Fish is assuming.

Fish's reading presupposes that Milton's poems are merely vessels for a reader's interiorizing of values already implicit in the reader. The only reason to reread them is to remind the reader of what they already possess. Fish's, in the end, is an interesting Platonic ideal of reading as anamnesis. It is also an ideal that (with some revision) can work in our attempt to tread the fine line between the text and the reader as the locus of meaning. On the whole *Paradise Regained,* after its induction, does not purport to offer the reader judgment and spirit. Rather, the main portion of the poem—the scenes of temptation—gives the reader the opportunity to sublimate and internalize a religious culture by allowing the reader to read Satan's offers from a place where that reader already enjoys the benefit of spirit and judgment.

In itself, Jesus' statement about the reader is not unlike Milton's in *Paradise Lost* in its hope to find a "fit audience." The difference is that the character, not the narrator, invokes that reader, and this particular character is also the exemplar of a "spiritual" reader. What Jesus does in reading Satan's offers is sublimate them into a spiritual kingdom; what we do as readers is imitate him. Jesus is able to read spiritually because he is himself the possessor of the Spirit's power, which he received at the Baptism (I, 29–31). We as readers are able to imitate him as spiritual readers insofar as we too possess spirit and judgment (which we do not get in the main portion of the poem). The question, then, is when and how may we gain that spirit?

We must revise Fish's Platonic reading ideal. Fish's reader is able to see the lower order of meaning in the text's formality only when the reader has gained spiritual understanding, which in *Paradise Lost* the reader gains in observing Michael's teaching Adam about Christ, who, Fish notes, represents in Milton's text the "position occupied by Plato's Supreme Good." Fish's readers perceive the "Truth" because they have observed Adam's education, especially the part played by Christ, whose action, Fish suggests, takes "place not there but everywhere, not at one point in time, but at all points" (p. 352). Because *Paradise Regained* does not educate the reader by representing a scene in which a fallen being receives instruction, the poem seems to have less potential for constructing an opportunity for the reader's recollection of the Supreme Good, or, in Milton's words, the "spirit" and "judgment" necessary to bring to the reading. What the brief epic does instead is use the form of the induction to "move" the reader to that place where he or she might gain a spiritual understanding.

The reader gains that spiritual understanding by observing the first scene of the poem, the Baptism, from three distinct perspectives. The ways the reader is moved from one perspective to another depends on the text's governing the reader's responses. Before we enter the scene of temptations in *Paradise Regained,* we are moved to a site where the spirit is available to us. That place is also defined in terms of a cosmic role. We as readers possess that spirit, I suggest, inasmuch as we participate in the angelic mode of perception. The scene in which God declares the potential relationship between representation and actuality, which I noted in the introduction, was a scene meant for the eyes of angels: "From them I will not hide / My judgments" (*PL* XI, 68–69). Taking into account Jesus' skeptical formulation of reading in his rejection of Athens, we must state the ways the poem articulates its reading site as a paradox.[21] In order to understand how a text becomes unnecessary to the spiritual reader, we must become spiritual readers. To become spiritual readers, we must assume the perspective of angels and to assume that vista we must attend to the way the text directs us to that site. The poem does not work by a simple paradox of the sort Sir Thomas Browne reveled in. Underlying its simple paradoxical form is a fertile field of epistemological and political questions. When Jesus states that the reader must bring the proper spirit for the text's comprehension, the text he is referring to is his own life — the life of Jesus. The understanding of that subject belongs, according to Milton's contemporaries, to the realm of meditative theory.

Louis de Granada writes that "the principall matter of meditation" is "all the pointes of the lyfe and passion of our Saviour Christ." Meditation is, of course, the mode of concentrated intellectual application to an object, such as the life of Christ. Attending to that life rigorously, according to Thomas à Kempis, gives the meditative soul an upright mind which in turn transforms the world into a "booke of godly instructions." Reading, moreover, is not just an act of discerning the world's finer elements from its more gross, but a way of apprehending the spirit in the world and using that energy to ascend out of the world. As Lorenzo Scupoli writes, "when thou doest reade, thou maist keepe our Lord in thy presence, ascend wyth thy thoughts to him, and beholde him under these words."[22] Learning to read the life of Christ, then, allows one to learn to read the world, which in turn allows one to escape that world, which is the basic principle of meditative theory.

The meditative theorists of the sixteenth and seventeenth centuries reach that principle from three basic premises: first, meditation works initially by transporting us away from the earth and into heaven; second, our transportation to heaven is truly a journey into ourselves — heaven is within us; and third, within ourselves the ideal perspective in meditation for viewing the life of Christ is that of the angels. *Paradise Regained* establishes its narrativity in its induction by following this program.

NARRATIVITY AND MEDITATION: THEORIES OF MOVING THE READER

In arguing that *The Pilgrim's Progress* is a meditative fable, U. Milo Kaufmann notes that there is a kind of "superimposition of static and linear development" in the narrative. This superimposition, moreover, leaves the reader with the impression that, within the story, the "movement is not movement at all."[23] But there is movement in *The Pilgrim's Progress*—slow and often subtle, but movement nonetheless. Like that in *Paradise Regained,* the movement in Bunyan's narrative involves interpretation and accretion of hermeneutic skills. Like Milton's poem, Bunyan's fable is also about the movement toward God. In this sense, the movement is both subtle—like the phoenix in *Samson Agonistes,* "vigorous most / When most unactive deem'd" (1705–06)—and, like the motion Raphael describes to Adam, directed toward the source of being. Meditation, according to its Renaissance theorists, involves a great deal of movement. Movement is intrinsic to the tradition of meditation that precedes and informs one mode of self-knowledge in *Paradise Regained*—what I call *meditative motion.* I must first note, however, two other meditative aspects—*meditative stance* and *meditative orientation.*

By meditative stance I mean the individual's mode of perception as it is revealed in the physical and mental posture of the meditating subject. In his study of the nature of religion, *The Sacred and the Profane,* Mircea Éliade suggests that we may contrast the act of inhabiting a house with the act of walking on a road. Living in a house "symbolizes the world of the family, of society, of getting a living." Walking signifies the desire to "leave the world" and to refuse any "worldly situation."[24] Jesus will conclude his career in this poem with a return to "his Mothers house" (IV, 635). In the interim, he is a walking subject whose ambulation is attended by his meditation: "Thought following thought, and step by step led on" (I, 185–92). Jesus here exemplifies the meditative stance, setting out, as he does, and led by the Spirit, "Musing and much revolving in his brest." This is Jesus' contemplative attitude; conversing with solitude he "His holy Meditations thus persu'd" (I, 195). This perambulating Jesus meditates on his autobiography in order to come to terms with the recent revelation of his status. The physical stance, the walking, the musing, the fasting signify the abstracted mental posture of the meditator.

Meditative orientation takes under its consideration the search for a binding paradigm most conducive to the meditation. The meditative orientation for Bernard, for example, is the Passion of Christ; it is the central feature of his meditations, the single originating monad from where all knowledge is deduced.[25] The difference between the meditative orientation and the meditative object is that whereas the object is an entity upon which the mind meditates, the orientation is the formal paradigm of perception within which sense is accessible and beyond which there is nonsense. While Bernard's meditation is christocentric, Milton's is theocentric. In *Paradise Regained,* Jesus ends his autobiographical meditation with complete intellectual submission to God: "What concerns my knowledge God reveals" (I, 293). He will end all but one of his replies to the temptations with that same acquiescent faith. Because God for Jesus is the origin of sense, he apprehends all Satan's offers as they relate to his theocentric epistemology. The meditative orientation, the origin of sense for Jesus, is simply God — and nothing else.

Meditative motion, then, may be seen as the mental resolution achieved by the contemplative mind as it concentrates on an object within the meditative orientation. The motion may be cathartic (in the case of considering the Redemption), or enervating (in the case of considering human strength in relation to God's) or, as I will describe it in relation to this poem, ascendant and interior. That the quality of resolution achieved in the meditating mind should be expressed in terms of movement is important, for meditation is not merely the static perception of an object, but a form of constantly changing discernment which allows the mind to move both deeper into the mysteries of the object and higher in the knowledge of divine things. In order to appreciate the premises underlying knowledge of celestial verities, we must first understand the role of reason in faith, a debate best approached through a consideration of the battle between flesh and spirit.

I

In his epistle to the Galatians, as in that to the Romans, Paul counsels the community to "Walk in the Spirit" in order to frustrate "the lust of the flesh. For the flesh lusteth against the Spirit, and the Spirit against the flesh: and these are contrary the one to the other" (Gal. v, 16–17). Using this scriptural verse as his text, William Perkins distinguishes four separate significations of spirit and flesh, and suggests an interpretation of the battle between them: (1) the battle of the soul against the body, (2) the battle between natural reason and natural appetite, (3) the battle between Christ's godhead and Christ's manhood, and (4) the battle between the holy and the unholy inclinations of the mind. Perkins writes, "the spirite signifieth a created quality of holinesse, which by the Holy Ghost is wrought in the minde, and affections of men: and the flesh, the naturall corruption or inclination of the minde, wil, and affections to that which is against the lawe." The lusting of the Spirit, he continues, is able "to beget good meditations, motions, inclinations, and desires in the minde, will, and affections."[26]

It would be hard to overstress the popularity of the topos of the battle between flesh and spirit in Christian letters. Joshuah Sylvester's poem, *Auto-Machia,* has for its secondary subtitle, *"man's* Strife with *man;* Our Flesh & Spirit in *Duel."*[27] In chronicling the "Christian warfare," John Downame stipulates that the crucial battle is waged between the flesh and the spirit.[28] But, as the various significations Perkins outlines suggest, flesh and spirit are primarily modes of cognition. Usually the difference is figured between fleshly knowledge and spiritual wisdom, or between reason and faith.

Joseph Hall provides us with a full elaboration of the place of rationality in a fideistic system of belief. Humans are blessed with three kinds of mutually exclusive vision, each with its hierarchical prerogative. Hall writes:

A faithfull man hath three eyes: The first of sense, common to him with brute creatures: the second of reason, common to all men: the third of faith, proper to his profession: whereof each looketh beyond other; and none of them medleth with others objects. For, neither doth the eye of sense reach to intelligible things and matters of discourse: nor the eye of reason to those things which are supernaturall and spirituall: neither doth faith looke downe, to things that may be sensibly seene.[29]

Hall makes a distinction between Christianity and Philosophy based on the modes of perception available to each. He writes,

The Schoole of God, and Nature, require two contrary manners of proceeding. In the Schoole of Nature, we must conceive, and then beleeve: in the Schoole of God, we must first beleeve, and then we shall conceive. He that beleeves no more than he conceives, can never be a Christian; nor he a Philosopher, that assents without reason. In

Natures Schoole, we are taught to bolt out the truth, by Logicall discourse: God cannot endure a Logician. In his Schoole he is the best Scholler, that reasons least, and assents most.[30]

Only the possession of the third eye of faith allows the faithful Christian to enroll in God's school. Elsewhere, though, Hall is not so dogmatic. In his contemplation on the Three Wise Men, he writes:

Those Easterlings were great searchers of the depths of nature, professed Philosophers, them hath God singled out to the honor of the manifestation of Christ: Human learning well improved makes us capable of divine; There is no knowledge whereof God is not the Author; hee would never have bestowed any gift, that should leade us away from himselfe; It is an ignorant conceit, that inquiry into nature should make men Atheous: No man is so apt to see the Star of Christ as a diligent disciple of Philosophy.[31]

Lest he appear to have gone too far, Hall adds, "Philosophie without this Starre, is but the wisp of errour," adding immediately after that this whole episode is beyond the pale of philosophy to discover: "These things goe not by discourse, but by revelation." There seems to be a correlation between faith and reason that requires an absolute surrender of the latter to assert the sincerity of the former. Hall suggests that nescience is at the heart of submission to the will of God: "There is not a more noble proofe of our Faith, then to captivate all the powers of our understanding and will to our Creator, and without all sciscitations to goe blind-fold, whither he will leade us."[32]

Hall would later argue a closer relationship between the three eyes of the faithful being than in his *Meditations*. In that tract he made the three eyes—of sense, reason, and faith—mutually exclusive; in *The Invisible World* he makes reason the link between the visible and invisible realms. "Now then, having taken a view of both worlds; of the materiall world, by the eyes of sense and reason; of the Invisible by the eyes of reason and faith; I cannot but admire God in both, and both of them in God; but the Invisible so much more, as it is infinitely beyond the other" (*The Invisible World*, p. 352). Fideism is not always antirational in Hall, and rarely so in Milton. Although in his prose works Milton tends to disagree with Hall's devaluation of reason, the difference is only of degree. Milton's fideism is more evident in his poetry, but never antirational. Perhaps Donne's two-handed ingenuity defines Milton's position most adequately: "Reason is our Soules left hand, Faith her right."[33]

The meditative motion, then, requires a combat of flesh and spirit, and, varying in different minds, a degree of antirationalist fideism. But reason is not supplanted by faith, either in Hall or in Milton. This motion, I have suggested, is both ascendant and interior. It is ascendant inasmuch as that is the tendency of human aspiration; all things, as Raphael says, "up to him return" (*PL* V, 470). It is interior inasmuch as human beings possess an inward spirit and as that is the place of the "paradise within." This motion is a dual motion, encompassing both ascendancy and interiority, because representation is the only form of self-knowledge available to fallen beings. The meditative soul undertakes to represent itself as if it were ascending in order to promote an internal desire to ascend. We begin by tracing the theorists' descriptions of the ascendant motion.

According to meditation theorists, the first motion necessary to ascent is the removal of oneself from earth and earthly things. Lancelot Andrewes suggests that there "is a Use of Dignity, when a man doth abstract himself from the earth, and by often prayer doth grow into acquaintance and familiarity with God." Andrewes reiterates this theme of abstraction and gives it a program of research: "Men do converse and enter into familiarity with God, by abstracting their minds from humane affairs, and sublevating them into heaven by a continuall meditation of God, and things pertaining to the life to come."[34] The earth is the base from which the meditating mind ascends, and perhaps the matter of the meditation that produces that ascent. Henry Church advises us to "Raise Heavenlie Discourse, from Earthlie things."[35] The idea of elevation is intrinsic to Bernard's devotional method; the subject is Christ's passion, but the ultimate aim of the meditating mind is heaven: "Although we have our bodies here beneath, yet wee may lift up our hearts above. Therefore let us runne, not with the steppes of the body, but with the affections, but with the desires, but with the sighes of the soule."[36] Chrysostom counsels the faithful searcher to seek out heaven by crucifying the self to the world: "Do not, because thy body is not translated into heaven, suppose that thou hast anything to do with the earth."[37]

Peter de Alcantara formulates a sequential paradigm for this ascension. Mental prayer consists of a subtle movement from meditation to contemplation to prayer:

> In this exercise of prayer we must joyne meditation to contemplation, seeinge one is, as it were a ladder unto the other. . . . [It is] the part of meditation, with diligent attention to consider and ponderate celestiall thinges. . . . It is the property of contemplation which followeth meditation, to enjoy this kindled fire, that is to say, to embrace that affection, which with much labour he hath sought and found.

This sequence of meditation leads one ultimately to the "taste of heavenly thinges."[38]

George Wither's meditative emblems offer a succinct and accessible summary of the ideas we have been discussing. The sequence of heart emblems in Wither's popular collection uncovers the narrative nature of the cordial life.[39] A variety of emblems featuring hearts occurs in episodic sequence in Wither's collection. Under an emblem of a heart with an eye looking up to the sun, he writes:

> A *Heart,* which bore the figure of an *Eye*
> Wide open to the *Sunne;* by some, was us'd,
> When in an *Emblem,* they would signifie
> A *Minde,* which on Celestiall Matters mus'd:
> Implying, by the same, that there is nought
> Which in this lower *Orbe,* our Eyes can see,
> So fit an Object for a manly thought,
> As those things, which in Heav'n above us be.

The musing of the seeing heart is the contemplation unique to the person possessing what Hall called the "eyes of faith," that discernment beyond the reaches of sense and human intelligence:

> God, gave *Mankinde* (above all other Creatures)
> A lovely *Forme,* and upward-looking *Eye,*
> (Among the rest of his peculiar *Features*)
> That he might lift his *Countenance* on high:
> And (having view'd the Beauty, which appeares
> Within the outward *Sights* circumference)
> That he might elevate above the Sphæres,
> The piercing Eye, of his *Intelligence.*
> Then, higher, and still higher strive to raise
> His *Contemplations* Eyes, till they ascend

> To gaine a glimpse of those eternall *Rayes,*
> To which all undepraved *Spirits* tend.

The battle of the flesh and spirit finds expression when Wither states his optimistic view of human inclination, its tendency to ascend:

> For, 'tis the proper nature of the *Minde*
> (Till fleshly *Thoughts* corrupt it) to despise
> Those Lusts whereto the *Body* stands inclin'd;
> And labour alwayes, *upward* to arise.

Wither concludes by suggesting that as one's thoughts tend in this life, so will one's soul in the next—either spirit or flesh. "Well-minded men" will go above to the celestial realm, while those who doted on the flesh will "bide below."

Under an emblem of a smoking and winged heart reposing on a book filled with Greek characters under a sun on whose hem resides a Tetragrammaton, Wither commends the meditative life in its ascent from the subject of natural history to divinity:

> The *Booke,* here shadow'd, may be said, to show
> The *Wisdome,* and *Experience,* which we know
> By Common meanes, and, by these *Creatures,* here,
> Which to be plac'd below us, may appeare.
> The *Winged-heart,* betokens those *Desires,*
> By which, the *Reasonable-soule,* aspires
> Above the *Creature;* and, attempts to clime,
> To *Mysteries* and *Knowledge,* more sublime:
> Ev'n to the *Knowledge* of the *Three-in-one,*
> Implyed by the *Tetragrammaton.*
> The *Smokings* of this *Heart,* may well declare
> Those *Perturbations,* which within us are,
> Untill, that Heavenly wisedome, we have gain'd,
> Which is not, here, below, to be attain'd;
> And, after which, those *Hearts,* that are *upright,*
> Enquire with daily studie, and delight.[40]

Enacting his own advice to turn to meditation in order to turn one's mind to the highest truths humanity can know, Wither concludes his contemplation of this emblem by representing the transformation of his early "desire" in the act of ascending to later "delight." The heart is transformed from its smoky being into an "upright" state.

Ascension would indeed seem to be the theme of a wide range of writers. Arthur Capel notes the combat between flesh and spirit, and the concomitant ascension achieved by the victory of meditation. "For what," asks Capel, "is mans *misery* but his own *disobedience* to himself? the *Flesh* daily warring against the *Spirit,* and innumerable impossible *desires* daily fighting against *Reason.*" He delineates human life in geometric terms:

> *Our life is but a moment of time,* between two *Eternities* of *infinite beginning* and *never ending.* It is the very *middle point* of a *perpendicular line;* and but a *punctum,* a thing of no *sensible* being, but *imaginary,* from which if we *ascend* by *holy meditations, Faith,* and *good works,* we shall attain to a never-ending *beatitude;* but if from it we *descend* by *carnall thoughts,* sensual *appetites,* and *evil actions,* we shall be perpetuated in everlasting *torments.*

Again we see the distinction between spiritual thinking (which promotes ascension) and carnal thinking (which leads to descent). A thinking being's trajectory determines its direction and, in the end, its status as a spiritual or a carnal being. I have borrowed Heidegger's term *being-toward* to describe this directionality. To give it a seventeenth-century accent, we can use two unlikely theorists. Hobbes gives us the argument that, in the "*Celerity of Imagining,*" the best thing to have is a "*steddy direction* to some approved end."[41] The direction in Milton, as in these theorists of meditation, is toward God; the end is God. The even less likely theorist is Moloch, who declares that "in our proper motion we ascend" (*PL* II, 75).

In moving toward heaven, though, the elect soul also moves into itself. For, according to the theory of spatial movement involved in meditation, heaven does not signify only the celestial abode after death but also the soul in life; not only the church triumphant but also the church militant. Andrewes, for instance, writes that "Heavenly meditation" teaches us to seek the kingdom of God not only above, but also within, for as "we know we shall have our part in heaven, so must we begin our heaven here on earth." John Norden counsels the "pensive man" to search above in order to develop within:

> It behoveth us carefully first and before all things to seeke the king-
> dom of God, the way, the means, and the guid therunto, which is not
> to be sought elsewhere, it is not in the inward viewe and therefore to
> be sought from above, to be inwardly received and comprehended by
> faith, it is the kingdom of the ministeries of God.

"Thy Kingdome," writes Henry Clapham, "is Spirituall and specially inward." John Preston suggests that the establishment of the
"new covenant" will be the result of a renovated "inward disposition and pronenesse put into the heart." The individual who establishes this new covenant internalizes God through meditation:
"There is nothing seemes so beautifull as Grace, as the Image of
God renewed in thy soule."[42] To Moloch's statement of the propriety of ascent, we now can add Michael's statement of the seat of the
new Eden—the "paradise *within*."

To get an idea, now, of how the ascending motion is also the
interior motion, we can turn to William Narne's exposition of the
act of praying:

> Prayer is a principall part of Gods service, wherein a true Christian,
> leaving the earth in his heart and affections, ascending into Heaven in
> his mind, approaching unto the throne of grace, presenting him selfe
> before the glorious God, hee conferreth, and speaketh familiarly with
> his Creator, hee offereth a spirituall sacrifice unto his Majestie, he
> wrestleth with the Omnipotent, he giveth a comfortable victorie, hee
> becommeth *the Temple of God, the holy Spirit dwelling in him,* and
> obtaineth *every good gift,* that is necessarie for him.

In working one's way up to God, one also establishes an internal
temple to God. Movement upward concludes its career in movement within. Moreover, Narne's upward-inward movement, like
Milton's, is part of a political program for self-government: "By
praying fervently, and by *seeking the Kingdome of God principally,*
thou . . . shall get power and dexteritie to rule thy selfe arightly."
Likewise, Peter de Alcantara, in his tractate on meditation, suggests, through an artful circularity in his language, that by rising
to God above the reader also achieves godliness within. He writes,
"Lett him elevate his understanding to God, consideringe his divine presence, with that due reverence and attention as is requisite,
and lett him imagine God Almightie himselfe to be presente in his
soule, as in verie deed hee is."[43] Within the space of this brief

paragraph Alcantara sends the meditating mind above, only to allow it to discover that it had been traveling within. Given that *Paradise Regained* is a narrative that deals with the theme of regaining external paradise by reforming the internal kingdom of God, the idea of heavenly ascent as a means of psychic ingress is superbly fit.

As a complete example of the various facets of meditative theory outlined above, Richard Baxter best shows the happiest marriage of puritan discursive rhetoric and meditative intuition. In the fourth part of *The Saints Everlasting Rest,* Baxter outlines a "Directory for the getting and keeping of the Heart in Heaven" by the use and exercise of "Heavenly Meditation." Baxter's is a simple directory meant for the new citizen of the commonwealth, but it consists of a complex intermixture of Renaissance psychology, puritan sensitivity to the motions of the life of the soul, and careful interest in meditative perspectives. Consider the way in which he suggests the interaction of the phenomenal world and the sensible saint: "Gods way to persuade their wills, and to excite and actuate their Affections, is by the Discourse, Reasoning, or Consideration of their Understandings, upon the Nature and Qualifications of the Objects which are presented to them." Meditation is to be conducted with such a force of concentration that we are rapt above like Elijah: "O blessed are the eyes that so see, and the ears that so hear, that the heart is thereby raised to this blessed heavenly frame."[44]

Baxter answers that vexed question of soteriology, the question of assurance, how one may know oneself saved, not by casuistry—as had been done from Perkins to Jeremy Taylor—but, following Zwingli, by a notional pietism: "Consider a heart set upon heaven, will be one of the most unquestionable evidences of thy sincerity, and a clear discovery of a true work of saving grace upon thy soul." The directory directs, "O Christian, get above"; "Reader, Heaven is above thee, the way is upwards." In response to the question "How can mortals ascend to heaven?," Baxter answers: "Faith hath wings, and Meditation is its chariot, Its office is to make absent things, as present."[45] Like Zwingli's notional pietism—that desire is indicative of fate—meditation, as I suggested at the end of the last chapter, is akin to the third form of self-knowledge in having its basis in representation. Meditation allows the meditating person to transmute desire into love, absence into presence, by representing one's self to one's self as being present.

Baxter allows us to see how meditation—the concentrated application of our discursive and intuitive powers—is able to fetch us
above and how heaven allows us a purview of the world, a prospect
that is present, ethically superior, and affective. Although at times
Baxter's language belies the fact, he directs his reader to an imaginary, internal heaven. As Bunyan's conflation of sacred and psychical
history in *The Holy War* demonstrates the agency of the individual
in the universal and, likewise, the macrocosmic in the microcosm,
Baxter's conflation of the heavenly and the visceral makes prescient
the state of glorification hereafter. In making what is absent present, what is invisible visible, Baxter directs us to a perspective of
faith where we can "look on the means and end together." That
perspective is, in Milton's theology, solely God's. The closest to it
would be that of the angels: "The good angels do not see into all
the secret things of God, as the Papists pretend," Milton writes.
But they do see a great deal nonetheless: "Some things indeed they
know by revelation, and others by means of the excellent intelligence with which they are gifted."[46] That perspective, although
not seeing the means and end together, is perhaps the most to
which a human may aspire. According to one tradition of meditative theory, it is a perspective that meditation helps establish.

II

The Jesuit, Louis Richeome, in making the distinction between
contemplation and meditation, suggests that contemplation, the
higher mode of understanding, enjoys "a vision which approach-
eth to the knowledge of Angels, who understand without discourse."[47] As the angel Raphael tells Adam, in describing how
Adam may work his body up to spirit, reason is the soul's being—
"Discursive or Intuitive; discourse / Is oftest yours, the latter most
is ours, / Differing but in degree, of kind the same" (*PL* V, 488–
90). Adam may aspire to an angelic view of things, Raphael tells
him, by accommodating his mode of reasoning from the discursive
to the intuitive, by attending to the "secrets of another World,"
and perceiving "what surmounts the reach / Of human sense"
(569, 571–72). Not only does Raphael use the trope of metaphor
to deliver his narrative of spiritual beings in a way comprehensible
to carnal sense, he also manipulates the articulation so that it
seems present: "For Time, though in Eternity, appli'd / To motion,

measures all things durable / By present, past, and future" (580–82). Adam enjoys an angel's perspective in Raphael's narrative.

In meditation, as Louis Martz's admirable survey shows, the meditator requires a certain dramatic presence, and never more than when one meditates on the life of Christ. The popular meditation of Bonaventura, for example, expects the reader to apprehend vividly each moment in the life of Christ, and from this to develop pious affections. Consider how Bonaventura prefaces his treatise:

> Wherfore thou that coveytest to feele truly, the fruyte of this presente booke thou must with all thy thoughte & thyne entent procure thee in thy soule present to those thinges that be here written, said, or done of our lorde Jesu. And that earnestly and respectively as thoughe thou heardest them with thy bodily eares or sawest them doone with thy bodily eyes.[48]

He emphasizes the need for presence—that the active bodily eyes and ears of the believing reader behold the scene immediately before them. Later in the book, Bonaventura will suggest that a heavenly presence is required for the meditator to appreciate the import of the Son's sacrificial offer: "Now take good heede and imagine in thy harte as if thou were present in the sighte of that blessed Lorde, with how great benignitie and gladness he speaketh these wordes." To appreciate the mercy of the Lord, to understand the tone of benign love with which He speaks, one must ascend to heaven. There, by being infused with the holiness of the place, the reader may appreciate the process of salvation unfolding. Bonaventura's rhetorical strategy requires a constant motion, from manger to heaven to wilderness. To find a more stable perspective, we must turn to the homiletic meditations of that Father whom Milton calls "holy *Chrysostome*" (CM IV, p. 299) and Joseph Hall names "sweet *Chrysostome*."[49]

In his *Homilies on the Gospel of Saint Matthew*, Chrysostom uses a rhetorical strategy that requires both a dramatic presence and an angelic perspective. He prefaces his narrative with an account of the difference between Moses' Law and Jesus' Gospel: "In the Old Testament, it was upon Moses' going up, that God came down; but here, when our nature hath been carried up into Heaven, or rather unto the royal throne, then the Spirit makes His descent." As was the case with Bonaventura, meditating on the life of Christ brings with it both a required angelic viewpoint and an opportunity for aspiring to that perspective. Chrysostom situates the reader among the angels:

> What then could ever be equal to these good tidings? God on earth, man in Heaven; and all became mingled together, *angels joined the choirs of men, men had fellowship with the angels,* and with the other powers above: and one might see the long war brought to an end, and reconciliation made between God and our nature, the devil brought to shame, demons in flight, death destroyed, Paradise opened, the curse blotted out, sin put out of the way, errors driven off, truth returning, the word of godliness everywhere sown, and flourishing in its growth, the polity of those above planted on the earth, those powers in secure intercourse with us, and on earth angels continually haunting, and hope abundant touching things to come.
>
> (My italics)[50]

This is the vision of Paradise regained; I shall argue it is also the perspective established in the induction to *Paradise Regained*.

The moment in the life of Christ which inspired Chrysostom to such pious meditation and opened the possibility for the conversation between humans and angels was the Baptism—the first event in the public ministry of Christ, the moment when the mystery of the Incarnation was manifestly declared. In his treatise on the Baptism, William Cowper notes that in that blessed event heaven and earth are indeed joined. In Jesus, he writes, "things which are in heaven and in earth, are now gathered together into one; by him, Angels come downe and doe service unto men; by him, men goe up to the Father, to worship him." This regenerate worship is now of such virtue and potency that "by it, not onely doe the heavens open unto men, . . . but men are also transported and carried up into heaven."[51] The Baptism, we recall, is also the moment when Jesus gains the power to be the spiritual reader he will become. It is also the moment when we as readers may assume something like that power.

Baptism, according to Wither, is the moment that allows for meditation, a moment when the soul is purified to the degree of being able to ascend to something like an angelic perspective. Under an emblem of Ganymede ascending to heaven perched on an eagle, Wither writes,

Though this be but a *Fable,* of their feigning,
The *Morall* is a *Reall truth,* pertayning
To ev'ry one (which harbours a desire
Above the Starry *Circles,* to aspire.)
By *Ganymed,* the *Soule* is understood,
That's washed in the *Purifying flood*
Of sacred *Baptisme* (which doth make her seeme
Both pure and beautifull, in *God's* esteeme.)
The *Ægle,* meanes that Heav'nly *Contemplation,*
Which, after Washings of *Regeneration,*
Lifts up the *Minde,* from thinges that earthly bee,
To view those *Objects,* which *Faith's* Eyes doe see.[52]

Faith, according to Baxter, gives the meditating soul the final perspective it hopes to achieve—a state which is the closest to enjoying God's view of things, and which in Milton is an angelic vista.
The Baptism is the beginning of Milton's meditation on the life of
Christ, and the induction to the poem in which that meditation
occurs assumes the perspectives we have so far outlined.

READING LIKE AN ANGEL:
THE INDUCTION TO *PARADISE REGAINED*

The meditative theorists suggest that the ideal subject position for
viewing the life of Christ would be a faithful, present, almost
angelic disposition. That angelic disposition is most effective because the angels possess a spiritual understanding that extends
beyond the human. But an angelic perspective, it is worth repeating, is of course an epistemic category. When Peter Sterry elaborates the structure of a tripartite soul, it falls into the categories of
the soul's "Sensitive, Rational, Intellectual, or Angelical" parts.
The last of these interests us. Sterry writes, "The Intellectual part
of the Soul, is the Orb or Sphere of Angels. This is the Souls
Angelical part. Here the Soul's *abstract,* and separate from the
Body, (which is called the *Divine Death* of the Soul) [and] beholds
the Intellectual Forms of things, the immortal Essences and Substances, the Angels in their own bright and universal Glories."[53] By
making an intellectual mode of perception an angelical one, Sterry
allows the reader to anticipate the heavenly in his or her own soul.

Not only the Cambridge Platonists, but the Italian humanists, too, represented an angelic epistemology.

In his *Oration on the Dignity of Man,* Giovanni Pico suggests that it is not the ability to discard a body that is the primary property of an angel, but rather "his spiritual intelligence that makes an angel." The way for human beings to aspire to that "spiritual intelligence" is by "emulating the Cherubic way of life." Such an imitation requires both an ascent and an interior motion. In order that "men might ascend to heaven and become angels," they need to go into their "own souls" and make them "the house of God." This, in the end, is the dignity of human beings and, Pico concludes, their way of gaining self-knowledge: "For he who knows himself in himself knows all things." Likewise, in his *Epistolae,* Marsilio Ficino maintains that because they are able to employ their reason and to undertake contemplation, human beings come "much nearer to the blessed angels." Intellect, in Ficino's epistemology, is the mediator between nature and supernature, between humanity and divinity. And, like Pico, Ficino sees in this intellection the beginning and the end of self-knowledge: "The intellect is prompted by nature to comprehend the whole breadth of being; in its notion it perceives all, and, in the notion of all, it contemplates itself."[54] In this way, then, does the induction to *Paradise Regained* promote the narrative model's scheme of self-knowledge. That scheme was first articulated in reference to the angels in *Paradise Lost.*

Milton establishes the narrativity of *Paradise Lost* by describing motions within the narrative that require certain perspectival shifts of the reader. Those shifts in perspective require the reader to assume novel spatio-temporal vistas within the cosmos of the narrative and also to acquire new affective responses to the action being viewed from a different perspective. If, as Blake would say, the eye altering alters all, we might add that the altering eye carries with it an emotional change too. The movement in the focalization in this narrative involves a parallax, wherein the object of vision seems apparently displaced because of a change in the point of observation.

The reader's perspective is altered (and with it the reader's affective response) with the subtle transitions in the microstructure of the induction to *Paradise Regained*. This distinction can be seen by differentiating between the tableaux and the transitions between them. These tableaux are something like what Louis Martz has called "panels" and Kenneth Burke labeled "fundamentals of structure."[55] There are four tableaux in the induction to *Paradise Regained*—seriatim, the invocation (1–17), the scene of the Baptism at Jordan (18–39), the devilish consistory (40–127), and the scene in heaven (128–81). The rest of the induction (182–293) is Jesus' autobiographical soliloquy, which I will discuss in the final section of this chapter. Although I mark it off as a significantly different part of the induction, it is nonetheless part of the *discipline* of the narrative, although it is also the transition to the *doctrine*.

We might distinguish the points of transition within the first part of the induction. These transitions occur between the tableaux, from invocation to Jordan, from Jordan to the consistory, and from the consistory to heaven. Each movement not only alters the reader's perception of the ensuing tableau, but also suggests to the reader an affective stance with which to view that tableau.

In the induction to *Paradise Regained*, that movement follows the program established by meditative theorists. The reader is elevated during the course of the induction in order to achieve something like an angelic perspective. Finding *Paradise Regained* to express an "actively compressed style" and to carry with it such "baroque packing," Alastair Fowler has felt himself reading as if he had "an angel's vista of things."[56] Although that is the perspective meditative theorists believed most apt for observing the life of Christ, it is a matter of more than style. That vista is the product of subtle transitions between tableaux. The assumption of that perspective begins in the place the theorists suggested it ought to begin: the Baptism.

I

The Baptism is the most important tableau of narrative discourse in this induction, and, moreover, the basis for the rest of the induction. In the consistory, Satan will attempt to interpret its significance; in heaven, God will alert the angels to this second symbol in the unfolding mystery of the Incarnation; and in his soliloquy, Jesus will attempt to reassess his previous life in terms of this new revelation. As we follow Satan's eristics, and God's ambiguously stated predictions, and the angels' artful chorus, we are also

involved in the interpretation of the significance of the Baptism—
especially the multiple role of the Spirit in that miracle. The first
tableau, then, allows the poet to invoke the Spirit (as muse); the
second to describe its all-important descent in the Baptism (in the
shape of a dove); the third, to delineate Satan's denial of the Spirit
in the consistory (as, literally, a dove); and the fourth to provide a
perspective for the reader undergoing acculturation.

The transitions between the tableaux work progressively to
raise us from earth to heaven. Between the second and third tableaux we follow Satan from Jordan, where we have been watching
the Baptism, to his gloomy consistory. The movement is from the
"flood Jordan" to "mid air"—a partial ascent. The transition between the third and fourth tableaux works in much the same way as
the transition in Book X of *Paradise Lost* where Sin and Death were
transformed abruptly from focalizers to objects of focus. As Satan
sets out for Jordan to find Jesus, the reader is again involved in an
ascendant motion, from "mid air" to a presence with the "most
High." Our perspective shifts as we look *at* Satan rather than
through him. From focalizer, he becomes the object of our focus.
The general motion, then, is one of ascension, as the reader rises
from Jordan to mid air to high heaven. The motion occurs around
the scene of the Baptism, that moment in cosmic history, we recall,
when Chrysostom thought that "men had fellowship with the angels."

The fourth tableau in the induction occurs in heaven and pre-
pares the reader for what I shall argue is his or her final situation in
the poem, a sort of angelic perspective. In heaven, we are allowed
to attend God's speech to Gabriel and the rest of the angels, parallel with the heavenly colloquy. By the end of God's speech we are
invited to share something like the angelic perspective.

God begins by taking up the issue which both the invocation
and Satan's speech have alerted us to—the issue of doubt and
proof. God says that Gabriel and the angels shall this day witness
the "verification" of the Annunciation, "by proof" (I, 130). He
refers to Jesus, paraphrasing Gabriel's Annunciation, as "a Son /
Great in Renown, and call'd the Son of God" (135–36). Although
the emphasis is on verification and dispelling doubt, there is no
assertion that this Son is *the* Son of God. The next clause of God's
speech tells us that Gabriel told Mary "doubting" of this miraculous conception (137). The ambiguity of "doubting" is quite art-

ful, referring either to Mary or to Gabriel, or to both. God then refers to Jesus as "this man born" (though of a "birth divine"), and informs us that he shall expose "this man" to Satan (140–41). God mentions that he will allow Satan the liberty of tempting Jesus and reminds us and the angels of a former occasion of allowed temptation, the episode of Job. The next sentence begins by informing us that Jesus is "a man / Of female Seed" and is Job's ethical superior, "far abler" (150–51). His ability, in fact, extends even to reversing the tide of cosmic history, winning "by Conquest what the first man lost" (154). But this all shall occur "at length" (152). In the present instance ("first"), God shall "exercise" Jesus in the desert to allow him to "lay down the rudiments / Of his great warfare," which he will need to "conquer" Sin and Death (155–59). The terms of warfare are suddenly recast when the next clause informs us that the rudiments are, and the conquest will be by, "Humiliation and strong Sufferance" (160). This abrupt alteration from physical, military terms to paradoxical, ethical terms (the strength of weakness) forces us to think anew of heroism, removing us from the carnal mode of knowing, which informed Satan's interpretation, to a spiritual mode of wisdom.

What happens next in God's speech is most important. God names the audience of this exercise in the wilderness and states the ethical imperative required of that audience:

> That all the Angels and Ethereal Powers,
> *They now, and men hereafter,* may discern
> From what consummate virtue I have chose
> This perfect Man, by merit call'd my Son,
> To earn Salvation for the Sons of men.
>
> (I, 163–67, my italics)

God's pronouncement suggests that we are meant to enter a certain communion with the angelic perspective—the prerogative of the meditating mind. Moreover, just as Milton plays with a recursive time scheme in Book X of *Paradise Lost*, returning the reader to a prelapsarian moment with Sin and Death in order to show how the Fall looked from a nonhuman perspective, so here also Milton returns us in time to the present scene. Baxter suggested meditating on the signifying Spirit in the Baptism as the way to wing our way to heaven: "So might a wise industrious Christian get his thoughts carried into Heaven, and receive, as it were, returns from thence again, by creatures of slower wings then Doves, by the assistance of the Spirit the Dove of God."[57]

Moreover, the angels are invited especially to view the "merit" and the "virtue" of the Son. In the *Christian Doctrine,* Milton maintained that any human who hoped to understand the "merit" of the Son had to be in a state of "imperfect glorification." That state involves being ingrafted in Christ in order to be allowed the epistemological habit of appreciating merit in its essence. Once ingrafted, humans are allowed the "comprehension of spiritual things, and the love of holiness." That, of course, is what the reader who has "spirit" and "judgment" possesses — an ability to perceive the spiritual text of Jesus' life (CM XVI, pp. 3–65). If we assume that the recursive time scheme of God's invitation here (164) permits us to assume a perspective Milton held to be angelic, then we too might be allowed to perceive the spiritual things Jesus will express in the action of the poem. Interestingly, in *Areopagitica,* Milton held that the ability to discern the spiritually good from the carnally dross is solely the angels' (CM IV, pp. 349–50). The reader is also asked to perform this sort of discernment in *Paradise Regained.*

The movements between the tableaux indicate that the reader is meant to ascend with the focalizing agent — something like my interpretation of the meditative motion of ascent. By emphasizing that angels and men see the same virtue, despite disparate time schedules, God echoes the call for presence, which is another important aspect of meditation. Throughout *Paradise Regained* there is an insistent call for presence, such as was not to be found in *Paradise Lost.* In the first epic, the reader is always reminded that Adam and Eve are original, and that nothing preceded them; in *Paradise Regained,* we are made to feel a personal involvement in the life of Jesus, and part of that involvement is achieved through a sense of immediate presence.

Now: the word makes itself felt throughout the narrative, from its beginning at the flood Jordan — "Now had the great Proclaimer" — to its conclusion at the angelic chorus's prophecy of salvation — "Now enter, and begin to save mankind" (I, 18; IV, 631). There is a persistent presence in the fable, a constant attention to being there and then. Jesus enters the desert "now"; Satan encounters him "now" (I, 193, 314). The time, Jesus recognizes, is "Now full" and he is "now by some rousing motions led" (I, 287, 290). At the first encounter, Jesus informs Satan that "God hath now sent his living Oracle" into the world (I, 460). Jesus "Now" hungers first (II, 244). And, finally, only after the final temptation Jesus "now" avenges Adam's loss, and founds "now" the fairer paradise (IV, 602, 609). Unlike the Fall, which was only a historical and local event, the Atonement, though a historical event, is for Milton pervasively eternal. Presence and angelic perspective are the two requirements for meditating on the life of Christ. Through careful rhetorical artistry, Milton places the reader there and then, or, perhaps better, in the here and now.

II

Narrative in general relies on and develops shifting perspectives. In their study of the nature of narrative, Robert Scholes and Robert Kellogg argue that the "reader gravitates always to what seems the most trustworthy viewpoint, depending on the criteria for trustworthiness which the narrative evokes."[58] In *Paradise Regained,* the most trustworthy perspective is the angelic. Through the movement of focalizers in the poem, the reader ascends to something like that perspective. Not only is this the vista most amenable to an uplifting moral meditation on the virtues of the Son, but it is also the one that provides the best prospect for whatever drama this poem offers.

A certain stance is expected of the reader, a certain degree of engagement that must be established before the combat commences. The essence of that engagement is, I believe, found in the chorus of the angels, the angelic moment:

> So spake the Eternal Father, and all Heaven
> Admiring stood a space, then into Hymns
> Burst forth, and in Celestial measures mov'd,
> Circling the Throne and Singing, while the hand
> Sung with the voice, and this the argument.
> Victory and Triumph to the Son of God
> Now entring his great duel, not of arms,
> But to vanquish by wisdom hellish wiles.
> The Father knows the Son; therefore secure
> Ventures his filial Vertue, though untri'd,
> Against whate're may tempt, whate're seduce,

Allure, or terrifie, or undermine.
Be frustrate all ye strategems of Hell,
And devilish machinations come to nought.
So they in Heav'n their Odes and Vigils tun'd. (1, 168–82)

There are a variety of interpretations of this choral song, ranging from Roger H. Sundell's assessment of it as a "hymn of triumph" to Thomas B. Stoup's suggestion that it is more assuring than triumphant in tone. Richard Douglas Jordan asserts that the angels have "no doubt of the outcome," while Burton Jasper Weber claims that the song serves "to suggest the reality of Jesus' struggle."[59]

The way in which this choral interlude may be read, and interpreted, is extremely important to how we measure the dramatic element of the Son's development. Is there a fluid certainty in this song? I would posit, to be truest to the tone, that it possesses a wavering confidence. The proclamation of victory and triumph is strong and rings clear with emotion. The Father knows the Son, they continue in their assertive manner, and the Father is "therefore secure" in venturing his filial virtue. Confidence, though, begins to flag somewhat in the next clause, and visibly weakens in the following lines. The Chorus notices that the Son, for all his Father's security in him, is nonetheless "untried." The sense, variously drawn out from one verse to the next, continues, and the confidence wanes. The want of trial is troubling, but the catalogue of the variegated types of trial is ominous. The repetition of "whate're," whether seductive or tempting, contains more than a whisper of doubt. The next verse fulfills this emotion. The catalogue is difficult to read; it can hardly be called "liquid" in its presentation.[60] For such a short poetic space — indeed only five items are named — there is a pervading sense of the many forms of evil: "Against whate're may tempt, whate're seduce, / Allure, or terrifie, or undermine." The final two verses are disquieting as well. Consider the possible tone of such a hopeful declaration. The angelic choir addresses the very strategems and machinations of hell. By addressing these inanimate objects, the Chorus may be showing signs of troubled concern. The source of all this evil is never mentioned in their song. It is "hellish wiles," not Satan, that the Son will vanquish; it is "whate're," not whoever, may tempt him, and against which (not whom) he must venture his filial virtue. These final two lines, then, are but the conclusion to what has been a troubling unwillingness to mention the devil. And it is not untoward, I think, to discern a tone more hopeful than confident: "Be frustrate all ye strategems of Hell, / And devilish machinations come to nought."

One final point: Following God's speech, the angelic choir, indeed "all Heaven / Admiring stood a space" before bursting into heavenly hymns. We need only compare this with the angelic choir that met the Son's original offer of sacrifice in the third book of *Paradise Lost:*

> Loud as from numbers without number, sweet
> The multitude of Angels with a shout
> Loud as from numbers without number, sweet
> As from blest voices, uttering joy.   (*PL* III, 344–47)

The most notable difference, of course, is the lack of immediate response in *Paradise Regained*'s angelic chorus. The angels have been taken aback; they have, for one brief moment, perhaps only the second time in heavenly history, been struck dumb. This is not insignificant, especially as an answer to those who maintain that there is no tension in the poem.

As to the readers' situation, then, we would infer that they are meant to share this perspective, doubtful, hopeful, aware of the forces involved. The discomfort felt by the angels as they survey the scene acts as a control for our own emotional responses. Of all the perspectives through which the reader has traveled, none is more fit. The bardic perspective of the invocation effected a temporal shift for the reader, who is cast on the shores of Jordan—the first "Now." The Baptism, the first scene of the narrative, allowed the reader to enjoy the earthly perspective. Standing on the shores of the river Jordan, the reader sees people flocking from all around in response to the Baptist's call and sees the Spirit/dove descend from heaven attended by God's pronouncement. Taken from those shores into the satanic perspective, the reader rises to midair and is infested with some doubt about Jesus' identity. Another ascent takes our reader to heaven, where God's speech allays but does not wholly remove this doubt. The reader then finds himself or herself included in a present perspective that in some intangible way involves an angelic prospect. The angelic choral hymn is not resounding in confidence. It heightens the awareness of the wiliness of satanic machinations and the weakness of human flesh. Drama is not wholly dispelled, but rather anticipated.

In an essay emphasizing the "ritual" of *Paradise Regained,* Jackson I. Cope claims that there is "no drama" in the poem. Part of his reading is based on the perspective of this undramatic scene. The perspective, Cope writes, is that of God: "We watch, as we always watch in ritual acts, with God. We stand not in the tortured question marks upon Satan, not even in the fresh discoveries vouchsafed the angels, for we have always known what God announces to them. We watch knowledge exfoliate itself in the metaphoric mask of history." I have argued against this point of view. As readers, participating in the rites we are about to watch, we are situated in a temporal and spatial framework where we have not always known what God tells the angels. Furthermore, it is quite doubtful that ritual is ever viewed through God's eyes; ritual, in most cultures, is the activity of a community's attempt to pacify its god, or their attempt to enact a myth or belief in order to please that god. God, in either case, is always the ultimate spectator and all human participants in the rites are part of the spectacle. The purpose is to transmit the mythical content from one generation to another, not to expose the workings of the religion from an omniscient viewpoint. To think that one is watching any culture's ritual acts "with God" is to accede to a rather dangerous and epigone fantasy that the Other's rituals are what we are able to understand because it is what we have evolved beyond. What Milton is suggesting is that the "ritual" must be renewed and seen through eyes cleared of the malaise of tradition; what Jesus sets out to do is reformulate the conditions of the ritual. What we are asked to assume here is the perspective from which we will choose to view that act. Cope, I would suggest, is not only assuming a perspective that the poem has not offered as a viable solution, but is assuming one that helps dispel everything this poem has to offer in terms of its attempts to articulate a novel culture and to present its action in a somewhat dramatic way.

Cope's reading does not focus on ritual at all, but rather on myth, which Cassirer has noted is the "epic element" in any religious culture. Rite, Cassirer continues, is "the *dramatic* element"; this poem, which recounts the initial rite of Jesus' public ministry, might best be read from the perspective which rite requires—that is, a perspective which does not dispel the "*dramatic* element."[61]

Meditation is also informed by a kind of drama, based on a dialectic between modes of apprehension and the intellectual movements required through comprehension. Milton's poems pursue the same sort of drama. His artistry was always attuned to the subtleties of shifts of perspective, to the wavering refluxes that play within humanity, to the indefinable interplay of human liberty and divine sanction. It would indeed have been a very strange reader in 1671 who picked up any of Milton's major poems and expected to be surprised by the *outcome;* and it is a reader Milton did not cater to. The drama of *Paradise Regained,* like that of *Paradise Lost* and *Samson Agonistes,* consists not in whether or not a thing will happen; the outcome is undeniably known. Milton's poetic and dramatic achievement is in tracing the internal dialogue between reason and passion, between wisdom and desire, between self and godliness. We are not surprised at the outcome of any of Milton's masterpieces; we are alert to the ways the conditions for a new culture have been articulated and exemplified (either negatively, as in *Paradise Lost,* or positively, as in *Paradise Regained*). *Drama,* therefore, is not truly a fit term to use in describing *Paradise Regained* or *Paradise Lost* or even *Samson Agonistes.* If by *dramatic* we mean the tension that exists between possible outcomes, there is some of that in *Paradise Regained,* though muted. If by *drama* we mean Aristotelian anagnorisis, then we must insist that *Paradise Regained* not be called dramatic. It is more meditative, more concerned with its expression of the ways cultures are born. Its most dramatic appeal, perhaps, is its violation of the essential gesture of drama—the way it does not present a scene of anagnorisis. Its process of engagement is what in the following chapter I will call the "dialectics of spirit."

Dialectic has, of course, its own type of drama: pedagogical and discursive. Our interest in this section has been to see how we become situated before the dialectic commences, how our perspective is translated from whenever and wherever we are to the eternal present of holy heaven. The induction involved us in an elevating motion based on the interpretation of the significance of the Baptism. We are, then, situated in a contemplative perspective for the imaginary meditation of the life of Jesus. In the final section of this chapter, we may, from the perspective in which we have been situated, "as far as Angels' ken" (*PL* I, 59), watch the intellectual meditation of the Son as he contemplates his vocation in terms of the knowledge he has gained at the Baptism.

While Jesus is formulating his role in cosmic history by meditating on the Baptism, we, as readers, are invited to enter into his
meditative soliloquy. The final movement of meditation, according
to its sixteenth- and seventeenth-century theorists, is interiority.
Jesus' soliloquy, an overt meditation with all its constituent parts,
allows the reader to enact that final movement within the narrative.
For, in the end, the theory of meditative movement serves our
understanding of *Paradise Regained* in only a limited way. The
most obvious signs of that limit rest on the fact that meditation
does not share the presuppositions of narrative; it does not attempt to suggest a way of creating a new world in its discursive
practice. Rather, meditation works as a method of transcending the
perceivable world — with all its political traumas, its oppositional
antinomies, and its basic human problems — and reaches to an unknown world that is specifically not an *alternative* world, but rather
what meditation considers *the* real world. For the meditating mind,
indeed for the religious mind as Eliade portrays it, the accession to
the sacred in terms of meditative motion is posited on the assumption that the world one transcends is unreal and the world one
ascends to is real. This, perhaps, is a roundabout way of saying that
meditation is intuitive where narrative — the act of imagining an
alternative world within the cultural space of the political world —
is not. Meditation, then, belongs properly to the realm of the
lyrical.[62] Needless to say, *Paradise Regained* is no lyric; it is resolutely narrative. The Son's soliloquy is the point of transition between the induction and the content, between the discipline of
reading and the doctrine of reading. The soliloquy makes that
transition by reworking our sense of how to read a life — *the* life, in
fact, that is going to serve as the paradigm for regaining paradise.
So, while the elevating part of the induction taught the value and
the process of meditative ascendancy, the reading part of the induction teaches the practical method of meditating on the life of
Jesus; it teaches us the process of meditative interiority.

Thus, because the Baptism is the scene of contested interpretation, one must move beyond Satan's eristics into the realm of Spirit
in order to determine the event's significance. As Baxter wrote,
"When the *heavenly-minde* is above with God, he may far easier
from thence discern every danger that lyes below, and the whole
method of the devil in deceiving" (p. 612). By being situated in an
angelic perspective, the reader may discern Satan's self-deception

about the Baptism's significance and therefore appreciate Jesus' candid reading of it. In meditation, the ascendant motion signals the movement within. Again, "because meer Cogitation of it be not prest home, [and] will not so pierce and affect the heart, Therefore we must here proceed to a second step, which is called Soliloquy, which is nothing but a pleading the case with our own souls" (p. 749). In this narrative, though, the soliloquy is Jesus' and our attendance on it marks both the shift from meditation's upward motion to its inward and our engagement with the dialectic. It also marks, as I suggested, the end of the induction and the beginning of the narrative.

CONVERSING WITH SOLITUDE: READING A LIFE

As I suggested in the introduction, meditation plays a significant role in Milton's poetic as one significant way each of his characters attains a degree of self-knowledge. Adam begins his conscious life by meditating on his origins in order to determine his allegiance. Waking up to find that he has a self, Adam begins to meditate on "who I was, or where, or from what cause" (*PL* VIII, 270). Samson begins the final part of his career with a lengthy meditation on how his previous self has undergone alteration and tries to determine his new self—"what once I was, and what am now" (*SA*, 22). Jesus, too, begins his mission by pursuing "holy Meditations" on what he once was and what he is now by dint of the knowledge he gained at the Baptism (*PR* I, 195). The type of meditations Adam, Samson, and Jesus employ would fall into the narratological category of the "hypodiegetic" or "metadiegetic" level of the narrative.[63]

The difference between the brief epic and the other two works is that Jesus' hypodiegetic soliloquy not only establishes ways of knowing (as does Adam's) and ways of being (as does Samson's), but also articulates the basis of a new culture; for that is what Jesus' life becomes when he narrates it—the foundation of a renovated religious culture. His articulation of his life as an object of examination acts as a mediation between the two capacities of humanity: as ontic being and epistemic being. For what Jesus does in representing his career as a symbolic expression is both gain self-knowledge and objectify his life.

According to Ernst Cassirer, symbolic expression fulfills the task of "objectification," which is necessary for establishing a "life" as a thing to be an "object" of *imitation*. In effect, Jesus represents his life to himself in his opening soliloquy. By representing his life to himself, he forms an object, which becomes a model to be imitated for whoever is conscripted to work toward establishing a renovated culture. The process is aptly described by Cassirer:

> In language we objectify our sense-perceptions. In the very act of linguistic expression our perceptions assume a new form. They are no longer isolated data; they give up their individual character; they are brought under class-concepts which are designated by general "names." The act of "naming" does not simply add a mere conventional sign to a readymade thing — to an object known before. It is rather a prerequisite of the very conception of objects; of the idea of an objective empirical reality.

When applied to religious cultures, however, as Eliade says, objective reality needs to be more than empirical. Symbols "awaken individual experience and transmute it into a spiritual act, into metaphysical comprehension of the world." Reality, then, for the religious culture is founded on the accession to the sacred. For the religious being, as drawn by Eliade, "human existence realizes all of its potentialities in proportion as it is religious — that is, participates in reality."[64]

So, then, Jesus' soliloquy will demonstrate how he achieves self-knowledge (which is the preparation for confronting the Other) at the same time as he establishes the premise for the confrontation with the Other, which is the object of his life. Jesus' life in Milton's narrative assumes all the importance of being three interrelated functions — the means for his own self-knowledge, the formal paradigm of the new culture, and the object of contention between the protagonist of the new culture and the antagonist of the old. I must stress the difficulty involved for Jesus in narrating his life — a difficulty that exists not only because of the far-reaching political ramifications of the final object (his life), but also because he must displace himself from the life he is telling in order to make it an object. As Peter Brooks notes, how "we narrate a life — even our own life to ourselves — is at least a double process, the attempt to incorporate within an orderly narrative the more devious, persistent, and powerful plot whose logic is dictated by desire."[65] One of the strongest desires acting against the narration of our own lives would be the desire to maintain the integrity we believe we have when we do not explore our past—a desire that might be categorized as wishing to remain *infans* (in every sense of the word). Moreover, as Jacques Lacan makes pointedly clear, the expression of desire relegates us to the sphere of the "primary language," inwhich the subject reveals as much unwittingly as he or she does consciously. Within that sphere, the subject loses subjectivity precisely in the way Cassirer noted: "This subject, who thinks he can accede to himself by designating himself in the statement, is not more than such an object." This is the classic problem of self-knowledge, from the Delphic oracle to Foucault: Put in modern terms, what relation exists between the signified and the signifier, especially when the subject enunciating the signifier is signifying himself or herself? Lacan phrases the question as follows: "Is the place that I occupy as the subject of a signifier concentric or excentric, in relation to the place I occupy as subject of the signified?—that is the question." Like a modern Hamlet, Lacan asks where the self is in a discourse of self-revelation. Unlike Hamlet, he asks the question about only the sort of death obtaining for the realm of the Symbolic.[66] What Jesus does in his soliloquy is ask the question in order to resolve it in another sphere altogether—one in which, simply put, the meditation of a life gives way to the narrative of a life, which narrative in turn gives way to an accession to the sacred. I will demonstrate this process in my examination of Jesus' soliloquy.

First of all, we might note the political gesture that Milton makes, rather pointedly, in terms of presenting his Jesus as a *meditating* being. To appreciate how much of a gesture it may have been, we should turn to a historic encounter of scriptural annotators. In 1582, the English College of Rheims published an annotated New Testament "out of the authenticall Latin." Infuriated by the Catholic annotations, Queen Elizabeth and Parliament ordered Thomas Cartwright to answer the Rhemes Bible. In that same year (1583), Cartwright received both a letter from influential Cambridge dons requesting a response and one hundred pounds from Sir Francis Walsingham, which enabled him to furnish himself with books. Despite the urgency of these requests, Cartwright's reply was not published for thirty-five years—posthumously in 1618. In the interim, William Fulke, one of the Cambridge dons who signed the letter to Cartwright, published a response to the Rhemes translation in 1601.[67] The dialogue between the Catholic

Rhemes College translators and Fulke, a Protestant, gives us an idea of how each church conceives of meditation.

The Rhemes Bible uses Christ's solitude in the desert to suggest the scriptural warrant for hermitages and monasteries:

> As John the Baptist, so our Saviour by going into the desert and there living in contemplation even among brute beasts, and subject to the assaults of the Divel for our sinnes, giveth a Warrant and example to such holy men as have lived in Wildernesse for penance and contemplation, called Eremites.

Initially, William Fulke responds by confuting the Rhemes reading. "Christ went into the wildernes," he writes, "neither for penance, nor contemplation, but as the text sayeth, that he might be tempted of the devil." But he then palliates his answer somewhat. Although contemplation was not Christ's intention in the temptation sequence, Fulke and his party held that meditation was not wrong in and of itself: "And yet condemne we not the contemplative life of them, that of old went into the wildernes."[68]

Milton, though arguably of Fulke's party, disagrees with the Protestant annotator. Jesus is, in *Paradise Regained,* a "glorious Eremite," whose entrance into "the bordering Desert wild" allows him to pursue "holy Meditations" (I, 8, 193–95). Nor does he quit his contemplative stance when confronted with the temptations. In Book II, Jesus again, "tracing the Desert wild," feeds himself with "holiest Meditations" (II, 110–11). But, likewise, Milton rejects the Catholic tradition as outlined by the Rhemes annotators. Jesus' entry into the desert gives no warrant for either a cloistered or a fugitive existence. Meditation is, in Milton's conception of it, a process of thinking (and, what comes to be the same, acting) under adversity in the taskmaster's eye. When he meditates on Satan's offers, his contemplative act helps establish the eternal kingdom. When he meditates on his own life, his act helps found the base of that kingdom.

Of course, Milton was not alone amongst Protestants in believing in Jesus' contemplative life; nor, for that matter, can the division between meditative theory and church sect be made as strictly as it has been made. For instance, Daniel Dyke, a Protestant, claims that Christ spent the forty days of fasting in "sweet soliloquies," in "heavenly and spirituall meditations, and contemplation, and talking secretly with his Father." On the other hand, we ought not to think that even within a sectarian unity there is any unity.

There is also the problem of political affiliation. For instance, John Stradling exploits the whole of Christ's life to suggest the propriety and warrant for the courtly life. In a poem beginning with an encomiastic dedication to Charles I and concluding with a cloying epitaph on James I, Stradling uses Christ's presence at the marriage in Galilee, his miracle of turning water into wine, to suggest a rather different *imitatio Christi:*

> He left a patterne of civilitie,
> To such as should his holy Faith embrace:
> To shun all churlish harsh rusticitie,
> And frame them selves to persons, time, and place.

As Christopher Hill has long ago noted, and as Joseph Wittreich has recently reminded us with an extended case study, the seventeenth-century interpretation of scriptural characters and scenes was based on a variety of hermeneutic strategies and founded on a variety of political categories. Stradling's Christ, based as he is on a casuistical, courtly existence (nothing of the Shepherd here), it would be safe to say, has little relation to Milton's Jesus, based on a rigorous self-examination and self-rule (and wholly the "Eremite"). Notwithstanding the radical difference between his Christ and everyone else's, Stradling also points out that Christ was a meditative being during the Temptation: "Full fortie dayes he spent in meditation."[69] One wonders, though, about how different a form meditation may take from one person to another.

In any case, the main object to which Milton's Jesus applies his meditative talents is the Baptism. In light of the knowledge he gained from that event, under the guidance of the Holy Spirit, Jesus undertakes to recreate his life story in order both to see how he reached the state he has reached and to lay down the pattern of a political life. Local knowledge gained from such an epiphany acts to unify the discrete moments of his past life. The Spirit attends Jesus at this particular time—it is his "secret weapon," as Georgia Christopher puts it. Jesus, as Milton elsewhere writes, is at the moment of the Baptism invested with his mission and the divine power to perform it.[70] The spirit allows Jesus a form of certitude that offers us a corrective to Satan and answers some of our persistent questions about authority, station, and time—questions which Satan had troubled us with by his dubious explication. God, as we have seen, did not allay the doubts to which Satan gave rise, but rather cast the burden of faith on the angels, and, by implication, on us. Nor is this to say that at the end of Jesus' speech the doubts of the reader will be dispelled and all future narrative activity be rendered undramatic. The burden of faith is one borne until the narrative effects its own satisfactory resolution. No character speaks with enough authority to make dialogue redundant—both between characters or within the reader's imagination. This is true for all narrative, even a narrative in which an omniscient character speaks. In Milton's poems this is always the case. His God was as Arminian as he.[71]

Having received his baptism, Jesus muses and revolves in his heart the best way of commencing the "mighty work . . . Of Saviour to mankind," and how first to publish his "God-like office now mature" (I, 186–88). Jesus confronts, that is, the two problems of optimum means and optimum time. It is unnecessary to stress the tension between *best* and *first* which informs the temptations and indeed the narrative. Satan relies upon this tension, upon which all human activity and obedience rests. As to time, Satan will advocate immediate action: "Not when it must, but when it may be best" (IV, 473). As to means, Satan will urge greatness: "Aim therefore at no less then all the world, / Aim at the highest" (IV, 105–06). There is a dialectic of resolution in Jesus' long autobiographical musing, a speech dramatically enacting the movement of the mind called to action, revealing the process from earthly to heavenly reliance, from old dispensation to new. And that historical movement pursues a trail through the life of this exalted man. Thus, Jesus interprets his previous life before tracing the effect of the Baptism on his future. In terms of time and means, the soliloquy is concerned with both potential and fulfillment, with discovering possible means to possible ends. It is also a search for sanction, what I previously called the *meditative orientation,* the monad of sense. We see Jesus, then, in a meditative retrospection of his previous life and an inquiring anticipation of his future life—a contemplation attentive to the one authority to which this poem ostends.

I

I will trace the movements of the soliloquy as they develop, repudiate, or revise preceding movements. In structure, the speech may be easily divided into three main movements: (1) Jesus' rehearsal of his childhood and early maturity (196–226), (2) his reiteration of Mary's biography of him and his activity following this revelation (227–67), and (3) the relation of the Baptism and Jesus' interpretation of its significance (268–93).

There are, Arnold Stein notes, four distinguishable "stages of knowledge" in the soliloquy. Stein regards both the 1671 poems as treatments of "heroic knowledge"—how it is attained and how it is rendered into action. His reading of Jesus' autobiography is certainly attentive to what he believes is this overarching theme.

The first stage of heroic knowledge according to Stein is the "intuitive," the desire to "learn-know-do." The second stage is the "discursive and disciplined," which is marked by the study of the Law. The third stage is that of "human intuition," wherein an "aspiration of knowing-doing-promoting to fulfill specific ends" is demonstrated. The fourth stage is that of redefining "public good in terms of knowledge." It is the stage of circularity in which a bridge is formed between intuitive knowledge and discursive practice, between "the truth of righteous things and real public good." The "fourth stage returns to the original intuition, but has the support of a fuller human discipline of reason and intellectual experience." The problem with Stein's reading is that he reaches this conclusion after a close reading of only thirty-one of the ninety-seven-line soliloquy. To insist on reifying Jesus' ethical education at this stage of the soliloquy not only misrepresents the overall scheme of perception Jesus promotes, but leads to a quite limited understanding of Jesus' final gestures. The rest of the soliloquy, Stein holds, is "not a further stage" and does not develop Jesus' thoughts on knowledge any more profoundly. The whole poem must be considered in order to define the specific terms of the ethical education involved in the fourth stage, Stein notes, but, nonetheless, the "fourth stage is the final one." Herein lies my disagreement with Stein. His reading of the first thirty-one lines of the soliloquy is perceptive, but his subordination of the next movements of the soliloquy as merely variations on the theme of time is troubling.[72] A reading which follows the soliloquy through from beginning to end reaches, I believe, a quite different conclusion.

Within what I call the first movement, Stein notes four distinguishable "stages." Syntactically, there are two sentences in this first movement, the first introducing the mind of the speaker and the tension under which he speaks and the second developing all four stages of knowledge which Stein explicates. We might best approach the first movement by respecting this syntactical division and also attending to the inflections of the two voltas within the second sentence.

The first sentence runs:

> O what a multitude of thoughts at once
> Awakn'd in me swarm, while I consider
> What from within I feel my self, and hear
> What from without comes often to my ears,
> Ill sorting with my present state compar'd.   (I, 196–200)

The great speech of Samson as he begins his self-revelation must come to mind ("restless thoughts, that like a deadly swarm / Of Hornets arm'd, no sooner found alone, / But rush upon me thronging" [SA, 19–21]), and perhaps also the introduction to Satan's anguished address to the Sun as he surveys Eden for the first time ("Now conscience wakes despair" [PL IV, 23]). But the thoughts that swarm within the Son's mind are vastly different. He does not suffer, as Satan does, from ill thoughts in a pure environment or, as Samson does, from ill thoughts reflecting on previous actions that have created the present evil environment. These are swarming thoughts provoked by an external, jarring discord which plays upon a serene internal concord; truly a state of *concordia discors,* which Dr. Johnson defines as "that suitable disagreement which is always necessary to intellectual harmony."[73] The tension of public demands — the news of distress and necessity — acts on the internal knowledge, the knowledge he has a few days before received of his Messianic vocation. Milton believed this tension necessary for any poetic exhibition of *proairesis,* the tension between fortune from without and the "wily suttelties and refluxes of mans thoughts from within" (CM III, p. 239).

The immediate response to these swarming thoughts — the attempt to resolve the external flux with the interior calm — leads to an autobiographical exposition. The autobiography of the Son begins with his childhood love of learning:

> When I was yet a child, no childish play
> To me was pleasing, all my mind was set
> Serious to learn and know, and thence to do
> What might be publick good; my self I thought

Born to that end, born to promote all truth,
All righteous things: therefore above my years,
The Law of God I read, and found it sweet,
Made it my whole delight, and in it grew
To such perfection that, e're yet my age
Had measur'd twice six years, at our great Feast
I went into the Temple, there to hear
The Teachers of our Law, and to propose
What might improve my knowledge or their own;
And was admir'd by all.   (I, 201–14)

The third line above deserves closer examination. It develops the thought from the line preceding and tells what the mind was set on. The tripartite structure of the sense is divided by the caesura since the first two verbs are verbs of knowledge and the third is of action. Knowledge must be accumulated before action is undertaken: "and thence to do." And do what? The break at the end of the line, the hanging sense of action, leaves us suspended in our understanding of the application of knowledge in action. Nor is the answer to the question one of resounding confidence: "What *might* be public good" (my italics). Not only is the sense of action weakened by having to wait on the line break; it is muted by the sense of possibility involved. The rest of the passage bears this out. The Son only *thinks* that this is the end to which he was born. The visit to the temple is not undertaken by the scholar full of himself. The suggestions he plans to propose are what *might* improve either the general knowledge or his own. And the description of the response he receives is glorious in its simplicity: "And was admir'd by all." We will not discover that he was pursuing his Father's business at the temple from him. Only when Mary delivers another version of the Son's history do we learn this (II, 95–99). What has been accomplished in this stage of the dialectic is this: Knowledge has been elevated, but not at the expense of revelation; the desire to know and promote truth is still the product of an earthly desire, a thought. Action toward the public good has been examined and, though not found wanting, has not been elevated to an end in itself; this public good is an ambiguous entity (one does not always know what it *might* be).

The quotation was cut off to emphasize the movement of the dialectic. I quote again, repeating the first clause of the verse:

> And was admir'd by all: yet this not all
> To which my Spirit aspir'd; victorious deeds
> Flam'd in my heart, heroic acts, one while
> To rescue *Israel* from the *Roman* yoke,
> Then to subdue and quell o're all the earth
> Brute violence and proud Tyrannick pow'r,
> Till truth were freed, and equity restor'd:
> Yet held it more humane, more heavenly first
> By winning words to conquer willing hearts,
> And make perswasion do the work of fear;
> At least to try, and teach the erring Soul
> Not wilfully mis-doing, but unware
> Misled: the stubborn only to subdue.   (I, 214–26)

As learning was primal to the second part of Jesus' self-revelation, so the question of power and heroics is basic to this third. The themes of the temptations Satan offers the Son are already in the Son's mind, "much revolving in his breast." And though the Son, as we shall see, does come to a resolution apropos the potentials of knowledge (the rejection of the kingdom of Athens ought not to surprise after one has seen the Son's early examination of the limits of knowledge) and of power (*qua* Parthia and Rome), it is nonetheless a stressful situation when Satan offers these things.

We must not disregard the tension within the Son in his replies to the temptations; he is, after all, rejecting things which had, at some time, appealed to him. At this point in his autobiography, Jesus' mind is imbued with a type of physical heroism. He thinks of "heroic acts," whereas we know his destiny is "Above Heroic." The verbs Jesus uses are those that belong to an older heroic tradition of the Homeric and Virgilian characters: "rescue," "subdue," "quell."[74] Truth and justice, of course, ought to be free and reigning, respectively. Nor is this a point that jars with Jesus' ultimate mission. Nonetheless, both are entities which are liberated by actions and perhaps for motives which must be rejected. Verbs of action must give way to verbs of mediation. Truth will be freed and equity restored not by one who subdues and quells, but by one who mediates by persuasion.

Then comes that volta, the pause of the thought on "Yet." The mind has developed from this concept of heroic acts to means "more humane, more heavenly." The sole verb of action is now sandwiched in a line that will not allow it to dominate. *Conquer* is in itself a word that would have fit with the preceding heroic thoughts. But placed, as it is, between its sweet determining force—"winning words"—and its pleasing ductile subject—"willing hearts"—it cannot but be redefined. The softness of the line, with its abundance of *w*'s, brings to prominence and softens the word and the concept; this is a conquest above heroic. The exception, of course, is the concern for the "stubborn," who will yet be subdued.

The whole of the proposition is involved with possibility. The effort is what is positively asserted: "At least to try, and teach." Suasive rhetoric joins heroic action, public good, and knowledge as things that *might* be of value in establishing a new kingdom. There has been no statement yet of guaranteed application, only an examination of possible ones. This is the process of "growing thoughts," and the organic metaphor is very nice: thoughts not yet budded, thoughts that may, for the benefit of the whole plant, yet be pruned.

What is important to notice is that Jesus attempts to understand his life first of all through the prism of the Old Testament. When he turns to the "Law of God," and reads it in light of his disposition (his "Spirit") to be knowledgeable and to be heroic, he alters the significance of the text. The first act of his recorded life, then, is the act of reading and interpreting the political text he is about to supersede, in fact the political text which will be superseded *by* his life's assuming its textual place. Here, then, is the beginning of the revisionist impulse in his narration of his life. By casting as only potential what is Law, what is indeed written law, he expresses the enabling conditions for exceeding that law.

The next movement of the autobiography is significant in that it is held at a further remove and that it is, moreover, the only instance of human mediation that Jesus enjoys in the entire poem. Jesus attempts to understand his "growing thoughts" by reflecting on the story his mother told him about his origins. Like most stories mothers tell their children when their children become adults, the implications of the child's exploits seem to lead inescapably to the mother's definition of the adult's self. When the adult repeats that story internally, it is most often done to prove the personality's continuity to oneself, its coherence in its history as revealed by the mother, and therefore attesting to the mother's interpretation. On the other hand, of course, the adult may tell the mother's story in order to renounce its implications, in order to discover the rupture in the homogeneity of a life and therefore establish the grounds for a new beginning. In either case, the story assumes its importance by being an object that requires immediate interpretation. In all discursive instances, repetition *is* interpretation, and Jesus' relation here is no different.

> These growing thoughts my Mother soon perceiving
> By words at times cast forth inly rejoyc'd,
> And said to me apart, high are thy thoughts
> O Son, but nourish them and let them soar
> To what highth sacred vertue and true worth
> Can raise them, though above example high;
> By matchless Deeds express thy matchless Sire.
> For know, thou art no Son of mortal man,
> Though men esteem thee low of Parentage,
> Thy Father is the Eternal King, who rules
> All Heaven and Earth, Angels and Sons of men,
> A messenger from God fore-told thy birth
> Conceiv'd in me a Virgin, he fore-told
> Thou shouldst be great and sit on *David's* Throne,
> And of thy Kingdom there should be no end.
> At thy Nativity a glorious Quire
> Of Angels in the fields of *Bethlehem* sung.   (I, 227–43)

The only way we can discover Jesus' method of interpreting his mother's story—as indeed the only clue we have to what any individual does when he or she repeats a narration—is to attend to the persistent concerns that seem valorized over others. Here Jesus seems to show a concern with highlighting the divine symbols in his mother's story of his birth: the celestial Annunciation, the wise men led by the "Star new-grav'n in Heaven," the angelic choir, the prophecies of Simeon and Anna, the foretold ascension to the throne of David, the kingdom *sine fin,* and, of course, Jesus' divine paternity. There is a significant alertness in this retelling of Mary's speech that heightens the miraculous elements involved in the story. It is fit that Jesus would be interested in the symbols attending his birth, especially given his situation *now,* after the Baptism. He has just received the divine Word pronouncing who he is; as he recasts his mind to things his mother told him, his interest will presumably be on the evidence that supports the pronouncement lately heard.

Paradise Regained does of course allow Mary to tell something of her own history and her relationship to her son. While it is a different story from the one Jesus repeats, it is nonetheless informative of the differences in the interpretive strategies mother and son employ. If we look ahead to Mary's history in the second book we may see how an altered perspective leads to an altered emphasis. Her speech is raised by motherly concerns and is based on the terrestrial travails that have occurred since the fateful annunciation: "Hail highly favour'd." She spends a good portion of her narrative describing the night of the birth and its concomitant pains:

> While I to sorrows am no less advanc't,
> And fears as eminent, above the lot
> Of other women, by the birth I bore,
> In such a season born when scarce a Shed
> Could be obtain'd to shelter him or me
> From the bleak air; a Stable was our warmth,
> A Manger his.   (II, 69–75)

This might fruitfully be compared with Jesus' remembrance of the story his mother told him. As the wise men come following the star, they are directed to "the Manger, where thou lais't, / For in the Inn was left no better room" (I, 247–48). The simplicity of the declaration, with absolutely no concern for the quality of pain involved, shows how the interpreter foregrounds other aspects. This simple description of the place of birth is preceded by the rich description of the angelic choir and proceeds to the ornate reference to the novel star in heaven—two symbols pertaining to the divine meaning of his birth. The beautifully pathetic description that informs Mary's narrative, the pain of the season, the unavailability of abode, the insistence on the poor quality of their lodgings, is simply encapsulated by Jesus in one reductive verse: "For in the Inn was left no better room."

After hearing what his mother tells him, Jesus returns to the Old Testament to discover who he is. If his first reading of the Law had served the purpose of mediating his desires to be a scholar and a hero—that is, defining him by a role he wishes to play—this second reading serves the purpose of defining him in relation to history. If we say that he is the subject of his reading, then we may

designate his first reading as synchronic and his second as diachronic. And it is important that his attempts at self-definition
issue from his reading, his textuality, as it were. His mother's story
about who he is, in effect, is merely a human introjection into his
textually defined personality. It is highly significant that from her
words he immediately returns to the Law:

> This having heard, strait I again revolv'd
> The Law and Prophets, searching what was writ
> Concerning the Messiah, to our Scribes
> Known partly, and soon found of whom they spake
> I am; this chiefly, that my way must lie
> Through many a hard assay even to the death,
> E're I the promis'd Kingdom can attain,
> Or work Redemption for mankind, whose sins
> Full weight must be transferr'd upon my head.   (I, 259–67)

His mother tells him that he is the "Messiah" (245), but Jesus
nonetheless searches for textual proof of his role. He does not
mistrust his mother's ability to interpret God's signs; rather, Jesus
needs to be able to discern his life as it is prerecorded. The knowledge Mary gives him is significant. His first reading of the Law did
not reveal to him who he was; he was able to do so only after his
mother gave him both the signs and the semiotic system with
which to reread the Law. But he must reread it because he will not
only live out its directions, but will, by doing so, reorient both its
significance and the mode of interpretation through which that
significance will be drawn. What Jesus does, according to Milton,
is create the conditions for true liberty by "dissolving the whole
law into charity" (CM IV, p. 76). The way he begins that process
here is by imbricating his experience into the fabric of the Old
Testament. The significance of that act—of placing his life in an
exegetical relation to the Law—is, I would go so far as to say, what
Milton considered the single most revolutionary feature of Christianity.

The one thing Jesus learns beyond Mary's relation is the fact of
death. Insofar as we can tell, Mary believes that Jesus will accede to
David's throne, to the kingdom of Israel (240, 254). She does not
understand the conditions of that kingdom nor, at least here or in
her own soliloquy, does she express her full understanding of the
crucial condition by which Jesus will rule—that is, by dying (II,

66–104). His first reading of the Old Testament showed him the Law as a way of conducting one's life; as a text it is a piece of ethical scholarship. His second reading of the Old Testament teaches him the Law that governs his life and death; as a text, it becomes existentially bound to his identity. The significance of his discovering the fact of his death is not be rushed over. To get a fuller understanding of its significance, though, we must first of all attend to the way Jesus establishes the very conditions of understanding. To do that, we must continue our analysis of the soliloquy to its end.

Having attended to both the internal impulses, those leading him to consider his role in the pursuit of public good, and the external, the information his mother gives him of his high "Parentage," and having read the Law of God twice, each time finding in it material for governing the course of his life, Jesus turns now to the historical event that initiates him into a public role.

One would think Jesus' knowledge before he attends the Baptism to be complete. He has heard from his mother of his "matchless Sire"; he has felt within himself, even as a child, the desire to promote "public good"; he has had his aspirations of "heroic acts" transformed into a resolution of the "more humane, more heavenly" role of mediator; and he has searched out the scriptural evidence of his messianic status. Despite this evidence, he still approaches the Baptism waiting for the prefixed time. The Baptist recognizes him, but it is the ultimate revelation, both spiritual and auditory, the descending Spirit from heaven, and, "last the sum of all," the voice of the Father, that gives Jesus the knowledge of who he is. Even approaching the Baptism with maternal, scriptural, and prophetic knowledge of himself, the Son must still wait on the spirit and word of God.

> But as I rose out of the laving stream,
> Heaven open'd her eternal doors, from whence
> The Spirit descended on me like a Dove,
> And last the sum of all, my Father's voice,
> Audibly heard from Heav'n, pronounced me his,
> Me his beloved Son, in whom alone
> He was well pleas'd; by which I knew the time
> Now full, that I no more should live obscure,
> But openly begin, as best becomes
> The Authority which I deriv'd from Heaven.

> And now by some strong motion I am led
> Into this Wilderness, to what intent
> I learn not yet, perhaps I need not know;
> For what concerns my knowledge God reveals.   (I, 280–93)

The sentiment of the final line of this passage, then, is both a recapitulation of the process of his self-discovery and a statement of the complete reliance on God that will mark his future exercise: "For what concerns my knowledge God reveals." In fact, Jesus had not dared presume even to express his own identity until God had given him the revelation of it.

Led by "some strong motions," the Son has assayed within himself the qualification of the messianic calling—examining, at times muting, possible means of fulfilling his great calling. The most important aspect of the whole passage is Jesus' unrelenting reliance on God. Everything is examined in the context of God; nothing in itself is good; all are "things indifferent." The potential, not the entelechy—the modal, not the substantial—occupies the Son, for realization is always unerringly directed by God the Father. Thus, no means is too base to be unworthy of consideration, and, by the same token, no means is in itself worthy to be considered outside of the theocentric vision.

This is the autobiography of Jesus, and its significance to his later exercise should not be understated. A great part of the temptations Satan offers depends on the subtlety with which he manipulates desires that the Son has himself examined, and likewise, a great part of our consciousness of the failings of these tempting offers has been heightened beyond Satan's because we have been privy to the Son's examination of their basis.

Jesus' interpretation of his history has been concerned with the problem of authority. The knowledge of his uniqueness—"in whom alone"—gives Jesus the knowledge that he is indeed the chosen one, and that the time is now full for the publication of his mission. Jesus has answered the question of the significance of *Son of God*, a question that will recur throughout the whole narrative, with an assertion of his uniqueness. By partial revelation, by the accretion of perspectival interpretation, the narrative has effected a dialectic concerning the questions of authority and station. The divine declaration as first given is simple—this is the beloved Son of God (I, 32). Satan acts upon this text with his infernal rhetorical energies, but manages to elucidate an important clause as to God's "pleasure" in his Son (I, 85). Jesus, as the object and addressee of the declaration, asserts that he is not only the delight of his Father, but his sole delight (I, 285–86). This makes Satan's insistence on the polysemy of the term—his unwarranted distinction between "his Son" and "His first begot" (I, 88–89) redundant. And the knowledge of his uniqueness answers the two questions with which the soliloquy was introduced: the questions of optimum means and time.

Here, then, we may finally turn our attention to the epistemology on which Jesus' narrative is premised, and the one which it establishes. In answering the questions of the best means and the best time to promote God's mission, Jesus uses terms that are irreducibly ineffable. Jesus' knowledge is that he relies on God; this is all he knows and all he needs to know. There is an unmistakable circularity in the last seven verses of his soliloquy (283–89) — a circularity some might see as vicious and others as a mark of acquiescence. In either case, this circularity is demonstrated through theocentricity: the energetic and infinite movement from God to human to God. From a modern philosophical point of view, this may seem epistemologically wrongheaded, but this irreducible inscrutability of reference is at the basis of Milton's theology.[75]

The first one and a half verses credit the voice heard with authority—the Father's voice, from heaven, and the "sum of all" (283–84). The next three lines enact the declaration, using a ritual repetition of "me his, / Me his" to ensure a continuity of message (284–85). John had earlier used repetition to the same purpose: "Me him / Me him" (I, 276–77). The repetition is, in effect, the granting of authority to Jesus. The next three lines interpret the significance of this declaration in relation to the persistent questions of optimum time and means. The two questions, as we shall see, are conflated through the movement of the poetry.

Jesus recognizes that the time is now full immediately after he recognizes his uniqueness (285–87). Having gleaned his uniqueness, his origin, and the certainty of his station, Jesus assays the knowledge of time. The line takes up the relationship of the knowledge of station—"by which"—and aligns it to the knowledge of time: "I knew the time." The enjambment leaves us hanging and awaiting the object of Jesus' knowledge at the beginning of line 287. The time, he says he knows, is "Now full." There is a certain threshold reached with this knowledge, and the significance of the threshold is assayed in the clause immediately following: It is now time to publish his office. The answer to the question of optimum time has resolved itself into the question of means: "as best becomes." Again, the line break forces us to await the knowledge as delivered through the "process of speech," and the answer, where we would have expected a resolute and concrete one, is ineffable. The best means is that which best becomes the "Authority" derived from heaven.

Satan interprets the voice from heaven with a degree of skepticism and attempts to make diffuse the singular sense of the announcement, "Son of God." Jesus recognizes the uniqueness of the term through a celestial definition, for, as Milton notes, "Definition is that which refines the pure essence of things from the circumstances" (CM IV, p. 100; cf. CM XI, p. 261). An understanding of "essences" presupposes a sense that is able to apprehend spiritual entities. Describing his view of the symbolic dove, Satan reports seeing only a physical bird and interprets that with dubiety: "A perfect Dove descend[ed], what e're it meant" (I, 83). Jesus sees the spirit, the tenor in the vehicle: "The Spirit descended on me like a Dove" (I, 282; cf. I, 30–31). This variation in perceptual skills is the difference, Milton held, between the true "christian arbitrement of charity" and the false "way of a literal apprehension" (CM IV, pp. 136, 9). In this aspect, Satan and Jesus differ radically, and I trace the themes of this difference in the next chapter. In the interim, we must notice how Jesus' life has become, already, the *object* of interpretation. Both Satan and Jesus apply their hermeneutical abilities to that object and the way they apply them—charitably or literally, candidly or maliciously—spells the difference between the old and the new cultures Milton is showing in conflict.

The movement of the verse offers us a good clue to the movement of Jesus' mind and, as we shall shortly see, the movement of universal history. His mind ranges over the potential modes of applying one's energies to ameliorate one's culture, yet is always attuned to the essential origin of derived authority. This is the same movement we discovered earlier in this soliloquy in our examination of line 203—the hesitant analysis of possibilities. But whereas at that point in the soliloquy Jesus was rehearsing a childhood love of the Law, at this point Jesus has passed a threshold that, in effect, makes him the first antinomian.

If Milton's conception of the historical movement from the old dispensation to the new remained constant from *Paradise Lost* to *Paradise Regained,* then this stage of the latter poem effects that all-important shift. Michael informs Adam of this future history:

> So Law appears imperfet, and but giv'n
> With purpose to resign them in full time
> Up to a better Cov'nant, disciplin'd
> From shadowy Types to Truth, from Flesh to Spirit,
> From imposition of strict Laws to free
> Acceptance of large Grace, from servile fear
> To filial, works of Law to works of Faith.   (*PL* XII, 300–06)

In this soliloquy Jesus enacts that movement—from law to faith, from the concrete to the ineffable. Jesus has no canon of law to which he may direct his attention and from which he may derive the authority of his actions. He has only one authority, derived immediately from heaven and possessing as yet no coherent constitution. Nor will it, until the life of Jesus itself becomes that constitution:

> Our Saviour for whom that great and God-like work was reserv'd, redeem'd us to a state above prescriptions by dissolving the whole law into charity. And have we not the soul to understand this, and must we against this glory of Gods transcendent love towards us be still the servants of a literall indightment? (CM IV, p. 76)

The liberation of humanity is twofold, from legal and mortal bounds, and this liberation is effected in the same passionate act of Jesus, his life.

Jesus must, Michael tells Adam, fulfill justice by fulfilling that in which Adam failed: "Obedience to the Law of God" (*PL* XII, 397). Obedience and love will fulfill the Law of God, though love alone is enough. Love and obedience to God will cause Jesus to suffer a "reproachful life and a cursed death," a death suffered "for bringing Life." He is condemned to death and nailed to the cross, Michael tells Adam, "But to the Cross he nails thy Enemies, / The Law that is against thee, and the sins / Of all mankind (*PL* XII, 415–17).

Michael has implicitly made the distinction of laws: that of the old dispensation, which can evince depravity but not remove it, which is the Mosaic covenant; and that of the new dispensation, which is obedience and love, the eternal covenant of God, under which Adam failed and which through Jesus is reinstated in the fullness of time. Because of ethical principles which obtain for the new dispensation, all answers must now be transmuted into theo-centric queries. The canon of Mosaic Law had a reference unto itself; to it and from it answers and questions may be posed and resolved. Now, at the fullness of time, all questions are posed immediately to God, and each of the faithful elect enters into a dialectic circularity with divinity: "For what concerns my knowl-edge God reveals."

The new covenant made God's grace universal,

> for from that day
> Not only to the Sons of *Abraham's* Loins
> Salvation shall be Preacht, but to the Sons
> Of *Abraham's* Faith wherever through the world.
> (*PL* XII, 446–49)

But it also made God's grace intensely personal. The Mosaic cove-nant, the legal lapidary text that had hitherto been the conductor of communion between God and his creatures, united the entire nation. The Christian covenant, the ineffable legal code whose only constitution is the life of Jesus, leads the believer into direct communion with her or his creator. In pursuit of such direct com-munion, freed from ecclesiastical institution and restraint, Milton, we know, concluded his religious quest alone, in his church of one. His hero establishes the pattern for that singularity by beginning it alone, conversing with solitude.

Solitude, Montaigne wrote, is not merely a state of physical separation, but a state of desire: "Therefore it is not enough, for a man to have sequestred himselfe from the concourse of people: it is not sufficient to shift place, a man must also sever him-selfe from the popular conditions, that are in us. A man must sequester and recover himselfe from himselfe." So Montaigne meditates: "The greatest thing of the world, is for a man to know how to be his owne."[76] For Jesus, though, solitude was a state in which one communed with God, and his meditation might have refined Mon-taigne's insight with something like Joseph Hall's: "I am not mine owne, while God is not mine."[77] Jesus' self-knowledge, then, is intimately governed by his epistemological premise that what he needs to know is revealed to him by God. What God reveals to him, audibly, is that he is his Son. What that relationship entails is the one thing Jesus discovers beyond his mother's story and before his Father's pronouncement—the fact of his death.

II

Having now a better understanding of the epistemology Jesus establishes in this soliloquy and its historical import as the first step in the dissolution of the Mosaic law, we may turn finally to the importance of that principle discovery Jesus alone makes in this soliloquy—his recognition of death. He expresses the knowledge of death as the culmination of his second reading of the Law and as the defining feature of his identity: "of whom they spake / I am; this chiefly, that my way must lie / Through many a hard assay even to the death" (262–64). The discovery comes between his mother's and his Father's voices, between the discourses of his earthly and his heavenly parent. For a critic given to structuralist topographies, this discovery might mark the transition from horizontal discourse to vertical intuition. Given the process of Jesus' discourse, it might well mean such a transition. But this discovery also bears immense possibilities for a richer understanding of Milton's christology and for explaining the tension that exists in this soliloquy. Treating it as a means into what is in Milton a rather occluded area, we might begin with a brief analysis of death as a function in the Miltonic cosmos.

Adam, to begin at the beginning, did not know what death could possibly be. When rehearsing to Eve God's sole interdiction, he concludes by reflecting on the irony of having the Tree of Life so close to the Tree of Knowledge: "So near grows Death to Life, whate'er Death is, / Some dreadful thing no doubt" (*PL* IV, 425–26). It is hard to be ironic when one is innocent, and Adam's ruminations are somewhat superficial here. When he is a little closer to death, a week later, his meditation is more suggestive in its exploration of the potential ways of dying (X, 720–844). Beginning his analysis with the question of what death means in relation to a total entity composed of both soul and body, Adam in Eden, as Milton was later to do in Chalfont, concludes with the doctrine of mortalism: "All of me then shall die" (792). Having established what portion of the total human being will perish, Adam next assays the problem to which he offers no solution—the question of what dying means in temporal terms:

> But say
> That Death be not one stroke, as I suppos'd,
> Bereaving sense, but endless misery
> From this day onward, which I feel begun
> Both in me, and without me, and so last
> To perpetuity; Ay me, that fear
> Comes thund'ring back with dreadful revolution
> On my defenseless head; both Death and I
> Am found Eternal, and incorporate both.   (808–16)

Adam does not come to any resolution about the temporal limits of death. When he finally encounters a visual presentation of death, he responds with renewed horror that is eventually palliated into something like patience: "Henceforth I fly not Death, nor would prolong / Life much" (XI, 547–48).

If death is fairly insubstantial in *Paradise Lost,* as some critics have noted, then what may we say of its presence in *Paradise Regained,* where the only mention of it is in this momentary epiphany in Jesus' soliloquy?[78] To answer that question we must again return to *Paradise Lost,* but this time to the Son's reflections on death. Having accepted the role of sacrificial redeemer, the Son maintains that he will "yield" to death for a season in order to vanquish it: "Death his death's wound shall then receive" (*PL* III, 252). As Maurice Kelley has argued, the whole of this passage in *Paradise Lost*—and especially the phrase "All that of me can die" (246)—reflects the uncertainty Milton was entertaining about the question of Christ's divine nature dying in the period when Picard was his amanuensis. Eventually, in his second assay on the problem in the *Christian Doctrine*—and I would add in *Paradise Regained*— he would conclude that Christ's divine nature died also.[79] The scene in heaven is certainly a more detailed analysis of how death shall meet its demise than anything found in *Paradise Regained.* In fact, there are only two other allusions to death in the later poem. In the first instance, God maintains that Jesus will conquer Death along with Sin (I, 159). Secondly, in the scene most critics have rightly located as the fullest metaphoric elaboration of the Passion, Satan offers the storm in the desert as a "sure fore-going sign" of the dangers, adversities, and pains Jesus must suffer on his way to Israel's throne (IV, 448–80).[80] What Satan seems unwilling to say, or is ignorant of, is that the greatest adversity—death—is also the way Jesus will assume that throne. In the passage that will direct us to an appropriate context for appreciating the importance of death to the universe of *Paradise Regained*, Satan says,

> Did I not tell thee, if thou didst reject
> The perfet season offer'd with my aid
> To win thy destin'd seat, but wilt prolong
> All to the push of Fate, persue thy way
> Of gaining *David's* Throne no man knows when,
> For both the when and how is no where told,
> Thou shalt be what thou art ordain'd, no doubt;
> For Angels have proclaim'd it, but concealing
> The time and means: each act is rightliest done,
> Not when it must, but when it may be best.
> If thou observe not this, be sure to find,
> What I foretold thee, many a hard assay
> Of dangers, and adversities and pains,
> E're thou of *Israel's* Scepter get fast hold.   (IV, 464–77)

Satan understands that Jesus is searching for the optimum means and the optimum time in which to fulfill his mission. What he fails to understand is that the "way" he is going to do so is indeed by withstanding all "hard assays." And on those two key words, we may return to Jesus' soliloquy.

When Jesus says that his "*way* must lie / Through many a hard *assay* even to the death," he not only preempts Satan's feeble attempt to understand how humiliation may lead to exaltation, but he also alludes to what I will suggest is the preponderant emotion he feels in determining his sense of selfhood in the soliloquy. As Walter MacKellar has noted, the "assay even to the death" echoes Isaiah: "He was cut off out of the land of the living" (liii, 8). More than that, though, Jesus in *Paradise Regained* states what Christ is going to say just before the Crucifixion: "My soul is exceeding sorrowful, even unto death" (Matt. xxvi, 38). In fact, this is the passage Milton uses in the *Christian Doctrine* to argue that Christ's divine soul died along with his body (CM XV, pp. 230–31).[81] Its importance in this soliloquy, then, cannot be understated. Not only does it help us better appreciate the immanence of death in the soliloquy, but it also helps us establish Jesus' emotional state in the act of objectifying his life.

Jesus affirms his ultimate destiny (even unto death) before he hears his Father's voice, which had allowed him to affirm his identity. In the unfolding of his soliloquy, and his life, the sense of death precedes the sense of self. Moreover, Jesus never affirms this sense of self as if he were an autonomous being; in the end his relationship to his Father defines him ("me his, / Me his"). This sense of a sliding selfhood—evinced in Jesus' hesitancy about affirming his status in relation to God until he has sanction to do so—might be characterized as *anxiety*. It is, admittedly, a word very infrequently used by Milton, in fact infrequently used by anyone in the seventeenth century, but in its modern sense it is the word most capable of describing the way Milton presents Jesus in this soliloquy. In both Matthew and Mark, the word used to describe Christ's "sorrow unto death" is *tristis*. It was translated as "sorrowful" in Wycliffe's Bible (1380), the Rhemes translation (1582), and the Authorized Version (1611). It was translated as "heaviness" in the Tyndale Bible (1534), the Cranmer version (1539), and the Geneva translation (1557). Both *sorrow* and *heaviness* would have suggested to a seventeenth-century reader a more profound existential emotion than the terms do to a modern reader; they would, I suggest, have been read to signify something like *anxiety*. Closer to our own day, we may note that, when Kierkegaard turned to this particular verse in the gospels of Mark and Matthew, he established that Christ was "anxious unto death." Even more recently, Norman O. Brown suggested that "anxiety is the ego's incapacity to accept death."[82] Although the term *anxiety* may not have been current in the age, the concept itself suffered no neglect from so astute a thinker on the human condition as Milton.

When Milton defines death in the first of its four degrees, it takes on many of the qualities we associate with anxiety in our post-Freudian age. According to Milton, death in its first degree signifies "all evils whatever, together with every thing which in its consequences tends to death." The five qualities characterizing death include (1) "guiltiness," (2) "terrors of conscience," (3) "the sensible forfeiture of the divine protection and favor," (4) "pollution," and (5) "shame." The second degree of death is "spiritual death," the third "the death of the body," and the fourth and final one the "death eternal" (CM XV, pp. 202–05; 202–51).[83] This first degree of death, then, which is a preparation for an ultimate bodily dissolution in the third degree, is a dying in life, a preparatory function in the spirit's progress. It is, as Freud would characterize anxiety, a "particular state of expecting the danger or preparing for it, even though it may be an unknown one." Anxiety characterizes the ways Adam responds to the visions of death in Michael's presentation. Although I am sure it would be possible to draw a schematic homology between the five qualities of death in its first degree which Milton names in the *Christian Doctrine* and the various responses of Adam in *Paradise Lost,* it is more worth our while here to attend to the ways in which Jesus in *Paradise Regained* uses death—which is the principle by which he defines his life—to articulate a code of liberty. For that, we might turn to modern analyses of the relationship between anxiety, death, and freedom.

According to Heidegger's tracing of Dasein's ways of "Being-in-the-world," anxiety (*angst*) is what attends the moment when Being directs itself: "Anxiety makes manifest in Dasein its *Being towards* its ownmost potentiality-for-Being—that is, its *Being-free for* the freedom of choosing itself and taking hold of itself. Anxiety brings Dasein face to face with its *Being free for (propensio in . . .)* the authenticity of its Being, and for this authenticity as a possibility which it always is." The most distinctive possibility of Dasein's being turns out to be its "Being-towards-Death," which, Heidegger maintains, "is essentially anxiety," and which expresses itself in the last instance as "freedom towards death." That, interestingly, is how Kierkegaard defines *anxiety*—"anxiety is freedom's actuality as the possibility of possibility," which of course reaches its furthest possibility in Christ's anxiety unto death. The response toward death is anxiety because the human being is made up of both soul and body, as both Milton in his ruminations on Christ and Kierkegaard in his on humanity determined, and only in the dialectic between finitude and infinitude may anxiety assume what Kierkegaard calls its educative function. Moreover, once it assumes that function, anxiety promotes faith, freedom, and ultimately godliness: "With the help of faith, anxiety brings up the individuality to rest in providence."[84]

Milton asserted that the Baptism was, for Jesus, a metaphoric signification of death; the "baptism was intended to represent figuratively the painful life of Christ, his death and burial, in which he was immersed, as it were, for a season" (CM XVI, pp. 184–85). Of course, for Jesus, death does not possess the same types or degrees of anxiety as those Milton delineates for sinful beings, but for him death was nonetheless a reality attended by another kind of anxiety. Milton insisted that Jesus felt the terror of death, "he felt even his divine nature insufficient to support him under the pains of death" (CM XIV, pp. 330–31). But his death, as Michael tells Adam, as Paul told the Corinthians, as Donne told Death, changed death from an end into a means. Put simply, as Milton puts it, Jesus' death led to human liberty from death. Again, then, we find that same amalgamation of ideas as we find in Kierkegaard and Heidegger—death's involvement with freedom and possibility. But Jesus expresses his anxiety (in his being unto death), his sense of possibility (as we saw in his analysis of the ways of winning souls), his sense of liberty (the "Authority" he derives from heaven), and his sense of finitude always in relation to the infinite God in this soliloquy—"what concerns my knowledge God reveals." His anxiety, then, occurs in a discourse of self-revelation that transforms his life into an objective symbol.

Cassirer alerts us to the ways that discourse objectifies the subject of its semantic content and gives it a symbolic quality. Eliade shows us how the symbolic becomes meaningful only insofar as it relates to the divine. The Incarnation, Eliade continues, "guarantees the validity of symbols." When Jesus objectifies his life by casting it into a discursive structure, he is both establishing the basis for his life's symbolic quality as a form to be imitated and grounding its significance in its death. This is what Lacan argues concerning the relationship between discourse and symbols: "When we wish to attain in the subject what was before the serial articulations of speech, and what is primordial to the birth of symbols, we find it in death, from which his existence takes on all the meaning it has." The representation of that mortal grounding occurs in "the endless circularity of the dialectical process that is produced when the subject brings his solitude to realization."[85] What is produced when Jesus brings his "solitude" into realization is the dialectical process I suggested characterizes Milton's antinomian epistemology—the acquiescent circularity between the divine and the human—as well as the object that is his life. And the fullest realization of that solitude for Jesus is that he will die.

This realization that he will die occurs to Jesus before he finally defines his identity as God's Son. It occurs at the moment after he rereads the Law, which he does after he has heard his mother tell him his true parentage. It occurs, that is, after he discovers not only that he is a being made up both of soul and body in the usual sense, but also that he is a being literally born out of that division, as even Satan recognizes: "His Mother then is mortal, but his Sire, / He who obtains the Monarchy of Heav'n" (I, 86–87). His knowledge of death, then, comes to him literally between the knowledge he gets from his mother and that which he gets from his Father, between his understanding of the relationship obtaining between his human and divine being, between his public and his private life. Moreover, and more importantly, Milton has Jesus recognize the fact of his death at the beginning of his career. This, I think, has deep implications for understanding Milton's christology. For Calvin, for instance, the relationship of Jesus' career to humanity is simple enough: "Our salvation may be thus divided between the death and the resurrection of Christ: by the former, sin was abolished and death annihilated; by the latter, righteousness was restored and life revived, the power and efficacy of the former being still bestowed on us by means of the latter."[86] For Milton, to judge by both his representations of and his silences about Christ, the effective workings of Christ's mission lay in his teachings rather than in his death or resurrection. Again, let me emphasize that this is not to say that Milton did not believe in the efficacy of Christ's death and resurrection, but that he chose to represent his Jesus—both as the Son of God in *Paradise Lost* and as the incarnate being in *Paradise Regained*—always in the role of one *anticipating* his death. That is, he always represents Jesus as anxious in his being unto death. And in that anxiety, Jesus acts out the role of the primary educator of humanity. We may say that if for Calvin, in terms of emphasis in representation, Christ's significance lay in his death and resurrection, then for Milton, under those same terms, Jesus' significance lay in his life. That life for Milton is doubly significant, both in the articulation of its anxiety—which helps make sense of each human life—and in its articulation as a *life*—the model and constitution of Milton's ideal polity.

Finally, what we have in this soliloquy, which started its reflection on what it means to be called the "Son" of God and by beginning with a meditation on when the Son was "yet a child," is the meaning of maturity. Milton characterized the historical epoch that dissolved the old dispensation into the new as mature. Not only, he argues, does the New Testament herald "the end and fulfilling of the Law" but also "our liberty" from the Law (CM III, pp. 196–97). And that is why, Milton goes on to say, "the Gospell is our manhood" (p. 363). Or, as he phrases it in a slightly less masculinist moment,

> Christian liberty is that whereby we are loosed as it were by enfranchisement, through Christ our deliverer, from the bondage of sin, and consequently from the rule of the law and of man; to the intent that being made . . . perfect men instead of children, we may serve God in love through the guidance of the Spirit of truth. (CM XVI, pp. 152–53)

That is the end of a process that began when God "adopts" us as children, Milton concluded (CM 16, 50–53). We become adults in the new dispensation, and its enactment in its first instance is found in the way Jesus records his life, from childhood to adulthood.

As I suggested in the introduction, one theory of psychoanalysis makes the claim that a personal, narrative revisionism is the pathway to curing mental disequilibrium. In one form, that theory proposes a renewed maturity by allowing the patient to choose his or her parentage. As Erik Erikson proposes,

> To be an adult means among other things to see one's own life in continuous perspective, both in retrospect and in prospect. By accepting some definition as to who he is, usually on the basis of a function in an economy, a place in the sequence of generations, and a status in the structure of society, the adult is able to selectively reconstruct his past in such a way that, step for step, it seems to have planned him, or better, he seems to have planned *it*. In this sense, psychologically, we *do* choose our parents.[87]

It would be inappropriate to say that Jesus chooses his parents in this poem. However, he does choose how to define himself in terms of each of his parents. And more significantly, he chooses the basis of his identity in terms of the sphere by which he defines each parent. Jesus' mother tells him about his childhood and paternity privately ("my Mother . . . said to me apart"), while he hears his Father publicly ("my Father's voice, / Audibly heard from Heav'n").

In that tension between the private and public spheres, he will articulate his life. Moreover, this poem signifies in that same tension.

Jesus will go about "His Father's business" publicly, as his mother well knows (II, 96–100); he will, however, not do so in this poem, which persistently defers the moment of his public entry. We recall the number of times the word *now* resounds throughout this poem. Ironically, each moment of possible presence—each *now*—marks only one more moment of deferral. He recognizes that the time is now full for him to enter into his public ministry and that he should no more "live obscure" but rather publish his Father's mission (I, 288). Nonetheless, he concludes this poem by deferring that mission and going back to his mother and the private sphere: "Home to his Mothers house private return'd" (IV, 635). The representation of his career in this poem has him beginning and ending in solitude and obscurity. In comparing Milton's vision of Christ to Calvin's, I suggested that the main difference lay between whether to valorize Christ's death or Jesus' life as symbolic. By deferring Jesus' entry into the public realm, but nonetheless having him express the conditions of his political establishment in the relative privacy of the wilderness, Milton emphasizes not only that the life is what is important, but he expresses, moreover, that the beginning of politics is found in the private and internal life of the individual.

The first temptation concludes with Satan's autobiographical confession, and Jesus' corrective interpretation of it (I, 358–405, 407–64), and with each discerning the other (I, 356). The second temptation will define the various levels of that mutual discernment. But in the first book, in the first temptation and the biographical encounters before and after it, the protagonist and antagonist are developed, and developed, moreover, in terms of each one's biographical and interpretive skills—in terms of each one's career. For both Jesus and Satan will offer a narrative of what each one's life represents. Satan will tell about how his life is the standard by which the world is measured: "I gain'd what I have gain'd, and with them [humans] dwell / Copartner in these Regions of the World, / If not disposer" (I, 391–93). In his representation, Jesus sets up a new standard of judgment, a new spirit of disposition. God, says Jesus, has sent "his living Oracle" into the world to teach the Father's final will. He also establishes simultaneously, Jesus suggests, the epistemological foundations for that will's being understood.

> And sends his Spirit of Truth henceforth to dwell
> In pious Hearts, an inward Oracle
> To all truth requisite for men to know.   (I, 462–64)

By the end of Book I, everything has been put into place. The epistemology Jesus established in his soliloquy has now been installed into the human psyche. Jesus' life, as the primary object of knowledge, has been articulated. And we the readers have been offered the spirit we need to have in order to discern both the Son's merit and the product of that merit—a renovated culture in which self-government precedes civil.

Finally, the most important development in Book I is the way Jesus presents his life as the base of future knowledge and of future being—the way, that is, that he has narrated his career as a cultural artifact. *Career* can mean both motion and vocation. And each of these terms can again mean, in the case of the first, either the process of recognizing grace or the flux and reflux of human activity. In the case of the second, *career* can mean either the form of the process of grace or the form of human activity. But in each case in Milton's universe, God is the ultimate reality. One can career toward or away from, but always in relation to him. He is, in other words, the center of sense—cognitive and emotive. The icons of the two main characters at the end of Book I allow us to visualize their respective careers. The Son is the "Morning Star then in his rise," Satan a dissimulating, nocturnal, airy entity "Into thin Air diffus'd" (I, 294, 502). Ascension and diffusion, the one rising in meditative confidence toward heaven, the other a self-consuming inactivity: they are careering movements and the movements of career. In their distinct trajectories, the two icons also signify the motion each agonist will bring to bear when they meet in confrontation.

3

Confronting the Other:
The Art of Hermeneutics

I N THE KEY perspectival shift in Book X of *Paradise Lost,* Sin and Death are displaced from the role of focalizers into the objects of focus within God's vision. I suggested that, like all such shifts, this shift carries with it an affective response; in this case, Milton seems to be directing us to an optimism in the eventual order of things. Sin and Death occupy the world, God says, only as a necessary prelude to establishing a new heaven and a new earth. In *Paradise Regained,* Satan is the character displaced in this way. His displacement also suggests something about the telos of the poem's vision of eternity, but something slightly different than that signified by his offsprings' displacement. Whereas in *Paradise Lost* the displacement of Sin and Death had led to God's prophesying the eventual renovation of the world, in *Paradise Regained* Satan's displacement signifies the evanescence of his world in the process of Jesus' establishing the conditions of a radically new culture. Put another way, whereas Sin and Death are in the world for the purpose of razing its old order and God is looking through them to the new order, Satan is in the world for the purpose of allowing the new order to be articulated. As God says in the later poem, Satan will "exercise" Jesus' ability to "lay down the rudiments / Of his great warfare" (I, 156–58). The metaphor of battle will give way in the course of this poem to the metaphor of state formation. Satan allows, then, the constitution of the new world to be drawn up.

At the end of Book I, moreover, the conditions of the dialectic in which the main portion of the poem will be engaged are established, and the stability of the dialectical contestants is represented. Early in the induction Satan is presented as physically out of sync with the new world order; his instability is represented in two key metaphors. As I argued at the end of the previous chapter, the first book of the poem suggests that Satan is being displaced *spatially* when it concludes with his fading into nothingness— "Into thin Air diffus'd" (I, 499). At the same time, Jesus has been presented as the "Morning Star then in his rise" (I, 294). It is an apt opposition—one fading into night, the other rising into morning. This opposition suggests the process of Jesus' articulating the conditions for his new religious culture; a world is born while another fades from the light of day.

There is, however, another way in which Satan is displaced, and a way that has rich ramifications for our understanding of his epistemic capacity. At the moment when God's perspective subsumed Satan's (and indeed Satan), Satan was displaced *temporally*. Satan had set out from the consistory with the intention of finding Jesus at Jordan and tempting him. He is in a devilish rush; indeed, we recall, he suggested in the consistory that they had hardly enough time to debate adequately the question of who should subvert Jesus' mission (I, 95, 109–10). Satan, despite his rush, will not come upon Jesus for something like forty-three days. Between the time Satan sets out to find Jesus and the time he actually finds him, Jesus will lodge "some days" in Bethabara, and then go on to meditate for "Full forty days" (I, 183, 303). Only after forty and some days does Satan enter the scene (I, 314).

This is the same Satan, we must remember, who in *Paradise Lost* had flown from hell to earth in only a few hours (*PL* II, 920–1055). This, too, is the same Satan who managed to fly around the Earth circling the "Equinoctial Line" three times and the polar line four more in a mere "seven continu'd Nights" (*PL* IX, 63–66). While it is true, as many critics have noted, that Satan in the brief epic has slowed down in his old age, no amount of senescence could account for such a change. The more plausible reason, and here one hears the voice of Thomas Newton, may be that Milton simply was "not very exact in the computation of time."[1] Milton might have avoided this indecorum by presenting the satanic consistory after Jesus had concluded his forty days in the desert. The overzealous critic might better impute Satan's temporal lag to Milton's error than Milton's art.

However, precisely the same sort of temporal displacement occurs in the next book of *Paradise Regained*. As Satan sets out from his second consistory and takes his flight toward the desert (II, 241), he finds himself frustrated of reaching Jesus until after eighteen more hours. Jesus is enjoying his second meditation when Satan sets out (II, 245–59). He will conclude it, go to sleep, dream "as appetite is wont to dream," wake up, and walk until noon, before Satan finally confronts him again (II, 298). Satan's quick dispatch is again mocked by the ways he is lost in time at each instance of Jesus' meditations. One suspects that there is something more profound at work here than Milton's inability to keep his story straight in time, as Newton thought.[2] The critic, now no longer overzealous but rather cautious, decides that once was error, twice art.

Narrative, we saw, has primarily a function of creating worlds — "the supreme function of the human mind," as Jameson puts it. In narrative, of course, as Scholes and Kellogg maintain, "time is a major structural element." Paul Ricoeur devotes three volumes to studying the various ways time plays a role in the experiencing and creation of narrative worlds. Not only does he study the "fictive experience of time," but also the "temporal world" that is unfolded in every narrative work. Indeed, in a preliminary essay to the full-blown study, Ricoeur goes so far as to say that narrative and time have a reciprocal relationship: "temporality . . . [is] that structure of existence that reaches language in narrativity and narrativity . . . [is] the language structure that has temporality as its ultimate referent."[3] In our analysis of *Paradise Regained* we need not go so far as Ricoeur; time is not the ultimate referent of this narrative, but only one of a variety of signs in its articulation of its own symbolic system. What is important to note here, rather, is that the time the Son is meditating, during which Satan cannot gain access to him, is what Eliade would characterize as "sacred time." Time, then, is not the narrative's ultimate referent, but one aspect of the world on which the narrative works to make it symbolic.

Sacred time is "primordial mythical time made present," and it finds its expression in the Christian liturgy which represents for the believer, Eliade writes, "a historical time sanctified by the incarnation of the Son of God." This sense of time, however, is

available only to the believer: "This transhuman quality of liturgi-
cal time is inaccessible to a nonreligious man." The purpose of
occupying this time for the religious person is to recreate the
original moment of salvation and thereby to renovate the present
world in reference to the moment of its cosmic turning point.
Stating this process as a diurnal exercise, Blake writes:

> There is a Moment in each Day that Satan cannot find,
> Nor can his Watch Fiends find it; but the Industrious find
> This Moment & it multiply, & when it once is found
> It renovates every Moment of the Day if rightly placed.[4]

It is worth pointing out that in Blake's poem it is the moment
Ololon enters in search of Milton.

In Milton's poem that moment is part of the strategy of representing the renovation not just of a day, but of a culture (and one
Blake would in his turn attempt to renovate differently). Satan's
displacement suggests his inability to understand that renovation.
What Milton does is displace Satan *in time* in order to demonstrate
Satan's flagging epistemic capacity and register in a metaphoric
way the antagonist's inability to perceive the significance of Jesus'
realm and the conditions by which it is established. This displacement is also, as I will suggest below, part of Milton's strategy to
articulate a scene of anagnorisis beyond the end of the poem. The
confrontation between Satan and Jesus is never quite simply a
confrontation. Not only does Satan have a tough time trying to
arrive at where Jesus is, literally and temporally, but he also has a
distinct gap between his ability to see what is before him and his
ability to understand it. In this chapter, I will attempt to describe
the ways that Satan employs (and becomes the dupe of) such epistemic inabilities in the scenes of confrontation.

There is now critical consensus that *Paradise Regained* is a
poem about a "hermeneutical combat."[5] That is, the dialectic of
the narrative is generated through the individual interpretations of
Satan and Jesus as they perceive the same objects and posit the
significance of each object in relation to the world each inhabits;
for they do, as is made progressively clearer in their encounters,
inhabit different worlds. For the most part, the contestants are
diametrically opposed in their interpretations, and this opposition
has its basis in their interpretive creeds, which in turn have their

bases in their epistemologies. Each begins fully to articulate his epistemological presuppositions in the first encounter, which putatively is the temptation to bread but is in actuality the temptation to hermeneutical ethics. However, that first encounter is only a further development of the interpretive creed each has already posited as his governing method in each one's reading of the Baptism. To discover in what salient ways Satan's and Jesus' interpretive orientations differ, we may turn to the Baptism, and from there to the temptation of the kingdoms to discover in what ways each one's interpretive creed enables the development of the world each inhabits. The way each character chooses to read the world governs the world that he comes to inhabit. Furthermore, that original choice not only constitutes the world he inhabits, but eventually the world he chooses to inhabit will govern his perception of it—it will constitute him. In the first chapter I looked at one side of Blake's dictum, that the eye altering alters all, to suggest that the alteration includes emotive change in the perceptival. In this chapter, we might look at the other side of Blake's saying and suggest that when the altering eye alters all, it also alters the very eye that is the perceptive organ. In other words, not only does perception constitute the world perceived, but the world perceived will, in turn, constitute the faculty of perception. That, simply put, is what the second temptation demonstrates—that the ways of confronting the Other produce the self.

The Other in *Paradise Regained,* moreover, is not simply Satan (for Jesus) or Jesus (for Satan), but also the world for each. Each constructs a world, only one of which stands. Obviously, that world is the one Jesus constructs—the world of spirit. And the reader who is invoked only after that world has been constituted is the reader who has the "spirit and judgment" to perceive the qualities of that world. What interests us here is not so much which world eventually stands while the other falls, but the process by which each world is constructed and the epistemological postulates developed in each construction. In the first chapter I suggested that Jesus approaches the problem of self-knowledge by defining himself in a variety of directions—toward society, the Law, his mother and the private sphere, death, and, finally, his Father and the public sphere. He does not simply dismiss one direction when he begins anew to define himself in relation to the next; he does not, for example, give up the self he has defined as being toward death when he defines another self as being toward God. The composite nature of his self-definitions is as important as their progressiveness. Because his life is objectified doubly, both in discourse and as the constitution of a new culture, the transitions in self-knowledge are as significant as the end product, which is, of course, itself multiply defined. In this chapter, we will see how Jesus defines himself by employing a different set of directions. His self-knowledge now, in this second temptation, is not only the process (and product) of defining himself in relation to Parthia, Rome, and Athens, but more of how he defines himself in relation to three modes of understanding—skepticism, enigma, and what Jung called "assimilation" and what I'll be calling the "dialectics of spirit." Satan will also define himself in relation to these three modes of understanding in order to construct his world, which is the obverse world to Jesus'.

"IN DUBIOUS BATTLE": THE USE AND ABUSE OF SKEPTICISM

No single aspect of *Paradise Regained* has assumed such a prominent place in the criticism of the poem as that referred to as the "doubt motif." *Paradise Regained,* writes Joan Malory Webber, is "suffused with the language of doubt." Led into the desert by the Spirit as a "glorious Eremite," Jesus will emerge from that wilderness "By proof the undoubted Son of God." This man, "late of woman born," Satan tells his compeers, was baptized and received the "testimony of Heaven" so that the "Nations may not doubt." This man, "call'd the Son of God," God tells Gabriel, will "this day by proof" emerge victorious from his exercise and "verifie that solemn message" which Gabriel had but lately delivered to Mary "doubting." Linking the perspectives of narrator, Satan, and the angels is a degree of doubt as to the status of the Incarnate Son. Even God refers to him nominally—"call'd the Son"—and the force of that "call'd," Earl Miner notes, "carries something of the dubiety of a Spenserian 'seem'd'."[6]

The traditional interpretation of the doubt motif deals almost exclusively with the figure of Satan. The question critics pose—whether or not Satan is aware of Jesus' identity at the last—and the answers they give to that question are simply inadequate to the complexity of Milton's theological and epistemological concerns. For doubt is not simply one of Satan's poses, nor is it simply a matter of dramatic decorum. By suggesting that the resolution of the "doubt motif" rests solely on Satan's final recognition of the Son on the pinnacle, critics ignore two other forms of skepticism presented in the poem to offset Satan's pyrrhonic machinations. By appreciating these two validating epistemologies, and therefore understanding Milton's soteriology, we come anew to the question of Satan's recognition of Jesus as Son of God and derive alternate answers.

I

When Satan offers the learning of Athens to Jesus, he outlines five schools of philosophy: the Socratic (including Platonic under the "Academics old and new"), the Peripatetic, the Epicurean, and the Stoic.

> To sage Philosophy next lend thine ear,
> From Heaven descended to the low-rooft house
> Of *Socrates,* see there his Tenement,
> Whom well inspir'd the Oracle pronounc'd
> Wisest of men; from whose mouth issu'd forth
> Mellifluous streams that water'd all the schools
> Of Academics old and new, with those
> Sirnam'd *Peripatetics,* and the Sect
> *Epicurean,* and the *Stoic* severe.   (4, 269–77)

Jesus, though, answers the five offered with six criticized, and the addition is not only an important alteration between the offer and rejection, but an important distinction between the modes of apprehension of the tempter and the tempted:

> The first and wisest of them all profess'd
> To know this only, that he nothing knew;
> The next to fabling fell and smooth conceits,
> A third sort doubted all things, though plain sence;
> Others in vertue plac'd felicity,
> But vertue joyn'd with riches and long life,
> In corporal pleasure he, and careless ease,
> The Stoic last in Philosophic pride.   (4, 290–97)

What Jesus does, then, is criticize a school of philosophy that Satan has not offered him, the Pyrrhonian one: "A third sort doubted all things, though plain sence."[7] Jesus' sly remark, moreover, arguably ties together two interrelated and important themes in the narrative: the role of doubt in this exercise, and the presuppositions of "sence."

We are quickly and poignantly made aware of the difficulty of apprehension in the action of this poem. And here we find the essential tension in Milton's theology. Belief rests on knowledge, but a form of knowledge that is not easy to glean; for it is most emphatically never merely a matter of facile acceptance. Such easy belief belongs to the "heretick in the truth," that putative Christian unable to pursue his or her saving knowledge to the fount of its origin, and by this inability depotentiates it of its salvationist quality. This entire argument rests, of course, on how closely Milton aligned knowledge with salvation.

We may best appreciate how radically Milton's epistemology and soteriology cohere by contrasting his soteriology with Calvin's. As is well known, Milton did not follow Calvin in the doctrine of predestination, differing from him in at least two ways: (1) Milton believed predestination to refer only to election, not to reprobation, and (2) Milton did not believe anyone predestined to reprobation for all eternity (CM XIV, pp. 91–175). In *Divine Dialogues* (1668), Henry More suggested the term *preterition* to replace *reprobation* (that "dark *Dogma*"), the former meaning "no designment of [the persons] to sin and damnation."[8] Milton, demonstrating admirable humanism, refutes even this milder form of reprobation because it too is based on a judgment for all eternity: "*Atque hinc præteritionis ab aeterno . . . redarguuntur*" ("Hence may be refuted the notion of a preterition . . . from all eternity"). Knowledge is the basis of Milton's theology, and grace, he argues in *Christian Doctrine,* must be catholic in offering everyone the potential "at least sufficient for attaining *knowledge* of the truth and final salvation." The distribution of grace is not equal, and Milton stresses this point, for mercy must be tempered with justice, but "there are none to whom he does not vouchsafe grace sufficient for their salvation" (CM XIV, pp. 102–03, 146–47).

One would be mistaken to argue that Milton ascribed a capability of attaining saving knowledge to human merit, for grace, that irresistible and absolutely necessary force, is basic to his, as to all, Christian doctrine. But we may see that Milton allows, within the human bailiwick, a greater activity in determining the degree of saving knowledge each individual may attain. He summarizes his conclusions regarding predestination as follows: "Thus much, therefore, may be considered as a certain and irrefragable truth: that God excludes no one from the pale of repentance and eternal salvation, till he has despised and rejected the propositions of sufficient grace, offered even to a late hour" (CM XIV, pp. 152–53; cf. pp. 156–57). Milton concludes his chapter on predestination by admonishing those who have not made the important and "proper distinction between the punishment of hardening the heart and the decree of reprobation" (CM XIV, pp. 174–75). The latter decree presupposes an absence of grace determined from eternity, whereas the former punishment is based on an economic principle in which in the same measure as grace is denied the punishment of obduracy is applied. Knowledge is the quiddity of salvation, and obduracy is imposed only on those who reject the saving knowledge.

Three forms of skepticism may be found in *Paradise Regained*. The first represents the lapsed human condition unable to comprehend the majesty of divinity ("thir minds / How dark'n'd"). The second is a remnant of that healthy skepticism Milton employed in his intellectual career: a noble purity of vision that proceeds from questioning the validity and limitations of human traditions to apprehending the suprarational essence of faith in God. Finally, there is the doubt of desperation, the skepticism Jesus criticizes in rejecting Athenian philosophy, that which doubts everything though "plain sence."

II

Citing 1 Corinthians viii, 10–11, William Ames notes that, "Doubting that doth diminish only assent may stand with a weake Faith." "But not," he continues, citing James i, 6-8, "that doubting which takes away assent." As historian of the Christian warfare, John Downham noted that even after election and up to the threshold of justification, the religious warrior may be prone to doubt. Faith, he continued, was the fruit of the spirit, and doubt of the flesh; and, moreover, as faithless flesh was prone to obduracy, so was doubt prone to despair. The unsteady Christian would be "tossed up and downe with the waves of doubting" till at last he was dashed "against the rockes of despaire." As William Gouge, the outfitter of the Christian warrior, noted, true faith may stand with doubting. Indeed, one may even despair and yet be revived, for there are two types of despair—one that is obdurate and one that is holy. Richard Sibbes eased the hearts of English puritans by observing that a "holy despaire in our selves is the ground of true hope," and that nothing "is so certaine as that which is certaine after doubts."[9]

For created beings bereft of the original rectitude that had allowed them immediate comprehension of divine precepts, doubt was a part of lapsed existence. As Milton contends, doubt, "to which even the pious are sometimes liable," is superable through hope and faith (CM XVII, p. 59). And so the pious are liable and so forgiven. In *Paradise Regained,* this first form of doubt is exemplified by Andrew and Simon. They, discovering Jesus "So lately found, and so abruptly gone, / Began to doubt, and doubted many days, / And as the days increas'd, increas'd thir doubt" (II, 10–12). Andrew and Simon doubt because they do not understand either the majesty of the king or the type of the kingdom to which he will accede. Expecting a mundane kingdom to be restored to Israel immediately, they wonder at the retirement of the king they expected to restore it. They doubt God's mode of deliverance, but they resolve that doubt into a joyful patience: "Thus they out of their plaints new hope resume" (II, 58). Mary likewise doubts—her fears raising some "troubl'd thoughts"—and in the same way resolves her thoughts into patience: "Meekly compos'd awaited the fulfilling" (II, 109). These, then, are the earthly perspectives on the incarnate Jesus, wondering at the divine majesty spiriting forth from carnal man, yet doubtful as to the type of strength he might be capable of applying toward the restoration of Israel's monarchy. This is the form of doubt representing the human condition—feeble because reliant on sensual phenomena, but strong because of an ability to transcend that reliance in an act of patience and faith.

III

The second type of skepticism is that wherein doubt is used to dispel dogma without attempting to raze all authority, whether sensual or intellectual. Milton belonged to an age in which doubt was a useful tool for dismantling dogmatism, whether of natural, religious, or divine history. Bacon begins and ends the aphorisms outlining the four idols of the mind with the warning that skepticism is but a heuristic device, and not in any way an end in itself. Bacon's directions, as the subtitle to *The New Organon* tells us, concerned the "interpretation of nature." Were we to alter the book of nature to the Book of Revelation, and "the authority of the senses" to the authority of the Scriptures, we would have Milton's theological organon. Milton, as Herschel Baker noted, fully agreed with Bacon, Chillingworth, Browne, and Descartes, that the first step to wisdom is doubt.[10]

Descartes likewise, in outlining his methodical evolution of knowledge, claimed that though skepticism serviced his desire for certainty, it was not in itself a desirable mode of perception. He writes:

> Reflecting especially upon the points in every subject which might make it suspect and give occasion for us to make mistakes, I kept uprooting from my mind any errors that might previously have slipped into it. In doing this I was not copying the sceptics, who doubt only for the sake of doubting and pretend to be always undecided; on the contrary, my whole aim was to reach certainty.

The career of that healthy skepticism was finally the solipsism of *cogito ergo sum:* "And observing that this truth '*I am thinking, therefore I exist*' was so firm and sure that all the most extravagant suppositions of the sceptics were incapable of shaking it, I decided that I could accept it without scruple as the first principle of the philosophy I was seeking."[11]

Joseph Glanvill thought "the *method* of the most excellent *Des-Cartes* not unworthy its Author; and (since *Dogmatical Ignorance* will call it so) a *Scepticism*, that's the only way to *Science*." This final phrase evidently pleased Glanvill for it became the subtitle to the second edition, retitled *Scepsis Scientifica: Or, Confest Ignorance, the way to Science* (1665). But though doubt was useful for science, Glanvill averred, it was not the path to divinity: "In *Theology*, I put as great a difference between our *New Lights*, and *Antient Truths*; as between the *Sun*, and an unconcocted evanid *Meteor*. Though I confess, that in *Philosophy* I'm a *Seeker*; yet cannot I believe, that a

Sceptick in *Philosophy* must be one in *Divinity*."[12] While the beginnings of philosophy were in a "Crepusculous obscurity" the gospel
began in its zenith, in the very meridian of its strength and lustre.

Although the gospel began in brightness, Milton might have
written, sixteen centuries had done nothing but obscure the primitive glory of its origins in dogmatic idolatry and superstition.
What he might have counseled, and did practice, was a healthy
skepticism toward orthodox traditions. Led by this skepticism, he
entered the lists against the Episcopalians, emerging from thence
into the heated battles of the divorce controversy, and concluding
his career by dismantling the orthodoxy of Trinitarianism. The
search for primitive truth led Milton through forays that might
have disillusioned lesser humans. The path of that primitive truth
required an attendant doubt as to the traditions of human construction. And so Milton applied his mind to the task. Scripture
and Providence his guides, with wandering steps and slow he took
his solitary way through England's heated intellectual battles.

In *Paradise Regained,* Jesus uses this type of doubt to body
forth his suprarational theosophy. We have seen how the doubts of
Andrew, Simon, and Mary deliver us from thoughts of a worldly to
those of an otherworldly kingdom. We might turn to Jesus' second
soliloquy to discover how he delivers us from a worldly to an
otherworldly logic. Jesus begins his soliloquy:

> Where will this end? four times ten days I have pass'd,
> Wandring this woody maze, and humane food
> Nor tasted, nor had appetite; that Fast
> To Vertue I impute not, or count part
> Of what I suffer here; if Nature need not,
> Or God support Nature without repast
> Though needing, what praise is it to endure?
> But now I feel I hunger, which declares,
> Nature hath need of what she asks; yet God
> Can satisfie that need some other way,
> Though hunger still remain: so it remain
> Without this bodies wasting, I content me,
> And from the sting of Famine fear no harm,
> Nor mind it, fed with better thoughts that feed
> Mee hungring more to do my Fathers will.   (II, 245–59)

Jesus establishes the presuppositions of virtuous behavior in this soliloquy. Virtue does not exist, or at least is not imputed, without necessity. Without endurance there is no praise. Praise is deserved when someone endures something, that is, goes without some necessary thing. Without hunger, then, there is no laudable virtue exercised in the fast. The implications of this situation will necessitate an examination of the dialectic of the soliloquy as a set piece.

Charles S. Jerram, the 1877 editor of *Paradise Regained,* offered a reading of the soliloquy in which it becomes a simple, logical exercise. He paraphrases, "*either* nature may not feel need at all, *or,* though she may do so, God can satisfy her by other means than food. But my feeling hunger tells me that the former alternative is not true, therefore the second remains."[13] The fault with this is, paradoxically, its logic. In a desire to discover a logical progress in the soliloquy, Jerram has ignored the verses themselves. What Jesus says, in effect, is that God can satisfy the "need"—the crux of heroic endurance—in a way by which hunger and need are differentiated: need is satisfied, though hunger yet remains. This is a curious shift, and not warranted by worldly logic; "hunger" is the "need," and so a distinction between hunger and need is not a simple division of content and form. Jesus makes an essential difference, which knows not, cares not, and trafficks not in the logic of the world's ways. This distinction between "need" and "hunger" is not noted by Jerram. Only by ignoring this impossible distinction can logic be imputed to the soliloquy. Its logic, I would argue, is of another sort. What is intimated here, I think, is that the logic pertaining to acquiescence in an inscrutable Being is as mysterious as it is laudable.

Given this alogical gesture, then, the concluding two verses of the soliloquy ought not to surprise us. His need satisfied, though his hunger yet remains, Jesus is, he claims, "fed with better thoughts that feed / Mee hungring more to do my Father's will." The sense of these two lines is not easily accessible. There is no way around the difficult fact that Jesus is saying, in heterodoxy to biological functions, that he is fed to be hungered. And again this flaunts worldly logic with an otherworldly dialectic. In the commerce of the earth, any feeding has a satisfying effect: it satisfies the need of hunger. Jesus separates hunger from need and states that the meal he enjoys is one that causes him to hunger more. Finally, given the definition of virtue with which this soliloquy began, what Jesus does here is nothing less than an act of sublime humility. Though suffering the need of hunger, because his need and his hunger are divided, and his need satisfied, his action, according to his own definition, is not laudable: It deserves no praise because there is no need. That is perhaps in accord with divine logic, but through earthly eyes we can only admire the virtue and the humility informing this exalted man. The logic is otherworldly, based on divine prerogative, not human needs and functions. At its basis are the defining qualities of virtue and faith. "True Vertue," wrote John Smith, is the basis of insight "in heaven's Logick." "Faith," wrote Thomas Adams, is properly "the Christians Logick."[14]

Jesus' first soliloquy, his long autobiographical exposition in the first book, ends, as dusk descends, with intellectual acquiescence: "What concerns my knowledge God reveals." This second soliloquy ends, as the hour of night approaches, with another statement of acquiescence. The foundation of Jesus' heroism is theocentricity, and the means of establishing a theosophic dialectic is by scrutinizing skeptically the mode of worldly logic. In rejecting Athenian logic, Jesus says that he who receives "Light from above, from the fountain of light, / No other doctrine needs, though granted true" (IV, 286–87). Whoever would have true learning, not intoxicate or superficial—"As Children gathering pibles on the shore"—must bring to their erudition a "spirit and judgment equal or superior." Jesus' "secret weapon," argues Georgia Christopher, is the Holy Spirit, the inspiring force enabling him to interpret the various crises of his life.[15] The comprehension of spiritual things, Milton wrote, comes through the grace of the Holy Spirit. Although we have but an imperfect comprehension of these spiritual things, Milton concludes, it is nonetheless incumbent upon us, and necessary to our salvation to attain to even that imperfect knowledge (CM XVI, pp. 6–9). Jesus is the beneficiary of that Spirit, from its descent in the form of a dove at the Baptism, through his autobiographical reinterpretation of his worldly ambitions in light of that spiritual knowledge, to his rejection of worldly logic in favor of theosophy. With the theological tradition of the Holy Spirit in mind, we may discuss the final form of skepticism in *Paradise Regained,* that denial of sense which is solely Satan's prerogative. Before turning to the final form of skepticism in the poem, we must review the traditions of the doubt motif in hermeneutics on the Temptation.

IV

The presentation of the doubt motif as it applies specifically to Satan's capacity for knowledge about the divine reality of the Son brings with it numerous questions. First there is the issue of Satan's knowledge. On the one hand, was Satan ignorant of Jesus' identity? If so, was his ignorance sincere? Was, then, the temptation sequence an identity contest, in which Satan attempts to clear himself of ignorance by knowing Jesus' status, and Jesus answers with such ambiguity as to keep him from that knowledge? Or, on the other hand, was Satan not ignorant? If so, why did he pretend to ignorance? Was the temptation sequence not an identity contest? And if not, what was it?

Second, there is the issue of what exactly Satan wished to discover. Did he wish to know the mystery of the Incarnation? Did he wish to know whether the man clothed in fleshly tabernacle before him now was also the ineffable second person of the Trinity? Did he wish to know whether Jesus was God?

Third is the issue of whether or not Satan achieved the knowledge after which he strove. For those who argue that the temptation sequence was an identity contest, it is imperative that Satan should not discover Jesus' identity. For those who argue that Satan knew but maliciously pretended ignorance of Jesus' identity, it is imperative that Satan should discover Jesus' identity. In one case, knowledge is victory, in the other defeat. There are parallel traditions here, and to appreciate them both helps us to understand the subtlety of the plot of *Paradise Regained*. For Milton, I will argue, reforms both these traditions into something unique.

Jesus' forty-day fast immediately follows the Baptism, and the incongruity between the open proclamation of the former event and the obscure trial of the latter leads Satan to doubt the verity of the baptismal announcement. As Chrysostom wrote, Satan

> was thenceforth in perplexity, and neither could believe that He was mere man, because of the things spoken concerning Him; nor on the other hand receive that He was Son of God, seeing Him as he did in hunger. Whence being in perplexity he utters ambiguous sounds.

Chrysostom accepts that Satan was sincerely perplexed and that the uttered "ambiguous sounds" evinced a heartfelt confusion.

From this conception arose the idea that the temptation sequence was an identity contest. On the one hand, Satan begins in perplexity and offers the temptations in order to achieve certitude, while on the other, Jesus answers the temptations with sufficient ambiguity to conceal his identity. Christ, Chrysostom concluded, "even when these things are said, doth not yet reveal Himself."[16]

The Chrysostom tradition, based on the idea that Satan's doubts were sincere, and that he was therefore motivated to tempt Jesus in order to discover his true status, arrived in the seventeenth century intact. Richard Ward writes that "some say" Satan tempted Jesus "because he doubted whether hee were or not" the Son of God. Jesus answers Satan's temptations, then, in order to delude him: "Christ would not suffer the Divels to beare witnesse of him, but rebukes them, when they acknowledge him."[17] Chrysostom received widespread but not universal approbation on this theme, and a subtle shift in the interpretation of Chrysostom's interpretation concerning Satan's knowledge occurred. Another tradition concerning Satan's knowledge had gained ascendancy in English commentary. This tradition suggested that Satan knew who Jesus was, but maliciously pretended ignorance in his attempt to corrupt Jesus.

There was evidence concerning Jesus' identity preceding the fast, and this evidence, commentators believed, must have been available to Satan. The bishop of Galloway, for example, paraphrases Satan's purpose:

> His purpose here, is to impugne that notable Oracle sounded from Heaven at Christs Baptisme: *This is my beloved Son, in whom I am well pleased:* so said the Father. But this cannot bee now (saith Satan,) that voyce hath been but a delusion; for the Sonne of God is the Heyre of all things, and hath the Angels for his Ministers and Servants: but it is not so with thee; for, here thou art among wild beasts, in great necessitie, like to perish for hunger.

Satan, Cowper continues, "knew that Jesus was the Sonne of God, and afterwards he confesseth it; yet such is the malice of his nature, that hee fighteth against his knowne light" (pp. 613–14). Sincere perplexity becomes malicious pretense, and ignorance willful nescience. Joseph Hall notes that the evidence available to Satan ought to have been enough to dispel any doubts that Jesus' present afflictions may suggest to him: "His very supposition convinces him: The ground of his temptation, answers it selfe."[18]

Thomas Fuller, writing in 1652, pays more attention to the dynamics of the narrative than any other commentator. Satan, Fuller begins, "must needs know that Christ was the Son of God, by what he had seen and heard." Fuller cites the Annunciation, the angelic chorus to the shepherds, the prophecy of Simeon, and the dove at the Baptism as evidence to which Satan must have been privy. He concludes his summary as follows:

> All these did only amount to vehement suspitions, whereby Satan might probably conjecture, but could not certainly conclude him *the Son of God*. I mean, thus he could not hereby collect, That Christ was the second Person in the Trinity incarnated . . . He knew him to be the Son of God by grace and adoption, such an one as *David* and other men were . . . He knew also that he was the Redeemer of *Israel*, such as *Moses, Joshua,* and the rest of the Judges were: all of them Saviours of their people by temporal deliverances from their enemies: But he knew not certainly (though he shrewdly suspected) that he was the only Son of God by eternal generation . . . Wherefore the devil did not wholly despaire, but tempted Christ with some probability of success.

When Fuller sets out to explicate the first temptation, he surveys the possible interpretations of Satan's use of the conditional. "Some conceive," he writes, "that Satan herein dissembled his knowledge . . . though assured Christ was the Son of God . . . But *cui bono?* For what conceived good to himself should the devil disguise his knowledge herein?" "Others conceive," he continues, "that as an angry dog bites a stone out of sheer madness, though knowing he shall sooner break his teeth, then batter the stone: so Satans malice so far transported and blinded his judgement that he tempted Christ, though (knowing him for the Son of God) his temptations would prove ineffectual." Finally, Fuller states his own opinion: "I rather cast the grain of my opinion into the Scale of those Divines, who conceive the devil unsatisfied in this point, and therefore his *if thou be the Son of God* proceeded from his desire of more perfect information therein." Fuller uses this as proof to conclude that Satan has a confined and limited knowledge. Indeed, Satan returned "such ridling Oracles [as the Delphic] meerly to palliate his own ignorance." But though Satan is honestly ignorant he does not demur from passing on his doubts through his queries: "It is Satan's master-piece, to make Gods children first doubt of, and then deny their sonship." By the final temptation, Fuller writes, Satan "(who long had look'd for that which he was loath to finde, *viz. whether Christ was the Son of God*) was now, to his great sorrow, sufficiently satisfied in the *affirmative,* that he was so; and therefore desisted from farther inquiry therein."[19]

John Gumbleden, chaplain to "Robert, Earl of Leicester, Viscount Lisle, Lord Sidney of Pensehurst," might be expected, with such a family to edify, to be attentive to the narrative aspects of the gospel. Writing in 1657, he produced an extremely astute commentary on the temptation sequence. The questions of doubt and Satan's knowledge are a leitmotif in his commentary. Immediately, Gumbleden establishes that Satan knows from the Baptism that Christ is the Son of God. He paraphrases Satan's first speech to Christ: "Thou was not long since declared at *Jordan* to be *the Son of God,* which I make a doubt of." Satan "doubted (*if thou be*) whether he whom he then *tempted* were that *Person* or not; he doubted: yet surely, more out of *malice* then out of *ignorance.*" Satan must know because Christ was revealed by the prophets and was proclaimed at the Baptism. The authority of the voice at the Baptism was "a true saying, and worthy of all acceptation, though it were of *no credit* at all with *Satan,* who here *subtilly* pretends *ignorance.*" At the first temptation, then, Gumbleden notes, Satan was "*not convinced,* even when he *was convinced,* not *satisfied,* as he pretended, that, *Person* whom he *tempted* was the *Son of God,* even when there was no just cause to be *dissatisfied,* having evidence enough." At the end of the second temptation, Satan remains convinced but reticent: "and *therefore the Son of God,* which that *other unclean spirit* acknowledged *expresly, Mark* 1:24. and surely was not now doubted of by *this unclean spirit* here, although in words he would not *acknowledge* it." At the end of the third temptation, Satan is *confounded, conquered, convinced,* and *satisfied.* And this is evinced, Gumbleden concludes, by Satan's "deep silence."[20]

Gumbleden's commentary lacks the sense of dramatic movement to be found in Fuller's. No small part of the reason is because Fuller chooses to follow a plot in which Satan begins in ignorant doubt and ends in dismaying knowledge while Gumbleden chooses one in which Satan begins in malicious pretense at doubtful ignorance and ends in satisfied and silent defeat. There is no alteration in Satan's knowledge in this latter interpretation, whereas there is a sense of progression in the former. Milton, it has often been argued, follows the Chrysostom tradition, in which Satan begins in ignorance and ends in dismaying knowledge. But we have seen how the *English* tradition altered the orientation of Chrysostom's reading by assuming Satan's earlier knowledge of Jesus' status at the baptismal proclamation and by applying Satan's later avowed recognition of the Son's power at the miracle at Capernaum into its search for the degree of Satan's knowledge during the temptation sequence. Chrysostom had anticipated this reorientation in a way. When discussing the Baptism, he points out that the multitude will not believe the efficacy of the event. Without ever referring to Satan, however, Chrysostom notes that certain types of knowledge are accessible only to the faithful, especially knowledge of miracles and symbols. When a "soul is uncandid and perverse, and possessed by the disease of envy," he writes, "it yields to none of these things [miracle and symbolism of Baptism]; even as when it is candid it receives all with faith, and hath no great need of these."[21] In the terms of the debate we are tracing, then, Chrysostom would suggest that Satan, being one of the uncandid souls, begins in incomprehension and ends in confusion. He is granted no satisfaction.

Critics of *Paradise Regained* generally follow the tradition best exemplified by Fuller, that Satan begins in doubting and ends in recognizing Jesus' Sonship. But this reading, it seems to me, simply does not agree with either Milton's theology or his narrative. Milton made an important distinction between the decree of predestination and the punishment of hardening the heart. Now, recalling that knowledge is central to salvation, we may see in Milton's final narrative, in the character of Satan, the process of rejecting knowledge, the obduracy proceeding from this denial, and the end to which it leads. It is the third type of skepticism, that which is neither laudable nor redeemable.

V

Although doubt is allowable in Christian doctrine, even to the degree of a type of desperation, there is one form of doubt which represents a trespass beyond salvation: the sin against the Holy Ghost. This malign sin, Perkins writes, is "so called, because it is

done contrarie to the immediate action, namely, the illumination
of the Holy Ghost." It contains "a voluntarie, and obstinate deniall
of, and blasphemie against the Sonne of God, or that truth which
was before acknowledged concerning him." Gouge defines it thus:
"A despitefull rejecting of the Gospell, after that the Spirit hath
supernaturally persuaded a mans heart of the truth and benefit
thereof." These reprobrates blaspheme "against all *probabilitie* and
possibilitie, yea against *their own judgement* and opinion."[22]

Perkins points out that the archetypal sinner against the Holy
Ghost is Satan. "We have an example of this sin," he writes, "partly
in the divel, who albeit he knew well enough that Jesus was that
Christ, yet he never ceased both wittingly and willingly with all his
power to oppugne the sacred Majestie of god."[23]

Milton differed from Perkins and Gouge in the same measure as
he was an Arian to their orthodox Trinitarianism.[24] The "dreaded
sin against the Holy Spirit," Milton boldly argued, is "in reality a
sin against the Father, who is the Spirit of holiness." Though there
is an alteration in its orientation, the sin remains largely the same:
that "whereby the Father enlightens us through the Spirit," which
"if any one resist, no method of salvation remains open to him"
(CM XIV, pp. 394–97). Andrew, Simon, and Mary, we saw, resolved their doubt into hope and faith. Jesus uses doubt to transcend the logic of the phenomenal world. The final form of skepticism belongs to Satan.

Satan's first interpretive effort in the narrative concerns the
Spirit's descent "in likeness of a Dove" (I, 30). Relating the Baptism to his peers, Satan states that a "perfect Dove" descended on
the Son's head. The dove becomes in Satan's mind a literal bird and
is interpreted with a willful nescience—"what e're it meant" (I,
83). Jesus interprets the same event in his autobiographical soliloquy with attention to the spiritual significance of the symbol: "The
Spirit descended on me like a Dove" (I, 182). Satan lacks that
unerring paraphrase of Christian love that would enable him to
transcend the literal and appreciate the spiritual significance of a
symbol.[25] But this is not simply a case wherein Satan does not
possess the interpretive capacity to appreciate the symbol; rather,
he chooses to delude himself. We must remember Milton's theological position here. The reprobate sense is not predestined, but
willed by an inveterate obstinacy in the face of undeniable evidence.

As in *Paradise Lost* the devils achieve an "insensate" state by their own malice, so in *Paradise Regained* Satan progressively denies the spiritual evidence of Jesus' Sonship and, in doing so, achieves a final senselessness (*PL* VI, 789–98). His interpretation of the dove is one example. I must stress the point that Satan has opportunity enough to recognize exactly who Jesus is in the early part of the narrative, for *Paradise Regained* is not based on Satan's honest ignorance, nor on a kind of drama in which Satan is kept from the knowledge of Jesus' Sonship through the wiles of the author and the protagonist (as in the Chrysostom tradition). Milton has Satan attend the Baptism and see the Spirit descend and hear God pronounce Jesus his Son. He then has Satan discuss this evidence with his fallen angels. In that gloomy consistory, Milton has Satan demonstrate the process of rejecting the evidence that would give him the knowledge of Jesus' identity.

Satan's speech in the consistory turns on a single word. Having defined precisely the role Jesus is to play in history—to regain the kingdom Adam and Eve lost—and the majesty of his bearing in his "youths full flowr, displaying / All vertue, grace and wisdom," Satan, relating the Baptism to his peers, states that Jesus went to Jordan,

> Not thence to be more pure, but to receive
> The testimony of Heaven, that who he is
> Thenceforth the Nations may not doubt.   (I, 77–79)

On that key word, "doubt," Satan's rhetoric takes a new turn. Before that word, all his relation had been offered in an impersonal mode. The next words change the perspective into an intensely private one: "I saw." He recounts the dove's descent and interprets it doubtfully: "what e're it meant." He then says, "I heard" the voice out of heaven and interprets the obvious message—"This is my Son belov'd"—doubtfully. Satan rejects the latently spiritual in favor of the manifestly literal. He notices the spirit residing in Jesus—"in his face / The glimpses of his Fathers glory shine"—but denies the inevitable conclusion to be drawn from that fact: "Who this is we must learn" (I, 84–91). On this point, John Smith's comment is apposite:

There is a *knowing of the truth as it is in Jesus,* as it is in a *Christ-like nature,* as it is in that sweet, mild, humble, and loving Spirit of Jesus, which spreads itself like a Morning-Sun upon the Soules of good men, full of light and life. It profits little to know Christ himself after the flesh; but he gives his Spirit to good men, that reacheth the deep things of God.

But Satan attempts to know Jesus only after the flesh: the spirit he rejects. Doubt is the essential instrument of Satan's hermeneutics, one he uses in order to delude himself.[26] In his doubtful interpretation in the consistory, Satan blasphemes against the Holy Ghost.

At the first encounter Jesus openly recognizes Satan and claims that Satan recognizes him: "Why dost thou then suggest to me distrust, / Knowing who I am, as I know who thou art? (I, 355–56). There is, of course, a difference in their knowledges, for while Satan attempts to keep his knowledge superficial—valorizing the bodily lineaments over the glimpses of the spirit resident within— Jesus' knowledge is profound, even to recognizing Satan's motivation.

Here we might examine the disparate interpretive methods of the two combatants. We may best do that by comparing Satan's relation of the Job incident with Jesus' interpretation of it. Whereas Satan claims to have tempted Job to "prove him, and illustrate his high worth," Jesus claims that Satan's "malice" moved him to "misdeem / Of righteous *Job*" (I, 370, 424–25). In the scriptural story of Job, Satan does not strike one as immediately malicious. He goes to heaven where, upon hearing of the perfect and upright Job, he suggests that Job's uprightness is due to his comfortable situation. Satan suggests that, were Job to lose his possessions and loved ones, "all that he hath," then he would undoubtedly curse God to his face. God sends Satan to the task to disprove this accusation. In the poem, Jesus interprets this story not by its surface effects but by its substructure of motivation. Satan's malice lies in the offers, the inability to behold uprightness and appreciate it, to leave well enough alone, one might say. When Satan tells his version of the Job incident he offers a straightforward narrative (I, 368–70). When Jesus tells his version, he goes beyond the narrative surface and delivers an interpretive version, taking into account facts of motivation. Jesus does not concern himself merely with the manifest surface detail of the narrative but with the structure of meaning latent in it, the spiritual and transcendent significance of the text. Satan's original and malicious "misdeeming" becomes the originating center or kernel of the narrative, from which the interpretation of his further cruelty emerges. Satan's version of the Job narrative lacks the psychological depth to show the motivations of the actors involved in it. Jesus' interpretation begins with that psychological motivation and interprets the surface action accordingly. It is the place of divine wisdom to do so. Arthur Capel writes, "As *Light* not only discovers the gross *substances* of things, but their *figures* and *colours;* so *wisedome* not only perceives the *actions* themselves, but the *affections* with which, and *intents* to which they were done." George Downame makes the distinction between acts and motivations the basic theme of his *Christian Warfare*. God, he writes, "respecteth not so much our actions as our affections." And in the anatomy of the spirit, "affections . . . are the feete of thy soule" as "faith is the mouth of the soule." Satan, in this consideration, is both amputated and mute. And through his bootless attempts to corrupt Jesus he is ultimately silenced.[27]

Satan has now shown himself recalcitrantly unwilling to make the transition from carnal to spiritual interpretation. Confronted with undeniable evidence of Jesus' status, he denies it nonetheless. Given a chance to declare that he knows who Jesus is, he refuses it. Instead he demonstrates a capacity for retaining only the superficial qualities of an event—in this instance, the story of Job. From this point on, and only from this point on, once Satan has demonstrated his unwillingness to recognize the spiritual, Jesus confuses him with enigmatic answers to his carnal questions.

Following Jesus' interpretation of Satan's version of the Job narrative, Satan claims to be a boon to mankind in the form of oracular aid (I, 387–96). Jesus notes that the ambiguity with which Satan had tempered these oracular prophesies, by "mixing somewhat true to vent more lyes," made them useless: "Ambiguous and with double sense deluding." No passage of Scripture, Milton wrote, "is to be interpreted in more than one sense." Satan's present "double sense deluding" will continue to his final attempt at comprehending the spiritual significance of the phrase "The Son of God, which bears no single sence" (IV, 514). Satan's duplicity is based on his interpretive creed. "There is a *double head,* as well as a *double heart,*" notes John Smith. "Mens corrupt hearts will not suffer their motions and conceptions of divine things to be cast

into that form that an higher Reason, which may sometimes work
within them, would put them into."[28]

Satan, as seventeenth-century theologians noted, employed a
hermeneutics of malice. Satan is an interpreter who sometimes
aggravates facts or speeches, writes Taylor, which "charity would
give a favourable construction onto." Daniel Tuvil adds that there
is a form of discourse common to old men, "limited with doubts,
and suppositions. . . . They are for the most part left-handed (that
is to say) malicious, and apt to conster all things to the worst
sense." Satan, it would appear, is just this sort of old man. Likewise, Joseph Hall writes, "There is no word or action, but may be
taken with two hands; either with the right hand of charitable
construction, or the sinister interpretation of malice, and suspicion: and all things doe succeed, as they are taken."[29] In terms of
this two-handed hermeneutics, Satan's malice in the face of spiritual evidence bespeaks nothing less than the sin against the Holy
Ghost.

Now Satan has determined his fate to a dubious sense because
he first refused and now is unable to recognize the spiritual content of any material thing, or the spiritual significance of any
enigmatic statement. The reader, on the other hand, must see the
words Jesus henceforth addresses to Satan through the unerring
paraphrase of Christian charity. The reader, who has just been
granted an inward oracle to allow him or her that necessary ascen-
dance, may determine the spiritual significance of Jesus' enigmatic
scheme of answering Satan (I, 460–64).

We might turn, then, to the offer of the banquet to see how
Jesus' answer is meant to inform us of his capacity for miraculous
activity but exclude Satan from that comprehension. "What doubts
the Son of God to sit and eat?" Satan inquires. To which Jesus
answers:

> Said'st thou not that to all things I had right?
> And who withholds my pow'r that right to use?
> Shall I receive by gift what of my own,
> When and where likes me best, I can command?
> I can at will, doubt not, as soon as thou,
> Command a Table in this Wilderness,
> And call swift flights of Angels ministrant
> Array'd in Glory on my cup to attend.   (II, 379–86)

"Doubt not," Jesus tells Satan, but Satan, he knows, will doubt yet. For though Jesus has just told Satan that he (Jesus) is capable of any miracle, and of commanding angels, Satan continues to offer him mundane trivialities (wealth, glory, and then the kingdoms). Satan, that is, has not understood what Jesus has just told him.

Critics have generally followed Elizabeth Marie Pope's reading of this passage:

> The declaration of Christ's rank is evidently meant to be entirely hypothetical: the one positive statement he makes is covered by the rush of questions which precede and follow it, nor does Satan take it as the proof or affirmation which he is trying to obtain. As usual, the Lord has neither denied nor acknowledged his real identity: he has merely put the whole question aside without committing himself.[30]

To argue that Jesus is not asserting his powers, but merely answering Satan within the logical framework Satan has himself provided, is to ignore the crucial question of why Jesus should assert these things at all. It is my argument that Jesus asserts his powers because the other auditor, the faithful reader, will understand the spiritual significance of the statement.

The crucial line, which Pope sees "covered" by the rush of questions before and after it, is a direct answer to Satan. "What doubts the Son of God to sit and eat?" Satan asks. "I can at will, doubt not," Jesus asserts. And it is an assertion. Jesus is not merely seeing how far he may confute Satan's offer within the logical terms Satan has posed. There is nothing conditional or hypothetical in Jesus' reply—it is outright declaration. He does commit himself, but Satan is unable to understand because, for his carnal mind, it is an enigma beyond comprehension. Furthermore, Satan does not take it as the proof he is trying to obtain because he cannot: he has already rejected that opportunity. Never again in the scheme of this narrative will Satan accept any of Jesus' declarations as proof. He has been given the proof and, having refused it, he is now denied the spirit to comprehend it. For the reward of malice in affairs of the spirit is unmitigated ignorance and pervading carnality. Whoever blasphemes the Holy Spirit is irredeemable, and redemption, Milton held, was involved with the ability to apprehend spiritual things.

Satan, having used his skepticism to doubt the essential spirit residing in the Son, concludes the temptation sequence ignorant of Jesus' identity. In the final section of this chapter, I will argue that, as the Son stands on the pinnacle and Satan, "smitten with amazement," falls, Satan can recognize only the physical station, and not the spiritual status, of the Son. Like his interpretation of the dove, and because of it, his understanding of the Incarnation is limited to external facts. Having donned the garment of skepticism in his first attempt at interpreting the status of the incarnate Son, Satan finds it, like Hercules's shirt, an external garment that becomes, by dint of wear, a consumptive part of the body it adorns. Or, to use the metaphor I suggested at the outset of this chapter, having constituted his world by employing an illegal form of doubt, Satan finds himself in turn constituted as a being of some dubiety.

VI

This sense of the dynamic movement from malice to wilfull ignorance is a development of the mature Milton. In earlier works he had yet to develop an epistemology in which one could relegate oneself to obduracy. There is a sense of election in *A Mask,* for example, when the Lady says to Comus,

> Thou hast not Ear nor Soul to apprehend
> The sublime notion and high mystery
> . . . .
> And thou art worthy that thou shouldst not know
> More happiness than this thy present lot.
> (784–85, 788–89; cf. 792)

This is the early Milton. The later Milton has a less hostile attitude toward his antagonists. Satan has more accessibility to sublime knowledge, only to waste both the knowledge and the potential for aspiring to it. As Satan stands looking at the beautiful Eve, his malice is overawed by her angelic and heavenly form:

> That space the Evil one abstracted stood
> From his own evil, and for the time remain'd
> Stupidly good, of enmity disarm'd.   (*PL* IX, 463–65)[31]

For a moment in time and space, Satan is able to comprehend goodness, to return to his days of heavenly rectitude and apprehend the beauty of virtue in all her various charms. But the will to corrupt overcomes his abstraction, and he is rapt to evil designs. Now we turn to the final Milton. As Satan looks at the "exalted man," the recipient of heaven's voice and spirit, the first thing he feels is "wonder." But that innocent admiration gives way immediately to envy and rage. He flies to the consistory, uses a rhetoric of dubiety to cast his compeers and himself into doubt's boundless sea, and continues his career toward senselessness. Milton's sensibilities do not harden in this last work, as some critics have argued. In this last narrative he is alive to the beneficial issues of a skeptical attitude, and he concludes his career without settling into any easy dogmatism or compromising the liberty of thought for whose defense he had entered heated battles. But he is also aware of the possible malice of skepticism, aware of the dangers to which the Pyrrhonian is prone, and aware of the transcendent fideism necessary to the Christian religion he had made his life's work to promote in its primitive purity.

The presentation of the debate in the desert, the conclusion of the Miltonic effort, offers an examination of the tension between terrene and heavenly minds, between the use and abuse of skepticism, and of the relationship of doubting to sense. "A third sort doubted all things, though plain sence," Jesus tells Satan. Sense, we have seen, is singular if viewed with an accommodating spirit and an honest reason. "When *Reason* once is raised by the mighty force of the Divine Spirit into a converse with God," John Smith wrote, "it is turn'd into *Sense*." When once it is debased by a malicious interpretive skepticism, it turns into a "double sense deluding." Like a Pyrrhonian, Satan is skeptical about appearances and resolutely unwilling to affirm anything about essences.[32] While Satan articulates his doubt about appearances—"thou seem'st the man"—even as he alters his visage, Jesus articulates his knowledge of essences—"I discern thee other then thou seem'st"—while retaining the same appearance; moreover, by referring to his own interior demeanor, he demonstrates that Satan's doubts are unfounded. It is "plain sence" that Jesus is the Son of God. Not only does the glimmering spirit shine forth in his conversation and countenance, but he has been the recipient of a heavenly symbol and pronouncement. Satan is the archetypal blasphemer against the Holy Ghost because he doubts the efficacy and source of those divine miracles. At the first encounter, Satan confesses:

> though I have lost
> Much lustre of my native brightness, lost
> To be belov'd of God, I have not lost
> To love, at least contemplate and admire
> What I see excellent in good, or fair,
> Or vertuous, I should so have lost all sense.   (I, 377–82)

But goodness, fairness, and virtue exist in Milton's theocentric universe only as they are derived from God. To love these virtues and to hate God is simply a contradiction. But Satan attempts to extradite sensibility from the origin of sense, and for that reason he loses all sense. The loss of sense, however, does not make Satan mad; it makes him ineducable. Having constituted a world where doubt—to the degree of doubting the Spirit—is an epistemological norm, Satan is in turn constituted as a being incapable of employing the spirit and judgment necessary to understand Jesus' construction of his world—the world of the spiritual kingdom within. The construction of that world is an ongoing process I have called the "dialectics of spirit." First, however, we must determine the new communicative norms governing that dialectic. For once Satan employs doubt to the degree he has, Jesus begins to employ the obscurity of enigma.

THE POETICS OF ENIGMA: A WORLD BEYOND ROME

Mary's touching maternal soliloquy delivering us from the doubts of Andrew and Simon to the certitude of Jesus' self-descent—"and at once / All his great work to come before him set"—concludes with a recollection of the last time Jesus had disappeared, at the temple in his twelfth year.

> But where delays he now? some great intent
> Conceals him: when twelve years he scarce had seen,
> I lost him, but so found, as well I saw
> He could not lose himself; but went about
> His Father's business; what he meant I mus'd,
> Since understand; much more his absence now
> Thus long to some great purpose he obscures.   (II, 95–101)

Mary's apprehension lags behind Jesus' acts and words. At his precocious claim of age twelve, she muses first then understands later what he means. At the present disappearance, she finds the significance much more perplexing. Obscurity is no small part of the career of Mary's Son. He appears at Jordan "obscure" (I, 24), and then realizes in the fullness of time that he must no longer "live obscure" (I, 287). And yet, as Mary notes, he still "obscures." Hall contemplates the paradox of obscurity and revelation in Christ's birth: "In an obscure time (the night) unto obscure men (shepherds) doth God manifest the light of his Sonne, by glorious Angels." Thomas à Kempis, in his *Imitatio Christi,* obscurely tells the would-be emulator that, if he "wilt be learned, and knowe indeede, then [he must] studie to be unknowne, and to be obscure." Thomas Fuller, commenting on the forty days Christ spent in the desert, notes that Christ was wont, after performing some eminent act, "presently to cloud himself in obscurity," and to "eclipse himself."33

I hope to penetrate a slightly different kind of obscurity here, a means Jesus has of presenting information so that it puzzles a certain portion of its audience for a certain period of time. For example, although Mary was at first puzzled at Jesus' statement that he was going about his Father's business, she eventually comes to understand its significance. Likewise in the Gospel, many of Jesus' parables will be obscure, difficult to understand, artfully teasing the auditors out of their habitual mode of thought and into another mode of comprehension. In the case of the confrontation between Satan and Jesus, Jesus presents the conditions of his kingdom in a way that is obscure to Satan because Satan has established himself in a mode of skepticism that has affected his ability to understand anything beyond the literal. This form of obscurity, this method of presenting information that is beyond the apprehension of the present audience of characters within the narrative, and available to only a limited audience of readers of the narrative, I name *the poetics of enigma.* This poetics has an unappreciated tradition, which I hope to delineate below, and is, moreover, an important element in Milton's overall poetic. I believe that an understanding of the poetics of enigma will allow us at once to appreciate the artistic method of *Paradise Regained,* to discern the characterization of Jesus in the narrative within a more sympathetic context than it has usually received, and, finally, to understand how Milton represents Satan's anagnorisis beyond the end of the narrative.

I

Of the evangelists, John delights the most in enigma. Consider the crucial scene in which Jesus is called before Pilate, at the instigation of the multitude who accuse him of calling himself "Christ a King." Pilate asks Jesus, "Art thou the King of the Jews?" In Luke, Mark, and Matthew, Jesus replies, "Thou sayest." In John, Jesus answers, "Sayest thou this thing of thyself, or did others tell it thee of me?" (xviii, 34). To this, Pilate replies that the chief priests of the nation said "this thing." Jesus renews his answers: "My kingdom is not of this world: if my kingdom were of this world, then would my servants fight, that I should not be delivered to the Jews; but now is my kingdom not from hence" (36). Pilate asks again, "Art thou a king then?" To which Jesus answers,

> Thou sayest that I am a king. To this end was I born, and for this cause came I into the world, that I should bear witness unto the truth. Every one that is of the truth heareth my voice.
> Pilate saith unto him, What is truth? (37–38)

One is not quite sure what to make of Pilate's final remark.[34] Like the rest of the relation in John's version of this incident, there is an irreducibly enigmatic substructure to the dialogue. Christ's final words, that everyone who is of the truth will hear, that is, understand his voice, allow us to infer that Pilate is not one of those elected to this knowledge. It is a statement to which there is no reply, only silent assent. John delights in the enigmatic, in the knowledge only the elect may glean. His gospel begins by reveling in the paradoxical and developing thereby a theory of the epistemology of the elect:

> He was in the world, and the world was made by him, and the world knew him not.
> He came unto his own, and his own received him not.
> But as many as received him, to them gave he power to become the sons of God, *even* to them that believe on his name.
> Which were born, not of blood, nor of the will of the flesh, nor of the will of man, but of God. (John i, 10–13)

That knowledge is allowed to the select few chosen by God is the key to the poetics of enigma; for it is the purpose of enigma to exclude from the whole of the audience the majority whose apprehension is incapable of appreciating the subtlety or orientation of the knowledge available in the enigmatic statement.

In Matthew, just before the interview with Pilate, Jesus is taken before the chief priest. Two false witnesses come and accuse Jesus: "This *fellow* said, I am able to destroy the temple of God, and to build it in three days" (xxvi, 61). The false witnesses falsely interpret the words Jesus delivers in John ii, 19. And, I hope to demonstrate, on this verse in John we may establish the precepts conditioning the poetics of enigma.

Having whipped the money changers in the temple, Jesus tells the merchants to depart and debase the temple no longer: "Make not my Father's house an house of merchandise" (John ii, 16). The narrative ensues as follows:

> Then answered the Jews and said unto him, What sign shewest thou unto us, seeing that thou doest these things?
> Jesus answered and said unto them, Destroy this temple, and in three days I will raise it up.
> Then said the Jews, Forty and six years was this temple in building, and wilt thou rear it up in three days?
> But he spake of the temple of his body.
> When therefore he was risen from the dead, his disciples remembered that he had said this unto them; and they believed the scripture, and the word which Jesus said. (ii, 18–22)

The false witnesses are the first to interpret this sequence, and the construction they put on it is possible. Christ stands before the temple when he says this, and the Jews believe that he refers to this material building. The false witnesses reiterate this belief. In the conclusion to this scene Jesus does not disabuse the Jews of their belief. The narrative voice of John informs us, the later readers, and not the Jews, proleptically of the hidden significance of Christ's enigmatic statement.

Chrysostom uses this sequence to pose and answer some questions on the nature of the understanding:

> Wherefore then did He not resolve the difficulty and say, "I speak not of that Temple, but of my flesh"? Why does the Evangelist, writing

the Gospel at a later period, interpret the saying, and Jesus keep silence at the time. Why did He so keep silence? Because they would not have received the word; for if not even the disciples were able to understand the saying, much less the multitudes.

There are, according to Chrysostom, two diverse audiences to the present scene, the disciples and the multitude. The disciples were disabled from apprehending the true sense of Christ's saying by two things: "one the fact of the Resurrection, the other, the greater question whether He was God that dwelt within; of both which things He spake darkly when He said, 'Destroy this Temple, and I will rear it up in three days'." The multitude, "because they were foolish, . . . gave no heed at all to part of what was said, and part they heard with evil frame of mind. And therefore Christ spoke to them in an enigmatic way." Aside from the two present audiences, one of whom would remain benighted because of an "evil frame of mind," the other of whom would become enlightened by the historical unfolding of Christ's life, there is also the future audience, from the evangelist John, whose interjection at verse 21 — "But he spake of the temple of his body" — was the enlightened comment of a later interpreter, to those who, according to Chrysostom, would later understand those sayings of Christ which were "not intelligible to His immediate hearers."[35]

Reading the story from a historical perspective, Augustine comments on the various audiences to Christ's statement, noting each audience's capacity for understanding:

Flesh they were, fleshly things they minded, but He was speaking spiritually. But who could understand of what temple He spake? But yet we have not far to seek; He has discovered it to us through the evangelist, he has told us of what temple He said it. "But He spake," saith the evangelist, "of the temple of His body." And it is manifest that, being slain, the Lord did rise again after three days. This is known to us all now: and if from the Jews it is concealed, it is because they stand without; yet to us it is open, because we know in whom we believe.

Here Augustine establishes two levels of enigma: the first, which is incomprehensible to the Jews in the narrative, and the second, which is beyond the knowledge of those who "stand without." Augustine elsewhere openly asserts the usefulness of enigma: "He gives us what is plain, for food; what is obscure, for exercise." Boccaccio would establish a new aesthetic on this foundation in order to defend secular poetry.[36]

The proliferation of commentaries on this scriptural passage in seventeenth-century England is worth surveying. The annotations to the translation of the gospel by Theodore Beza suggested that the Jews were given this dark answer because they requested a miracle, and it is "not good crediting them which stand only upon miracles." John Diodati cites reasons why Christ need not perform a miracle, and then asserts that the purpose of the enigmatic saying is that the understanding was meant to be referred to the future:

> Christ will not shew them any miracle, as well because the doing of it depended upon his good will and pleasure, as because that in that act which he had done, it being evidently good and laudable, there needed no extraordinary proof; and also, because they through their incredulity were unworthy of it. And therefore hee refers them to his resurrection and glorification; by which the truth of his person and office would clearly appear.

The Puritan annotators of the 1645 *Annotations* followed Chrysostom in the distinction between the disciples and the multitude: "Those things he spake, not plainly, because he knew they would not have believed, the disciples could not yet, how much lesse the vulgar?" Henry Hammond paraphrases Jesus' enigmatic statement in a way that ensures the eradication of enigma: "Jesus said unto them, The signe that is to be shown to you is this, that when you have put me to death, I now tell you, that I shall within three daies rise again." He then annotates it to explain the enigma: the Jews "mistook his [Christ's] meaning, and thought he had spoken of the Temple of Jerusalem."[37]

George Hutcheson most fully captures the spirit of Augustine and Chrysostom:

> These Jewes mistaking Christs speech, do again carp, supposing he had meant of the material Temple. But *John* cleareth Christs meaning, whereas they (as would appear) were left to their mistakes. *Whence learne*, It is Gods judgement on haters of truth, that Christ speaketh in parables to them; and that they are given up to mistakes and carp at him, and are left in their mistakes.

They are left in their mistakes, Hutcheson argues, because the obstinacy of "wicked men, and especially polluters of the House of God, will hardly be reformed, however they be convinced." Thomas Taylor writes, "Christ will not purposely make himselfe knowne to such as hee knowes will make no right use of him." And he uses parables so that "such as would not make a right of his holy doctrine, might not understand."[38]

With Calvin, as we might expect, we find the most definitive distinction between the elect who understand and the reprobate who remain ignorant because unworthy. At this juncture, Calvin writes, Christ uses an "allegorical expression." Moreover, "Christ deliberately spoke so obscurely because He reckoned them unworthy of a direct reply—just as elsewhere He declares that He speaks to them in parables because they cannot grasp the mysteries of the Kingdom in Heaven." There is a mystical quality to enigma, in that it dissipates immediately upon expression but reappears later at the fulfillment of the prophesied event: "The disciples did not understand Christ's saying; but the teaching which seemed to have vanished uselessly into thin air produced fruit in its own time." Enigma, moreover, allows Christ to exclude the unbelievers without entangling himself into a rhetoric of contempt: "He hints this [the Resurrection] figuratively because he does not judge them worthy of a clear promise. In short, He treats unbelievers as they deserve and at the same time frees Himself from all contempt."[39] For Calvin, then, enigma is both a poetics of emplotment, in allowing Christ to speak obscurely of a future event whose onset will clear the obscurity for the elect, and a poetics of characterization, in allowing Christ to condemn the reprobate without resorting to a tone of contempt.

Richard Baxter's interpretation follows the tradition in which enigma is at service to historical unfolding. He paraphrases, "He [Christ] told them enigmatically what should be after plainly expounded. Many Prophecies written darkly, are not intended to be presently understood, but when they are fulfilled."[40]

Augustine, as we saw, pointed out that the Jews were unable to comprehend Jesus' wisdom because of their carnality of mind: "*Caro erant, carnalia sapiebant.*" In the intellectual combat of flesh and spirit, or nature and grace, both flesh and nature are made blind to the ethereal wisdom which spirit and grace are able to perceive. The Cambridge Platonist, John Smith, writes, "There is an inward sweetness and deliciousness in divine Truth, which no sensual minde can tast or rellish." Those possessing "terrene minds" and "terrene affections" are blind to the beauties of divinity. There are "hidden Mysteries in Divine Truth, wrapt up one within another, which cannot be discern'd but only by divine *Epopists*." By delivering an enigmatic dictum, Christ offers a statement that is at once comprehensible to the spiritual person and incomprehensible to the carnal. Nathaniel Ward, for example, argues that the weaponry of the spirit is not only unavailable to the natural creature, but unknowable: "Now to a naturall man, spirituall weapons are like the Armour of *Saul* to *David,* hee is not acquainted with them, he knowes not how to weld them by no meanes."[41]

In the poetics of enigma, as deduced from the Judeo-Christian tradition, the characters who are unable to perceive the facts, unable to understand the spiritual significance residing in opaque statements, are unhappily relegated to the realm of obdurate reprobation. Those who comprehend only the phenomenal world are doomed never to comprehend the spiritual. Concerning the ultimate vision of that spiritual world — God — Augustine writes that "men see Him just so far as they die to this world; and so far as they live to it they see Him not." And as Richard Sibbes writes, "god delights to confound carnall wisedome."[42]

Carnal wisdom, moreover, is not only confounded; it is made representative of a type of intellectual dysfunction. The fullest and most eloquent tract on this theme is Thomas Adams's *Mysticall Bedlam*. There are, writes Adams, two types of madness: "*corporall* and *spirituall*. The object of the former is *Reason:* of the latter, *Religion*. That obsesseth the *braine,* this the *heart*." The second of these affects all three faculties of mind, the understanding, reason, and will. "*Spirituall madnesse* is a depravation, or almost deprivation of all these faculties, *quod coelestia;* so farre as they extend to heavenly things." In this inability to comprehend the spiritual heavenly things of the world, in remaining attentive to only the sensible world, the person spiritually mad careens toward a doom of nonsense. Calvin also traces the path from malignancy to hardness of heart to madness. Sin is punished, William Perkins likewise notes, within the soul by a terrible sequence of "trembling of conscience, care, trouble, hardnes of heart, and madnesse." Elsewhere, he writes, "every offence imprints a blot in the soule . . . till the light of nature be extinguished, & men come to a reprobate sense." Joseph Hall notes that sin "dimmeth and dazeleth the eie, that it cannot behold spirituall things."[43]

Fallen angels are prime examples of spiritual madness. Hall points out that, though they know much, yet "they are kept off from those divine illuminations," that is, the illuminations into the "invisible world" as it is discovered to "spiritual eyes." Fallen angels, Henry Lawrence writes in his history, are unable to "see things, as the good Angells and holy people doe, (to wit) the beauty of holinesse, the evill of sin, the lovelinesse of God in Christ, the glory of God, as Father to his elect, such sights as might gaine and winne them to God, they are perfectly blinde in, and understand nothing of."[44] Such reflection, of course, is more good evidence for suggesting, as I did in the second chapter, that the position we as auditors of *Paradise Regained* are expected to occupy is that of the good angels.

Calvin, we noticed, saw in the art of enigma a means for Jesus to condemn the reprobate without using a tone of contempt. Bernard saw in Christ's tone to the malignant multitude an example of confuting by courtesy:

> Hee heard the Sophisticall and subtle questions of the Scribes and Pharises, and taught them to see their errors, but they were wilfully blinde, and rejected his wholesome doctrine: and lest hee should seeme unto them to checke them in a fit of his fury, and to reprehend them in the heat of his choller, hee confuted their grosse infidelitie and venemous malice with great lenitie and much patience.

It must be noted, however, that Bernard is meditating on Christ in the Passion week, a period in which Jesus exercised only his meekness. At other points in Christ's career, as we noted above, he is not patient; his whipping the money changers is but one example. Daniel Tuvil, citing a passage in which the Pharisees question Jesus, notes that Christ answers those who approach him in the mood of "a deceitfull and captious interrogatorie" with a "Dilemma," a "two-edged argument" with which he cuts the "throate of their inquisitivenesse." Hall, elaborating on the episode of the woman taken in adultery, observes that "sometimes taciturnity and contempt are the best answers." There are times when Christ responds, William Perkins notes, with "indignation and detestation." Although Christ mostly uses a reasonable, meek, and modest tone,

Thomas Taylor adds, he can be roused to anger to demonstrate the "hatefulnesse and detestation of that sinne of idolatrie."[45]

To sum up, then, we have noted how the art of enigma makes accessible to the elect who have spiritual vision and faith an insight into the world of futurity and redemption while excluding the reprobate lacking such vision and faith from that purview. The carnality of mind the reprobate suffers disallows him or her clarity of vision into the heavenly world. And the poetics of enigma is directly related to how one perceives Christ's tone, ranging from Calvin, who hears nothing harsh in it, to Hall, who notes the cadences of contempt.

II

Milton criticism has also noted a variety of tones in the Jesus of *Paradise Regained,* from the alleged "coldness" of his replies to the "wittiness" of his answers. Georgia Christopher traces the variety of tonal fluctuation ranging "from plaintive bewilderment to icy reticence to flaming denunciation." Critics as diverse as A. E. Dyson, Hilaire Belloc, and W. W. Robson have used the word "rude" to describe Milton's Jesus. E.M.W. Tillyard, attending to the rejection of Athens, complains of the "tone of anger" for which he fails "to make dramatic propriety or historical precedent account."[46] With this critical debate in mind, and also our present concern with the poetics of enigma, we may now turn to Milton's prose to see how he develops a theory of the usefulness and proper occasion for obscurity.

The *Tetrachordon* seems to me to contain Milton's most cogent statements on the art of hermeneutics, and on what is now called narratology. Because of the controversial subject, divorce, and his hope to reform the tradition of interpreting the "foure chief places in Scripture, which treat of Mariage, or nullities in Mariage," Milton elaborates the decorum of his interpretive creed with admirable clarity. The first thing an interpreter must do, he notes, is to pay regard to the perspective of each speaker and thereby grant each due authority. In the case of Genesis, for example, when God and Adam differ, we must remember that "*Adam* spake like *Adam*" while "God spake like God" (CM IV, p. 93). And Christ, as we shall note shortly, speaks like Christ.

The text is Matthew xix, 3–12. The scene is Judea, the cast a multitude of Pharisees and Jesus. The Pharisees "came unto him, tempting him, and saying unto him, Is it lawful for a man to put away his wife for every cause?" (Matt. iii, 3). Milton interprets, "The manner of these men comming to our Saviour, not to learne, but to tempt him, may give us to expect that their answer will bee such as is fittest for them, not so much a teaching, as an intangling" (CM IV, p. 141). There is a lesson here for every educator, Milton deduces. Act with innocence and attempt to educate your fellow human beings until they demonstrate a marked tendency to deceive you. Then you must put on a wiser countenance.

> No man though never so willing or so well enabl'd to instruct, but if he discerne his willingnesse and candor made use of to intrapp him, will suddainly draw in himselfe, and laying aside the facil vein of perspicuity, will know his time to utter clouds and riddles.

This is the essence of the poetics of enigma. And the audience to whom it is most directed, the opponents of Christ—in this instance the Pharisees—are treated thus because of their obdurate unwillingness to learn and their evil motivation to corrupt.

Milton then interprets Christ's answer to the Pharisees within the context the narrative demands. The statements Christ makes are enigmatic because the audience to whom they are directed, *in the context of the narrative,* are undeserving of anything more.

> Christ stirr'd up in his spirit against these tempting Pharises, answer'd them in a certain forme of indignation usual among good authors; wherby the question, or the truth is not directly answer'd, but som thing which is fitter for them, who aske, to heare. . . . So Christ being demanded maliciously why *Moses* made the law of divorce, answers them in a vehement *scheme,* not telling them the cause why he made it, but what was fittest to be told them, that *for the hardnes of their hearts* he suffer'd them to abuse it. (CM IV, p. 168)

I have italicized *the context of the narrative* for a reason. The poetics of enigma may superficially seem to be a new name for an old idea—dramatic irony—where the audience, having knowledge superior to the actors, looks on the scene with something akin to omniscience and fully appreciates the irony of actions which the performers commit possessing only partial knowledge. But there is a profound difference, and it is worth noting here.

Were this scene of Christ and the Pharisees only a dramatic situation, for example, we would presuppose only a limited context outside the world of the drama. The dramatist generally assumes an audience comprised of people equally capable of appreciating the irony of his characters' actions. But the poetics of enigma does not posit such an homogeneous audience. Besides the characters within the context of the scene — Jesus and the Pharisees — there are characters within the context of the audience — the elect who understand the residing spirit and the reprobate who interpret with carnal literalness. Within the dogma of reprobation and election, the poetics of enigma would seem a fit vehicle for Christian narrative art. It may appear less humane than Shakespearean drama, and in large part this is true, but we are dealing here with a poet whose humanity was based first and foremost on his Christianity, and the dogma of election is implicit in Christianity, although Milton, as we have seen, tempers it with his distinctive form of humanism.

Because the scene between the Pharisees and Jesus was not merely dramatic, Milton, following Augustine especially, does not assume an audience homogeneously capable of understanding the scene's significance. So, not only does Milton note that Christ answers the Pharisees with "the *trope* of indignation, fittest account for such askers," but Milton himself answers the reprobate hermeneut with similar indignation, as he describes the

> vulgar expositor [who,] beset with contradictions and absurdities round, and resolving at any peril to make an exposition of it, as there is nothing more violent and boistrous then a reverend ignorance in fear to be convicted, rushes brutely and impetuously against all the principles both of nature, piety and moral goodnes; and in the fury of his literal expounding overturns [the many ways of understanding how God allowed liberty for divorce].

Milton later calls these hapless expositors "crabbed *masorites* of the Letter, as not to mollifie a transcendence of literal rigidity," and the individual of that rabble an "obdurat *Cyclops*, to have but one eye for this text" (CM IV, pp. 169, 174).[47]

The reception to *Tetrachordon* did nothing to mollify Milton's opinion of the interpreting population. His *Sonnet XI*, "On the Detraction Which Followed Upon My Writing Certain Treatises," records that though the treatise "walk'd the Town a while, / Numb'ring good intellects," it no longer or seldom is "por'd on" in this age of ignorance and bigotry. His next sonnet, "On the Same," characterizes more fully the audience which did not number among the good intellects:

> I did but prompt the age to quit their clogs
> By the known rules of ancient liberty,
> When straight a barbarous noise environs me
> Of Owls and Cuckoos, Asses, Apes, and Dogs.
> . . . .
> But this is got by casting Pearl to Hogs
> That bawl for freedom in their senseless mood,
> And still revolt when truth would set them free.
> License they mean when they cry liberty;
> For who loves that, must first be wise and good;
> But from that mark how far they rove we see.   (1–4, 8–13)

Milton's England, it turned out, had more Pharisees than Miltons. And the lesson was not lost on him. By his thirty-eighth year, in 1646, Milton believed in only the church of one, the church of "Ioannes Miltonvs Anglvs." For our present interest, the publication of *Tetrachordon,* which is itself a condemnation of the reception of *The Doctrine and Discipline of Divorce,* marked an alteration in Milton's conception of the natural human capacity to interpret both Holy Scriptures and his writings. Henceforth Milton knew, appreciated, and accounted for the different interpretive constructions capable of being put on linguistic structures. Though Milton addressed the hieratic auditor, he knew the demotic would also signify: "And what the people but a herd confus'd." Henceforth, it is safe to say, Milton bid his muse, "fit audience find though few."

Few phrases could so succinctly summarize the credo behind the poetics of enigma, and coming, as it does, in the middle of the poem, it alerts us to the fact that Milton did not believe all readers of *Paradise Lost* equally capable of comprehending the significance transcending the poem's "literal rigidity." For the twentieth-century critic, this may be an unpleasant reminder of a theology which, whether the terms *reprobation* (Calvin) or *preterition* (More) were used to describe its active exclusion, seemed not to hesitate in declaring fit a scheme in which the majority of humans were doomed to existential ignorance and immortal suffering.[48] The semblance between Calvin and Milton, however, is deceptive, for while Calvin held predestination to operate from eternity, Milton held that everyone received potential "at least sufficient for attaining knowledge of the truth and final salvation." As I pointed out in the previous section of this chapter, Milton emphasizes the essential difference between reprobation and obduracy, the former being something foreign to true Christian doctrine and presupposing an absence of grace determined from eternity, while the latter is based on an economic principle in which in the same measure as grace is denied the punishment of obduracy is applied (CM XIV, pp. 146–47).[49]

Within the pale of the poetics of enigma, then, Milton's terms of predestination are more humane than Calvin's. Christ still makes enigmatic statements, and they are still incomprehensible to the multitude, be they Jewish or Pharisaical, but the incomprehension, Milton makes clear, is based on an opportunity for knowledge that the multitude had hitherto squandered. Present ignorance presupposes previous malice.

So when Milton turns his attention to the scriptural passage upon which the poetics of enigma may be established, John ii, 19, he follows the tradition in his usual reforming way. Where Christ "spake briefly and enigmatically, without explaining his meaning to enemies who were unworthy of a fuller answer," Milton argued, Christ also "thought it unnecessary to mention the power of the Father" (CM XIV, pp. 236–37). Milton applies the poetics of enigma, characteristically, to strengthen his Arian arguments.

The following important themes should be kept in mind as we turn to *Paradise Regained:* (1) Milton's dismissal of reprobation in favor of a theory of obduracy based on unwillingness to accept saving knowledge potentially available to all; (2) Milton's use of the poetics of enigma to demonstrate the *effects* of the hardening of the heart; (3) Milton's use of the poetics of enigma to justify his interpretation of those scriptural passages traditionally applied to the anti-Arian case; (4) the doctrinal presuppositions of Milton's call for a "fit audience"; and (5) Milton's perception regarding the tone Christ employs in the situation of duress.

III

Milton cites the case of Christ's answer to the Pharisees in order to propose both how enigmatic statements are applied to confuse the obdurate audience and how enigmatic statements must alert the careful expositor to ascend to the spiritual significance of that statement. Jesus spoke, Milton writes,

> in that fiercenes and abstruse intricacy, first to amuse his tempters and admonish in general the abusers of that Mosaic law; . . . [and] that his Disciples and all good men might learne to expound him in this place, as in all other his precepts, not by the written letter, but by that unerring paraphrase of Christian love and Charity, which is the summe of all commands, and the perfection.

This is the call of the poetics of enigma: (1) comprehending the form of discourse in which the auditor is unable to apprehend the "abstruse intricacy"; and (2) defining the "fit audience"—that reader who approaches the poetry armed with the capacity to use the "unerring paraphrase of Christian love and Charity" in order to transcend the "literal rigidity" and appreciate the spiritual quality of the verse. Moreover, the characters within the scene and the expositors outside it are interdependent. The Pharisees are "amused"— and "amused" here means "confounded" (OED, 2)—because they literally interpret Mosaic Law under the covenant of grace. The expositor who sympathizes with the Pharisees, the reader who is too literal to appreciate the spirit residing in the text, will likewise be amused (CM IV, p. 186).[50]

The prototype of the literal-minded Pharisee is, of course, Satan. John Gumbleden, for instance, catalogues the scribes, Pharisees, Jews, priests, elders, Judas, the false witnesses, Herod, Caiphas, and Pilate as Satan's "fit instruments." Perkins and Taylor also suggest that Jesus is tried by "Satans instruments." Lawrence writes, "As he dealt with the Divell in himself, so he dealt with the Divell in the Scribes and Pharises . . . So hee answered them, and confounded them."[51] Keeping in mind, then, the tone and fate appropriate to the literal-minded, we come to *Paradise Regained.*

Satan and Jesus have interpretive creeds that are as different as flesh from spirit, as malice from candor. I have argued in the previous section that the important moment in defining each one's hermeneutic style is Satan's autobiographical confession. While Satan's interpretations are "Ambiguous and with double sense deluding," Jesus' interpretation is singular and sufficient.[52] Whereas Satan repudiates the Spirit residing in the dove and in Jesus, Jesus recognizes the Spirit in the symbol and evinces the Spirit within himself in his conversation (I, 83, 91–93). Satan is allowed to see the Baptism in order to see the Spirit descend in the form of a dove, but he chooses to ignore the spiritual significance and attend only to the literal vehicle. In this choice, he shows his malice and is punished thereafter with obduracy.

Relating the story of Job, Satan tells a partial truth, that he tempted Job when God bid him to do so. Jesus recognizes Satan's motivation, the "malice" that moved him to misdeem Job originally (I, 368–70, 424–26). Malice, Thomas Taylor notes, drives Satan to "aggravating with vehemency of words, facts or speeches, which charity would give a favourable construction unto."[53] Candor, Milton writes, is the opposing virtue, "whereby we cheerfully acknowledge the gifts of God in our neighbour, and interpret all words and actions in a favorable sense" (CM XVII, p. 311).

Raphael tells Adam the narratives of the War in Heaven and the Creation in juxtaposition in order to allow Adam to choose between the destructive energy of Satan and the creative spirit of the Son. In this narrative, the battle is one of interpretation, and the juxtaposed modes of apprehension between which the reader must choose are carnal malice and spiritual candor. The choice is allowed the reader when, at the silencing of one oracle, another is given voice. Jesus proclaims,

> God hath now sent his living Oracle
> Into the World, to teach his final will,
> And sends his Spirit of Truth henceforth to dwell
> In pious Hearts, an inward Oracle
> To all truth requisite for men to know.   (I, 460–64)

This dual threshold, the emergence of the living oracle "now sent" and the inward oracle "henceforth to dwell," suggests that both Jesus, in the temptations he will be offered, and the readers, who will watch him encounter and defeat the tempter, are endued with the "Spirit of Truth" or the spirit enabling us to recognize the Spirit of Truth.[54]

In the scriptural story upon which the poetics of enigma is based, Christ answered the Jews regarding the temple and prophesied his resurrection; so Jesus, in this narrative, answers Satan in prophetic and enigmatic fashion. The reader, possessing the inward spiritual oracle, is able to comprehend the significance of these enigmatic answers, and, in the various answers to the offer of the kingdoms, the reader finds the establishment of Jesus' spiritual kingdom. Let us examine, then, the temptation of the kingdoms.

To Satan's offer of Israel, Jesus replies that he will wait on God's time. Jesus concludes this speech with five rapid questions:

> But what concerns it thee when I begin
> My everlasting Kingdom, why art thou
> Sollicitous, what moves thy inquisition?
> Know'st thou not that my rising is thy fall,
> And my promotion will be thy destruction?
>
> (III, 198–202)

The rapidity and poignancy of the questions leave Satan "inly rackt," and his reply is interesting, mostly because Jesus does not answer it. The critical debate concerns Satan's rhetoric, whether, as Stein notes, the passage evinces his sincerity, or, as Lewalski notes, manipulates it. The passage, it seems to me, is riddled with contradictions. Satan says he has no hope, yet he is hopeful (204, 214). He says he has no fear, yet he is fearful (205, 220). He wishes to reach his ultimate repose, yet expects Jesus' reign to prevent that (209–10, 215–22). Satan wishes to reach his ultimate repose, and expects Jesus' reign will effect that (209–10, 223–26). He has somewhat conflated the issues of his ultimate end with Jesus' kingship, but also separated them ("whether thou / Raign or raign not"). The contradictions riddle the speech, and, I must admit, make one doubt its sincerity.[55] The speech is not an easy one to assess; its tone is undoubtedly artful, yet one is reluctant to deny any latent sincerity it may have.

One does not need to choose between Stein and Lewalski because their readings are not incompatible. There is, as Stein notes, a genuinely moving rhythm controlling the speech. But there is also, as Lewalski notes, a sense of "appalling apprehension" as we realize that Satan is manipulating his own emotions to lead into another temptation.[56] I believe the speech reveals Satan's confusion, his inability now to understand anything about the kingdom Jesus is to found. He does not know whether the kingdom will lead to his end, his salvation, his fear, his hope, his deposition, or his triumphant return to the fold. There is rhetoric at work, but there is more confusion, the response to the enigmatic questions of the kingdom about which Satan has so little understanding.

To the offer of Parthia, Jesus makes the distinction between the logic he follows and the logic the world follows. The armed force of Parthia is, he tells Satan, "Plausible to the world, to me worth naught" (III, 392). It is the "world" Satan represents. The carnal kingdoms he offers, the carnal interpretations he makes of spiritually significant things, reveal the logic by which he discerns the world. But to Jesus these things are worthless. His is a logic governed by another orientation. The logic by which Jesus interprets the temptations, by which he interprets everything presented to his mind in this narrative, is theocentric. He concluded his autobiographical soliloquy with an absolute reliance on God's informing power: "What concerns my knowledge God reveals." In the course of each temptation but one, Jesus refers to God. In the case of Parthia, as in the case of Israel, he leaves the founding of the kingdom "To his due time and providence" (III, 439).

I refer to Jesus' theocentricity now so we may appreciate the significance of the sole speech Jesus makes which has no reference to God. The concluding verses of that reply contain the most pointedly enigmatic statement Jesus makes:

> Know therefore when my season comes to sit
> On *David's* Throne, it shall be like a tree
> Spreading and over-shadowing all the Earth,
> Or as a stone that shall to pieces dash
> All Monarchies besides throughout the world,
> And of my Kingdom shall be no end:
> Means there shall be to this, but what the means,
> Is not for thee to know, nor me to tell.   (IV, 146–53)

As noted above, Milton thought that when Christ "spake briefly and enigmatically, without explaining his meaning to enemies who were unworthy of a fuller answer," Christ also "thought it unnecessary to mention the power of the Father." For the power of the Father has effectively allowed the Son and the fit reader to apprehend the kingdom whose inner means is beyond Satan's knowledge.[57]

Jesus' most confident statement, which is also his most enigmatic, comes in his answer to the offer of Rome. Not only is Rome the only historically relevant kingdom offered to Jesus, it is also the epitome of a kingdom suffering the tyranny of an intemperate leader. Jesus lives and dies under the kingdom of Rome and under the rule of Tiberius. Rome represents what for Milton constituted historically and presently the greatest compromises of Christianity. "Popery," we recall, is one of the two things which Milton does not grant freedom of press to in *Areopagitica* (the other being whatever is impious or absolutely evil). By rejecting Rome, Jesus refuses to allocate for himself, and therefore limit himself to, a local historical epoch. Rome, Virgil had prophesied some fifty years before the action of *Paradise Regained* takes place, was to last forever: "No limits have I fix'd, of time, or place, / To the vast empire of the godlike race." In the reign of Augustus's carnal and lascivious stepson, Jesus is born, a king who will instill the spirit into another kingdom, and whose kingdom shall be of the spirit. In this poem, set in 29 a.d., and which purposely echoes the Virgilian beginning of the *Aeneid*, that political poem of national aetiology, Jesus repudiates the Virgilian dream, rejecting Rome as carnal ("vile and base"), and choosing the spiritual kingdom truly limitless.[58]

As Thomas Greene has recently argued, Rome represented for the Renaissance its own alien face. Writers as diverse as Joachim Du Bellay and Ben Jonson responded to the image of Rome with what Greene defines as a "double gesture" akin to a pathological act. The figure who responded most fully and with the greatest sense of need to the face of Rome was, of course, Petrarch. He, according to Greene, pursued a deeper historical reality beneath what were frankly unpromising modern appearances by essentially "reading" an order into the Roman wilderness and the Roman ruins. Petrarch's gesture is rightly praised by Greene as the first step in establishing the basis of a radical critique of his culture— "not the critique that points to a subversion of declared ideals, but rather the kind that calls ideals themselves into question." That radical critique begins in what Greene calls Petrarch's "creative inquisitions" of the landscape and history of Rome. By imagining the possibility of a cultural alternative, Petrarch set the standard for appreciating the depths of time, and he set the image of the Renaissance as an age of archaeology, of disinterment.[59] When Milton turns his attention to Rome, at what has been characterized as the end of the Renaissance, he finds a different way of posing a radical critique of his culture. Not only because of religious affiliation but also because of his deeply ambivalent feelings about Rome, Milton uses the city to establish the enigmatic core of the spiritual kingdom. In the answer to the offer of Rome, Jesus reaches the depth of enigma; beyond this—which, after all, for Milton in 1671 would have been the place Satan would have been most comfortable—there is no greater puzzle. Satan, like many people in Rome, this grandson of an adamant recusant must have thought, has willed himself into a state of blindness that cannot be answered. Because of this, the construction of the spiritual kingdom works *through* him.

The enigmatic distich concluding Jesus' speech—"Means there shall be to this, but what the means, / Is not for thee to know, nor me to tell"—is a fit answer in terms of the poetics of enigma we have traced. By answering the offer of Rome directly with an enigmatic and elevated counteroffer, whose means of establishment are beyond Satan's comprehension, Jesus states for the final time in the narrative the time and means for the founding of his kingdom. The time is in God's hands—the season will make itself manifest—and the means is in the inner being. The irony, it seems to me, is that whereas Jesus says now that he must be reticent about the means, the whole of the temptation sequence preceding this enigmatic statement has been just such an elaboration of that means. The answer of internal government, of internal liberty, in sum, of the kingdom within, has been unfolded in the dialogue between the two adversaries in the desert. Temperance, love of God, obedience, patience, virtue with humility: are not these the means of establishing the kingdom within? Michael, we recall, tells Adam that the means of possessing the "paradise within" is through faith, virtue, patience, temperance, and charity (*PL* XII, 581–87). Moreover, the inward oracle graciously granted to us in Book I signifies that we might comprehend those virtues so beyond Satan's sense.

In conclusion, then, we might cast a skeptical glance at the critical theory that *Paradise Regained* is, in the words of Earl Miner, a "detective story," and suggest, instead, how fully it participates in the tradition of the poetics of enigma. If Milton, as Elizabeth Marie Pope suggests, "was working under the influence of the tradition that Christ deliberately withheld from Satan all evidence of his identity," then quite simply Milton failed, or, what I would argue is more plausible, Milton failed to be sufficiently influenced. To the offer of the kingdoms, Jesus taunts Satan:

> And dar'st thou to the Son of God propound
> To worship thee accurst
> . . . .
> Wert thou so void of fear or shame,
> As offer them to me the Son of God,
> To me my own.   (IV, 178–91)

This is hardly withholding of evidence. The theory that this poem is a detective story has reigned in critical history for as long as any other misconception in Milton studies, and it is, moreover, one of the great hindrances to appreciating Milton's mind. The revelations at the Baptism, at the offer of the banquet, and here, do not lead one to conclude that Jesus was hiding his identity from Satan. Rather, given the manifest clarity of the Son's declarations of his Sonship, might we not be better advised to ask how it is that Satan manages to maintain a posture of ignorance in the face of all this evidence? We might indeed give up the idea of the detective story theory and attempt to observe more closely the inner workings of Satan's epistemological dysfunction.[60]

But in terms of the poetics of enigma, we find nothing dissatisfying in the evidence before us, considering we have traced a precedent tradition, a Miltonic justification of that tradition, and, arguably, an application of that tradition in this narrative. Satan has willed himself into a state of carnal wisdom and is incorrigibly bound by that limited mode of perception, so bound, indeed, that the fittest answer for him is enigmatic. The difference between treating the poem within the one tradition—that Christ deliberately withheld from Satan all evidence of his identity—and the other—that because Satan has willed himself to folly, his career is one of unimpeded ignorance in terms of spiritual things—is the difference between Calvin and Milton. Moreover, the second tradition, which I have called the poetics of enigma, makes sense of Jesus' obscurity in a framework where he is not always obscure (as in his forthright statement that he is the Son of God). Because Satan had wasted the potential opportunity he had to recognize the Spirit latent in Jesus and the dove, he falls into a mental dysfunction, an inability to apprehend the spiritual significance of statements Jesus makes thereafter. In this way, Jesus does not have to withhold his identity from Satan because Satan will not understand it. Even after Jesus states outright that he is the Son of God, Satan's sense is duplicitous: the term, for him, "bears no single sence" (IV, 514). There is, then, a certain dynamic quality to the narrative — not a melodramatic one in which the villain learns the identity of the hero, but one in which he who wills himself to ignorance careers to nonsense. This is arguably the typical Miltonic narrative process. The "delusion" the fallen angels suffer in Book X is "like in punishment, / As in thir crime" (544–45). Finally, the poetics of enigma allows Milton to demonstrate his characteristic concern for the "fit audience," those readers who respond to Jesus' refined sense of spirit with the unerring paraphrase of Christian charity.

At the temple, Jesus confounds the Jews while enlightening future Christians. For the Jews, as for the false witnesses, the temple is the material building in this carnal world. For the later Christians, the temple is the body of Christ, that mystical form whose death and resurrection is the basis of faith — the temple of the "upright heart and pure." Foretelling the Resurrection obscurely, Christ's statement at the temple, as Calvin put it, seemed to have vanished uselessly only to bear fruit in its own time. For paradise to be regained, Satan, Milton says, must be foiled, defeated, and repulsed. William Cowper writes that the early career of Christ, comprising his genealogy, his baptism, and his temptation,

> makes up unto us a complete doctrine of Christian comfort. . . . In his Genealogie, we have seene what manner a man Christ Jesus is. In his Baptisme we have learned, how hee is become ours; and now in his tentation wee see, how he begins to worke the worke of Satans confusion, and our Redemption.[61]

Satan's confusion plays no small part in regaining paradise in Milton's narrative.

The spiritual significance is wholly clear to the spiritually minded, Augustine said, and wholly obscure to the carnally minded. Irony in *Paradise Regained* is most manifest when the "Spiritual Foe" looks with unfeigned repugnance at Jesus, the man "enshrin'd / In fleshly Tabernacle" through whose "lineaments" only glimpses of spirit shine, and asks querulously, "What dost thou in this World?" What Jesus is doing in this world, he might have answered Satan, but only if he had any desire to be explicit, is establishing a constitution—his new law, his body—that is answerable to Satan's old constitution and will supersede Satan's old world order. The way he will do so, in the final assessment, is by articulating a spiritual, internal kingdom. Moreover, his articulating the conditions of that kingdom is both an answer to Satan's contentions and beyond Satan's comprehension. For that reason, I must say that Jesus' new constitution is built upon a dialogic confrontation with Satan but also transcends the materials of that confrontation as well as Satan's epistemic capacity. I have termed this process of transmuting the materials of Satan's offers into a spiritual kingdom the *dialectics of spirit*. At the heart of this dialectic is an ethics of communication that relies on our understanding of the three modes of thought I have outlined so far.

First of all, the dialectics is based on the same sort of mental movement that governed meditation—the interiorization and elevation of earthly materials in an act of transforming contemplation. In the case of *Paradise Regained,* what Jesus does is what Milton ascribes to him in *A Treatise of Civil Power:* "Christ's government . . . deals only with the inward man and his actions, which are all spiritual and to outward force not lyable . . . [H]is spiritual kingdom [is] able without worldly force to subdue all the powers and kingdoms of this world" (CM VI, p. 20). We will see, literally, in the second temptation the ways that Jesus does just that—*by thinking on* the kingdoms. In order for that thinking to have any meaning, however, we must be sure that Jesus actually does perceive and apprehend in all its significance each offer of Satan. That, in Milton studies, is a point of some contention, which I'll deal with below. Secondly, this dialectics is the final mode of apprehension following upon the modes of skepticism and enigmatics. As I suggested above, according to Milton's soteriology, any being who lapses to a degree of doubt that reaches blasphemy against the Holy Spirit is unalterably reprobate. Satan had demonstrated his skepticism in defiance of spiritual evidence and thereby doomed himself to a state of existential ignorance. Confronted then with an antagonist who was unwilling and is now unable to accept spiritual significations, Jesus begins to answer him with enigmatic replies. Jesus uses enigma as a way of reconstituting material things into spiritual. His riddles allow the disciples to understand—indeed, to bring to consciousness historically—the idea that the spiritual temple of the soul has a reality above the physical temple of Jerusalem. What the following section will argue is that Jesus, having employed a form of skepticism to work out a theosophic logic, and then having deployed a form of enigmatics to situate that logic within the material of Satan's offers, will finally produce an internal kingdom by applying a bi-level dialectic to his confrontation with Satan.

THE DIALECTICS OF SPIRIT: A WORLD BEYOND THE WORLD

Part of the reason Milton came to believe in the efficacy of enigma was that he came to disbelieve that his fellow citizens had homogeneously equipotent hermeneutical abilities. The historical time during which he lost that faith was, of course, the divorce controversy of 1644–45. What he perceived as idiotic responses to what he felt was an intelligent reading of the gospel's intention regarding the potential grounds for divorce caused him not only to repent having written the divorce tracts in the vernacular, but also caused him to controvert his earlier position about the innate capacity of any human being to understand the Truth. It might prove worthwhile to return to that earlier Milton to discern the sort of epistemology he proposed before he came to discredit certain human abilities. The passage most worth noting is the happy and justly famous one from *Of Reformation*, where Milton argues against those who maintain that the "obscurity" of the Bible is enough reason to turn instead to the patristic writers for clarification:

> The very essence of Truth is plainnesse, and brightnes; the darknes and crookednesse is our own. The *Wisdom* of *God* created *understanding*, fit and proportionable to Truth the object, and end of it, as the eye to the thing visible. If our *understanding* have a film of *ignorance* over it, or be blear with gazing on other false glitterings, what is that to Truth? If we will but purge with sovrain eyesalve that intellectual ray which *God* hath planted in us, then we would beleeve the Scriptures protesting their own plainnes, and perspicuity, calling to them to be instructed, not only the *wise*, and *learned*, but the *simple*, the

poor, the *babes,* foretelling an extraordinary effusion of *Gods* Spirit upon every age, and sexe, attributing to all men, and requiring from them the ability of searching, trying, examining all things, and by the Spirit discerning that which is good. (CM III, p. 33; cf. YP I, p. 566)[62]

Three years later, Milton would still maintain many of the same metaphors and many of the same sentiments. In *Areopagitica,* published in November 1644, Milton still felt that the bleariness of eye—by then phrased as "our eyes blear'd and dimm'd with prejudice and custom"—could be but a partial hindrance to discerning Truth. The activities of searching, trying, and examining would still be those efforts of "musing, searching, [and] revolving new notions" in the later tract.

One potential difference might be the way Truth is represented in the two tracts. In the first tract, Truth was to be discerned by the fit understanding of any person regardless of age, station, or sex; in the second, Truth seems to be a self-sufficient entity capable of fighting its own "wars" and needing no discerning of any sort. Milton hints at this prospect in the earlier tract when he asks what relationship exists between human cognitive limits and divine verity—"what is that to Truth?"—but there is nonetheless a marked difference when he poses that question in the later tract: "Who ever knew Truth put to the wors, in a free and open encounter?" The difference is that whereas Truth is presented as an "object" in *Of Reformation,* it possesses its own subjectivity in the latter tract. Of course, we cannot make too much of such local differences in the representation of Truth. Truth is still presented as an object of inquiry in *Areopagitica,* although we should not disregard the ways Truth is also presented as a subject of inquiry in this same tract. Within a few months, the most significant differences would appear between the early Milton, who believed the Spirit worked in all manner of people, and the late Milton, who believed in a much more discriminating Spirit. The one constant, however, is that the Spirit is still the agency by which "good" is discerned, and that remains a constant throughout Milton's life. So when we examine the famous metaphor in *Areopagitica* of the construction of the "Temple of the Lord," we find that what Milton has in mind for the building of the "great reformation" is something he calls "spirituall architecture" (CM IV, pp. 350, 347, 342). In *Paradise Regained,*

what Milton has in mind is something like a "spiritual constitution," for the last epic is Milton's final assay at demonstrating the
dialectic by which the Spirit may reveal the art of self-government.
Because, put bluntly, paradise in *Paradise Regained* is a kingdom;
and in the temptation to the kingdoms, we find how it may be
regained and governed anew.

I

"My kingdom," Christ tells Pilate, "is not of this world" (John
xviii, 36). To his disciples, he says, "the kingdom of God is within
you" (Luke xvii, 21; cf. Rom. xiv, 17). It was the height of impru-
dence, John Gumbleden wrote, for Satan to offer to Jesus *"all the
Kingdoms of the world,* whose *Kingdome* is not of this *world."* Even
more curious is the fact that Milton should develop the offer of the
kingdoms so fully in his narrative of the temptations, indeed to the
degree that Satan offers each of the kingdoms individually, then *in
toto,* causing some critics to wonder at the wisdom of Satan's or
Milton's economy.[63] Whether the redundancy of the offers is decor-
ous or not, Milton, in the offer of the kingdoms, establishes a code
of internal government through the spirit of the second Adam
countereffective to the carnal lapse of the first. When Adam falls,
the terms in which Milton describes his internal being are borrowed from politics:

> Thir inward State of Mind, calm Region once
> And full of Peace, now toss't and turbulent:
> For Understanding rul'd not, and the Will
> Heard not her lore, both in subjection now
> To sensual Appetite, who from beneath
> Usurping over sovran Reason claim'd
> Superior sway.   (*PL* IX, 1125–31)

The Fall of humanity was the fall of an internal political system, an
insurrection within the government Bunyan called "Mansoul." When
Michael describes the postapostolic times of superstition and idolatry to Adam, he uses political terms to express the new legality.
The "carnal power" shall appropriate under pretense "Spiritual
Laws" on every conscience; but the "Spirit within" shall direct the
faithful beyond the confining forms set by this secular rule (XII,
515–24). The external and internal governments are conflated here,

and it is difficult to say whether Mansoul or Israel is being described. And when Michael concludes the lesson, he promises Adam a "paradise within," attainable through virtue, patience, temperance, and charity (XII, 575–87). As angel and man descend from the "top / Of Speculation" Michael has counseled Adam to forego sidereal knowledge in favor of visceral. This is the last mount in *Paradise Lost,* but not the ultimate mountain in Milton's poetic career.

Gumbleden noted that there are four important peaks in the life of Christ, the first being the mountain from which Jesus views the kingdoms. The rest follow in order: "our Saviour Christ himself, not long after his *tempting preached* on a *Mount;* and after that, was *transfigured* on a *Mount;* and last of all, *Ascended* into Heaven from a *Mount.*"[64] Jesus chooses, in each instance, a natural mount from which to aspire even higher (beyond nature), and in each case with a degree of transforming spirit: by words in the sermon on the mount, by typological fulfillment in the transfiguration on the mount, and by atonement in the Ascension. The third of these mounts is most useful for our purposes here.

In the transfiguration, Christ communes with Moses and Elias, both of whom are invoked in the narrative. In "the Mount," Jesus answers Satan's first temptation,

> *Moses* was forty days, nor eat nor drank,
> And forty days *Eliah* without food
> Wandred this barren waste, the same I now. (I, 351–54)

In terms of historical progression, the Temptation was seen by almost all commentators as the fulfillment of the types of Moses and Elias (Luke ix, 28–37; Mark ix, 2–13; Matt. xvii, 1–13). So Thomas Taylor writes, "As *Moses* fasted 40. dayes at the institution of the law, and *Elias* at the restitution of it, so would Christ here at the manifestation of the Gospel."[65] A new covenant is established at the end of the fast, and the spiritual constitution of the kingdom toward which this covenant leads is drafted in this second temptation, on this first of the mounts in the life of Jesus. The second mount fulfills the type of the first hill, described as the highest in Eden:

> Not higher that Hill nor wider looking round,
> Whereon for different cause the Tempter set
> Our second *Adam* in the Wilderness,
> To show him all Earth's Kingdoms and thir Glory.
>
> (XI, 381–84)[66]

I would like to argue that the second Adam is set on the mount not for "different cause," but for the same cause as Michael had Adam ascend the hill: to teach the virtues necessary for regaining the primitive internal government the first Adam had lost. The difference is that whereas Adam was educated on the first mount and the reader (as is noted by Fish and others) is a supplementary pupil, only the reader is educated on the second. The reader's education is, like Adam's, on the art of establishing the kingdom of God within.

"As in the kingdoms of the world there is an art of courtship, a skill and mystery teaching to manage them," wrote John Hales, "so in the spiritual kingdom of God and of Christ, there is an holy policy, there is an art of spiritual courtship, which teaches every subject there how to demean and bear himself." Elaborating on Christ's statement to Pilate that his kingdom is not of this world, Hales suggests that Christ's "words seem like the Parthian horsemen, whose manner was to ride one way, but to shoot another way." Although the words "seem to go aspace towards Pilate," in a transcendent sense they

> aim and shoot at another mark. . . . Though these words be spoken to a Samaritan, to an infidel, to Pilate, yet their face is toward Jerusalem; they are a lesson directed to the subjects of his spiritual kingdom, of that Jerusalem which is from above, and is the mother of us all.

Though "from above," this kingdom, Hales makes abundantly clear, is within: "Heaven, that is the inward and spiritual man." And the establishment of that kingdom within is solely the prerogative of the Savior: "To rule the inward man in our hearts and souls, to set up an imperial throne in our understandings and wills, this part of our government belongs to God and to Christ: these are the subjects, this is the government of his kingdom."[67] The kingdom within, like the paradise within, is the countereffective political settlement to the loss of the sovereignty of reason to passion. And not only is it established, Hales intimates, in a dialogue where one partner does not fully understand the significance of the pointed words being hurled at him (Pilate), but it is established because those words strike at another auditor altogether—"the subjects of his spiritual kingdom." This, we noted, was the presupposition of the poetics of enigma: That which Jesus speaks is meant to unfold

its significance at a later epoch and to another subject. This unfolding is what I am suggesting happens in the final process of understanding available to the reader of *Paradise Regained*.

While Satan attempts to corrupt Jesus in the temptation of the
kingdoms, the Son meditates on the offers and answers Satan in
such a way as to establish the constitution of the kingdom within,
which is the foundation of the paradise regained. Two postulates
must then be presented—first, that Milton has Jesus *meditate* on
the offered temptations and, secondly, that in that act of meditation Jesus develops the foundation of a renovated religious culture.
That is, we need to see that there is an authentic confrontation (a
dialectic) and that this confrontation goes toward establishing the
kingdom within (of spirit).

To suggest that temptations may be an object of meditation
may seem to go against a long tradition that holds that evil enters
into the mind through a prolonged delectation on the enticements
of evil. The most succinct summary of that *topos* is given by Adam:

> Evil into the mind of God or Man
> May come and go, so unapprov'd, and leave
> No spot or blame behind.   (*PL* V, 117–19)

Adam speaks, of course, of the time of innocence, when the blameless mind was so because of its inherent purity. Since the Fall,
though, "as the state of man now is," in the words of *Areopagitica*,
there is in the human mind a basic impurity that precludes a
prolonged and disinterested consideration of temptations. But part
of Jesus' task is to take upon himself the pains and trials of humanity, and that, Milton thought, entailed meditating on the temptations to which humans are prone, and, by meditating, altering the
orientation within which temptation leads to sin or to virtue.

Thomas à Kempis writes of the process of *delectatio morosa:*
"For first commeth into our minds a bare cogitation of evill, then
followeth a strong imagination, out of which proceedeth a won-
derfull delectation, wicked motion, and assent unto sin." But, in an
interesting precedent for the basic theme of *Areopagitica*, à Kempis
also considers that, whoever "onely outwardly shunneth tentations, and plucketh not up the root from whence they doe spring,
is so far from escaping them, that they assaile him the sooner, &

make him much worse then he was before." This is a strong conception of the impurity of a "blank vertue," and one Milton would allow and admire. To "see and know, and yet abstain" from evil is the formation and exercise of virtue in this postlapsarian world. For Milton, indeed, the very stuff of evil is also, properly understood, the stuff of goodness: "The knowledge and survay of vice is in this world so necessary to the constituting of human vertue, and the scanning of error to the confirmation of truth" (CM IV, pp. 311, 320).[68] The gaze of the meditating subject is able to transform what is putatively evil or indifferent into what is virtuous and good.

In *Paradise Regained,* the form of this "survay of vice" is the second temptation. And the meditative attitude of Jesus as he discerns Satan's temptations with "answer meet" allows him the progressive enlightenment into the quality of the unending kingdom. The kingdoms, John Gumbleden writes, "were by the Divel set before the *imagination* and *understanding* of our Saviour, to *contemplate* on." Meditation, argues Baxter, is indeed a fit way to dispel all temptations:

> When thou art cast into perplexing troubles of minde, through suffering, or fear, or care, or temptations, then is it seasonable to address thy self to this duty. When should we take our cordials but in our times of fainting? When is it more seasonable to walk to heaven, then when we know not in what corner on earth to live with comfort? or when should our thoughts converse above, but when they have nothing but grief to converse with below?

Tracing the pains and tribulations to which humans are liable in this world is part of the meditative directory. Baxter now points us to the second level of conversation:

> The Meditation that I now direct you in, is onely of the end of all these, and of these as they refer to that end: It is not a walk from Mountains to Valleys, from Sea to Land, from Kingdom to Kingdom, from Planet to Planet: But it is a walk from Mountains and Valleys, to the Holy Mount *Zion;* from Sea and Land, to the Land of the Living; from the Kingdoms of this world, to the Kingdom of the Saints; from Earth to Heaven; from Time to Eternity.

Walking from earth to heaven is, as we have seen, the meditative motion. First despise the things of the earth, then ascend to the glories of heaven: These are the two levels of conversation to which the meditating mind is directed. The terms of direction Baxter uses, from the kingdoms of the world to the kingdoms of the saints, is revealing. For earlier he had written on the *contemptus mundi* theme with precisely this scene in mind: "If Satan should take thee up to the Mountain of Temptation, and shew thee the Kingdoms, and glory of the world; he could shew thee nothing thats worthy thy thoughts, much less to be preferred before thy Rest." And the "Rest," the saint's everlasting abode, is heaven: "Reader, Heaven is above thee, the way is upwards." That the meditative soul should "walk" allows us to transfer our attention to the ambulating meditative hero of Milton's narrative: "Thought following thought, and step by step led on . . . His holy Meditations thus persu'd" (I, 192–95). "Meditation is like perambulation," William Fenner muses, "the perambulation of the soule."69

Concerning the first level of conversation, we have noted the importance of representing Jesus and Satan in confrontation. There must be a controversial, adversarial relationship between them: Satan must offer the kingdoms to Jesus, and Jesus must not merely reject them, but must debate with Satan about them. Just as in *Areopagitica* Truth and Falsehood meet in a "free and open encounter," so in *Paradise Regained* do Jesus and Satan "encounter" each other: "So fares it when with truth falshood contends" (III, 442; CM IV, p. 347). It is, however, not a critical consensus that they do contend, that there is a confrontation between them that is not superficial, but genuine. Before turning our attention to how a dialectic can lead to a spiritual state, then, we might first ensure that there is a dialectic in the confrontation between Satan and Jesus by examining the most recent argument against such a view.

II

Contrasting Milton with Donne, Thomas O. Sloane determines that whereas there is a radically adversarial nature in Donne's poetry, there is only an ostensibly adversarial form in Milton's. That *Paradise Regained* allegedly presents us with a sterile and nonconfrontational politic is no new insight in the critical history of the poem. Harold Fisch has argued that Jesus rejects Satan's offers with "a blank wall of indifference" to such a degree that dialogue itself is nullified. Cary Nelson has also argued that Jesus' responses "deny the existence of confrontation." Sloane's insight has thrust because he traces Milton's metaphysical formalism back to his alleged Ramism. Sloane is not the first to intimate that Milton's poetic is somehow related to his Ramist dialectic, but Sloane's is certainly the most ambitious and most thorough analysis of *Paradise Regained* as a Ramist exercise in monologue. Milton, notes Sloane, "was no precise Ramist. But there is Ramism *in* Milton, and it's deeply expressive of the kind of confidence that runs counter to humanism."[70] I will argue, on the contrary, that there is no Ramism in Milton's art, for when it came to poetry Milton would brook no theorist as dogmatic as Ramus.

When establishing the curriculum to his academy, Milton overturned Ramus's basic ordering of subjects. Whereas Ramus would have the program of education proceed from the "thin gruel of poets and orators" through to mathematics and finally to physics, medicine, jurisprudence, and theology, Milton offers the order of "organic arts" in almost diametrical opposition. He begins with logic, moves to rhetoric, and ends with the sublime art of poetry: "To which poetry would be made *subsequent, or indeed, rather precedent,* as being less subtle and fine, but more simple, sensuous, and passionate" (CM IV, p. 286 [my italics]). Diametrically opposed to Ramus's denigration of the poetic arts, Milton emphasizes how poetry is doubly significant to his educational curriculum. Poetry is the most important art in being the end of all studies in the schedule of the student's career (it is "subsequent"), but it is also the most significant because the other arts gain their meaning from its origin (it is "precedent"). Whereas Ramus believed his "method" to be a "transcription of the divine order," and therefore a means of getting "in contact with all the multitude of things as these are in God's mind," Milton believed that education must proceed by a sort of Pauline "conning over the visible and inferior creature" to attain but an imperfect knowledge of God. The "same method," he concludes somewhat piquantly, "is necessarily to be followed in all discreet teaching" (CM IV, p. 277).[71] It would appear that Ramus's gnosticism did not appeal to Milton's sense of dialectic—the sense of the necessity of human cognition to work *through* the world.

Finally, because Ramus had an unflattering view of poetry,

making it a "homiletic monologue" through the application of his method, Milton concluded his recension of Ramist dialectic by rejecting the universal applicability of the Ramist method. The final argument of the *Art of Logic* concerns the "crypsis of method," that is, the art by which oratory and poetry attempt to allure or please the auditor through heterogeneity of true method, digressions, lingerings, and inversion of order. At this point Ramus and Ramists stop. Milton adds in conclusion: "But their own doctrine of method is to be turned over to the orators and poets, or at least to those who teach oratory and poetics" (CM XI, p. 485). Milton has not been guilty of originality throughout this recension, but he is wholly responsible for this final sentence. Walter J. Ong writes, "This completely overturns the Ramist cart. Ramus had insisted that all method of any kind belonged not to rhetoric or to poetry but to logic and to nothing else. It appears that Milton is not so sure" (YP VIII, p. 204). Although Sloane acknowledges Milton's disagreement with Ramus as to the universal applicability of method, he nonetheless tends to attribute to Milton precisely this dogmatism of Ramism, which Milton is innocent of.[72]

Although his ascription of Ramism to Milton is somewhat facile, Sloane's understanding of the presuppositions of Ramism is sound and helpful. Ramist method, like meditation, is a mode of perceiving things divine, and therefore a mode of transcending the sensual and rational in favor of the mystical. Ramism, as Sloane points out, is intuitive in ways that are damaging to discursive humanist rhetoric. Ramist Truth, he writes, "in its proper form is intuitive, impersonal, clear of emotion, and ultimately nonverbal." Like meditation, another "highly complex mode of communication," Ramism has a tension between the discursivity necessary to rhetoric and the intuition which is "not just anti- but nonrhetorical":

> Any communicative mode that is at heart intuitive is at heart unsystematic; its surface procedures are incantatory, or ritualistic, using words in the service of a nonverbal reality. Here is the greatest paradox of the Ramist system: it is outwardly systematic and verbal, inwardly unsystematic and nonverbal. Meditation has the same kind of paradox.[73]

Not all meditation, however, is incantatory and nonverbal. In the first chapter, I traced the various ways theorists of meditation have accorded reason its place in contemplative action and pointed out that there was certainly no uniform agreement as to the degree to which reason might govern faith or faith work within the bounds of discursive reasoning.

Richard Baxter, for example, in his exemplary contemplation, invokes an enthusiastic style, leading from incantation to silent assent: "O blessed Grace! O blessed Love! O the frame that my soul will then be in! O how Love and Joy will stir! but I cannot express it! I cannot conceive it!" But Baxter also believes that meditation requires more than mere intuition. Why, he asks, "do we give our senses leave to be chusers of our Happiness, while Reason and Faith stand by?" Reason and faith stand together against the senses, for reason is part of God's gift to humanity: "Gods way to persuade their wills, and to excite and actuate their Affections, is by the Discourse, Reasoning, or Consideration of their Under-standings, upon the Nature and Qualification of the Objects which are presented to them." A Christian's joy, he argues, "should be a grounded rational Joy." But even rational judgment must give way to the suprarationality of fideism: "There is in a Christian a kinde of spiritual taste, whereby he knows these things, besides his meer discursive reasoning power."[74] That there is a tension between the discursive and the intuitive faculties in humans is undeniable, but only by denying the tension and arguing only for the intuitive resolution may one assert the lack of discursive reasoning in con-templation. Ficino, for instance, does not negate the sensible pro-cess of apprehension when he is attempting to assert the intuitive; he works through them on his way to asserting the potency of the self-reflective intellect. Nor should we deny the ways Baxter comes to the intuitive. Milton's is not as simple an epistemology as Sloane makes it out to be; perhaps examining its process will enable us to understand with a greater degree of accuracy its workings and its presuppositions.

We may turn first to Raphael's elaboration of the process of intellection. Raphael tells Adam that his intellectual system is based on a process of transcendental refinement, but he compares that intellect to the digestive system:

> Man's nourishment, by gradual scale sublim'd
> To vital spirits aspire, to animal,
> To intellectual, give both life and sense,

Fancy and understanding, whence the Soul
Reason receives, and reason is her being,
Discursive, or Intuitive; discourse
Is oftest yours, the latter most is ours,
Differing but in degree, of kind the same.

(*PL* V, 483–90)[75]

We should notice two things here. First of all, Milton is arguing a continuum from sense to intellect (something like Ficino, but perhaps more materially based). Milton was, we should remember, a mortalist, and his mortalism led him to make certain assumptions about epistemology. Secondly, Milton is asserting that discourse is but a mundane form of heavenly conversation, namely intuition.

The difference, he emphasizes, is one only of degree. When Sloane turns his attention to this passage, he notes that "*Intuitive* in Milton's lexicon had within it the Latin *intueor*—to gaze at, to contemplate. It was obviously nondiscursive, as Raphael's usage shows."[76] Is this not, however, precisely what Raphael's usage does not show? By suggesting that discursive and intuitive forms of knowledge differ only in degree, "of kind the same," and that just as the intuitive is sometimes used by humans, and the discursive by angels (for they use the intuitive only "most" of the time), Raphael makes quite clear that the intuitive is not "obviously nondiscursive." Raphael's narrative, moreover, demonstrates his ability to liken the "spiritual to corporal forms / As may express them best." Earth may be after all but the shadow of heaven (V, 563–76).

Having suggested that Milton eschews a discursive humanist rhetoric in favor of an intuitive, formal, and monologic meditation, Sloane then turns to *Paradise Regained* as his text case. He argues that the poem has no sense of opposition, no debate: "Jesus refuses to debate. *His* mode of thought and the narrator's are an escape from and an alternative to controversy, and thereby a pattern for our behavior toward Satan within or without."[77] Concerning Milton's alleged Ramism, and concerning Milton's own beliefs about the relationship of discourse to intuition, I believe I have shown Sloane to be wrong. Here, though, I wish to show how Sloane is partly correct in his reading of *Paradise Regained*. Jesus, as I suggested in my reading of his second soliloquy, does use a form of intuitive and suprarational thought. But, in confrontation with Satan, I will suggest below, he also uses a form of "contraversal" discourse. Like Raphael, Jesus ascends from discursive to intuitive forms of knowledge, and he demonstrates this in the very structure of his replies to Satan's offer of the kingdoms. In the structure of those replies, in the interstices of discourse and intuition, we find that process I have been calling the dialectics of spirit.

III

In the offer of wealth, Satan makes a variety of rhetorical gestures establishing the logic by which he works. First of all, he relies on the legal logic of antecedents. He gives examples of monarchs — Antipater and Herod — who acceded to the throne by lucre. Moreover, Satan works by presupposing that wealth is the sole means of acquiring power. First of all he states the relationship obtaining between wealth and power: "Money brings Honour, Friends, Conquest, and Realms." Then he states in an enthymeme what wealth may do for Jesus: "If at great things thou wouldst arrive, / Get Riches first, get Wealth." The implicit second premise in Satan's Aristotelian enthymeme is that wealth is uniquely the guarantor of power. If Jesus is indeed not interested in confronting Satan, as some have suggested, then he need only refer all of Satan's arguments to a higher court. Were Jesus as nondiscursive as some critics have made him out to be, then he would simply say, "No, Satan, God will give me all I need."

But, of course, Jesus does not. And it is, then, worth paying attention to what Jesus does do because only in the process of his thinking may we gather the evidence to make statements about his modes of thinking. What Jesus does first is answer Satan's legal logic with legal logic of his own. Jesus cites as his antecedents of monarchs who have come to power without money both the Hebraic examples of Gideon, Jephthah, and David and the classical examples of "*Quintius, Fabricius, Curius, Regulus*" (II, 406–86). This is a direct answer to Satan, not an escape from the logical standards Satan is using, not an intuitive nonreply to an offer he pays no attention to, not a monologic retreat from genuine confrontation. Jesus has *contraverted* Satan. We have seen that Satan posits the presupposition that wealth is the sole means of aspiring to a monarchy. First of all, by showing the precedents of those who became kings without money, Jesus has offered a damaging critique of Satan's insistence on wealth's unique status; implicitly, Jesus says that money is not the sole means of possessing power.

Only after contraverting Satan in a logical debate at the discursive level does Jesus begin to establish the conditions of his internal kingdom. First of all, he questions the very presuppositions of earthly monarchy itself: "Yet not for that a Crown, / Golden in shew, is but a wreath of thorns." Secondly, Jesus repositions his argument so that "kingship" is no longer an external state relying on force, but an internal state under the individual's governance:

> Yet he who reigns within himself, and rules
> Passions, Desires, and Fears, is more a King;
> Which every wise and vertuous man attains.   (II, 466–68)

The dialectic exists at two quite separate levels: (1) Jesus questions the supposed efficacy of wealth and the purposes and merits of kingship, and (2) Jesus transcends the idea of an earthly monarchy by setting greater value on an internal kingdom:

> To know, and knowing worship God aright,
> Is yet more Kingly, this attracts the Soul,
> Governs the inner man, the nobler part.   (II, 475–77)

At the first level of conversation Jesus *argues;* he examines Satan's case and offers damaging criticisms of it within the logical paradigm of the world. Unlike Hall's deity, Milton's can endure a logician.[78] Using history and juridical decorum (citing precedents against Satan), psychology (disputing the terms of happiness with Satan), and logic (questioning the unstated minor premise in the enthymeme) to make his case, Jesus debates with Satan in "contraversal" terms. After he has concluded this primary level of conversation, and only after, Jesus then begins to converse at a transcendent and interior level.

We discover the same bilevel rhetorical form in Jesus' answer to the temptation of glory. There Satan attempts to conflate earthly fame and glory with heavenly fame and glory. Satan first offers them together and then subtly sets glory apart in Platonic, archetypal terms. Consider the terms of his offer:

> The fame and glory, glory the reward
> That sole excites to high attempts the flame
> Of most erected Spirits, most temper'd pure
> Ætherial, who all pleasures else despise,
> All treasures and all gain esteem as dross,
> And dignities and powers but the highest?   (III, 25–30)

Fame suddenly disappears from the elaboration, and glory becomes a transcendent thing. But when Jesus answers the offer, he
begins by conflating the terms *fame* and *glory,* but disputing the
levels of their operation. At the earthly level, he asks, "What is
glory but the blaze of fame, / The peoples praise, if always praise
unmixt?" (III, 47–48). At the earthly level, fame and glory are
based on the whims and judgment of an inconstant rabble. Satan
had asked, why deprive "all Earth her wonder at thy acts," and
Jesus answers that the earth's terms of praise are empty: "They
praise and they admire they know not what." Jesus then rises to the
level of heavenly glory. If glory is the ethereal purity desired by
erected spirits, and nothing but the "highest," then it must have
nothing to do with the earth:

> This is true glory and renown, when God
> Looking on the Earth, with approbation marks
> The just man, and divulges him through Heaven. (III, 60–62)

Jesus counters with his historical precedent, Job, and uses that case
to make clear the division Satan had attempted to conflate:

> Famous he was in Heaven, on Earth less known;
> Where glory is false glory, attributed
> To things not glorious, men not worthy of fame.
> (III, 68–70)

Jesus then criticizes the glory earned by military conquest and
turns again to an interior and ascendant ethics. Glory may be
attained, he says, by "wisdom eminent, / By patience, temperance."
He ends by examining the historical cases Satan had made, notably
Scipio, and then concludes by stating that he seeks not his own
glory, but God's.

As we see, then, the dialectic operates on two levels. On the
first, the discursive level, Jesus debates with Satan. He disputes

Satan's arguments with earthly examples, earthly logical forms, and earthly definitions. From that discursive level, Jesus ascends to the intuitive level of the interior kingdom. But this is ascent, not escape. Faith is ultimately inscrutable, but it is not merely asserted without reason. Faith is the conclusion to a discursive examination of earthly alternatives. On the first level, Jesus demonstrates the inherent flaws of the satanic offer, its lack of consistency within its own defined terms. Then Jesus answers on the heavenly level, wherein he asserts that all truth, all meaning, all sense, is to be derived from the origin of being, God. Jesus attempts, that is, a reorientation of the notion of truth, posing a logic founded upon the primary axiom of God.

To see how Jesus begins to formalize this new notion of Truth, we must turn to what is arguably the most interesting of all the temptations and what is surely for generations of Miltonists the most troubling of all Jesus' rejections—the kingdom of Athens. I have suggested that the offer of Rome is the site of Jesus' most enigmatic reply as well as the one place in the poem where he does not refer to the power of God; in the next two chapters we will more fully examine why Rome is so important. But if the offer of Rome is the place where enigma is most evident, then clearly the offer of Athens is the place where the dialectic of spirit is most to be discerned. I have demonstrated above that the structure of Jesus' replies is based on the model in which Jesus first contraverts Satan's offers and then transcends them by an assertion of a spiritual kingdom. In his answer to the offer of Athens, Jesus begins by asserting the domain of the spirit and then turns his attention to debating Satan. One assumes that because it is the seventh reply to the offers of kingdoms, Jesus has now no need to demonstrate the conventional process of ascent to intuition. What is even more significant, though, is that, in the rejection of Athens, Jesus invokes the reader who had been situated at the beginning of the poem among the angels.

The reply to Athens begins by an assertion that the Spirit's enlightenment is sufficient to all things. Jesus states, "He who receives / Light from above, from the fountain of light, / No other doctrine needs, though granted true" (IV, 285–87). Jesus articulates here the conditions for a revolution concerning the grounding of truth. What is true is not what is measurable or accepted as true by empirical research—it is what is inscrutable and received from an infallible source. Here, then, Jesus simply does not debate with Satan. He answers Satan with a new formality, the formality of divine understanding from whose pale Satan is excluded. The concluding clause of this assertion—"though granted true"—ought not to trouble us much because Jesus has already made the distinction between human reason and divine intuition. Truth, as Jesus signifies it, belongs to the realm of "things indifferent." The Spirit discerns what is good, and the place of the Spirit in its working is what has importance.

Moreover, Jesus does not end his speech with this assertion of an inscrutable fideism. He continues, examining each item offered—poetry, philosophy, oratory—with exalted *human* reasoning powers. He disputes philosophy, especially Stoicism, because of its arrogance and because of each school's inconsistency within its own standards. The Socratic's claim to "know this only, that he nothing knew" is undercut because knowing "nothing" would entail not being able to claim knowledge of anything, including nescience (IV, 291). The Platonic is too much given to "fabling"—and here Milton might well be suggesting the inherent problem of Plato's republic as a story and a story in which storytellers are evicted. We examined the problem with the skeptical school in the first section of this chapter. The Epicurean school placed its virtue in material property, while the Stoic placed its in pride. The basic problem with all the schools, though, is that they are unable to articulate the means to self-knowledge:

> Alas what can they teach, and not mislead;
> Ignorant of themselves, of God much more,
> And how the world began, and how man fell
> Degraded by himself, on grace depending?   (IV, 306–09)

Jesus is able to offer the opportunity for self-knowledge because he has taught the conditions for establishing an inner kingdom of the Spirit. That is, knowing oneself requires first of all attempting to know God—the phrasing of the second line above suggests no less. Milton had long espoused this formula, from *Of Education* to *Paradise Regained*.

Immediately after this, Jesus invokes the reader:

Who therefore seeks in these
True wisdom, finds her not, or by delusion
Far worse, her false resemblance only meets,
An empty cloud. However many books
Wise men have said are wearisom; who reads
Incessantly, and to his reading brings not
A spirit and judgment equal or superior,
(And what he brings, what needs he elsewhere seek)
Uncertain and unsettl'd still remains,
Deep verst in books and shallow in himself   (315–24)

I suggested in chapter 2 that the reader who is here invoked would be the same as the one situated in heaven by the poem's induction. The reason the reader is invoked here, I would argue, is that he or she has now been given a demonstration of the ways to read the world properly. The epistemological constant in Milton's thought is that the Spirit is necessary for the discerning of Truth. The Truth is discerned by a process of meditative "conning over" from the earthly to the divine. The reader who has watched Jesus work through six of Satan's offers to kingship has probably learned that lesson. In the terms Milton used in 1641 and 1644, that reader's eyes have probably lost some of the blear that kept them from perceiving the Truth. Here, then, in the rejection of Athens, are all the elements necessary for establishing the conditions of Milton's epistemology.

First of all, the enabling condition for knowledge is access to the Spirit—"Light from above." Second, what that spiritual light gives is the ability to discern Truth beyond what custom and tradition would construe as "granted true." Third, the intelligent reader capable of reading the world in this way is the one who brings to his or her reading "spirit and judgment." That reader, I argued in the second chapter, would be the one already positioned in the heavens—where, after all, all competent meditation leads. Here, then, at the conclusion of the offers of kingdoms, the reader reenters the scene of the poem. As Hales had noted in examining Christ's replies to Pilate, when Christ speaks he is addressing an audience beyond the immediate hearer. *Paradise Regained* demonstrates this definitively. Satan does not understand what Jesus is saying. As much as he had not been able to reach Jesus when Jesus was meditating, so here Satan is still trying to get to where Jesus is while Jesus is meditating on his kingdom without end. Satan may not get there — and will not within this narrative, as I hope to show in the final section of this chapter — but we do. The reader understands the structure of Jesus' replies — the way they move from discourse to intuition, the way they reject the earthly trappings of monarchy while articulating the enabling conditions of an internal kingdom.

The replies proceed, then, on two levels. The first is the level of earthly reason, where Jesus and Satan achieve a "conversation meet," where worldly logic "by his own arms is best evinc't" (IV, 232). On this level, Satan and Jesus participate in a dialogue, a debate, where truth and falsehood contend. Here is the humanism Sloane finds wanting in Milton. The second level of reply is divine reason, where Jesus walks alone. On this level, the path to the kingdom within and without end, Satan cannot comprehend goodness, cannot comprehend his adversary, for they are not adversarial. In this, there is no dialogue; Jesus' language, the language of constituting an eternal kingdom, is to Satan "no more communicable." At this level, Jesus, the unified body of truth, converses only with solitude: "Thus the Son / Commun'd in silent walk" (II, 261). Baxter had asked, "When is it more seasonable to walk to heaven, then when we know not in what corner on earth to live with comfort?" It is an icon Milton uses to great effect: the meditating Son tracing the desert fasting, but fed with holy meditations. "Sathans temptations," Baxter adds, "are laid on the earth, earth is the place, and earth the ordinary baite: How shall these ensnare the Christian, who hath left the earth, and walks with God?"[79]

Mountains, we noted earlier, play an important part in Christ's public life. It was not on a mountain, but while discoursing around the dinner table that Adam first learned from Raphael how to ascend to godly knowledge:

> Well hast thou taught the way that might direct
> Our knowledge, and the scale of Nature set
> From centre to circumference, whereon
> In contemplation of created things
> By steps we may ascend to God.   (*PL* V, 508–12)[80]

But Adam and Eve trespass; they reject that organic scheme of ascending to divine knowledge, preferring to aspire to it directly

through disobedience. Adam then has to climb the hill of speculation to learn anew how to ascend to God from his fallen condition.
The proper ascent is serious and ambulatory, "by steps," whereas
the improper is flighty and imaginary: "They swim in mirth, and
fancy that they feel / Divinity within them breeding wings" (IX,
1009–10).

Milton's narrative on the regaining of Paradise, like his tractate
on education, proposes that the end of learning "is to repair the
ruins of our first Parents by regaining to know God aright." In the
poem, Jesus describes how to "know, and knowing worship God
aright" (II, 475). But this is no simple feat, "because our understanding cannot in this body found it self but on sensible things,
nor arrive so clearly to the knowledge of God and things invisible."
And so we must therefore aspire by "orderly conning over the
visible and inferior creature" (CM IV, p. 277). In "conning over"
the kingdoms of the earth, Jesus expresses an understanding of the
invisible kingdom within. In terms of his dialectic, the movement
is from the discursive to the intuitive. In terms of his mandate of
government, the movement is from the mundane to the heavenly —
the act of self-knowledge Milton recommended everywhere in his
narrative model. In this, he was at one with Ludovisus Vives:
"This is the course of most absolute wysedome, whereof the first
steppe is, *to knowe thy selfe,* and the laste of all, *to know god.*"[81]

The knowledge and survey of vice, Milton held, was necessary
to constituting human virtue, and the "scanning of error to the
confirmation of truth" (CM IV, p. 311). A proper dialectic would
refine and raise something true and virtuous from the mundane.
Milton felt, moreover, that the offer of the kingdoms was just such
an opportunity for this refining dialectic. The "substance of the
tempters words to our Saviour were holy," Milton wrote, "but his
drift nothing lesse" (CM III, p. 128). While Satan's drift in the
offer of the kingdoms is to corrupt, the essence of Jesus' answers,
like his drift, is to refine in order to regain.

The critics who hold that Jesus merely rejects the offer of the
kingdoms do not do justice either to Milton's narrative or to his
politics. He had written earlier, "To sequester out of the world into
Atlantick and *Eutopian* polities, which never can be drawn into use,
will not mend our condition; but to ordain wisely as in this world
of evil, in the midd'st whereof God hath plac't us unavoidably"

(CM IV, p. 318). That which does not contemplate evil is but a blank, excrementally white virtue. God placed us in this wilderness, Milton wrote, not without dust and heat, in order to allow us to work both from within to refine the world without and from without to refine the paradise within: "Wherefore did he creat passions within us, pleasures round about us, but that these rightly temper'd are the very ingredients of vertu?"

As Jesus sets out to meditate on how to best accomplish his mighty work, he feels revolving in his breast the disparity of his internal passions and the external world:

> O what a multitude of thoughts at once
> Awakn'd in me swarm, while I consider
> What from within I feel my self, and hear
> What from without comes often to my ears,
> Ill sorting with my present state compar'd.   (I, 196–200)

His thoughts are both "of things past and to come" (300). That which is past is the Baptism, which had inaugurated a new polity. Chrysostom writes of the dovelike Spirit's significance: "Henceforth He leads us away from the old to the new polity, both opening to us the gates on high, and sending down His Spirit from thence to call us to our country there." That which is to come is the Temptation, in which Jesus establishes the constitution of that new polity, neither utopic nor worldly, but virtuous and internal. Through the Temptation is established the "most perfect rule and patterne of godlines & vertue," Isaac Colfe noted. And in the same measure as the kingdom of God is raised, so is the kingdom of Satan razed: "To the beating downe of that cursed kingdome of Sathan, and to the enlarging and advancing of his most glorious kingdome."[82] By meditation, Jesus does precisely this: He establishes the constitution to govern the inner being and frustrates Satan's "conquest fraudulent." Although the first Adam lost Paradise, the loss was described in terms of government. Likewise, although the second Adam regains paradise, it is described in terms of the kingdom within. Offered the kingdoms of the world, Jesus answers with an offer of the kingdom of the spirit, an enigma the literal Satan can see only in the stars. Satan reads the "Starry Rubric" and concludes that "A Kingdom they portend thee, but what Kingdom, / Real or Allegoric I discern not" (IV, 376, 386–

90). Jesus does not answer this. He need not, for Satan can never discern the kingdom within.

The offer of the kingdoms is by far the longest meeting of the two contestants in the wilderness and the most important for Jesus' articulating the conditions of his kingdom—internal and eternal. What the temptation of the kingdoms represents, according to Carl Jung, is the political power of the Roman Empire. It was Christ's role to mediate this power. To see Jung's arguments about the Temptation will help us appreciate the political import of what I call the dialectics of spirit and its place in the political power of personality. Personality, wrote Jung, must be developed through conscious assent to an inner voice. Only in this way can an individual divine what is the collective psychology of his or her times. The "genuine personality" liberates the people by voluntarily sacrificing herself or himself to the necessary vocation, consciously translating into one's "own individual reality what would only lead to ruin if it were lived unconsciously by the group." Jung writes brilliantly on the Temptation, and might profitably be quoted at length:

> The story of the Temptation clearly reveals the nature of the psychic power with which Jesus came into collision: it was the power-intoxicated devil of the prevailing Caesarean psychology that led him into dire temptation in the wilderness. This devil was the objective psyche that held all the peoples of the Roman Empire under its sway, and that is why it promised Jesus all the kingdoms of the earth, as if it were trying to make a Caesar of him. Obeying the inner call of his vocation, Jesus voluntarily exposed himself to the assaults of the imperialistic madness that filled everyone, conqueror and conquered alike. In this way he recognized the nature of the objective psyche which had plunged the whole world into misery and had begotten a yearning for salvation that found expression even in the pagan poets. Far from suppressing or allowing himself to be suppressed by this psychic onslaught, he let it act on him consciously and assimilated it. Thus was world-conquering Caesarism transformed into spiritual kingship, and the Roman Empire into the universal kingdom of God that was not of this world.

Jung's "assimilation" into consciousness and "transformation" into spirit is something like the force which, as it is seen in *Paradise Regained,* I have called the dialectics of spirit.[83]

Jung notes that Christ does not reject; he transforms. Milton, too, saw the power of the psyche, the potential of personality. Milton, like Jung, knew of the irresistible power of the inner world of the mind. Jesus descends into himself—into his mind, his personality—in order to ascend through Satan's earthly kingdoms to his spiritual. It is, finally, an act of meditation.

Meditation, as I noted in chapter 2, strives to achieve the perception of the spiritual world, both in heaven above and within us. Suggesting the use of the eye beyond sense and reason, the most ethereal of the capacities unique to the human soul, the writers of this meditative tradition would have the meditating mind perceive God *through* his created universe. So Paul exhorted the Roman congregation: "For the invisible things of him from the creation of the world are clearly seen, being understood by the things that are made, *even* his eternal power and Godhead" (Rom. i, 20). As I suggested earlier, in the scenes of confrontation the Other is the world. Jesus applies his spiritual judgment to that material. At the first level of his dialectic he does address Satan and dispute his readings of the world, but on the second level he is working directly on the world.

Joseph Henshaw, articulating the distinction that runs deep between reason and faith, writes that "God made this world not barely to *looke* on, but to *contemplate* on, and of Him in it: here the Christian and the Philosopher part, *they* are led by *reason, we* by *faith*." Hall's "Invisible World" is seen through the eyes of faith:

> Every action, every occurent shall mind me of those hidden and better things: and I shall so admit of all material objects, as if they were so altogether transparent, that through them I might see the wonderful prospects of another world. . . . And certainly, if we shall be able so to withdraw our selves from our senses, that we shall see, not what we see, but what we thinke, (as it uses [*sic*] to be in the strong intentions of the mind) and shall make earthly things, not as Lunets, to shut up our sight, but Spectacles to transmit it to spiritual objects.

In his book of meditations, Augustine converses with the world in a way quite reminiscent of Adam's first glimmers of consciousness: "Then said I to the mass of the whole world, Tell me, art thou my God or no? And it answered with a mightie voyce, I am not: but through him I am whom thou seekest in me: Hee hath made mee: seeke him above me, by whom I am now ruled, and was once created."[84] To see *through* the earthly and carnal to the heavenly and spiritual, to treat the material of vice in such a way that it is made the stuff of virtue, to meditate on the world in order to ascend to heaven: these are the options available to the faithful being in the duress of temptation.

The contemplative person, as characterized by John Earle, must be a scholar of the "great University of the World," and no cloistered soul. The purpose of their study is to transform the earthly into the heavenly: "Hee lookes not upon a thing as a yawning Stranger at novelties; but his search is more mysterious and inward, and hee spels Heaven out of earth. He knits his observations together, and makes a Ladder of them all to climbe to God." Spelling heaven out of earth—that is what meditation accomplishes. What is more earthly than temptations, and what more heavenly than the rejection of them? This is the "good we have by our tentation," writes Richard Capel, "that we come to know our selves, to know Satan, and to know God; such is our estate, that the furthest about is the neerest way to heaven."[85]

Alluding to the Temptation of Christ, but confusing the second and third temptations, Henshaw writes:

> Earth is but our rode to Heaven, and the things of this world, like *high-way* fruit, are common to all. . . . There is another good, which is wholly the *Godly's,* and wholly to bee sought for the kingdome of *Heaven,* and the *righteousnesse* thereof: they whose kingdome is not of this world, can see the kingdomes of this world (with their saviour from the pinnacle) and contemne them, or at least not fall downe and worship them.[86]

They whose kingdom is not of this world, Henshaw might have added, may also, with Jesus on the specular mount, see the kingdom of the godly, the kingdom both above and within.

Meditation, however, is only the third of the intellectual faculties to be applied to the temptation of the kingdoms. First of all, doubt had to be assayed. Jesus used skepticism to formulate a theosophic epistemic capacity, while Satan used it to blaspheme against the Holy Spirit. Their willed contrary positions concerning the Spirit—Jesus acceding to its potency, Satan blaspheming it—determines their respective positions in the ensuing debate. The intellect filled with the Spirit will enigmatically address an intellect devoid of spiritual apprehension in order to address a different audience at a different level of understanding—the spiritual readers. In addressing them, Jesus, in dialogue with Satan, establishes the means for what this poem had set out to do—regain Paradise. Finally, Milton's unique achievement is to write a scene of Satan's anagnorisis beyond the book, as it were.

"LIKE AN AUTUMNAL STAR": BEYOND THE ENDING OF *PARADISE REGAINED*

So far, I have been concerned with demonstrating why Satan does not understand Jesus' mission. Here I wish to show the conditions under which Satan will come to understand, partially at least, some of the magnitude of that career he had hitherto not fully understood because of his displacement.

If there is "meaning" to be found in *Paradise Regained,* and I believe there is, it may be discovered in its plenitude in the second temptation. Meaning, as Victor Turner points out, is not merely cognitive hindsight, but rather "something existentially emergent from the entanglement of persons wholly engaged in issues of basic concern to the central or representative actors, the formulators of 'positions' or life-stances." In the case of our epic, the most thorough and significant entanglement is over the types of world each inhabits, and the ways that those worlds are both products and producers of the "life-stances" of each contestant. The first temptation had allowed each to articulate his life—and each had also assayed an interpretation of the other's life. Moreover, as Milton made clear, what each did in presenting his life and interpreting the other's is articulate an hermeneutical ethic, either candid or malicious. What each does after that is enter into the second temptation with a worldview, and, I would argue, emerges from that temptation with a world. As Nelson Goodman suggests, the "symbol systems we think in and employ in our world-versions determine the form of the worlds we think about and live in."[87] Satan uses a mode of Pyrrhonism to propose a material world devoid of spirit; Jesus uses a mode of doubt to reach a level of theosophy that allows him to inhabit easily and represent enigmatically a spiritual world.

But to whom is this world represented, then? If, after all, I am arguing that Satan is unable to perceive the world Jesus inhabits, then the "entanglement of persons" Turner speaks of might be relatively inconclusive. Of what value is Jesus' world if it is not perceived to be the superior one by Satan? One could suggest that it is rigorously undecidable which world the narrative holds to be superior. Because Satan has so far not given up his faith in the world he is inhabiting, the reader cannot simply assent to Jesus' world without making a clear choice for which there is no justification in the narrative. We cannot, for instance, say that it is "logical" that Jesus' world is better suited to promoting our moral lives than Satan's because Jesus' world is constructed out of a different form of logic than is Satan's. Likewise, we cannot say that we are justified because Jesus has shown the flaws in satanic logic by referring to the dialectic of spirit—where Jesus moved *through* Satan's logical forms to his own—precisely because Satan has not given up that logic. What we must say, whether we wish to use it as a means of affirming our decision or not, is that, as with any system, the standard of judging between structures within that system exists outside of the system. Or, applying Gödel's theorem to the cosmos of Milton and the case of *Paradise Regained,* God judges Jesus' world to be the absolutely correct one. Such is clearly the case, of course, but there is another way of approaching the problem of distinguishing the worlds which the narrative represents, and that is by returning to the process, returning to the ways of "world-making," to borrow Goodman's useful phrase.

Part of the way that the poem promotes one world over another, and indeed part of the way it negotiates between worlds, is by distinguishing between different ways of world-making. Moreover, it does so by referring to the reader. Concerning works of art, aesthetic objects "work when they inform vision; inform not by supplying information but by *forming* or *re*-forming or *trans*forming vision; vision not as confined to ocular perception but as understanding in general."[88] *Paradise Regained* works by informing our sense of understanding about the ways worlds are made and the ways worlds are destroyed. So, too, in the dialectic of this poem, is the reader entangled as much as the contestants are. The poem "works" on the reader, but the reader is not "intangled" in the way Fish or Iser believe. We recall that, when Milton used the phrase "not so much a teaching, as an intangling" in *Tetrachordon,* he was referring to the way Christ spoke beyond the comprehension of the Pharisees who were, after all, too literal minded to appreciate the meaning of his doctrine. When Fish transmutes this phrase into an epistemology of the reading mind, he eviscerates it of most of its derogatory intent. Intangling becomes, rather, a congenial, though frustrating, way for the narrator to involve the reader in the narrative. I would suggest that the reader's comprehension occurs the way Milton suggests it occurs—beyond the entangling of Satan. Entangling confronts Satan in such a way that another audience of a different order becomes the one authentically addressed. *Paradise Regained*'s audience, I have suggested, is the spiritual reader, the final transmutation of what in 1642 had been for Milton the "knowing reader," in the mid-1650s the "candid and judicious readers," and in 1667 the "fit audience."

By showing so far only the ways that Satan is excluded from knowledge, I have perhaps underemphasized the ways Milton allows Satan to understand some things. In attending, finally, to the process of Satan's knowledge, we may find another aspect to Milton's poetic that is, quite frankly, more congenial and humane than the one so far described.

So far I have shown how Milton follows with apparent rigor this principle of exclusion to its logical limits. Satan exists, insofar as understanding is a register of existence, in a different world. That, I will maintain, is what Milton does until after the pinnacle scene.[89] Critics who have attempted to propose that *Paradise Regained* is an "identity contest" have been working from a set of established questions first suggested in 1752 (in Newton's variorum edition) and since formalized into critical orthodoxy. After examining the presuppositions of those questions, both in their original and modern formulations, I conclude that Calton, the foremost annotator of that variorum edition, took his conclusion as his presupposition. Moreover, modern criticism has done much the same, especially with four key issues and one narratological condition. The four issues critics assert and I contest are (1) that it is humanly impossible for Jesus to stand on the pinnacle, (2) that Jesus is held on the pinnacle by a miracle, (3) that this miracle demonstrates that the Son is "divine," and (4) that this miracle gives Satan the knowledge of the Son's divinity. The narratological condition is that the final temptation is of an entirely different order than the previous two. I would argue that standing on the pinnacle is humanly possible, that Jesus does stand by dint of human abilities, that there is no miracle, nor apotheosis on the pinnacle, and that Jesus is "divine" only if we take "divine" to mean not coeternal or copotent to the Father. Furthermore, I make no distinction between the second and third temptations; the third temptation is as much a temptation as the first and second are, and therefore Jesus must operate by the same standards as he has done before.

When does Satan begin to acknowledge Jesus' world? I began this chapter by pointing out that Satan was displaced in time twice in the early part of the narrative, each time as Jesus was meditating. Whereas Satan dissolves into thin air, and indeed gets lost there, Jesus achieves an integrity of being by entering into himself. As he begins his second soliloquy in the second book, he,

> Sole but with holiest Meditations fed,
> Into himself descended, and at once
> All his great work to come before him set;
> How to begin, how to accomplish best
> His end of being on Earth, and his mission high
>
> (II, 111–15)

If, as I suggested in the introduction, self-knowledge is the signal theme of this poem, then we must say that few symbolic gestures so confidently assert self-knowledge as ably as the act of descending into oneself. Moreover, no gesture quite so articulately suggests the ways that the constitution of Jesus' mission on earth will be recorded—on his being, on his body, on his self. What Jesus does in setting before himself all his great work is, literally, set himself as his great work. That is why he does it in an act of self-discovery and self-inquiry. In this persistently interiorizing narrative, Jesus' act of descent into himself is the most rigorously political act of all, and, Milton maintains, the most necessary to any reforming of the Reformation. On the other hand, the Satan who is diffused in time and space represents the most reactionary of all politics; his is the way of the Restoration, an unquestioning return to the material kingdoms of the world. That is, to return to our interest in evaluating each one's world by judging the standards of each one's way of world-making, we may say that Satan's world is ephemeral because its proponent has run out of time, while Jesus' world is integral because Jesus is in himself collected.

Satan, moreover, gets an insight into this after the pinnacle scene. In that way, we may answer the apparent problem of Satan's world existing intact in the same sphere as Jesus'. To conclude the temptation sequence on the same premises as it had until now been conducted, Milton would have to present a Satan who did not know who was standing on the pinnacle. Following the skeptical route he had been pursuing, and was now careering in, Satan would not be allowed to understand the spiritual station of the person on the pinnacle. The same Satan who had denied the Spirit in the dove would see only a man standing on the pinnacle. The key word, as I have argued elsewhere, is "amaze" (IV, 559). Milton had suggested, in the *Doctrine and Discipline of Divorce,* that Christ answers the Pharisees with enigmatic riddles in order "to amaze them yet furder" because they were "not fit" to be told the spiritual facts (CM III, p. 456).[90] In the next chapter I will argue how crucial the concept of amazement is to *Samson Agonistes.* For now, I will note that Satan's "amazement" at Jesus' response is not an epiphany, but a blindness. *Amazement* here is as Dr. Johnson defines it: "Such a confused apprehension as does not leave reason its full force"—the apt conclusion to Satan's denial of the Spirit. He sees the physical man but cannot understand his mission. Not yet.

Although he does not understand the divine man at the pinnacle, Satan will comprehend to a degree the role the Son is to play in cosmic history, but only to a small degree. And, as I have stressed, he does not learn it during the temptation sequence. Only after he has fallen back into his consistory, after Jesus has completed the temptation exercise and been lifted off the pinnacle by the angels, will Satan be allowed a small degree of knowledge. To appreciate how Satan's epistemic functioning is presented in the final scene, we must return to that all-informative first encounter between the two contestants. In answer to Satan's boast of his oracular aid to humanity, Jesus declares that Satan cannot know God's expressed will:

> when his purpose is
> Among them to declare his Providence
> *To thee not known,* whence hast thou then thy truth,
> But from him or his Angels President.
>
> (I, 444–47, my italics)

Satan, that is, expresses oracular truths although he does not know them. God acts through Satan without Satan's conscious knowledge of the material he is passing on to the world. In the final scene of the angelic chorus, we find much the same thing. Having lifted Jesus from his uneasy station, fed him, and sung his victory, the angelic chorus addresses Satan:

> But thou, Infernal Serpent, shalt not long
> Rule in the Clouds; like an Autumnal Star
> Or Lightning thou shalt fall from Heav'n trod down
> Under his feet: for proof, e're this thou feel'st
> Thy wound, yet not thy last and deadliest wound
> By this repulse receiv'd,
> . . . .
>   *hereafter learn* with awe
> To dread the Son of God: he all unarm'd
> Shall chase thee with the terror of his voice
> From thy Demoniac holds, possession foul
> Thee and thy Legions, yelling they shall flye,
> And beg to hide them in a herd of Swine.
>
>   (IV, 614–26, my italics)

Satan has a chasm in his intellectual capacity which disables him from entertaining divine verities in their immediate manifestation. Physically, this mental chasm is represented by his dissolution into a spatio-temporal void. When God determines, Satan is suffered to express that truth in the same way he does all actions tending to promote providential designs—"contrary unweeting" (I, 126). Only after he has expressed the truth himself without understanding it (it is to him "not known") does the truth appear to make itself manifest to him. I say "appear" because there is no evidence that Satan does have the truth. He only claims to have it: "Then to thy self ascrib'st the truth foretold" (I, 453).

Satan does not comprehend any truth of God's Providence through its activity. He becomes aware of it only after ("hereafter learn") and only through either God or the angels. In the final scene of the narrative, Satan likewise does not learn the truth of Jesus' station through the Son's acting out of God's Providence, or through the Son's manifestation of that grace, but only at the very end, and only through the angels. This time, of course, the truth of God's "living Oracle" is expressed and only partially understood.

The angelic chorus alludes to the one scene in the Gospels in which Jesus will again meet the devils, where he exorcises them from the unclean man in Capernaum (Luke iv, 31–37; Mark i, 21–28). As Jesus approaches the possessed man, the devils call out, "I know thee who thou art; the Holy One of God." Jesus then commands them out. In both Mark's and Luke's gospel, this is the first of Jesus' miracles. The angels suggest that Jesus shall "command" the devils out of the possessed man into "a herd of Swine" as a prelude to the final debelling of Satan and his crew. Jesus has not manifested himself by miracle in the temptation sequence, and so Satan does not comprehend the Spirit residing within. By alluding to a scene outside the action of the narrative, and a scene in which Jesus will perform his first miracle, the angels demonstrate how Satan's intellectual capacities still lag behind. The devils will claim to "know" Jesus only after the action of *Paradise Regained,* only in a scene alluded to in the final moment of the narrative. The resolution of the doubt motif, then, is not effected within the action of *Paradise Regained.* Although we are made aware that he shall possess some degree of knowledge of the spiritual power of his queller, at a later time, in the narrative proper Satan concludes his career in a state of senseless amazement. The scene of anagnorisis is written into the narrative, but only in the form of a prophetic statement. The actual scene itself is beyond the bounds of this story.

Catherine Belsey has rightly noted that the poem most comparable to *Paradise Regained* is *Ode on the Morning of Christ's Nativity.* The concern of both poems, she writes, is the "Incarnation-as-signifier and the textuality of meaning." *Meaning* for Belsey is something akin to Turner's definition, which began this section. In the place of the "fixity of eternal truth," she writes, "differance and dissemination mobilize meaning, identify it as the location of a process of change in which we are all able to take part, since meanings are produced and not given."[91] Meaning is always a product of confrontation, of difference as well as "differance," and its process is in the entanglement of both adversaries and of the readers. The reason the Nativity ode is the fittest poem to compare to *Paradise Regained* is not just that both deal with the Incarnation, but because both deal with Christ's mission in a radically inconclusive way. In each poem a world is evoked and then placed in the future. In the Nativity ode, the world of classical mythology is first called forth and then made to flee in the face of a new world

order. Although it flees, it yet exists in some mystical way, charac-
terizable, I suppose, as a "trace." "But wisest Fate says no, / This
must not yet be so" (Nat., 149–50). In *Paradise Regained,* we have
that same confrontation between an old world and a new one, and
that same persistent deferral of the new one's inauguration in practice.

One might say that this deferral is intrinsic to Christianity and
also to those forms of political revolution based on Christian tenets. In a May 1843 letter, Marx wrote that Germany was a "dehu-
manized world." What it required to regain the human sense of
"self-esteem" necessary to a political revolution was to regain its
human "sense of freedom." "This sense," Marx notes, "vanished
from the world with the Greeks, and with Christianity it took up
residence in the blue mists of heaven, but only with its aid can
society ever again become a community of men that can fulfil their
highest needs, a democratic state." The young Marx proposed a
narrative model of self-discovery and self-consciousness, espousing freedom and directing those who would strive for it to a future
good. Moreover, to discover its sense of "freedom," humanity had
to tell itself a better story, to make the past meaningful for and
heading toward a future. "The reform of consciousness," he says in
the conclusion of his next letter, "consists *entirely* in making the
world aware of its own consciousness, in arousing it from its
dream of itself, in *explaining* its own actions to it." From that act of
coming to consciousness would emerge the fulfillment of the past:
"Our task is not to draw a sharp mental line between past and
future but to *complete* the thought of the past." What is most
interesting is the way Marx concludes the letter by employing, yet
again, religious terms to describe political acts: "What is needed
above all is a *confession,* and nothing more than that. To obtain
forgiveness for its sins mankind needs only to declare them for
what they are."[92]

Milton, with a little less Catholicism, also writes about how the
past requires the present to regard its sins and to reform them. The
act of coming to what Marx calls self-consciousness, and what we
have been calling self-knowledge, requires a use of the present. By
making Jesus' act of coming to self-knowledge and his act of confronting and defeating Satan available for the reader, Milton represents the paradigm of every individual's coming to self-knowledge.
And in that act of coming to self-knowledge, every individual

becomes a subject of the kingdom of God precisely because he or she helps in the destruction of the kingdom of Satan. When the individual doubts adequately and appropriately, that individual will learn to eschew the materialist world and understand the spiritual one behind the enigmatic pronouncements of Jesus. From doubt, and through enigma, the individual becomes a subject of the spiritual world. When the individual doubts inadequately and inappropriately, that individual will deny the spiritual world and accept the materialistic version of it. That individual falls prey to enigma instead of being exercised mentally by it, and that individual will become subject to the spiritual world. The crux, as I noted, is the sin against the Holy Ghost. Its resolution comes in that final prophecy of the angelic chorus foretelling Jesus' exorcising of the devils from the man at Capernaum.

The link between the crux and the resolution may be explicated by referring to a later point in Christ's career. Just after Christ has exorcised a blind and dumb man on the sabbath, the Pharisees accuse him of casting out devils only by employing the power of the prince of devils, Beelzebub. Christ's answer alerts us to how we may understand the conclusion to *Paradise Regained:*

> Every kingdom divided against itself is brought to desolation; and every city or house divided against itself shall not stand: And if Satan cast out Satan, he is divided against himself; how shall then his kingdom stand? And if I by Beelzebub cast out devils, by whom do your children cast *them* out? therefore they shall be your judges. But if I cast out devils by the Spirit of God, then the kingdom of God is come unto you. . . . Wherefore I say unto you, All manner of sin and blasphemy shall be forgiven unto men: but the blasphemy *against* the *Holy* Ghost shall not be forgiven unto men. (Matt. xii, 25–31)

Christ does not affirm whether he is casting out the devils by the power of Beelzebub or by the power of the Spirit. He leaves it up the Pharisees to decide. But he also names the cost of their decision: "Whosoever speaketh against the Holy Ghost, it shall not be forgiven him, neither in this world, neither in the *world* to come" (xii, 32). In either case, whatever power Christ might be using for exorcising the devils, the satanic world will be destroyed. If he is using Beelzebub's power, the satanic world will fall because it becomes divided against itself. If he is using the power of the Spirit, the satanic world will be destroyed because the "paradise within" will be installed in every individual who believes in Christ's power: "Then the kingdom of God is come unto you."

In the very midst of his confrontation with the Pharisees, between naming the powers of his exorcising abilities and naming the sin against the Holy Ghost, Christ states what has become the famous slogan of more than Christianity: "He that is not with me is against me" (Matt. xii, 30). This names the difference, one might say, between being a "subject of" and being "subject to." Its premise is the ability to gain self-knowledge — the ability to instate the kingdom of God within oneself and to become a subject of it. Jesus does this, and the angelic chorus concludes by showing us how we, too, can do it. The final remark to Satan, characteristically, is aimed at the reader. The religious kingdom within will be established, they say. It will be in the future, and it will be all-encompassing. The choice now is either to become a subject of that kingdom or to become subject to it. The process is either to accept the Spirit or to reject it. *Paradise Regained* is a narrative about how one accepts the Spirit and how one rejects it. Its companion poem is also an exploration of the narrative model of self-knowledge. And it is in the meaning to be discovered in the interaction between the two poems that we may best discern in what ways Milton came to his own self-knowledge and in what ways he is a cultural critic.

Both the Nativity ode and *Paradise Regained* represent most fully in Milton's work the process of ritual — that passing of liminal thresholds in a rite of passage which, Turner argues, is potentially a radical critique of the given culture. Rome, as Greene noted, represented that possibility for Petrarch. In the interstices of the 1671 volume — between Rome and Philistia — Milton finds the potential for his radical critique of English culture.

PART THREE

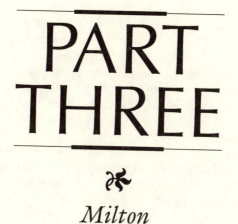

Milton

"I am not a poet, but a poem. A poem that is being
written, even if it looks like a subject."

—*Jacques Lacan (1976)*

4

Confronting the Book:
The Art of Liberty

ᘒ

THE MODERN CRITICAL tendency of studying Renaissance literary works as poems instead of as printed books
obscures the heterogeneity of discourses which Louis Adrian
Montrose considers to be an important aspect of the impact such
books were meant to have on their audiences. Spenser's *The Shepheardes Calendar,* for instance, is exemplary of the Elizabethan
printed book in its "tendency toward the proliferation and contam-
ination of genres, toward the inclusion within its covers of a variety of discursive forms characterized by distinctive modes of address to the readers." As a book, then, *The Shepheardes Calendar,*
like other Elizabethan "print-specific" works, manifests a "tendency toward the elaboration rather than the effacement" of its status
as a social—and not merely literary—production. Part of the importance of this reorientation is that it would allow us to see how a
poem is "not merely the *product* of a received ideology but it is
itself a distinctive *production* of ideology." The determination of a
poem's production of ideology involves seeing precisely in what
ways its author's subjectivity is represented in the book. So, in the
case Montrose is studying, Colin Clout's offering the lamb to the
infant mother-goddess allegorically represents Spenser's offering
the pastoral itself to his queen ("Aprill"). Thus does Spenser represent himself as subject in the two distinct ways Montrose notes
when he defines the process of subjectification. On the one hand,
Spenser represents himself as a locus of consciousness and initiator

277

of action (that is, as an author-subject), while on the other he also is represented as one who is positioned, motivated, and constrained within networks of power beyond his control or comprehension (that is, as subject to a monarch).[1]

If we may discover such a radical significance in *The Shepheardes Calendar* by returning to its original form (as book), then we might well wonder what reading of *Paradise Regained* we might be able to offer if we treated it in its original form, which is even more complex than that of Spenser's work. In its original form in 1671, *Paradise Regained* was published as one half of a book—the other being, of course, *Samson Agonistes*. In fact, neither work was published separately until 1779.[2] Each had its own title page, and each was separately paginated, but the two were bound together and the significance of that parataxis might be worth examining (and, as we shall see, has been recently the object of some examination). For precisely the same reason Montrose studies *The Shepheardes Calendar* as a book we might study the 1671 binary as a book—to see the process of subjectification in each work and between both works. This would entail seeing in what ways the two main characters share strategies of transforming a self into a representative subject, and in what ways they differ radically. It also entails seeing how each genre lends itself to the differences in each hero's process of subjectification—how each character defines himself in relation to possible discursive strategies and how each defines himself in relation to the division between the private and the public realm. By noticing these differences, we can begin to see the basis of Milton's politics, which, stated broadly and in a preliminary way, is concerned with the question of agency—the self's becoming the subject of ideology or subject to ideology. In the introduction, I suggested that Milton situates the question of agency in a complex of other related concerns regarding the enabling conditions of free will, the basis of agential liberty in the possibility of knowledge, and, especially important for our present study, the relationship between such agential liberty and self-knowledge.

We have seen how these questions—how a self gains knowledge and how self-knowledge can lead to cultural renovation—are treated in *Paradise Regained*. I will explore Milton's own treatment of these same questions as they involve his own, definitive politics. Milton's final exploration of a political ideal is found in his 1671 volume, and that volume's politics are based on the relationship existing between *Paradise Regained* and *Samson Agonistes* in terms of the concept Milton held to be the medial node between theology and politics — Christian liberty. We have already examined Milton's theological statements on the conditions of liberty, and we have also seen how his politics derive from those theological insights — generating what Spinoza called a "theologico-politics." Our concern, then, in these final two chapters, is with Milton's politics as they are represented in the final volume. In that act of representing his politics, Milton also follows the postlapsarian form of self-knowledge. By understanding Milton's coming to self-knowledge in his final volume of poetry, we will be able to discern his politics. In this chapter I will offer a reading of *Samson Agonistes* within the framework I established in the introduction — the process by which a self becomes either a subject of God or subject to God.

"TO WHICH IS ADDED": MILTON IN 1671

Critics have recently come to acknowledge that the publication of *Paradise Regained* and *Samson Agonistes* in a single bound volume was no accident. The volume is odd, to say the least, containing an epic that is arguably unepical and a tragedy that somehow defies its genre.[3] The first serious attempts to treat the two works as if they were purposefully and significantly in apposition were tentatively made in 1971. In the tercentenary celebration of the volume, two distinguished critics came forward with the bold thesis that the two works were published together for an artistic reason. But each of these critics felt he should preface his daring critical examination with a conservative hypothesis of a mundane nature. Balachandra Rajan asks:

> Does Milton really mean that his tragedy is an afterthought or that he is making up for the paucity of those four books and giving the reader due value for his splendid shilling? Or does he mean that the addition fulfills a larger integrity, that the two poems in a sense extend into each other and relate themselves to the poems that precede them, and that what is apparently thrown in for good measure is in fact indispensable to the pattern of the achievement?

In the same vein, Arthur Barker asks: "Is the addition a lapse, a

clumsy afterthought, a response to the booksellers' desire for a
sizable volume? Or does the collocation represent the imperfectly
resolved conflict of the later Miltonic moods which we can discern
in the poetic difficulties we encounter in the two pieces?" The
mood of Milton criticism of that decade was ably expressed by
William Kerrigan: "It is interesting to entertain (though folly to
prove) the possibility that the publication of *Samson Agonistes* and
Paradise Regained in one volume (1671) was no accident."[4] But
ours is another decade and another mood.

Joseph Wittreich's recent book on *Samson Agonistes* (1987) deals
with the work in the context of the 1671 volume. Not only does
Wittreich eschew any gestures of homely wisdom, such as those
made by Barker and Rajan who claim that the volume may contain
the two poems as much out of economic as artistic wisdom, but he
proceeds to deny the autonomy of either poem in the volume:

> *Paradise Regained* and *Samson Agonistes* have not a separate but a
> shared syntax; these poems together form a totality, with the individ-
> ual poems themselves becoming like fragments. The volume, that is,
> becomes the poem; *its* syntax, not that of the separate poems, governs
> the meaning; and the meaning itself derives from the concatenation.

And, true to the new critical spirit, William Kerrigan has argued
that it is the better part of wisdom (and not "folly") to prove that
the parataxis was intentional, not casual: Taken "together Christ
and Samson form the pattern of a guided life, its riddles solved by
attunement of intuition to divine will." In 1930, Tillyard saw the
1671 volume as an "accident of joint publication"; in 1983, John
Shawcross viewed it as the "wisdom of joint publication."[5]

We will keep in mind Montrose's suggestion that treating the
book as such allows us to see the variety of discursive modes within
it, the elaboration of processes of subjectification both within and
beyond it, and the ways in which the book itself is both subject to
and the subject of ideological forces. I will deal with the two works
of the 1671 volume as contrasting studies in precisely those three
interrelated themes. We have seen how Jesus represents himself as a
subject by reading his life and defining himself in terms of a variety
of directions—toward the Law, toward his death, toward God.
Moreover, we saw how the dialectic of the second temptation allowed Jesus to present a radical critique of his culture. To appreci-

ate how Milton writes his own subjectivity into this book, and how he articulates a radical critique of his culture, we must also see how Samson works at attaining subjectivity. Between the two works in the book—within the heterogeneity of genres, in the midst of the historical distance between Philistia and Rome—we might discover Milton's critique of England, his process of subjectification, and his production of ideology.

So far, we have noted how Milton treats self-knowledge in the brief epic. It is an activity of discovering the self's relation to God and thereby demonstrating the paradigmatic (that is, Christian) method of the self's achieving its subjectivity. Self-knowledge is the force of reason that allows the self to make that act of subjectification and therefore gain agential liberty. I will examine what I consider the crux of each poem—Jesus on the pinnacle, Samson at the pillars—in reference to the crux of the companion poem. I hope to account for verbal and iconic echoes in these crucial scenes in determining the relationship between the two poems.

The similarity in form between *Samson Agonistes* and *Paradise Regained* is remarkable. Each hero begins with a long soliloquy in which he confronts himself, each then goes on to a series of three confrontations with the Other, and each ends with a final climactic event. There, however, the similarities end, for I contend that because of Samson's failure in transforming his "self" into a subject of God, a failure caused by his inability to employ his reason in the act of self-knowledge, he loses his agential liberty and becomes, instead, subject to God. That is, simply put, Samson is a servant of God, and not a Son. To see why he was not able to become a Son, we have to begin at his opening soliloquy and trace the movements of his loss of reason.

"BREEDING ORDER'D AND PRESCRIB'D": SAMSON ALONE

The relationship of the two heroes becomes clearer if we appreciate the similarities and differences in their opening meditative soliloquies—both in the external and internal settings, and in the dialectic of each one's musing. In each of the speeches, the hero notes the discordance between inner and outer being. At once in his mind, Jesus says, a "multitude of thoughts" arises while he considers

> What from within I feel my self, and hear
> What from without comes often to my ears,
> Ill sorting with my present state compar'd.   (I, 196–200)

"I seek," Samson says,

> Ease to the body some, none to the mind
> From restless thoughts, that like a swarm
> Of Hornets arm'd, no sooner found alone,
> But rush upon me thronging, and present
> Times past, what once I was, and what am now.   (17–23)

Whereas Jesus escapes society the better to converse with solitude, Samson fears solitude because of the thoughts that pursue him. Samson is perturbed inside while enjoying a pleasant external environment: "The breath of Heav'n fresh-blowing, pure and sweet" (10). Jesus is calm inside while treading through the wilderness, "with dark shades and rocks environ'd round" (I, 194). While Samson is "dark, dark, dark, amid the blaze of noon" (81), Jesus is the "Morning Star" rising brilliantly, though his environment is "dusk with horrid shades" (I, 294–96). Samson is ensconced in thoughts of "Times past" and present—"what once I was, and what am now"—while Jesus thinks of how the past may provide the future: "things past and to come" (I, 300). Jesus' soliloquy is meditative, pursued with an unperturbed mind, while Samson's is troubled in tone, tortured in tenor.[6]

Samson is querulously inquisitive about the reasons for his nativity and his vocation: "O wherefore was my birth from Heaven foretold / . . . Why was my breeding order'd and prescrib'd" (23, 30). Jesus is calm and accepts the wisdom of divine prescription without repining: "Yet neither thus disheartn'd or dismay'd" (I, 268). Samson has an overwhelming sense of carnality; he thinks the body might have been better designed if strength did not reside in the hair nor sight in the eye. He is like the fallen Adam in this sense—he feels uncomfortable with his "corporeal Clod" of a body (PL X, 786). Jesus has no sense of body whatsoever. He speaks of the aspiration of his "Spirit" (PR I, 215), and he nourishes not his body, but his "thoughts" (230).[7] The only reference Jesus makes to his body is figurative. In order to work redemption for mankind, Jesus must have its collective sins "Full weight . . .

transferr'd upon [his] head" (267). In this way, the second Adam answers in spirit what the first Adam had asked in flesh:

> for what can I increase
> Or multiply, but curses on my head?
> Who of all Ages to succeed, but feeling
> The evil on him brought by me, will curse
> My Head. (*PL* X, 731–35)

Dream not of duels, or "local wounds / Of head or heel," Michael tells Adam, for the Son of God will take on his head the burden of obedience and love (*PL* XII, 386–465). The Son of God takes on flesh in order to transfigure it into spirit.[8] So far, then, it would appear that the differences between the two heroes is that Jesus is calm and reflective while Samson is perturbed and somewhat cantankerous. While this is true to a large extent, the difference is only superficial. Their more important difference concerns their disparate talents at attaining self-knowledge.

Jesus, we recall, defines himself in terms of directions. He represents himself as a being-toward. By defining himself in certain key directions—the Law, the private sphere, death, and the public sphere—he gained the degree of self-knowledge required to be a subject of God and therefore to be graced with agency. Samson's soliloquy in which he defines himself has an interesting lack of direction. In fact, the only way to characterize Samson's "self" as it is represented in this opening soliloquy is to say that he is labile. Let us examine the rhetoric of his soliloquy to see how each time he reaches a threshold potentially enabling him to direct himself toward God, he retreats into an act of desperate ambivalence.

He begins by being the recipient of heaven's "breath . . . fresh-blowing, pure and sweet" (10). I would agree with those arguments stating that heaven's breath here signifies the Spirit. As Georgia Christopher has recently argued, such Protestant thinkers as Luther argued that Samson was indeed the recipient of the Holy Spirit. Luther, for instance, numbers Samson among those Old Testament heroes "who were full of the Holy Spirit."[9] However, *pace* Christopher, I would do so only to suggest how much Milton does *not* present us with a "drama of regeneration." What this drama enacts is precisely Samson's inability to keep the Spirit—

that is, his inability to be a free agent. It is important, therefore, that Samson be offered the opportunity to receive the Spirit, and that the opportunity come early. Jesus was the recipient of the Spirit just before his reflective soliloquy: Jesus "walk'd alone, the Spirit leading" (I, 189, 290, 299). Samson asks to be led on by some unknown entity: "A little onward lend thy guiding hand" (1). It is interesting, too, that immediately after the mention of Heaven's "breath," Samson asks whatever or whoever guided him to that spot to leave him "to respire" (11). Surely Milton was too careful an artist to place heaven's breath and Samson's respiration in such a close relationship without intending for us to make some sort of association between the breath and the Spirit. The reason I stress the point is that Samson must be the recipient of the Spirit for Milton's politics of agency to be borne out in a just manner. What Samson does with the Spirit is another matter altogether.

Samson begins, as Jesus had done, by reflecting on his past. We already noted that whereas Jesus directs himself toward the future Samson remains inconsolably concerned only with the past. He then makes a transition, as does Jesus, to the question of his birth, his vocation, and his present situation:

> O wherefore was my birth from Heaven foretold
> Twice by an Angel, who sat at last in sight
> Of both my Parents all in flames ascended
> From off the Altar, where an Off'ring burn'd,
> As in a fiery column charioting
> His Godlike presence, and from some great act,
> Or benefit reveal'd to *Abraham's* race?
> Why was my breeding order'd and prescrib'd
> As of a person separate to God,
> Design'd for great exploits; if I must dye
> Betray'd, Captiv'd, and both my Eyes put out,
> Made of my Enemies the scorn and gaze;
> To grind in Brazen Fetters under task
> With this Heav'd-gifted strength? O glorious strength
> Put to the labour of a Beast, debas't
> Lower than bondslave! Promise was that I
> Should *Israel* from *Philistian* yoke deliver;
> Ask for this great Deliverer now, and find him
> Eyeless in *Gaza* at the Mill with slaves,
> Himself in bonds under *Philistian* yoke.   (23–42)

When Jesus heard from Mary that his birth had been foretold, he deferred his response about the possible meaning of the angelic pronouncement. He hears this and returns to the Law to see what it may mean. To be fair to Samson, he has no book to which he may refer and he does draw the significance of his calling with some degree of talent. We might be troubled by his insistence on the "greatness" of his calling in his eyes. It is difficult to tell to whom belongs the "great act" Samson refers to at line 28—the angel or Samson. In any case, within a couple of lines he asserts that he was called to perform "great exploits." But, even so, we should remember that Jesus, too, responded to his youth with a desire for greatness. What is more troubling is the alacrity with which Samson decides that his "great exploit" should somehow or other involve his death. Quite simply, he has no sanction for this discovery. His career as deliverer required him to free Israel; the idea that he must die to do so is his own addition. Moreover, and more importantly, Samson phrases the question of his death in relation to his imprisonment and as a querulous lament: "Why . . . if I must dye / Betray'd, Captiv'd." What is important to recognize, then, is that Samson's knowledge of his death is not part of his self-discovery, as was Jesus' of his; rather, his is a desire wrought of his present condition. Jesus realizes that death is part of his identity insofar as he is to accede to his kingdom; Samson desires dissolution and cannot understand how death might be productive of good: "Why was I born if I must die?"

Like Jesus' speech, Samson's has an important volta. Having lamented the irony of the great deliverer's release to his enemies, Samson begins to consider the possibility that he is blaspheming in questioning his Lord's will:

> Yet stay, let me not rashly call in doubt
> Divine Prediction; what if all foretold
> Had been fulfilld but through mine own default,
> Whom have I to complain of but my self?   (43–46)

Here we begin to hear the potential for growth in self-knowledge. When Samson thinks that he might be to blame, he is on the threshold of authentic discovery. This would be repentance. But repentance in Milton requires the utmost vigilance and a degree of sincerity that only a few of his characters ever demonstrate; Samson unfortunately is not one of them. When Satan begins to consider the possibility of repenting of his rebellion in the soliloquy on Mount Niphates, he immediately proceeds to think about how regaining heaven would only cause him to desire renewed rebellion (*PL* IV, 81–104). Quite simply, Satan is incapable of understanding what repentance is. He cannot fathom what it would mean to take the blame upon himself for what he has done; he cannot in the farthest reaches of his mind understand what it would be to submit oneself to God. For Satan, the only repentance he can imagine is "feign'd submission." Samson is not so insincere as Satan, but he is, nonetheless, incapable of knowing what repentance is and therefore is unable to repent.

Immediately after this brief moment of insight, Samson renews his lament. He does not consider the ways of repentance, but attempts to extricate himself from blameworthiness by representing himself in metaphors that deny his own agency. He suggests that he is a receptacle that has been violated. Even while he is putatively blaming himself, he uses images that suggest the blamelessness due to an inanimate vehicle:

> Who this high gift of strength committed to me,
> In what part lodg'd, how easily bereft me,
> Under the Seal of silence could not keep,
> But weakly to a woman must reveal it.
> O'recome with importunity and tears.
> O impotence of mind, in body strong!
> But what is strength without a double share
> Of wisdom, vast, unwieldy, burdensom,
> Proudly secure, yet liable to fall
> By weakest suttleties, not made to rule,
> But to subserve where wisdom bears command.
> God, when he gave me strength, to shew withal
> How slight the gift was, hung it in my Hair.   (47–59)

Strength is placed in him, and taken out of him. His being had a seal of silence that was broken; he was violated and, consequently, not responsible for revealing the secret he was supposed to keep. There is in Samson, if I may so term it, no overarching consciousness that we might expect to find in a "self"; he tends to represent himself as a disintegrated being. We saw earlier how Jesus reaches a state of anxiety that is educative by discovering the tension between his spiritual being and his corporal. When Samson begins to discover that tension, he presents it as a division: "O impotence of mind, in body strong!" The sort of anxiety Samson feels is the sort that also comes from recognizing the essential disparity in the human makeup, but his, unlike Jesus', is the sort that is fluctuating because it unreflectively and incessantly tends to rehearse the same grounds of its original sin. Kierkegaard defines precisely this sort of anxiety that is prone to this querulous rehearsing of its basis: "anxiety about sin produces sin."[10] It is the sort of anxiety that comes from an inability to consider the future; while Jesus thought of what would come, Samson retreats time and again to what simply had been. Moreover and more importantly, he represents that history as if he were not an agent in it, but rather a vessel of its becoming.

Immediately thereafter, though, Samson once again returns to the possibility that he is to blame for his downfall, and once more he attempts to reach a threshold of self-knowledge:

> But peace, I must not quarrel with the will
> Of highest dispensation, which herein
> Happ'ly had ends above my reach to know:
> Suffices that to me strength is my bane,
> And proves the sourse of all my miseries.   (60–64)

The retreat to lamentation is even quicker now. Three lines after considering the justice of his situation, Samson concludes abruptly that all his miseries may be traced back to his strength. Consider the complete sentence from lines 53 to 58. The entire sentence is about strength; "strength," as a matter of fact, is the subject of that sentence. It is "strength" that is liable to fall, that is incapable of ruling, that is meant to subserve. Where, one wonders, is "Samson" in relation to all of this free-floating strength? Samson here attempts to achieve what we might term a sort of false transcendence; he renounces his own agency in favor of ascribing a subjectivity to one facet of his being that it quite simply does not and cannot possess.

Let me use a later historical confrontation to demonstrate what Samson is doing here. Marx critiqued Hegel's doctrine of the state by tracing the problem back to Hegel's tendency to promote a certain type of abstraction:

If Hegel's starting-point had been *real mind,* then the 'universal end' would have been its content and the various powers would have been its mode of self-realization, its *actual* or *material* existence whose determinate characteristics would have emerged from the nature of its end. But as he begins by making the 'Idea' or 'substance' into the subject, the real essence, it is inevitable that the *real subject* should appear only as the *last predicate* of the abstract predicate.

The process of this subject/predicate inversion requires three gestures: (1) the "state" in Hegel's writing "becomes abstract reality or substantiality," (2) "its substantiality passes over into necessity, substantial reality," and (3) "this substantial reality" becomes "in fact *concept, subjectivity.*" Thus does an abstract entity, properly defined as the activity of other subjects, in itself acquire subjectivity. This is not strictly a nineteenth-century problem. Hobbes noted that the second form of absurdity is the ascribing of properties to things incapable of bearing those properties: "The second cause of Absurd assertions, I ascribe to the of giving names of *bodies,* to *accidents;* or of *accidents,* to *bodies.*" Typically, he uses this insight to argue that faith and spirit are given properties that they simply cannot possess because nothing can "inspire" anything else. In any case, Hobbes's insight helps us historicize Samson's absurdity in granting the "accident" of his "strength" its own body while treating the body of "Samson" as merely an "accident."[11]

Samson's "strength"—on which he places the full blame for all his miseries—has achieved just that sort of mystical subjectivity Hegel wished to assign the state. Strength is not, as Samson would have it, a subject in and of itself; strength is an activity through which Samson's agency is exercised. So that telling sentence beginning "What is strength" might alert us to the ways Samson is starting to avoid accepting blame for his actions by ascribing subjectivity to what is only an abstraction of his own activity. Had Samson truly understood the nature of repentance, he would have said "I am my bane; my actions are the source of my misery." But Samson is in the process of eschewing the sort of self-knowledge he requires to become a son of God. No small part of that self-knowledge is knowing that he must abide by and be responsible to the choices he has made—his agency is not to be denied when it backfires on him.

But if strength is the source of his miseries, blindness is the most trying of those miseries. There are few more moving passages in Milton's works than Samson's lengthy apostrophe to sight (67–110). We find in it the depth of Samson's despair, the degree to which he has abnegated his own agency, and the overweening pride with which he criticizes God. However, I also must admit to finding it quite difficult to trace the theological crimes Samson commits here, given that he is, after all, lamenting what we take so much for granted. To argue, for instance, that Samson commits a heinous indecorum bordering on blasphemy when he suggests that God's original constitution of the human body is imperfect—"why was the sight / To such a tender ball as th' eye confin'd?" (94–95)—is also to take the high moral road at a very great cost to our humanity. Whatever theological proprieties Samson may be breaking here, he is also in a position most of us won't find ourselves in. The measure of Milton's success, I think, is that we are forced to recognize that. Having recognized it, then, we must, in order to discover the process by which Samson loses the Spirit, still trace in what ways he renounces his subjectivity. Perhaps the only way to appreciate what other ways there are to respond to blindness we should see what the author of *Samson* did. In answering More's taunts in the *Second Defence,* Milton concludes his responses to the personal smears: "Would it were equally in my power to confute this inhuman adversary on the subject of my blindness! but it is not. Then let us bear it. To be blind is not miserable; not to be able to bear blindness, that is miserable."[12] To my mind, that last sentence is the most beautiful one Milton ever wrote. It is also a fine counterpoint to Samson's moving sentiments. Samson does not, as his author did in 1654, differentiate the misery from the agent able to bear it. He uses the misery to express his despair and renounce his agency: "Scarce half I seem to live, dead more than half" (80). Not only does he lose "half" the responsibility properly belonging to him, but he goes on to represent himself once more in the same sort of metaphor of a vessel, a receptacle: "My self, my Sepulcher, a moving Grave" (103).

Samson, then, to conclude the examination of his soliloquy, does not gain self-knowledge here because he insistently renounces the very idea of a self as an organized constitution having a degree of agency and reason. Each time he begins to seem to have the potential for recognizing a self that is blameworthy, Samson represents himself as being under the compulsion of some other abstract agency—either by using metaphors that indicate he is a vessel or by ascribing agency to what is only one facet of his activity. We recall that in *Paradise Regained* when Satan set himself to doubting the Spirit, he ensued upon a full career of radical Pyrrhonism. Although Samson is not like Satan, he nonetheless is abiding within the same theological structure defining agency. Because he squanders the opportunity to use the Spirit to gain self-knowledge, which is necessary to assuming the role of subject of God, Samson becomes to that degree less a reasonable being and therefore less an agential being. In this, he is exactly like Satan.

To state the case dogmatically, Samson chooses to give up reason, agency, and choice. Milton's theology finds its strength in the seeming paradox that it requires choice to give up choice. He manages to demonstrate how certain persons lose what God permits to all (free will) by showing how those persons exercise the very agency of free will (reason) in the losing of both. Samson has the opportunity to break out of his mode of despair. Had he just come to know himself by grasping fully those glimmers of his blameworthiness, those moments when he seems on the verge of theodicy, he, too, would have been a free agent. But Samson, as much as Satan, eschews the knowledge of self that the Spirit would have given him. Jesus, on the other hand, demonstrates just the sort of reasonableness required to gain self-knowledge, which, in turn, is required to maintain agency.[13]

I am suggesting that there is implicit in Milton's theology a system of relating agency back to self-knowledge, which in turn is traced back to the ability of the "self" to become a "subject." The way of proceeding in that self-knowledge is to progress from defining oneself in one direction to defining oneself in yet another direction—just the way Jesus defines himself. This is progress, though, not simply diffusion. In other words, the defining of self follows a trajectory or steadiness of direction. Progress, we must recall, is what Milton suggested is requisite to virtue in *Areopagitica*. According to Stanley Fish, *Areopagitica* represents the moment when Milton's theory of "personality" underwent a transformation. Before 1644, according to Fish, "persons" in Milton's works were self-contained and unchanging—"possessed of and by an inner certainty that renders them forever the same, no matter what the changes in external circumstances." In *Areopagitica*, though, Milton articulated a new concept of personality: "Fixity of mind and judgment is stigmatized as the sign of spiritual sloth." To an extent, this is quite correct and will prove very helpful to future Milton criticism. The way Fish phrases this insight, however, is not only troubling in and of itself, but it leads him to misrepresent Milton's theory of personality. Fish concludes his analysis of the alteration in Milton's thought by stating the conditions concerning the wayfaring Christian life in which Truth is always on the horizon and the wayfarer in "perpetuall progression": "In the context of such a life, constancy of mind is what one wants to avoid, while change, discontinuity, and endless transformation are what one avidly courts."[14]

Fish conflates *progression* and something like *inconstancy*, and that simply is not warranted by anything Milton says—before or after 1644. On this point, we might again invoke Hobbes. I suggested in chapter 2 that Hobbes pointed out how thinking required an "end" toward which the mind could direct itself. Hobbes goes so far as to say that "without Steddinesse, and Direction to some End, a great Fancy is one kind of Madnesse" (*Leviathan*, p. 136). In Hobbes's science, as in Milton's narrative, progress and constancy are not antithetical; in fact, they support each other. Inconstancy, on the other hand, is what leads to madness always in Hobbes and more often than not in Milton. In *Paradise Regained,* for instance, Satan is inconstant, Jesus progresses. In the late political tracts, the rabble are inconstant in their desire for a monarch; Milton progresses to another form of government of the spirit. More troubling, though, is that once "inconstancy" has replaced progression, Fish goes on to make an argument we will discuss more fully below—that Samson's infidelity is the highest form of faith. But Samson, as he represents himself in this opening soliloquy, is not "progressing," but "inconstant." He does not define himself by progressing from one direction to another, but wavers and fluctuates between defining himself as the predicate of the subject *strength* or as a vessel whose seal has been broken. Because Fish is quite correct in pointing out that "progression" is the mark of discernment in Milton's characters, it is equally important to note when these characters exhibit progression and when they are simply inconstant. On that distinction we may differentiate self-knowledge from self-centeredness in Milton's characters, and, with regard to each character's self-knowledge, we may attend to his confrontations with the Other.

Too many critics tend to dismiss the importance of Samson's soliloquy to his later encounters with Manoa, Dalila, and Harapha. The assumption that Milton presents Samson at the lowest stage of his being in order to show how he gains self-knowledge in his confrontations with the Others (and therefore regains the spiritual grace of God) is untrue to Milton's theology. It is also, and this is more significant, not borne out by the plot of the poem. *Samson Agonistes* is most emphatically not what has come to be called a "drama of regeneration." The argument that it is such a drama rests on the premise that Samson is somehow able to regenerate himself by regaining the Spirit, which I have just shown he lost in the opening soliloquy. The breath of heaven that Samson inhaled to open the play was exhaled in nothing but a fit of despair. The traditional argument suggests that Samson regains that spirit in the much-debated "middle" of the drama.

To give our discussion some focus, I will return briefly to the issue of death as it is raised and resolved in each of Jesus' and Samson's soliloquies. Jesus had intuited that death was the way to his kingdom — a fact he discovered between his representations of hearing his mother and hearing his Father, between what I defined as his private and his public aspects. Samson represents his calling as it was originally told to "both [his] Parents" and does not so much discover the fact of his death as desire it: "Why was my breeding order'd . . . if I must dye." Living as he does is "yet more miserable" than death (100–05). Death, then, is something desirable to Samson; it is, moreover, the primary register of his despair. So as we trace the so-called "middle" of *Samson Agonistes,* we will pay special attention to how Samson asserts or assuages this desire for suicide. It is, I think, the measure of how much the hero of this play undergoes a drama of regeneration.

"DEGENERATLY I SERV'D": BEYOND REGENERATION IN *SAMSON*'S MIDDLE

The traditional regeneration reading of the play suggests that, in the process of encountering Manoa, Dalila, and Harapha, Samson is roused from his servile apathy to a renewed heroism. In the words of Albert R. Cirillo, *Samson Agonistes* "is about human, moral endurance, or fortitude, and the manner in which this leads to the triumph over despair, which is regeneration."[15] Mary Ann Radzinowicz has declared that, since John Steadman's important essay, "'Faithful Champion': The Theological Basis of Milton's Hero of Faith," "it has become unnecessary to retrace the steps of Samson's gradual process of sanctification."[16] It seems to me, though, that it is most necessary to examine again the presuppositions of the regenerative reading. Critics have examined anew the steps to Samson's alleged "regeneration" and have determined that the very regeneration theory itself is suspect. I find myself in substantial agreement with these critics—notably Irene Samuel, John Carey, Joseph Wittreich, Stanley Fish, and the very first of these, G. A. Wilkes. When Wilkes first set out to interpret the play, John Steadman called his study "an attack on the 'regeneration theory.'"[17] It seems to me more an *exposé*. I hope to trace the movement of Samson's mind through the three encounters and also take account of the critical readings that suggest that this is a drama of regeneration. These critics, I believe, misconstrue Milton's theological claims for the process and effects of regeneration and misread Milton's play to make it fit this misconstructed theological pattern.

The play unfolds by emphasizing the hero's ongoing irresolution, his consistently uneasy lability of mind. Samson begins in a state akin to despair.[18] In each encounter, as in his soliloquy, Samson vacillates between expressed faith and latent infidelity. For instance, in his response to his father's concerns that Samson will be forced to go to the Temple of Dagon, Samson shows some degree of hope:

> This only hope relieves me, that the strife
> With me hath end; all the contest is now
> 'Twixt God and *Dagon*.   (461–63)

Yet, a little further on after his father departs, Samson shows himself to be so bereft of hope as earnestly to desire dissolution:

> Nor am I in the list of them that hope;
> Hopeless are all my evils, all remediless;
> This one prayer yet remains, might I be heard,
> No long petition, speedy death,
> The close of all my miseries, and the balm.   (648–52)

Samson will continue to vacillate; it is his nature to shift between hope and despair. But critics are unwilling to recognize (or allow for) this unsteadiness. They find a set pattern in which Samson is cured of his despair at one crucial moment in the play. The argument that the play is a drama of regeneration rests, after all, on the theory that the plot demonstrates a hero undergoing and expressing his regeneration, not one who wavers between despair and hope.

Most critics argue that the Harapha incident is the crux of Samson's regeneration. Samson, they claim, answers Harapha with his most confident statement as he finally begins to take some responsibility for his earlier actions:

> All these indignities, for such they are,
> From thine, these evils I deserve and more,
> Acknowledge them from God inflicted on me
> Justly, yet despair not of his final pardon
> Whose ear is ever open; and his eye
> Gracious to re-admit the suppliant;
> In confidence whereof I once again
> Defie thee to the trial of mortal fight,
> By combat to decide whose god is God,
> Thine or whom I with *Israel's* Sons adore.   (1179–88)

"With this speech," writes Don Cameron Allen, "we know that Samson will not die an apathetic death." Instead, Allen continues, we know that Samson is now back in God's good graces:

> Life has returned to him; and though he does not yet know how it will all be brought about, he is God's champion once more. There is no temptation in this scene and no comedy; it is the most important scene of all, for it is the hinge of the tragedy. By the victory over Harapha, who symbolizes all that is valiant in Philistia, God, working through Samson, has put Dagon down. It is, in truth, the final event of the tragedy in miniature.[19]

But consider that as soon as Harapha skulks off Samson returns to exactly the same sort of desperation of life that he had earlier demonstrated:

> But come what will, my deadliest foe will prove
> My speediest friend, by death to rid me hence,
> The worst that he can give, to me the best.   (1273–75)

The encounter with Harapha did nothing special to regenerate Samson. Samson still wavers between hope and despair (and, again, to the point of a desire for suicide). Allen cites these lines only to argue that somehow they are Samson's "last breath of despair." But surely having Samson utter such despair right after his confident outburst against Harapha indicates that he is not regenerated. As Wilkes argues, "at so critical a moment," the poem can certainly not "afford any ambivalence of attitude."[20] And yet the poem not only allows but highlights just such an ambivalence.

Steadman, whose article Radzinowicz saw as the sum of Milton's theology, does not cite these lines, but he does argue from lines 648 to 649 that Samson is one of those, like Abraham, "who against hope believed in hope" (Rom. iv, 18, 19). Steadman's case rests on two arguments. In the first, Steadman makes a curious division in kinds of hope: Samson's "hope in God stands, however, in striking contrast to the absence of personal hope."[21] The second is that Samson has full faith in God.

I can find nothing in the *Christian Doctrine* to warrant the distinction in kinds of hope. True, some, such as Richard Sibbes and William Perkins, hold that there is a "holy despaire" in each person that is commensurate with true faith in God, but I have not been able to find this distinction anywhere in Milton.[22] Moreover, Sibbes and Perkins note that effectually called persons despair in their own capacities. Samson never does this; his faith is in the living Samson, whatever he may say to the contrary. This leads to Steadman's second point, which strikes me as being untrue to the play; Samson simply does not demonstrate full faith in God. Whether Samson should fight Harapha or not is debatable. It seems to me, among others, that Milton suggests Samson fails in this encounter.[23] For, in expressing a willingness to fight Harapha, Samson lapses into infidelity. "My trust," he declares, "is in the living God" (1151). But his faith is, rather, in his physical prowess. Why, for example, should one so faithful suggest that some "narrow place enclos'd" be assigned to the fight? Does the "faithful Champion" need to circumscribe the power of his God? How, furthermore, ought we to react to Samson's ascription of visible and tactile qualities to the ineffable God: "Then thou shalt see, or rather to thy sorrow / Soon feel, whose God is strongest, thine or mine" (1165–66)? If this is faith, it is a puerile expression at best. This is not faith, though, because Samson is incapable of rousing himself to unwavering faith. He must be roused to it. He has lost the agency he requires to act properly—to will well, as Perkins puts it—because he does not have the reason to employ it.

But the "regeneration theory" is based not only on a misreading of the play but also on a commensurate misconstruction of Milton's doctrine of regeneration, which states that the being who is to be regenerated does not possess the power to do so but is, rather, regenerated by the power of God. Once again, the best way of seeing the subtlety of Milton's theology is to compare him on this point with William Perkins. Perkins argues that there is no logic of cause and effect in regeneration:

> For every cause is before his effect, if not in time, yet in priority of nature. The wil converted so soone as God hath begunne to renew it, wils to be renewed: and it could not will the conversion of it selfe, unless it had formerly tasted of the goodnesse thereof. And though we first feele the desire to be converted, before the grace of conversion, it is nothing: for sometimes we perceive the effect before the cause.[24]

Samson, it might then be argued, can will himself to a state of regeneration because he has "formerly tasted of the goodnesse thereof." But, Perkins is quick to add, even at this stage of renovation God is the principal mover in all three forms of grace: in "preventing grace," God gives power to work; in "working grace," God gives the will to will well; and in "co-working grace," God gives "deed" to the will.

Even after regeneration, for the will to do any work it requires a "double grace": first, the "assisting grace," whereby God preserves, confirms, and protects the regenerate; and second, the "exciting grace," whereby "God mooves and stirres up the will, that it may indeede will and doe the good to be done." This grace, Perkins concludes, "is ordinarily required to the effecting of every good worke."[25] Even though he intimates that somehow human will is able to bring forth good works "of it selfe," Perkins always makes God's activity a precondition, thus making humans but the vehicular expression of God's agency. We saw in the introduction how Milton contests Perkins's definition of liberty and asserts that the fallen will is able to will well, although feebly. The basis of Milton's assertion for the continued activity of the will is "reason." Agency accrues to those beings who are reasonable. What, though, of those beings who are not? Here, I would suggest, is where Milton's doctrine differs from Perkins's only in degree.

Regeneration, Milton writes, "appears to be to a certain degree in the power of the regenerate themselves" (CM XVI, p. 17). Two things stand out in this statement: first, that human power is only apparently in the power of the regenerate (*"esse videtur"*), and second, that it is apparently so only to a "certain degree," meaning, then, that regeneration *is* preponderantly in the power of God. Milton elsewhere derides the notion of *earned* regeneration. His interpretation "affords no countenance to the doctrine of human merit, inasmuch as both faith itself and its works are the works of the Spirit, not our own" (CM XVI, p. 41). Even were Samson faithful, which we have seen he is not, it would not be due to his activity but to that of the Spirit. And we have seen already to what degree Samson respired the Spirit. Reflecting both on Milton's theology and on the way he has presented his hero, we must view with skepticism such enthusiastic, because ill-informed, arguments as Morris Freedman's that Samson's "new strength is, simply, self-generated, self-controlled." This is simply untrue to Milton's doctrine and his drama. Samson is generated by what Perkins might have called "exciting grace," and what Milton called "rouzing motions." Approaching now Samson's fourth confrontation of the drama—the encounter with the Officer—we might reconsider what is signified by what Anthony Low has called these "obscure and ambiguously interpretable inner promptings."26

FROM "INTIMATE IMPULSE" TO "ROUZING MOTIONS": GOD IN *SAMSON AGONISTES*

Regeneration, according to those critics who read *Samson Agonistes* as a drama of regeneration, is given to Samson as a reward he has earned because he has regained his faith in God. Milton, as we saw above, does not countenance the idea of earned regeneration. If, then, we are to go on calling *Samson Agonistes* a drama of regeneration we must redefine the genre so that it accommodates the process of regeneration as it happens within the general guidelines of Milton's theology—that is, as the working of the Spirit *through* the regenerate being. This, I must stress, is not to deny Milton's Arminianism. As I noted earlier, Milton argues that agency belongs only to those who are reasonable beings; Samson does not number among that crowd. Thus, he is not an agent of the Spirit (or a subject of God or a Son of God), but rather a vessel of the Spirit (or subject to God or a servant of God). This is amply demonstrated at the key scene with the Officer.

The Officer enters and delivers the message of the lords, bidding Samson to come with him to the temple (1321–29). Samson claims that such attendance is against Hebrew law and denies the request: "I cannot come" (1330–32). The Officer renews his suit, and Samson again states his unwillingness: "I will not come" (1343). To the Officer's third brief appeal, Samson remains obdurate: "I will not come" (1353). Only after this triple denial does Samson receive his "rouzing motions" (1393). Immediately after this, at the Officer's return and reiterated request, Samson goes to the temple: "I am content to go" (1414). There is, as Wilkes rightly notes, "an unmistakable discontinuity" between the two scenes and a remarkable conversion in the hero that may be ascribed, I think, only to a force other than his mentality.[27] Of his own will, Samson does not go to the temple. He goes only after he receives the "rouzing motions." Until recently, no one gave very serious consideration to what the "rouzing motions" might signify; it was taken for granted that they represented the grace of God, just as they had done in *Paradise Lost,* when God sends his "motions" to work in Adam and Eve (*PL* XI, 91). However, with the new critiques of the regeneration reading, we might return to examine the supposition of those ambiguous motions.

Those who argue for the regeneration reading see the motions as a sign of grace that not only sanctions Samson's final act, but is the reward for his achieving renewed faith. For those who contest the regeneration theory, the motions are nothing more than a signifier of Samson's own personal desire. As Joseph Wittreich has recently argued, Samson is "confusing a physical with a spiritual stimulus and mistaking an internal impulse for a divine prompting." Wittreich is arguing from the earlier moment of Samson's receipt of God's "motions"—the "intimate impulse" leading him to marry the woman of Timna (224). Irene Samuel offers an eloquent case for this second argument. Using Charles Dunster's note on a passage in which Samson is discussing the reasons he married outside of his tribe (878–95), she notes "Samson's habitual confusion of his own impulse with 'divine compulsion.'" She cites Samson's former self-delusion—a "Samson self-deluded earlier about his divinely inspired impulse to marry Dalila"—as a good reason to suspect this "final impulse [which] may be as little divine in its inspiration." She then goes on to quote a passage from Milton's prose to show that he did not hold all "impulses" to be of certain origin: "Divine illumination . . . no man can know at all times to be in himself, much less to be at any time for certain in any other."[28]

There are several points to consider in Samuel's argument. First of all, the passage from *A Treatise of Civil Power* is taken seriously out of context. Milton begins by stating the two standards of authority common to all of the Protestant faith: "No other divine rule or autoritie from without us [is] warrantable to one another as a common ground but the holy scripture, and no other within us but the illumination of the Holy Spirit so interpreting that scripture." He then cites the passage quoted by Samuel above to argue *for* the individual conscience: "And these [Scriptures] being not possible to be understood without this divine illumination, which no man can know at all times to be in himself, much less to be at any time for certain in any other, it follows cleerly, that no man or body of men in these times can be the infallible judges or determiners in matters of religion to any other mens consciences but thir own." First of all, Samuel ignores that important historical placement—"in these times." In the time of judges, God regularly communed with his chosen vessels of destruction—like Gideon, for instance. Later, in *A Treatise,* he will distinguish the English Parliament's ability to govern the church from the ancient Israeli magistrates' ability precisely on those grounds: "Those magistrates under the law might have recours, as I said before, to divine inspiration" (CM VI, pp. 6, 26–27). On the eve of the Restoration, Milton must have thought, God's conversation was not so readily heard. Second, Milton does not use the argument that it is impossible to know certainly whether or not one possesses "divine illumination" to place the illumination itself in a suspicious light. He uses it to argue that, because of human limitation—and therefore any person's occasional inability to differentiate between divine illumination and self-desire—no individual may be given government over another's conscience. Each must rule herself or himself. But that does not deny Milton's belief in the validity of divine inspiration when it is truly divine.

Moreover, Samuel's contention about Samson's "habitual confusion" is not quite correct either. Samson does not confuse his impulses with divine compulsion, and he certainly doesn't do so habitually. Rather, Samson failed once to distinguish the temporal limits or the duration God sets on his divine commands. When we return to examine that failure, we find how authentic divine commands are differentiated from self-delusions. To appreciate the distinction between the limits of divine sanction and the perpetual unfathomableness of his personal desire, we might turn to what Samson has to say about the impulse that prompts him to marry the woman of Timna. God, he states, allowed him to marry her:

> The first I saw at *Timna,* and she pleas'd
> Mee, not my Parents, that I sought to wed
> The daughter of an Infidel: they knew not
> That what I motion'd was of God; I knew
> From intimate impulse, and therefore urg'd
> The Marriage on; that by occasion hence
> I might begin *Israel's* Deliverance
> The work to which I was divinely call'd.   (220–25)

The phrasing is ambiguous, to say the least, although Milton went out of his way to clarify at least one potential ambiguity. In the first printing of the poem, line 222 read "That what I *mention'd* was of God." Milton makes the change to "motion'd" in the list of errata, and that is a word Milton did not use lightly.[29] As Samson uses it, though, it is made somewhat ambiguous. The key word *motion* seems to belong to Samson's subjectivity — "what *I* motion'd was of God" — and does therefore create some suspicion about whose "intimate impulse" might be working on Samson's decision-making faculties. Certain critics have begun to explore that suspicion.

According to Stanley Fish, there are three answers to the question of the earlier motion's provenance. Samson believes that the first marriage was inspired by God, but the second was a mistake prompted by his own carnal desires misinterpreting God as their impulse. Manoa believes both marriages were mistakes. The Chorus believes that both marriages were inspired by God. Fish's reading follows that of Samuel and Wittreich in determining that the later "rouzing motions" could not have emanated from God because of the obscurity surrounding the earlier "intimate impulse." The three different and contradictory interpretations of those "impulses" creates a blurring not only of the "status of either or both of the marriages" but the status of the very "impulses" themselves. Fish concludes it "follows then that when he later reports on the 'rousing motions' he begins to feel, there is no way to be confident that those motions correspond to some communication that is occurring between him and God."[30]

Fish's reading strategy is extremely curious. Why should we think that all three interpretations are equally valid? We will soon enough see that none of them is. Moreover, why should the commerce between the three interpretations lead us to conclude that it is impossible to determine where the impulse came from? Surely contradictory statements may be resolved in a framework that establishes the truth-value for any given interpretation. Furthermore, Fish is factually wrong in his assessment both of the Chorus' and of Samson's understanding of the "intimate impulse." If the interplay of the three interpretations determines what sense we make of the "intimate impulse," then we might attend quite carefully to the ways *each* interpretation invalidates itself. For, in the end, I would argue, none of the three interpretations is correct. The key to determining the provenance of the impulse is to read between the interpretive versions.

The most skeptical observer in this play is Manoa:

> I cannot praise thy Marriage choises, Son,
> Rather approv'd them not; but thou didst plead
> Divine impulsion prompting how thou might'st
> Find some occasion to infest our Foes.
> I state not that; this I am sure; our Foes
> Found soon occasion thereby to make thee
> Thir Captive, and thir triumph. (421–27)

First of all, that opening line is not just the funniest in the whole drama, it also reveals the way Manoa thinks. Manoa's skepticism about Samson's claim to have felt divine impulse is based on his understanding of the visible outcome: "I state not that; this I am sure." Had Samson not been taken captive, Manoa would surely have believed in the divine impulse. For Manoa, quite simply, success is the measure of divine grace. Manoa is the obverse here of those Independents who equated Cromwell's military victories with

God's will—such persons as Marchamont Needham and Cromwell himself (YP V, p. 126). According to that logic, Cromwell's loss would have been taken to mean that the divine will was with the royalist army. Milton did not accept the equation Needham and Cromwell did, although William Empson claims that "Milton had long been printing the conviction that his political side had been proved right because God had made it win."[31] Milton nowhere prints this conviction; nor is it recorded anywhere else (except in Empson's book). As Milton stated as early as 1649, "Wee measure not our Cause by our success, but our success by our cause" (CM V, p. 307). He would add that it certainly is a "good confirmation" of God's will when a good cause does succeed, but the main force of his thought is that success is not the measure of the goodness of any cause. At the height of Cromwell's success in 1654, Milton still maintained that same tenet: "A cause is neither proved to be good, nor shown to be bad, by success: we demand not that our cause should be judged of by the event; but the event by the cause" (CM VIII, p. 185). Manoa, however, measures the quality of God's will directly by its visible results. His "I state not that" translates simply enough as "Well, that's good and fine, but *look* at you." This tendency in Manoa's thinking is shown to the fullest at the end of the play, when he distinguishes between Samson's heroics and Samson's degradations. Even though he feels Samson has fulfilled his life's aim in killing the Philistines, Manoa still laments "His lot unfortunate in nuptial choice, / From whence captivity and loss of eyes" (1744–45). Captivity and blindness, it has to be pointed out, are what allowed Samson to perform at the temple. Manoa, then, is indeed an agnostic, and for that reason we might decline to base our understanding of the "intimate impulses" on his interpretation.

Likewise, the Chorus is hardly any better an authority regarding the divine impulse. In their famous speech beginning "Just are the ways of God," they pretend to be appalled by those who would attempt to understand the many ways of God—those who would "confine th' interminable"—but in reality that is what they do:

> For with his own Laws he can best dispense.
> He would not else who never wanted means,
> Nor in respect of the enemy just cause
> To set his people free,

Have prompted this Heroic Nazarite,
Against his vow of strictest purity,
To seek in marriage that fallacious Bride,
Unclean, unchaste.   (315–22)

First of all, it is not so clear as Fish would make it that the Chorus
is talking about Dalila and the woman of Timna here. They mention only one "Bride," so the Chorus might be talking about either.
Moreover, because they undercut the very conditions of theodicy
they have just articulated, it is somewhat difficult to grant their
interpretation much validity.

Rather, we should turn directly to Samson, for in his *unwitting*
revelation of how he understands God's impulses we may make the
distinction between his desire and God's commands. The inter-
polation of his own desire is revealed when he begins to extend
God's command beyond its intention—that is, when he applies
God's command to marry the woman of Timna to his desire to
marry Dalila. Some critics, Radzinowicz foremost among them,
feel that Samson is divinely inspired to marry Dalila:

> He married outside his own tribe because he knew "from intimate
> impulse" that what he proposed "was of God" in that it provided the
> occasion to begin the liberation of Israel. He chose Dalila as his
> second wife in the same manner he chose his first, from among the
> overlord, unclean, and forbidden tribe, because of the earlier divine
> guidance and its recognized intention.[32]

But God did not sanction the marriage to Dalila, Samson did. He
says: "I thought it lawful from my former act" (232). First of all, it
goes hardly without saying, Samson is no great thinker. He takes
God's singular command, an impulse that was valid, and applies his
desire to it in a second instance. In grammatical terms, while God
states his command in the imperative (implying only a present
tense), Samson tends to hear it in the aorist—that is, indefinite,
without limitation. God says, "Marry this Philistine *woman.*" Samson thinks this licenses him to marry Philistine *women:* "I thought
it lawful from my former act." But Samson's error in thinking that
the first, divine impulse to marry carried with it an option for a
second, self-willed choice does not invalidate either the original
divine impulsion or any other clearly marked "motions."

In answer to Fish's argument, then, there is no reason to believe Samson *knows* that he is making a mistake in marrying Dalila; he only states that he thought it was lawful, and that it came to a rather bad end. He does not anywhere state that it came to a bad end because it was not divinely sanctioned. Here is where Fish's reading of the radical indeterminacy of the "intimate impulse" fails to account for itself. While there are three contradictory interpretations, it is not impossible to discover the grounds of those interpretations and choose between them. Manoa, we saw, determined the cause by the end, which means that he would naturally deny the divine impulse if the end does not agree with what he perceives to be the "best." The Chorus undermines its own theodicy by attempting to circumscribe God's will and makes ambiguous which "Bride" they intend, and so their interpretation is simply inadequate to the known facts. Finally, Samson, *pace* Fish, does not "assume" that his marriage to Dalila was a mistake. It is precisely on the grounds of his not knowing that he made a mistake that we can come to understand how to distinguish personal desire from divine sanction. Does the impulse come from a "motion" from God, or is it a product of Samson's "thinking"? Therein is the difference between divine impulse and human desire.

So when Samson receives the "rouzing motions" *after he has already done his thinking*—in declining to go the temple thrice—we might be inclined to believe that this is indeed divine impulse. The difference between Samson before receiving the "rouzing motions" and after is measurable by the "will" he states. Before the "rouzing motions," he says twice, "I will not come" (1343, 1353). After, he says,

> I begin to feel
> Some rouzing motions in me which dispose
> To something extraordinary my thoughts.
> I with this Messenger will go along.   (1392–95)

The difference between the "will" in the first and second instance is not, as Fish contends, the difference between the "fixed position of a fully formed and independent self" and a "self 'willing' to have its configurations transformed by a future it cannot read" (p. 579). The difference is between a Samson thinking through the prism of the law—"Our Law forbids at thir Religious Rites / My presence; for that cause I cannot come" (1331–32)—and a Samson whose present thoughts are beyond his normal capacities, whose thoughts are indeed "extraordinary." After the "rouzing motions," Samson's will is simply not his own. He has by now become the vessel he thought he was in his opening soliloquy.

So far I have been basing my argument against Samson's self-motivated regeneration on the question of his suicidal desire. Samson keeps insisting on his desire to die after each episode in which he is allegedly becoming regenerate; it would indeed be hard to propose that Samson's despair is somehow involved with his regeneration, as we saw. After he receives the "rouzing motions," then, according to the logic of my reading, Samson should no longer demonstrate a desire for death; he should not be desperate. But, as Samuel argues, Samson does still desire to die after the "rouzing motions": "The Samson we hear long for death through scene after scene can resolve his *agon* only with death for himself as well as his enemies."[33] If he still wishes to die after he has received divine impulse to act in God's wars, it would seem that he has not overcome his earlier suicidal desires, which, in turn, would suggest that God's "rouzing motions" were not effective in rousing Samson beyond his will. Samson, however, does not "long" for death:

> I begin to feel
> Some rouzing motions in me which dispose
> To something extraordinary my thoughts
> . . . .
> If there be aught of presage in the mind,
> This day will be remarkable in my life
> By some great act, or of my days the last.   (1392–1400)

Samson is not saying here is that he "long[s] for death"—which is what he had intimated in his earlier pronouncements at lines 648–52 and 1273–75—but that he is now "presaging" his death. And the difference is that between a willful and an inspired musing, between his previous ordinary and his present "extraordinary" thoughts. Samson is roused beyond thinking; his inability to generate self-knowledge led to his losing the agency of his will, and he has become now a vessel of divine wrath.

Whatever the differences in matters of tone and generic decorum between *Samson Agonistes* and *A Mask*, there is no difference in the theology regarding agency. As the Spirit "epiloguizes," "if Vertue feeble were, / Heav'n itself would stoop to her" (*A Mask*,

1022–23).[34] In Samson's case, virtue's weakness called for heaven's silent descent to rouse the hero to his final act. This, as Carey argues, is the final argument against the "regeneration theory": "With this old type of hero (unlike the new model hero of *Paradise Regained*) God still has to pull the strings." That is the difference between the two heroes of the 1671 volume. Whereas Jesus receives "strong motions" (I, 290) at the beginning of his career and lives out his agential liberty faultlessly, Samson must receive "rouzing motions" at the crucial point in his career because he has lost his agential liberty. It is very important not to ascribe the wrong sort of motion at the wrong time to either hero. For instance, Christopher Hill is incorrect in saying that Jesus receives "rousing motions," and William Kerrigan even more damagingly wrong in saying that "rousing motions come to Christ on the pinnacle."[35] In truth, Jesus receives only "strong motions" and that only at the beginning of his career. Samson, on the other hand, must be "rouzed" at the end of his career in order to fulfill its mandate; he is unable to express himself without a cue from stooping heaven.

William Perkins noted a difference in the types of grace necessary for willing well — that between "assisting grace" and "exciting grace" — which had as its basis the difference between remaining confirmed or being stirred to will a good act. So, for Perkins, "exciting grace" is "ordinarily required to the effecting of every good worke." Milton makes the distinction between "strong motions" and "rouzing motions" — the former being the continued activity of the Spirit in the sons of God who have the agency of choice, the latter being the instant act of the Spirit through the servants of God who have lost that agency in the display of their own unreasonableness. In effect, then, Jesus' success at self-knowledge allows Jesus to be an agent and Samson's failure at self-knowledge prevents it.[36] The final scene of the drama, and the point where the convergence of the two poems in this book is most interesting, is the scene of Samson at the pillars.

PILLARS TO PINNACLE:
THE CLOSE OF THE MILTONIC CAREER

There are several important things to note about the crux of *Samson Agonistes*. As had been the case in *Paradise Regained*, the crux is the point at which each character evinces whatever knowledge of the renovated culture he possesses. So as we saw, in the brief epic Jesus abides by the principles of his spiritual, internal kingdom and stands knowing the state of Israel while Satan falls in ignorance of the spiritual state of the kingdom to which Jesus will accede and in relative nescience about the king he sees standing before him. Satan's knowledge is inscribed as an event that will happen beyond the ending of the narrative—the moment of Jesus' first miracle. In *Samson Agonistes,* we find the same strategy of revelation. In examining the pillars scene, I will show what sort of knowledge Samson takes with him about the state of Israel he is about to deliver. I will also show what degree of knowledge the citizens of Philistia take with them to their deaths, as well as that which the Chorus takes beyond the tragedy's ending. For, precisely like the brief epic, the tragedy writes an anagnorisis beyond its close—"beyond the fift Act." The scene at the pillars, presented as a narrative, is doubly removed from us as a spectacle—first because it is related by the Messenger (1597–1660) and second because the Messenger is not privy to all Samson says (1631–32).[37]

At the crux of the play we find Samson, his "head a while enclin'd,"

> And eyes fast fixt he stood, as one who pray'd,
> Or some great matter in his mind resolv'd.
> At last with head erect thus cryed aloud.   (1637–40)

The image is meant to remind us of the opening portrayal the Chorus gives of Samson:

> See how he lies at random, carelessly diffus'd,
> With languish't head unpropt,
> As one past hope, abandon'd,
> And by himself given over.   (119–22)

Then Samson lifts his head "erect" and cries out his final speech. The image captures in essence the movement from Samson's original dejection to his hopeful activity, a movement that is possible only through providential sanction—leading him from unfruitful hopelessness to resolved prayer.

He lifts his dejected head "erect," which we know from *Paradise Lost* is the capital posture of devotion (*PL* VIII, 254–60; cf.

PL IV, 289, "Godlike erect"). He stretches his arms between the pillars, his head inclining between his broad and powerful shoulders. He lifts his head to address the worldly lords and tell them that his performance, thus far for their entertainment, shall now be conducted under the auspices of divinity. The image is essentially that of Jesus on the cross, head declined, until he raises it, bleeding from the crown of thorns, and cries with a loud voice to God: "*E-lo'i, E-lo'i, la'ma sa-bach-tha'ni?*" (Mark xv, 34). It is also the iconic portrayal Milton adumbrates with Jesus on the pinnacle in *Paradise Regained*.[38] Using echoing typological icons, Milton thus urges the reader to see the two cruxes in some sort of relation.

But, more importantly, there are verbal echoes resonating through the volume, signifying the quality of their relationship. In Samson's speech there are certain key words that may be meant to recall previous instances of these key words, both in the previous sections of the tragedy and at the crux in the epic preceding it in the 1671 volume. Samson stands at the pillars, lifts his head from prayer, and calls out to the audience:

> Hitherto, Lords, what your commands impos'd
> I have perform'd, as reason was, obeying,
> Not without wonder or delight beheld.
> Now of my own accord such other tryal
> I mean to shew you of my strength, yet greater;
> As with amaze shall strike all who behold.   (1641–46)

The speech falls into two distinct parts, marked by a temporal change: Hitherto / Now. The second distinction is made between the previous "commands" Samson was obeying, those of the lords, and the new command he is now obeying—"my own accord." The third distinction is between what we have noted to be the important elements of liberty in Milton's thought—*reason* on the one hand and its antonym, *amaze,* on the other. These three binaries will serve to demonstrate what we are to make of Samson's final act and what we may make of the two crucial scenes in the 1671 volume.

The most recent critics writing on the pillars scene have made a very strong case for reading it as a moment in which a bloodthirsty and self-motivated Samson murders the Philistines without any sanction from God. So far my argument has been that Samson is the vessel of God's will—implying that Samson has lost his agential liberty and that he is indeed working within God's sanction. I will elaborate my reading as it obtains for the pillars scene in relation to two critics, Joseph Wittreich and Stanley Fish. Wittreich writes: "What Samson does, by his own admission, is done of *his own accord;* he kills, and killing, we are told, is an act never coming from God, but 'meerely from Satan.'" Moreover, Wittreich continues, the "action is performed impulsively, without reflection on liberation and deliverance and without regard for the authority of inspiration such as displayed by Gideon in another of the inset narratives in the Book of Judges." Stanley Fish writes that Samson's final speech is "not of very much interpretive help." When Samson says that what he is about to do is of his "own accord," Fish suggests that Samson is about to perform an "action for which he has no final warrant except what he himself at the moment thinks best to do." The two critics differ, of course, in what they feel Milton might be suggesting by having Samson act of his own accord. Wittreich would have this moment exemplify Samson's transgression of Milton's moral code, while Fish would have it exemplify Samson's fulfillment of Milton's moral code in its post-1644 mode: "For Samson, God's power to dispense means that one can never figure out exactly (without doubt) what God is doing or what he wants us to do, and that therefore whatever we do we must do 'freely,' on our own, in the absence of any firm (unequivocal) evidence that it is what God wants."[39]

Before I trace the verbal echoes in the play to determine the meaning of Samson's final speech, let me disentangle certain other features of the two critical arguments. First of all, the brief quotation from Daniel Dyke in Wittreich's argument serves no real purpose, and it does not express something Milton held to be true.[40] Nowhere does Milton state a belief that the mandate for killing comes only from Satan. The often-cited passage from *A Defence* is exemplary of his ambiguous attitude toward motivations for murder:

Samson, that renowned champion, though his countrymen blamed him (Judg. 15, 'Knowest thou not that the Philistines are rulers over us?'), yet made war singlehanded against his rulers; and whether instigated by God or by his own valor only, slew not one, but many at once of his country's tyrants. And as he had first duly prayed to God to be his help, it follows that he counted it no wickedness, but a duty,

to kill his masters, his country's tyrants, even though the greater part
of his countrymen refused not slavery.

One would be rash to assert from this passage whether or not
Milton believed Samson was sanctioned by God (CM VII, p. 219).[41]
But it does show that Milton did not believe all instigation to
killing came only from Satan. The two sources for instigation he
names here are either God or Samson's valor.

Second, Wittreich's comparison of Samson to Gideon is misleading, for Gideon displays another kind of infidelity and is another sort of character. The series of Judges narratives manifests a
different judge at each juncture in Israel's history: a left-handed
Benjaminite, a woman, the son of a harlot, and, finally, a uxorious,
weak-minded, and somewhat blustering fool. Each, significantly,
appears unfit to the whoring and idolatrous nation to which he or
she is judge. For the Lord sees not as humans see: that is the theme
of Judges. Gideon was capable of such reflection—indeed, too
capable, one might think. For the memorable feature of Gideon's
career was his skepticism, his unwillingness to assent to divine
impulse without testing its author (Judg. vi, 36–40). It is difficult
to imagine what discourse Gideon might have delivered at the
pillars. And, likewise, it is untoward to expect Samson to contemplate the quality of his service as he stands surrounded by enemies.
Samson was no intellect; he rarely reflected except on his own
miseries. The difference between the two deliverers is such as exists
between Hamlet and Othello; neither is cast into a situation that is
suited to his particular genius. Moreover, and more importantly,
"reflection on liberation and deliverance" and "regard for the authority of inspiration" are two quite different things. Samson forgoes the former because of his limited mental capabilities, but he
has regard for the authority sanctioning his act, as I hope to demonstrate below.

Wittreich begins his quotation of Samson's last speech at line
1643—"Now." By not citing the first three lines of Samson's speech,
Wittreich gives the impression that Samson's final words are indeed
an expression only of extreme egocentricity and willful violence.
But, in the context of the whole speech as a set rhetorical piece,
Samson's egocentricity, while not obviated, is comprehensible in
light of his late "rouzing motions." As I argued earlier, the speech
in its full context falls into two distinct parts. Samson begins by

addressing the lords. "Hitherto," he says in the first part, I have obeyed you. But "Now," he says in the second, I will obey "my own accord." Once the distinction is made between the two parts of the speech, we can begin to trace the meaning of the speech more fully. For example, when placed in contradistinction with the "commands" of the Philistine lords, Samson's statement of doing what is of his "own accord" takes on a rather different meaning. We are indebted to Wittreich for the theory of the best way of proceeding in detecting those traces of intertextuality. His concept of the 1671 volume's "shared syntax" is potentially revolutionary and opens up opportunities for rich and novel reading strategies. Applying that theory in this practical instance will demonstrate the value of Wittreich's insight. I will follow the generation of the cumulative syntax of the 1671 volume by first tracing the use of the word *commands* in the tragedy and then tracing its development in the companion brief epic. With that syntax before us, we may be better able to determine the semantics of this important scene.

In the tragedy, the word *commands* occurs most significantly when Dalila tells Samson of one instance of the Philistine lords' successful "commanding." The lords, she tells Samson in describing the assaults, snares, and sieges she suffered, "Sollicited, *commanded,* threatn'd, urg'd, / Adjur'd" her into considering her public duty (853–54, my italics). Samson, on the other hand, claims that his "commands" come from an entirely different realm. He answers Harapha's hollow taunts by asserting that he (Samson) was "no private but a person rais'd / With strength sufficient and command from Heav'n" (1212–13). Here, then, are the types of "commands" followed by each of the spouses in this marriage hardly of true minds—Dalila following the commands of the Philistine lords and Samson following those commands coming from God. And so when Samson refuses to follow the Officer to the temple, with this reply,

> Can they think me so broken, so debas'd
> With corporal servitude, that my mind ever
> Will condescend to such absurd commands?   (1346–48)

we know that he has in mind the difference between the commands of the Philistine lords, which he is here rejecting, and which Dalila makes such a poignant example of succumbing to, and the "com-

mand from Heav'n" on which he knows he must act. In the exchange between the Chorus and Samson shortly after this, he makes
the distinction quite clear. The Chorus counsels political expedien-
cy in the form of insincerity: "Where the heart joins not, outward
acts defile not." To which Samson replies,

> Where outward force constrains, the sentence holds
> But who constrains me to the Temple of *Dagon*,
> Not dragging? the *Philistian* Lords command.
> Commands are no constraints.   (1379–83)

Samson establishes an important distinction between being forced
to go to the temple (which would be "constraint") and going out
of obedience to the Philistine lords' "commands."

The "rouzing motions" then descend shortly after this, and,
upon the renewed entreaty of the Officer, Samson sets off to the
temple. The Officer's querulous second attempt concludes with a
threat of bodily violence, to which Samson responds, initially, with
good humor, suggesting that the violence may prove more pernicious to the attacker than the attacked. Then Samson responds
with facetiousness:

> Masters commands come with a power resistless
> To such as owe them absolute subjection;
> And for a life who will not change his purpose?   (1415–17)

The artistry of this speech lies in the fact that, although the "Masters" to whom Samson refers are the Philistine lords, he phrases his
obedience to them as if they had Godlike powers. To whom else
would Samson owe "absolute subjection"—certainly not to the
government he has just said "no" to three times a few minutes
earlier? No, Samson owes such subjection to God. Compare here
Joseph Hall's usage: "The Lord of life and death speakes with
command." Or, in an instance more closely related to the present
situation, "What command soever wee receive from God, or our
Superiors, wee must not scan the weight of the thing, but the
authority of the commander."[42] Samson does weigh the authority
of his commands, and he chooses to follow the one he receives
from heaven over the one issued by the Philistine lords.

The use of this same word earlier in the play is also important.
In his opening soliloquy, Samson complains that his body and mind

have ever been at variance: "O impotence of mind, in body strong!" (52). The body, he states, ought "to subserve where wisdom bears command" (57). Thus Samson outlines his divided self, his inter-necine revolt, a revolt that must be quelled and resolved into some sort of divine integration before he may perform the work God has set for him. Here, then, the simple context of the drama itself has supplied the two significant aspects of the word before us: the impor-tant distinction between the lords' commands and the command from heaven. The body-mind dichotomy—that the body ought to obey the commands of wisdom—has also troubled Samson.

In this new context of the tragedy's cumulative syntax, Samson's "own accord," when taken as part of his whole speech, does not simply signify a willful act but his obedience to another set of "commands" which are the opposite of the "commands" given by the Philistine lords. Given that Samson has already mocked the lords' commands—"Masters commands come with a power resist-less" (1415)—and stated that his "command [comes] from Heav'n," it would appear that Samson is stating his "own accord" as a metonymy for the "command from Heav'n." Now to state this as such is not to discount the literal meaning of "own accord" as Fish and Wittreich have given it, but it is worth noting that Milton elsewhere uses the phrase to signify precisely that courageous act of a person defying what Samson calls "outward force." For in-stance, Milton writes of Paul in *A Treatise of Civil Power in Ecclesiastical Causes:* "Yet while he made himself servant to all, that he might gain the more, he *made himself so of his own accord, was not made so by outward force,* testifying at the same time that he was free from all men." To do something of one's own accord, in Milton's usage here, is contradistinct from doing something in response to dint of "outward force," not, as Wittreich and Fish take it, as contradistinct to public action. And the "outward force" signified in *A Treatise* is that "greevous yoke, the commandments of men" (CM VI, pp. 35, 29–30; cf. YP VII, pp. 267, 263).[43] Likewise, the "commands" of the Philistine lords in *Samson Agonistes* constitute for Samson the "outward force" which he must refuse to bow to in his obedience to the "command from Heav'n."

Samson's own "accord" now is an outcome of grace. He was not at accord with himself. His mind and his body had been at vari-ance. The flesh was not only willing, it was also commanding. The accord he has now is a result of the abatement of the internal war that had been raging between mind and body. "Wisdom bears command" indeed now, but the wisdom is distinct from the carnal selfishness of Samson, and the command is contradistinct from the command of the Philistine lords. So in the context of the drama at large, the "accord" is not simply Samson's willful desire for satanic murder. Without pressing too far the possibility that "accord" in this speech may intimate personal concord, it is worth noting that Milton thought grace promoted such an attitude of personal integrity. Adam and Eve are divided between themselves, and Adam divided within himself, before the motions of grace descend. The Fall causes "Discord" first, and not only among the creatures of earth, but "worse felt within" Adam (*PL* X, 707, 717). Adam and Eve regain a degree of their former integrity when the "motions" descend from heaven. As Saint Bernard wrote, "I am not united with God, and therefore I am divided in my selfe"; or, as Joseph Hall puts it, "I am not mine owne, while God is not mine."[44] But Samson does not achieve the sort of meditative unity Hall and Saint Bernard are defining here.

Samson's statement of doing what he does out of his "own accord," even when shown to be signifying an act opposed to the commands of the Philistine lords, is nonetheless a curious way of phrasing his accord with divine command. When Samson spoke of acting out the will of God before, he also phrased it in just such an egocentric formulation: "What I motion'd was of God." This way of phrasing what he does in obedience to God marks Samson's distance from the Miltonic ideal as it is found in the Jesus of *Paradise Regained*.

Satan's first temptation to Jesus is for Jesus to "Command / That out of these hard stones be made thee bread" (*PR* I, 342–43). Dyke emphasizes the point: Satan "sayes not, pray to God, but *command* that these stones be made bread."[45] Jesus answers that it is not bread alone by which people are fed, but by the word of God. The word of God, it turns out, is exactly what Satan is *commanded* to say to the idolatrous rabble at his temple, and he is, furthermore, commanded to inform these idolaters of the providential design *without himself being cognizant of it*. It is "not known" to Satan (I, 446, 449). Again what is emphasized, as at the pinnacle, is Satan's ignorance, his "unweeting" participation in the designs of Providence.

Just as Dalila represented the cost of obeying the Philistine commands—and by inference symbolizing what Samson might potentially become if he, too, were to succumb to their commands—so in the brief epic only the fallen angels obey Satan's command (II, 149). Jesus, however, obeys the command that does, indeed, come from the word of God:

> Shall I receive by gift what of my own,
> When and where likes me best, I can command?
> I can at will, doubt not, assoon as thou,
> Command a Table in this Wilderness.   (II, 381–84)

Why is Jesus' phrasing of his ability to command "selfless" while Samson's "of my own accord" is not? As I have pointed out throughout this study, the "self" in the Miltonic moral cosmos is transformed into either a "subject of God" (keeping its agential liberty and becoming, therefore, a son of God) or transformed into a being "subject to God" (losing its agential liberty and becoming, therefore, a servant of God). The basis of the transformation is reason, and especially the mode of reason applied to gaining self-knowledge. As I have argued, Jesus demonstrates his reasonableness, knows himself in relation to God, and becomes then a subject of God. When he pronounces himself capable of commanding, he is doing so in that role—which has no "self" in it. Samson, on the other hand, demonstrates his unreasonableness, does not know himself in relation to God, and becomes subject to God. When Samson acts, he is not a volitional agent but a vessel of God's Spirit. In this precise sense, whatever of Samson there is in the act constitutes a "self"—that is, the residue of unreason which prohibited him from becoming a subject of God. In that sense, Jesus is selfless in his pronouncement while Samson is self-centered in his. It also helps us explain the curious way Samson phrases his obedience to God's will: "What I motion'd was of God."

The word *commands* takes a prominent place in the crux of *Paradise Regained*. Satan, having noticed that Jesus does not obey the commands Satan tempts him to issue, now tempts Jesus at the pinnacle using precisely that with which Jesus had answered his first temptation and circumvented Satan's first command. On the pinnacle, Satan tempts Jesus with the Word of God: "For it is written, He will give command" (IV, 553). With the nocent subtle-

ty characteristic of the antagonist throughout the poem but, especially at this juncture, Satan has posited a situation where there
seems to be no hope for escape. Jesus had said, at their first encounter, that the command worth following is the Word of God. At
this final encounter, Satan offers him a command that is the Word
of God. Jesus' answer must avoid all possible pitfalls, and it does.
As I have argued elsewhere, the answer can be interpreted only as
meaning that one must not tempt God the Father. If we take it to
mean that one must not tempt the Son because he is the Lord, then
Jesus has shown his "Progeny," which is what Satan desires. Jesus'
answer is also the word of God, and so avoids the danger of a
secular response to a sacred command.[46] The final instance of the
word in the poem is in the angelic Chorus' address to Satan, in
which it predicts the episode where Jesus exorcises the devils from
the two men of Capernaum (IV, 622–28). The Chorus uses this
episode to figure the Second Coming, when the Son will "command them [the devils] down into the deep." The movement of the
poem completes, in its usual way by ostending into the future, the
cycle's coming around from Satan's commanding Jesus (unsuccess-
fully) to Jesus' commanding Satan (successfully). Joseph Hall notes
that "None ever offered to deale with Satan by a direct & primary
command, but the God of Spirits." Those who pretend to command as gods, Hall continues, are actually aligning themselves to
Satan: "If any created power dare to usurp a word of command, he
[Satan] laughs at their presumption; & knows them his vassals,
whom hee dissembles to feare as his Lords."[47] The lords of Philistia, we must remember, did just this.

The word *command*, then, aligns the two works in order to
demonstrate the difference in degree between the two heroes. Samson obeys the command from heaven, although he phrases it in
terms of his "own accord." Jesus obeys the command from heaven
with simple self-abnegation. In his final quotation from scripture,
"it is written / Tempt not the Lord thy God," Jesus refers only to
God the Father. This is the expression of sublime theocentricity,
and for theocentricity to be effective and sincere it requires a
conscious mind devoting itself to God. To argue, as Stanley Fish
does, that Jesus "is God to the extent that *he,* as a consciousness
distinguishable from God, is no more," is to make this instance of
Jesus' self-abnegation a fulfillment rather than a prefiguring of the
final consummation, when "God shall be All in All" (*PL* III, 341).[48]

As I have demonstrated, Jesus establishes his identity in relation to a series of directions, the last and most important of which is God. The sort of self-knowledge which he is aspiring to in his earthly form requires him to define himself as a "subject of God" to that extent that he may be said to have consciousness—"reason is but choosing." In this sense, then, Jesus represents something like *recta ratio* on the pinnacle by virtue of his insistent theocentricity, while Samson remains irreducibly self-centered even while operating under God's authority and as God's vessel.

Finally, then, with that very significant binary—"reason" / "amaze"—we might conclude our efforts in developing the "shared syntax" of the 1671 book. This distinction between the operation of reason and the results of its inoperability suggests a basis for Milton's soteriology, his doctrine of free will, and, indeed, his politics. In my reading of *Paradise Regained*, I stressed the importance of the word *amaze* in the description of Satan's nescience as he falls from the pinnacle. As I argued in the last chapter, we must see the "amazement" with which Satan is stricken to signify not a simple bewilderment or awe-struck wonder, but a complete absence of reason, a dysfunction in his cognitive abilities in a new epistemology governing a new world order. He is, for that reason, incapable of apprehending the station from whose presence he fell.

Thomas Bilson noted in 1604 that Christ may be "astonished" (as he is in Mark, chapter 14), but Christ may never be "amazed." For "all vehement amazing," writes Bilson, "for the time depriveth a man of *motion, sense,* and *speech*." It also deprives him, he continues, of "understanding."[49] Amazement is akin to madness in this sense, and madness—the disavowal of reality for a world of delusion—does not allow Satan to understand the Son's mission, career, or ultimate monarchy, which is, in a word, the Son's station and the renovated culture based on his constitution. Jesus, on the other hand, is the Son of God to the extent that he is Reason itself. He has worked through the forms of worldly logical inquiry in his soliloquies, especially the second, and established himself as operating with Godlike reason in his dialectical confutations of Satan's offers. Reason, as Milton everywhere insists, is the basis of choice (often synonymous with the ability to choose), and it is equally the foundation of agential liberty. At the pinnacle, then, Jesus operates as the utmost of reasonable beings, acts freely, and concludes his private career by establishing the new internal Eden in the consummation of his self-knowledge.

Samson begins his address to the Philistine audience at the temple by saying that what he had hitherto performed was done in obedience to the Philistine lords' commands—"as reason was" (1642). His marvelous acts had produced "wonder" and "delight" in those who "beheld" them. Now, he is about to perform something that will not be beheld with "wonder" or be done in accord with "reason," but rather his act "with amaze shall strike all who behold" (1645). I wish to stress that this "amaze" that Samson speaks of here refers to everybody involved in this scene, and that includes the Philistines, Samson himself, and those both telling the narrative (the Messenger) and those hearing it (Manoa and the Chorus of Danites).

The "amazement" at the conclusion of *Paradise Regained* obtains only for Satan; he alone is incapable of understanding the world order Jesus has, according to the angels, "founded now" and remains disabled as the narrative concludes (IV, 609). The "amaze" at the conclusion of *Samson Agonistes,* on the other hand, obtains for both the actor and the audience—although in differing degrees. The first and greater kind of amazement is that of the faithless, those who are excluded from the pale of eventual knowledge because of their obduracy—which is the amazement of the Philistines. The second kind of amazement is that of the actor who does not know what he has just done, who is acting out a script whose outcome he does not altogether comprehend. That is the amazement of Samson—the amazement of God's "agonist." It is also the "amazement" of the tribe of Danites.

The Philistine audience demonstrates the first kind of amazement. Among the Philistines, according to the Chorus' relation, God sends a "spirit of phrenzie" which "hurt thir minds." Their "mad desire" causes them to "call in haste for thir destroyer":

> They only set on sport and play
> Unwittingly importun'd
> Thir own destruction to come speedy upon them.
> . . . .
> Insensate left, or to sense reprobate,
> And with blindness internal struck.   (1670–87)

The madness of the Philistines is that of obduration, the same madness that seizes Satan and the rebel angels at the sight of the

Son's rehabilitation of heaven (*PL* VI, 785–97). This madness is of the reprobate, the mind hurt by that which it cannot comprehend—God. Like Satan in *Paradise Lost* and in the brief epic, they have lost their "sense."

Samson demonstrates the second kind of amazement, which is the agonistic madness of God's player—not a wrathful frenzy, but a spiritual captivity. The most unrelentingly self-referential play of the English Renaissance can help us understand this distinction between the audience's amazement and the actor's amazement. As Hamlet ruminates on the departing players he has just asked to act *The Murder of Gonzago* for the king, he ponders the talents of a player who is able to "force his soul so to his own conceit." Hamlet then goes on to distinguish between the actor who performs for Hecuba—"distraction in his aspect"—and the actor who has the motive and cue for passion that Hamlet has—the actor who can "make mad the guilty" and "*amaze* indeed / The very faculties of eyes and ears." This motivated actor not only "amazes" the audience but is himself distracted—and not merely in "aspect," but in very soul. Although both actor and audience would be amazed by this actor's performance, each would be amazed in differing degrees. The audience would be amazed to the extent of being made "mad" if guilty or "appalled" if free, while the actor would be only partially amazed to the degree of drowning the stage with tears and cleaving the "general ear with horrid speech." The actor would *express* his amazement, while the audience would be affected with amazement. The actor, according to Hamlet's distinction, which is also one that I am suggesting works for *Samson Agonistes,* has a mind "infatuated" in his acting, precisely the sort of amentia that Tolstoy called the artist's "infection."[50] That is, to take Tolstoy's metaphoric usage more literally, the actor is not immune while he is the carrier.

In Samson's case, the actor, God's agonist, must release himself from his mundane reality to accept his role in the divine script. Before this, Samson, as "reason was, obeying," followed his life instinct and acted out the role prescribed for him by the Philistine audience. As he said earlier, and playfully, "for a life who would not change his purpose?" (1417). Now, renouncing reason, on which he had always had but a tenuous grip, he follows a higher instinct. Had he been more capable of wit at precisely this point in his life, he might have said, "for a death who would not change his purpose?" On that turn in Samson's final moment—between acting out what would keep him alive ("as reason was"), and acting out his death ("as with amaze")—I would invoke Freud's distinction between the "pleasure principle" and the "death instinct."

According to Freud, the "pleasure principle" is the most simple activating force of any organism—the instinct that leads it to avoid pain and embrace whatever produces pleasure. The "reality principle" is what operates at a higher level, whereby the organism postpones immediate satisfaction in order to create whatever requires creation. The "death instinct," finally, is the effect of every organism's ultimate recognition that every animate being had been inanimate *prior* to its animated state. The organism recognizes that before life there was death, and therefore the final instinct is one that is basically "conservative" in its desire to return to its inanimate state. The death instinct, then, is expressed as "a need to restore an earlier state of things." The ways any individual wards off what is already immanent is a sign, according to Freud, that "the organism wishes to die only in its own fashion." By fashioning his or her own death, the individual comes to achieve that final and irrevocable integrity of being. We may take Manoa's words to mean this when he says that "*Samson* hath quit himself / Like *Samson*" (1710–11). In this death, and likewise in this simile, the tenor and the vehicle are one and the same. Samson, from his opening soliloquy, had desired his death while at the same time representing himself as an inanimate being, a vessel. Unlike Jesus' educative anxiety, Samson's was selfish and self-promoting. Although Norman Brown does not make the Kierkegaardian distinction between the types of anxieties, he nonetheless does point out that "anxiety is the ego's incapacity to accept death."[51] But the ego—and that word is precisely the one to use in describing Samson—can face its own death when it loses its agency and becomes instead a vessel. This vessel is both amazing to those who behold it and amazed in itself. Jesus on the pinnacle, in the adumbration of his Passion, transforms his anxiety about death into a spiritual love for God and operates as a reasonable being in the crux of his existence. Samson at the pillars, however, transcends his anxiety about death by acting as a vessel of God, as one who is outside the pale of reason.

I have argued that Samson's seemingly willful "of my own accord" is less willful than it at first appears, when it is seen in context of the whole play and the whole book. In the penultimate line, it might appear that Samson is still acting out of undeviating self-motivation: "I mean to show you of my strength, yet greater" (1645). Wittreich and Samuel's point is that Samson is so obviously egocentric at this final moment that we cannot imagine him acting toward a public good or acting out of anything but selfish and murderous desire.[52] However, Samson's insistent use of the first-person pronoun is palliated by the final clause in this penultimate line. After the opening "I" and the possessive "my," he goes on to assert that this strength is "yet greater"—which I take to mean it is "yet greater" than *his* strength. The suggestion that this final performance is beyond even Samson's capacity is made more explicit in the final clause of his speech where he states that the "trial" shall strike as with amaze all who behold. I have argued that Samson amazes himself as well as the Philistines. His own accord, that is, goes against even himself.

I would agree with the objection that there yet remains something irreducibly egocentric about Samson's final speech. He does not have the selflessness of Jesus. And I believe that Milton meant to convey this complex duality—a hero whose *act* is selfless to the degree of dying, and yet whose *being* is selfish to an irreducible level. That is the condition of being subject to God.

Just as Satan had represented himself as a skeptical being to the point where he actually became a skeptical being, so too does Samson represent himself so much as a vessel that eventually he becomes nothing but a vessel—at the end, a vessel of divine energy. God has done this deed *through* Samson, and the vessel is amazed at his own act. Jesus, on the other hand, has represented himself as being a rational person and an agent of change. More importantly, he represents his rationality in terms of the single monad of sense in the Miltonic cosmos—God. In his first soliloquy, he surrendered his knowledge to God's will: "For what concerns my knowledge God reveals" (I, 293); because of his selflessness, he expresses Godlike merit. This is the new person of the new covenant—beyond history, in personal communion with God. Samson, as type of Jesus, is obviously more carnal, for that is the movement of typology: "From shadowy Types to Truth, from Flesh to Spirit" (*PL* XII, 303). Samson is that tenebrous and carnal figural type, as Jesus is the veritable spiritual fulfillment. Jesus, as Hall proclaims, is "our true *Samson*."[53]

Samson, however, is not the only one who is amazed. The Chorus of Danites and Manoa, and indeed the Messenger, are all amazed to a degree. Of course, our only access to the scene of Samson at the pillars is the Messenger. It is worth attending to the Messenger's amazement in order to determine what sort of knowledge he brings with him about the old world Samson has just destroyed and the new world Samson has placed as a possibility for the tribe of Dan. I have so far demonstrated the important shift in Samson's speech between his previous actions ("Hitherto") and his present ones ("Now"). One of the more important signifiers of that change is Samson's shift in tenses when he presents himself as a spectacle. Whereas he had before been "beheld" with wonder, the audience must now "behold" him with "amazement." Moreover, I have argued that the "all" in this speech refers both to Samson and to the audience. So, when the Messenger describes the affect of the "horrid spectacle" he describes his "dire imagination" as being in the grasp of both tenses—"Which earst my eyes beheld and yet behold" (1544). Likewise, he presents himself as being of "sense distract" (1557). It would appear, then, as Samson says, that "all" who have dealings with the "great event"—whether they saw, acted out, or are about to narrate this event—are "amazed."

Likewise, there is a certain distracted sense in the final scenes which involve the Chorus and each of the Semichoruses. Even though the Chorus has not been privy to the scene at the pillars, it feels quite comfortable relating the scene's smallest particulars to the very person who has just related all it should be able to claim knowledge of. As the Messenger concludes his story at line 1660, the Chorus describes Samson's death: "Among thy slain self-kill'd / Not willingly, but tangl'd in the fold, / Of dire necessity" (1665–67). The first Semichorus then describes the amazement of the Philistines—along with a few choice descriptions of their meals ("fat regorg'd of Bulls and Goats") and their singing ("Chaunting thir Idol"). The second Semichorus describes Samson's "great event" with two similes (1688–1708). After this quite celebratory speech, Manoa attempts to raise the Chorus' spirits: "Come, come, no time for lamentation now" (1709). What is curious about the ending of the play is that nobody seems to be paying any attention to what anyone else is saying. Immediately after the Messenger completes his narrative about Samson, the Chorus turns around and tells him what has happened at the temple. Immediately after the Chorus praises Samson by comparing him to a triumphant dragon, an assailant eagle, and an undying phoenix, Manoa suggests it cheers up. This lack of communicative clarity is itself revealing because, like *Paradise Regained,* this tragedy inscribes within itself a moment of lucidity beyond its close.

"BEYOND THE FIFT ACT": THE POLITICS OF *SAMSON AGONISTES*

Here again a comparison with Hamlet proves informative. Hamlet, like Samson, is a character who spends a good portion of this play desiring dissolution, yet in the end he does not die by his own hand but dies, rather, in the grasp of another form of dire necessity—"this fell sergeant, Death, / Is strict in his arrest" (V, ii, 325–26). It would not be very difficult to formulate the complex of Hamlet's desire, deferral, and death in the interplay of the pleasure principle, the reality principle, and the death instinct, and it probably has been done before. But when we consider that Hamlet is also the Renaissance stage's most thorough theorist, we might begin to pay closer attention to some of the possible reasons for this interplay. A brief survey of how Hamlet's comments on the nature of dramatic presentation inform the play's politics will help us approach *Samson Agonistes* with a sense of how to read significant instances of auto-referentiality in that play.

First of all, when told to swear to act, and thereby initiate the action of the play, Hamlet addresses the motivating source—the ghost of his father—as part of the stage machinery: "You hear this fellow in the cellarage" (I, v, 151). Thereafter, of course, Hamlet puts on an "antic disposition"—which is to say he begins *acting at acting,* which makes his apostrophe on the insincerity of the player who plays for Hecuba somewhat curious (which is precisely what it is supposed to be, I guess).

As Kenneth Burke rightly points out, the dramatic "moment of decision-making" which usually occurs at the end of the first act is delayed in *Hamlet* until the end of the second act.[54] The reason for this deferral may be, as Laurence Olivier so dogmatically stated it in his film production, that this is the story of a man who couldn't make up his mind; but it also may be because this is a story of a man whose death instinct is nonetheless palliated by the reality principle.[55] In effect, for Hamlet death and pleasure become equal-ly and almost synonymously the objects of his desire. His first soliloquy on his desire for his flesh to "melt" and "resolve itself into dew" is one example of how Hamlet conflates pleasure and death (I, ii, 129–30). In his third soliloquy he likewise expresses his idea that death is a "consummation / Devoutly to be wished" (III, i, 63–64). But the reality principle is what postpones the satis-faction of that desire for death and pleasure—"There's the respect / That makes calamity of so long life." For Hamlet, the reality prin-ciple *is* the play. The "play's the thing" in every sense for this sublime theorist of the stage. Not only has he made the audience poignantly aware of the metafictional nature of his acting, and indeed of his acting out his acting, but he has also employed a play within a play to determine the truth value of the ghost's story. And we must remember that the ghost's story is the initiator of the play's action and also how Hamlet immediately addressed the very material stage after the ghost told his story. Hamlet desires death (which would be pleasure), but in the act of postponing that desire he creates the possibility of the play bearing his name. In *Hamlet,* then, the reality principle operates to delay Hamlet's desire to die and therefore allows for the possibility of the play. So, when Ham-let does die, it is not unfitting that he should once more make a metafictional commentary on the nature of the drama which con-sisted of his life, depended on his living, and ends with his death.

At the end of this play the dying Hamlet turns to the audience and does two significant things. What is surprising is that he does *two* things, one of which does not concern the world of the theater. First of all, he promises to tell a story that he cannot tell and then appoints a narrator to do the job for him. And he does this while addressing the audience and his fellow players:

> You that look pale and tremble at this chance,
> That are but mutes or audience to this act,
> Had I but time—as this fell sergeant, Death,
> Is strict in his arrest—O, I could tell you—
> But let it be. Horatio, I am dead;
> Thou livest; report me and my cause aright
> To the unsatisfied.   (V, ii, 324–29)

Recognizing his inability to narrate a story beyond the drama,

Hamlet appoints Horatio to do so. Of course, Hamlet is here merely following the conventional decorum of the tragic hero in appointing for his story to be told. But Hamlet does more.

Secondly, and I think more profoundly, Hamlet spends his final breath in a political act; he does not name the next king of Denmark, but supernaturally prophesies his election: "But I do prophesy th' election lights / On Fortinbras. He has my dying voice." Moreover, the story Horatio is to tell of Hamlet's life is now especially directed to Fortinbras's ears: "So tell him, with th' occurrents, more and less. / Which have solicited—the rest is silence" (V, ii, 344–47). In *Hamlet,* then, the *narrative* of the "occurrents" of Hamlet's life and death, more or less, occupies the place of a political manifesto; it is to be told to the next political force in Denmark for whatever value they might make of it. What Shakespeare does so brilliantly in *Hamlet* is promise a narrative which we will not get—but which we expect Fortinbras to receive, and which has something to do with Denmark's political future. For us, though, the "rest is silence."

Samson Agonistes is by no stretch of the imagination as self-referential a play as *Hamlet,* nor is its lead character nearly as bright a theorist of the dramaturgical arts as is Hamlet, but there are significant similarities that will help us understand the interplay of narrative and drama in Milton's tragedy. The similarities begin with the fact that both Hamlet and Samson bring with them, almost from the beginning of each play, a strong desire for death, and each suffers an anxiety preventing him from "self slaughter." The differences begin with Samson's reluctance to put on an "antic disposition" as contrasted with Hamlet's eagerness to do so. In declining to go the temple the first time, Samson asks the Officer what need they have of him:

> Have they not Sword-players, and ev'ry sort
> Of Gymnic Artists, Wrestlers, Riders, Runners,
> Juglers and Dancers, Antics, Mummers, Mimics,
> But they must pick me out[?]   (1334–37)

He takes up his role as "agonist" only after he is "rouzed" to it. After Samson becomes an actor, the drama is placed in relative abeyance. Samson leaves the stage at line 1437 and, like Hamlet, ends his stage career with a promise for a story:

Happ'n what may, of me expect to hear
Nothing dishonourable, impure, unworthy
Our God, our Law, my Nation, or my self,
The last of me or no I cannot warrant.   (1434–37)

Whereas in *Hamlet* the story is not for us to hear, in *Samson Agonistes* we do get that story from the Messenger, who takes on the form of a Danite Horatio. What is significant, then, is that the story of Samson's end—"occurrents, more or less"—is part of the tragedy. And, like *Hamlet,* that story has some political significance for the future of the country.

Finally, also like Hamlet, Samson turns from mere actor to metafictional actor when he commences addressing the audience in his final breath. At the key moment when he is resting during an "intermission" (1630), Samson turns from his role, as it is appointed by the Philistines, and addresses the audience he is performing for. He will now, he says, take a "yet greater" role for which God has fitted him. The tragedy's boundaries, which had been narrowed by the scene at the theater and more focused by the relation of the Messenger at the scene, suddenly collapse—and there is a suddenness in it—as do the walls, the pillars, the actor, and the spectators. From the rubble of the theater rises, phoenix-like, a glimpse—but only a brief glimpse—of the stage that is eternity.[56] Samson, the actor who brought down the theater, does not know what that stage looks like. He is part of the historical dialectic that paves the way to it. More important, however, is that the story of that action—of Samson's "great event"—is part of *Samson Agonistes* and, therefore, part of the political future of the tribe of Dan.

Had we access to an imaginary sixth act of *Hamlet,* we would probably find Horatio telling the story of Hamlet's life to Fortinbras in order to teach him something about Danish politics. The Messenger in *Samson Agonistes* is telling the story of Samson's end to the Chorus and to Manoa (and, to judge by the way he tells the story, even to himself) in order to teach them something about the possibility for Israel's future politics. The Messenger is telling the story to the tribe of Dan, who are in a position to assume their own sovereignty. The captivating culture of Philistia is, as Manoa rather unsympathetically puts it, "not in plight to say us nay" (1720). The Messenger's narrative, then, occupies a place of prolepsis *within* the drama. As Montrose had noted about *The Shepheardes Calen-*

dar, there is some significance to the heterogeneity of discourses. Likewise, as Fredric Jameson notes about the significance of this heterogeneity in such forms as the "novel" (for Jameson) or the "book" (for Montrose), these "generic discontinuities" reveal "their own specific and contradictory ideological meaning."[57] And the audience of the Messenger's narrative does attend to its political implications. After the Messenger concludes his "Relation more particular and distinct" (1596), Manoa remarks on his son's deed and its political significance. Samson has freed Israel, Manoa notes, but it is up to Israel to find the courage to "lay hold on this occasion" (1717). The *narrative* of Samson's end gives birth to a political thought of a continuing freedom from Philistine bondage, but in the summary of this *tragedy* we discover why this freedom would be lost.

On this point, we might well attend to what Stanley Fish has to say about the operation of "spectacle" and "evidence" in *Samson Agonistes*. Fish has persuasively demonstrated that every character in the play "will go to any length in their joint effort to piece together a story that can be read as a confirmation of the reasonableness (and therefore the predictability) of events in the world." Each character reads Samson in order to tell a story about him that makes sense, more often than not by erasing the Samson that the character avoids beholding. A mark of that desire to tell what one doesn't want to see is the number of times characters deny the "spectacle" before them in drawing out the "evidence" they need to complete their tale. At the end, this tendency to tell a story about Samson takes on an almost manic quality. Each is so eager to tell a story that nobody pays attention to the others' versions. According to Fish, there is an emergent narrative turn in *Samson Agonistes* because the author would "blur" the climactic scene of the play by having the Messenger relate it and by having it recast by two Semichoruses and Manoa after it is related. The playwright effects that blurring in order to frustrate the reader's desire not to behold "the lack at the heart of the story."[58]

So far I have shown that there is not so obvious a "lack" as Fish has been intent on arguing—at least insofar as the "rouzing motions" and the "intimate impulse" are concerned. Here, the effect of having the Messenger deliver the story of Samson at the pillars is to suggest something about the limitation all the characters in this play suffer—their basic inability to perceive the possibility for a different culture. What the Messenger's relation does is offer the Chorus an opportunity to see how the "life" of Samson might serve its political aims. But, like a lame Fortinbras, the Chorus does not gain that knowledge from the Messenger, and neither does Manoa. To see, first of all, how Manoa misunderstands the possibilities for a new world, we need to compare what happens to each hero in the 1671 volume at the close of his career.

In the aftermath of the slaughter of the Philistines, Manoa decides to go get his son. He tells himself the story he wants to believe about Samson and makes a crucial remark about the future political status of the Israelites:

> To *Israel*
> Honour hath left, and freedom, let but them
> Find courage to lay hold on this occasion,
> To himself and Fathers house eternal fame.   (1715–18)

In the hope of a promising political future, Manoa sets off to retrieve Samson's body; Samson's body, then, is taken back "Home to his Father's house" (1734). Jesus, on the other hand, must resist the temptation to enter his "Fathers house" and must instead return "Home to his Mothers house" (*PR* IV, 549, 635). Not only is there an explicit contrast between the publicity of Samson's return and the privacy of Jesus', but there is, moreover, an echo between the two heroes and the two works on what it means not to occupy the private sphere. For, in the final analysis, Milton held that it was very important to define oneself by one's relation to the private sphere. And that is what Samson insistently failed to do. He never once mentions his mother; he defines himself only in relation to his father. In doing so, he reveals something about his loss of liberty and his inability to gain the sort of self-knowledge acquired by Jesus in the companion poem.[59]

By defining themselves in discourse, both Samson and Jesus have constituted a separate reality, as Jerome Bruner suggests is true of all discursive moments: "Part of that reality is the stance that the language implies towards knowledge and reflection and the generalized set of stances one negotiates creates in time a sense of one's self." By expressing the discursive conditions obtaining for the possibility of knowledge in that moment of discourse, as we suggested earlier, the self of that discourse finally constitutes a subjectivity. This use of language, Bruner concludes, is best characterized as "culture creating." In his soliloquy, Jesus has constituted himself in relation to three discourses—the written Law, his mother's private relation, and his Father's public pronouncement. The Law represents a mediation between the public and the private realms in two distinct ways. First, Jesus reads the Law privately, but it is also the reason for his first public act—going to the temple at age twelve to listen to and educate the "Teachers of our Law." Second, Jesus uses the Law as a mediation between his mother's revelation and his Father's—between privately knowing he is the Son of God and having it publicly affirmed by his Father. And, of course, the lone piece of knowledge he takes from the text—the one act that will radically transform the meaning of that text—is the recognition of his death.

William Kerrigan has suggested that in "its passage to the sacred, the superego acquires" what he calls its "feminine aspect—not in the vulgar sense that women are intuitive, which is a lesser way to think, but in the sense that intuition in all people, men and women, is a form of knowing or being rooted in the early matrix of sudden attunements and shared promptings."[60] It is worth considering whether Milton might have imitated his Jesus in defining himself between the two discursive spheres Jesus locates in his soliloquy, between the early (private) matrix and the mature (public) patrimony. For Jesus' discovery of his being and his identity between the private maternal voice and the public divine one also follows Milton's representation of his accession to the public and to the sacred.

In an autobiographical reminiscence in 1654, Milton, remembering a moment in 1638, represented the moment of leaving the private sphere of home and his entry into the public sphere as a traveler on the grand tour, on the basis of one tragic absence in his life: "I had the curiosity, after the death of my mother, to see foreign countries." Milton's references to his mother, as all biographers testify, are infrequent and often conventional. For example, twenty lines earlier in the *Second Defence*, he refers to her as "an excellent woman" known throughout the neighborhood for her charity (CM VIII, pp. 118–21). It is praise enough, I suppose, but it lacks the vigor with which Milton presented his father in, say, *Ad Patrem,* where he pointedly rejects the trite in order to praise his father appropriately: "I will not mention a father's usual generosities, for greater things have a claim on me." What is interesting is what the "greater things" turn out to be:

It was at your expense, dear father, after I had got the mastery of the language of Romulus and the graces of Latin, and acquired the lofty speech of the magniloquent Greeks, which is fit for the lips of Jove himself, that you persuaded me to add the flowers which France boasts and the eloquence which the modern Italian pours from his degenerate mouth . . . and the mysteries uttered by the Palestinian prophet.

Milton's father gave him all the polite languages of Western civilization. Now, as is well known, when Milton finally did decide what he would write to achieve the undying fame he knew would be his, he wrote it in his mother tongue.[61]

Ad Patrem was written in 1637, the year Milton's mother died. Seven years later, Milton translated Martin Bucer's tract on divorce in what the stationers recorded as his second public appearance (YP II, pp. 416–20). At the conclusion of his translation, Milton excuses himself from the art of "Englishing" what belongs to another: "My mother bore me a speaker of what God made mine own" (CM IV, p. 60). When it came to another sort of entry into another sort of public sphere—that of writing—Milton premised that entry if not on his father's absence, at least very much on his mother's invocation. And it is not untoward, I think, to suggest that Milton here had both "mother" and "God" in mind as his parents. In 1671, Milton would represent Jesus in the act of defining himself between his mother and God as he (Jesus) is on the threshold of public activity. In 1642, Milton represents himself in an act of self-definition between his mother and God as he is on the threshold of public activity.

This alerts us to two things. First of all, it demonstrates that the premise of Lacan's model of the entry into the realm of the Symbolic, being the absence of the mother, is somewhat incapable of capturing the tension Milton feels between his mother's being and his linguistic capacities.[62] And, second, we may see how Milton's own definition of himself as speaker falls not only into that gap between his mother tongue and the languages his father has purchased for him, but also in that space between two parents—one of whom is his mother, the other God. When Jesus defines himself in relation to the private sphere, then, he is not just deferring his entry into the public realm but, rather, establishing one important direction for self-knowledge. Mary did teach Jesus how to reread the Law by pointing out how to look for signs of his parentage in it. In this light, and under the conditions Jesus himself suggests between the public and the private sphere, the meaning of Jesus' return to the mother's house at the end of this poem might bespeak something more complex about the question of *subjectification*. It might perhaps mean what Timothy Reiss suggests about the "freedom" of Montaigne's "subjects": "The freedom of the individual resides in keeping a space for the private while at the same time lending oneself to the public order, to the requirements of the law—which moreover is the condition *sine qua non* for maintaining this private freedom."[63]

Freedom for Milton, as we have seen throughout, rests on reason, which Milton insistently defines as a function of the internal person, the conscience beyond the laws of civil power. Early in his career, Milton also suggested that because the public being could not always be "contemplative, or pragmaticall abroad," he or she must always have a domestic sphere to which he or she might have recourse. Now, while it is true that Milton felt that this domestic sphere ought to provide leisure, "wherein the enlarg'd soul may leav off a while her severe schooling," he nonetheless would not have denied that this time of leisure would allow for another sort of "schooling"—less severe but nonetheless concerned with knowing oneself in relation to an intimate Other (CM IV, p. 86). For Jesus in *Paradise Regained*, as for the Milton of the Martin Bucer divorce tract, that intimate Other could well be residing in the domestic sphere designated as the "Mothers house." For Jesus certainly, and for Milton perhaps, the knowledge he gets from his mother is knowledge that helps him understand how to define himself in terms of his parents and in terms of his own death. From Mary, Jesus learns how to read the Law and from that he learns what it is going to take to give humanity its lost freedom. From Sarah Milton, John Milton learned to speak what God made his own—and that was a profuse amount of prose and poetry concerned with defining three species of liberty. From the domestic spheres of two mothers, two sons taught their respective cultures how not to be servants.

Here, again, we find Samson on the other side of the fence. For Samson forgoes the knowledge of himself and, therefore, that freedom belonging to the private sphere, inasmuch as he does not acknowledge his mother's presence in his life. Not only did Samson

refuse to mention his mother or the private sphere in his autobiography, he continues to eschew any sense of selfhood based on
being a private person—"I was no private but a person rais'd . . .
To free my Countrey" (1222). As Jackie DiSalvo suggests, there is
an undeniable "gender split" in Samson's very "male psyche." There
is also, moreover, an insistent denial of his intuitive abilities. Samson cannot achieve self-knowledge while he persists in denying one
half of his parentage and while he refuses to explore his "self" as it
exists in the domestic sphere. So, in the end, Manoa's taking his
son's body back to his "Fathers House" is a fit enough conclusion
for his father's son. It does not, however, bode well for the Israel
Manoa thinks Samson freed. And to get a better idea of how
ominous it looks for Israel, we should turn to another echo between the two poems that occurs in the concluding choral song of
each work.

To understand the way that the Chorus in *Samson Agonistes*
demonstrates the limited possibilities for seeing this new culture,
we may turn to the wonderful close of the tragedy:

> All is best, though we oft doubt,
> What th' unsearchable dispose
> Of highest wisdom brings about,
> And ever best found in the close.
> Oft he seems to hide his face,
> But unexpectedly returns
> And to his faithful Champion hath in place
> Bore witness gloriously; whence *Gaza* mourns
> And all that band them to resist
> His uncontroulable intent,
> His servants he with new acquist
> Of true experience from this great event
> With peace and consolation hath dismist,
> And calm of mind all passion spent.   (1746–59)

The Chorus is myopic in its ability to perceive the possibility for a
new world. The "true experience" that the tribe of Dan takes from
Samson's great act will not be altogether applied to Israel's political
establishment. Historically, according to its analogue, the Book of
Judges, this very Chorus will soon be as idolatrous as ever. For, this
tragedy does not present a "lack" in its final scenes, but a proleptic
glance at a moment beyond its close. In this way is the relation of

the Messenger the fulfillment of what Horatio might have done. And it is precisely in the "silence" between the two poems in this 1671 production that we can best trace the ways the tribe of Dan fails to learn what they claim to have learned—"highest wisdom."

This final choral song is also an echo of its parallel song in *Paradise Regained*. To get an idea of the sort of dialectic that occurs between these two poems, we might turn to the brief epic and see how it concludes. The angelic chorus sings that with the Son's victory, his "great event," "A fairer Paradise is founded now / For *Adam* and his chosen Sons" (IV, 609–10). "Sons or Servants," we saw, was Milton's distinction between those who reasonably participated in agential liberty and those who unreasonably lost it. In the chorus' interpretation of God's will, who acquires the "new acquist / Of true experience"? Quite simply, the "servants" of God, says the chorus. They don't know yet how to escape a far more damaging servitude than that they suffered under the Philistines— which is the servitude they suffer to their own desires. The tribe of Dan believes in God's "uncontroulable intent," and they are therefore his "servants." Who acquires the "highest wisdom" in the brief epic? The "Sons" of God, say the angelic chorus. And the way to that regained garden is to reign within oneself, to shed that servitude to one's own desires first and foremost. This ending in *Samson Agonistes* alerts us to the ending choral song in *Paradise Regained*. The tribe of Dan did not acquire the "highest wisdom" they could. They and theirs would be servants for a few more generations. Those who read *Paradise Regained* with "spirit and judgment" see another world, a regained paradise fit for the sons of God. Furthermore, we ought then to be aware of the historical distance within the "book." Like *Paradise Regained,* this tragedy adumbrates a moment of recognition beyond itself which requires an understanding of the historical interlude between these two poems. Here we might turn to what this tragedy is silent about, but what it nonetheless inscribes very much into its workings—and that is its analogue, the Book of Judges.

In the analogue, Samson is the last of the important judges. After Samson's death the tribe of Dan follows the idolater Micah, then the Levite and his concubine, which finally leads to the slaughter of the men of the tribe of Benjamin. Running as a haunting refrain from the seventeenth to the twenty-first chapters of the Book of Judges is the phrase Milton might well have had prominently in mind as he composed his Restoration tragedy: "In those days there was no king in Israel" (Judg. xvii, 6; xviii, 1; xix, 1; xxi, 25). From the first to the end of the sixteenth chapter, from the first judge Ehud to the final significant judge Samson, the usual refrain runs: "And the children of Israel did evil again in the sight of the Lord" (Judg. iii, 12; iv, 1; vi, 1; xiii, 1). One has difficulty denying that for Milton the shift from "evil" to "king" would be an especially poignant reminder of the end of the Republic. Of course, the next book of the Bible describes the birth of Obed, the grand-father of David, the king of Israel whose line would be inter-rupted. The next set of books after that, Samuel and Kings, shows how Israel came to be burdened with a monarchy. In fact, if we think now of the 1671 book as a whole, we notice that Milton ends the tragedy at the point where Israel is about to become a mon-archy, and he begins the brief epic at the point when that monarchy is transmuted to heaven.

When Milton sang of the Republic in the *Second Defence* in 1654, he suggested that he was going to imitate an epic poet precisely so that he could be reticent:

> But as the poet, who is styled epic, if he adhere strictly to established rules, undertakes to embellish not the whole life of the hero whom he proposes to celebrate in song, but, usually, one particular action of his life, as for example, that of Achilles at Troy, or the return of Ulysses, or the arrival of Æneas in Italy, *and leaves alone the rest;* so likewise will it suffice for my duty and excuse, that I have at least embellished one of the heroic actions of my countrymen. *The rest I pass by.* If, after achievements so magnanimous, ye basely fall off from your duty, if ye are guilty of any thing unworthy of you, be assured, posterity will speak, and thus pronounce its judgment: The founda-tion was strongly laid, the beginning, nay more than the beginning, was excellent; but it will be inquired, not without a disturbed emo-tion, who raised the superstructure, who completed the fabric! To undertakings so grand, to virtues so noble, it will be a subject of grief that perseverance was wanting. It will be seen that the harvest of glory was abundant; that there were materials for the greatest operations, but that men were not to be found for the work; yet, that there was not wanting one, who could give good counsel; who could extort, encourage; who could adorn, and celebrate, in praises destined to endure forever, the transcendent deeds, and those who performed them. (CM VIII, pp. 252–55; my italics)

Milton's will to silence in 1654 is ominous; his silences in the 1671 volume are revealing. What Milton chooses not to present—in leaving "alone the rest" which might well be compared to Hamlet's "the rest is silence"—is the state of Israel after its history under the judges and before its history under Jesus—precisely the period of Israel under monarchy. By having the Messenger narrate a glorious deed, Milton suggests that within the world of the tragedy there is potential for a renovated culture, for creating a world out of a significant and heroic life. Samson's life, unfortunately, was not enough of an example, and it would take the life of the hero in the companion narrative and his "transcendent deeds" to give the volume its revolutionary quality.

The two works within the 1671 volume enjoy a commerce that up to this time had been noticed but not sufficiently traced; and there yet remains, I think, more subtle nuances and more significant relationships between the two poems. For my purposes, it is enough to suggest that in the interchange between the two poems, and especially in the silence about the history spanning their events, there is reason enough to turn to the analogue to see what would be the political significance of a culture that still described its individuals as "servants." In the analogue, we find inscribed in the Old Testament the reason Manoa's advice to his fellow Danites to "lay hold on this occasion" goes for naught. To see, finally, why this is so, we must return to the two similes concluding each of the works in the 1671 volume.

"TO COMPARE SMALL THINGS WITH GREATEST": JESUS IN *SAMSON AGONISTES*

At the conclusion of the third temptation in *Paradise Regained*, as Jesus remains standing and Satan plummets to his consistory below, the narrator uses two similes to describe the Son's victory:

> But Satan smitten with amazement fell
> As when Earths Son *Antæus* (to compare
> Small things with greatest) in *Irassa* strove
> With *Joves Alcides,* and oft foil'd still rose,
> Receiving from his mother Earth new strength,
> Fresh from his fall, and fiercer grapple joyn'd,

Throttl'd at length in the Air, expir'd and fell;
So after many a foil the Tempter proud,
Renewing fresh assaults, amidst his pride
Fell whence he stood to see his Victor fall.
And as that *Theban* Monster that propos'd
Her riddle, and him, who solv'd it not, devour'd;
That once found out and solv'd, for grief and spight
Cast her self headlong from th' *Ismenian* steep,
So strook with dread and anguish fell the Fiend.
                                        (IV, 559–73)

Barbara Lewalski has offered a pertinent reading of the significance of these two similes. The Antaeus allusion refers to the
traditional association of Jesus as the second Hercules, while at the
same time alluding to the traditional allegorical reading of Hercules's victory over Antaeus as the victory of reason over passion.
The Sphinx simile alludes to Jesus' attainment of true wisdom.
"Oedipus defeated the Sphinx by solving the riddle whose answer
is 'Man,' and Christ defeats Satan because he possesses true self-
knowledge and knowledge of the human condition." Kathleen Swaim
has gone further yet in her interpretation of these two similes. She
maintains that their significance can be gleaned only from probing
the "myths" which each allusion represents enigmatically. For instance, Swaim maintains that the Hercules simile, when probed to
its mythical kernel, can yield the meaning that Jesus was inaugurat-
ing a new dispensation from that time forward. Because the simile
alludes to the myth, and because in the myth Hercules slays Antaeus on his way to free Prometheus, the "source and pattern of all
humanity," we can conclude that Jesus frees humanity analogically
in the same way Hercules frees Prometheus.[64]

The term *Joves Alcides* refers to Hercules only in terms of his
relationship to Jove—that is, as a Son of God—and we have seen
the manifold significance of that filial relationship to Milton's
theology. The second simile refers to Jesus as "Man" in the two
senses detected by Lewalski and Swaim: first, in that Oedipus
the solver of the Sphinx's puzzle is a man, and secondly in that
the answer to the puzzle was "man." In this way, we find yet
further support for not determining that Jesus was "divine." He
was, at the pinnacle, as he was throughout the poem, both man
and Son of God. He is, as God says at the beginning of the poem
with little ambiguity, "This perfect Man, by merit call'd my

Son" (I, 166). Moreover, both similes refer to Jesus; this is not the case in the companion tragedy.

At the end of the Messenger's relation of Samson's final act, the Chorus is mystically invested with a degree of prophetic insight. Without seeing the event or the Philistine audience's response to it, they are able to comment on both. They begin by elaborating on Samson's motivations and excuse the "dire necessity" which entailed his death in this "work." They then divide into two semichoruses. The first defines the frenzy of the Philistine audience—something they have not seen—while the second offers two distinct images of avian avengers. They claim that Samson was illuminated with inward eyes,

> His fierie vertue rouz'd
> From under ashes into sudden flame,
> And as an ev'ning Dragon came,
> Assailant on the perched roosts
> And nests in order rang'd
> Of tame villatic Fowl; but as an Eagle
> His cloudless thunder bolted on thir heads.   (1691–97)

In describing how Samson's virtue was "rouz'd," the Chorus invokes the dragon and the eagle who also perform their dreadful deeds just as Samson had done, by being the recipient of "rouzing motions." The other bird simile, though, presents us with a pacific and self-creating phoenix. The dragon and the eagle are simple similes referring to Samson (the Chorus begins each simile with an "as"). The phoenix is not a simile of Samson, but, if anything, a simile of the simile of Samson. In describing Samson's regained "virtue," the Chorus uses an odd double simile formula to introduce the second simile, "as seem'd, / Like":

> as seem'd,
> Like that self-beggot'n bird
> In the *Arabian* woods embost,
> That no second knows nor third,
> And lay e're while a Holocaust,
> From her ashie womb now teem'd,
> Revives, reflourishes, then vigorous most
> When most unactive deem'd,
> And though her body die, her fame survives,
> A secular bird ages of lives.   (1699–1708)

This phoenix simile alludes to Jesus, who knows no second, whose vigorous activity in the wilderness seemed passive to Satan, and who died to bring "ages of lives."[65] The Chorus has offered dualities before this, notably the two forms of heroism available to Samson: invincible might or patience of mind (1279–1308). They counseled the second because of Samson's blindness, but Samson acted out the first. The vision of the Chorus was dull in that instance. It is now inspired, but not wholly clear—still shadowy and somewhat carnal.

In the fulfillment of his type, Jesus is the second phoenix and regains paradise by the second form of heroism. Patience, the Chorus in the tragedy notes, makes "each his own Deliverer" (1300). Patience, Jesus tells Satan in the epic, is also the means of establishing the kingdom within:

> What if he hath decreed that I shall first
> Be try'd in humble state, and things adverse,
> By tribulations, injuries, insults,
> Contempts, and scorns, and snares, and violence,
> Suffering, abstaining, quietly expecting,
> Without distrust or doubt, that he may know
> What I can suffer, how obey? who best
> Can suffer, best can do; best reign, who first
> Well hath obey'd; just trial e're I merit
> My exaltation without change or end.   (III, 188–97)

This display of patience, God tells the angels, is an exercise that helps the Son prepare for the great work of salvation. He is both the way and the example. God displays him in the wilderness so that angels "now, and men hereafter may *discern*" his consummate virtue. By meditating on the only time of unsullied purity of virtue—the three years of public ministry that would establish the means of eternal spiritual dialectic with God—Milton discerns and allows his reader to discern the paradigm of ethical behavior.

Returning to the final similes of *Samson Agonistes,* we notice that the phoenix is female. In her reading of the significance of what Christopher Grose calls this "emphatically feminine phoenix," Jackie DiSalvo suggests that the phoenix palliates the absolutist distinctions in gender that Milton is prone to describing. Taken together with the "masculine eagle," the final product of the Chorus' similes is an "androgynous bird" analogically signifying a self "beyond all contraries of gender, a fully human self."[66] I have suggested, however, the difficulties involved in taking the phoenix to refer to Samson at all. But when we allow that it may refer to Jesus, the fact that the phoenix is feminine supports in yet another way how Milton maintains the importance of resolving gender relations, and domestic relations, in the gaining of self-knowledge and therefore in the attaining of freedom. To be a Son of God, the hero must know who his mother is and what she signifies in his life. Jesus does; Samson does not. Moreover, in being "self-be-gott'n," the phoenix refers in one more way to the role of the Son before the Incarnation—which is what role he would have had in 1120 b.c.

Christ, then, is not absent from the world of *Samson Agonistes,* whether we agree with Fish that his presence can be traced back to 1949 or to 1671.[67] But the possibility that this presence is of any political value for the tribe of Danites is immediately lessened when Manoa responds to the hopeful simile of the phoenix with an uncomprehending call for the Chorus to desist being so pessimistic: "Come, come, no time for lamentation now" (1709). Once again we have this curious lack of communicative clarity between all the characters at the end of the play. Here is a tribe that simply is not able to understand itself. At each point where one communicates to the other, the other demonstrates a persistent lack of ability to understand. The importance of this moment to the world of the tragedy at large is that when Manoa misunderstands the hope extended in that simile of the phoenix, he also denies the presence of both Samson's feminine aspect and the possibility for comprehending the Spirit that the Son exerted even in the time of the Law. As Milton wrote in his *Christian Doctrine,* Christian liberty was "not unknown to the descendents of Abraham, even under the law of servitude." He draws his evidence from the fact that "they were still called sons of God" (CM XVI, pp. 52–55; cf. pp. 150–53).[68] So there existed, even in the time of the Law, the distinct possibility for Samson to become a son of God. But Samson did not become a son of God precisely because, as we saw, he foreclosed the opportunity for self-knowledge leading to agential liberty. Moreover, Manoa also denies the tribe of Dan the possibility of aspiring to self-knowledge by foreclosing the opportunity to appreciate the hopeful presence of the feminine phoenix. Manoa calls for the tribe to help him bring Samson "Home to his Fathers house" (1734). By continuing to deny the presence of the mother as Samson had done, both Manoa and the tribe of Dan ensure that they will continue to be denied the sort of complete self-knowledge that Jesus brings with him from his mother's words and takes with him "Home to his Mothers house" (IV, 635). Likewise, Manoa misses the point about how the simile of the phoenix relates to the simile of the dragon—the simile of a simile—and thereby would have allowed the possibility for comprehending the spiritual force at work in Samson's "great event." Instead, Manoa proclaims, with little understanding of how to generate a good simile, that "*Samson* hath quit himself / Like *Samson*" (1710–11).

Although the Spirit was available to those who lived before Christ, as was the possibility of being adopted sons of God and having agential liberty, Milton maintained that the Christian dispensation truly brought those possibilities to the forefront. For Milton, the Christian dispensation meant the victory of grace over the tyranny of law:

> Christ having cancell'd the hand writing of ordinances which was against us and interpreted the fulfilling of all through charity, hath in that respect set us over law, in the free custody of his love, and left us victorious under the guidance of his living Spirit, not under the dead letter.

This liberty, Milton made clear, was not only for individuals but for nations:

> To follow that which most edifies, most aides and furders a religious life, makes us holiest and likest to his immortall Image, not that which makes us most conformable and captive to civill and subordinat precepts; whereof the strictest observance may oftimes prove the destruction not only of many innocent persons and families, but of whole Nations. (CM IV, pp. 74–75)

Satan, we saw, was unable to comprehend the Spirit of the new covenant; his carnal apprehension of things leads to his defeat. He cannot understand the premise of temperance: the beauty of reigning within.

In the *Second Defence*, as almost everywhere else in his prose and poetry, Milton states that internal government must be antecedent to any lasting civil liberty. In *Paradise Regained* Jesus offers the paradigm of that internal renovation. By demonstrating exalted temperance, Jesus, by merit more than birthright, also establishes the new covenant. In this dispensation, the Law is within—like the locality of government and the reward of paradise. The Law for Samson, on the other hand, is an established code of behavior. He does not go to the temple at the Officer's first command because of the Law: "Our Law forbids at thir Religious Rites / My presence; for that cause I cannot come" (1331–32). The "rouzing motions" lead him to a degree of antinomianism. He is directed by God to disobey that particular law—not to attend. But Samson says that he will nonetheless do nothing else "Scandalous or forbidden in our Law" (1420, cf. 1396–97). He is directed to rise above the Law in this one instance; he is otherwise still living and dying in the dispensation of the Law. Milton, it is worth noting, held that some people "of renowned vertu have sometimes by transgressing, most truly kept the law" (CM IV, pp. 75–76).[69]

In *Paradise Regained,* although the Law is destroyed by the exalted man, the liberty established by the dispensation of grace is not to be had by all. As Milton said in his doctrine, reason is the basis. Reasonable beings transcend the literal law, understand the enigmatic quality of the kingdom within, and therefore occupy the paradise regained. Unreasonable beings, such as Satan and the rabble, are limited by doubting to a carnal understanding, do not comprehend the enigma of a spiritual and internal kingdom, and therefore remain outside the paradise regained. This distinction based on intellectual capacity is true not only of those delivered but also of those who act as their deliverers.

In 1671, he presents one hero who is not reasonable and who, therefore, acts out the role of servant in God's ongoing revelation, and another hero who is the essence of reason and therefore the Son of God. The crucial difference between Samson and Jesus is that whereas Jesus displays a liberty of will in pursuing his vocation, Samson must be roused to his work. They differ not only as Old Testament judge to New Testament messiah, but also as unreasonable actor to reasonable hero. Jesus, that is, was a free agent because he was a reasonable being; Samson was neither. This does not come down to a debate between Calvin and Arminius; it comes down to the tension we found earlier in Milton.[70]

Samson, despite or maybe because of his limited intellectual powers, appeals to us in the way that Irene Samuel has noted:

Because Samson is so much better than those among whom we find him, we want him to be better still—to win through to some total comprehension, to be redeemed by his intolerable suffering, to recognize the sheer futility of a Dalila, a Harapha, to rise above his own brute strength and learn what deliverance means. And like tragic agents generally, he is too deeply enmeshed in snares of his own and others' weaving to break wholly free.

This desire is raised and then defied by the tragedy, and in that dialectic is the lesson to be gleaned. Violence is made intrinsic to the tragedy so that both the violence and tragedy may be dissipated: "Sowr against sowr, salt to remove salt humours" (*SA, 3*). As René Girard points out concerning the reciprocal violence of the bacchanal, the "rite is not oriented toward violence, but toward peace. The tragic demystification discloses a bacchanal that is pure frenzy, naked violence. And the process of tragic demystification is itself violent, for it cannot but weaken the rites and contribute to their 'going wrong'."[71] In the 1671 volume, Samson represents the formality of a violent and retributive deliverance—one that marked the history of Israel, especially under the judges. In the companion poem, a new and wholly spiritual form of deliverance is inaugurated. In the interim, Samson is part of the dialectic of history—born to act a role in the shadowy path to the future.

As God's agonist, Samson expresses one aspect of the tension between God's prescience and human freedom. Samson was unable to fulfill God's plan of his own free will. Had he been able to do so, Samson would have shown himself a reasonable being. It is a circular argument, perhaps even unfairly so, but this is the sense of career to be discovered everywhere in Milton's thought—as true of a nation as of an individual, who stumbles falls and who falls keeps falling. As we saw in chapter 3, Milton disagreed with Calvin on the question of the universality of salvation. Milton believed salvation available to all, but he knew that not all would choose salvation.

Between the Milton of the *Second Defence* and the Milton of the 1671 volume, we find the same tension between hope and fear, between optimism in the potential and troubled concern in the presentiment of his fellow countrymen. In 1671, Milton believed as much as he did in 1641 that the way to liberty was by eradicating the "double tyrannie, of Custom from without, and blind affections within" (CM V, p. 1). Both heroes of the 1671 volume confront thoughts from within and encounter the crust of custom from without. The difference is that Samson in his opening soliloquy has only "restless thoughts" of himself and his own history while Jesus in his opening soliloquy has a "multitude of thoughts" of things both "from within" and "from without" (*PR* I, 196–99; *SA* 18–22). Samson destroys the tyranny of custom by destroying the culture responsible for its imposition in this local instance (1120 b.c.). Jesus, by contemplating the two forms of tyranny, destroys them both and establishes the culture within, able to withstand any imposition at any time.

The volume offers two images of each hero, the iconic and the poetic. One iconic image is of Samson at the pillars, arms outstretched and head erecting. The other iconic image is of Jesus at the pinnacle, suffering the wiles of Satan as he will suffer from birth to Passion. One poetic image is of Samson as the hero whose race is run, the hero in his final return. The other poetic image is of Jesus as the hero whose race is yet to run, the hero whose return is his beginning. In this lies the optimism of the 1671 volume.

In order to enter that regained paradise with his or her savior, the citizen of England in 1671 had to return to the fount of his or her faith, to meditate on the two forms of delivery, and to choose between filiality or servitude. Milton noted in *Tetrachordon* the relationship between a "nation" and the individual "families" making it up and the individual "persons" making up those families. He had early in his career thought that "one family, one man endowed with knowledge and wisdom, like a great gift of God, may be sufficient to reform a whole state" (CM XII, p. 259). The gift of God would be clarified in Milton's developing theological politics as the "Spirit." The knowledge and wisdom he early regarded as the significant achievement of any individual and the necessary basis of any civil reform would remain constant. Moreover, Milton still emphasized the important relationship between state, family, and individual person. In the 1671 volume, Milton stressed a model of individual self-knowledge that not only relied on the "gift of God," but also emphasized the importance of familial relationships to any form of self-knowledge. In his 1671 volume, as I suggested at the outset of this chapter, we may find inscribed Milton's political subjectivity. Having now proposed a reading of *Samson Agonistes* sufficient to our purposes, having before us an interpretation of how Jesus articulates his subjectivity in the brief epic and how Samson attempts to do the same in the companion tragedy, we may turn, finally, to a discussion of how Milton articulates his subjectivity, his politics, and his model of reform in this volume.

5

Confronting the Author:
The Art of Politics

I N ALMOST THE same breath with which he pronounces Milton the "greatest English political poet," Fredric Jameson also states that *Paradise Regained* is "post-political." The basis of his reasoning generally is that religion, even when it presents itself as a revolutionary force, must at a certain moment in its political process become reactionary. In the case of Milton specifically, he traces that reactionary moment to the final two books of *Paradise Lost* and the whole of *Paradise Regained*. When Milton begins what Jameson calls an "inward turn—a displacement from politics to psychology and ethics," he leaves the world of "collective praxis" and enters one concerned only with "personal, private salvation."[1] That turn, for Jameson, no longer constitutes politics but rather what he calls "post-politics." One may, of course, contest Jameson's definition of "politics," and do so by employing even the Marxist tenets on which he is establishing the distinction between the individual subject and collective action. In fact, Jameson himself had three years earlier adapted an Althusserian conception of the subject in order to suggest one possible point of convergence between the subject and the collective. In a passage which he later edited out of his essay on Lacan he writes, "The ideological representation must rather be seen as that indispensable mapping fantasy or narrative by which the individual subject invents a 'lived' relationship with collective systems."[2] This earlier formulation of

Jameson's allows that representations of individual experiences might signify a relationship to collective forces; that is, it opens up a space for appreciating a potential point of intersection between the representation of persons and politics. Jameson's later formulation, on the other hand, forecloses that critical space.

Several things are worth noting about Jameson's critical gestures. First of all, his argument that there is a discernible "break" between an earlier "political" Milton and a later "post-political" Milton is by no means original; it is, in fact, the conventional reading of Milton's political career. Second, the conditions by which Jameson defines what is "post-political" fail to account for much that is considered "political," both in seventeenth-century England and in contemporary America. The major lesion he suggests between what is personal and what is political seems blind to many feminist arguments about the ways the personal is imbricated with the political and vice versa; and, in our present case, he does not even attempt to account for Milton's own arguments that the originary place of all political action is the personal subject. Third, even though he maintains that religion may act as a revolutionary force, and that even in its precapitalist modes it might be considered a "*distorted* anticipation of historical materialism," Jameson nonetheless considers it merely a "figural mode" and not a cognitive system. All in all, then, Jameson does not *dispute* Milton's definition of the site of politics or Milton's insistence that religion is a revolutionary force, he merely replaces what Milton considers the preconditions for his political science with his own. One cannot deny that it is useful to discern a given thinker's politics by deploying a political code different from one's own, but it is unwarranted to use that foreign code then to deny the status of that thinking as politics.

How did Milton define "politics" in the years when there is little controversy about his being political, and how did he depart from that early definition? I will work from his native definitions and see if Milton's late works may be called political by his own standards. In what ways are Milton's ideas on religion and the individual subject political? By placing Milton in a dialogue with a contemporary who is undisputedly political, we will be able to discern whether or not Milton's ideas can be considered political. This second argument will be concerned with Milton's politics in dialogue, the first with Milton's politics in soliloquy. By employing both methods we are able to discover whether Milton in his late career is political by either his own conditions or those of his age. We should, then, be able to dispute or corroborate that traditional reading of Milton's late career.

As Jameson noted, in Milton's career there is a "break" that most critics date at the Restoration of May 1660. The break itself is inscribed as a "turn" from a material concern with active, collective politics to a spiritualized concern with a personal, internal dialectic with God. Several questions arise from this characterization and its dating. What may be said about Milton's "politics" before the Restoration? What is meant by "politics" in this instance—and how does this differ from Milton's thinking on the same issues after the Restoration? What evidence exists to demonstrate that the Restoration is the most feasible date to fix on this alleged "break" in his politics? Concerning Milton's late politics, what is the relationship between subjection and subjectivity? And what is the relation of either to self-knowledge? The exploration of these questions requires several distinct arguments. First of all, we must understand what is meant when a critic uses the word *politics* to characterize one instance of Milton's career and denies it as descriptive of another instance. Then we may see whether this critical distinction between what is political and what is not holds for Milton's last two poems.

Milton's final two works are political in precisely the same way that Milton's writing of the early to middle 1650s is political. Briefly put, Milton's politics are concerned with (1) the ways individuals, families, and states are interlocking structures; (2) the place of the individual subject in relation to God and in relation to the state; and (3) the role of self-knowledge and of self-government in both individuals and nations. For various reasons, over and above having to argue for Milton's politics in soliloquy and in dialogue, this argument has to be circuitous.

First of all, I have to make the case for what constitutes Milton's politics against a long line of critics who have characterized Milton's thought as apolitical. Politics is what I suggested as the method for determining the ratio of knowledge and experience inasmuch as knowledge transforms experience. In relation to the third form of selfhood, based on the postlapsarian or representational form of self-knowledge, politics would be the way of determining the relationship between self-representation and self-knowledge. To understand Milton's politics, then, we have to understand Milton's self-knowledge as it is articulated in the 1671 volume. To understand Milton's act of coming to self-knowledge, we likewise have to understand his acts of self-representation in the volume.

Second, to demonstrate that Milton inscribes his self-representation into his 1671 volume, I will use a form of critical inquiry that has long and unjustly been decried as "biographical fallacy." To prevent my argument from being dismissed on a charge of misrepresentation, I will demonstrate the shortcomings of New Criticism's invalidation of the use of biographical criticism.

Third, I will refer to three interdependent levels of tropical discourse—simile, allegory, self-representation—in order to make this argument about Milton's self-representation.

In sum, the argument will deal with issues of critical characterization, theoretical propriety, and discursive modalities. It might be helpful in that case to state both the general argument of this chapter as well as its overall structure. Generally, I wish to see what sort of political self-knowledge *Milton* reaches in the 1671 volume, and I will do so by discerning the ways he inscribes his own subjectivity in the two works at the level of "political allegory." The overall structure of my argument will be as follows.

I will discuss some of the implications of both the critical characterization ("retreat") and the historical chronicling of Milton's late politics ("1660"). Second, I will suggest that we may develop a better understanding of what I have been calling Milton's "politics" by pointing out his ideas on the evolution of social forms, and in this way discern the ways the personal and the political interact in Milton's political thought. Third, I will argue that it is not the Restoration of May 1660, but rather the *Second Defence* of 1654 that we might posit as the key date and event in Milton's late politics. Indeed, it is my intent to argue that the *Second Defence* plays a quite prominent role in both *Paradise Regained* and *Samson Agonistes*.

In order to argue for this intertextuality, I will be working from what I'll tentatively characterize as the tropological to what I'll call the modal. The mode is what Jameson calls "political allegory," and the trope is the use of similes in the 1671 volume. Mostly my argument about Milton's "political allegory" will be concerned with his inscription of his *subjectivity* into his book. Given that the formal proofs I will be bringing to bear on this act of self-inscription are what New Criticism would call "extrinsic evidence"— evidence therefore falling into the category of the so-called "biographical fallacy"—I will preface my interpretation of the relationship of the 1654 and the 1671 books by confronting the residue of that facet of New Criticism.

Finally, I will turn my attention to discovering the potential significance of Milton's self-representations in his 1671 volume and what that self-representation suggests about Milton's late politics. I will then demonstrate how Milton's politics are to be understood when he is placed in an implicit dialogue with Thomas Hobbes. Having discerned what Milton has to say about political subjectivity, I will attempt to discover what Milton has to say about political *subjection*.

PART ONE: MILTON'S POLITICAL SOLILOQUY

Milton and the Restoration: Some Conjectures

Like *author*, a word whose significance I will be discussing below, *politics* is not a word that can be used unproblematically. Milton is not a politician in the strict sense of one actively engaged in the theorizing or creating of the material conditions of state policy. Milton is certainly not a politician in the way Cromwell was a politician. But Milton does deserve consideration as a political theorist in the way that Hobbes is so considered; that is, as one who writes about the theoretical conditions of state policy. Milton did not attempt to deal with the intricacies of government issues at the level of economic or judicial reform. He was concerned mostly with broadly defined questions of certain liberties and how those liberties were affected in the interaction of various forms of state apparatus. That, I take it, is how most critics who write on Milton's politics define them, and with that I have no quarrel. The term I have been implicitly suggesting for characterizing Milton in his political mode is *cultural critic*, in the same way Thomas Greene, for instance, characterized Petrarch's role in fourteenth-century Italy. Both have an interest in the human aspects of cultural transformation, not the economic. Like Petrarch's critique of Italy, Milton's criticisms of English culture take on the form of implicit or explicit comparisons with ancient cultures—most notably Israel and Rome.

The level at which Milton feels most comfortable discoursing on active politics is always the ethical, the personal, the subjective. So, for example, just as Milton's presentation of the Fall is an act of political commentary, so might any instance of Milton's political commentary refer directly to the Fall. Locke will refer to the Fall as the moment when political economy underwent a significant change, but in doing so he delineates the Fall as an instance of economic transgression. For Milton it is always an act only of ethical transgression, and for that reason his politics unfailingly are to be discerned most fully at the level of ethics. Given this anthropological bent in his political thinking, I would posit an anthropologist's definition of politics for our purposes: "For cultural analysis and criticism, the contesting of the meaning of things or events is what centrally constitutes politics." Cultural critique of this sort constitutes a politics that operates at the level of hermeneutics. However, that does not make it apolitical. Being interpretive does not make it merely historical, in the sense Jameson poses: "Milton's poem is historical, even though . . . it fails to be political." We ought to remember Benjamin's thesis about the personally transformative power of history. The interpretation of the past is in itself a political act; in Milton it is emphatically so. Moreover, none of Milton's late poems is only historical; each and every one of them is also theoretical. As I have been suggesting throughout this book, in his narratives, especially *Paradise Regained,* Milton theorizes and demonstrates the preconditions required for the establishment of a new culture. Thus, *Paradise Regained* is theoretical and therefore political, not in the sense by which Althusser defines *theory*—"something which in a certain way anticipates a science"—but rather in the way Marx defines the power of theory—"a material force once it has gripped the masses." "Theory," Marx continues, "is capable of gripping the masses when it demonstrates *ad hominem,* and it demonstrates *ad hominem* as soon as it becomes radical."[3] The radix in Milton is not economic alienation but spiritual alienation, but that, for the reading masses of the seventeenth century, would have been as *ad hominem* as *ad hominem* gets. In the end, Milton's politics is not only interpretive and theoretical, it is also preparatory. Not only does Milton read the failure of the English Revolution in the allegory of the Fall, or trace the reasons for its failure in the results of the Fall, but he also documents and prescribes the necessary knowledge and conditions for a renewed revolution.

So when Michael tells Adam that national subjection follows the paradigm of personal failure in self-knowledge, he is both interpreting one failure of maintaining national liberty and articulating the necessary conditions for a renewed attempt at regaining that liberty. Michael is both historian and theorist. This is not only a subtle distinction between two blurred points on a continuum of what constitutes "politics," it is a necessary premise to understanding why Milton is, as Jameson correctly states, the "greatest English political poet." Critics have long been interested in seeing how Milton inscribes his politics into his final three poems. Richard Corum attempts to argue that Milton's major poems can be said to be "private confessional texts, admitting under the covering and displacing trope of sacred story, the failures of the private life." Critics before Corum spent their energies searching for the ways that Milton admitted the failures of his public, political life under the trope of sacred story. I suggest that the place to find Milton's politics is between the public and the private. We saw how important the integration of public and private was to our reading of both the opening soliloquy of *Samson Agonistes* and the tragedy's close. When critics of various political persuasions turn to *Paradise Regained,* they almost unanimously consider the poem to be a "retreat" from the active politics of Milton as he was in *Paradise Lost* and *Samson Agonistes,* as well as the Milton of the prose writings from 1641 to 1660.[4]

According to Jameson, for instance, the "political" Milton is found mostly in Books 1 to 10 of *Paradise Lost.* The final two books of *Paradise Lost* and all of *Paradise Regained* open up what he calls "that privatized and post-political world . . . with its characteristic failure of hope following upon the failure of the revolution." It is worthwhile clarifying what Jameson is implicitly assuming about politics as a mode of human endeavor. Jameson distinguishes between politics, which is a matter only of "collective praxis," and post-politics, which deals with an "inward turn—a displacement from politics to psychology and ethics." So in the case of Milton, there is a return to an emphasis on "personal, private salvation and the repudiation of millenarianism." Put into a more contentious form, according to Jameson, the personal is not the political. And that, he argues, is the case in the last two books of *Paradise Lost* and the whole of *Paradise Regained.*[5]

A rigorous Marxist, in an Althusserian cast of mind (at least here), Jameson does not hold that what operates within the "organizational framework of the individual subject" should rightly be called "politics," but properly constitutes the turn away from politics. That, of course, at least according to Althusser, is the idea of the Marx of *Capital* (1867), not the Marx of the *Critique of Hegel's Doctrine of the State* (1843) or the Marx of the *Economic and Philosophical Manuscripts* (1844). In other words, Jameson traces the "break" in Milton's politics according to Milton's conception of the subject, using as his definition of politics only the late Marx's theory of subjectivity. According to Althusser, Marx came into his own and founded the continent of History as a Science when he eschewed all Hegelian tenets *but* the one that states, according to Althusser, that "history is a process without a subject."[6] Conversely, according to Jameson, Milton came into his own when he left the realm of collective praxis and returned to the conception of the emergent bourgeois subject in relation to individual salvation; inasmuch as in his "break" Marx became "political" did Milton in his become "post-political." I have discussed in the introduction what the place of the subject is in terms of Milton's theology and in terms of Milton's conception of self-knowledge. In this chapter I will discuss the place of the subject in terms of Milton's politics — the politics of the author.

One way of answering Jameson's contention is to refigure his conflation of textual politics and practical politics. Even though Milton appears to have written about personal salvation, the representation in the text need not be about only personal salvation. At the level of "political allegory," the text might be "figuring" a collective praxis (and this, as I suggested above, is something Jameson would have allowed in 1977). To state the case in the language of seventeenth-century theology, Milton's representation of Jesus in the wilderness is also a figural representation of the beginnings of the collective church — in fact, of its metaphorical head at the outset of his mission. The concepts of "political allegory," of "figuration" as the mode of religion's imposition of a "master-code" on its "political content," and indeed of reading representations of religion as "*distorted* anticipations of historical materialism" are all Jameson's. But he chose not to apply them as rigorously to *Paradise Regained* as he might have done, and the reading he arrives at of its retrograde political character is the result of that choice. In fact, if we read *Paradise Regained* through Jameson's admirable concepts, we will reach a reading that finds the poem insistently political in Jameson's own sense of the term.[7]

Although Hugh Trevor-Roper is on quite the other side of the political spectrum from Jameson, his reading of Milton's late politics almost precisely replicates Jameson's. Insofar as he would be willing to characterize Milton's thinking as "politics," Trevor-Roper argues that by "1660" Milton's "ideology had disintegrated" and Milton could do nothing "except retreat still further into his ego and bring out at last the riches buried in it." But Trevor-Roper is here making a distinction Milton goes out of his way to deny, and which his works resist. We have seen how Milton's position, on this basic point anyway, is not much different from that of Althusser, who argues that "the category of the subject is constitutive of all ideology . . . insofar as all ideology has the function (which defines it) of 'constituting' concrete individuals as subjects." The difference between Milton and Althusser on this question is that whereas Althusser sees the subject as the only category of being, and that subject as always-already interpellated in ideology, Milton argues the possibility for two modes of being, either the subject's fullness of being or privation of being. That is, Milton insists on the category of *choice,* and thereby ensures that no subject is always-already interpellated into ideology, but that every *individual* has the choice to be the "subject of" or "subject to" God. That, in any case, is Milton's theory of subjectivity at the level of his theology. What his theory may have been at the level of state politics will be explored in this chapter.

Returning to Trevor-Roper's contention, we must assert that Milton's "ideology" did not "disintegrate" in 1660; nor did he "retreat" anywhere. His politics, from as early as we wish to define them, are always imbricated with the questions we have just noticed throughout this study. What role does self-knowledge play in the process of *subjectivity?* What role does failure to negotiate self-knowledge play in the role of *subjection?* What place does self-discipline have in the government of nations? Of course, as I have been arguing so far, Milton's ideology belongs to the sphere of his religious beliefs. His idea of the subject's "interpellation" is more rightly that of Althusser's Christian model.[8] It is only here that we may begin to discuss them at the sheerly political level. Trevor-Roper's reading of Milton's politics serves us well because it articu-

lates the two separate problems involved in this critical assessment
of the late Milton. One concerns the question of how Milton's
politics as expressed in *Paradise Regained* are critically represented
("retreat"), the other about what date is established for the alleged
"break" between the old and the new politics ("1660").

Arthur Baker's comments exemplify both problems. Milton in
1671, he argued, gave up the political fervor of, say, 1649, to return
to a "radically spiritualized" ideal as expressed in 1641. Barker
presents us with a Milton who is "in blindness and defeat under
the Restoration monarchy." The Restoration of May 1660 symbolizes, both emotionally and materially, what Christopher Hill calls
Milton's "experience of defeat." It is Hill, most of all, who deals
with specific dates for determining the changes in Milton's politics.
He argues that for Milton "1660 was arbitrary, unjust, unfair,
unpleasant—but true." Milton, indeed, was forced to reevaluate his
Arminian presuppositions because the "Restoration of 1660 had
brought back the spectre of the God of will." Hill presents the
sixteen weeks in 1660 when Milton's life hung in the balance—
when his name was proposed for exemption from the Act of In-
demnity, when two of his books were doomed to the fire by the
House of Commons—with admirable and appropriate pathos.
However, it is equally important to trace Milton's political beliefs
to his expressed discontent before 1660. Far too judicious a historian to argue from public dates to private responses, Hill does
trace Milton's political beliefs back to an earlier date. He points
out that Milton's "disillusionment with the politics of the Parliamentarian revolutionaries" led him "to believe that a convergence
of the human with the divine would be necessary before a good
society could be built." That disillusionment and that belief, he
would guess, came "after the Restoration." Hill does concede,
however, that Milton probably realized the impossibility of establishing God's kingdom in England "long before 1660," but the
earliest he seems willing to allow would be two years before that
determinate date. The revolution's "failure must have been manifest to Milton by 1658, when he probably began writing *Paradise
Lost.*"

When Hill turns his attention to *Paradise Regained,* he sees a
certain "pragmatic approach to politics." Jesus rejects those things
that had led the English revolutionaries astray—"avarice and ambi-
tion, the false politics of compromise with evil, clerical pride or

ivory-tower escapism, the urge for instant solutions." Moreover, Hill is quite right to note that the poem is anti-Erastian in the extreme. But the conclusion he draws from that fact—that this explains Jesus' "dismissal of political solutions"—is simply inadequate to the sheer complexity of Milton's theologico-politics. Hill is correct in noting that Milton's espousing of Christian liberty as an internal function is "not a quietist doctrine." Later critics would not be so astute.[9]

After Hill, critics such as Michael Wilding, Herman Rapaport, and Andrew Milner have suggested to varying degrees just how spectacular Milton's alleged "retreat" might have been. For Wilding, in *Paradise Regained* Milton rejects "political and public aims in favour of the individual, private, and moral aims." According to Milner, Milton attempted to assess the "relative merits of both quietistic and activistic responses to political oppression" in his brief epic. In that sense, Milton may be said at least to have kept open the possibility of political activism, although Milner finally does conclude that Milton was espousing a "doctrine of quietism." Finally, Rapaport sees in Milton's work a denial of politics and the beginning of the experience of "proto-facism," an argument developed on the basis of an absolutism which he traces not just to Milton, but to Christianity. Joan Bennett has attempted to answer these critics by suggesting that, at certain points in this poem, Milton presents a Jesus who is not an object of imitation, but rather, and quite simply, the Redeemer. She reads Jesus' rejection of Satan's political offers in two ways. Initially, because Jesus is setting for himself the role of the unique Mediator, he does not need Satan's political tools, and in this role Jesus is not to be imitated. Second, because Jesus is not presented here as a pattern of the reader's imitation, there is no reason to affirm that his rejection of political activism need dictate the reader's attitudes toward public activity.[10] While I find Bennett's distinction useful and her readings of these earlier critics perspicacious, I think, nonetheless, that an appreciation of how Milton inscribed his political subjectivity in his final volume would allow us to come to yet another viable conclusion.

We could better understand the politics of *Paradise Regained* by seeing how the poet represents himself in the 1671 volume. To appreciate the degree to which his final volume of poetry is suffused with self-representation, we have to return to the two landmark prose tracts of the early to middle 1650s. For it is not only by 1658, as Hill suggests, that Milton had begun to reevaluate his hope in the ability of civic politics to transform England. As early as 1651, Milton was inscribing hints about his loss of hope in the political establishment of the republic, and by 1654 he was expressing ominous reservations about Cromwell's protectorate. The remarks of 1671 have a longer history than eleven years.

As early as the 1651 *A Defence,* we can hear in Milton a troubled concern with the Independents' government, especially as it concerns the church. By 1654, it seems to me, Milton had long lost belief in the government of Cromwell; it is there, in the *Second Defence,* that we might trace the "break" in Milton's politics, if that is what it is to be called. I have reservations about the term *break* because it is inadequate to the task of describing what is, after all, the political thought of an unsystematic thinker in politics. There are important strands of continuity in Milton's politics, and there is no such thing as Milton's politics divorced from his theological ruminations. We would search in vain to find in Milton anything like the systematic sophistication in political theory of a Hobbes or a Locke or a Winstanley. Nowhere in Milton can we find anything resembling Hobbes's diagnosis of an emerging "possessive market society." Milton never develops his political thought to the extent of considering the importance of recognizing the conditions allowing for the alienability of labor, as would Locke. He would not, as Winstanley did, consider that the basis of political reform might be economic reform (but, then again, nobody in the seventeenth century but Winstanley was so astute about this tenet). We do not even find in Milton so thorough an examination of the standards of suffrage as we do in the Levelers.[11]

Milton's political thought is more that of a prophet-poet than a political scientist or a political activist. Milton never considered his role in the achievements of the republic to be more important than when he represented himself as the recorder and prophet of the glorious deeds leading to its establishment. His political thought was not concerned with the basics of the science of government, precisely because he would come to eschew the very idea of the state, as David Quint points out. Moreover, as Quint argues, that state which seems to be uppermost in Milton's mind is Hobbes's *Leviathan* with its centralized government and its tenet of absolute subjection. As Quint suggestively concludes his study, "Hobbes' could be the name for that which all the various political strategies of *Paradise Regained* converge to resist." That resistance, I would argue—against Quint's characterization of it as "passive individualism"—involves an act of Milton's writing his *subjectivity* that in itself contests the Hobbesian notion of *subjection*.[12] That act of writing is for Milton, as it was for Spenser, an act of self-representation allegorically figuring the political life of the author. Thus Milton's politics may be defined at the level of the personal—the authorial self-representation of an interplay between subjectivity and subjection. Milton's theory of the place of politics is based on his theory of the evolution of social forms—the way the political collective finds its origin in an act of the prepolitical subject's self-knowledge.

From Adam to Israel: Milton's Concept of the Evolution of Social Forms

The statement with which I closed the previous chapter—that a single individual or a family may be capable of reforming an entire state—comes from Milton's *Prolusion* VII. It is universally acknowledged as Milton's most brilliant collegiate performance and it seems the most mature piece of thinking of the early works. Not only will he go on to elaborate the thought of how the individual, the family, and the state are interlocking structures, but he also begins to define the process of meditation as the Platonic soul's search for the happiness knowledge gives it, to develop the theory of the interrelationship of intellect, virtue, and will, and to establish the importance of self-knowledge to self-government. Indeed, there is a great deal in this prolusion that could be characterized as the germ of much of the philosophy of the mature poems. Milton's early thinking on the concept of self-knowledge is of interest to us here. He suggests that those persons who have complete self-knowledge are those who enjoy in turn a "kingdom in themselves far more glorious than any earthly dominion." On this point, we can hardly see any difference between the seventh prolusion and *Paradise Regained*. Moreover, Milton suggests that self-knowledge is also the primary principle involved in the evolution of society. Having described primitive humanity in its precultural form, he goes on to suggest how humans came to be political animals: "Then of a sudden the Arts and Sciences breathed their divine breath into the savage breasts of men, and instilling into them the knowledge of themselves, gently drew them to dwell together within the walls of cities" (YP I, pp. 288–306, esp. pp. 291, 293, 297, 299). There are a few notable points to be made about this statement. First of all, self-knowledge is intricately related to social formations, but it, as an idea, is nonetheless *prior to* any social formations. The savage people first knew themselves and then gathered together in cities. Second, and what is a constant in Milton's thought, self-knowledge cannot be divorced from the gifts of the Spirit—the "divine breath" Jesus inhales and Samson sniffs at.

The process of the evolution of social structures may be seen at work in *Paradise Lost*. At the Creation, the first human being was endued with "Sanctity of Reason" and made therefore capable of "self-knowing" (*PL* VII, 508–10). Adam's first instinct when he rises from his creation is to know himself by attempting to know where he is and by what cause: "But who I was, or where, or from what cause, / Knew not" (VIII, 270–71). Adam is still alone in his precultural state when God tests his ability to gain self-knowledge in their initial colloquy. Adam is found successful, as God says, because God found him "knowing not of Beasts alone, . . . but of thyself, / Expressing well the spirit within thee free" (VIII, 438–40). So, as Milton had suggested to his collegiate audience, self-knowledge issues from the exercise of the heavenly spirit and precedes any social formations. After this test, God grants Adam his wish of "Social communication" (VIII, 429). When Adam does fall, much as he would like to blame "society," he finds himself blameworthy because he had failed in self-knowledge, as the Son unambiguously pronounces. You would not have fallen, says the Son, "hadst thou known thyself aright" (X, 156). We have then in this brief historical enactment of social evolution, an initial period of primitive glory in a precultural state, followed by a period of individual self-knowledge requiring the prevenient Spirit of God for its working, which is followed by a period of society, and finally leading to a failure of society premised on a failure in individual self-knowledge. We should not underemphasize the relationship between individual self-knowledge and political society, what God calls "Social communication." For Adam's fall—which does not symbolize but *is* a failure in self-knowledge—is also the pattern of the decline and fall of nations.

That is the lesson Adam learns from Michael when he receives the future history of the world. As Michael prophesies, nations will fall precisely by the same process and for the same reasons as Adam fell—they too will not achieve the self-knowledge required of them. To see the degree to which nations are implicated in patterns of individual behavior, we have to turn to Michael's exploration of the first kingdom in the world. In response to Adam's horror at the spectacle of Nimrod, the first of tyrants, Michael says,

> Justly thou abhorr'st
> That Son, who on the quiet state of men
> Such trouble brought, affecting to subdue
> Rational Liberty; yet know withal,
> Since thy original lapse, true Liberty
> Is lost, which always with right Reason dwells
> Twinn'd, and from her hath no dividual being:
> Reason in man obscur'd, or not obey'd,
> Immediately inordinate desires
> And upstart Passions catch the Government
> From Reason, and to servitude reduce
> Man till then free. Therefore since hee permits
> Within himself unworthy Powers to reign
> Over free Reason, God in Judgment just
> Subjects him from without to violent Lords;
> Who oft as undeservedly enthral
> His outward freedom: Tyranny must be,
> Though to the Tyrants thereby no excuse.
> Yet sometimes Nations will decline so low
> From virtue, which is reason, that no wrong,
> But Justice, and some fatal curse annext
> Deprives them of thir outward liberty,
> Thir inward lost.   (*PL* XII, 79–101)

There is a complex structure to Michael's response. He begins by abhorring Nimrod's political act (79–82), and then gives a lengthy explanation of how rational liberty was lost ("thy original lapse"), using terms belonging to both psychology and politics ("And upstart Passions catch the Government" 82–90), before returning to the question strictly of politics—the question of subjection. However, even in the delineation of political subjection, Michael still speaks of two interrelated realms of being. First of all, he describes how individuals become subject to violent lords (90–96), and then, finally, he delineates how this same process works for nations (97–

101). That is, in both individuals and in nations, external servitude is always preceded by internal loss of liberty, which is "reason." Subject to "inordinate desires," the individual will become subject to tyranny. Unable to be virtuous ("which is reason"), countries will lose their democratic liberties and become subject to tyrants.

One tempting though slightly misleading way of phrasing the relationship between individual and national subjection is to say that, for Milton, "the personal is the political." If the phrase when applied to Milton does not have quite the sort of revolutionary resonance it has when applied by feminist theorists to women's experience in a patriarchal world, it does nonetheless allow us to suggest something about the sort of relationship Milton imagined to exist between individuals and nations, between personal politics and civic politics. As Teresa de Lauretis has defined the phrase, "the personal is the political because the political becomes personal by way of its subjective effects through the subject's experience."[13] There is no political force like the one de Lauretis defines—including patriarchy, racism, and heterosexism—which is imbricated in Milton's experiences.

However, the personal is political for Milton in two other senses. First of all, in his insistence that nations are capable of self-knowledge, he is giving political structures a personality. Unlike Hobbes, who presented a state which is wholly impersonal—a series of covenants established in an atmosphere of fear and mistrust— Milton held to an idea of the state which had its own subjectivity.[14] Milton does not go so far as Hegel in granting subjectivity to the state apparatus, nor does he do it as an apologist for that state's power. If anything, as we see by what Michael says to Adam about Nimrod, he does it to assert the importance of personal probity in the continuance of civil liberty. In this second sense we can most accurately say that the personal is the political for Milton. Milton found wholly unappealing the idea of the state's governing its citizens and ensuring order by regulating citizens' liberties. He preferred a model in which discipline operated at the personal level; that is, the actual politics of regulating conduct should be at the level of the person, not the state's judicial apparatus. In this second sense Milton is arguing for a theory of the relationship between the state and the person that is based on cohesion (the state survives so long as its citizens are able to regulate their own inordinate desires) and not on regulation (the state survives so long as it sets limits on its citizen's desires). That we now consider this to be unfeasible, if not outright nonsensical, is a testament to how right Hobbes may have been about human nature. That we would consider apolitical a theorist who proposed such a model is a testament to how far we are from the subject of seventeenth-century politics.

What is consistent, then, from Milton's early thought (from at least the seventh prolusion) to his post-Restoration thought (at least as late as *Paradise Lost*) is that he believed in an integral relationship of individual self-knowledge leading to a sound libertarian state. That, of course, is also very much the trajectory of Jesus' teaching in *Paradise Regained*. Although this is clear enough, what is not clear is how Milton defined his self-knowledge in his later years. How, that is, did Milton negotiate from a "self" to a "subject" in the 1671 volume? Numerous critics, including Tillyard, have noted that "Christ's description of his own childhood" in *Paradise Regained* echoes Milton's reflections on his own childhood so much that it appears to be "a bit of covert autobiography." Or as Don Wolfe wrote, "Milton painted himself in his characterization of Jesus in *Paradise Regained*" (YP V, p. 82). On the other hand, there are those like Hugh Trevor-Roper who claim "Samson is Milton." To get a better idea of Milton's "politics," it will be necessary to explore in what ways Milton inscribed his subjectivity in both works in the 1671 volume. For, as we have just seen, it is in terms of the "personal" that we may best understand Milton's "politics."[15] Admitting that premise, we can contest many of the recent readings of Milton's post-Restoration politics. So far we have seen that in Milton's thought the nation follows the pattern of the individual. The individual in turn, we may now say, follows the pattern of the "book."

One of Milton's severest criticisms of licensing is that a licensed book disables the author from teaching with authority, "which is the life of teaching." And teaching with authority, according to Milton, means enabling the author to present himself as "a doctor in his book." For the "book," according to Milton, is not an absolutely dead thing, but contains a "potencie of life" that is as active as the soul whose progeny it is. It seems worthwhile to attempt to discover Milton in Milton's 1671 volume—especially given this poet who hoped to write something that would not be allowed to die, who believed a book to contain the life of its author, who, in his most haunting words, believed that a "good Booke is the pretious life-blood of a master spirit, imbalm'd and treasur'd up on purpose to a life beyond life," and who elsewhere argued that an author's political opinions could be discovered in his or her characters' mouths.[16] We might, then, examine what hints exist in the 1671 volume that could provide an inroad to discerning the poet in his poems.

"A Doctor in his Book": Milton's Political Simile

I have suggested that the two similes in the second of the two concluding semichoral songs of *Samson Agonistes* adumbrated the presence of Jesus, the hero of the companion poem, in the tragedy itself. What prevented the tribe of Danites from working from that shadowy knowledge toward any substantial liberty was the remarkable lack of communicative clarity demonstrated by all the characters at the end of the play. The tribe of Dan did not recognize its own prophecy of its ultimate deliverer because each of its members was too attentive to creating his own story of Samson's significance. None, that is, understood Samson as a type of Christ, but each insisted on seeing in Samson a type of Samson—typified most fully by Manoa's tautological simile, "*Samson* hath quit himself / Like *Samson*" (1710–11). This desire for telling a story which is inattentive to a future good is itself an indicator of a much more important failing in the Danites, their inability to free themselves from what is truly enslaving them—their own desires.

The Danites do not transform their transient desires into an enduring love of God, which is the only way to answer desire in the Miltonic cosmos. Rather, they display precisely the unruly strength of their desire in those reiterative stories about Samson *as* Samson. The chance for them to assume Sonship and liberty is available—in simile, as it were—but they do not grasp it. The simile signaling the presence of Jesus in *Samson Agonistes* is, like the Spirit in the form of the dove in *Paradise Regained,* an opportunity for the characters to demonstrate their hermeneutical abilities. Manoa's attempt shows us his carnal limitations; the Chorus' closing song, with its insistence on necessity and servitude, adequately represents for us their intellectual incapacities. Not only are the similes in the tragedy linked to the similes in the brief epic because Jesus is allegorically represented in the phoenix simile, but also because the similes used to describe Samson represent the "rouzed" hero (the servant) while the similes used to describe Jesus represent the hero who is man and Son of God. According to the distinction we find in Milton's theology, each of the poems ends with a simile describing its hero as either a son of God or a servant of God. The similes in *Samson Agonistes,* then, are one more piece of evidence for reading these two poems as parts of one book. Moreover, the similes in *Paradise Regained* suggest that this book should be read in conjunction with another of Milton's books.

Joan Bennett has recently noted how Milton is fond of using the Sphinx to represent those who would attempt to justify monarchy. Not only does he employ the image in *Eikonoklastes* (1649), where the defenders act the part of the unsuccessful assayers of the Sphinx's riddle (YP III, p. 413), but he also uses it in *A Defence* (1651), in which the defenders act the part of the Sphinx to Milton's Oedipus (YP IV, p. 390).[17] However, his *Second Defence* (1654) gives a more pertinent example of Milton's fondness for using the Sphinx in simile. In answering More's representation of him, Milton expresses contempt for More's inconsistency. More, he says, compares him at one point to a dwarf and at another to Antaeus. Approximately nine lines of Latin later, Milton compares More to the indeterminate Sphinx because he did not put his identity on the title page of the *Clamor* (CM VIII, p. 77; cf. YP IV, pp. 591–92). That Milton should think of Antaeus and the Sphinx together in so short a space of time would be in itself just an interesting observation about what sorts of associations he might be prone to make in any given situation. But these two similes not only parallel their counterparts at the conclusion of Milton's brief epic, they occur in a veritable flood of phrases and set rhetorical speeches in the prose tract that can be traced almost exactly to certain equivalent phrases and set pieces in *Paradise Regained.* Milton places these two allusions in the very midst of his autobiographical digression in the prose tract. That there are similarities of expression between Milton's autobiographical examination in the *Second Defence* and his hero's in *Paradise Regained* has been suggested before, although always with a degree of tentativeness.[18]

The two similes occurring in both *Paradise Regained* and in the *Second Defence* do not just signify a simple parallelism, but denote a much more profound affiliation between Milton in 1654 and Milton in 1671. The basic level of significance is the author's self-representation in the two books. Critics such as Wolfe and Tillyard primarily have in mind the Milton of the autobiographical digression in the *Second Defence* when they suggest that Milton patterned his Jesus after himself. The reason he did so is to represent *his* subjectivity. Just as Spenser in the allegorical figure of Colin Clout in *The Shepheardes Calendar* inscribed himself as a humble citizen of Elizabeth's England (subject to her government and within her control) and also as a locus of discursive consciousness (the subject of his own aesthetic will and making her subject to his art), so does Milton inscribe himself in both *Paradise Regained* and *Samson Agonistes* in the form of a "political allegory." To see the extent and significance of that self-representation, we must turn now to and make the case for what has been described as the "allegorical" content of the "book."

From Trope to Mode: Milton's Political Allegory

In an often-cited letter to his brother and sister, Keats wrote that "Shakespeare led a life of Allegory: his works are the comments on it." It was an apt time for Keats to begin thinking about how to resolve any relationship life and letters might have one to the other, for the reviews of *Endymion* were becoming, as he menacingly put it, "more and more powerful." In any case, what Keats says of Shakespeare he was willing to apply to any great poet: "A Man's life of any worth is a continual allegory—and very few can see the Mystery of his life—a life like the scriptures, figurative—which such people can no more make out than they can the hebrew Bible." The application of this theory to Keats' immediate situation is clear enough; the critics, he must have thought, could not figure him out. How might we apply this theory of the allegorical life to Milton? It might be worthwhile—again—to consult the works as allegorical figurations of their author's self-representation. The primary legacy of the Romantics to Milton scholarship is that they suggested that Milton can be found in his works. As Coleridge so succinctly phrased it, "John Milton himself is in every line of the Paradise Lost."[19] The allegory that is of more recent and pressing interest is what Jameson calls the "political allegory."[20]

Before Keats, and perhaps as an analogue to this instance of Keats's creativity, Milton had remarked on the relationship of life and works: "And long it was not after, when I was confirm'd in this opinion, that he who would not be frustrate of his hope to write well hereafter in laudable things, ought him selfe to bee a true Poem" (CM III, pp. 303–04). Unlike Keats's inscrutable Hebrew Bible, which is beyond the figuring of, say, the review editor of the *Quarterly Review* or other "nameless blots," Milton's "true Poem" is readable and based on a theory of authorial self-representation that suggests a fruitful way of approaching his final published volume of original verse. What I will do here is trace the poem "Milton" in Milton's final two poems. Elsewhere Milton espoused such a methodology of reading for whoever would determine the political opinions of his authors; he also stated the inherent dangers in that methodology. In *A Defence,* Milton takes Salmasius to task for confusing the sentiments of one of Aeschylus's baser characters with the author's own more republican ideals. We must "not regard the poet's words as his own, but consider who it is that speaks in the play, and what the person says." For characters, he continues, "speak not always the poet's opinion, but what is most fitting to each character." In our modern critical idiom, Salmasius failed to contextualize the given character's speech within the narrative or drama in which it occurs and account for its significance within the political ideas of the implied narrator or dramatist. After doing so, Milton contends, we might be able to determine how "poets generally put something like their own opinions into the mouths of their best characters" (CM VII, pp. 306–07, 326–27).[21] That is a critical methodology we might find fruitful when we set out to discover which of Milton's "own opinions" might be said to exist in the 1671 volume, and, more properly speaking, to see how he figures his subjectivity as a political allegory in the companion poems.

Of the variety of ways of elucidating Milton's self-representations or of reading his political allegory in his mature poetry, perhaps the least helpful is that in which the critic simply notes how one instance of Milton's discourse contradicts another—such as suggesting, for example, that, while Jesus rejects Athenian learning in 1671, Milton wrote in 1655 that there could be "nothing more absurd, more inconsistent, than that I hold Grecian learning in contempt." The obverse of this method would be to note local instances of corroboration in order to argue how one instance of Milton's discourse suggests an affinity between the author and any of his characters—such as suggesting, for instance, that Samson's address to Dalila as "Hyæna" might reflect Milton's own attitudes when he himself calls More a "Hyæna."[22] Such parallels, whatever value they may have, are of limited help when we are interested in seeing the author's inscription of his political subjectivity in any given work. To discover that requires rather more complex methods of reading.

Christopher Hill is the most thorough of exegetes when it comes to Milton's political allegory, as indeed we might expect of the very best historian of the English Revolution. Hill dismisses the idea of a consistent allegorical structure to *Paradise Lost,* and with that dismissal one can have few reservations. Instead, he asserts that we must "distinguish between allegory, in which characters have a single and consistent significance" and the "allusive method [which] gave full rein to Milton's ambiguity." Allusion, however ambiguous, must be understood in reference to some context and Hill provides one for his systematic discussion of Milton's last three works. In all "three poems Milton is grappling with the problems set by the failure of God's cause in England." Hill strives to maintain that argument through at least two levels — both treating the Fall as "an allegory of man's inability to live up to his own standards" and also discerning local moments in the epic as veiled references to historical events of the English Revolution. It is in Hill's attempt to maintain some sort of consistency at this second level that I find him least persuasive. For one thing, Hill wishes to argue that the same portion of narrative can refer to an almost limitless number of "historical events." He suggests that the War in Heaven, having taken two days, might represent the "two decades" of the civil war. The Restoration might be figured in the mention of the time when "doubtful conflict" reigned. The opening of Book IX of *Paradise Lost,* Hill maintains, "emphasizes the *political* aspects of the Fall." The lines in question—

> foul distrust, and breach
> Disloyal on the part of Man, revolt.
> And disobedience: On the part of Heav'n
> Now alienated, distance, and distaste,
> Anger and just rebuke, and judgment giv'n.   (IX, 6–10)

—Hill sees as describing the "events of 1660 no less than those of 4004 B.C." Concerning Michael's description of the time of the

Apostasy (*PL* XII, 507–35), Hill writes, "the reference to Restoration England could hardly be more explicit." I personally do not hear these particular echoes nor see the immediate references, and likewise I am not convinced of the sheerly political overtones Hill argues are there. For that reason, I find the entire methodology of tracing such polysemous allusions somewhat less persuasive than I might. Of course, I must also admit to not having the enviable frame of reference about seventeenth-century English history Hill has (nobody but Hill has that!), and there is, moreover, Hill's quite persuasive argument (made elsewhere) about how the allusive method is one of the few ways of avoiding the limitations censorship attempted to impose on political expression in the seventeenth century.[23]

Even so, Hill's argument that Milton turned to "the story of the Fall to explain the failure of a revolution" is not especially furthered by his tracing the local instances of veiled allusion. Although the poem does have a few slight and obscure allusions to the political situation of England, there is nothing in *Paradise Lost* to compare to the sustained integrity of parallel significance between two levels of narrative (one Israeli, the other English) that, say, *Absalom and Achitophel* demonstrates, nor are there such indecorous and blatant references such as that odd moment in Cowley's *Davideis* when the angel Gabriel admonishes the antimonarchists of "Albions stubborn Isle."[24] More significantly, when Milton does allude to England's political situation it is almost always done in reference to himself. For instance, in the most famous of those moments, in the invocation to Book VII, the allusion may well be to England after the Restoration, but the context of the reference is nonetheless Milton:

> More safe I Sing with mortal voice, unchang'd
> To hoarse or mute, though fall'n on evil days,
> On evil days though fall'n, and evil tongues;
> In darkness, and with dangers compast round,
> And solitude.   (VII, 24–28)

Because Milton's political allusions are almost always imbricated in autobiographical references, it might be worth heeding Milton's own reading methodology and attempt to discover the author's political opinions by tracing a whole series of the various points of convergence between the poet who represents himself as a true poem and his autobiographical self-representations as they appear in the two poems. I would argue that, in the fuller context of Milton's intertextual self-representations, we will find the richest and most interesting example of Milton's political allegory.

I will argue that Milton's self-representation in his 1671 volume has immediate implications for our understanding of his late politics. There is one theoretical problem I must confront before setting out on this final adventure. To discover in what ways Milton represented himself in his two poems, I will marshall evidence from his autobiographical digressions in his prose writings, especially those of the middle to late 1650s. For anyone schooled in New Criticism, it will be clear that I am going to rely on what is termed *external evidence,* and that perhaps I might even be treading the unholy ground of the "biographical fallacy." To ease the mind of my reader, let me say that this is precisely what I am going to do. As a preliminary step to eschewing the conventional critical decorum regarding a critic's warrant for making assertions about the potential relationship of any author to his or her work, I would like to examine the theoretical confusion that has lent credence to the dismissal of what used to be called by those who believed in it "biographical evidence" and by those who did not, "biographical fallacy." For it is on the questionable foundation of much theoretical confusion that critics who believed in the method have been inclined to disvalue the quality of their own findings about authorial self-representation with the disingenuity of conjecture, and for those who did not believe in the method simply to disregard entirely the validity of other critics' findings with the disingenuity of dismissing the critical method. To appreciate that confusion and to understand how it has helped foster the anathema against arguing from biographical evidence, I must turn to the debate wherein the confusion is most manifest—that resounding anathema issued by Wimsatt and Beardsley against the "intentional fallacy."

Apologia Pro Vita Critica Vitae:
The Value of Biographical Criticism

Biographical criticism of the sort Coleridge might have indulged in—such as his comment in 1833 that "in every one of his poems . . . it is Milton himself whom you see; his Satan, his Adam,

his Raphael, almost his Eve . . . are all John Milton"—has long
been eschewed by the critical institutions in which we work. It
would be hard to fix a particular date for when this happened in
general, or when it happened in Milton criticism in particular, but
we may safely say that it had much to do with the founding of New
Criticism. Indeed, we can say that W. K. Wimsatt's strictures on
"intentional fallacy" also heralded the beginning of the end of
biographical criticism. The question of biographical criticism and
the question of intention have become almost one and the same
because Wimsatt and Beardsley created the ideal conditions for
confusing a variety of issues which, properly speaking, have to be
distinguished. Gerald Graff has rightly noted how they confused
the questions of "knowability" and "desirability" in the act of
anathematizing "intention" as a category of critical inquiry. Second, and in the same moment of argument, they also confuse the
question of critical inquiry with the question of axiology. Consider
the sentence in which they declare their argument: "The design or
intention of the author is neither available nor desirable as a standard for judging the success of a work of literary art." Graff's point
about their first confusion is borne out. Their confusion between
critical inquiry as discovery and critical inquiry as axiology should
also be noticed here. Moreover, and this is the problem that bears
directly on our argument, they also confuse the question of "intention" as the "design" in the author's mind with the question of
what material conditions are necessary for a poem to come into
being. The "intentional fallacy" may be disputed on this confusion,
or, to put it more precisely, here is where we must distinguish what
Wimsatt and Beardsley conflated.[25]

There are two points in the essay where Wimsatt and Beardsley
explicitly mention the uses and abuses of "biographical evidence."
The first occurs when they argue, reasonably I think, that "the use
of biographical evidence need not involve intentionalism" (p. 11).
But on the next page they begin to cloud the issue. The two crucial
sentences in their argument are worth quoting and examining:

> There is a gross body of life, of sensory and mental experience, which
> lies behind and in some sense causes every poem, but can never be and
> need not be known in the verbal and hence intellectual composition
> which is the poem. For all the objects of our manifold experience, for
> every unity, there is an action of the mind which cuts off roots, melts

away context—or indeed we should never have objects of ideas or anything to talk about. (P. 12)

There are a variety of confusions in this passage. First, they maintain that earlier equation of possibility ("can never") with desirability ("need not"). Second, it is not clear what they mean by a "unity" as it is expressed here; what I think they mean to signify is the poem "as in itself it really is." But such "unities" are, of course, the reconstructions of our own critical methods and desires. When Wimsatt and Beardsley define a "poem" they assume that completeness means inviolability: "Poetry succeeds because all or most of what is said or implied is relevant; what is irrelevant has been excluded, like lumps from pudding and 'bugs' from machinery" (p. 4). What is "relevant" is naturally, according to Wimsatt and Beardsley, what is "internal" to the poem; and never what is "external" (p. 10). But what if what is "relevant" exists as precisely "external evidence" which is referred to in the "internal" part of the poem? Let me use *Paradise Regained* to demonstrate the sort of Epimenides paradox that exists when this argument is taken to its logical conclusion.

When Milton opens *Paradise Regained,* he begins by referring his reader to his previous work, notably *Paradise Lost.* The very first line of the poem — "I who e're while the happy Garden sung" — directs us to "evidence" that exists outside of the poem, that is "external evidence." To argue that the reference to *Paradise Lost* assumes its "relevance" only as it belongs solely to the world of *Paradise Regained* is to do precisely what Wimsatt and Beardsley would have us do—inflict the critical desire for an "object" onto what is not so easy to objectify. When we follow their advice in this instance, we are willing to deny the continuum of an author's self-representation (I realize the question of "author" is being begged here, and I will return to it presently). There is not the "unity" in *Paradise Regained* that Wimsatt and Beardsley would have us believe there is. Its unity belongs to a larger context, which is one of those "contexts" that Wimsatt and Beardsley claim is "melted away" by critical desire. According to the very standards by which Wimsatt and Beardsley were conducting their argument, if we believe that *Paradise Regained* is a "unity" which has its own "internal evidence" allowing its reader to determine its meaning, we are at the very first line of that "unity" directed to a piece of "external evidence"—namely, *Paradise Lost*. The only way to maintain the argument is by imposing the critic's desire. As critics we all bring to bear our own desires in our readings; that is part of what makes critical activity worthwhile. But when that desire becomes the mainstay of a critical argument, then we might begin to question it. Wimsatt and Beardsley's critical desire to melt away contexts falls into that category.

In order, then, to make the case for a poetic world as a "unity," the critic replaces the author's desire with his or her own. This is where the earlier confusion between possibility and desirability assumes its noxious state. The critic's desire, expressed at first as simply acceding to what was after all impossible, now assumes the most prominent place in critical inquiry. The critic's desire determines the boundaries of inquiry. That leads to the third point in the passage. The "action of mind" refers to a critical desire to designate what is an "object"—which, like a "unity," has its own inviolate system of self-regulation—in order to keep critical conversation alive. Otherwise, the rest would be silence.

The second explicit reference to "biographical evidence" occurs at the close of the essay, where it is taken to mean the act of asking the still-living author what he or she meant (p. 18). But what happens between these two explicit references is where the confusion occurs. Wimsatt and Beardsley have done nothing less than make authorial self-representation part of the baggage of the biographical fallacy. To ensure that poetic worlds remain inviolate, they remove any authorial comment that requires reference to a world outside of the poem for it to make any sense. The "Milton" of the first word of his brief epic ("I") is simply elided. The "biographical fallacy," in its inherited form, refers to the act of critically justifying one particular reading by reference to what authors have elsewhere written about themselves or their work, or using some given psychological or physiological fact written about the author's life by someone else to justify that same reading. It belongs to the realm of evidence Wimsatt and Beardsley denominate as "external." I have already attempted to show how certain linguistic functions within the world of one poem destroy the illusion of that poem's inviolate integrity and make problematic what is "internal" and what "external."

With the question of our critical tendency to make objects—and the conflation of two separate activities involved in that tendency—I will demonstrate the confusion inherent in Wimsatt and Beardsley's argument in its turn from the issue of intention to the basis of biographical evidence. When Louis Montrose makes the case that Spenser inscribes his subjectivity in the "Aprill" eclogue of *The Shepheardes Calendar,* he is asserting the validity of that argument on the basis of an "allegory" of Spenser's "life." The argument that Spenser represented himself as Colin Clout and Elizabeth as the goddess is based on a second level of significance having to do with what we know of Spenser's political life. Let me stress that Montrose's argument has nothing to do with "intention." He could care less what Spenser "meant" when he represented himself, or even whether Spenser "meant" to represent himself; his argument is simply that Spenser did represent himself and that this representation is significant. Montrose's main argument is concerned only with demonstrating that Spenser represented himself as subject to his monarch. He can persuade us to read Colin Clout's act as symbolizing Spenser's own by showing us the persistent parallels between Spenser's activity (writing an eclogue, presenting it to his queen) and Colin Clout's (raising a lamb, offering it to the mother-goddess). The basis of his understanding of the "Spenser" in his argument involves reference to a world of evidence beyond the poem. If we did not know that Spenser was a subject of the monarch Elizabeth, we obviously could not make this argument about the poem's significance. And Spenser's political life belongs to that realm where we may trace the "causes" of poems—that place Wimsatt and Beardsley call the "gross body." Montrose is able to argue for Spenser's self-representation without arguing for his intention because he implicitly makes a distinction that Wimsatt and Beardsley unquestionably confuse. Making it explicit will help us get beyond Wimsatt and Beardsley's dogmatic strictures.

So, to use another example in order to clarify what Wimsatt and Beardsley confuse, referring to Keats's pulmonary tuberculosis as a way of understanding his sonnet "When I Have Fears" would constitute "biographical criticism"; but it does not, properly speaking, have much to do with "intention" because it is a fact that only helps us appreciate the sense of imminent death that both the persona of the sonnet and the author of that sonnet share. It falls into the second category of Wimsatt and Beardsley's argument—the "gross body" behind the poem—but not the first. To cite the similarity between Keats's condition and that of his persona is not a way of explaining the structure or design of the sonnet. What we know, then, about Keats's medical history need not determine what the poem's "intention" may be (which, with Wimsatt and Beardsley, I would admit is unknowable), but what we do know about Keats's medical history is informative about the way Keats might have inscribed himself into the poem. To avoid the confusion Wimsatt and Beardsley inherited and promulgated, I would tentatively make the distinction between the "intention" of a work (which has to do with factors beyond our knowledge) and the "authorial self-representation" in a work (which, I would argue, is not unknowable, but does require referring to so-called "external evidence"). Granting, of course, that knowledge itself is indefinitely contestable, and that knowledge of literary works is infinitely so, I would still assert that we must distinguish between what is a transcendent category ("intention") and a mode of intertextual examination (such as determining the author's self-representation). Once we make that distinction, we are in a better position to read the political allegories of our poets. This distinction allows Montrose's argument to stand as exemplary, and will allow me to make the case I am about to make.

When contemporary critics work at establishing some sort of relationship between the author of the work as a political subject and the work itself as a product (and production) of ideology, they often take an unnecessary precaution of palliating the evidence they draw on to demonstrate their cases. For example, to invoke two of the finest critics writing today, when Stephen Greenblatt and Fredric Jameson use what we might consider "biographical" or "extrinsic" evidence, each goes out of his way to suggest that what he is doing is excusable. Greenblatt's comments on Spenser are an apt first example. Greenblatt argues that in the shift from the age of the age of Wyatt, More, and Tyndale to the age of Spenser, Shakespeare, and Marlowe, we can trace the possibility for self-fashioning within more "fully realized fictional worlds" and the possibility of conceiving of literary activity as the primary part of professional identity. Therefore, when literary production achieves this new valency, Greenblatt writes,

> it becomes easier to discuss the formation and undermining of identity *within* individual works without formally referring beyond them to

the lives of the creators, though we must remind ourselves that the very existence of such apparent inwardness depends upon the lived experience of a self-fashioning culture.

Without invoking the "lived experience" of those individuals occupying this new culture, Greenblatt still wishes to argue that we ought not to forget that literature is a product of cultural definitions, an object having its basis in the ways certain cultures allow certain modes of production, or, especially, a thing made by an individual whose cultural experience may be expressed within it. It is an odd double gesture—at once wishing to assume that "gross body" of the political subject while also eschewing any question of "intentionality."

So, too, we find this same double gesture in Jameson's work on Balzac. When Jameson discusses Balzac's "life" in relation to certain characteristics of his work, he situates himself somewhere between noticing and transgressing what he calls with some irony the "taboo against biographical criticism":

> In the preceding pages, the 'life' of the historical individual Balzac has been used, neither as a set of empirical facts, nor as a textual system of characteristic behavior, but rather as the traces and symptoms of a fundamental family situation which is at one and the same time a fantasy master narrative.

Earlier in *The Political Unconscious,* Jameson had expressed his distaste for the idea of autonomous fictional worlds (the New Critical legacy) and suggested that each such "printed text" must be placed in a dialogical system where the silenced voice of the repressed class would be restored or artificially reconstructed. For Jameson, though, this reconstruction must involve *disembodied* voices—which might appear to be a curious idea in a materialist theory, but is not at all curious so long as one accepts Jameson's linguistic materialism, or what he calls the "materialistic philosophy of language." According to his earlier formulation of such a materialistic philosophy of language, the critic must make a rigorous distinction between the signified and the referent, and the study of the referent should deal with "what is and must remain incommensurable with individual expression." Under these conditions, then, Balzac's voice is heard only as a trace with no real relationship to the alleged "life." In other words, "Balzac" is an *effect* and not an *instance* of a larger order of conflict; that is his attitude in 1981, in any case.

When Jameson writes on Milton in 1980, he finds himself in much the same double bind—a double bind traceable at least analogously, one might suggest, to the tension concerning subjectivity between the early and the late Marx. At one point, reflecting on Eve's desire to be "sometime superior," Jameson wisely notes that this moment is the "classic inscription of Milton's own sexual anxiety." Within ten lines, again to prevent the idea that the author might somehow be implicated at the level of subjectivity, Jameson notes that "those personal biases and ideological opinions of the biographical individual John Milton are not really what is at stake here." In his arguments on Milton in 1980, Jameson is still maintaining the same sort of equivocation attending his use of biographical evidence. In each instance, Jameson's dual gestures involving transgression of and obedience to the taboo against biographical criticism are simply unsatisfying. We have to return to an earlier Jameson to find a revolutionary theory of biographical criticism.

What Jameson's 1980 comments on Milton, like his 1981 comments on Balzac, demonstrate is that at least he is struggling with what he had attempted to resolve as early as 1977, when he wrote that "it is perhaps time to have a closer look at the ideological function of that taboo [on biographical criticism]." In 1977, he went as far as he would ever go in exploring the ideology behind that taboo, and he set there, at least, the standards by which I am arguing my point here:

> It should be observed that where the older biographical criticism understood the author's life as a context, or as a cause, as that which could explain the text, the newer kind understands that "life," or rather its reconstruction, precisely as one further text in its turn, a text on the level with the other literary texts of the writer in question and susceptible of forming a larger corpus of study with them.

That is, employing different terms, a newer method of biographical criticism should make the distinction I earlier made between intention and authorial self-representation and the forms of evidence we may draw on to support the latter but not the former. That, though, is only Jameson's *theory;* practically speaking, he did not, either in 1981 or in 1980, attempt to situate his readings within this framework of the newer kind of biographical criticism.

In each instance, instead of being proactive in asserting his "newer" method of biographical criticism, he is defensive against what he perceives to be the still valid taboo against the old method. It is time, I think, that we began to give up that defensive pose.[26]

In being defensive in this specific way, both Greenblatt and Jameson do a sort of what I'll call the Lutheran two-step. They say, "here I stand, I cannot do otherwise," while standing neither here nor there and doing otherwise. It would seem, then, that whenever a critic wishes to discuss the politics of some author, as do both Greenblatt and Jameson, without, however, wishing to return to some simplistic notion of the "author," the critic must make just such a double gesture.[27] To avoid that double gesture, I suggest something more to the point: The critic should simply make that important distinction between the discursive modes available for the author's self-representation and the critic's discerning of that self-representation on the one hand, and "intention" on the other. So, when I am arguing that Milton inscribed himself as a political subject within both *Samson Agonistes* and, especially, *Paradise Regained*, the Milton I have in mind—the "true Poem"—is the "Milton" who inscribed himself into both his *Defence of the People of England* and his *Second Defence*—that is, Milton the person as we can know him only in his texts.

Perhaps in response to the confusion in Wimsatt and Beardsley's argument, many critical structures were soon after developed to create situations in which a critic could talk about an author without referring to intentionality, indeed without referring to "extrinsic" evidence. By "Milton," one could say in 1962, after Wayne Booth made it respectable, I mean of course the "implied author." By "Milton," one could say in 1969, after Barthes's funeral oration on the author, I mean clearly the "instance writing." By "Milton," one could say in 1970, after Foucault answered his titular question "What Is an Author?," I mean without doubt the "author function" in the realm of certain discourses. At one level, these critiques of the idea of natural presence in the text are quite useful and incontestable on their own grounds. By "Milton," critics have always signified a certain construction of textuality. Nor is it altogether helpful to attempt to argue for "Milton" as a being beyond the text, some sort of presence one can invoke beyond the realm of the medium through which one has access to him and his thoughts.[28] The textual Milton is all we know and all we need to know. My interest lies elsewhere, and that is in seeing how Milton represented himself and his *subjectivity,* especially as it obtains for his mature political thought and how that is determined by his autobiographical representations in his last poems. That is, in full agreement with Greenblatt, my interest is in that fictional structure, the "self-fashioned" Milton.

One final objection must be met before I leave the question of biographical criticism, and that has to do with the question of autobiographical discourse itself. Paul de Man suggests that autobiography is best considered "a figure of reading or of understanding that occurs, to some degree, in all texts." So *Paradise Regained* is in this sense autobiographical to some degree, as is the *Second Defence,* say. Of course, de Man does add, enigmatically enough, that "just as we seem to assert that all texts are autobiographical, we should say that, by the same token, none of them is or can be." This negation of what might be considered the "purity" of autobiography as a genre (which status de Man denies it) especially concerns two points. For one thing, de Man argues, autobiography demonstrates the impossibility of closure (and, one assumes, that closure is somehow related to "coming into being," which in turn is somehow related to the value or truth of autobiography). Second, and more to our present interest, the very question of autobiographical self-knowledge is tested by the notion of the "tropological structure that underlies all cognitions, including knowledge of self." Now, one might wish to take issue with de Man's strictures here. After all, that there are horizons of self-knowledge that are determined by textual systems does not argue against self-knowledge itself as performed in an autobiographical instance. Nor does the fact that these horizons are themselves both indeterminate and always on the horizon (that is, incessantly deferred) necessarily mean that all self-knowledge's being partial makes it not self-knowledge. It would be a curious notion of "self-knowledge" that required absoluteness or transcendence from the tropological nature of cognitive systems to be called self-knowledge, and it would be premised on a concept of selfhood one would not expect to ascribe to de Man.

The basis of de Man's whole argument is that he posits an inherent desire in the nature of the autobiographical subject that may or may not be part of that subject's psychical makeup. He states that the study of autobiography is "caught in this double motion, the necessity to escape from the tropology of the subject and the equally inevitable reinscription of this necessity within a specular model of cognition."[29] Suppose, however, that the subject of the autobiographical act had no desire to "escape" the tropology inherent in all linguistic and cognitive functioning. Indeed, suppose the subject wished precisely to inhabit those very structures in order to inscribe a subjectivity within the text operating under that very "specular model of cognition"? We have seen, for instance, that Spenser used the tropes available to him in order to represent his subjectivity in his book. Likewise, we may find in Milton the same happy use of tropology in order to represent himself in his book in the act of coming to self-knowledge. I have already argued that the similes at the conclusion of *Samson Agonistes* refer us back to the companion poem and its hero, and that the similes at the conclusion of that companion poem refer us back to the *Second Defence*. I will now develop the case that, from this tropological gesture, we may read Milton's political allegory.

"Collected in Himself": *The Symptoms of Political Discourse*

Earlier, I noted that one of the least effective ways of reading Milton's political allegory is to trace sheer parallels between simple instances in his poetry and supporting or subverting instances in the autobiographical moments in his prose. Although these simple instances of sheer parallelism might alert us to which significant points of convergence are worth exploring, in and of themselves they are unpersuasive. And this, naturally, includes my tracing the similes of the Sphinx and Antaeus between the 1671 and 1654 volumes. We must discern a consistent mode of discourse at the level of formal parallels in order to argue at a political allegorical level. To do that, it would be necessary to define Milton's wonted mode of discourse in politics in order to make any sort of argument about his political self-representation in his poetry.

As is the case with any politician or political thinker, there are in Milton's works discernible patterns of thinking that suggest something not only about his train of associations but also about his political premises and resolves. With Milton, I think, we should attempt to define those persistent gestures he makes in his political writings and then see if they are discernible in his poetic works. In this way, the political allegory of the author will be traced at the level of his discursive habits. The formal parallels between the Milton of 1654 and the Jesus of the 1671 brief epic exist at the level of the symptomatic gestures the author and his hero are prone to making in a given situation. The place to diagnose these gestures is ideally in the time of Milton's most extreme stress—and that is March 1660. Let me emphasize that I am not asserting this date as one of great significance in Milton's political evolution, but only as a point of diagnosing his habitual mode of political discourse. For one thing, it is useful to be able to trace the most salient alterations between two editions of the same text in order to see how the changes Milton makes are symptomatic of his discursive strategies. In fact, when we turn our attention to the two editions of *The Readie and Easie Way,* we find that the alterations Milton makes between them recapitulate in precise detail those gestures he had been making over the last nine years of his political life.

In four significant changes from the first (February 1660) to the second edition of *The Readie and Easie Way* (April 1660), Milton demonstrates his usual mode of expressing his ideals in times of political ferment. The first change is not truly part of Milton's discursive habit, but it alerts us to Milton's diagnosis of the political demise of the republic. In the significant change between the first and second edition, Milton inscribes his distinct loss of hope for the continuation of liberty from monarchy. Whereas he had concluded the first edition with the hope that the "children of libertie" (YP VII, p. 388) may yet keep what they have, he ends the second edition by lamenting their "expiring libertie" and hoping only for a future in which the "children of reviving libertie" may "reclaim" that which they are on the verge of losing (YP VII, p. 463). Milton, that is, proclaims how the false republic must give way to a renewed servitude that may, he hopes, finally be shed by those children of "reviving libertie" who would have gleaned from their predecessors' errors why the first republic was false. In terms of this given political situation, Milton makes three other significant changes.

The first change occurs in the characterization of the rabble. Although Trevor-Roper is somewhat right in saying that Milton's "hatred of . . . the common people" was a regular feature of his work from 1649, it is worth noticing when his denunciation of the rabble becomes more exorbitant, and also for what ultimate reason he expresses his disdain for the "common people." So we find in the

second edition of *The Readie and Easie Way* this denunciation of
the rabble as a premise and symbol of the individual's right to
maintain liberty: "More just it is doubtless, if it com to force, that
a less number compell a greater to retain, which can be no wrong
to them, thir libertie, then that a greater number for the pleasure
of thir baseness, compell a less most injuriously to be thir fellow
slaves" (YP VII, p. 455). This passage is not in the first edition of
February 1660.[30]

The second significant change between the two editions involves reference to Rome. In the first edition, Milton refers to the
shame of the commonwealth if it should fail to maintain itself. In
doing so, he implicitly suggests that the ideal of a republic is to be
found in Rome: "Where is this goodly tower of a Common-wealth
which the *English* boasted they would build, to overshaddow kings
and be another *Rome* in the west?" (YP VII, p. 357). The passage
runs unaltered in the second edition also (p. 423). But what the
second edition has in addition to this reference to Rome is an
interpolated passage in the section in which Milton is justifying a
grand council that would sit perpetually. In the first edition, Milton writes, "In *Rome* the Senat, consisted of members chosen for
term of life; and by that means remain still the same to generations" (p. 371). In a passage added to the second edition, Milton
severely qualifies the model of Rome as exemplary of the utility of
continuing parliaments. He attempts to refute the argument that
the Roman tribunes ruined democracy—"brought them to such a
licentious and unbridl'd democratie" because of their "excessive
power"—by arguing that this happened only because the common
people were allowed to contend with the senate (pp. 438–40).
Rome is no longer the model of democracy it had been in the first
edition, but it is now a model of England in its degeneracy from
democracy to monarchy. As I will suggest below, this change in the
presentation of Rome should not be interpreted to signify Milton's
changing attitudes toward the idea of Rome; it merely indicates
which aspect of Rome he seems willing to present and hide in any
given political moment.

The third significant change between the two editions involves
Milton's explicit inscription of himself in his tract. In the first
edition, at the beginning of the famous "The whole freedom of
man consists either in spiritual or civil liberty" speech, he had
alluded to the written work available for anyone who doubted the

importance of separating the church and state in order to ensure liberty of conscience. This fact, he writes, "hath been heertofore prov'd at large in other treatises" (YP VII, p. 380). In the second edition, he inscribes himself fully and explicitly at this point in that same speech. This fact, he writes, "I have heretofore prov'd at large in another treatise" (p. 456). The dissociated voice of the first edition gives way to the profoundly self-conscious voice of the second edition. This is just what happens at the beginning of *Paradise Regained:* "I who e're while the happy Garden sung." Finally, Milton, as he always does, invokes, in both editions of *The Readie and Easie Way,* Christ as the eternal king who will supercede parliament or monarchy:

> They shall so continue (if God favour us, and our wilfull sins provoke him not) even to the coming of our true and rightfull and only to be expected King, only worthy as he is our only Saviour, the Messiah, the Christ, the only heir of his eternal father, the only by him anointed and ordaind, since the work of our redemption finishd, universal Lord of all mankind. (YP VII, pp. 374, 445)

These, then, are the gestures Milton persistently makes in the discursive strategies of his political polemics. To state it schematically, in times of political stress Milton tends (1) to establish the premise of the significance of the individual in any theologico-political activity by denouncing the idea of the majority; (2) to compare the present political establishment to what is for Milton both the potential and the danger of a republic, Rome; and (3) inscribe himself into the work as the political model of individual resolve. Over and above all this, he always invokes Christ as the eternal king of the world. This does not happen serially, of course, but it is the consistent *mode* of Milton's political engagement. Now we might see how this pattern holds for our examination of Milton in the early to middle 1650s.

Performing Milton: From 1651 to 1671

The main purpose of identifying a habitual discursive strategy in an author is to be able to trace the ways that his or her "performing" of politics is an act of self-knowledge. As Victor Turner writes, "performances are, in a way, *reflexive,*" and that "in performance," the performer "reveals himself to himself."[31] That revelation of Milton to Milton occurs in the third moment of his discursive strategy—the moment of inscribing his subjectivity into his political tract. It is integrally related to Milton's patterning the life of the individual after the life of the book. Quite literally, Milton, when his hopes for the republic decline, inscribes himself more rigorously into his prophesies of its decline. And that does not happen first in 1660. It happens earlier in his 1658 additions to the 1651 *Defence;* and it happens in his 1654 *Second Defence.*

Just as he was to do in April 1660, Milton in 1651 expressed his disillusionment with the present political system. Toward the end of *A Defence,* Milton concludes his attack on Salmasius and addresses the people he is defending:

> One thing yet remains, haply the greatest, and that is, that ye too, my countrymen, yourselves refute this adversary of yours, which to do I see no other way than by striving constantly to outdo all men's bad words by your own good deeds .... After so glorious a deed, ye ought to think, ye ought to do, nothing that is mean and petty, nothing but what is great and sublime. This praise that ye may attain, there is but one path to tread: as ye have subdued your enemies in the field, so shall ye prove that unarmed and in the midst of peace ye of all mankind have highest courage to subdue what conquers the rest of the nations of men—faction, avarice, the temptations of riches, and the corruptions that wait upon posterity; and in maintaining your liberty shall show as great justice, temperance, and moderation as ye have shown courage in freeing yourselves from slavery. (CM VII, pp. 550–53; cf. YP IV, p. 535)

At the very end of the 1651 edition of the *Defence,* Milton suggests that if the people of England did not regulate their moral lives in the time of peace, they would soon lose God's favor and become indeed but another example of a culture unable to extricate itself from idolatry and superstition: "But if you prove to be of other mind—which may the good God forbid forever! ... ye will find God far more wrathful against you than either your adversaries have found him embittered, or ye have found him aforetime gracious and favorable beyond all other nations at this time on earth" (CM VII, pp. 554–55; cf. YP IV, p. 536).

These are the last words Milton wrote in 1651; the 1658 additions to the *Defence* indicate that the tract Milton wrote was going to live beyond 1658, and not the government of the country for which he wrote it. "I believe that now, though more briefly than I had intended, I have finished my task. Such as it is, this memorial, I see, will not easily perish." That "memorial" is not England's republic, but Milton's "task" — in fact, Milton's *Defence*. As he was to do in the second edition of *The Readie and Easie Way*, Milton inscribes himself (and his writing) more explicitly into those tracts, expressing his discontent with the present government. He ends the 1658 additions with the promise that he is writing "yet greater things" (YP IV, pp. 536–37; cf. CM VII, pp. 556–59). At least as early as 1651, Milton had some severe doubts about the abilities of his fellow citizens to maintain their liberty. That ominous final paragraph, with its threat of divine perdition, does not represent Milton's usual tone or his usual rhetorical gambits. Milton hardly ever resorted to fire and brimstone; he usually left that sort of thing to Prynne. The additions to 1658 do not continue in that tone, but they nonetheless suggest an uneasiness worth noting because they conform to that paradigm we have already discerned in Milton's tendencies in times of political stress.[32]

Even so, the most we may confidently say about Milton's 1651 comments is that they are not especially hopeful; in them we see a note of doubt about England's capacity for rising above the idolatry and superstition of monarchy. However, three years later, at the end of the *Second Defence,* the hint of despair is not so subtle. Milton concludes his admonishment of the people of England to gain self-knowledge as a collective body with the prophesy that they will not be able to do so. In that act we begin to see the full expression of Milton's individualism:

> As for myself, to whatever state things may return, I have performed, and certainly with a good will, I hope not in vain, the service which I thought would be of most use to the commonwealth. . . . If our last actions should not be sufficiently answerable to the first, it is for themselves to see to it. (CM VIII, p. 253)

He continues with the suggestion that he will, like an epic poet, "leave alone the rest." This will to silence, I suggested in the previous chapter, is quite revealing in the 1671 volume. In 1654, it suggests that Milton did not think the future after 1654 worth singing about. That is the date, if one is to be proposed, where we should begin to explore what sorts of changes were occurring in Milton's late politics.[33]

As early as 1651, then, Milton hints of unease with the English republic, which by 1654 become ominous and broad doubts. In each instance where the hints occur, the author begins to inscribe himself more resolutely into his prophesies. Thus, we can trace in Milton's writing in the 1650s the same two symptoms we traced in April 1660—a diagnosis of "expiring liberty" followed by a more self-consciously authorial self-representation within the tract. In 1654, of course, we have the most extended moment of auto-biographical prose in Milton's career. As William Haller points out, Milton's autobiographical moments, discrete as they are, to-gether form his "spiritual autobiography."[34] I have suggested a political motive for those moments of especially determined self-inscription, and the *Second Defence* is just such a moment. More-over, it is worth reading that autobiographical digression in direct comparison with Jesus' autobiography in *Paradise Regained*. The sheer number and quality of the parallels are striking.

In 1654, the first publication of the blind Milton occurred, and in that tract we find the prophet Tieresias begin his transformation into the poet Maeonides. Tillyard has called the *Second Defence* the "greatest of Milton's prose works and one of the greatest of the world's rhetorical writings." In terms of our interest, the prose epic demonstrates the most closely woven of Milton's arguments on what is essentially the method of his brief epic—in the words of Louis Martz, "the movements of the meditative mind as it defines the nature of the Son of God."[35] In both works, moreover, Milton attempts to delineate the qualities of Sonship in juxtaposition to the qualities of servitude. Let's now see how Milton and his Jesus perform politics.

First of all, both the autobiographical author in the *Second Defence* and the hero in *Paradise Regained* begin with a description of what Kenneth Burke calls the "pre-political childhood": "De-voted even from a child to the more humanizing studies, and always stronger in mind than in body," writes Milton, "I set an inferior value upon the service of the camp . . . and betook myself to those occupations, where my services could be of more avail." The protection of Truth, he thought, required "reason—the only defence which is truly and properly human." The hero of *Paradise Regained* began his autobiographical soliloquy by stating that, when he was "yet a child," he was of a mind wholly devoted "to learn and know." He considers the utility of military prowess in the freeing of Truth, but decides in the end on the "more humane, more heavenly" method of persuasion (*Def,* p. 11; *PR* I, 201–22).[36]

Second, Milton recounts the conditions surrounding his writing of the first *Defence*. He was asked by the Independents to write an apology against Salmasius, but told by his doctor that he could lose his eyesight in the strain of doing this task. He placed before himself the two destinies and compared himself to Achilles having to choose between conservation and duty, between safety and glory. The comparison with Achilles is merely a superficial gloss on what Milton considers to be operating within. For, as he says, he feels a "diviner moniter within." The comparison with Achilles suggests another facet of Milton's life, however. Milton explicitly mentions that it is Thetis, Achilles's mother, who goes to consult the oracle at Delphi and brings back the choice to her son; in fact, Achilles is named only in reference to his mother (*Thetidis filius*). Likewise, Jesus feels the "Spirit" operating within him and helping him choose his career. Moreover, he not only receives an internal monitor, but also inaugurates the covenant when historically that "inward Oracle" replaces the very Delphic oracle Thetis had consulted (*Def 2,* p. 69; *PR* I, 290, 460). So, too, Mary, like Achilles's mother, plays a prominent role in helping her son find the way of understanding his career.

Third, what Milton receives by giving up his sight in service to his country is nothing less than an "inward and far surpassing light." That light reflects both in his countenance and in his epistemological abilities. In his darkness, "the light of the divine countenance does but the more brightly shine." Furthermore, he says that although he is blind he is nonetheless able to perceive in his "mind's contemplation whatever is real and permanent." Finally, blindness also allows Milton to claim the strength of weakness: "For then I shall at once be the weakest and the most mighty." Jesus, too, God tells us, will have such paradoxical strength: "His weakness shall o'recome Satanic strength." Moreover, Jesus enjoys the light of God in both his countenance and his epistemological abilities. In Jesus' countenance his "Fathers glory shine[s]." Moreover, we have seen at length how Jesus is able to meditate in his mind what is lasting and real, his kingdom (*Def 2,* pp. 73, 71; *PR* I, 161, 93).

Fourth, Jesus' most significant act is his willing to God to reveal whatever is necessary for his knowledge: "For what concerns my knowledge God reveals." On this act of submission, I have developed the basis of how self-knowledge leads to becoming a Son of God. Likewise, Milton submits himself to God: "I acquiesce in his divine will, for it is he himself who comforts and upholds my spirit." The act of making oneself a Son of God is consistent between the hero of the brief epic and the author of the prose epic (*Def 2*, p. 71; *PR* I, 293). Immediately after this, Milton alludes to Antaeus and the Sphinx, who are the two main characters of the final similes of the poem.

Fifth, Jesus transmutes the definitions of fame and glory as Satan offers them into a form of divine worship that depends not on grasping occasion's forelock, but on waiting for the "time prefixt." So, too, does Milton redefine fame as that which exists only in relation to promoting God's designs and is worth pursuing only in terms of God's schedule: "But I was not eager for fame, who is slow of pace; indeed, if the fit opportunity had not been given me, even these things would never have seen the light. It was not the fame of every thing that I was waiting for, but the opportunity." And he redefines "greatness" to belong only to those who "make this life of ours happy, or . . . which lead to another and happier life." Just as Jesus had rejected the usefulness of wealth without virtue, valor, and wisdom, so does Milton reject wealth without "virtue," "industry," and "patience of labour" (*Def 2*, pp. 113, 97, 243; *PR* III, 43; II, 430).[37]

We have seen now the numerous and telling comparisons between the Milton of the *Second Defence* and Jesus in *Paradise Regained*. It would be difficult to deny that, as Don Wolfe writes, "Milton painted himself in his characterization of Jesus in *Paradise Regained*." We have also seen how Milton's self-inscriptions tend to follow upon his moments of political disappointment (in 1654, 1658, and 1660). That was one gesture I determined belonged to Milton's habitual political method. A second gesture involves the denunciation of the rabble as an act of establishing the importance of the individual in any theologico-political activity. This second gesture is the final significant parallel between the 1654 and the 1671 books. Jesus and Milton both eschew the value of earthly fame because of the unreliability of those who would be judges. Jesus answers Satan's offer of glory with a bitter attack on the rabble:

> For what is glory but the blaze of fame,
> The peoples praise, if always praise unmixt?
> And what the people but a herd confused,
> A miscellaneous rabble, who extol
> Things vulgar, & well weigh'd, scarce worth the praise,
> They praise and they admire they know not what;
> And know not whom, but as one leads the other;
> And what delight to be by such extoll'd,
> To live upon thir tongues and be thir talk,
> Of whom to be disprais'd were no small praise?
>
> (*PR* III, 47–56)

Many critics have noted how it is difficult to reconcile the meek Savior of the Gospels with the vehement speaker of these lines. It is not difficult, however, to reconcile these lines with the author who expressed exactly the same sentiments in 1654:

> They praise or blame, without choice, without discrimination, without judgment or measure, now princes, now plebeians, alike the learned and unlearned, honest men and knaves, as prompted by caprice, — as inspirited and transported by the bottle, by the hope of getting a little money, or by their own senseless fury; heaping together from all sides inconsistencies, both in words and things, so threadbare and of colours so incompatible, that it would be better far for the person praised to be passed by in silence, and to live, as the saying is, on the sneers of contempt than to be thus praised: nay, he who has incurred their blame, may take it to himself as no ordinary honour. (*Def 2*, p. 79)

By 1654 Milton had long foregone any hope of establishing a wide-based electoral body in England. Whenever he defined the "majority" he did so in reference only to those he considered to be free of self-desire, and by referring only to the very small minority who fell into that category. Although it might appear Milton defined England's "majority" in the same way that today's public evangelists define what they call America's "moral majority," we must palliate this somewhat by adding that Milton used this gesture of renouncing the rabble in order to define any minority's rights to pursue their liberty in defiance of a majority wishing to pursue servitude.

We have seen, now, that in 1654 and 1671 Milton followed the same general political method as that which existed between the two editions of *The Readie and Easie Way*. In a moment of disappointment with the political establishment, Milton inscribed himself into the work of prophecy and expressed disdain for the rabble who were incapable of generating the sort of individual self-knowledge required for maintaining national liberty. The final gesture involves the use of Rome as an idea in Milton's political thought. What role, then, does Rome play in Milton between 1654 and 1671?

"Queen of the Earth": Jesus, Milton, and Rome

By pointing out the different attitudes expressed toward Rome between the first and the second editions of *The Readie and Easie Way*, I do not intend to suggest that Milton underwent anything resembling a change of mind about Rome during March 1660. He did not. Rome for Milton was always tainted, from at least as early as 1640. In his *Commonplace Book*, Milton described the process of Rome's decline from democracy with pretty much the same sort of language he would use some thirty years later:

> The form of state to be fitted to the peoples disposition some live best under monarchy others otherwise. so that the conversions of commonwealths happen not always through ambition or malice. as amoung the Romans who after thire infancy were ripe for a more free government then monarchy, beeing in a manner all fit to K[ing]s. afterward growne unruly, and impotent with overmuch prosperity were either for thire profit, or thir punishment fit to be curb'd with a lordly and dreadfull monarchy; which was the error of the noble Brutus and Cassius who felt themselves of spirit to free an nation but consider'd not that the nation was fit to be free, whilst forgetting thire old justice and fortitude which was made to rule, they became slaves to thire owne ambition and luxurie. (YP I, p. 420)[38]

In the first edition of *The Readie and Easie Way*, Milton ignored some of the factors of Rome he had already well considered earlier in his life; and, in the second edition, he simply articulates those failings of Roman democracy he had already diagnosed some twenty years earlier. The only importance we might attach to Milton's using the example of Rome as one of his persistent political gestures is that Rome comes to symbolize, at various times in significant ways in his political career, what we may for simplicity's sake call either the *potential* or the *destiny* of England. Rome would represent in Milton's thinking something like that register which T. S. Eliot called an "objective correlative."

So, for instance, in the *Defence of the People of England* (1651), Milton compares England to Rome rather triumphantly as one instance of success to another instance of failure. Like the Roman Senate, which had sent envoys to Antony in spite of Cicero's protests, certain members of the English Parliament had wished to send proposals to Charles. The ends of each country would have been the same, Milton notes, "but that it pleased God Almighty to order it otherwise — to deliver *them* into slavery, but to assert our liberty." Accordingly, in 1651, Milton's references to the "people" were equanimous and his belief in the collective power of reform strong. In the *Second Defence,* however, Milton's view of the "people" had undergone the sea change which we have already noted, and his references to Rome's purpose as an analogy to English politics likewise indicated something other than they had three years earlier. In 1654, Rome for Milton represented not so much England's *potential* — the "Rome in the west" — as England's *destiny:*

> But last of all, it is not to be forgotten, that those who are unworthy of liberty are commonly the first to show their ingratitude towards our deliverers. Who would now fight, or incur the least danger, for the liberty of such men? It does not suit, it does not fall to the lot of such men to be free. However they may bawl and boast about liberty, they are slaves [*servi*] both at home and abroad, and yet perceive it not. . . . They may make the same attempt by arms again and again; but they will make no progress: they may change their slavery perhaps; but they will never be able to shake it off. This is what very frequently happened even to the ancient Romans, after they had become effeminate and unnerved through luxury. (CM VIII, pp. 248–49)[39]

As we saw to be the case between the first and second editions of *The Readie and Easie Way,* Rome is transformed from an example of England's potential in *A Defence* to what we might call, following Raphael's usage, a "terrible Example" of England's destiny in the *Second Defence* (*PL* VI, 910).

In *Paradise Regained,* Rome is quite simply the most important offer Satan makes to Jesus. For all intents and purposes, the offer of Parthia does nothing but highlight the importance of the offer of Rome.[40] Satan makes sure that, even as he is offering Parthia first, Rome is always at hand:

> But say thou we'rt possess'd of *David's* Throne
> By free consent of all, none opposite,
> *Samaritan* or *Jew;* how could'st thou hope
> Long to enjoy it quiet and secure,
> Between two such enclosing enemies
> *Roman* and *Parthian?* therefore one of these
> Thou must make sure thy own, the *Parthian* first
> By my advice
>
> . . . .
>
> Maugre the *Roman*.   (III, 356–67)

In no other temptation does Satan attempt to suggest to Jesus that there are other options available should he choose not to accept this one. Here, however, he keeps Rome available while he offers Parthia. Also, in his answer to the offer of Parthia, Jesus is brisk and not really concerned with showing its demerits. In fact, after briefly dismissing Parthian military might in seven verses (III, 386–92), Jesus turns his attention for eight more verses to the more general question of the means and time for his mission (393–401) before turning his attention at length to what appears to be the most significant feature in his response to the offer of Parthia, which is his description of the tribes of Israel (402–39). Finally, when Satan does get around to offering Rome, he discounts the only other historically relevant kingdom — Parthia. Rome, he says, "thou justly may'st prefer / Before the *Parthian*" (IV, 84–85). Rome is also the kingdom Jesus knows the most about, and the only one he outdoes Satan in describing.

I suggested in chapter 3 that Rome represents a variety of political ideals for the Renaissance. As Thomas Greene so aptly suggested, Rome was the object of the Renaissance artist's archival study and likewise the deterrent to his belief in a historical continuity. For Milton, as for Petrarch, Rome offered the possibility of a radical critique of his culture. For the Rome represented in *Paradise Regained* is the Rome of the *Second Defence* and the Rome of the second edition of *The Readie and Easie Way* — that is, Rome as destiny, not as potential.[41]

Rome is, of course, the culture enslaving Israel in 29 A.D. In answering the offer of Rome, Jesus tells Satan why this once noble nation is enslaved to its own desires. He was not sent to free Tiberius or Sejanus or Rome, he says:

Let his tormenter Conscience find him out,
For him I was not sent, nor yet to free
That people victor once, now vile and base,
Deservedly made vassal, who once just,
Frugal, and mild, and temperate, conquer'd well,
But govern ill the Nations under yoke,
Peeling thir Provinces, exhausted all
By lust and rapine; first ambitious grown
Of triumph that insulting vanity;
Then cruel, by thir sports to blood enur'd
Of fighting beasts, and men to beasts expos'd,
Luxurious by thir wealth, and greedier still,
And from the daily Scene effeminate.
What wise and valiant man would seek to free
These thus degenerate, by themselves enslav'd,
Or could of inward slaves make outward free?   (IV, 130–45)

This is a description of England as Milton perceived it in 1654 as much as it is of Rome in 29 A.D. Milton had used Rome's luxury to suggest the reasons for their political demise in 1640 in the comment in his *Commonplace Book*. He had kept silent about that luxury when he used Rome as an example of England's republican potential in those moments of optimism, saving that description for his moments of political pessimism.

Milton's 1801 editor, Henry John Todd, suggested that Milton may have had in mind the Restoration monarchy when he described the "superlatively extravagant luxury of the Romans (possibly not without a glance at the manners of our Court at that time)." An earlier editor with an obviously different political perspective, Robert Thyer, felt provoked by this passage to comment on the difficulty of reconciling Milton's libertarian sentiments with his support of Cromwell. In a note on this passage in the 1752 variorum edition, Thyer writes:

No one had ever more refin'd notions of true liberty than Milton, and I have often thought that there never was a greater proof of the weakness of human nature, that he with a head so clear, and a heart I really believe perfectly honest and disinterested, should concur in supporting such a tyrant and profess'd trampler upon the liberties of his country as Cromwell was.

While I do not wish to suggest that Thyer is simply wrong in his description of Milton's attitudes toward Cromwell, I do think that his noticing this passage as a particularly interesting point of departure with Cromwellian politics is astute. What Milton had in mind in this passage, I think, is not the Restoration court, although that is quite plausible, but rather the England of 1654.[42]

The description of Rome in Jesus' reply as self-enslaved by its luxury and effeminacy sits well with the description of Rome in the *Second Defence;* it also agrees wholly with the Rome Milton wrote about in his *Commonplace Book.* The significant point of comparison, however, is that Jesus claims that he will not free the Romans because they are self-enslaved to their own desires. The way for them to see the potential for liberty involves a moral revolution. When Satan suggests that Jesus might "expel this monster" who is corrupt and corrupting, Jesus answers him with the pointed suggestion that he might "Expel a Devil who first made him such" (IV, 100, 129). That would be the moral revolution making possible the renewed freedom of the noble Romans. In the comment in the *Commonplace Book,* it was Brutus and Cassius who were not able to alter the Roman political establishment because they were not able to reform the moral integrity of the Roman people.

In *The Second Defence,* Cromwell assumes the place of Brutus. Neither man, according to Milton, is capable of leading his country to liberty without a wholesale internal revolution: "No man, not even Cromwell himself, not the whole nation of those deliverers the Brutuses, if it should revisit us, either could, if it would, or would, if it could, deliver you again" (CM VIII, pp. 244–45). What was needed, as he made abundantly clear, was a revolution of the spirit—as he said very early in his career, "the reforming of the Reformation it self" (CM IV, p. 340). In *Paradise Regained,* he chose to represent the inauguration of that political potential. He argues in the *Second Defence* that, without a firm moral basis in each individual in the state, the state itself was doomed to regress to servitude. In the terms he had used to make the distinction between freedom and servitude in his theological debate, if the English would not act like Sons of God, they would become servants of God:

> To be free is precisely the same thing as to be pious, wise, just, and temperate, careful of one's own, abstinent from what is another's, and

thence, in fine, magnanimous and brave — so, to be the opposite of these, is the same thing as to be a slave; and by the wonted judgement, and as it were by the just retribution of God, it comes to pass, that the nation, which has been incapable of governing and ordering itself, and has delivered itself up to the slavery of its own lusts, is itself delivered over, against its will, to other masters — and whether it will or no, is compelled to serve. (*Def,* pp. 248–51)

For Milton, nations assume the place of sons or servants in exactly the same way and by precisely the same process as individuals. The same act of will is either allowed its maintenance or revoked because of its misuse. And, as with individual theology, so it is with national politics. A nation that does not use its will and right reason to achieve national self-knowledge and make itself a subject of God will, to that extent, lose its will and become subject to another nation. "Do you, therefore, who have the wish to continue free," he writes, "either begin with being wise, or repent without delay" (p. 251). Rome is the last offer Satan makes before offering the kingdoms as a package. Jesus' reply to the offer is, as I noted in chapter 3, both the most enigmatic of his replies and the only one in which he does not refer to the power of God the Father. One possible reason he does not do so may be that in the very next reply to the kingdoms as a whole he refers so insistently on the power of God the Father that it might have been artistically uneconomical for Milton to have him mention the Father here. But, more importantly, I think, is that in the offer to Rome we find Jesus' most powerful statement of the foundation of his kingdom:

> Know therefore when my season comes to sit
> On *David's* Throne, it shall be like a tree
> Spreading and over-shadowing all the Earth,
> Or as a stone that shall to pieces dash
> All Monarchies besides throughout the world,
> And of my Kingdom there shall be no end:
> Means there shall be to this, but what the means,
> Is not for thee to know, nor me to tell.   (IV, 246–53)

The kingdom is both enigmatic and extremely potent. This is where it is simply inappropriate to call Milton's late politics passive or quietist. Milton hits this note in early 1659 when, in *A Treatise of Civil Power,* he likewise describes Christ's rule: "Christ hath a government of his own, sufficient of it self to all his ends and purposes in governing his church. . . . [Which] deals only with the inward man and his actions." This internal government, Milton continues, is "able without worldly force to subdue all the powers and kingdoms of this world, which are upheld by outward force only" (YP VII, p. 255). This is the insistent note in Milton's political comments in 1659 and 1660.

Milton argued in both editions of *The Readie and Easie Way* that Christ would eventually come to reign, and hoped only that the government he would supercede might be a parliament and not a monarchy. It is a political thought and not only a religious belief, as Milton insists. Surely God, he writes, "hath not chosen the force of this world to subdue conscience and conscientious men, who in this world are counted weakest; but rather conscience, as being weakest, to subdue and regulate force, his adversarie, not his aide or instrument in governing the church" (YP VII, p. 257). To say with Christopher Hill that this is not quietist doctrine is not to say quite enough; to say that it is divorced from active politics is simply inaccurate. For Milton did not "retreat" into this belief after the Restoration, as almost all critics intimate. It was his belief of what could prevent the Restoration, a belief he held as early as 1654, and it is a belief of what sort of political revolution had to occur in order to disestablish the monarchy, a belief he held as late as 1671. It is, let us make no doubt about it, the same belief. In the *Second Defence,* just after he counsels the way to wisdom through national self-knowledge, he begins to see the end of the republic: "If after achievements so magnanimous, ye basely fall off from your duty, if ye are guilty of any thing unworthy of you, be assured, posterity will speak, and thus pronounce its judgment: The foundation was strongly laid, the beginning, nay more than the beginning, was excellent; but it will be inquired, not without a disturbed emotion, who raised the superstructure, who completed the fabric!" (*Def 2,* p. 255). In 1654, Milton began to see the end of the republic. Its demise was not dependent on the external imposition of monarchy, but on the internal failure in the nation's attempt at self-knowledge.

I have so far suggested that the *Second Defence* and *Paradise Regained* share Milton's wonted strategy of political discourse. First, each has established the initial premise of reform at the individual level in resounding critiques of the rabble. Second, in each, Milton inscribes himself into the workings of the poem—in the *Second Defence* by the long autobiographical digression, in *Paradise Regained* by what are almost exactly the same autobiographical facts in the mouth of his hero. Third, both employ Rome as an analogy for England's destiny. More important, their similarities run to the most profound level of Milton's thinking. Without attaining self-knowledge as individual subjects, a nation could not retain its civic liberties for long. Politics, Milton insisted, had first to operate at the level of the individual person; reformation had first to return to the basic principle by which a self became a subject of God. In this we may find the consistency between the seventh prolusion, the 1654 *Second Defence*, and the 1671 volume. All these political ideas of the Milton of 1671 are those of the Milton of the 1654 *Second Defence*. So, we may trace Milton's consistent political thought from 1671, not just to the Restoration of 1660, not just to the death of Cromwell in 1658, but as early as 1654 and perhaps 1651. Both in terms of its dating and in terms of its characterization, the critical debate on Milton's late politics is misrepresentative.

What Milton was counseling in 1654 and in 1671 was a return to a prepolitical state in order to reform the political state. He advocated the necessity of self-knowledge at the level of the individual as the basis of the formation of the state. That for him was truly reformation—internal and civic. Liberty, as he writes in the middle of the *Second Defence*, "is to be sought for not from without, but within, and is to be obtained principally not by fighting, but by the just regulation and by the proper conduct of life" (*Def 2*, p. 131).

Between 1671: Milton's Third Defence of the People of England

Succinctly put, what Milton says in 1654—that the just regulation of life is the way to substantial and lasting liberty—is the message Jesus gives in the brief epic. Jesus offers that answer of how to regulate the inner soul and thereby ensure substantial liberty in his reply to the offer of Parthia, while reflecting on the enslaved tribes of Israel:

> As for those captive Tribes, themselves were they
> Who wrought their own captivity, fell off
> From God to worship Calves, the Deities

Of *Egypt, Baal* next and *Ashtaroth,*
And all the Idolatries of Heathen round,
. . . .
Should I these of their liberty regard,
Who freed, as to their antient Patrimony,
Unhumbl'd, unrepentant, unreform'd,
Headlong would follow; and to thir God perhaps
Of *Bethel* and of *Dan?* no, let them serve
Thir enemies, who serve Idols with God.
(III, 413–17; 426–31)

Like Rome, Israel is captive to its own desires. This is as true of
Israel in 29 A.D. as it had been in 1120 B.C. Such nations incapable
of self-knowledge "serve" their enemies, and one of the two tribes
Jesus names shows us how the 1671 volume is consistent in so
many ways.

The judge of the tribe of Dan articulates this opinion of Milton's. In rebuking the Chorus for the nation's inability to act with
him in destroying the Philistines at an earlier juncture of their
history, Samson answers their query about why "*Israel* still serves
with all his Sons":

Had *Judah* that day join'd, or one whole Tribe,
They had by this possess'd the Towers of *Gath,*
And lorded over them whom now they serve;
But what more oft in Nations grown corrupt,
And by thir vices brought to servitude,
Than to love Bondage more than Liberty,
Bondage with ease then strenuous liberty.   (*SA* 266–72)

To the Chorus's query, Samson's reply might be paraphrased: Israel
had no "Sons." There were none who had attained self-knowledge,
who mastered themselves in terms of desire, who loved liberty
wholly and passionately. That pronouncement, in one sense, includes Samson himself. For liberty, as Milton stated in the *Second
Defence,* is to be sought within. And within is where Jesus goes in
his opening meditative soliloquy; but it is not where Samson goes
in his. There are two forms of tyranny, Milton wrote in 1649:
"Custom from without, and blind affections within" (CM V, p. 1).
In *Paradise Regained,* Jesus discovers within himself what affections he must forego in pursuing a more radical critique of his

culture and what external devices he must reject in establishing a profoundly novel religious and political culture. In *Samson Agonistes,* Samson retains all his internal affections and simply destroys the external theater and nobility of Philistia. Cromwell, like Brutus, like Samson, could deliver a nation from custom; only Jesus in his role as perfect model of how to attain self-knowledge could deliver a nation from its blind affections. Joan Bennett argues that Jesus is presented here as the only Redeemer and is therefore not to be imitated; his reflections on political activism, therefore, are not presented to the individual reader as a pattern of the political life. I suggest, in contrast, that Jesus is presented as just that model. The way to national political liberty is through precisely the form of self-knowledge Jesus gains at the individual level.

Milton comes to know himself in 1671 through his representation of both Samson and Jesus. The words of Samson that when nations grow corrupt they are enslaved to their own desires express Milton's political opinions. Jesus' words about the degree of radical critique and self-knowledge as a requirement to lead nations back to liberty also express Milton's political opinions. What both heroes discern is that the individual must, in an act of self-knowledge, in a moment of extended soliloquy examining his early and recent life, become a subject of God. Whereas Jesus succeeds in attaining this subjectivity, Samson fails. Samson is unable to understand how one act of heroism is insufficient for the moral overhaul required for true liberty. Samson's act, then, is like Cromwell's; it frees Israel for a time. A momentary political revolution, Milton comes to realize, will not succeed until the ethical conditions are right. While Samson's *theory* of what happens when nations grow corrupt does indeed express Milton's political opinion, Samson's *action* of freeing Israel by an external moment of force demonstrates Milton's final critique of the limits of premature revolutionary action. The end of *Samson Agonistes* tells us that Milton thought there had to be certain ethical preconditions before, but also only as a prelude to, a renewed civil liberty.

Those preconditions are the subject of the companion poem — which is, in the end, where Milton represents most fully in all his works the act of coming to self-knowledge. Both in Jesus' striving for self-knowledge and in his own, Milton articulates the style of those preconditions (the basis of civil liberty in personal ethics) and the order of political action. This "inward turn" is by no means an ultimate retreat, but an order of priority. Without an ethical substructure of the sort Jesus articulates, there could be no lasting peace or liberty. Thus, although at the end of *Samson Agonistes* there is external freedom for Israel, they are still captivated to their internal desires which shortly will lead to yet another form of colonization. Ironically, even though at the end of *Paradise Regained* Israel is still subjected to the Roman empire, the state now has the preconditions for enduring liberty from all political restraints. Superimposed on the life of Jesus as the paradigm of the political establishment of that ethical ideal is the life of John Milton as an example of the very act of self-knowledge that is the necessary precondition to England's ultimate freedom. Milton works from *Samson Agonistes* to *Paradise Regained,* exploring two modes of political action—one strictly collective and the other representatively personal. The tribe of Dan will fail to retain its freedom because even though they are a collective they are nonetheless not educated in the ways of keeping liberty. Although Jesus acts alone, he establishes the way every individual must come to recognize his or her place in the maintenance of political freedom. Milton represents himself in the brief epic as one of those who comes to self-knowledge and becomes a subject of God.

It might appear, then, that for Milton being "subject to God" in its theological sense equates to being subject to a state in a political sense. In other words, perhaps only Jesus attains subjectivity while Samson suffers political subjection. That, however, is not the case. Samson is not merely a model of inadequate self-knowledge, of servitude, or of failed political action. He is, over and above that, nonetheless an agent of God, although a somewhat unwilling vessel, and therefore he is not subject to any state. Even though Samson represents Milton's radical critique of premature political activism and Jesus represents his ideal of patiently awaiting the proper preconditions for political action, neither hero must undergo subjection *to the state.*

What did Milton have in mind as an idea of the state, and what did he theorize about subjection? It is hardly sound political theory to suggest that national liberty may be maintained at the level of ethics, or that a state's freedom resides in the ability of its citizens to gain self-knowledge. Politics, as it is usually understood in reference to national structures, refers to the policing of any public deviations from what the state decides is appropriate ethical behavior. The state does not concern itself with private thinking, only with public action. But rather than characterize Milton's insistence on establishing political stability at the individual level as a "retreat" from politics, we might see what Milton was arguing about the state and in response to what theories he was positing his own. For, in the end, Milton was not divorcing ethics from politics, as is so often suggested, but was promoting a certain order of politics that involves a restructuring of political activity. Thus, there is no other term to describe Milton's late writing than *politics*.

Milton's idea of the state, I believe, can be found in the choice he made to present two liberators in two national situations. Their similarity is that each liberator is called to free the state of Israel from its present colonized status — Israel as it was colonized by the Philistines in 1120 B.C. and Israel as it was colonized by the Romans in 29 A.D. In this space between two presentations of Israel, we find Milton's most complete thoughts on the state of England and his theories on the idea of the state itself. The political thinker Milton seems to have in mind in his 1671 volume is Thomas Hobbes.

PART TWO: MILTON'S POLITICAL DIALOGUE

John Aubrey wrote in his minutes on the life of Milton that Elizabeth Minshull told him that while Milton would acknowledge that Hobbes was a "man of great parts, a learned man," he nonetheless did not "like him at all." The reason is not hard to guess, but Aubrey records it anyway: "Their Interests & tenets were diametrically" opposed. Above this, Aubrey records that their ideas "did run counter to each other."[43] In the second part of this chapter, I will discern in what ways we can make sense of what I have so far insisted on calling Milton's politics in relation to the theories of Hobbes. Hobbes serves my purpose here because there are so many interesting points of intersection and contradiction between his thinking on politics and Milton's. By seeing the way Milton attempts to resolve issues first raised by Hobbes, we may at yet one more level dispute that reading of Milton's late career as the process of fleeing politics and retreating into some egotistic ethical self. The Milton in implicit dialogue with the writer who is, after

all, the first modern practitioner of political science is not in retreat from politics; he is involved in it at the most profound level.

"And Seems a Moving Land": Milton and Hobbes

I have suggested the ways that Milton differs radically from
Hobbes on the question of politics. Whereas in Hobbes, as in
Foucault, the individual is always "subject to" either internal consciousness (in Hobbes, "desire") or external control, in Milton the
individual becomes either a "subject of" God or "subject to" God—
in Milton's phrasing a "Son of God" or a "Servant of God." In
chapter 2 I read Jesus' autobiography as an example of the type of
defining one's subjectivity that Milton held to be salutary, wherein
the "self" in an act of self-knowledge accedes to becoming a "subject of God." In chapter 3 I showed the sort of dialogue that was
possible between one who was a subject of God and one who had
eschewed the process of understanding required to become a subject of God and therefore became, against his will, subject to God.
The dialogue was part of Jesus' program of establishing the conditions for a new political culture in which self-government was both
the premise and the model of national government. In chapter 4, I
demonstrated how the operative distinction between sons and servants could help us appreciate the intertextuality in the 1671 volume, in which we are presented with contrasting studies of a
servant and a son. Now it is time to see how that distinction
between sons and servants does not belong just to Milton's theology but also to his politics. Milton's concerns in the end are still the
same—the question of subjectivity, as it integrally involves the
questions of liberty, agency, and self-knowledge. They are played
out now, though, at the level of the idea of the state, and they are
displayed in dialogue with Hobbes.

To begin the exploration of what I am calling an "implicit
dialogue" between Hobbes and Milton, I will define what I mean
by an "implicit dialogue." As far as we know, Milton probably read
Hobbes, which is why he did "not like him at all," according to
Aubrey's account. But it is not on the basis of his having read
Hobbes that I am interested in seeing on what points of convergence and contradiction Milton might be disputing Hobbes's political ideas. Rather, I am going to suggest that their imaginary
dialogue exists as a confrontation between two sets of what Fou-

cault calls "discursive formations," the units of systematization of a series of "statements." At the level of the "statement," Foucault argues, we can best understand how different thinkers might engage in dialogue. Statements, according to Foucault, are the constituent units of discourse, and any articulation becomes a statement only when it is "related to a whole adjacent field."[44] So, in our present case, Hobbes and Milton are in implicit dialogue between two discursive formations—the rules governing the state of Leviathan, and the rules governing Jesus' regained paradise. The confrontation between these two formations occurs on the field of statements concerning the status of the political subject. Finally, the statements deal with the individual's relationship to four interrelated structures of power.

The first structure is the status and composition of individuality. What, for Hobbes or for Milton, constitutes an individual? The most important question concerning this individual is his or her relationship to desire. The second structure is the composition of the family. What is the function of the family in the regulation of an individual's becoming a subject? The most important question concerning the family is about the place of the mother in relationship to the family's most significant function—the individual's striving for self-knowledge. The third structure is the state. What does the subject owe the state, and what does the state owe the subject? Under what conditions does the state lose its authority over the subject? The most important question here is the site of Law in relation to the state. The fourth and final structure is the church. What is the church—a visible and subordinate state apparatus or an invisible and superordinate epistemic structure? The most important question concerning the church is its relationship to the other state apparatus. Hobbes and Milton are implicated in dialogue at the level of their statements concerning these four interrelated structures—the individual, the family, the state, and the church.

1. The Church

Milton, as we saw, has a habitual mode of discoursing on political questions. Hobbes has his own polemical practice and we may discover his political agenda in its habits. Most readers usually object to Hobbes's bullying rhetorical strategy in his political writing. He states simply and insistently that any swerving from his idea of an absolutist sovereignty will return the commonwealth to that state he calls either a "Warre of every one against every one" (p. 189) or, what is the same thing, a state of "meer Nature, (which is a condition of Warre of every man against every other man)" (p. 196). Against this backdrop of absolute anarchy, Hobbes proposes the peace and commercial possibilities of the absolute sovereignty. Likewise, Milton had an idea of anarchy against which he established his ideal state. For Milton, directly contrary to Hobbes, absolute sovereignty, the rule of any single person over the commonwealth, represents the state of anarchy. Against this notion of anarchy, Milton proposed his aristocratic democracy. If this political expedient were not taken, he warned in 1659, England would return to a state of monarchy (which is anarchy). Each goes on to establish the impossibility of conducting commercial business under that condition of anarchy (whether "meer Nature" or a "single government by any one person") (YP VII, p. 336). Each also had an idea of what purpose the church could play in the state—either as part of the state apparatus or as one potential leverage against an absolutist state.

In a discussion of seventeenth-century politics, it is impossible to divorce the question of the status of the state from the question of the status of the church. As Althusser points out, "all ideological struggle, from the sixteenth to the eighteenth century, starting with the first shocks of the Reformation, was *concentrated* in an anti-clerical and anti-religious struggle" precisely because the church was the "one dominant Ideological State Apparatus." Even in an emergent capitalist system, such as England was in the seventeenth century, the church was the nodal point of contention. Foucault suggests that "Christianity is the only religion which has organized itself as a Church," and the church is "a very special form of power." In fact, he even suggests that the modern state be conceived of as either "a modern matrix of individualization, or a new form of *pastoral* power."[45] Given the significance of the church in relation to the state in seventeenth-century political discourse, what Hobbes and Milton had to say about the church is part of each one's *political* program.

In his attempt to establish a theory of a peaceful, absolute sovereignty, Hobbes considered the church to be his radical nemesis. In his arguments for the revolutionary quality of the church, Milton considered absolute sovereignty to be the reactionary enemy. Each had much to say about the church, either as a potential force of reformation or as a potential source of disturbing seditious sentiment. Milton, we recall, held that "Christ hath a government of his own, sufficient of it self to all his ends and purposes in governing his church" (YP VII, p. 255). It was an institution—the true and invisible church—that could overturn any and all kingdoms upheld by mere outward force. In Milton's mind, it was simply the most potent revolutionary force in the world. Hobbes, on the other hand, felt that the church should be wholly governed by the absolute sovereign in order to ensure that no such reformations would occur. All reformations, sniffed Hobbes, were to be attributed to the same cause—"unpleasing Priests" (p. 183). In light of that prognosis, Hobbes sets up a political program dependent on his ability to depotentiate the church of its revolutionary power.

In order to see the degree of radical difference between these two thinkers on the question of the church, as indeed on any political question, I will first note the two points in which they *appear* to be in agreement. Both Hobbes and Milton seem to agree that tithing as a method of church maintenance is simply wrong in and of itself (this is Milton's argument throughout his life; it is Hobbes's at the very end of the *Leviathan,* p. 714; cf. pp. 565–66). Second, neither thinker has much respect for what Milton called the "heretic in the truth," that person who does not examine the tenets of his or her faith, but accepts them on implicit reliance on the pastor. As Hobbes notes in derision, "And wee see daily by experience in all sorts of People, that such men as study nothing but their food and ease, are content to beleeve any absurdity, rather than to trouble themselves to examine it; holding their faith as it were by entaile unalienable" (p. 677). In reply to this form of implicit faith, he ends his brief history of church government in England by suggesting that the method following the loss of power of the Presbyterians—the method closest, he thought, to primitive Christianity—"is perhaps the best," for "there ought to be no Power over the Consciences of men, but of the Word it selfe, working Faith in every one" (p. 711). On this point, there appears to be hardly any disagreement between Hobbes and Milton. The radical difference is operative in the way each writer defines faith, the Word, and, finally, the church.

For Hobbes did not say that faith ought to be a matter of

individual conscience until after he had eviscerated Scripture of all its revolutionary significance. Whereas Milton held that the Word of God was to be interpreted only with reference to the individual's guiding spirit and thereby liberate into play its revolutionary political doctrine, Hobbes had already made interpretation the prerogative solely of the institution of the Sovereign: "The interpretation of the Bible [is] authorized by the Common-wealth" (p. 479). Just a few pages before Hobbes apparently allowed individual conscience some freedom of play (p. 711), he repeats the tenet against interpretive liberty: "For a Private man, without the Authority of the Common-wealth, that is to say, without permission from the Representant thereof, to Interpret the Law by his own Spirit, is another Error in the Politiques" (p. 700). Moreover, Hobbes also removed any political efficacy from the New Testament. Because Jesus claimed that his kingdom was not of this world, Hobbes insisted that the revolutionary tenets of the New Testament were not to be followed publicly, but only privately: "For internall Faith is in its own nature invisible, and consequently exempted from all humane jurisdiction" (pp. 550–51). In fact, Hobbes argues that Christ's whole mission involved the lesson of subjection to one's sovereign: "For our Saviour Christ hath not given us new Laws, but Counsell to observe those wee are subject to; that is to say, the Laws of Nature, and the Laws of our severall Sovereigns" (p. 611). Finally, then, both Christ and Scriptures are co-opted as part of the civil state apparatus in Hobbes's final assessment: "And are not the Scriptures, in all places where they are Law, made Law by the Authority of the Common-wealth, and consequently, a part of the Civill Law?" (p. 701). Against this, we must set Milton's tenet that Christ's kingdom would overthrow all kingdoms—a tenet he held both in his prose and his poetry.

In the end, then, what appears to be a point of agreement between Hobbes and Milton actually proves to be a place of radical difference between the two thinkers. But what is especially worth noticing is that Hobbes's main political opponent in his argument for absolute sovereignty is the church. The church is a political force in Hobbes's scenario precisely in its ability to induce individuals to depart from civil law. Hobbes attempts to situate the church as a powerless institution within the absolute sovereignty. Milton, on the other hand, argues for the church's revolutionary place in human politics. He sees Christ's mission as founding the condi-

tions for establishing a new state, both in the hereafter and in the
here and now. Milton insists that Christianity is not just an argument for ecclesiastical or religious freedom, but also "even civil
liberty" (CM VIII, pp. 146–47). In an echo of Hobbes, Milton
wrote in 1659 that force ought not to subdue conscience, but
conscience ought to subdue and regulate force (YP VII, p. 257).
Of course, for Hobbes, faith is what individuals are allowed to act
out as their sovereign sees fit, while for Milton faith is untempered
by any worldly bridles and is what may indeed challenge any worldly
restraint. Notice what political force the church has in Hobbes's
argument; it makes wholly invalid the criticism that Milton in his
late works is retreating from politics because he returns to defining
the conditions of individual ethics. Hobbes fears that precisely
these individual ethics will be the most potent revolutionary forces
bringing about the demise of the state. According to what is implicit in Hobbes's scenario, then, Milton's arguments about how
Christ's mission is revolutionary is *political* (unless, of course, one
concedes that Hobbes, the midwife of political theory, was, say,
"post-political").

The primary point of difference between Hobbes and Milton
on the question of the place of religion in politics may be traced to
how each interprets Matthew xxiii, 21: "Render therefore unto
Cæsar the things which are Cæsar's; and unto God the things that
are God's." Hobbes takes the first clause at its face value and writes
that this is a simple declaration by Christ validating paying civil
taxes to the king when the king determines it necessary: "And that
the Kings word, is sufficient to take any thing from any Subject,
when there is need" (p. 259). Milton takes the second clause to
subvert the first and writes that Christ intends to say, rather, that
not all things belong to Caesar: "If indeed stamping or writing
availed so much to establish royal right, kings could instantly turn
all our property over to themselves by merely writing their names
upon it." Neither Hobbes nor Milton is attempting to suggest that
this passage refers just to taxes. From this interpretation, we see
that Hobbes writes that the subject must give up "any thing" to
the sovereign who so deems it necessary. And that "any thing," as
Hobbes develops his politics from this foundation, includes liberty: "The Liberty of a Subject, lyeth therefore only in those things,
which in regulating their actions, the Sovereign hath prætermitted" (p. 264). Milton was trying to prevent precisely this sort of

argument in his reading of the verse in question: "Our liberty is not Cæsar's, nay but God's own birthday gift to us; and to render unto any Cæsar you like this which we got not from him were an action most foul, most unworthy the origin of man" (CM VII, pp. 150–53). For Hobbes, then, the State ("Cæsar") must be superordinate to the church ("God"), while for Milton the order is exactly reversed. What is for Hobbes a part of the state apparatus is for Milton one of the few ways to contest the state's rights.

2. The State

Each thinker develops the liberties the subject of the state may be allowed in reference to his distinct interpretation of Matthew xxiii, 21. The basis of their hermeneutical differences concerns another question altogether—the properly political question regarding representation and authority. Each, that is, asks what the status of the person is in light of the state as a structure of power. For Hobbes, all citizens are subject to the absolute sovereign who becomes representative of their person and their authority. A person, Hobbes writes, "is he whose words or actions are considered, either as his own, or as representing the words or actions of an other man" (p. 217). If the words and actions are one's own, then the person is "Naturall." If the words and actions are representative of another, then the person is "Artificiall." Hobbes then makes the distinction between "Actor" and "Author." Whoever owns his or her own actions and words is the author; if the words and actions are owned by another, then the person is merely an actor. The state is the effect of reducing the many persons—actors and authors—to one person who then represents all (pp. 218–20). That happens with the establishment of the primary covenant of the commonwealth:

> The only way to erect such a Common Power . . . is, to conferre all their power and strength upon one Man, or upon one Assembly of men, that may reduce all their Wills, by plurality of voices, unto one Will: which is as much as to say, to appoint one man, or Assembly of men, to beare their Person; and every one to owne, and acknowledge himself to be the Author of whatsoever he that so beareth their Person, shall Act, or cause to be Acted, in those things which concerne the Common Peace and Safetie; and therein to submit their Wills, every one to his Will, and their Judgements, to his Judgment. (P. 227)

Simply put, what every citizen must do is give up his or her *will* and *judgment* and accept responsibility for whatever act the sovereign performs. The terms of the covenant Hobbes establishes run exactly counter to what Milton believed to be the basis of any covenant between a person and his or her God. The primary covenant between the person and the state representative, for Hobbes, runs as follows: "I Authorise and give up my Right of Governing my selfe to this Man." In the end, then, the least we may say about *Paradise Regained* is that Milton's insistence on self-rule is as much a statement of political activism as Hobbes's insistence on each citizen's renouncing self-rule.

Milton's ideas about representation, authority, and the place of individual responsibility run quite contrary to Hobbes's. Milton held that each person ought not to be represented by and therefore responsible for the actions of a single, absolute sovereign. In effect, this is God's pronouncement, and in his language he seems to be directly answering Hobbes. Adam and Eve, he says, "trespass, Authors to themselves in all / Both what they judge and what they choose" (*PL* III, 122–23). They are not "authors" of another's actions, but of their own, and nobody else can fulfill that authority. There exists no covenant in which they may submit their wills ("what they choose") or their judgments ("what they judge") to another. The possibility of that spurious covenant does not emerge until they lose their ability to maintain self-knowledge and until this failure is enacted at national levels. Hobbes had maintained that the liberty any citizen of the commonwealth might be entitled to is determined by the sovereign's will—this is the condition of being "subject to a sovereign." No citizen, Milton felt, should be "subject to" another human being; and, likewise, no human being should be responsible for subjecting another to his or her rule. Only God can make a human subject to his power. On the other hand, what Hobbes felt was the liberty only of the king, Milton felt was the liberty precisely of any person who had, by obeying God and gaining self-knowledge, made herself or himself a "subject of God." As Hobbes defines this regal prerogative, the sovereign "never wanteth Right to any thing, otherwise, than as he himself is the Subject of God, and bound thereby to observe the laws of Nature" (p. 265). Only the laws of nature limit the rights and powers of the absolute sovereign. In fact, to give us an idea of how loosely restrictive those laws of nature are, Hobbes states imme-

diately thereafter that a sovereign may command one of his innocent subjects to death for no reason without doing that subject any
"Injury." The idea behind each one's idea here is the question of
where law is properly constituted.

Whereas Milton maintains that the monarch is liable to civil
laws — and that therefore the execution of Charles was a legitimate
exercise of justice — Hobbes maintains that the sovereign "is not
Subject to the Civill Lawes" (p. 313). That is, Milton holds that
laws exist beyond an individual's jurisdiction of them while Hobbes
feels that the body of the sovereign was itself the constitution of
the law: "For to be subject to Lawes, is to be subject to the
Common-wealth, that is to the Sovereign Representative, that is to
himselfe; which is not subjection, but freedome from the Lawes"
(p. 367). In reply to precisely this idea, Milton answers with his
antinomian Christ. First of all, Michael tells Adam of the process
of being freed from the Mosaic Law: "to the Cross he nails thy
Enemies, / The Law that is against thee" (*PL* XII, 415–16). Second,
in *Paradise Regained,* Jesus' life becomes the constitution of the
antinomian state, and the major political statement of that life is
the importance of ruling oneself (precisely what Hobbes would
have every citizen forego). We can then understand why in *A Defence* Milton held that the king was subject to the law because he
could no longer rule himself. Quoting the ancient legal authority
Bracton, Milton notes: "Where passion rules, there is neither king
nor law" (YP IV, p. 492).[46] In Milton's political program, freedom
from the law, which is obtained by self-rule, which is in turn the
result of self-knowledge, is not the prerogative only of monarchs,
but of each and every citizen in the commonwealth: "He who
reigns within himself, and rules / Passions, Desires, and Fears, is
more a King" (*PR* II, 466–67). For Hobbes, the state is a formation based on the renunciation of each citizen's will and judgment
and self-government — in a word, each citizen's subjectivity. For
Milton, on the contrary, the state was a formation only insofar as it
allowed each citizen to express his or her will and judgment — that
is, only insofar as it did not interfere with a prior and more significant covenant between the individual and God. Their debate finally
comes down, then, to the question of the individual subject and
the place of that subject in relation to his or her "Passions, Desires,
and Fears."

3. The Individual

Hobbes held two things to be unconditionally durative—one at the personal level, and the other at the level of the commonwealth. First, he believed that all humans are desiring beings: "Life it selfe is but Motion, and can never be without Desire, nor without Feare" (p. 130). Hobbes manipulates human fear to argue for the usefulness of absolute sovereignty, and he uses desire as an incitement to that state. The other unconditionally durative thing in Hobbes's theory is subjection to the sovereign. The citizens of the commonwealth, having authorized the sovereign to rule over them, lose all rights to renounce that subjection. The citizen may not claim a covenant with God because the sovereign has now become the mediator between the citizen and God:

> And whereas some men have pretended for their disobedience to their Soveraign, a new Covenant, made, not with men, but with God; this also is unjust: for there is no Covenant with God, but by mediation of some body that representeth Gods Person; which none doth but Gods Lieutenant, who hath the Soveraignty under God. (P. 230)

There is, once the covenant is taken, no way of escaping it, even if the sovereign should commit horrendous iniquities, precisely because Hobbes has redefined any action of the sovereign's to be legal (and therefore not an iniquity). Therefore, as Hobbes triumphantly notes, "none of his Subjects, by any pretence of forfeiture, can be freed from his Subjection" (p. 230).

In Hobbes' scheme, then, the two things that appear to last the whole of the course of human life are personal desire and political subjection. In fact, according to Hobbes, desire and subjection come to an intersection at the level of language. "Law in generall, is not Counsell, but Command" (p. 312; cf. pp. 303, 346–47, 370–71). "The language of Desire . . . is Imperative . . . which when the party is obliged to do, or forbeare, is *Command*" (pp. 128–29). The key word, *command,* as we will see presently, is not only where desire and subjection meet, but where the differences regarding the relationship of desire and subjection between Milton and Hobbes are most manifest. Both thinkers agree that the two concepts reside well together, although for quite different reasons. According to Hobbes, because humans are "subject to desire novelty," they must be held under unending subjection to an absolute sovereign. Should they be able to pursue novelty—such as another form of government—the commonwealth would dissolve and they would return to the state of "meer Nature." As Hobbes writes, "the nature of this offence, consisteth in the renouncing of subjection; which is a relapse into the condition of warre" (p. 360; cf. p. 368).

Milton always held that the more thoroughly enthusiastic a royalist was, the more sacrilegious he seemed to be (see CM VIII, pp. 94–95). Salmasius, like Hobbes, suggested that Charles was the rightful mediator between humanity and God. Milton attempted at each stage of his career to free the church from that sort of civil mediation, and at the end of his career he found that he was left with a church of one person, subject to no civil body of restraint or mediation. In the end, Milton held that every individual must have his or her own covenant with God, and in *Paradise Regained* he offered the formal paradigm of that covenant's establishment. Like Hobbes, he felt he had to negotiate between the question of subjection and desire.

As I mentioned in chapter 1, the sort of charity Michael advises Adam to foster, and the sort of love Adam himself describes, has as its basis the potential for representing oneself to be in the presence of God (and therefore for imagining God to be in one's presence). What this sort of love entailed was precisely a transcendence of "desire." Hobbes stated that, "by Desire, we always signifie the Absence of the Object," and "by Love, most commonly the Presence of the same" (p. 119). Likewise, Adam answered Michael's final vision of the Second Coming with his new knowledge that it was best to "love with fear the only God, to walk / As ever in his presence" (*PL* XII, 562–63). His "love" allows him to imagine the "presence" of God and thereby allows him to attempt to allay all other transient "desires" based on "absence." God being imagined present, all other desires become, to that extent, undesirable (inasmuch as their Creator is present). That, in sum, is the sort of liberty Jesus advocates in *Paradise Regained*—the liberty from desire. Milton is answering Hobbes's insistence that such transcendence is impossible because, as Hobbes puts it, "to have no Desire, is to be Dead." Hobbes might be said to be in agreement with Milton inasmuch as the act of transcending desires involves a form of what early Christianity first termed "mortification," but it is hard to imagine that Hobbes would countenance that agreement very much. Hobbes maintains that a life without desire is truly death and no kind of life at all, while Milton holds that a life in which the individual mortified his or her desires was the only kind of life imaginable and the only way to true liberty.

We may define the direction each of these writers takes precisely on the issue of what sort of felicity is allowable and knowable in this life. Hobbes bases his assertion that life *is* desiring by referring only to this world and to the unknowability of the next: "What kind of Felicity God hath ordained to them that devoutly honour him, a man shall no sooner know, than enjoy" (p. 130). Milton, on the other hand, bases his assertion that we can transcend desire itself in our ability to transmute all instances of desiring (all our intimations of absences in our lives) by referring to the immediate presence of God in our selves precisely because of our ability "to know . . . God aright" (*PR* II, 475). Moreover, Milton feels that this knowledge and its attendant transformation of desire is the basis of liberty. In almost precisely the obverse argument, Hobbes maintains that such "deliberation," as he calls it, is just that—a "de-liberation," a loss of freedom operative on the individual's willing toward some action that would satisfy his or her appetite: "And it is called *Deliberation;* because it is a putting an end to the *Liberty* we had of doing, or omitting, according to our own Appetite, or Aversion" (p. 127).[47]

For Hobbes, desire is the condition of life, and subjection to an external sovereign that limits the liberties of an individual is one way to contain the desire for novelty, which, if taken far enough, can lead to a state of mere nature. Desire for Milton, although it is not always and in every way the condition of life, has a way of leading to subjection when taken to its limits. This is why every culture becomes externally enslaved only when it has already become enslaved to its own desires. Any culture's inability to *imagine* the presence of God—and instead requires the immediate illusion of his presence in the form of idols—is a form of desire that leads first to superstition and then, consequently, to political subjection. The way to avoid such subjection to an external force is to regulate internal desire at the personal and the national levels, and that is to make a covenant with God. An example of precisely this sort of covenant is found in *Areopagitica* when Milton proclaims: "How great a virtue is temperance, how much of moment through the whole life of man!" The regulation of desire, for Milton as for Hobbes, is where the personal and the political intersect.

For Hobbes, then, desire is regulated at the site of the sovereign, for Milton at the site of the church—and the "church" here for Milton, we must remember, is an individual relationship with God. To be a subject of God, for Milton, meant being subject to no other earthly power. For the individual who had gained self-knowledge by "knowing God . . . aright," there was no other mediator necessary; that subject had only to await the coming of Christ's kingdom. The model of that citizen was Jesus, the subject who rejected the kingdoms and established both the first covenant with God and the pattern of all future covenants. For Milton, then, the possibility of a heavenly politic made it necessary to resist any earthly force that might delimit the liberties of that citizen who was a subject of God. Hobbes was in full agreement with Milton on the point that nothing was more deleterious to civil authority than the hope of God's kingdom. But Hobbes attempted to limit the revolutionary power of this subject of God by proscribing any person's being a citizen of both England and heaven.

To those who argued that the soul was subject to higher authorities than the monarch, Hobbes first noted that, if this were the case, two separate kingdoms would have to share the same subjects: "There must needs be two Common-wealths, of one & the same Subjects; which is a Kingdome divided in it selfe, and cannot stand. For notwithstanding the insignificant distinction of *Temporall,* and *Ghostly,* they are still two Kingdomes, and every Subject is subject to two Masters" (p. 370). In such a situation, there would be two powers contesting their juridical authorities in maintaining two sets of laws, which would necessarily lead to a state of "Civill warre" (p. 371). In response to that potentially disruptive situation, Hobbes gives the authority for interpreting Scripture, indeed for deciding what is canonical in Scripture, solely to the sovereign. He pretends to grant God absolute authority over all things, but he places the grounds for discerning that authority within the power of the earthly sovereign:

It is true, that God is the Soveraign of all Soveraigns; and therefore, when he speaks to any Subject, he ought to be obeyed, whatsoever any earthly Potentate command to the contrary. But the question is not of obedience to God, but of *when,* and *what* God hath said; which to Subjects that have no supernaturall revelation, cannot be known, but by that naturall reason, which guided them, for the obtaining of

Peace and Justice, to obey the authority of their severall Common-wealths; that is to say, of their lawfull Soveraigns. (P. 415)

Because the interpretation of Scripture belongs solely to the sovereign, the way of knowing God's commands is limited to his mediation. Scripture was written, Hobbes writes, in order to "shew unto men the kingdome of God; and to prepare their mindes to become his obedient subjects" (p. 145). All this preparation, however, can occur only at the behest of the "Civill Soveraign" because he is the "Supreme Pastor, to whose charge the whole flock of his Subjects is committed" (p. 569).

In this extremely Erastian state, the Petrine Church becomes nothing but a cornerstone in a civil power structure. Commenting on Matthew xviii, 18, Hobbes notes that whatever power Christ granted Peter (in the role of church), in reality he granted only to the supreme monarch: "But howsoever this be interpreted, there is no doubt but the Power here granted belongs to all Supreme Pastors; such as are all Christian Civill Soveraignes in their own Dominions" (p. 579). And therefore, he continues, "Christian Kings have their Civill Power from God immediately" (p. 594). The recurrent phrase that Hobbes employs to justify his interpretation of Scripture is Christ's saying, "My kingdom is not of this world" (John xviii, 36; *Leviathan,* pp. 445, 447, 514–16, 625–26, 646). Because Christ's kingdom is not of this world, Hobbes argues, "by the *Kingdome of God,* is properly meant a Common-wealth, instituted (by the consent of those which were to be subject thereto) for their Civill Government" (p. 445). In the end, the Hobbesian state has made all revolutionary forces subordinate to the absolute sovereign. His power is the only recognizable power in the state, in matters of religion, and even in questions of life and death.

Milton, on the other hand, challenged the Erastian establishment because of its effect on the revolutionary power of the church, and he questioned the very concept of what Hobbes calls a "Christian King." In *A Defence,* written the same year as the *Leviathan,* Milton notes that "a king either is no Christian at all, or is the people's servant: if he would be lord and master out and out, he cannot at the same time be Christian" (CM VII, pp. 158–59). The absolute sovereign Hobbes is presenting as a Christian king is precisely one who would, according to Milton, be neither a king nor a Christian, but simply a tyrant. Moreover, Milton contests

Hobbes's reading of Christ's mission. Whereas Hobbes felt that Christ came to promote individual subjection to the reigning monarch (p. 611), Milton insisted that Christ came not only to offer inward freedom, but also political: "Who does not know that he put himself into the condition not only of a subject, but even of a servant, that we might be free? Nor is this to be understood of inward liberty only, to the exclusion of civil liberty" (CM VII, pp. 144–45). Religion, then, is not for Milton simply concerned with that "inward turn," but is also concerned with civil liberties, which properly belong to the realm of politics. And we should not miss the importance of the link between internal freedom from desire and external liberty from subjection, which is Milton's political theory from 1651 to 1671. What frees humanity from internal enemies and civil restraints is, of course, Christ's Crucifixion. And, we must recall the importance of Mary in the representation of the crucial moment in *Paradise Regained* when Jesus understands that his death is requisite for the liberation of humanity. In that moment of radical self-knowledge, Jesus is aided by his mother. In the question of family politics, too, Milton is in dialogue with Hobbes.

4. The Family

At the end of *Samson Agonistes,* Milton presents us with the state of Israel just after its liberation and just before its next subjection. It would become subject to another colonizing power, and eventually to an absolutist monarchy because of its inability to gain the self-knowledge which would allow it to transcend its own desires. Its subjection is related wholly to its being enslaved to desires that it cannot rule. Part of that subjection, as I argued in the last chapter, has to do with the patriarchal family structures obtaining for Samson and the Danite chorus. When the Chorus presented the two similes of the masculine dragon/eagle and the feminine phoenix, Manoa chose to regard only the masculine symbol, to dismiss the hope represented in the feminine simile of Jesus, and to invoke the ancient heroic model of the male's return "Home to his Fathers house" (S 1734). Jesus' self-knowledge, on the other hand, is complete because he is able to understand the role both his parents play in his life. The completeness of his self-knowledge is evinced at the end when he acknowledges Satan's offer of his "Fathers house" and yet returns "Home to his Mother's house" (*PR* IV, 549, 635).

According to its social historians, the European family by the sixteenth and seventeenth centuries had become the primary institution for regulating control over the individual subject. As Norbert Elias writes, only "then does the social dependence of the child on its parents become particularly important as a leverage for the socially required regulation and molding of impulses and emotions." In this period of European history, as Philippe Ariès maintains, we may begin to trace the family's utilitarian function — "to ensure disciplined, rational manners."[48] These "manners" are part of what Elias calls the "civilizing process," part of what we might call the legal apparatus ensuring maintenance of the law. We might compare Milton's Jesus and Samson with Hobbes's model of the family as a unit of political activity in particular reference to each one's family and each one's relationship to the law.

In the *Leviathan*, Hobbes argues for an interlocking relationship between family and state structures. Hobbes writes that "Dominion" is acquired by one of two ways, either by "Generation" or by "Conquest." The former interests Hobbes because it is the one that will allow him to make the case for the covenant involving the citizens of the commonwealth:

> The right of Dominion by Generation, is that, which the Parent hath over his Children; and it is called paternall. And is not so derived from the Generation, as if therefore the Parent had Dominion over his Child because he begat him; but from the Childs Consent, either expresse, or by other sufficient arguments declared. (P. 253)

Hobbes then employs his usual rhetorical gambit by distinguishing between the state of "Civill Law" and the state of "Civill warre." Here is where Hobbes's other formulation comes into more pertinent play. Hobbes now states that the state of "meer Nature" is the state of an absolute matriarchy:

> If there be no Contract, the Dominion is in the Mother. For in the condition of meer Nature, where there are no Matrimoniall lawes, it cannot be known who is the Father, unlesse it be declared by the Mother: and therefore the right of Dominion over the Child dependeth on her will, and is consequently hers. (P. 254)

The state of "meer Nature" now takes on its final anarchic form in Hobbes's political theory. What had been first presented as a war of every man against every man now becomes a matriarchal situation in which every child's survival depends on the whim of its mother, and no man's child is his own. That, Hobbes must have thought as he addressed England's patriarchs, was the clinching case for the viability of the absolute sovereign.

Having established this sharp distinction between the state of civil society and the state of nature in gendered terms, Hobbes goes on to argue that there is a covenant involved in this familial structure. The mother may choose to nourish or to expose the child; in the case of the former, she gains dominion over the child because the child owes obedience to whoever maintains its life. If she exposes the child, whoever saves and nourishes the child gains dominion over it because, as Hobbes writes, "preservation of life being the end, for which one man becomes subject to another, every man is supposed to promise obedience to him, in whose power it is to save, or destroy him." Whoever has dominion over the child also has dominion over all offspring issuing from that child when he or she matures. In this way, succession of subjects is ensured. After Hobbes concludes the analogy between the state and the family, he dismisses the thoroughness of the analogy by suggesting that, in some ways, every family is a "little Monarchy; whether that Family consists of a man and his children; or of a man and his servants; or of a man, and his children, and servants together: wherein the Father or Master is the Soveraign" (p. 257). The one possibility Hobbes refuses to consider is that of the mother's dominion.[49] In the Hobbesian cosmos, matriarchy is anarchy. Put another way, in this Hobbesian state, each citizen must, like Samson at the end, go "Home to his Fathers house."

Milton presents us with two different family structures and in implicit comparison with Hobbes we begin to see a pattern developing. The sort of patriarchal rule which Philistia is imposing on Israel will continue because of Israel's insistence on "Paternall dominion." The sort of revolution Israel might have been able to raise when Samson demolished the Philistine temple required precisely the self-knowledge they deny themselves by returning to traditional patriarchal values. The feminine phoenix suggests the hope of liberation that Jesus will instate—liberation from both internal and external subjection. But that feminine phoenix just does not signify for Manoa. Samson is taken back to his father's house, and the Chorus still sees Israel's citizens as "servants." In *Paradise Regained,* Jesus articulates another code of behavior, and it is one that requires embracing the significance of the mother. Jesus returns to his mother's house, he discovers his ultimate mission only by understanding what she has told him, and he is represented, in simile, as a feminine phoenix in the companion poem. Certainly it would be farfetched to say that *Paradise Regained* espouses matriarchy; it does not. But each example of Hobbes's "little Monarchy" was premised only on a father's rule; in each household, that is, the mother was simply written out, which is true of *Samson Agonistes* as well. Not only is this not the case in *Paradise Regained,* Mary, in fact, plays a prominent part in the narrative. This "little Monarchy" disputes every familial model Hobbes offers.

Each hero understands what the Law means in his life by reference to his family structure. Jesus reads the Law the first time unaided by any family member; what he discovers in it is an ethical guideline from which he develops his theory of the two ways of altering the state. He may either "subdue and quell" the enemies in order "to rescue *Israel* from the *Roman* yoke" through heroic acts or he may make winning words conquer willing hearts, and "make perswasion do the work of fear" (I, 210–26). When he reads the Law the second time, after his mother has told him what to look for, he discovers the truth of the Law by gaining an insight into who he is. This is the most radical act of self-knowledge Jesus undertakes, and this instance of self-knowledge allows him to recognize his mission, his destiny, and his role in cosmic history. That role becomes accessible to him only because his mother taught him how to read. And when he assumes that role, ironically, it will be in order to overturn the Law in which he discovered himself writ.

Samson, on the other hand, has received his information about the Law only from his father. And so, in an echo of Jesus' line, he can see only one way to act heroically: "Promise was that I / Should *Israel* from *Philistian* yoke deliver" (38–39). "Deliverance" for Samson always involves a show of strength; he never considers the option for intellectual persuasion of the sort Jesus will undertake. When a parent does offer advice to Samson about how to read his situation, it is neither helpful or comforting advice, but advice worried about only one thing:

> So *Dagon* shall be magnifi'd, and God,
> Besides whom is no God, compar'd with Idols,
> Disglorifi'd, blasphem'd, and had in scorn
> By th' Idolatrous rout amidst their wine;
> Which to have come to pass by means of thee,
> *Samson,* of all thy sufferings think the heaviest,
> Of all reproach the most with shame that ever
> Could have befall'n thee and thy Fathers house.   (441–48)

Manoa's concern is always the same throughout the tragedy—the "Fathers house" which the living Samson has shamed and to which the dead Samson will triumphantly be returned. As opposed to the parental advice that allows Jesus to gain a profound self-knowledge, Samson receives from Manoa only an incitement to further despair and a reiteration of the importance of the glory of the "Fathers house." It is, of course, precisely this "Fathers house" which Satan tempts Jesus with (IV, 549). In the end, both Samson and Jesus show their "Progeny"—one able to transcend the Law, the other obedient to its letter until his death.

After Hobbes has used the family analogy (and questioned its limits) to develop the case for dominion by generation, he takes up the other form of dominion by conquest. The analogy he employs here is that of a master-servant relationship:

> This Dominion is then acquired to the Victor, when the Vanquished, to avoyd the present stroke of death, covenanteth either in expresse words, or by other sufficient signes of the Will, that so long as his life, and the liberty of his body is allowed him, the Victor shall have the use thereof, at his pleasure. And after such Covenant made, the Vanquished is a servant, and not before." (P. 255)

The absolute sovereign, in this analogy, has unrelenting power over this servant/subject:

> The Master of the Servant, is Master also of all he hath; and may exact the use thereof; that is to say, of his goods, of his labour, of his servants, and of his children, as often as he shall think fit. For he

holdeth his life of his Master, by the covenant of obedience; that is, of owning, and authorising whatsoever the Master shall do. And in case the Master, if he refuse, kill him, or cast him into bonds, or otherwise punish him for his disobedience, he is himselfe the author of the same; and cannot accuse him of injury. (P. 256)

Hobbes concludes the chapter by using the scriptural scene in which God allows Israel a monarch (1 Sam. viii) to argue that monarchs must have absolute power: "This is absolute power, and summed up in the last words, *you shall be his servants*" (p. 258).

In sum, then, Hobbes presents us with a model of government in which citizens assume the positions either of sons or servants — either dominion by generation or dominion by conquest. But in either case there is unrelenting *subjection*. Hobbes concludes with two significant gestures. First of all, he states the only way of avoiding subjection to an absolute sovereign is to subject oneself to an even more absolute sovereign: "And whosoever thinking Soveraign power too great, will seek to make it lesse; must subject himselfe, to the Power, that can limit it; that is to say, to a greater" (p. 260). Second, he declares that political science has just been born: "The skill of making, and maintaining Common-wealths, consisteth in certain Rules, as doth Arithmetique and Geometry; not (as Tennis-play) on Practise onely: which Rules, neither poor men have the leisure, nor men that have had the leisure, have *hitherto* had the curiosity, or the method to find out" (p. 261, my italics).[50] In summary, then, Hobbes develops the theory of dominion by generation using the analogy of the family and presents the theory of dominion by conquest using the analogy of the master-servant relationship in order to articulate the conditions for escaping subjection by only more abject subjection and to claim the birth of a truly political science.

In offering as the sole alternative to an absolutist state an even more absolutist state, Hobbes was making his case unassailable. What Milton espoused, in response to this form of argument, is a subjectivity to what he considered the greatest power — God. That is, Milton argued that there was another form of revolution — and it is, indeed, the one on which Hobbes is consistently trying to foreclose the possibility — which consisted of foregoing subjection to the state by becoming a subject of God. Hobbes concluded the whole of *Leviathan* by returning to this point:

And because I find by divers English Books lately printed, that the Civill warres have not yet sufficiently taught men, in what point of time it is, that a Subject becomes obliged to the Conquerour; nor what is Conquest; nor how it comes about, that it obliges men to obey his Laws: Therefore for farther satisfaction of men therein, I say, the point of time, wherein a man becomes subject to a Conquerour, is that point, wherein having liberty to submit to him, he consenteth, either by express words, or by other sufficient sign, to be his Subject. (P. 719)

It is not clear whether Hobbes is suggesting submission to the republic or not, because he will go on to argue that some acts are required to cause the enemy's disequilibrium, but what is clear is that subjection is required for peace. Milton presented two models of the subject—Samson as the servant subject to God and Jesus as the Son who is a subject of God. Not only does Milton's usage of sons (dominion by generation) and servants (dominion by conquest) echo and answer Hobbes's, but in either case each hero eschews *subjection* to a state.

Samson scoffs at the notion of "absolute subjection" to the Philistines even as (and because) he is subject to God: "Masters commands come with a power resistless / To such as owe them absolute subjection" (1415–16). Jesus rejects the kingdoms because he is a subject of God. Subjection, he tells Satan, is the fate only of those who do not attain self-knowledge or strive for self-government, but instead *serve* their desires: "Subject himself to Anarchy within, / Or lawless passions in him which he serves" (II, 471–72). But, for either hero, Jesus or Samson, subjecting oneself to a higher power allows one to escape subjection to the state—Philistia or Rome. The escape for this subjection occurs at the level of the individual subject (Samson or Jesus), within a family structure (Manoa or Mary), in relation to a church-state power struggle, involving all four structures of power. We have seen how for Milton liberty from state subjection requires the transcendence of individual desire, involved with an act of significant self-knowledge, which is premised on a balanced familial situation. In the end, after the individual subjects have dealt with their own desires, and fit themselves into a complete family structure, the debate between the state and the church took on meaning at the level of the "Person."

Hobbes argues that the commonwealth must be represented by

one "Person," and whoever "carryeth this Person, is called sover-aigne" (p. 228). In this "Person" is reduced all the authority of each citizen of the commonwealth, "every one to owne, and acknowl-edge himselfe to be Author of whatsoever he that so beareth their Person, shall Act" (p. 227). Hobbes had also considered the one condition under which a church could refer to a single person: "And in this last sense only it is that the *Church* can be taken for one Person; that is to say, that it can be said to have power to will, to pronounce, to command, to be obeyed, to make laws, or to doe any other action whatsoever" (pp. 497–98). Hobbes quickly goes on to discount this definition by establishing another in which the church exists only at the sovereign's behest; that is, only the sover-eign can command, will, and be obeyed. Hobbes has reduced the church of one person to the person of the absolute sovereign. Against this Erastian state of personality, Milton responded two ways.

First, he discounted the absolute sovereign and argued that each person does indeed become a church of one precisely because each person is capable of willing and of judging; both Adam and Eve are "Authors to themselves," and Samson claims he is "Sole Author" (377). Second, Milton also reduced the commonwealth from a collective structure to a personal one, but, unlike Hobbes, he did so not by reducing the state to one "Author," but by making each "Author" a state. In 1654, Milton noted that the actions of one's fellow citizens, that is the actions of one's country, could be held with a degree of honor as reflective of one's own aspirations: "Who is there who considers not the honourable achievements of his country as his own" (CM VIII, pp. 6–7). The actions a state authors might be of significance to the person who is a citizen of that state, but by the end of the *Second Defence*, Milton will have already begun to repudiate those actions and to remove himself from their stain. In a private letter written twelve years later, Milton articulates what was implicit by the end of the 1654 tract and what becomes his consistent thinking thereafter — that, just as much as he considered himself to be a Church of One, so, too, did he consider himself to be a State of One: "One's country is wherev-er it is well with one" (CM XII, p. 115). *Contra* Hobbes, Milton does not reduce the church to the state and the state to a person who is sovereign, but rather situates both the state and the church in each person — or, more precisely, both in John Milton.

In his intricate self-representation between two heroes, one a subject of God the other subject to God, and neither subject to a state, Milton set down in an orderly fashion the preconditions not just for a reformed church, but also for a reformed state. Each individual is a church and a state, under the direct government of the only person who can govern the church and the final state of his kingdom—Jesus. Finally, then, the inward turn is not an escape from collective praxis; that praxis is exerted at a level of persons who are churches and states, persons whose self-knowledge will allow them collective salvation from subjection to the external state. In the end, then, perhaps Milton's final political act is to erect the state in the person. That is the notable shift from Milton in 1654 to what we may now, with renewed appreciation for his persistent politics, call the subject of late Milton. The person, then, in both Hobbes and Milton, is a site of political struggle. And the authority of that person comes down, finally, to the power of commanding. Also involved with the question of the authority of commanding are two other questions which I mentioned at the conclusion of chapter 1—the question of history and the question of reading.

The Empty Garden

Hobbes uses the scriptural account of the fall and its aftermath (Gen. iii) to develop the case that all subjects are subject to the commands of those who have the power to command them, masters or parents: "the Commands of them that have the right to command, are not by their Subjects to be censured, nor disputed" (p. 259). Hobbes wished to give the absolute sovereign mediation over all knowledge of God's will because he did not wish to posit two separate authorities contending over two sets of commands:

> Law, in generall, is not Counsell, but Command; nor a Command of any man to any man; but only of him, whose Command is addressed to one formerly obliged to obey him. . . . Which considered, I define Civill Law in this manner. civill law, *Is to every Subject, those Rules, which the Common-wealth hath Commanded him, by Word, Writing, or other sufficient Sign of the Will, to make use of, for the Distinction of Right, and Wrong; that is to say, of what is contrary, and what is not contrary to the Rule.* (P. 312)

If Christ's kingdom is allowed to exist contemporaneously with the absolute sovereign's, "both will have their Commands be observed as Law" (p. 371; cf. pp. 346–47, 291, 303). If the commands are contrary to each other, as Hobbes doubtless thought they would be, then the commonwealth would dissolve into factions and thereby return to a state of "meer Nature."

When setting up a scenario in which God's command might be obeyed in disobedience to the absolute sovereign's, Hobbes first notes that "God [is] our King, whom we are obliged to obey" when he commands (p. 306). Therefore, when God commands obedience, it must be done, "whatsoever any earthly Potentate command to the contrary." However, as he goes on to elaborate, God's command can be known only through the sanction of the earthly potentate, who is certainly not going to authorize a command contrary to his absolute power. Hobbes's final word on the interpretation of supernatural command is simple enough. Initially, he grants that "God may command a man by a supernaturall way." Whoever receives supernatural command must obey it once he or she has fully determined that the command does indeed come from God, which of course can be done only by referring to the absolute sovereign's interpretation of the status of that command. This, as I argued in the last chapter, is the political scenario of *Samson Agonistes*. There, too, Milton was demonstrating the difficulty of discerning which "commands" are to be obeyed.

Samson is confronted with the "command" of the Philistine lords and the contrary "command from Heav'n" in the form of the supernatural "rouzing motions" (*SA* 1641, 1213). He must choose which command is properly to be obeyed and to obey it. Hobbes attempted to prevent the sort of action Samson engages in by arguing that it is impossible to know whether or not commands come from heaven:

> It is manifest enough, that when a man receiveth two contrary Commands, and knows that one of them is Gods, he ought to obey that, and not the other, though it be the command even of his lawfull Soveraign (whether a Monarch, or a soveraign Assembly,) or the command of his Father. The difficulty therefore consisteth in this, that men when they are commanded in the name of God, know not in divers Cases, whether the command be from God, or whether he that commandeth, does but abuse Gods name for some private ends of his own. (P. 609)

Hobbes would suggest that God's commands are radically indeterminate; therefore, the only institution capable of ensuring that personal desire is not at the root of some delusion of being inspired is the absolute sovereign. Milton, on the other hand, shows how God may command perdition and destruction to such a "sovereign Assembly" as the Philistines through some of his servants. It is not so important for Milton whether the commands are wholly knowable or not, but that the state has no power to authorize them one way or the other. For that reason, Samson articulates his divine sanction enigmatically but solidly in contradiction to the state's commands.

So when the Philistine Officer issues the lords' request, his phrasing echoes Hobbes: "Dar'st thou at our sending and command / Dispute thy coming" (1405–06). Of course, the Philistine lords' commands prove to be mere fodder for Samson's last vestiges of wit: "Masters commands come with a power resistless / To such as owe them absolute subjection" (1415–16). That is what Milton had to say about the commands of those who had no right to command, and that, for Milton, as we shall see shortly, includes all human commands. Whereas Hobbes argues that supernatural revelation is radically indeterminate and makes it thereby impossible to assert divine sanction as an impetus to political action, Milton makes problematic the opposing question of the right of any person or group to command. In *Samson Agonistes,* the Philistine lords' commands are pathetic acts, even though these lords lead an absolutist colonizing force. The only effective command in the play is God's, and it is made through the receptacle of a rather self-centered Samson. In the companion poem, Satan's commands are futile except in governing his fallen angels. It is worth noting that Jesus is the only one able to command successfully in either poem.

Moreover, this "Assembly" of Philistines in its colonizing situation is precisely the model Hobbes had earlier presented when he first defined *monarchy*. When a people are "governed by an Assembly, not of their own choosing, 'tis a Monarchy; not of *One* man, over another man, but of one people, over another people" (p. 247). Samson is not just overthrowing a colonizing power, but a monarchy in the Hobbesian sense. When Milton discusses the liberty a subject of God enjoys, he explicitly condemns that very "command" which an earthly potentate might have over that subject. It would hardly be right, Milton scoffs in *A Treatise of Civil*

Power, "that our freedom should subject us to a more greevous yoke, the commandments of men" (YP VII, p. 263).[51] Samson is the representation of that anti-monarchical freedom from the "commands" of earthly potentates.

For Hobbes, on the other hand, Samson is not a model of either antimonarchical or anticolonizing force. He is an example of what sort of "extraordinary Zeal, and Courage" God might inspire in his servants in order that they might free God's people from servitude (p. 331). What is interesting is that Hobbes chooses not to use the word *commands* in his discussion of Samson or any of the judges. He thereby avoids giving historical examples of God's "command" contradicting that of an earthly potentate. More importantly, he uses the Book of Judges to demonstrate the validity of the absolute monarch. No matter what sort of "extraordinary Zeal" God gives to his judges, he does not thereby give them any authority over the "Sovereign Power" (p. 507). The priests, including the judges, still owe their allegiance to the absolute sovereign, "in all matters, both of Policy and Religion." Milton's representation of Samson suggests, *pace* Hobbes, that God does "command" certain individuals to act against the absolute sovereign and to overthrow that very sovereignty, which thereby does not possess authority in "all matters." Second, Hobbes uses the Book of Judges as an unassailable proof that monarchy is sanctioned by the Old Testament. Using that haunting phrase that concludes Judges — "there was in those dayes no King in Israel" — Hobbes argues that the onset of monarchy in Israel is a testament to God's willing an Erastian power to monarchs: "To the Judges, succeeded Kings: And whereas before, all authority, both in Religion, and Policy, was in the High Priest, so now it was all in the King" (p. 507). Milton maintains silence about what succeeded the judges; instead, he simply registers his reticence by having the Chorus allude both to the continuing servitude of Israel and to the companion poem, which delineates the preconditions for the end of that servitude.

Milton's Samson, when situated within Hobbesian political theory, becomes a political force against monarchy. His obedience to the "command from Heav'n" against the "command" from the Philistine lords is an act of civil disobedience of the sort Hobbes attempted to prevent. What allows Samson to act against the Philistine monarchy is the knowledge that Israel had historical precedent of being free. There was a time when there was no "*Philistian* yoke." Likewise, Jesus knows that there was a time when there was no "*Roman* yoke." What each of these references alludes to is what for both Hobbes and Milton constitute a primary site of disagreement—the "Norman yoke" and its historical significance in the modern political establishment—that is, the power to command rests on the historical right of the commander. Whereas Milton was silent about what occurred between the end of the judges and the birth of Jesus while Hobbes reported that history triumphantly, Hobbes now attempts to erase the history of the Norman yoke while Milton indulges in exploring its political significance.

Subjection for Hobbes requires one tacit agreement—and that is the willingness to forget the past. Since conquest means the *possession* of power, what had to be abrogated was the historical conditions of the origins of that possession. For history, in this sense, leads only to renewed conflict; if there was one conquest in history that subjected this people to this particular monarch, and this people were conscious of that historical development, then there could just as well be another conquest, this time by the people over this particular monarch. C. B. Macpherson suggests that the only flaw in the Hobbesian model's correspondence to the English possessive market society is Hobbes's failure to allow for the existence of "politically significant unequal classes."[52] To this we might tentatively add that the only flaw in the Hobbesian model's correspondence to the English political establishment is Hobbes's failure to determine when historical excavation was warranted (as in his establishing a covenant for the English nation) and when it was not (as in his political opponents' searching history to dispute that covenant). The ambiguity of his final expression of this point serves to suggest his uneasiness with it:

> One reason whereof (which I have not there [ch. 29] mentioned) is this, That they will all of them justifie the War, by which their Power was at first gotten, and whereon (as they think) their Right dependeth, and not on the Possession. As if, for example, the Right of the Kings of England did depend on the goodnesse of the cause of *William* the Conquerour, and upon their lineall, and directest Descent from him; by which means, there would perhaps be no tie of the Subjects obedience to their Sovereigns at this day in all the world: wherein whilest they needlessely think to justifie themselves, they justifie all the successful Rebellions that Ambition shall at any time raise against them, and their Successors. Therefore I put down for one

of the most effectuall seeds of the Death of any State, that the Conquerours require not onely a Submission of mens actions to them for the future, but also an Approbation of all their actions past; when there is scarce a Common-wealth in the world, whose beginnings can in conscience be justified. (Pp. 721–22)

What Hobbes seems to be saying here is that national amnesia is about the only way of maintaining any order. If a conquering power attempts to justify its conquest it only alerts the conquered of the possibility for a later conquest of its own. So in the very act of requiring the subjects' acquiescence to its assumption of power it leaves open the door for a future power struggle. However, Hobbes is not mentioning here that his own model of the covenant that establishes the Leviathan is based on a historical moment. When defining that historical moment, Hobbes uses the model of a commonwealth established by "Institution," by mutual agreement of the sort Milton had in mind in the seventh prolusion. But the English monarchy was historically established by conquest, by what he calls a "Common-wealth by *Acquisition*" (p. 228). This late reference to the actual historical conditions of England's monarchy—William the Conqueror—is not wholly disingenuous.

For Milton, although he is inconsistent in his 1649–1650 comments on the Norman yoke, did indeed in 1651 spend some space examining William the Conqueror's conquest. He concluded that, although William gained dominion by conquest, he did not presume to establish dominion by generation. In *A Defence,* Milton answers Salmasius's musings on William's covenant by citing the *Elogiorum Civium Cadomensium Centuria Prima* (1609):

His [William's] own words at his death, which I report as transcribed from the Caen book—a thoroughly trustworthy document—remove all doubt. "I appoint no man," says he, "heir of the kingdom of England." By which words that right of conquest and that right of inheritance were at once and together officially bewailed as dead, and buried together with the dead Conqueror. (CM VII, pp. 412–13; cf. YP IV, p. 480)[53]

Here Milton contests both means of establishing dominion, either by generation or by conquest. Like Hobbes, he knows that few commonwealths have been established in a justifiable manner. Whereas Hobbes would simply employ a conservative amnesia and keep things as they are, Milton undertakes an historical exploration in order to challenge the way things are. Nor is that his political method only in 1651.

In the 1671 volume he makes the same political gesture by recalling two historical episodes in the life of Israel. In one instance, he represents the overthrow of what Hobbes defines as a monarchy—the colonizing Philistines. In the other instance, he represents the establishment of Jesus' kingdom—and it is a kingdom, Milton intimates, whose establishment will stand up to historical examination. The Hobbesian state involves enduring political subjection and is based on an initial conquest and a continuing generation whose history ought not to be examined. In contrast, Milton presents us with a state involving a desire for self-knowledge and self-government and which is based on a covenant whose history must be remembered. It must be remembered because that, for Milton, is the way to reformation—the only way to see "primitive Christianity" clearly in spite of the muddy pool of custom. The key moment in the establishment of the covenant between humanity and God occurs when Jesus rejects the first of Satan's offers and notes the silencing of the oracles:

> henceforth Oracles are ceast,
> And thou no more with Pomp and Sacrifice
> Shalt be enquir'd at *Delphos* or elsewhere,
> At least in vain, for they shall find thee mute.
> God hath now sent his living Oracle
> Into the World, to teach his final will,
> And sends his Spirit of Truth henceforth to dwell
> In pious Hearts, an inward Oracle
> To all truths requisite for men to know. (*PR* I, 456–64)

By silencing the Delphic oracle and replacing it with an inward oracle, Jesus suggests the supercession of an Apollonian self-knowledge by a strictly Christian self-knowledge. Jesus attains that self-knowledge by reading the Law twice through and finding himself in it: "of whom they spake, / I am" (I, 262–63). It is a process of coming to self-knowledge that Milton enacted in his self-representation in the 1671 volume, and it is an act of self-knowledge that Milton was exhorting his readers to imitate. Such a premise of reading as an act of coming to self-knowledge is, of course, part of the humanist rhetorical tradition. Victoria Kahn astutely describes this tradition: "Reading is a form of prudence or of deliberative rhetoric and . . . a text is valuable insofar as it engages the reader in an activity of discrimination and thereby educates the faculty of practical reason or prudential judgment which is essential to the active life."[54] Both Hobbes and Milton were working within this tradition, and both Hobbes and Milton were contending for the same reader—the reader whose active political life would be one either of subjection or subjectivity.

It is just on the question of the reader's relationship to the *Leviathan* that we have one of the more interesting near-contemporary responses to Hobbes. In his *Characteristics,* Shaftesbury attempts to undermine the whole of the *Leviathan* by suggesting that when Hobbes offers the reader a book about how human nature is characterized by only self-interest, Hobbes is, in fact, showing a generous public spirit and thus undercutting his own premise about human nature: "'Tis directly against your interest to undeceive us and let us know that only private interest governs you, and that nothing nobler, or of a larger kind, should govern us whom you converse with." Indeed, he asks, is it "possible that one who has really discovered himself such, should take pains to communicate such a discovery?"[55] Shaftesbury, I think, is too eager to find a paradox in Hobbes. By publishing his political theory and its basis in a theory of human nature, Hobbes was not undermining that basis, but attempting to construct it by constructing two distinct readers.

It is true that Hobbes was working from his own self-examinations and expressing that act of self-knowledge as a text for public perusal. As I noted in chapter 1, he translates the Delphic phrase *Nosce Teipsum* as "Read thy self" (p. 82). He claims he has read himself and come to the conclusion that he could act as a pattern of such self-knowledge. The curious thing is that he is a pattern to be read not just by any citizen of the commonwealth, but by the absolute sovereign. Consider the address to the final reader of the *Leviathan:* "He that is to govern a whole Nation, must read in himself, not this, or that particular man; but Man-kind: which though it be hard to do, harder than to learn any Language, or Science; yet, when I shall have set down my own reading orderly, and perspicuously, the pains left another, will be onely to consider, if he also find not the same in himself. For this kind of Doctrine, admitteth no other Demonstration" (p. 83). We are left with this ambiguity about whether the reader is the absolute sovereign or any citizen — whether the lesson is that everyone must be subject to the sovereign or that the sovereign must subject everybody to his power. It is difficult to decide one way or the other by the evidence in the book. As Victoria Kahn has pointed out, part of the rhetorical strategy of the *Leviathan* is to involve the reader to the extent that reading the text mirrors the process of constructing the commonwealth.[56]

If Hobbes's task were indeed to perform this rhetorical feat, and I agree with Kahn that it was, then he had to construct a reading situation in which both the sovereign and the citizen could read themselves. In answer to Shaftesbury's question, then, we would have to posit Hobbes's theory about the epistemic capacity of the common citizen, a theory later expressed in more famous form by John Locke. The "Common-peoples minds," Hobbes wrote, "are like clean paper, fit to receive whatsoever by Publique Authority shall be imprinted in them" (p. 379). The reason Hobbes does write about selfish human nature is not to demonstrate his own generosity, but to imprint the idea of the Leviathan on the minds of those who would otherwise be influenced by other political pens. Given the premise of a reader who is a "blank sheet," Hobbes's text constructs a political subject. Every citizen must read in himself or herself what Hobbes read in himself — that durative subjection to a state power is the best and perhaps only way of maintaining peace. Also, the absolute sovereign must read in himself what degree of power he must exert in maintaining his subjects' subjection. Each of the readers of the *Leviathan* assumes a place in the commonwealth by assuming a reading relationship to the text theorizing its establishment. A crucial point of these two readers' intersection is the passage I quoted above concerning the dangers of historical exploration. Monarchs should not wish to explain the origins of their power, nor ought citizens to inquire into those origins. Against this point, Milton establishes his theory about his ideal reader.

I have already mentioned that Milton believed every individual should have the rights Hobbes felt were solely the absolute sovereign's — the right to obey natural law, to will, and to judge. So, in this instance, Milton produces his text so that every individual would know what Hobbes wanted only the absolute sovereign to know — the origin of the power to command.

The example of such historical inquiry is Jesus. In his answer to the offer of the kingdoms, he excoriates Satan's suggestion about what sorts of power these kingdoms would give him, and instead refers to the one source of all commands: "It is written / The first of all Commandments, Thou shalt worship / The Lord thy God, and only him shalt serve" (IV, 175–77). The only text on which Jesus draws is Scripture. The only command to be obeyed is God's. The inward oracle Jesus had earlier invoked provides the "spirit" required to gain true self-knowledge, the kind of self-knowledge that has God as its ultimate source and destination and the kind of self-knowledge eventually leading to true self-government, where everyone commands himself or herself. As I argued in chapter 2, the ability to read with "spirit" characterizes the ideal, angelic reader of *Paradise Regained*. Now we see that reading with "spirit" is precisely what is necessary as a means of escaping the "material" state of Hobbes's Leviathan.

In that spirit, the readers of *Paradise Regained* are presented not only with an ideal reader in Jesus, but also with the object of their own historical excavations—his life. Unlike Hobbes, then, Milton does invoke history as a means of discovery. Jesus' life may be examined and reexamined without endangering the power of his state. Milton would agree with Hobbes that most political establishments cannot withstand overhard scrutiny; the history of the assumption of power is always displeasing to those subject to that power. Scrutinizing the life of Jesus, as Milton represents it, is rewarding only because it shows each individual the path to subjectivity. Just as Jesus reads about himself in the Law, so does Milton suggest that in *Paradise Regained* every reader would find himself or herself. In his representation of the politics of the regained paradise, unlike the politics of the Leviathan, Milton does not construct readers under subjection and proscribed from analyzing history; rather, he constructs readers who are subjects and who will discover that in the analysis of history. It is, in the end, the reason Milton's mature political statements take on narrative form. As Peter Brooks has written of the politics of narrative design, "it is important to consider not only what a narrative is, but what it is for, and what its stakes are: why it is told, what aims it may manifest and conceal, what it seeks not only to say but to do." The final dynamic of such narrative art is its transference, "in which the reader is solicited not only to understand the story, but to complete it."[57]

In 1654, Milton concluded his *Second Defence* by invoking the citizens of England to complete the fabric of their republic; in 1671, Milton concludes his *Paradise Regained* by invoking the citizens who would occupy the regained paradise to do so by imitating the object of their historical study. For, in the end, Milton's representation of Jesus does not differ in motive from Thomas à Kempis's *Imitatio Christi*. As à Kempis writes, "Verily, there I am where my cogitation is." To imitate Christ, à Kempis notes, is the way to gain true self-knowledge: "For that is true victory, to triumphe over a mans selfe."[58] Self-knowledge as self-rule—that might be the summary description of the personal-political program of Milton's final work:

> But to guide Nations in the way of truth
> By saving Doctrine, and from errour lead
> To know, and knowing worship God aright,
> Is yet more Kingly, this attracts the Soul,
> Governs the inner man, the nobler part,
> That other o're the body only reigns,
> And oft by force, which to a generous mind
> So reigning can be no sincere delight.   (II, 473–80)

Christ's kingdom, Milton would agree with Hobbes, is not of this world, but it has ramifications for this world, and first and foremost of these is that whoever is a subject of God is never going to suffer subjection to a state power. Conscience, in the end, will always subdue force.

It would be helpful to remind ourselves of the hermeneutical definition of politics I cited earlier: "For cultural analysis and criticism, the contesting of the meaning of things or events is what centrally constitutes politics." With due respect to Jameson, then, we must conclude that Milton's *Paradise Regained* is not "postpolitical." It situates itself, first of all, as political by this hermeneutical definition. Milton explores the meaning of two historical events, against the proscription of historical exploration Hobbes attempted to issue, in order to contest the notion of enduring subjection. It is also political, in the second instance, by a definition of politics Jameson attempted to deny, by Milton's situating the political in relation to the familial and the personal. There are "inward turns" in *Paradise Regained,* no doubt, but their meaning is not what Jameson suggests; they do not just signify a concern with personal salvation. The inward turn of the oracle argues for a Christian self-knowledge that will promote a Christian self-government, and this self-government is necessary for avoiding subjection to desire or to an absolutist state:

> Yet he who reigns within himself, and rules
> Passions, Desires, and Fears, is more a King;
> Which every wise and vertuous man attains:
> And who attains not, ill aspires to rule
> Cities of men, or head-strong Multitudes,
> Subject himself to Anarchy within,
> Or lawless passions in him which he serves.   (II, 466–72)

The way to national liberty is through personal probity. Without that inward turn, without a renewed self-knowledge at the personal level, civil liberty just would not endure. At the end of the 1654 *Second Defence,* Milton addresses the nation as a whole and advises it to gain self-knowledge if it would remain free from monarchy: "If it be hard, if it be against the grain, to be slaves, learn to obey right reason, to be masters of yourselves" (CM VIII, pp. 250–51). He presents in 1671 a model of that right reason and of self-mastery, a model that has constantly to be read and reread.

Hobbes requested his readers to peruse the book in order to see how they might find Hobbes's act of self-knowledge also "the same in himself. For this kind of Doctrine, admitteth no other Demonstration." Milton, like Hobbes, was representing himself and his self-knowledge in this narrative. Hobbes, however, would have his two readers—the citizen and the sovereign—read for radically different purposes: one to learn subjection, the other to learn how to subject. Milton writes only for the spiritual and angelic reader, who will learn subjectivity. The reader will learn to be a subject of God in precisely the same way that the angels learn. As Raphael states this practice of education, God habituates his angels to obey and to love him:

> But us he sends upon his high behests,
> For state, as Sovran King, and to enure
> Our prompt obedience.   (*PL* VIII, 238–40)

This is a succinct expression of Milton's politics. The state worth being a subject of is God's, and only God's. Moreover, each subject's final conception of selfhood is a product of one's self-representation in relation to God. By the time Satan reaches Mount Niphates, he can say only "Myself am Hell" because he cannot imagine himself loving God. Adam will regain a "paradise within," Michael tells him, precisely by loving God. Each reader of *Paradise Regained*, Milton intimates, will enjoy that same "paradise within," which is the precondition for substantial liberty and enduring political action when that reader reads like an angel.

It is fit, then, that the angelic chorus which had introduced us to the action—which had become our focalizer—should be the same agent for summing up the lesson of that action, which is represented in its use of imagery. The angels end the narrative with a song of victory in which they sing that Jesus has avenged the supplanted Adam, and now "regain'd lost Paradise" (IV, 602–04). From here on in, Satan will dare not set foot in Paradise to tempt:

> For though that seat of earthly bliss be fail'd,
> A fairer Paradise is founded now
> For *Adam* and his chosen Sons, whom thou
> A Saviour art come down to re-install.   (IV, 608–11)

Here, then, in this poem that made the representation of time problematic—in the way Satan was displaced in time both epistemologically and literally, in the way that presence was consistently invoked ("Now"), and in the way that the scene of anagnorisis was written beyond the temporal frame of the narrative—is the confusing temporal setting of this final statement. Satan's snares are broken, and he will henceforth tempt no one in Paradise—a paradise which has just been "founded now." But though founded now, it is both without occupant and without security from Satan. The angelic chorus frustrates the promise of the present with a reiterated sense of futurity. This fairer paradise is "Where they shall dwell secure, when time shall be / Of Tempter and Temptation without fear" (IV, 612–13). The hymn, as Barbara Lewalski astutely points out, prefigures Jesus' entire mission and office in history "by ambiguities of tense and conflations of time, by means of which Christ's nature is celebrated as already fully manifested, and his office is celebrated as already achieved but also as just beginning."[59] So, after his combat and victory, Jesus is sent away with the echoing sound telling of another threshold he must cross: "Now enter, and begin to save mankind" (IV, 631).

The garden, then, is empty—save for the exalted second Adam. The restoration of Paradise does not mean its repopulation—not yet. Thomas Playfere notes that this crucial moment in cosmic history may be appreciated by considering the movement between covenants in terms of gardens: "Truth it is, touching the Synagogue of the Jewes, Christ saith, My sister, my spouse is as a garden enclosed . . . But now . . . this enclosed garden hath beene turned into an open field . . . of *all* the whole world."[60] For Milton, the garden was now open to Adam's *chosen* children. Potentially available to all, the garden would be populated, when the time came, by only a few. In the interim, it is empty save for the exalted man. Naturally, the garden and the wilderness play a crucial role in Judeo-Christian thought. Thomas Taylor allows us some insight here:

> In opposition to the first *Adam*, who was tempted in paradise, a place in all the world the strongest and fittest to resist temptation in; and beeing overcome was cast out thence into the wildernes, as all the world was in comparison. But the second *Adam* to recover this losse, encountreth with Satan in a wildernesse; the fittest place in the world to be overcome in, and overcoming restoreth us to the heavenly paradise againe.

But, as David Masson notes, there "was no restored Eden upon earth even while Milton lived and wrote."[61] Not yet, Milton might have answered. First of all, each reader must read this symbolic narrative and strive to attain self-knowledge at the individual level. The return to an empty garden is a return to the person, to the self in the act of becoming subject. This empty garden is the symbol, finally, for the reordering of political action.

In 1651, Milton celebrated the political act of a collective, an act that was in past ages the prerogative only of individual heroes: "The people dared to perform in common such an act as in other lands is thought possible only for great-hearted men of old" (YP IV, p. 336; cf. CM VII, pp. 64–65). In 1654, Milton saw that this celebration of collective praxis was premature. The "people" could not maintain the freedom resulting from their initial act because they had not yet, as individuals, come to an adequate degree of self-knowledge. Addressing the same state that had been heroic in his eyes three years before, Milton advises returning to a renewed attempt at national self-knowledge: "A nation which cannot rule and govern itself, but has delivered itself into slavery to its own lusts, is enslaved also to other masters whom it does not choose, and serves not only voluntarily but also against its will" (YP IV, p. 684; cf. CM VIII, pp. 250–51). In 1651, Milton praised the movement from individual heroes to collective praxis; in 1654, Milton proposed a movement from collective praxis based on no solid foundation to individual acts of self-knowledge. In 1671, Milton reoriented politics back to that personal level; the empty garden which only the chosen subjects would inhabit is the symbol of that meditative act of self-knowledge.

At the very end of his meditation on the Incarnation, Milton left his contemplative hero physically at the threshold of his mother's house, historically at the onset of a new dispensation, and morally alone in a regained paradise. This is the fit conclusion to a meditative poem and the fit repose of a contemplative hero. The foremost exponent of the native English meditative tradition wrote: "Christ was used to a solitary garden."[62] In his greatest poem, Milton described how the garden came to be empty; in his second greatest poem, he outlined the means by which it could be regained. The garden, like the kingdom with which it had been in constant association throughout this narrative, would remain empty until a sufficient number of readers might begin to inhabit it, until the nation gained the sort of self-knowledge Jesus demonstrates and Milton enacts.

This is for both hero and author, emphatically, the third form of self-knowledge, the knowledge of a represented self, the self-knowledge Milton arrives at in the dialogue between the two final works of his poetic career and in the implicit dialogue with the scientific model's foremost theorist. Hobbes proclaimed he reached this self-knowledge in reading himself. In either case, the author is soliciting our political engagement; in each case, the author is forming each of us as a cultural subject. Hobbes is saying, "Know yourself to be determined and act as if you were." Milton is responding, "Know yourself to be free and act as if you were." Both are suggesting that knowledge can transform experience, and hence both are political in the same way. Hobbes and Milton are suggesting that self-knowledge, in our world, can take on only its third form, that of representation. The basic difference, the difference between the culture of the Leviathan and the culture of the empty garden, is that Hobbes declared in a tract of political science that all subjects were under subjection to their absolute sovereign, while Milton demonstrated in a political narrative why all subjects have a choice about their subjectivity.

NOTES

INDEX

NOTES

"The greatest part of a writer's time is spent in reading, in order to write: a man will turn over half a library to make one book."

—*Dr. Johnson (1775)*

A NOTE ON TEXTS

Parts of the second section of chapter 2 are taken from my essay, "Of *Paradise Regained:* The Interpretation of Career," which appeared in quite different form in *Milton Studies* XXIV, ed. James D. Simmonds (Pittsburgh, 1988), pp. 253–75. Most of the first section of chapter 3 is from my "'In Dubious Battle': Skepticism and Fideism in *Paradise Regained,*" which appeared in somewhat revised form in *The Huntington Library Quarterly* LIII, no. 2 (1990), 95–118. Scattered paragraphs throughout chapter 4 are taken from my "According to Samson's Command: Some Contexts of Milton's Tragedy," *Milton Quarterly* XXVI, no. 3. I would like to thank the editors, James D. Simmonds, Guilland Sutherland, and Roy Flannagan, respectively, for their kindness in allowing me to reprint the material here.

All quotations from *Paradise Regained* and *Samson Agonistes* are taken from the 1671 edition. Unless otherwise noted, all quotations from Milton's other poetry are taken from *John Milton: Complete Poems and Major Prose,* ed. Merritt Y. Hughes (Indianapolis, 1957). Sometimes I will cite from *The Poems of John Milton,* ed. John Carey and Alastair Fowler (London, 1968). Unless otherwise noted, quotations from Milton's prose are taken from *The Works of John Milton,* 18 vols., ed. Frank Allen Patterson et al. (New York, 1931–38). This edition will be cited as CM in the text and notes. I will also cite from *The Complete Prose Works of John Milton,* 8 vols., ed. Don M. Wolfe et al. (New Haven, 1953–82), which will be cited as YP in the text and in the footnotes. I will be citing all quotations from the poetry parenthetically using the traditional abbreviations: *PL* for *Paradise Lost*, *PR* for *Paradise Regained, SA* for *Samson Agonistes,* and *Nat.* for the Nativity ode.

The marginal line indicators in both poems in the 1671 volume are often incorrect. Rather than silently emend the compositors' mistakes, I have faithfully registered the erroneous line numbers in my citations. In this way, anyone wishing to refer to the 1671 edition will find it easier to do so. Briefly, the compositors' mistakes are as follows in *Paradise Regained:* in Book III, the marginal notation for line 270 is set beside verse 271 and is correspondingly incorrect until the end of the book; in Book IV, the marginal notation for line 210 is set beside verse 212, for 220 beside 223, and for 600 beside 604. In *Samson Agonistes,* there are a variety of these same errors (which are not worth noting). On the whole, though, I do not think my references will disorient the reader who refers to a modern edition.

Quotations from Chrysostom and Augustine are usually, but not always, taken from the *Select Library of Nicene and Post-Nicene Fathers,* cited as *NPNF* in the notes. All quotations from the Bible, unless otherwise noted, are taken from the Authorized Version. All translations, unless otherwise noted, are mine.

I have retained the original spelling and punctuation in quotations from seventeenth-century texts. I have, however, brought into conformity with modern usage the orthography of *i-j* and *u-v,* as well as silently inserting the appropriate *m* or *n* when the diacritical mark on the preceding vowel signifies such a value.

NOTES TO PREFACE

1. I must explain my comments about Rowse because I may actually tempt someone to read the book by making it sound more enticing than it is. As to the first desire, that Milton thought he was God, Rowse has pronounced, in *Milton and the Puritan: Portrait of a Mind* (London, 1977) with the sort of intuitive knowledge that belongs to his subject, that, for Milton, "'God' was but a projection of his own ego"; "God . . . God . . . God: we have seen that this is a simple equation with Milton" (pp. 58, 97). As to the second desire, let me indulge myself a bit. As is well known, John Philips noted in *The Life of Mr. John Milton* in *The Early Lives of Milton,* ed. Helen Darbishire (London, 1932), that when Milton woke up he had a mind full of verses to recite to his amanuensis. When the amanuensis was tardy, Milton would complain, saying that "hee

wanted to bee milkd" (p. 633). To this comment, responds our sage Rowse: "Isn't there something unconsciously feminine about that?" (p. 279). Ah, here is criticism of the old school—there is nothing to be found of that foolishness of distinguishing between the characteristics of the feminine and the bovine, not for the good professor. Here, we get the epitome of womanhood—ambulatory lactation. Here, more seriously, we get what I like to offer to my students as an example of what *can* be done with a mind.

2. Clifford Geertz, *The Interpretation of Cultures: Selected Essays* (New York, 1973), p. 49. Mircea Eliade, *The Sacred and the Profane: The Nature of Religion,* trans. Willard R. Trask (San Diego, 1959), p. 21.

3. Mary Douglas, *Purity and Danger: An Analysis of the Concepts of Pollution and Taboo* (London, 1966), p. 128.

4. Kenneth Burke, *A Grammar of Motives,* in *"A Grammar of Motives" and "A Rhetoric of Motives"* (1945; rpt. Cleveland, 1962), p. 508.

5. Walter Raleigh, *Milton* (London, 1900), p. 88. Fredric Jameson, "Religion and Ideology: A Political Reading of *Paradise Lost,*" in *Literature, Politics, and Theory: Papers from the Essex Conference, 1976–84,* ed. Francis Barker et al. (London, 1986), pp. 35–56, esp. p. 35.

1. CONFRONTING THE SUBJECT: THE ART OF SELF-KNOWLEDGE

1. Raymond Williams, *Keywords: A Vocabulary of Culture and Society,* rev. ed. (1976; rpt. New York, 1983), pp. 87–93; Frank Lentricchia, *Criticism and Social Change* (1983; rpt. Chicago, 1985), p. 14; Milton, YP VII, p. 460.

2. The passage in the first edition of *The Readie and Easie Way* (February 1660) runs as follows: "This would soon spread much more knowledge and civilitie, yea religion, through all parts of the land: this would soon make the whole nation more industrious, more ingenuous at home, more potent, more honourable abroad" (p. 384); YP 7, pp. 383, 458.

3. The Latin is as follows: "restitutum nempe civilen liberúmque vitæ cultum, per urbes, per regna, pérque nationes disseminare." The Yale translator renders "cultum" as "civilization" instead of "culture" (YP IV, p. 556).

4. Mary Douglas, *Purity and Danger: An Analysis of the Concepts of Pollution and Taboo* (1966; rpt. London, 1984), p. 128; Matthew Arnold, *Culture and Anarchy: An Essay in Political and Social Criticism,* ed. Ian Gregor (1869; rpt. Indianapolis, 1971), pp. 5–6. This definition is, of course, only the first and most famous of Arnold's attempts to circumscribe "culture"; to arrive at his fullest definition requires tracing the accretions he makes to this original one. It is important for my interest

only that we have before us the interrelatedness of thought and habit, which Arnold explicitly expresses here. Raymond Williams, *Culture and Society 1780–1950* (1958; rpt. Harmondsworth, 1963), pp. 17–18. See also Williams, *Keywords*, p. 127: "experience" is "part of that general movement which underlies the development of culture."

5. Fredric Jameson, *The Political Unconscious: Narrative as a Socially Symbolic Act* (Ithaca, N.Y., 1981), pp. 10, 19; Sigmund Freud, *The Future of an Illusion* (1927) and *Civilization and Its Discontents* (1930), both in *The Pelican Freud Library*, 15 vols., trans. and ed. James Strachey (Harmondsworth, 1973–1986), vol. XII, 183–241; pp. 251–340. All quotations from Freud's works will be taken from this edition, which hereafter will be cited as *PFL;* Burke, *Grammar of Motives*, pp. 74–75.

6. William James, "Brute and Human Intellect," in *The Works of William James*, 17 vols., ed. Frederick H. Burkhardt et al. (Cambridge, Mass., 1975–88), vol. XIII, pp. 1–37; Jerome Bruner, *Actual Minds, Possible Worlds* (Cambridge, Mass., 1986), pp. 11–43. Compare Hayden White, *The Content of the Form: Narrative Discourse and Historical Representation* (Baltimore, 1987), p. 26:

> whatever else a science may be, it is also a practice that must be as critical about the way it describes its objects of study as it is about the way it explains their structures and processes. Viewing modern sciences from this perspective, we can trace their development in terms of their progressive demotion of the narrative mode of representation in their descriptions of the phenomena that their specific objects of study comprise.

Burke, *Grammar of Motives*, pp. 29, 73, 147, 188, 225–26, makes his distinction between "dramatism" (which he also calls "dialectic") and "scientism." Although what I am calling "narrative" does not conform exactly to what Burke calls "dramatism," nor does what I am calling "science" to what he calls "scientism," I am generally indebted to his *Grammar of Motives,* and specifically indebted to his distinction between the two forms of knowledge.

7. On the actor-activity ration and the setting-actor-activity ratio, see Burke, *Grammar of Motives*, pp. xvii–xxv, 3–11, 127–274. Clifford Geertz, *The Interpretation of Cultures* (New York, 1973), pp. 33–54, expresses succinctly the basic premise implicit in anthropology as a discipline: "there is no such thing as a human nature independent of culture."

8. Ernst Cassirer, *An Essay on Man: An Introduction to a Philosophy of Human Culture* (New Haven, 1962), pp. 1–22; Sir John Davies, *Nosce Teipsum* [1599], in *Silver Poets of the Sixteenth Century*, ed. Gerald Bullett (London, 1947), pp. 343–401.

9. Cassirer, *Essay on Man*, pp. 4–5, 6–9, 10–12. Heraclitus's dictum is fragment 101 in H. Diels' *Die fragmente der Vorsokratiker*, 5th ed., ed. W. Kranz (Berlin, 1934), 1, 173. I have used the translation in G. S. Kirk and J. E. Raven, *The Presocratic Philosophers: A Critical History with a Selection of Texts* (Cambridge, 1957), p. 212. Cassirer translates the Greek as "I have sought for myself" (p. 4). The Heraclitian logos is described in fragments 1, 2, and 50; see Kirk and Raven, *Presocratic Philosophers*, pp. 187–88. Plato, *Phaedrus*, 230a, in *The Collected Dialogues of Plato*, ed. Edith Hamilton and Huntington Cairns (Princeton, 1961), pp. 476–525. For the Platonic logos, see *Republic*, Book 6, 511a–e, and *Philebus*, 58b–67b, both in *Collected Dialogues*, pp. 746–47, 1014–50. I will discuss the Christian model of self-knowledge throughout this study. For the distinction between "l'esprit géométrique," and "l'esprit de finesse," see Pascal, "De l'esprit géométrique, and the *Pensées*, ed. Charles Louandre (Paris, 1858), p. 231; quoted in Cassirer, *An Essay*, p. 10*n*15.

10. Freud, *Three Essays on the Theory of Sexuality*, in *PFL* VII, pp. 39–169: "There are thus good reasons why a child sucking at his mother's breast has become the prototype of every relation of love. The finding of an object is in fact a refinding of it" (pp. 144–45). Freud's additions to the 1920 edition of this treatise begin to contradict this argument (see esp. p. 158); see also Freud, *On Transformations of Instinct as Exemplified in Anal Erotism*, *PFL* VII, pp. 295–302, in which defecation begins to assume a more prominent place in the baby's perceptual distinction between self and the voided Other. I discuss Freud's arguments about the perceptual distinction between self and Other in terms of defecation in another article, "A New Emetics of Interpretation: Swift, His Critics, and the Alimentary Canal," *Mosaic: A Journal for the Interdisciplinary Study of Literature* XXIV, nos. 3–4 (1991), 1–32.

11. Miguel de Cervantes, *The Adventures of Don Quixote*, trans. J. M. Cohen (Harmondsworth, 1950), p. 682. For a study of the self/Other distinction in this novel, see René Girard, *Deceit, Desire, and the Novel: Self and Other in Literary Structure*, trans. Yvonne Freccero (1961; rpt. Baltimore, 1965), pp. 1–82. Specifically on the theme of enchantment as a device for self-representation, see Erich Auerbach, *Mimesis: The Representation of Reality in Western Literature*, trans. Willard R. Trask (1946; rpt. Princeton, 1953), pp. 334–58. It is worth noting that the most famous reversal of this primary distinction, Bishop Berkeley's reformation of the order of perception, does not alter the basic principles involved in this first act of self-definition. When Berkeley insists that "esse est percipi" ("to be is to be perceived"), he only changes the priority of the self and the Other; he does not in any way alter the fact that perception is the primary act of becoming subjective. Another example of this primary distinction is what Heidegger calls Dasein's "de-severance," which "dis-

covers remoteness; and remoteness, like distance, is a determinate categorical characteristic of entities whose nature is not that of Dasein." See Martin Heidegger, *Being and Time,* trans. John Macquarrie and Edward Robinson (Oxford, 1962), pp. 139–45.

12. A. R. Luria, *The Man with the Shattered World: The History of a Brain Wound,* trans. Lynn Solotaroff (1972; rpt. Cambridge, Mass., 1987), p. 66; cf. pp. 141, 99: "I've become a completely different person." For Luria's diagnosis, see pp. 21–35.

13. George Herbert Mead, *Mind, Self, and Society: From the Standpoint of a Social Behaviorist,* ed. Charles W. Morris (Chicago, 1934), p. 142: "The self, as that which can be an object to itself, is essentially a social structure, and it arises in social experience" (p. 140). The most brilliant literary employment of this concept is Richard Lanham's discussion of *sprezzatura;* see *The Motives of Eloquence: Literary Rhetoric in the Renaissance* (New Haven, 1974), pp. 144–64.

14. William James, *The Principles of Psychology,* 2 vols. (1890; rpt. New York, 1950), vol. II, pp. 321.

15. Werner Jaeger, *Paideia: The Ideals of Greek Culture,* 2 vols. (Oxford, 1941), vol. II, p. 144; Lanham, *Motives of Eloquence,* pp. 1–35. Lanham, following and developing on Jaeger's distinction between philosophy and rhetoric, calls this model the "rhetorical ideal of life."

16. I refer to the sort of legal philosophy that proposes, in a variety of ways and with a variety of vocabularies, that the "self" being punished for a crime committed earlier in that self's career is not the same "self" that committed the crime. For the classical restatement of the opposite philosophy, that of legal retribution, see Robert Nozick, *Philosophical Explanations* (Cambridge, Mass., 1981), esp. pp. 363–97. For an interesting, although not altogether critical, analysis of the presuppositions concerning concepts of selfhood underlying the classical theories of legal retribution, see Steven Knapp, "Collective Memory and the Actual Past," *Representations* XXVI (Spring 1989), 123–49.

17. Michel Foucault, *The Order of Things: An Archaeology of the Human Sciences* (New York, 1970), p. xxiii; Jameson, *Political Unconscious,* p. 125.

18. Fredric Jameson, "Imaginary and Symbolic in Lacan," in *The Ideologies of Theory: Essays 1971–1986,* vol. 1 of *Situations of Theory* (Minneapolis, 1988), pp. 75–115. I will discuss some of the problems of Jameson's reading of Lacan below.

19. Louis Althusser, *Lenin and Philosophy and Other Essays,* trans. Ben Brewster (New York, 1971), pp. 39, 11, 38; Karl Marx and Friedrich Engels, *The German Ideology,* ed. C. J. Arther (New York, 1970), p. 103.

20. Louis Althusser, *For Marx,* trans. Ben Brewster (1965; rpt. London, 1990), pp. 34–35. Louis Althusser and Étienne Balibar, *Reading*

Capital, trans. Ben Brewster (1968; rpt. London, 1979), pp. 31–32, 139. For Althusser's ambivalence regarding the practice of philosophy, see *Lenin and Philosophy,* pp. 26–27, 63, 65, 68, 107–09. The eight essays in this volume were written between April 1966 and April 1969. Unless there is good reason to alert the reader of a change in Althusser's thinking within these three years and mentioning which essay contains which belief, I will simply be citing from the book as a whole. Most of my exploration of Althusser's ideas of synchronic subjection will be based on a reading of the major work in the piece—the famous "Ideology and Ideological State Apparatus (Notes towards an Investigation)," (January–April 1969), in *Lenin and Philosophy,* pp. 127–86. Like Lentricchia, *Criticism and Social Change,* p. 95, I do not see the same "break" in Marx's corpus of work as does Althusser: "I am insisting, against Louis Althusser, that we read with no break inserted between *Capital* and the work prior to 1845"). I will discuss this presently.

21. Althusser, *Lenin and Philosophy,* p. 94, 122; cf. pp. 119, 123, 218.

22. Arthur C. Danto, *Narration and Knowledge* (New York, 1985), p. xi; Fredric Jameson, *Late Marxism: Adorno, or The Persistence of the Dialectic* (London, 1990), p. 99.

23. Even Derrida himself, in a lecture delivered in New York in 1968, had acknowledged that the term was not original with him. He quotes a passage from Heidegger's *Sein und Zeit*—"*we always already* conduct our activities in an understanding of Being" (p. 6; Derrida's italics)—in order to posit at least one earlier origin of this phrase. The German equivalent of "*toujours déjà*" does not occur on page six, but in an entirely different passage from *Sein und Zeit:* "We must always bear in mind . . . that these ontological foundations can never be disclosed by subsequent hypotheses derived from empirical material, but that they are always 'there' already" (*immer schon 'da'*) (p. 50). See Jacques Derrida, *De la grammatologie* (Paris, 1967), p. 13 and *Of Grammatology,* trans. Gayatri Chakravorty Spivak (Baltimore, 1974), p. 4; Derrida, "The Ends of Man," in *Margins of Philosophy,* trans. Alan Bass (Chicago, 1982), pp. 109–36. Bass notes that his translation of this passage is taken from the Macquarrie and Robinson translaton of Heidegger, but Macquarrie and Robinson, *Being and Time,* p. 25, has only "we always conduct"; Heidegger, *Sein und Zeit* (1931; rpt. Tübingen, 1967), p. 50; Heidegger also intimates that he may be invoking Husserl (see *Being and Time,* p. 490, note x [Heidegger's note]).

24. Karl Marx, *Grundrisse: Introduction to the Critique of Political Economy,* trans. Martin Nicolaus (New York, 1973), p. 227. The original German is as follows: "In diesem ersten Abschnitt, wo Tauschwerte, Geld, Preise betrachtet werden, erscheinen die Waren immer als vorhanden" (*Grundrisse kritik der politschen ökonomie* [Berlin, 1953], p. 138); Jameson, *Late Marxism,* p. 99. It is interesting to note that Jameson himself had a decade

earlier used the phrase on the same page as he had proclaimed "Always historicize" (*Political Unconscious*, p. 9). An imaginary Althusserian equivalent would be something like the meaningless "Always already historicize." To conclude the brief survey, we note that the phrase had enough currency for James Baldwin, *Giovanni's Room* (1956; rpt. New York, 1980), p. 223, writing in Paris for an American audience, to be able to conclude his 1956 novel by invoking it: "the journey to corruption is, always, already, half over."

25. As part of his elucidation of the concept of a "differential temporality," Althusser discusses, albeit briefly, Marx's comments on the dislocations in the capitalist mode of production (*Reading Capital*, p. 104). I don't have the space or the time to consider Althusser's interpretation of Marx's comments here, but I would direct the reader to the passages relevant to Marx's concept of temporality, especially in relation to the differential between what Marx calls "a specifically capitalist mode of production" and "the formal subsumption of labour under capital." See Karl Marx, *Capital: A Critique of Political Economy*, vol. 1, trans. Ben Fowkes (Harmondsworth, 1976), p. 1021.

26. Karl Marx, *The Poverty of Philosophy* (New York, 1963), pp. 110–11. Althusser, *Reading Capital*, p. 107.

27. *Ibid.*, p. 147. Etienne Balibar has also proposed that Marx's claim to have turned Hegel on his head ought rightly to be applied to the Hegelian concept of time (although with not the same meaning I am here suggesting). "Instead of the structures of history depending on those of time, it is the structures of temporality which depend on those of history." Like Althusser, Balibar notes that these structures operate in theory: "In Marx's theory, therefore, a synthetic concept of time can never be a pregiven, but only a result" (*Reading Capital*, p. 297). For Balibar's reading of Althusser on the synchrony/diachrony distinction, see *Reading Capital*, pp. 294–302.

28. White, *Content of the Form*, p. 20, proposes another way of defining the "historical fact": "In order to qualify as historical, an event must be susceptible to at least two narrations of its occurrence."

29. For the best succinct consideration of the structure/subject debate in Marxism, see Perry Anderson, *In the Tracks of Historical Materialism* (Chicago, 1984), pp. 32–55.

30. Hayden White, *Metahistory: The Historical Imagination in Nineteenth-Century Europe* (Baltimore, 1973), p. 286; cf. p. 310.

31. Frederick Engels, "Engels to J. Bloch in Königsberg (London, September 21 [-22], 1890)," in *Karl Marx and Frederick Engels: Selected Works* (Moscow, 1968), p. 692.

32. Althusser, *Lenin and Philosophy*, pp. 127–33, 143–45, 167, 183. I am concerned here with Althusser's most mature expression and defini-

tion of "ideology," found in the April 1969 essay. For earlier definitions, see Althusser, *For Marx,* pp. 231, 233, 235–36.

33. Theodor Adorno, *Negative Dialectics,* trans. E. B. Ashton (London, 1973), p. 198.

34. Karl Marx, *A Contribution to the Critique of Political Economy,* trans. S. W. Ryazanskaya (Moscow, 1970), p. 21; Karl Marx, *Critique of Hegel's Doctrine of the State,* in *Karl Marx: Early Writings,* trans. Rodney Livingstone and Gregor Benton (New York, 1975), pp. 58–198; Marx, *Grundrisse,* p. 687. Although this use of "fetishism" has some interesting relationships to Marx's more famous use of the term in *Capital,* the two ideas are not the same. For Marx's ideas on the "fetishism" of commodities, see *Capital,* pp. 164–65. For Marx's statements on the Hegelian idea of the state, see *Economic and Philosophical Manuscripts of 1844,* in *Karl Marx: Early Writings,* pp. 280–400. Marx argued that Hegel's formulation of alienation as a creative process rested on an untenable subject-predicate inversion (p. 396). On the same basis of this tendentious subject-predicate inversion, Marx criticizes Hegel's granting subjectivity to state apparatus in his 1843 *Critique of Hegel's Doctrine,* pp. 64–73. I will be using Marx's comments from this early tract in chapter 4 to discuss Samson's conception of subjectivity.

35. Burke, *Grammar of Motives,* pp. 59–61, 324–331. For a finer distinction between metonymy and synecdoche, see pp. 504–11. Habermas argues that because the sequence of concrete social formations in history is essentially contingent, we must distinguish between a "developmental logics" and a "historiographic *narrative.*" In fact, Habermas goes on to argue, "Evolution-theoretic explanations not only do not *need* to be further transformed into a narrative; they *cannot* be brought into narrative form." This is Perry Anderson's reading of Habermas's arguments; see Anderson, *Tracks of Historical,* pp. 58–67, esp. pp. 62–63. Anderson bases his reading on two of Jürgen Habermas's texts: *Communication and the Evolution of Society* (London, 1979), pp. 120–23, whose translation Anderson modifies; and *Zur Rekonstruktion des historischen Materialismus* (Frankfurt, 1976), pp. 244–45, whose translation Anderson provides. For Habermas's theories of subjectivity, see Peter Dews, "Power and Subjectivity in Foucault," *New Left Review* CXLIV (March 1984), 72–95.

36. Kenneth Burke, *The Philosophy of Literary Form: Studies in Symbolic Action* (1941; rpt. Berkeley and Los Angeles, 1973), p. 391; Burke, *Language as Symbolic Action: Essays on Life, Literature, and Method* (Berkeley and Los Angeles, 1966), p. 206; Burke, *Grammar of Motives,* pp. 430–40; cf. Burke, *A Rhetoric of Motives,* p. 537; Burke, *Language as Symbolic Action,* pp. 251; cf. 381; Marx, *Capital,* pp. 874–75; on the ideological state apparatus, see p. 899.

37. Michel Foucault, "Afterword: The Subject and Power," in Hubert L. Dreyfus and Paul Rabinow, *Michel Foucault, Beyond Structuralism and Hermeneutics* (Chicago, 1982), pp. 208–226. See also Dews, "Power and Subjectivity in Foucault," 72–95.

38. Jacques Lacan, *The Four Fundamental Concepts of Psycho-Analysis,* trans. Alan Sheridan, ed. Jacques-Alain Miller (1973; rpt. New York, 1981), pp. 8, 9, 39, 53, 265, 231. My reading of Lacan mostly will be based on this set of seminars, his eleventh, delivered in 1964. I will also refer to some of the essays in *Écrits: A Selection,* trans. Alan Sheridan (1966; rpt. London, 1977), especially the famous report to the Rome Congress in 1953. I distinguish between Lacanian psychoanalysis and Freudian psychoanalysis in the same way I distinguish between Marxism and Althusserian Marxism, and for the same reasons (see note 40). Althusser, "Freud and Lacan," in *Lenin and Philosophy and Other Essays,* pp. 195–219, also makes the claim that "a science is only a science if it can claim a right to an object of its own." On the Cartesian ambiguity of *expériences,* see René Descartes, *Discourse on the Method* in *The Philosophical Writings of Descartes,* 2 vols., trans. John Cottingham, Robert Stoothoff, and Dugald Murdoch (Cambridge, 1984–1985), vol. I, p. 143*n1*. Lacan's term is "*La science,*" which Sheridan renders "Science *itself*" (p. 231*n1*).

39. Lacan, *Four Fundamental Concepts,* pp. 22, vii, 29. Freud, *The Unconscious* (1915), PFL XI, p. 191. Freud, *Beyond the Pleasure Principle* (1920), PFL XI, p. 299. Freud, *The Interpretation of Dreams* (1900), PFL IV, pp. 775–76. Freud, "'A Child is Being Beaten' (A Contribution to the Study of the Origin of Sexual Perversions)" (1919), PFL X, p. 192.

40. Lacan, *Four Fundamental Concepts,* pp. 34, 31, 26, 63. Lacan, "The Function and Field of Speech and Language in Psychoanalysis," in *Écrits,* pp. 30–113; cf. pp. 51, 57, 77; also Lacan, "The Direction of the Treatment and the Principles of Its Power," in *Écrits,* pp. 226–80. Lacan, *Four Fundamental Concepts,* pp. 180–81, 26; cf. pp. 46, 176, 246. My general point of disagreement with Lacan here concerns the way he reduces the dynamic Freudian stages into a static synchronic monad. My interpretation of Freud is more in line with those readings that emphasize the dynamic quality of the Freudian stages and the diachronic interplay of the Freudian agents of id-ego-superego. Erik H. Erikson, *Childhood and Society* (1950; rpt. New York, 1985), stresses the diachronic stages of human development and identity formation in the Freudian theories. Norman O. Brown, *Life Against Death: The Psychoanalytical Meaning of History* (1959; rpt. Middletown, Conn., 1985), emphasizes the dramatic nature of Freudian thought in the dialectic of eros-death-sublimation. Burke, *Grammar of Motives,* p. 317, also disputes the "mechanistic" reading of Freud and discerns an "underlying dramatistic nature." Cf. Burke, *Language as Symbolic Action,* p. 75: "Freud is so thoroughly Dramatistic."

Although Lacan also refers to "Freud's dramatism," he has something in mind that is hardly "dramatic," let alone "dramatistic" (see Lacan, "The Subversion of the Subject and the Dialectic of Desire in the Freudian Unconscious," in *Écrits*, pp. 292–325, esp. p. 297). Jerome Bruner has also pointed out the importance of Freud's contribution to the dramatic concept of human functioning; see his two essays, "Freud and the Image of Man," and "Psychology and the Image of Man," in *On Knowing: Essays for the Left Hand* (1962; rpt. Cambridge, Mass., 1980), pp. 149–58, 167–89. Finally, Peter Brooks, *Reading for the Plot: Design and Intention in Narrative* (Oxford, 1984), has recently devised a narratological model of dynamic interplay based on the dramatistic reading of Freudian psychoanalysis: "Since psychoanalysis presents a dynamic model of psychic processes, it offers the hope of a model pertinent to the dynamics of texts" (p. 36). Given these readings of Freudian psychoanalysis as dynamic, as dramatistic, or even as expressing what we are calling a "narrative model of self-knowledge," I question Lacan's emphasis on Freud's psychoanalytical model as static and synchronic.

41. Lacan, *Four Fundamental Concepts*, pp. 182, 184, 105, 282; cf. p. 76–77, where Lacan mentions that the "gaze may contain in itself the *objet a* of the Lacanian algebra where the subject falls."

42. Lacan, "The Direction of the Treatment," in *Écrits*, p. 255. Lacan, *Four Fundamental Concepts*, pp. 126, 184. This conception of the unconscious is fundamentally the same model Lacan had articulated in the report to the Rome Congress in 1953. See Lacan, "The Function and Field of Speech," in *Écrits*, pp. 42, 49, 55, 58–59, 65, 80–86, 90.

43. Heidegger, *Being and Time*, p. 206. For a more ambivalent reading of where the self and Other may intersect in the act of hearing, see Julian Jaynes, *The Origin of Consciousness in the Breakdown of the Bicameral Mind* (Boston, 1976), p. 97.

44. Lacan, *Four Fundamental Concepts*, pp. 198–99. On how the "other" becomes the "Other" see Lacan, "The Agency of the Letter in the Unconscious or Reason since Freud," in *Écrits*, pp. 146–78; Lacan, "The Signification of the Phallus," in *Écrits*, pp. 281–91; and Lacan, "Subversion of the Subject," in *Écrits*, pp. 304–05, 322. For an earlier, cryptic version of this analogy, see Lacan, "On a Question Preliminary to Any Possible Treatment of Psychosis," in *Écrits*, pp. 179–225. On the meaning and history of the term *aphanisis*, which signifies the disappearance of sexual desire, see Lacan, "Signification of the Phallus," in *Écrits*, pp. 283, 291.

45. Jacques-Alain Miller, "Suture," *Screen* XVIII, no. 4 (1977); qtd. in Paul Smith, *Discerning the Subject* (Minneapolis, 1988), pp. 75–76.

46. Jameson, "Imaginary and Symbolic in Lacan," pp. 111–13; Lacan, *Four Fundamental Concepts*, pp. 154, 89.

47. Lacan, *Four Fundamental Concepts,* p. 246; cf. p. 269: "The analyst, that is to say, to the subject who is supposed to know." Lacan, "The Function and Field of Speech," p. 105, called the analyst the "mediator between the man of care and the subject of absolute knowledge" ("comme médiatrice entre l'homme du souci et le sujet du savoir absolu").

48. Lacan, *Four Fundamental Concepts,* p. 265. Earlier, Lacan made another link between Descartes and Freud:

> Opposite this certainty, there is the subject, who, as I said just now, has been waiting there since Descartes. I dare to state as a truth that the Freudian field was possible only a certain time after the emergence of the Cartesian subject, in so far as modern science began only after Descartes made his inaugural step. (*Four Fundamental Concepts,* p. 47)

Lacan, "The Agency of the Letter," in *Écrits,* pp. 164–66, also attempted to "correct" Descartes.

49. Descartes, *Meditations on the First Philosophy* (1641), in *The Philosophical Writings of Descartes,* vol. II, pp. 3–62, esp. pp. 32–36. The letter to Mersenne is taken from René Descartes, *Oeuvres de Descartes,* rev. ed., 12 vols., ed. Charles Adam and Paul Tannery (Paris, 1964–1976), vol. I, p. 152; the translation is that of the editors of *The Philosophical Writings of Descartes,* vol. II, p. 32n1. For the Latin text of the *Meditationes de Prima Philosophia,* see *Oeuvres de Descartes,* vol. VII, pp. 1–90. Cf. Descartes, *Discourse on the Method,* pp. 111–51.

50. Descartes, *The Principles of Philosophy* (1644), in *The Philosophical Writings of Descartes,* vol. I, pp. 179–291. See Spinoza, *The Ethics,* in *The Works of Spinoza,* 2 vols., trans. R.H.M. Elwes (New York, 1955), vol. II, pp. 43–271, esp. pp. 86, 120–27: "Will and understanding are one and the same thing."

51. Descartes, *Principles of Philosophy,* p. 206; John Hicks, *Evil and the God of Love* (1966; rpt. New York, 1985), p. 281. Dennis Richard Danielson, *Milton's Good God: A Study in Literary Theodicy* (Cambridge, 1982), esp. pp. 119–20, deserves credit for bringing Hicks's general work on theodicy and, especially, the concept of epistemic distance as a premise of that work to the attention of Miltonists; Descartes, *Meditations on the First Philosophy,* p. 36.

52. Thomas Hobbes, *Leviathan,* ed. C. B. Macpherson (1651; rpt. Harmondsworth, 1968), p. 261. All future quotations from the Leviathan will be taken from this edition. Hobbes, *The English Works of Thomas Hobbes,* ed. W. Molesworth (London, 1839-1845) pp. 1, ix; qtd. in C. B. Macpherson, *The Political Theory of Possessive Individualism Hobbes to Locke* (Oxford, 1962), p. 88. Hobbes, *De Cive, The English Version,* ed. Howard

Warrender (1642; rpt. Oxford, 1983), pp. 229, 255. Hobbes, *Leviathan,* p. 686.

53. Hobbes, *Leviathan,* pp. 719, 259, 313, 265, 667–68. See Catherine Gallagher, "Embracing the Absolute: The Politics of the Female Subject in Seventeenth-Century England," *GENDERS* I (Spring 1988), 24–39, where she marks the same distinction between "subjection" and "subjectivity" in the works of Margaret Cavendish. On the question of the category of the subject in relation to contemporary literary studies of the Renaissance, see Carol Thomas Neely, "Constructing the Subject: Feminist Practice and the New Renaissance Discourses," *ELR* XVIII, no. 1 (1988), 5– 18.

54. Hobbes, *Leviathan,* pp. 173, 370–71, 143, 431, 428–42, 433, 689, 505; the summation of Hobbes's materialistic premise is found on pages 689–90. Henry More, *Divine Dialogues,* 2 vols. (London, 1668), vol. I, p. 124; the speaker of these lines is the pious Philopolus.

55. Before C. B. Macpherson's *The Political Theory of Possessive Individualism,* such a view was possible. According to Macpherson, the "best-known students of Hobbes have taken the view that his political theory was not derived from his materialism" (p. 10). He cites the works of G. C. Robertson, *Hobbes* (Edingurgh and London, 1886); John Laird, *Hobbes* (London, 1934); and Leo Strauss, *The Political Philosophy of Hobbes, Its Basis and Genesis* (Oxford, 1936). He disputes this view in *The Political Theory of Possessive Individualism,* pp. 10, 76–79. While wholeheartedly in agreement with Macpherson's reading, my own interpretation of Hobbes's materialism rests on a different foundation—Hobbes's persistent attempts to subordinate spirit to state.

56. Hobbes, *Leviathan,* pp. 479, 605, 607. Milton, *Of True Religion, Hæresie, Schism, Toleration* (1673), in CM VI, pp. 167–68. I discuss more fully the differences between Hobbes and Milton on Erastian ideals in chapter 5.

57. Hobbes, *Leviathan,* pp. 228, 227. The Leviathan Hobbes is here instituting owes much of its evocative power to the famous description of the Leviathan in the Book of Job. In fact, Hobbes says later that he is basing his state of Leviathan on the last two verses of the Job, chapter xli: "There is nothing, saith he, on earth, to be compared with him. He is made so as not to be afraid. Hee seeth every thing below him; and is King of all the children of pride" (33–34) (p. 362, Hobbes's translation). The Leviathan is important in Job because God asks, "Canst thou draw out leviathan with an hook?. . . . Will he make covenant with thee?. . . . None is so fierce that dare stir him up: who then is able to stand before me?" (1–10). In other words, God uses this occasion to tell Job that rights come from power. The state Hobbes describes implicitly asks these same questions. In answer to Hobbes's Leviathan, Milton could pose another verse

from Job, one in which God says "whatsoever is under the whole heaven is mine" (11). Hobbes attempts to preempt the ramifications of that statement; I will discuss that attempt in chapter 5.

58. Hobbes, *Leviathan*, pp. 127–28, 139, 622, 395, 349. Compare p. 697, where Hobbes mocks the disinctions humans make to feign to themselves their possession of free will.

59. Descartes, *Principles of Philosophy*, pp. 179–291. Hobbes, *Leviathan*, p. 232. Hobbes's relationship to Descartes is unfortunately beyond the scope of this study. Hobbes does supply the third set of "Objections" to Descartes's *Meditations*. See Descartes, *Objections and Replies*, in *The Philosophical Writings*, vol. II, pp. 121–37.

60. Mary Ann Radzinowicz, "The Politics of *Paradise Lost*," in *Politics of Discourse: The Literature and History of Seventeenth-Century England*, ed. Kevin Sharpe and Steven N. Zwicker (Berkeley and Los Angeles, 1987), pp. 204–29.

61. Maurice Kelley, *This Great Argument: A Study of Milton's "De Doctrina Christiana" as a Gloss Upon "Paradise Lost"* (1941; rpt. Gloucester, Mass., 1962), pp. 22–27. I am counting both editions of *The Readie and Easie Way* in my tabulation of Milton's final flurry of political prose.

62. Milton, *A Defence of the People of England* (1651) in YP V, p. 374. I prefer the Yale translation here over the Columbia (see CM VII, pp. 144–45).

63. Joseph Hall, *Contemplations Upon the History of the New Testament* in *The Works of Joseph Hall*, 2 vols. (1628–1634), vol. I, p. 31; cf. 36, 41, where Hall refers to "Our Sonneship." I will hereafter be citing from this edition of Hall's works. Hall, *Meditations and Vowes* in *Works*, vol. I, p. 51. Henry Lawrence, *An History of Angells, Being a Theologicall Treatise of our Communion and Warre with Them* (London, 1649), p. 131. John Preston, *The New-Covenant, or the Saints Portion* (London, 1629), vol. II, pp. 108–09.

64. Milton, *A Treatise of Civil Power* (1659), in CM VI, p. 31 (cf. YP VII, pp. 264–65). Milton, *Christian Doctrine*, in CM XVI, pp. 152–55. The word most commonly used by Milton in Latin in terms of contradistinguishing *son* is *servus*, which the Columbia translator renders as "servant" and the Yale as "slave." Although I appreciate the point made by William J. Grace that *servus* "by itself means 'slave'" and that the Greek used in the New Testament (*dolous*) "emphatically means 'slave'," I nonetheless would maintain that, in this instance, we should refer back to the parallelism Milton himself makes in English, which, as seen in the *Treatise*, is "servant" (for Grace's point, see YP IV, p. 374*n*4). Milton, *A Defence*, in CM VII, 148. This is my translation of the phrase "filius fuit Petrus, et proinde liber."

65. It ought to be noted that even though the distinction between

sonship and servant is quite clear as attested by these passages, there is some difficulty in describing the Jesus of the brief epic as a Son while rejecting that he is also a servant, for Milton maintained elsewhere that Christ assumed the place of "a servant that we might be free"—and, moreover, that Christ assumed "servitude for himself" in order to establish "liberty for us, even civil liberty" (CM VII, 144–47). It would seem, then, that Milton's Christ would be both servant and Son. A few points are worth making against this reading, however. First of all, as I will argue in chapter 3, Milton presents Jesus in *Paradise Regained* before his public assumption of servitude in order to highlight the time when he was a Son of God and not a servant; and secondly, Milton would hold that even though Christ assumed the place of a servant, he "never failed to preserve the heart of a liberator" (YP V, p. 375; the Columbia translator renders "liberatoris" as "deliverer," whereas it seems to me the Yale translator's choice of "liberator" fits the political sense Milton is here stressing). Thus, Jesus in *Paradise Regained* acts out the role of liberator both in his being (that is, he is the Son of God) and in his actions (which are, in a word, paideutic, and teaching us to be free).

66. William Perkins, *A Golden Chaine* in *The Workes of that Famous and Worthy Minister of Christ in the University of Cambridge, Mr. W. Perkins,* 3 vols. (Cambridge, 1616–1618), vol. I, p. B₂. I will hereafter cite from this edition of Perkins's works; Perkins, *Golden Chaine,* in *Workes* I, p. 105. Cf. Calvin, *Institutes of the Christian Religion,* trans. Henry Beveridge (Grand Rapids, Mich., 1983), vol. II, pp. 202–58. I will compare Milton's and Calvin's soteriologies in chapter 3, contrasting Milton's insistence on the universality of salvation to Calvin's resolute denial of this. Perkins, *Golden Chaine,* in *Workes* I, p. 107, comes firmly down on Calvin's side. In this discussion, I am more interested in the role of free will in salvation, again contrasting Milton to the staunchest (though not necessarily least confused) Calvinist of England. I will briefly note the basis of Perkins's confusion below.

67. Perkins, *Golden Chaine,* in *Workes* I, p. 110: the second error of late divines is that they do not ascribe to God the agency and permission for the Fall (cf. p. 16: "God is not onely a bare permissive agent in an evill worke, but a powerfull effectour of the same"). R. T. Kendall, *Calvin and English Calvinism to 1649* (Oxford, 1979), pp. 30–31, 55. The Synod of Dort applied the unwieldly word, *supralapsarianism,* to define Bezan soteriology; the OED cites its first English use in 1633. Milton followed Arminius on this point in disapproving of the Bezan idea, although perhaps for different reasons; see CM XIV, pp. 102–03; for Arminius, see Carl Bangs, *Arminius: A Study in the Dutch Reformation* (Nashville, 1971), pp. 347–48, and A. W. Harrison, *Arminianism* (London, 1937), pp. 11–12, 48–50.

68. CM XIV, pp. 102–03: "The apostasy of the first man was not decreed, but only foreknown by the infinite wisdom of God." Cf. *PL* III, 95–128: God says, "Foreknowledge had no influence on their fault." *PL* VII, 173: wherein God says, "what I will is Fate," and that (interestingly) before the Creation, seems to contradict the preceding, but in reality (that is, the coherence of Milton's theology) it does not. According to *Christian Doctrine*, CM XIV, pp. 62–63, the Creation and the removal of the curse from the ground (Gen. viii, 21) are "among his [God's] sole decrees." In any case, Milton argued, "it is absurd to separate the decrees or will of the Deity from his eternal counsel and foreknowledge, or to give them priority of order" (CM XIV, pp. 64–65). See Danielson's *Milton's Good God*, pp. 82–83, 86, 132–49, for a wise assessment of Milton's Arminianism, and especially an elaboration of Milton's use of an "incompatibilist model of freedom."

69. Perkins, *A Treatise of Gods Free Grace, and Mans Free-Will*, in *Workes* I, 729; Calvin, *Institutes* I, p. 255; CM XIV, pp. 204–15; Kendall, *Calvin*, pp. 20–21, states that in Calvin the will is "effaced" (citing the above, Bk. II, iii, 6, "voluntatem dico aboleri"); it might be noted that Calvin palliates this somewhat in fuller context: "I say the will is abolished, but not in so far as it is will."

70. CM XV, pp. 206–07; Sumner's translation does not account enough for the mitigating adverb: "quae voluntatis *quasi* mors est" (my italics).

71. CM XV, pp. 208–11; it is significant, also, that Milton holds that this efficiency to do some good works follows vocation ("vocantis Dei"). Perkins, *Golden Chaine*, in *Workes* I, pp. 95–99, held that, not until the "Second Justification," the fourth stage of predestination, may any good works be attempted. John Downame, *The Christian Warefare* (London, 1604), pp. 563–79, who also, incidentally, holds that "universall redemption . . . is an idle dreame of mans braine" (p. 279), states that good works are the fruits of justification, the third stage of predestination.

72. Perkins, *A Treatise*, in *Workes* I, pp. 728–29.

73. CM XV, pp. 212–15. Cf. Don M. Wolfe, YP IV, p. 46: "To Milton freedom of conscience in religion was far more crucial than freedom of conscience in political expression."

74. Downame, *The Christian Warfare*, p. 68. Perry Miller, *Errand Into the Wilderness* (Cambridge, Mass., 1956), pp. 48–98, esp. 74, delineates the crux of the Puritan dilemma: "Men struggling in the coils of their doctrine, desperately striving on the one hand to maintain the subordination of humanity to God without unduly abasing human values, and on the other hand to vaunt the powers of the human intellect without losing the sense of divine transcendence."

75. CM XIV, pp. 62–79. Cf. the debate between Hylobares and Philotheus on God's immutability in More's *Divine Dialogues* I, pp. 73–78.

76. CM XIV, pp. 82–83; CM IV, p. 319; *PL* III, 108. For fuller discussions of Milton's concepts of "Sonship," see Northrop Frye, "The Typology of *Paradise Regained*," in *Milton's Epic Poetry: Essays on "Paradise Lost" and "Paradise Regained*," ed. C. A. Patrides (Harmondsworth, 1967), pp. 301–21; Louis Martz, *The Paradise Within: Studies in Vaughan, Traherne, and Milton* (New Haven, 1964), pp. 171–201; Hugh MacCallum, *Milton and the Sons of God: The Divine Image in Milton's Epic Poetry* (Toronto, 1986); and Joan S. Bennett, *Reviving Liberty: Radical Christian Humanism in Milton's Great Poems* (Cambridge, Mass., 1988), pp. 166–67.

77. Spinoza, *The Ethics*, pp. 113, 260, 255, 237.

78. CM VII, pp. 442–45. The terms Bracton uses in *De Legibus et Conseutudinibus Angliae* (1640), are *"vicarius et minister Dei"* and *"diaboli minister.*" See YP IV, p. 492*n*64; CM VII, pp. 476–79; cf. YP IV, p. 505; CM VII, pp. 532–33; cf. YP IV, p. 528.

79. Augustine, *Confessionum*, in *Patrologiae Cursus Completus,* Latin Series, ed. J-P Migne (Parisiis, 1841), vol. XXXII, col. 849; bk. 13, chap. 11. I am indebted to Kenneth Burke's reading of the *Confessions* for this insight about the workings of the Augustinian Trinity; see his *The Rhetoric of Religion: Studies in Logology* (1961; rpt. Berkeley and Los Angeles, 1970), pp. 43–171, esp. pp. 111, 165. The Spirit in the Augustinian Trinity represents not only "knowing," but also "loving." For a fuller exploration of the Spirit's role in self-knowledge, see Augustine, *De Trinitate*, in *Patrologiae Cursus Completus,* Latin Series, ed. J-P Migne (Parisiis, 1845), vol. XLII, cols. 971–77, bk. 10, chaps. 1–4. See also *De Trinitate,* cols. 1088–89, bk. 15, chap. 21.

80. Plato, *Laches,* 193e, *Collected Dialogues,* p. 137. Cf. Hans-Georg Gadamer, "*Logos* and *Ergon* in Plato's Lysis," in *Dialogue and Dialectic: Eight Hermeneutical Studies on Plato,* trans. P. Christopher Smith (New Haven, 1980), pp. 1–20.

81. Plato, *Charmides,* 164e, 166e–167a, in *Collected Dialogues,* pp. 110–11, 112–13.

82. Logos, as I discussed it above, is a key concept to Western philosophy, from Heraclitus to Marx. For Heraclitus, see fragment 197 in Kirk and Raven, *Presocratic Philosophers,* p. 187. For Marx, see Althusser, *Lacan and Philosophy,* p. 171. In his attempt to argue for his notion of interpellation in Christian terms, Althusser maintains that "ideology" might adequately replace "logos" in the Pauline quotation; as he writes, "it is in the 'Logos,' meaning in ideology, that we 'live, move and have our being.'"

83. Though they are certainly not minor characters and they certainly do conform to this paradigm, I exclude Eve and Satan from this list because Adam can be more fully explicated within this paradigm and Jesus and Samson are the subjects of later chapters.

84. Lanham, *Motives of Eloquence*, p. 152. Lanham describes the conditions of enselfment in relation to Castiglione's "sprezzatura." The term is probably older than Lanham (although this is the place I remember seeing it first), and its basic form, as Lanham points out, is found in George Herbert Mead's *Mind, Self, and Society*. Two recent studies have helped me form my ideas about how rhetoric or representation works in acts of self-knowledge: Thomas O. Sloane, *Donne, Milton, and the End of Humanist Rhetoric* (Berkeley and Los Angeles, 1985) and John M. Steadman, *The Hill and the Labyrinth: Discourse and Certitude in Milton and His Near-Contemporaries* (Berkeley and Los Angeles, 1984). I am more indebted to Victor Turner's anthropology, Lanham, *Motives of Eloquence*, Burke, *Grammar of Motives*, and Stephen Greenblatt, *Renaissance Self-Fashioning* (Chicago, 1980) for my representational reading of Milton.

85. See Simone de Beauvoir, *The Second Sex*, trans. H. M. Parshley (New York, 1974), esp. pp. 78–88.

86. Spinoza, *The Ethics*, pp. 120–21, 134, 137. Cf. Descartes, *Discourse on the Method*, pp. 123–24. The model of "triangular desire" is René Girard's; for its basic workings and for its Christian basis, with God as mediator for the subject's desiring of the object, see his *Deceit, Desire, and the Novel*, pp. 1–52, 294–98.

87. Sir Thomas Browne, *Religio Medici*, ed. James Winny (Cambridge, 1963), p. 81; my italics.

88. More, *Divine Dialogues* II, p. 53. Cf. Calvin, *Institutes* I, pp. 446–47, a passage I will discuss in the next chapter. William Ames, *The Marrow of Sacred Divinity* (London, 1642), p. 70. Cf. Peter Bulkeley, *The Gospel-Covenant; or, The Covenant of Grace Opened* (London, 1646), pp. 32–33. For a study of the covenant theology school, see Miller, *Errand Into the Wilderness*, pp. 48–98. Miller's readings of the puritan divines has been strongly contested, but usually on the basis of his not choosing representative puritans; the claim that he tends to focus on the academic elite, such as Preston, Ames, Bulkeley, and Cotton, does not, in my mind, invalidate his interpretations of this particular school, although it does limit the value of his explication of what the various strands of puritanism might have collectively argued. On covenant theology in general, see John Coolidge, *The Pauline Renaissance in England: Puritanism and the Bible* (Oxford, 1970), pp. 99–140. On the relation of covenant theology to the institutions of the pulpit and the school, see John Morgan, *Godly Learning: Puritan Attitudes Towards Reason, Learning, and Education, 1560–1640* (Cambridge, 1982), esp. pp. 24–35, 220–44; Morgan criticizes Miller for using "a very few puritans who were especially attached to the universities and to higher learning" (p. 45). To see the differences in their interpretations of puritanism, see Miller, *The New England Mind: The*

Seventeenth Century (Cambridge, Mass., 1939), pp. 200–01; and Morgan, *Godly Learning*, pp. 45–54. For modern Milton criticism on the question of local salvation or eternal mediation, see MacCallum, *Milton and the Sons of God*.

89. On Beza and the Heidelberg School's thinking on 2 Peter i, 10, in contrast to Calvin's reticence, see Kendall, *Calvin*, pp. 8, 25, 34–37; on Perkins's confusion between the Bezan and Calvinistic doctrines, see pp. 55, 60–62, 66; on Beza and the Heidelberg School as the origins of "federal or covenant theology," see pp. 38–41. Perkins, *A Declaration of True Manner of Knowing Christ Crucified*, in *Workes* I, pp. 626–34; qtd. in Kendall, *Calvin*, pp. 61–62. Arminius, *Declaration of the Sentiments of Arminius, Delivered Before the States of Holland*, in *The Works of James Arminius*, 3 vols., trans. James Nichols (London, 1825), vol. 1, pp. 516–668, esp. p. 603. Cf. Bangs, *Arminius*, pp. 347–48.

90. On the contrast between the Augustinian and the Irenaean theodicies, see Hick, *Evil and the God of Love*, pp. 37–89, 211–18. Hick suggests that the Irenaean theodicy was in abeyance from the fourth to the nineteenth centuries (p. 219). On how Milton may have employed the Irenaean theodicy, see Danielson, *Milton's Good God*, pp. 164–72.

91. William James, *The Varieties of Religious Experience* (1902; rpt. New York, 1958), p. 302; cf. pp.67–71, 216–20. Burke, *Grammar of Motive*, p. 332; cf. p. 334. On the question of "substance," certainly one of the key points of Burke's critique of the scientist model of accounting for motivation, see pp. 21–58.

92. Hayden White, *Tropics of Discourse: Essays in Cultural Criticism* (Baltimore, 1978), pp. 87, 99; Edward Said, "Molestation and Authority in Narrative Fiction," in *Aspects of Narrative: Selected Papers from the English Institute*, ed. J. Hillis Miller (New York, 1971), pp. 47–68, esp. p. 48. Cf. Said's remarks on narrative in his *Beginnings: Intention and Method* (1975; rpt. New York, 1985), pp. 82, 100; and *Orientalism* (1978; rpt. London, 1985), p. 240. David Lewis, *On the Plurality of Worlds* (Oxford, 1986). Nelson Goodman, *Ways of Worldmaking* (1978; rpt. Indianapolis, 1988). Nelson Goodman, *Of Mind and Other Matters* (Cambridge, Mass., 1984). Cf. Danto, *Narration and Knowledge*. For a critical discussion of the applications of Lewis's "plurality of worlds" to narrative theory, see Thomas G. Pavel, *Fictional Worlds* (Cambridge, Mass., 1986). On how narrative theory has been lagging behind theories of subjectivity, see Smith, *Discerning the Subject*, esp. pp. 90, 158.

93. Walter Benjamin, *Theses on the Philosophy of History*, in *Illuminations: Essays and Reflections*, ed. Hannah Arendt, trans. Harry Zohn (1968; rpt. New York, 1969), pp. 253–64, esp. pp. 261, 263; Perry Anderson, *Considerations on Western Marxism* (London, 1976), pp. 89–90.

2. CONFRONTING THE SELF:
THE ART OF MEDITATION

1. Jacques Derrida, *Of Grammatolog*, trans. Gayatri Chakravorty Spivak (1967; rpt. Baltimore, 1976), p. 158; Roland Barthes, "The Death of the Author," in *Image-Music-Text,* trans. Stephen Heath (London, 1977), p. 148.

For the critical confusion the concept of the Derridean "text" has caused, one need only examine a selection of the contrary interpretations of the phrase. See, for example, Louis A. Montrose, "Professing the Renaissance: The Poetics and Politics of Culture," in *The New Historicism,* ed. H. Aram Veeser (New York, 1989), pp. 15–36, esp. p. 16, and Robert Scholes, *Protocols of Reading* (New Haven, 1989), p. 2. Some clarity in what Derrida means by a "text" might be found in the dialogue between the essay written by Anne McClintock and Rob Nixon and Derrida's response to that essay. McClintock and Nixon, "No Names Apart: The Separation of Word and History in Derrida's 'Le Dernier Mot du Racisme," in *"Race," Writing, and Difference,* ed. Henry Louis Gates, Jr. (Chicago, 1985), pp. 339–53, esp. p. 339, which is a response to Derrida's "Racism's Last Word," in *"Race," Writing, and Difference,* pp. 325–38, suggest that the "strategic value" of Derrida's "method has to be seriously considered." What his method had apparently foreclosed was the opportunity, as they say, to "point to something beyond the text." Derrida, "But Beyond . . . (Open Letter to Anne McClintock and Rob Nixon)," in *"Race," Writing, and Difference,* pp. 354–69, esp. pp. 366–67, responds with some heat to this questioning of the political efficacy of his method. Derrida noted that McClintock and Nixon's comment on "beyond the text" was, as he put it, "a clever, oh so clever, nod in the direction of something I once said." That something, of course, is the famous comment in *Of Grammatology:* "There is nothing outside of the text." He corrects what he perceives to be the fundamental error his critics make: "Text, as I use the word, is not the book." Text, as he uses the word, refers to "a field of forces: heterogeneous, differential, open, and so on." And deconstruction, he goes on to assert, has a political agenda: "Deconstructive readings and writings are concerned not only with library books, with discourses, with conceptual and semantic contents. . . . They are also effective or active (as one says) interventions, in particular political and institutional interventions that transform contexts without limiting themselves to theoretical or constative utterances even though they must also produce such utterances." As such, then, Derrida's "strategic reevaluation of the concept of text" allows him to bring together "in a more consistent fashion, in the most consistent fashion possible, theoretico-philosophical necessities with the 'practical,' political, and other necessities of what is called deconstruction." Deconstruction, in the words of the inventor of the word, method, and program, is emphatically not what everyone thought it was—that is, "a turning inward and an enclosure by the limits of language."

2. M. R., *The Mothers Counsell or, Live within Compasse. Being the last Will and Testament to her dearest Daughter* (London, 1630[?]), p. 8, my italics.

3. Francis Bacon, *Essays*, ed. Michael J. Hawkins (1625; rpt. London, 1973), p. 150; Edmund Spenser, *The Faerie Queene*, ed. A. C. Hamilton (London, 1977), p. 737, my italics; the letter is appended to the first publication of the first three books of *The Faerie Queene* (1590), and it is dated January 23, 1589 (1590, N.S.).

4. Scholes, *Protocols of Reading*, p. 27; cf. pp. 1–49, 89–155. Roland Barthes, "Day by Day with Roland Barthes," in Marshall Blonsky, *On Signs* (Baltimore, 1985), pp. 98–117, esp. p. 101; cf. Scholes, *Protocols*, p. 10. Wolfgang Iser, "The Reading Process: A Phenomenological Approach," *New Literary History* III (1972), 279–99, esp. 295. Kendall Walton, "Do We Need Fictional Entities? Notes Towards a Theory," in *Aesthetics: Proceedings of the Eighth International Wittgenstein Symposium* (Vienna, 1984), p. 179; qtd. in Thomas Pavel, *Fictional Worlds* (Cambridge, Mass., 1986), p. 55; cf. pp. 86–89. Alastair Fowler, *Kinds of Literature: An Introduction to the Theory of Genres and Modes* (Oxford, 1982), p. 63. Wayne C. Booth, *The Company We Keep: An Ethics of Fiction* (Berkeley and Los Angeles, 1988), p. 259; cf. pp. 227–60. It ought to be mentioned, and is probably well known, that Iser's term, *entanglement*, is one first applied to the reading process by Stanley Fish in *Surprised By Sin: The Reader in "Paradise Lost"* (1967; rpt. Berkeley and Los Angeles, 1970), pp. 1–56; Fish, in turn, took it from Milton's *Tetrachordon* (1645) (CM IV, p. 141), and transformed it to mean something utterly different than what Milton meant. I take an infinite amount of pleasure in quoting a sentence that Milton writes five lines after the phrase Stanley Fish made famous by incorporating into his reading strategy—"not so much a teaching, as an intangling." The sentence runs, "If he be not lesse wise then that noted Fish, when as he should bee not unwiser than the Serpent." The Yale editor annotates the "noted Fish" to be the squid (YP II, p. 642*n*23); I leave it up the reader whether Milton knew better.

5. CM XIV, pp. 12–13; John Carey translates this phrase to read "my unprejudiced and intelligent readers" (YP VI, p. 123). Teresa de Lauretis, *Technologies of Gender: Essays on Theory, Film, and Fiction* (Bloomington, Ind., 1987), p. 118. The term *narrativity* was developed by Bremond, explaining Propp's suggestion about the abstractness of the formal properties of stories, to name an elusive "immanent story structure." See Shlomith Rimmon-Kenan, *Narrative Fiction: Contemporary Poetics* (Lon-

don, 1983), pp. 7–8. Hayden White, *The Content of the Form: Narrative Discourse and Historical Representation* (Baltimore, 1987), pp. 14, 24, uses the term to mean at least two distinct things: (1) "narrativity . . . is intimately related to, if not a function of, the impulse to moralize reality, that is, to identify it with the social system that is the source of any morality we can imagine"; and (2) "the means to track such shifts of meaning, that is, narrativity." White does describe the process de Lauretis calls "narrativity," but he calls it the "ideological element" (p. 87). De Lauretis has changed the usage to refer to the ways that narratives both implicate the sentient being reading them as well as construct an abstract narratee within them. I will assume her usage and her definition.

    6. Barbara Lewalski, *Milton's Brief Epic: The Genre, Meaning, and Art of "Paradise Regained"* (Providence, 1966), p. 133. Earl Miner, *The Restoration Mode from Milton to Dryden* (Princeton, 1974), pp. 275–76.

    7. William E. Cain, "Learning How to Read: A Note on *Paradise Regained* IV.321–30," *MQ* XIII, no. 3 (October 1979), 120–21.

    8. John Barth, *Sabbatical: A Romance* (1982; rpt. London, 1984), p. 61. Terry Eagleton, *Literary Theory: An Introduction* (Oxford, 1983), p. 138. Wayne C. Booth, *The Rhetoric of Fiction* (1961; rpt. Chicago, 1983), pp. 137–44, 177–82. Gerald Prince, "Introduction à l'étude du narrataire," *Poétique* XIV (1973), 178–96. Christine Brooke-Rose, *A Rhetoric of the Unreal: Studies in Narrative, Especially of the Fantastic* (Cambridge, 1981), pp. 105–27. Stanley Fish, *Is There a Text in This Class?: The Authority of Interpretive Communities* (Cambridge, Mass., 1980), pp. 21–67, esp. 48–49. Wolfgang Iser, *The Implied Reader: Patterns of Communication in Prose Fiction from Bunyan to Beckett,* trans. David Henry Wilson (Baltimore, 1974); Gerard Genette, *Narrative Discourse,* trans. Jane E. Lewin (Oxford, 1980), p. 260, has also used *implied reader.* Walter J. Ong, *Interfaces of the Word: Studies in the Evolution of Consciousness and Culture* (Ithaca, N.Y., 1977), pp. 54–81.

    9. Wolfgang Iser, "The Reading Process," pp. 279, 286–87. Karl-heinz Stierle, "The Reading of Fictional Texts," trans. Inge Crosman and Thekla Zachrau, in *The Reader in the Text: Essays on Audience and Interpretation,* ed. Susan R. Suleiman and Inge Crosman (Princeton, 1980), pp. 83–105, esp. p. 100. Tzvetan Todorov, "Reading as Construction," trans. Marilyn A. August, in *The Reader in the Text,* pp. 67–82, esp. p. 77. For the basis of Iser's early position, see Georges Poulet, "Phenomenology of Reading," *New Literary History* I (1969), 53–68.

    10. Northrop Frye, *The Return of Eden* (Toronto, 1965), p. 32. Christopher Grose, *Milton and the Sense of Tradition* (New Haven, Conn., 1988), pp. 110–11; cf. pp. 128, 140. Robert Crosman, *Reading "Paradise Lost"* (Bloomington, Ind., 1980), p. 58. Stanley E. Fish, *Surprised by Sin:*

The Reader in "Paradise Lost." All citations from this book will be noted parenthetically in the text.

11. Fish, *Is There a Text in This Class?*, p. 40. Cf. Fish, *Surprised by Sin*, pp. 340–56.

12. Fredric Jameson, *The Political Unconscious* (Ithaca, N.Y., 1981), pp. 98–99. Jonathan Culler, *Structuralist Poetics: Structuralism, Linguistics, and the Study of Literature* (London, 1975), pp. 109, 120. Barbara Herrnstein Smith, *On the Margins of Discourse: The Relation of Literature to Language* (Chicago, 1978), p. 182. Cf. Kenneth Burke, *Counter-Statement* (1931; rpt. Berkeley and Los Angeles, 1968), pp. 124–49, for a consideration of the relationship between literary form and readerly desire.

13. Especially useful in terms of this explication is Mary Nyquist, "The Genesis of Gendered Subjectivity in the Divorce Tracts and in *Paradise Lost*," in *Re-membering Milton: Essays on the Texts and Traditions,* ed. Mary Nyquist and Margaret W. Ferguson (New York, 1987), pp. 99–127. See also Janet E. Halley, "Female Autonomy in Milton's Sexual Poetics," and Lynn E. Enterline's "'Myself / Before Me': Gender and Prohibition in Milton's Italian Sonnets," in *Milton and the Idea of Woman,* ed. Julia M. Walker (Urbana, Ill., 1988), pp. 230–53 and 32–51, respectively; and Catherine Belsey, *John Milton: Language, Gender, Power* (Oxford, 1988), esp. pp. 85–89. I have reviewed *Milton and the Idea of Woman* in *Ariel: A Review of International English Literature* XXI, no. 1 (January 1990), 89–92.

14. Sir Philip Sidney, *An Apology for Poetry,* in *Criticism: The Major Statements,* ed. Charles Kaplan (New York, 1975), pp. 126, 124. Agricola, *De inv. dial.* (Parisiis, 1529), Lib. II, cap. iv, p. 167; qtd. and trans. in Walter J. Ong, *Ramus: Method and the Decay of Dialogue* (Cambridge, Mass., 1958), p. 103. Sidney, as Ong points out, is one of the primary agents of the second infusion of Ramism into England (p. 302). Of supplementary interest would be the ways theorists of psychical structures in the Renaissance began to introduce motion as one of mentation's constituent elements. For instance, Frances A. Yates, *The Art of Memory* (1966; rpt. London, 1984), p. 176, has shown how the "most significant aspect" of Ramon Lull's revolution in the art of memory is his introduction of the idea of movement as part of the structural working of the psyche.

15. The most thorough study of this phenomenon is Elizabeth Ely Fuller, *Milton's Kinesthetic Vision in "Paradise Lost"* (Lewisburg, Va., 1983).

16. E. M. W. Tillyard, *Milton* (1930; rpt. New York, 1967), p. 207; cf. p. 212. Fish, *Surprised by Sin*, p. 341.

17. My concept of "tableaux" is indebted somewhat to Louis Martz's

concept of "panels." See his *Poet of Exile: A Study of Milton's Poetry* (New Haven, 1980), pp. 203–18. My concern is more with shifts in locale rather than parallel scenes of instruction. I am also indebted to Wolfgang Iser's more recent theory about reader response, elaborated in his "Interaction Between Text and Reader," in *The Reader in the Text,* pp. 106–19. What Iser calls "moments" or "segments within the referential field" (115), I call "tableaux."

18. Iser, "Interaction Between Text and Reader," p. 115.

19. A very good critique has recently been made against the *felix culpa* tradition as it is putatively expressed in *Paradise Lost.* See Dennis Richard Danielson, *Milton's Good God: A Study in Literary Theodicy* (Cambridge, 1982). I use the term *felix culpa* to suggest the ways that the Fall leads to an optimistic recasting of the process of the world's being renewed (the new *felix culpa* tenet). For the fullest elaboration of the theme of *chronos* and *kairos,* see Edward W. Tayler, *Milton's Poetry: Its Development in Time* (Pittsburgh, 1979). *Chronos* is time as it is ordinarily apprehended, *kairos* as it is apprehended under the aspect of eternity (p. 17).

20. Fish, *Surprised by Sin,* pp. 350–51; Cf. Fish, "Things and Actions Indifferent: The Temptation of Plot in *Paradise Regained,*" in *Milton Studies* XVII, ed. Richard S. Ide and Joseph Wittreich (Pittsburgh, 1983), pp. 163–85.

21. Warburton simply called Jesus' statement at *PL* IV, 320– 22 a sophistry; see *"Paradise Regain'd": A Poem,* ed. Thomas Newton (London, 1752), p. 165.

22. Louis de Granada, *Of Prayer, and Meditation,* trans. Richard Hopkins (Douay, 1612), p. 326. Thomas à Kempis, *Of the Imitation of Christ,* trans. Thomas Rogers (London, 1617), p. 79. [Lorenzo Scupoli], *The Spiritual Conflict,* [trans. J. Gerard] (Rouen, 1613), p. D_8^v.

23. U. Milo Kaufmann, *"The Pilgrim's Progress" and Traditions in Puritan Meditation* (New Haven, 1966), pp. 107, 112. Cf. Stanley Fish, *Self-Consuming Artifacts: The Experience of Seventeenth-Century Literature* (Berkeley and Los Angeles, 1972), pp. 224–64, for a reading which accepts Kaufmann's premise but contests his conclusions.

24. Mircea Eliade, *The Sacred and the Profane: The Nature of Religion,* trans. Willard R. Trask (San Diego, 1959), pp. 183–84.

25. Cf. Bernard, *Saint Bernard, His Meditations: Or Sighes, Sobbes, and Teares Upon our Saviours Passion,* 4th ed., trans. W. P., (1608; rpt. London, 1631), pp. 299–334; Thomas à Kempis, *Imitation of Christ,* pp. 66–67; Louis de Granada, *Of Prayer, and Meditation,* p. 326.

26. William Perkins, *Two Treatises: The First, Of the Nature and Practise of Repentance. The Second, Of the Combate of the Flesh and Spirit* (1593; rpt. London, 1621), pp. 112–14. Cf. Perkins, *A Treatise of Gods Free Grace, and Mans Free-Will* (1602) in *The Workes of . . . Mr. W. Perkins,* 3 vols.

(Cambridge, 1616–1618), vol. I, [p. 730], misnumbered as p. 746. Perkins, *Two Treatises,* p. 120.

27. Joshuah Sylvester, *Auto-Machia: Or, The Self Conflict of a Christian* (N.p., n.d.).

28. John Downame, *The Christian Warfare* (London, 1604), p. 240.

29. Joseph Hall, *Meditations and Vowes, Divine and Morall* (1605) in *The Works of Joseph Hall,* 2 vols. (London, 1628–1634), vol. I, p. 34. Cf. Peter de Alcantara's *A Golden Treatise of Mentall Praier,* trans. G. W. (Bruxelles, 1632), p. 159. Cf. Joseph Hall, *The Great Mystery of Godliness, Laid Forth by Way of Affectuous and Feeling Meditation. Also, The Invisible World, Discovered to Spirituall Eyes, and Reduced to Usefull Meditation* (London, 1652), p. 92.

30. Hall, *Meditations and Vowes* in *Works* I, p. 25. Cf. Nicholas Breton, *Characters Upon Essaies Morall and Divine* (London, 1615), p. 1.

31. Hall, *Contemplations Upon the Historie of the New Testament,* in *Works* II, p. 13.

32. Hall, *Contemplations,* p. 8; "Sciscitations" means "questioning." This is the first recorded instance in the OED.

33. John Donne, "To the Countesse of Bedford," in *Complete Poetry of John Donne,* ed. John T. Shawcross (New York, 1967), p. 220. On Milton's *via media* between fideism and rationalism, see Lee A. Jacobus, *Sudden Apprehension: Aspects of Knowledge in "Paradise Lost"* (The Hague, 1976); Jacobus aligns Milton with the Cambridge Platonists in "employing reason in religious matters," while also admitting that the ultimate ways of knowing God transcend rational understanding (pp. 17, 197, 209). One of the Cambridge Platonists, John Smith, *A Discourse Concerning the True Way or Method of Attaining to Divine Knowledge* in *Select Discourses* (London, 1660), p. 16, uses Hall's metaphor to good effect to suggest that fideism is not necessarily antirational: "We must shut the Eyes of Sense, and open that brighter Eye of our Understandings, that other Eye of the Soul, as the Philosopher calls our Intellectual Faculty."

34. Lancelot Andrewes, *Nineteen Sermons Concerning Prayer* (Cambridge, 1641), pp. 110, 131, 198. Prayer is often synonymous with meditation in the writings of meditative theorists; Alcantara, in *Golden Treatise,* p. 134, writes, "in this exercise of prayer we must joyne meditation to contemplation." Cf. pp. 3, 5, 108–09, 115–18. Cf. Antonia de Molina, *A Treatise of Mental Prayer* ([St. Omers], 1617), p. 3. Cf. Hall, *The Art of Divine Meditation,* in *Works* I, p. 113: "Prayer maketh way for Meditation."

35. Henry Church, *Miscellanea Philo-Theologica, or God, & Man* (London, 1637), p. 55.

36. Bernard, *Most Devout and Divine Meditations of Saint Bernard: Concerning the Knowledge of Humane Condition,* trans. W. P. (London, 1632), p. 56

37. Chrysostom, *Homilies on the Gospel of Saint Matthew,* trans. George Prevost, in *The Nicene and Post-Nicene Fathers,* ed. Philip Schaff (Grand Rapids, Mich., 1975), vol. X, p. 78. Hereafter I will be using this edition of Chrysostom, abbreviated as *NPNF* in the notes.

38. Alcantara, *Golden Treatise,* p. 134, cf. pp. 3, 4, 5. On the subtle differences between contemplation and meditation, see Louis L. Martz, *The Poetry of Meditation: A Study in English Religious Literature of the Seventeenth Century* (New Haven, 1954), pp. 3–70, esp. 56–57.

39. See Barbara K. Lewalski's *Protestant Poetics and the Seventeenth-Century Religious Lyric* (Princeton, 1979), pp. 179–212, esp. 194–95, on the widespread use of heart emblems. For emblem literature in general, see Karl Jösef Holtgen's introduction in the facsimile edition of Henry Hawkin, *The Devout Hart: or Royal Throne of the Pacifical Salomon,* ed. John Horden (1634; rpt. London, 1975).

40. George Wither, *A Collection of Emblemes, Ancient and Moderne* (London, 1634–1635), pp. 43, 91.

41. [Arthur Capel], *Daily Observations Or Meditations, Divine, Morall* (N.p., 1634), pp. 6, 14–15; all italics are Capel's. Hobbes, *Leviathan,* ed. C. B. Macpherson (Harmondsworth, 1968), p. 134.

42. Thomas Taylor, *Christs Victorie over the Dragon: Or Satans Downfall* (London, 1633), p. 642, argues that the figure of the church in Revelation, chapter xii, represents the struggles and victory of the church militant: "By the heavens and those that dwell in them are meant the Church on earth and the Saints and Beleevers." Cf. p. 654: "They are in heaven, and inhabitants of heaven; so are wee." Andrewes, *Nineteen Sermons,* pp. 154, 200, 203; cf. pp. 273, 275. John Norden, *The Pensive Mans Practise Or, The Pensive Mans Complaint and Comfort,* 3rd ed. (1584; London, 1600), p. A$_{10}$^{r}. Henry Clapham, *A Tract of Prayer* (London, 1602), p. B$_2$^{v}. Alcantara, *Golden Treatise,* pp. 103–05; cf. 137. John Preston, *The New-Covenant, or The Saints Portion* (London, 1629), pp. 186–88.

43. William Narne, *The Pearle of Prayer Most Precious* (Edinburgh, 1630), pp. 206–07. All italics are Narne's. I have outlined elsewhere the idea of prayer's internal function in seventeenth-century thought; see Ashraf H. A. Rushdy, "'At Heav'n's Door': Prayer and Faith in *Lycidas,*" *Cithara: Essays in the Judaeo-Christian Tradition* XXIX, no. 2 (May 1990), 20–37, esp. 22–26. Alcantara, *Golden Treatise,* pp. 103–05.

44. Richard Baxter, *The Saints Everlasting Rest* (London, 1649–50), pp. 557, 600. On Baxter, see Martz, *Poetry of Meditation,* pp. 153–75; Kaufmann, *Traditions in Puritan Meditation,* pp. 197–216; and Thomas O. Sloan, "Rhetoric and Meditation: Three Case Studies," *The Journal of Medieval and Renaissance Studies* I (1971), 45–58, esp. 55.

45. Baxter, *Saints Everlasting Rest,* p. 604. On casuistry, see Camille

Wells Slights, *The Casuistical Tradition in Shakespeare, Donne, Herbert, and Milton* (Princeton, 1981), pp. 3, 10, 13–14, 62. On Zwingli's pietistic soteriology, see Roland Bainton, *The Reformation of the Sixteenth Century* (Boston, 1952), pp. 77–94. On the debate between Calivinistic and Bezan soteriology, see R. T. Kendall, *Calvin and English Calvinism to 1649* (Oxford, 1979), pp. 3–41. Baxter, *Saints Everlasting Rest,* pp. 607, 661, 621.

46. Cf. John Bunyan, *The Holy War,* ed. James F. Forrest (Oxford, 1980). Mansoul represents both an archetypal individual and the human race in cosmic history. Baxter, *Saints Everlasting Rest,* p. 626. Milton, *Christian Doctrine,* CM 15, 106–07; Book I, ch. ix.

47. Louis Richeome, *The Pilgrime of Loreto,* trans. [E. W.] (1604; rpt. Paris, 1629), p. 50; qtd. in Martz, *The Poetry of Meditation,* p. 17.

48. Louis L. Martz, "Meditations on the Life of Christ" in *The Poetry of Meditation,* pp. 71–117. Cf. Lewalski, *Protestant Poetics,* pp. 166–68, on the tradition of meditation as a means of apprehending the glories of heaven. Martz, *The Poetry of Meditation,* pp. 73, 75. Bonaventura, *The Myrroure of the Blessed Lyfe of Jesu Christe,* trans. N. Love (Douai, ca. 1606), p. 14. The status of this text is dubious from start to finish. See Pollard and Redgrave STC #3268, 3259 and Martz, *The Poetry of Meditation,* p. 72n4. I am citing from the imperfect copy in the Cambridge University Library, shelf no. Syn.8.60.57. The passage occurs in Bonaventura's preface; it is omitted in John Heigham's translation, *The Life of Our Blessed Lord and Savior Jesus* (St. Omers, 1622).

49. Bonaventura, *The Myrroure,* p. 43. Cf. Bonaventura, *The Life of Our Blessed Lord,* p. 73. Hall, *Contemplations,* in *Works* II, p. 180.

50. Chrysostom, *Homilies on the Gospel of Saint Matthew,* in *NPNF* X, p. 2, col. 1; X, p. 2, col. 2; cf. X, p. 78, col. 1.

51. William Cowper, *The Baptisme of Christ* (1612) in *The Workes of Mr. William Cowper* (London, 1623), pp. 600, 599.

52. Wither, *A Collection,* p. 156.

53. Peter Sterry, *A Discourse of the Freedom of the Will* (London, 1675), p. 107.

54. Giovanni Pico della Mirandola, *Oration on the Dignity of Man* (1486), trans. Elizabeth Livermore Forbes, in *The Renaissance Philosophy of Man,* ed. Ernst Cassirer, Paul Oskar Kristeller, and John Herman Randall, Jr. (Chicago, 1948), pp. 226, 229, 232, 235. Marsilio Ficino, *Epistolae,* bk. II, no. 1 (Venice, 1495 [Hain 7059]), fols. xxxviii ff.; translated as *Five Questions Concerning the Mind,* trans. Josephine L. Burroughs, in *The Renaissance Philosophy of Man,* pp. 211, 200, 199; cf. pp. 201, 204.

55. Martz, *Poet of Exile,* pp. 203–18. Kenneth Burke, *The Philosophy of Literary Form: Studies in Symbolic Action* (1941; rpt. Berkeley and Los Angeles, 1973), pp. 73–74. I am turning on its head Burke's notion that

understanding the "eventfulness" of the poem helps us to make basic discoveries about its "structure." For a critique of Burke's notion of "fundamentals of structure," see Wayne C. Booth, *Critical Understanding: The Powers and Limits of Pluralism* (Chicago, 1979), pp. 124–26.

56. Alastair Fowler, "*Paradise Regained:* Some Problems of Style," in *Medieval and Pseudo-Medieval Literature,* ed. Piero Boitani and Anna Torti (Cambridge, 1984), p. 184.

57. Baxter, *Saints Everlasting Rest,* p. 679.

58. Robert Scholes and Robert Kellogg, *The Nature of Narrative* (Oxford, 1966), p. 264.

59. Roger H. Sundell, "The Narrator as Interpreter in *Paradise Regained,*" in *Milton Studies* II, ed. James D. Simmonds (Pittsburgh, 1970), pp. 83–101, esp. p. 89. Sundell argues that the "episode of the baptism presents . . . the human perspective within which the reader will naturally view the poem's events, regardless of the availability of additional perspectives" (p. 86). Why should the reader be so willful if other perspectives are available? Cf. Don Cameron Allen, *The Harmonious Vision: Studies in Milton's Poetry* (Baltimore, 1970), pp. 117–18, who argues that Milton "takes us to Heaven" in order to "turn our imaginations in a new direction." But, seemingly in defiance to this insight, and somewhat illogically, "We are told that a duel is about to begin that will be worth watching; but since we must watch it as men, it is a man whom we shall see." The other duelist, we must remember, is a "Spiritual Foe" (I, 10). But why, in the first place, should the spectator's being *determine* the spectacle's in the way Allen suggests? Thomas B. Stroup, *Religious Rite and Ceremony in Milton's Poetry* (Lexington, Ky., 1968), pp. 51, 53. Cf. Jon S. Lawry, *The Shadow of Heaven: Matter and Stance in Milton's Poetry* (Ithaca, 1968), p. 308, who refers to the "jubiliant response of the angelic chorus," which is "reassuring." Richard Douglas Jordan, "*Paradise Regained* and the Second Adam," in *Milton Studies* IX, ed. James D. Simmonds (Pittsburgh, 1976), pp. 261–75, esp. p. 264. Burton Jasper Weber, *Wedges and Wings: The Patterning of "Paradise Regained"* (Carbondale, Ill., 1975), pp. 85–86.

60. On the "liquid texture" of Milton's verse, see Christopher Ricks, *Milton's Grand Style* (Oxford, 1963), pp. 81–87.

61. Jackson I. Cope, "*Paradise Regained:* Inner Ritual," in *Milton Studies* I, ed. James D. Simmonds (Pittsburgh, 1969), pp. 51–65, esp. p. 63–64. Ernst Cassirer, *The Myth of the State* (New Haven, 1946), p. 28.

62. Cf. Rosemond Tuve, *Elizabethan and Metaphysical Imagery* (Chicago, 1947), p. 349*n19*. Most contemporary studies focus on the lyrical poetry of the age—as both Martz and Lewalski do—as the most obvious examples. On the other hand, there are notable exceptions, such as Kaufman's study of *The Pilgrim's Progress.*

63. Rimmon-Kenan, *Narrative Fiction,* pp. 91–92, calls this level of internal narration "hypodiegesis." Genette, *Narrative Discourse,* pp. 228–34, calls it the "metadiegetic" level. Both terms signify the level of narration within primary narration. I will hereafter use Rimmon-Kenan's term.

64. Cassirer, *The Myth of the State,* p. 45. Eliade, *The Sacred and the Profane,* pp. 211, 202.

65. Peter Brooks, *Reading for the Plot: Design and Intention in Narrative* (Oxford, 1984), p. 281.

66. Jacques Lacan, *Écrits: A Selection,* trans. Alan Sheridan (London, 1977), pp. 81, 315, 165.

67. *The New Testament of Jesus Christ, Translated Faithfully Into English out of the Authenticall Latin, . . . In the English College of Rhemes* (Rhemes, 1582); Thomas Cartwright, *A Confutation of the Rhemists Translation, Glosses and Annotations on the New Testament* (N.p., 1618); William Fulke, *The Text of the New Testament of Jesus Christ* (London, 1601).

68. *Rhemes Bible,* p. 10. Fulke, *The Text of the New Testament,* p. 11; cf. Cartwright, *A Confutation,* p. 16.

69. Daniel Dyke, *Michael and the Dragon, or Christ Tempted and Sathan Foyled* in *Two Treatises* (London, 1616), p. 236. Cf. John Gumbleden, *Christ Tempted: The Divel Conquered. Or, A Short and Plain Exposition on a Part of the Fourth Chapter St. Matthew's Gospel* (London, 1657), p. 16, who suggests that the forty days were spent in "heavenly meditations, in devout prayers and supplications to his Father." John Stradling, *Divine Poems* (London, 1625), pp. 90, 91. Christopher Hill, *Society and Puritanism in Pre-Revolutionary England* (1964; rpt. Harmondsworth, 1986), p. 142. Joseph Wittreich, *Interpreting "Samson Agonistes"* (Princeton, 1986). The major proponents of the critical debate concerning the importance of sectarian alliance and meditative practice are, of course, Barbara Lewalski and Louis Martz. In *The Poetry of Meditation,* Martz makes the case that English Protestant poets were indebted to a tradition of Catholic meditative theory which writers as diverse as Donne (implicitly) and Baxter (explicitly) attempted to amalgamate with Protestant spirituality. In *Protestant Poetics,* Lewalski argues strenuously that the same poets "owe more to contemporary, English, and Protestant influences than to Counter Reformation, continental, and medieval Catholic resources." My point is that there is an earlier, irreducible tradition which is implicit in both Protestant and counter-Reformation theorists of meditation. The idea of meditation as a "dialectics of spirit" is rooted not in Christianity, but in Platonism, and operates under presuppositions which, according to Bertrand Russell, *Mysticism and Logic* (1917; rpt. London, 1986), pp. 20–48, esp. p. 36, may be traced back to as early as Parmenides; see G. S. Kirk and R. E. Raven, *The Pre-Socratic Philosophers: A Critical History with a Selection of Texts* (Cambridge, 1957), pp. 263–85.

Meditation, in this scheme, is a practical process through which the truths of realism are intuited. It was *inherited* by Paul and Augustine, and belongs as much to Bernard of Clairvaux as to Lancelot Andrewes, and as much to Peter de Alcantara as to Joseph Hall. For my purposes, then, I treat meditation as an epistemological category — a means by which seventeenth-century theorists develop a structure of cognition enabling mundane minds to discover divine realities. On Milton's Platonism, see the diametrically opposed arguments of Irene Samuel, *Plato and Milton* (Ithaca, 1947), and William Madsen, *From Shadowy Types to Truth: Studies in Milton's Symbolism* (New Haven, 1968).

70. Georgia Christopher, *Milton and the Science of the Saints* (Princeton, 1982), pp. 204–05: "The hero's first soliloquy seems designed to show the difference before and after receiving the gift of the Spirit." On the significance of the Baptism, see CM XIV, p. 367. See Ashraf H. A. Rushdy, "Standing Alone on the Pinnacle: Milton in 1752," in *Milton Studies* XXVI, ed. James D. Simmonds (Pittsburgh, 1990), pp. 193–218 on the question of Jesus' "divinity."

71. Earl Miner, "The Reign of Narrative in *Paradise Lost*," in *Milton Studies* XVII, ed. Richard S. Ide and Joseph Wittreich (Pittsburgh, 1983), pp. 3–25, esp. p. 9, has argued the same point regarding *Paradise Lost*.

72. Arnold Stein, *Heroic Knowledge: An Interpretation of "Paradise Regained" and "Samson Agonistes"* (Minneapolis, 1957), pp. 38–40, 40–41. I have touched on Stein's reading elsewhere, in Ashraf H. A. Rushdy, "Of *Paradise Regained*: The Interpretation of Career," in *Milton Studies* XXIV, ed. James D. Simmonds (Pittsburgh, 1988), pp. 253–75. John T. Shawcross, *"Paradise Regain'd": Worthy T'Have Not Remain'd So Long Unsung* (Pittsburgh, 1988), pp. 62–63, reads the soliloquy through the prism of Erik Erikson's *Childhood and Society* (New York, 1950) in order to determine its mythic substructure.

73. Samuel Johnson, *Rambler 167*, in *The Works of Samuel Johnson*, ed. Walter Jackson Bate and Albrecht B. Strauss (New Haven, 1969), vol. V, pp. 123–24.

74. The final word of I, 226 is *destroy* in the 1671 text; it was altered to *subdue* in the list of errata.

75. We might recall here the importance of the fideistic epistemology to the grounds of meditation (which I demonstrated using Hall). In the next chapter I will discuss how Jesus establishes a theosophic logic in his final soliloquy.

76. Michel de Montaigne, "Of Solitarinesse" in *The Essayes. Or Morall, Politicke and Millitarie Discourses*, trans. John Florio (London, 1603), pp. 119, 121.

77. Hall, *Meditations and Vowes* in *Works* I, p. 56.

78. William Empson, *Milton's God* (1961; rpt. Cambridge, 1981), p.

68, for instance, says that "in Milton's world death is a very subtle or almost meaningless term." I imagine he means to refer only to the world of *Paradise Lost*.

79. Maurice Kelley, *This Great Argument: A Study of Milton's "De Doctrina Chrisiana" as a Gloss Upon "Paradise Lost"* (1941; rpt. Gloucester, Mass., 1962), pp. 31–32. Kelley gives his fullest exploration of Milton's affirmative answers to that same question on pp. 150–55.

80. Cf. Stein, *Heroic Knowledge*, pp. 112–34, esp. pp. 118–24; Lewalski, *Milton's Brief Epic*, pp. 303–06.

81. Walter MacKellar, *A Variorum Commentary on the Poems of John Milton: Volume Four: "Paradise Regained"* (London, 1975), p. 81; cf. p. 284. The passage from Matthew is also in Mark xiv, 34, and John xii, 27.

82. The word *anxiety* occurs only five times in Milton—*PL* VIII, 185; *SA*, 659; *Second Defence*, CM IX, p. 199 (twice); and in *Christian Doctrine*, CM XVII, p. 226 (*anxietas*). The six translations are taken from *The English Hexapla* (London, 1841), for Mark xiv, 34. Søren Kierkegaard, *The Concept of Anxiety*, trans. Reidar Thomte (Princeton, 1980), pp. 155, 253n2. Heidegger's translators suggest that although *angst* might be translated as "anxiety" or "dread" its best modern equivalents would be "uneasiness" or "malaise"; see Heidegger, *Being and Time*, trans. John Macquarrie and Edward Robinson (Oxford, 1962), p. 227. Norman O. Brown, *Life Against Death: The Psychoanalytical Meaning of History* (1959; rpt. Middletown, Conn., 1985), p. 112; cf. pp. 77–109.

83. Freud's fullest exploration of anxiety is found in *Inhibitions, Symptoms, and Anxiety* (1926), in *PFL* X, pp. 237–333, esp. pp. 302–04. Freud also expresses the process of the move toward the death instinct in terms of anxiety; see *Beyond the Pleasure Principle* (1920), in *PFL* XI, pp. 275–311.

84. Freud, *Beyond the Pleasure Principle*, in *PFL* XI, pp. 281–82. Heidegger, *Being and Time*, pp. 232, 310–11. Kierkegaard, *The Concept of Anxiety*, pp. 41, 155, 161. On anxiety's educative function and its ways of individuation in the dialectic between finitude and infinitude, see Kierkegaard, *The Concept of Anxiety*, pp. 156–60. For Milton's discussion of the twofold nature of Christ, see CM XV, pp. 250–83.

85. Eliade, *The Sacred and the Profane*, p. 137. Lacan, *Écrits*, p. 105.

86. John Calvin, *Institutes of the Christian Religion*, 2 vols., trans. Henry Beveridge (Grand Rapids, Mich., 1983), vol. I, pp. 446–47. Cf. Calvin, *Commentary on the Gospel According to St. John*, 2 vols., trans. T.H.L. Parker (Edinburgh, 1959), vol. II, p. 183.

87. Erik H. Erikson, *Young Man Luther* (1958; rpt. New York, 1962), pp. 111–12.

3. CONFRONTING THE OTHER:
THE ART OF HERMENEUTICS

1. *Paradise Lost,* ed. Thomas Newton (London, 1749), note to Book XI, 135; qtd. in *The Poems of John Milton,* ed. John Carey and Alastair Fowler (London, 1968), p. 443.

2. The studies of time in *Paradise Regained* have generally been concerned with demonstrating how Satan lives out cyclical time while Jesus lives out Christian time (*kairos*). See A. B. Chambers, "The Double Time Scheme in *Paradise Regained,*" in *Milton Studies* VII, ed. Albert C. Labriola and Michael Lieb (Pittsburgh, 1975), pp. 189–205; and Laurie Zwicky, "*Kairos* in Paradise Regained: *The Divine Plan,*" *ELH* XXXI (1964), 271–77. Cf. also A.S.P. Woodhouse, "Theme and Pattern in *Paradise Regained,*" *UTQ* XXV (1956), 167–82.

3. Fredric Jameson, *The Political Unconscious: Narrative as a Socially Symbolic Act* (Ithaca, 1981), p. 123. Robert Scholes and Robert Kellogg, *The Nature of Narrative* (Oxford, 1966), p. 170; cf. p. 235. Paul Ricoeur, *Time and Narrative,* 3 vols. (Chicago, 1984–1987), esp. vol. I, p. 3 and vol. 2, p. 6. Ricoeur, "Narrative Time," *Critical Inquiry* VII (1980–81), 169–90, esp. 169.

4. Mircea Eliade, *The Sacred and the Profane: The Nature of Religion,* trans. Willard R. Trask (San Diego, 1959), pp. 68, 72. Cf. Edward W. Tayler, *Milton's Poetry: Its Development in Time* (Pittsburgh, 1979), pp. 148–84. Tayler calls Jesus a "chronometrical hero" (158). William Blake, *Milton, a Poem in Two Books,* in *Blake: Complete Writings,* ed. Geoffrey Keynes (Oxford, 1966), p. 526.

5. See Mary Ann Radzinowicz, "*Paradise Regained* as Hermeneutic Combat," *University of Hartford Studies in Literature* XVI, no. 1 (1984), 99–107; Mary Nyquist, "The Father's Word / Satan's Wrath," *PMLA* C, no. 2 (1985), 187–202; and Roger H. Sundell, "The Narrator as Interpreter in *Paradise Regained,*" in *Milton Studies* II, ed. James D. Simmonds (Pittsburgh, 1970), pp. 83–101.

6. Joan Malory Webber, *Milton and His Epic Tradition* (Seattle, 1979), p. 171; Earl Miner, *The Restoration Mode from Milton to Dryden* (Princeton, 1974), p. 272.

7. Satan offered Aristotelian philosophy, under the surname of Peripatetics, as the third school. It is relegated in Jesus' answer to the fourth, the "Others," under which also is answered the offer of the school of Epicurus. Cf. *Paradise Regain'd,* ed. Thomas Newton (London, 1752), pp. 162–63; *Paradise Regained,* ed. Charles Dunster (London, 1795), pp. 226–29; *The Poems of John Milton,* ed. Carey and Fowler, p. 1151; Walter MacKellar, *A Variorum Commentary on the Poems of John Milton,* (London, 1975), vol. IV, pp. 211–12.

8. John Calvin, *Institutes of the Christian Religion,* 2 vols., trans. Henry Beveridge (Grand Rapids, Mich., 1983), vol. II, pp. 202–58; Henry More, *Divine Dialogues,* 2 vols. (London, 1668), vol. II, pp. 71–73.

9. William Ames, *The Marrow of Sacred Divinity* (London, 1642), pp. 226, cf. 267–69; John Downham, *The Christian Warfare* (London, 1604), pp. 187–88, 190, 199–200, 541, 555; William Gouge, *The Whole-Armor of God,* 2nd ed. (London, 1619), pp. 238, 241; Gouge defines the other type of despair: "The temptation of Satan, tending to doubt and despaire" (p. 282). Richard Sibbes, *The Bruised Reede, and Smoaking Flax* (London, 1630), pp. 43, 68.

10. Francis Bacon, *The New Organon* I.xxxvii, in *The Works of Francis Bacon,* 14 vols., ed. James Spedding et al. (Boston, 1857–1874), vol. VIII, p. 98; cf. I.lxvii. Herschel Baker, *The Wars of Truth: Studies in the Decay of Christian Humanism in the Earlier Seventeenth Century* (Cambridge, Mass., 1952), pp. 154, 161.

11. René Descartes, *Discourse on the Method,* in *The Philosophical Writings of Descartes,* 2 vols., trans. John Cottingham, Robert Stoothoff, and Dugald Murdoch (Cambridge, 1985), vol. I, p. 125.

12. Joseph Glanvill, *The Vanity of Dogmatizing* (London, 1661), pp. 73–74. For an account of Glanvill's evolution from Cartesian mechanical rationalism to Baconian empiricism between this first edition of the essay and its second edition as *Scepsis Scientifica* (London, 1665), see Baker, *The Wars of Truth,* pp. 349, 361. This particular passage passed unrevised between the two editions. Cf. Glanvill, *Scepsis Scientifica,* pp. 55–56; Glanvill, *The Vanity of Dogmatizing,* pp. 186–87; *Scepsis Scientifica,* pp. 139–40.

13. *Paradise Regained,* ed. Charles S. Jerram (London, 1877), p. 109; cf. MacKellar, *Variorum Commentary,* p. 122.

14. John Smith, *Select Discourses* (London, 1660), p. 4. Thomas Adams, *Three Divine Sisters* in *The Works of Tho. Adams* (London, 1629), p. 139.

15. Georgia Christopher, *Milton and the Science of the Saints* (Princeton, 1982), p. 202.

16. Chrysostom, *Homilies on the Gospel of Saint Matthew,* in *A Select Library of Nicene and Post-Nicene Fathers,* trans. George Prevost, ed. Philip Schaff (Grand Rapids, Mich., 1975), vol. X, pp. 81–82. Hereafter cited as *NPNF.*

17. Richard Ward, *Theologicall, Dogmaticall, and Evangelicall Questions, Essays, Upon the Gospel of Jesus Christ, According to St. Matthew* (London, 1640), p. 97. An asterisk beside "some" directs us to "Chrysostom" in the margin.

18. William Cowper, *The Combate of Christ with Satan* (1609) in *The Workes of Mr. William Cowper* (London, 1623), p. 613; Joseph Hall, *Contemplations Upon the Historie of the New Testament,* in *The Works of Joseph*

Hall 2 vols. (London, 1628–34), vol. I, p. 33. Cf. John Lightfoote, *The Harmony of the Foure Evangelists* (London, 1647), p. 20.

19. Thomas Fuller, *A Comment on the First Eleven Verses of the Fourth Chapter of S. Matthew's Gospel* (London, 1652), pp. 10–11, 39–40, 177. Cf. Isaac Colfe, *A Comfortable Treatise Concerning the Temptations of Christ* (London, 1592), p. 54. It was universally accepted that Christ's fast was miraculous. See, amongst numerous others, Cowper, *The Combate*, p. 611, and Ward, *Theologicall*, p. 62–64, 89, 101.

20. John Gumbleden, *Christ Tempted: The Divel Conquered* (London, 1657), pp. 21–24, 28, 53–54, 65–66. Cf. p. 28: "A doubtful speech, as he delivers it; but surely not doubtfull as he understood it."

21. Chrysostom, *Homilies on the Gospel of Saint Matthew*, in *NPNF* X, p. 76.

22. Matthew xii, 31, Luke xii, 10, Mark iii, 28–29. Cf. Calvin, *Institutes* I, pp. 528–31. John Hales, *A Tract Concerning the Sin Against the Holy Ghost* in *The Works of . . . Mr. John Hales,* 3 vols. (Glasgow, 1765) vol. I, pp. 31–50, disputes Calvin's rigid reading and, following Augustine and Ambrose, poses a rather more humanistic interpretation, including a digression on the uses and abuses of doubt (pp.43–46). His definition runs as follows: "The blasphemy against the Holy Ghost, was an evil speaking of, or slandering of the miracles which our Saviour did, by those, who though they were convinced by the miracles, to believe that such works could not be done by the power of God, yet they did maliciously say, they were wrought by the power of the devil" (32); Perkins, *A Golden Chaine* in *The Works of . . . William Perkins,* 3 vols. (Cambridge, 1616–1618), vol. I, pp. 106–07; Gouge, *Whole-Armor,* pp. 567, 598.

23. Perkins, *Golden Chaine,* in *Works* I, p. 107; cf. Richard Capel, *Tentations: Their Nature, Danger, Cure,* 3rd ed. (London, 1636), pp. 262–65. Capel, oddly, says that "could the blasphemer against the H. Ghost repent, hee must have his pardon," assuming, I imagine, that, like Satan, the blasphemer has no thoughts of repentance (p. 281). Ambrose, though, does believe that the sin against the Holy Ghost could be pardoned by repentance; see Hales, *Works* I, p. 42.

24. The debate as to Milton's Arianism is too long to survey here, but the cases made for Milton's heterodoxy by Maurice Kelley, *This Great Argument: A Study of Milton's "De Doctrina Christiana" as a Gloss Upon "Paradise Lost"* (Princeton, 1941) and Michael Bauman, *Milton's Arianism* (Frankfurt am Main, 1987), I find more persuasive than those made for Milton's orthodoxy by William Hunter, J. H. Adamson, and C. A. Patrides, collected in *Bright Essence: Studies in Milton's Theology* (Salt Lake City, 1973).

25. Cf. CM IV, p. 186. Milton suggests that Christ spoke in such a way "that his Disciples and all good men might learne to expound him in

this place, as in all other his precepts, not by the written letter, but by that unerring paraphrase of Christian love and Charity, which is the summe of all commands, and the perfection."

26. Smith, *Select Discourses,* p. 8; see *Paradise Regain'd,* ed. Newton, pp. 10–11; James R. McAdams, "The Pattern of Temptation in *Paradise Regained,*" in *Milton Studies* IV, ed. James D. Simmonds (Pittsburgh, 1972), p. 186: "Satan wills to understand neither the conception of providence nor the portent of the dove at the Baptism." Cf. Nyquist, "The Father's Word / Satan's Wrath," 196.

27. [Arthur Capel], *Daily Observations Or Meditations, Divine, Morall* (N.p., 1654), p. 48; Downame, *The Christian Warfare,* pp. 120, 364, 658. Cf. Gouge, *Whole-Armor,* p. 256: "This extent of a good conscience respecteth rather the integrity of the heart, than the perfection of the work." On this Lutheran theme, see CM XVI, pp. 2–49 and XVII, pp. 3–73: "An action . . . is generally considered in the light of an effect, not of an instrument; or perhaps it may be more properly designated as the less principal cause" (XVI, pp. 34–37); critics have long recognized the design of silencing Satan running through the poem. See Leonard Mustazza, "Language and Weapon in Milton's *Paradise Regained,*" in *Milton Studies* XVIII, ed. James D. Simmonds (Pittsburgh, 1983), pp. 195–216; Stanley Fish, "Inaction and Silence: The Reader in *Paradise Regained,*" in *Calm of Mind: Tercentenary Essays on "Paradise Regained" and "Samson Agonistes" in Honor of John S. Diekhoff,* ed. Joseph Anthony Wittreich, Jr. (Cleveland, 1971), pp. 25–47; Robert L. Entzminger, *Divine Word: Milton and the Redemption of Language* (Pittsburgh, 1985), pp. 103–16; and Steven Goldsmith, "The Muting of Satan: Language and Redemption in *Paradise Regained,*" *SEL* XXVII, no. 1 (1987), 125–40.

28. Smith, *Select Discourses,* p. 6.

29. CM XVI, pp. 262–63. Milton does suggest in *Areopagitica* that truth may have more than one shape (CM IV, p. 348), and he allows for a "compound of the historical and typical" senses in Old Testament hermeneutics; Thomas Taylor, *Christs Combate and Conquest* (Cambridge, 1618), p. 27; Daniel Tuvil, *The Dove and the Serpent* (London, 1614), p. 54; Hall, *Meditations,* p. 67. On Satan's pretense and use of doubt as a mode of interpretation and temptation, see Don Cameron Allen, *The Harmonious Vision* (Baltimore, 1970), pp. 111–12, 115, 116; Webber, *Milton and His Epic Tradition,* pp. 171, 199; A.S.P. Woodhouse, *The Heavenly Muse,* ed. Hugh MacCallum (Toronto, 1972), pp. 328–29

30. Elizabeth Marie Pope, *"Paradise Regained": The Tradition and the Poem* (Baltimore, 1947), p. 78. Arnold Stein, *Heroic Knowledge: An Interpretation of "Paradise Regained" and "Samson Agonistes"* (Minneapolis, 1957), pp. 58, 221n7, follows Pope in this interpretation. Commenting on the scene, without overt agreement or disagreement, are Barbara

Kiefer Lewalski, *Milton's Brief Epic: The Genre, Meaning, and Art of "Paradise Regained"* (Providence, 1966), pp. 226–27, and Burton Jasper Weber, *Wedges and Wings: The Patterning of "Paradise Regained"* (Carbondale, Ill., 1975), pp. 35–36.

31. Milton, *A Mask*, 784–85, 788, cf. 792, "Thou art not fit to hear thyself convinc't." Daniel Tuvil, *Vade Mecum* (London, 1629), pp. 82–84, in reference to the beauty of Virtue: "Her Beauty hath amazed damnation; the very Glances of it have stroake such terrour in the hearts of those that have conspired her over-throwe, that they have seemed unmindefull of their Wicked resolution, and in an instant altered their intention." Cf. Smith, *Select Discourses*, p. 14: "As Truth does not alwaies act in good men, so neither doth Sense alwaies act in wicked men: they may sometimes have their *lucida intervalla*, their sober fits; and a Divine spirit blowing and breathing upon them may then blow up some live sparks of true Understanding within them; though they may soon endeavour to quench them again, and to rake them up in the ashes of their own earthly thoughts."

32. Smith, *Select Discourses*, p. 16. For the full program of the classical types of skepticism, see Sextus Empiricus, *Outlines of Pyrrhonism*, trans. R. G. Bury (Cambridge, Mass., 1933). The four are the Zetetic, the Ephetic or Suspensive, the Aporetic or Dubitative, and the Pyrrhonean (pp. 4–7). Milton would be criticizing and Satan employing this final mode. The Pyrrhonist "assents to nothing that is non-evident" and employs terms that "are virtually cancelled by themselves" (pp. 10–11). As such, then, the Pyrrhonist begins to doubt only when anything is affirmed beyond "appearance itself." In the famous excursion on honey, Sextus maintains that honey "appears to us to be sweet," but we can never know from appearances that "it is also sweet in its essence" (pp. 14–15). The fullest exploration of Pyrrhonism in action anticipates David Hume in its concern about the possibility of naming anything as a cause of anything else (pp. 336–45).

33. Joseph Hall, *Contemplations*, in *Works* II, p. 12. Thomas à Kempis, *Of the Imitation of Christ*, trans. Thomas Rogers (London, 1617), p. 5. Thomas Fuller, *A Comment on . . . Christ's Temptation* (London, 1652), p. 17.

34. Matthew xxvii, 11, Mark xv, 2 ("Thou sayest it"), and Luke xxiii, 3 (as Mark). Bacon, "Of Truth," in *The Works* VI, p. 377, contends that "jesting Pilate" would "not stay for an answer," implying that he might have understood it had he stayed. Cf. Hales, *Christ's Kingdom Not of This World* in *The Works* II, p. 292, who argues that when Pilate took Christ's kingship as an idle report, Christ puts him "out of doubt" and "assures him, that he is a king, but of such a kingdom as he could not skill of."

35. Chrysostom, *Homilies on the Gospel of St. John*, in *NPNF* XIV, pp. 81–82.

36. Augustine, *Homilies on the Gospel of John,* in *NPNF* VII, p. 73; cf. *Patrologiæ Cursus Completus,* Latin series, ed. J. P. Migne (Parisiis, 1844–1903), vol. XXV, col. 1472: "Hoc modo omnibus nobis notum est: et si Judæis clausum est, quia foris stant; nobis tamen apertum est, quia novimus in quem credimus." Augustine, *Homilies on the Gospel of John,* in *NPNF* VII, p. 251. Elsewhere, Augustine asserts that the "manifold obscurities and ambiguities" of Scriptures were "divinely arranged for the purpose of subduing pride by toil, and of preventing a feeling of satiety in the intellect, which generally holds in small esteem what is discovered without difficulty" (*Christian Doctrine,* in *NPNF* II, pp. 537, 577, 581–82). Boccaccio, *Boccaccio on Poetry,* trans. Charies G. Osgood (1930; rpt. Indianapolis, 1956), pp. 58–62. These pages represent the *Genealogica Deorum Gentllium,* Bk. XIV, ch. 12.

37. *The New Testament of Our Lord Jesus Christ Translated Out of the Greek by Theod. Beza . . . Englished by L. Tomson* (London, 1576), p. 141. The annotators are Beza, Joachim Camerarius, P. Loseler, and Villerius. John Diodati, *Pious and Learned Annotations Upon the Holy Bible* (1642; rpt. London, 1648), pp. 82–83. Lancelot Andrewes, *Seven Sermons Upon the Temptation of Christ in the Wilderness,* in *The Works of Lancelot Andrewes,* 10 vols. (Oxford, 1865), vol. V, p. 503, writes that Christ performed the miracle of turning water into wine so "that His disciples might believe in Him. That was the reason that moved Him to the working of that miracle, and because there was no such cause here He did it not. For the devil would not believe in Him, He knew, though He had done it." Cf. Daniel Dyke, *Michael and the Dragon, or Christ Tempted and Sathan Foyled* (London, 1616), pp. 244–45: "Miracles are for the confirmation of faith, but the Divell is uncapable of faith." *Annotations Upon All the Books of the Old and New Testament* (1645; rpt. London, 1657), q.v. John ii, 19. Henry Hammond, *A Paraphrase and Annotations Upon All the Books of the New Testament* (London, 1653), p. 299.

38. George Hutcheson, *An Exposition of the Gospel of Jesus Christ According to John* (London, 1657), pp. 29–30. Taylor, *Christs Combate and Conquest,* pp. 116, 118.

39. John Calvin, *Commentary on the Gospel According to St. John,* 2 vols., trans. T.H.L. Parker (Edinburgh, 1959), vol. I, pp. 55, 57.

40. Richard Baxter, *A Paraphrase on the New Testament, with Notes Doctrinal and Practical* (London, 1685), p. A_3^v.

41. Smith, *Divine Knowledge,* in *Select Discourses,* pp. 4, 8, 9; cf. Smith, *Of Prophesie,* in *Select Discourses,* p. 176; and Smith, *A Christians Conflicts and Conquests,* in *Select Discourses,* p. 480: "As God will onely be convers'd withall in a way of Light and Understanding; so the Devil loves to be convers'd with in a way of Darkness and Obscurity." N. W. [Nathaniel Ward], *Nature and Grace in Conflict* (London, 1638), p. 119.

42. Augustine, *Christian Doctrine,* in *NPNF* II, p. 538. Sibbes, *The Bruised Reede,* p. 106.

43. Adams, *Mysticall Bedlam,* in *The Workes of Tho. Adams,* p. 492. Cf. Adams, *Heaven-Gate,* in *The Workes of Tho. Adams,* p. 657. Calvin, *Institutes* I, pp. 10, 47, 53, 54, 57, 91. William Perkins, *Golden Chaine,* in *Works* I, p. 23. Perkins, *A Treatise of Gods Free Grace, and Mans Free-Will,* in *The Works of. . . William Perkins* I, p. 721. Hall, *The Art of Divine Meditation,* in *The Works* I, p. 107.

44. Hall, *The Great Mysterie of Godliness . . . Also, The Invisible World* (London, 1652), pp. 281–87. Henry Lawrence, *An History of Angells* (London, 1649), p. 62. Cf. CM XV, p. 111.

45. Bernard, *Saint Bernard His Meditations: Or Sighes, Sobbes, and Teares, Upon Our Saviours Passion,* trans. W. P. (1608; rpt. London, 1632), pp. 32–33. Daniel Tuvil, *The Dove and the Serpent* (London, 1614), pp. 12–14. Hall, *Contemplations,* in *Works* II, p. 191. Perkins, *The Combate Betweene Christ and Devill Displayed,* in *The Works of. . . William Perkins* III, p. 401; Thomas Taylor, *Christs Combate,* pp. 110, 333. Cf. Jeremy Taylor, *The Life of Our Blessed Lord and Savior Jesus Christ* in *The Whole Works of. . . Jeremy Taylor,* 15 vols., ed. Reginald Heber (London, 1822), vol. II, p. 199; John Udall, *The Combate betwixt christ and the Devill* (London, [1588]) p. I$_8^r$, who both mention the "zeal" and "heat" of Christ's answer to the offer of the kingdoms. I have outlined this tradition in Ashraf H. A. Rushdy, "'The Fatal Influence of Frigorifick Wisdom': Warming Up to *Paradise Regained,*" *MQ* XXIV, no. 2 (May 1990), 49–57.

46. The list of critics who have used the word *cold* to describe Jesus and his tone in the criticism of this poem is unhappily too long to survey here, though I have surveyed this critical trend elsewhere; see "'The Fatal Influence of Frigorifick Wisdom'." Arnold Stein, *Heroic Knowledge,* p. 24, notes the "wittiness" of Jesus and aligns it to Renaissance Neoplatonism; Christopher, *Milton and the Science of the Saints,* p. 216. Hilaire Belloc, *Milton* (London, 1935), p. 266: "Our Lord is very rude to the Devil"; W. W. Robson, "The Better Fortitude," in *The Living Milton: Essays by Various Hands,* ed. Frank Kermode (London, 1960), pp. 128–29; A. E. Dyson, "The Meaning of *Paradise Regained,*" *TSLL* III (1961), 197–211. The whole of Dyson's essay is an exercise demonstrating an ignorance of theology, of narrative art, and, saddest of all, of decorum. Dyson's mistakes begin with the immodesty of his title, and reach a zenith when he suggests that Satan and Jesus are interchangeable: "If you reversed their positions, would not both be still basically the same?" Dyson also calls Jesus' tone "insolent" (209, 202). E.M.W. Tillyard, *Studies in Milton* (London, 1951), p. 106.

47. The "masorites" to whom Milton refers are those Jewish scholars

who contributed to the Masorah (modern spelling, "Masorete"). It would seem that, in *An Apology,* Milton made them synonymous with "Fools who would teach men to read more decently then God thought good to write" (CM III, p. 316); cf. Milton's usages in *The Doctrine and Discipline of Divorce* (CM III, p. 376) and *Pro Se Defensio* (CM IX, pp. 110–11).

48. Milton criticism, however, is perhaps the one form of discourse in English letters where critics do not hesitate to judge the "fitness" of their predecessors. Stanley Fish, *Surprised by Sin: The Reader in "Paradise Lost"* (1967; rpt. Berkeley and Los Angeles, 1970), pp. 2–3, quite clearly directs his arguments to the school of "anti-Miltonism" made up of those he considers unfit readers. In return, Earl Miner, *The Restoration Mode,* p. 207*n*9 says of Fish, "I think Milton would have included him among the few "fit" readers". Through the centuries critics have implied or used overtly Calvinistic language in repudiating their opponents. Marvell perhaps set the trend when he suggested that *Paradise Lost* "Draws the Devout, deterring the Profane."

49. For their differences, see Calvin, *Institutes* II, pp. 202–58; CM XIV, pp. 91–175.

50. "Amuse" means to "confound, distract, bewilder, puzzle" (OED, 2); Dr. Johnson records only the instances in which it means, as in our modern sense, to entertain.

51. Gumbleden, *Christ Tempted,* p. 76; Perkins, *The Combate,* p. 407; Taylor, *Christs Combate,* p. 73. Lawrence, *History,* p. 175.

52. Cf. CM XVI, pp. 262–63: No passage of Scripture "is to be interpreted in more than one sense."

53. Taylor, *Christs Combate,* p. 26.

54. For seventeenth-century commentators on the silencing of Satan, see Thomas Bilson, *The Survey of Christs Sufferings* (London, 1604), p. 306; Dyke, *Michael and the Dragon,* p. 274; Gumbleden, *Christ Tempted,* pp. 65–66; and Taylor, *Christs Combate,* p. 243. On the "spirit," see Christopher, *Milton and the Science of the Saints,* pp. 208–10.

55. Stein, *Heroic Knowledge,* pp. 83–88; Lewalski, *Milton's Brief Epic,* p. 258; the two modern variorum editors, Carey and MacKellar, both agree with Stein, but are equally unfair to Lewalski. MacKellar, *Variorum Commentary* IV, p. 157, ignores her comments entirely, although echoing some of her points, while directing us to and agreeing with Stein., Carey, *The Poems of John Milton,* p. 1124, adds an unwarranted adjective, "mere," before "rhetorical craft," which is neither present nor implied in Lewalski's text. Satan's nature, of course, is to be notoriously self-contradictory in *Paradise Lost.* Cf. Taylor, *Christs Combate,* p. 279: "desperate and yet hopeful of victory."

56. Stein, *Heroic Knowledge,* p. 88, notes that there is no temptation following this speech: "No offer is made, and no pause to permit a

counter-offer," but then the speech may be meant, like the banquet, to allow for a continuance of discourse. And Satan does immediately take Jesus to another temptation.

57. Milton says (CM XIV, pp. 394–97) that the sin against the Holy Spirit is truly a sin against the Father, so Satan's failure to acknowledge the dovelike spirit is a form of atheism.

58. Lewalski, *Milton's Brief Epic,* p. 278, notes that the confidence is wrought from Jesus' full knowledge of his kingly office. Carey, *The Poems of John Milton,* p. 1143, comments on the "flashes of confidence" in this speech. Allen, *The Harmonious Vision,* pp. 119–20, argues that when Jesus is alone he is human, and when he is confronted by Satan he assumes divinity; in terms of character development, as Satan's fears increase, Jesus' "sense of his own divinity increases and the human side of his nature becomes more obscure." MacCallum, *Milton and the Sons of God* (Toronto, 1986), pp. 231–32, argues against Allen's interpretation. Virgil, *Aeneid* I, 278–79, in *The Works of Virgil,* 4 vols., trans. Christopher Pitt, ed. Joseph Wharton (London, 1778): "Imperium sine fine dedi" (II, pp. 84–85); the translator's lines are I, 371–72. On the pseudo-Virgilian opening to the *Aeneid* in the invocation of *Paradise Regained,* see Stein, *Heroic Knowledge,* pp. 7–8; Lewalski, *Milton's Brief Epic,* pp. 116–17, 386.

59. Thomas M. Greene, *The Light in Troy: Imitation and Discovery in Renaissance Poetry* (New Haven, 1982), pp. 235–36, 88–92.

60. Miner, *The Restoration Mode,* pp. 281–82, also comments on the "mystery-story atmosphere" of the poem. Elizabeth Marie Pope, *The Tradition and the Poem,* p. 39. I have elsewhere attempted to demonstrate the historical groundings for the sorts of questions asked at the beginnings of the formalization of *Paradise Regained* criticism in order to show how those original questions of 1752 have forced certain misreadings of the poem as a whole and the pinnacle scene in particular; the detective story theory stands foremost as one of those misleading questions. See Ashraf H. A. Rushdy, "Standing Alone on the Pinnacle: Milton in 1752," in *Milton Studies* XXVI, ed. James D. Simmonds (Pittsburgh, 1990), pp. 193–218.

61. William Cowper, *The Combate,* p. 606. Cf. Dyke, *Michael and the Dragon,* p. 341; Udall, *The Combate betwixt christ and the Devill,* p. $K_4{}^r$.

62. For Milton's comments about the language in which he wrote the divorce tracts, see his letter to Leo van Aitzema, February 5, 1655, where he counsels van Aitzema against having the first divorce tract translated into Dutch: "I should really prefer that you were having it translated into Latin, because I know by experience with these books how the common herd is wont to receive uncommon opinions" (YP IV, pp. 871–72); cf. *Second Defence,* CM VIII, p. 112. For Milton's reference to the anonymous author of *An Answer,* see *Colasterion* (1645), in CM IV, pp. 233–73, esp.

p. 250: "I mean not to dispute Philosophy with this Pork, who never read any." Cf. Lowell W. Coolidge, YP II, pp. 719–58, for how Milton responded to the anonymous author's tract point for point.

63. Gumbleden, *Christ Tempted*, p. 55. *Paradise Regained*, ed. Newton, p. 150, gave birth to the issues still alive in modern criticism. He notes that "there is nothing in the disposition and conduct of the whole poem so justly liable to censure as the awkward and preposterous introduction of this incident in this place." *Paradise Regained*, ed. Dunster, p. 107, attempted to answer Newton by suggesting that Satan's desperation is herein evinced, which only begs the question. Modern critics, Stein, *Heroic Knowledge*, pp. 92–93, and Lewalski, *Milton's Brief Epic*, p. 260, tend to agree with Dunster, although differing slightly in their estimations of Satan's conscious designs. Newton's objections have generally been neglected rather than confronted, and seem to me unanswerable.

64. Gumbleden, *Christ Tempted*, p. 50. Cf. Andrewes, *Seven Sermons*, in *The Works* V, pp. 516–17, on the "assumptions" in Christ's life, to the pinnacle, to Jerusalem to suffer, and to heaven; Hall, *Contemplations*, in *Works* II, p. 181: "I am wont to reckon up these four principall wonders of his life: Incarnation, Tentation, Transfiguration, and Agonie: the first in the wombe of the Virgin, the second in the Wildernesse, the third in the Mount, the fourth in the Garden."

65. Thomas Taylor, *Christs Combate*, p. 51; cf. Andrewes, *Seven Sermons*, in *The Works* V, p. 491; Colfe, *A Comfortable Treatise*, pp. 51–53; Cowper, *The Combate*, p. 611; Fuller, *A Comment*, pp. 19–20; Gumbleden, *Christ Tempted*, p. 18; Hall, *Contemplations*, in *The Works* I, pp. 32–33; Udall, *The Combate*, p. C$_6$^{v}; Ward, *Theologicall, Dogmaticall, and Evangelicall Questions*, p. 89; John Mayer, *A Commentarie Upon the New Testament*, 2 vols. (London, 1631), vol. II, p. 79.

66. For an interesting reading of the significance of mountains as symbols in Milton's poetic, from *Lycidas* to *Samson Agonistes*, see Balachandra Rajan, "To Which Is Added *Samson Agonistes*" in *The Prison and the Pinnacle: Papers to Commemorate the Tercentenary of "Paradise Regained" and "Samson Agonistes," 1671–1971*, ed. Balachandra Rajan (London, 1973), pp. 91–96, 98, 99, 102. Mountains, he notes, allow comprehension of an intuitive (visionary) sort, beyond the boundaries of discursive knowledge. In the long history of persons climbing mountains in order to aspire to a higher state of contemplative knowledge—both of God and self—we need only mention two notable instances: Bonaventura's imitating St. Francis and climbing Mt. Alverna, and Petrarch's imitating Philip of Macedon and climbing Mt. Ventoux. See Bonaventura, *The Mind's Road to God*, trans. George Boas (Indianapolis, 1953); and Petrarch, *The Ascent of Mont Ventoux*, trans. Hans Nachod, in *The Renaissance Philosophy*

of Man, ed. Ernest Cassirer, Paul Oskar Kristeller, and John Herman Randall, Jr. (Chicago, 1948), pp. 36–46.

67. John Hales, *Christ's Kingdom Not of This World,* in *The Works* II, pp. 286, 290, 301–02. On the Parthian horsemen, see *PR* III, 305–25: "Of equal dread in flight, or in pursuit." Cf. John Preston, *The New Covenant* (London, 1629), vol. II, pp. 132–37: "When men have so much strength within themselves, that they can guide and rule themselves, and walke in the way of righteousnesse, now they are made Kings, and such Kings the Lord makes all those that come to him."

68. Thomas à Kempis, *Imitation of Christ,* pp. 26, 25. The role of the *delectatio morosa* theme in Patristic thought is superbly delineated by James F. Forrest, "The Fathers on Milton's Evil Thought in Blameless Mind," *Canadian Journal of Theology* XV (1969), 247–67.

69. Gumbleden, *Christ Tempted,* p. 52. Although Gumbleden argues that the kingdoms were presented in a vision, he also adds that this is not "positively determinable from the Text." A debate arose as to Satan's method of presenting the kingdoms. Some commentators held that the kingdoms were available to Jesus only in external reality, some only in Jesus's imagination, some both in external reality and Jesus's imagination, and some felt it "were curious to enquire." Baxter, *The Saints Everlasting Rest,* pp. 706, 694–95, 639, 652. William Fenner, *A Divine Message to the Elect Soule* (London, 1647), p. 3.

70. Thomas O. Sloane, *Donne, Milton, and the End of Humanist Rhetoric* (Berkeley and Los Angeles, 1985), pp. 1–63, 209–78, 219. "Donne's *practice* is humanist, as Milton's *pronouncements* are" (p. 63, cf. p. 214). Harold Fisch, *Jerusalem and Albion: The Hebraic Factor in Seventeenth-Century Literature* (London, 1964), pp. 128–47. Cary Nelson, *The Incarnate Word: Literature as Verbal Space* (Urbana, Ill., 1973), p. 87. Cf. Rosemond Tuve, *Elizabethan and Metaphysical Imagery* (Chicago, 1947), pp. 331–53. Sloane states that Donne's "Good Friday 1613. Riding Westward" is essentially "contraversal," that is, wrought out of debate (pp. 34–41). William H. Halewood, *The Poetry of Grace: Reformation Themes and Structures in English Seventeenth-Century Poetry* (New Haven, 1970), pp. 26–29, finds that there is "no debate" in the poem. Whereas Sloane argues that *Paradise Regained* was discursive only to a limited extent, being rather intuitive in a "nondiscursive" way (pp. 225–30), William Kerrigan, *The Sacred Complex: On the Psychogenesis of "Paradise Lost"* (Cambridge, Mass., 1983), p. 89, calls *Paradise Regained* "relentlessly discursive."

71. On the curriculum of Ramus and Ramists, see Walter J. Ong, *Ramus: Method, and the Decay of Dialogue* (Cambridge, Mass., 1958), pp. 282–83. For an interpretation of the significance of the three adjectives to Milton's poetic, see Ruth Wallerstein, *Studies in Seventeenth-Century*

Poetic (Madison, Wis., 1950), pp. 107–09. Although underestimating the role of discursive reason in her analysis of "simple," Wallerstein concludes correctly that Milton's Platonism kept him from the parallel dangers of formalism and didacticism. Ramus, *Dialecticae institutiones* (1543), fols. 38–39; qtd. in Ong, *Ramus,* p. 189; Perry Miller, *The New England Mind: The Seventeenth Century* (Cambridge, Mass., 1939), p. 140, cf. pp. 493–501.

72. Sloane, *Humanist Rhetoric,* pp. 222–23, but on p. 219, for example, he quotes Abraham Fraunce, who notes that natural method "onely, and none other is to bee observed, so often as wee teach any art or science, or take upon us to intreate perfectly of any generall matter," and adds, "Milton agreed." Milton, as we have just shown, and as Sloane notes three pages further, does not agree.

73. Sloane, *Humanist Rhetoric,* pp. 137–44, esp. 138, 141, pp. 217–18; cf. Ong, *Ramus,* pp. 189, 192, 207. Sloane, *Humanist Rhetoric,* p. 143. Cf. Sloane's earlier position on meditation, "Rhetoric and Meditation: Three Case Studies," *The Journal of Medieval and Renaissance Studies* I (1971), 45–58, where he argues that the paucity of rhetorical theory in the seventeenth century was compensated for by the proliferation of tracts on the art of meditation: "Rhetoric and meditation taken together constitute the true rhetorical theory of the age . . . meditation became rhetoric." See Louis L. Martz, *The Poetry of Meditation: A Study in English Religious Literature of the Seventeenth Century* (New Haven, 1954), p. 39: "Meditation focused and disciplined the powers that a man already possessed, both his innate powers and his acquired modes of logical analysis and rhetorical development."

74. Baxter, *The Saints Everlasting Rest,* pp. 790–838, 792, 561, 557, 609, 615. For an extremely interesting study of the use of apostrophe in lyric exclamations, see Jonathan Culler, *The Pursuit of Signs: Semiotics, Literature, Deconstruction* (London, 1981), pp. 135–54.

75. For a perceptive reading of the relationship of food to knowledge in *Paradise Lost,* see Kerrigan, *Sacred Complex,* pp. 207–45. Cf. Baxter, *The Saints Everlasting Rest,* p. 685: "As Digestion is the turning of the raw food into chyle, and blood, and spirits, and flesh: So Meditation rightly mannaged, turneth the Truths received and remembered, into warm affections, raised resolution, and holy and upright conversation." In terms of the Second Adam theme, whereas Eve dreamt of eating and subsequently ate, Jesus dreams of eating and subsequently resists the offer of the banquet. Jesus is "fed with better thoughts that feed" him "hungring" more to do his Father's will; he is also with holiest meditations fed (II, 258–59, 110).

76. Sloane, *Humanist Rhetoric,* p. 230.

77. *Ibid.,* p. 250. The question of how efficacious Reason was in

resisting temptations alone is a vexed one. Richard Capel, *Tentations,* pp. 106–07, suggests, "the tentation is a spirituall thing; reason, a naturall weapon: now a naturall thing, can have neither stroke not force against a spirituall, and therefore reason is a false weapon." But Milton allows reason greater power.

78. Hall, *Meditations,* in *Works* I, p. 25.

79. Baxter, *The Saints Everlasting Rest,* pp. 706, 612.

80. Diane Kelsey McColley, *Milton's Eve* (Urbana, Ill., 1983), p. 101, points out that, while in Eve's dream, Satan's "imagery of ascent is foggily transcendental"; here, Raphael offers imagery that is "accommodatingly organic." The dream, she further notes, cautions against two opposed abuses: "the wanton sensuality of libertinism and the contempt of this world for the sake of contemplative ecstasy of Counterreformation mysticism." Milton's treatment of contemplation as a development of reason, and Jesus' unwillingness to reject the kingdoms out of hand without a refining interpretation of their merits support this view.

81. Ludovisus Vives, *An Introduction to Wysedome,* trans. Rychard Morysine (N.p., 1540), p. L$_8$v.

82. Chrysostom, *Homilies on the Gospel of Saint Matthew,* in *NPNF* X, p. 78. Isaac Colfe, *A Comfortable Treatise,* pp. 46, 31. Cf. Preston, *New Covenant,* p. 184: "Now, when Christ teaches the right knowledge, when hee reveales his truth to us, as a Prophet, hee takes away the roote, the bottome and foundation of a lust, and when the foundation is taken away, the worke of the Divell is dissolved in us, it fals to the ground."

83. Carl G. Jung, "The Development of Personality," in *The Collected Works of C. G. Jung,* 20 vols., ed. Herbert Read et al. (Princeton, 1953–1979), vol. XVII, p. 180. Jung also deals briefly with the Temptation scene in *Psychological Types,* in *Collected Works* VI, p. 53; see pp. 412–13 for definitions of "assimilation" and its correlative, "apperception."

84. Joseph Henshaw, *Horae Succisivæ Or, Spare Houres of Meditations* (1630; rpt. London, 1640), pp. 204–05. Hall, *Invisible World,* p. 356. [Augustine], *A Precious Booke of Heavenly Meditations,* trans. Thomas Rogers (London, 1629), p. 153. Cf. Fenner, *A Divine Message,* pp. 2–3, 4, 48; Henry Hawkins, *The Devout Hart or Royal Throne of the Pacifical Salomon* (N.p., 1634), pp. 5, 11; Lancelot Andrewes, *Nineteen Sermons Concerning Prayer* (Cambridge, 1641), pp. 154, 200, 203, 236, 273, 275; Henry Clapham, *A Tract of Prayer* (London, 1602), p. B$_2$v: "The Kingdome is Spirituall, and specially inward." Cf. William Narne, *The Pearle of Prayer Most Pretious* (Edinburgh, 1630), p. 288; John Norden, *The Pensive Mans Practise* (1584; rpt. London, 1600), p. A$_{10}$r. Kempis, *Imitation,* p. 70; Hall, *Invisible World,* pp. 98, 104.

85. [John Earle], *Micro-cosmographie. Or, A Peece of the World Discovered; in Essayes and Characters* (1628; rpt. London, 1629), p. K$_1$v. The

author's name on the title page is Edward Blount. The STC and others cite Earle as the author. Capel, *Tentations*, p. 234.

86. Henshaw, *Horae Succisivoe*, pp. 240–41.

87. Victor Turner, *The Anthropology of Performance* (New York, 1987), p. 33. Nelson Goodman, *Of Mind and Other Matters* (Cambridge, Mass., 1984), p. 28.

88. Goodman, *Of Mind and Other Matters*, p. 180.

89. I will not spend much time on the pinnacle scene itself because I have written on it elsewhere. See Ashraf H. A. Rushdy, "Of *Paradise Regained:* The Interpretation of Career," in *Milton Studies* XXIV, ed. James D. Simmonds (Pittsburgh, 1988), pp. 253–75; and "Standing Alone on the Pinnacle," pp. 193–218.

90. The next few paragraphs are taken from my "Standing Alone on the Pinnacle."

91. Catherine Belsey, *John Milton: Language, Gender, Power* (Oxford, 1988), pp. 104–05.

92. Karl Marx, "Letters from the Franco-German Yearbooks," in *Karl Marx: Early Writings,* trans. Rodney Livingstone and Gregor Benton (New York, 1975), pp. 199–209, esp. pp. 201, 209. The letters are both to Arnold Ruge.

4. CONFRONTING THE BOOK: THE ART OF LIBERTY

1. Louis Adrian Montrose, "The Elizabethan Subject and the Spenserian Text," in *Literary Theory / Renaissance Texts,* ed. Patricia Parker and David Quint (Baltimore, 1986), pp. 303–40, esp. pp. 320, 322, 306. I am referring to *The Shepheardes Calendar* as it is in *Shorter Poems of Edmund Spenser,* ed. William A. Oram et al. (New Haven, 1989), pp. 74–76.

2. Joseph Wittreich, *Interpreting "Samson Agonistes"* (Princeton, 1986), p. 332.

3. Ralph Waterbury Condee, "Milton's Dialogue with the Epic: *Paradise Regained* and the Tradition," *Yale Review* LIX (1970), 357–75, argues that the action of the poem "is not merely non-epic; it is specifically anti-epic." Cf. Stuart Curran, "*Paradise Regained:* Implications of Epic," in *Milton Studies* XVII, ed. Richard S. Ide and Joseph Wittreich (Pittsburgh, 1983), pp. 209–24; and E.M.W. Tillyard, *Milton* (1930; rpt. New York, 1966), p. 269: "It is not an epic, it does not try to be an epic, and it must not be judged by any kind of epic standard." For the play, see David Daiches, *Milton* (New York, 1957), p. 248: "Not to deny that *Samson Agonistes* is a remarkable play. But it is not, in the full sense of the word, a great tragedy. We lack a name for the kind of play which it is."

4. Balachandra Rajan, "To Which Is Added *Samson Agonistes,*" in *The*

Prison and the Pinnacle: Papers to Commemorate the Tercentenary of "Paradise Regained" and "Samson Agonistes," ed. Balachandra Rajan (Toronto, 1973), pp. 82–110, esp. p. 96. Arthur E. Barker, "Calm Regained Through Passion Spent," in *The Prison and the Pinnacle,* pp. 3–48, esp. pp. 13–14. William Kerrigan, *The Prophetic Milton* (Charlottesville, Va., 1974), p. 268*n*5.

5. Joseph Wittreich, *Interpreting "Samson Agonistes,"* p. 331; cf. 330. William Kerrigan, *The Sacred Complex: On the Psychogenesis of "Paradise Lost"* (Cambridge, Mass., 1983), p. 125. E.M.W. Tillyard, *Milton,* p. 255; John T. Shawcross, "The Genres of *Paradise Regain'd* and *Samson Agonistes:* The Wisdom of their Joint Publication," in *Milton Studies* XVII, ed. Richard S. Ide and Joseph Wittreich (Pittsburgh, 1983), pp. 225–48. Shawcross agrees with Wittreich's interpretation (p. 240), though he makes the same gesture as Barker and Rajan earlier (p. 226): "The addition of *Samson Agonistes* to the 1671 volume could have been a publisher's strategy." Christopher Grose, *Milton and the Sense of Tradition* (New Haven, 1988), pp. 3, 6, 117, 201, 208, has likewise explicitly argued that the 1671 volume might be read as a whole. Only the explicit comments regarding the volume's intertextuality begin, so far as I can tell, in 1971. See Arnold Stein, *Heroic Knowledge: An Interpretation of "Paradise Regained" and "Samson Agonistes"* (1957; rpt. London, 1965), pp. 138, 207.

6. Cf. Wittreich, *Interpretin "Samson Agonistes,"* pp. 351–52, on Jesus' "untroubl'd mind" (IV, 398) and Samson's "troubl'd mind" (186); and Barker, "Calm Regained," pp. 12, 13, 35, on the theme of "perturbation" in the two poems. Whereas Jesus' is a meditative, Samson's is an uncontemplative isolation.

7. I have discussed how Jesus transforms biological function into divine dialectic in chapter 3. He is fed with meditations at *PR* II, 111, and with better thoughts at *PR* II, 258. And at the end of the ordeal, Jesus shall break his fast on "Celestial Food" and "Ambrosial drink" (IV, 585, 587).

8. See chapter 3 for the "dialectics of spirit." For a different interpretation of Jesus' relation to his body, see Cary Nelson, *The Incarnate Word: Literature as Verbal Space* (Urbana, Ill., 1973), pp. 80–100.

9. Martin Luther, *Luther's Works,* 55 vols., ed. Jaroslav Pelikan et al. (Philadelphia, 1955–1976), vol. XXVI, p. 109. Georgia Christopher, *Milton and the Science of the Saints* (Princeton, 1982), pp. 225–26. Luther's point is that those imbued with the Spirit could fall "into huge sins" and also regain their place. For a severe critique of Christopher's argument, see Wittreich, *Interpreting "Samson Agonistes,"* pp. 26–34. I am, on the whole, sympathetic to Wittreich's argument about Milton's heterodoxy, but there are several points in which I find myself disagreeing with him (which I'll develop below). The point right now that deserves some men-

tion is whether or not heaven's breath may signify the Spirit. Louis Martz, *Poet of Exile: A Study in Milton's Poetry* (New Haven, 1980), pp. 272–91, esp. 273, suggests that heaven's breath "will suggest the presence of a higher power, still to be revealed." John Spenser Hill, *John Milton: Poet, Priest, and Prophet* (London, 1979), p. 156, says that the breath "is emblematic of the secret operation of inspiring grace." For a contrary reading, see Jon S. Lawry, *The Shadow of Heaven: Matter and Stance in Milton's Poetry* (Ithaca, N.Y., 1968), p. 354.

10. Søren Kierkegaard, *The Concept of Anxiety,* trans. Reidar Thomte (Princeton, 1980), p. 73.

11. Karl Marx, *Critique of Hegel's Doctrine of the State* (1843), in *Karl Marx: Early Writings,* trans. Rodney Livingstone and Gregor Benton (New York, 1975), pp. 58–198, esp. 73. For the points Marx is critiquing, see Georg W. F. Hegel, *Philosophy of Right,* trans. T. M. Knox (Oxford, 1952), pp. 164–79, para. 270–74. Hobbes, *Leviathan,* ed. C. B. Macpherson (Harmondsworth, 1968), p. 114.

12. *Second Defence,* CM VIII, pp. 62–63: "non est miserum esse caecum; miserum est caecitatem non posse ferre." The Columbia edition uses the 1809 George Burnett translation (revised by Moses Hadas), which is both truest to the Latin and the most euphonious. Cf. Helen North's translation in YP IV, p. 584; and Robert Fellowes's in *The Prose Works of John Milton,* 3 vols., ed. J. A. St. John (London, 1848), vol. I, p. 236.

13. Cf. Irene Samuel, *Plato and Milton* (Ithaca, 1947); Samuel, "The Regaining of Paradise," in *The Prison and the Pinnacle,* pp. 111–34, esp. p. 120$n9$, also refers to the "supremely rational hero of *Paradise Regained.*"

14. Stanley Fish, "Spectacle and Evidence in *Samson Agonistes,*" *Critical Inquiry* XV, no. 3 (Spring 1989), 556–86, esp. p. 576. The phrase "perpetuall progression" occurs in *Areopagitica,* CM IV, p. 333 (cf. YP II, p. 543). For Fish's more thorough reading of *Areopagitica,* see his "Driving from the Letter: Truth and Indeterminacy in Milton's *Areopagitica,* in *Re-membering Milton: Essays on the Texts and Traditions,* ed. Mary Nyquist and Margaret W. Ferguson (London, 1987), pp. 234–54.

15. Albert R. Cirillo, "Time, Light, and the Phoenix: The Design of *Samson Agonistes,*" in *Calm of Mind: Tercentenary Essays on "Paradise Regained" and "Samson Agonistes" in Honor of John S. Diekhoff,* ed. Joseph Anthony Wittreich, Jr. (Cleveland, 1971), pp. 209–33, esp. p. 209. Cf. Morris Freedman, "Waiting for Samson: The Modernity of *Samson Agonistes,*" MQ XIII (1979), 42–45, esp. p. 43: Samson's "new strength is, simply, self-generated, self-controlled"; cf. Sherman Hawkins, "Samson's Catharsis," in *Milton Studies* II, ed. James D. Simmonds (Pittsburgh, 1970), pp. 211–30; Hill, *John Milton,* pp. 151–74; Anthony Low, *The Blaze of Noon: A Reading of "Samson Agonistes"* (New York, 1974), pp.

168–72; W. R. Parker, *Milton's Debt to Greek Tragedy in "Samson Agonistes"* (Baltimore, 1937), p. 240; Mary Ann Radzinowicz, *Toward "Samson Agonistes": The Growth of Milton's Mind* (Princeton, 1978), p. 344; Tillyard, *Milton*, p. 298. Further discussions of the play as a study in regeneration are listed in John M. Steadman, *Milton and the Renaissance Hero* (Oxford: Clarendon Press, 1967), p. 188n1.

16. Radzinowicz, *Toward "Samson Agonistes,"* p. 344; Steadman, "'Faithful Champion': The Theological Basis of Milton's Hero of Faith," *Anglia* LXXVII (1959), 12–28; rpt. in *Milton: Modern Essays in Criticism,* ed. Arthur E. Barker (Oxford, 1965), pp. 467–83.

17. G. A. Wilkes, "The Interpretation of *Samson Agonistes*," *HLQ* XXVI (1963), 363–79; Steadman, *Renaissance Hero*, p. 188n1. In his recent work, Steadman has demonstrated more open-mindedness; cf. *The Wall of Paradise: Essays on Milton's Poetics* (Baton Rouge, 1985), p. 108: "The hero's spiritual regeneration, strongly affirmed by some commentators and as emphatically contested by others, may or may not be a precondition for the divine impulse that directly leads to the catastrophe of the drama, but it does (in retrospect) lend probability and verisimilitude to Samson's final and climactic *aristeia*."

18. The fullest reading of Samson's near-despair is still Don Cameron Allen, *The Harmonious Vision: Studies in Milton's Poetry* (1956; rpt. Baltimore, 1970).

19. Allen, *Harmonious Vision*, p. 93. Cf. John Hill, *John Milton*, p. 166; Tillyard, *Milton*, p. 290; M. M. Mahood, *Poetry and Humanism* (New York, 1970), pp. 211, 237–38; Louis L. Martz, *Poet of Exile*, p. 286: "The hero is fully restored."

20. Allen, *Harmonious Vision*, p. 93; cf. Radzinowicz, *Toward "Samson Agonistes,"* p. 51, who transfigures the despair of these verses into something akin to intellectual spirituality: "When the mind is master of itself, threats are of no matter." Cf. Georgia Christopher, *Milton and the Science of the Saints*, p. 243. Wilkes, "The Interpretation of *Samson Agonistes*," 366; cf. John Carey, *Milton* (New York, 1970), p. 144.

21. Steadman, "Theological Basis," p. 473.

22. Milton argued that despair is opposed to trust and takes place only in the reprobate (CM XVII, pp. 58–59). Richard Sibbes, *The Bruised Reede, and Smoaking Flax* (London, 1630), p. 43, notes that "A holy despaire in our selves is the ground of true hope." Likewise, William Perkins, *A Golden Chaine*, in *The Workes of . . . Mr. W. Perkins*, 3 vols. (Cambridge, 1616–18), vol. I, pp. 78–79, suggests that "an holy desperation of a mans own power, in the obtaining of eternall life" is one of the "foure principall hammers" for bruising a stony heart; bruising the heart is part of the process of effectual calling.

23. Lawrence W. Hyman, *The Quarrel Within: Art and Morality in*

Milton's Poetry (New York, 1972), p. 107, argues that Samson's challenge to Harapha is a challenge to God. William Madsen, "From Shadowy Types to Truth," in *The Lyric and Dramatic Milton*, ed. Joseph H. Summers (New York, 1965), pp. 95–114, esp. p. 104, notes that whether or not "we regard Harapha's visit as a temptation, it is clear that Samson's response is seriously flawed."

24. William Perkins, *A Treatise of Gods Free Grace, and Mans Free-Will* in *Workes* I, pp. 734–35. Christopher Hill, *Society and Puritanism in Pre-Revolutionary England* (1964; rpt. Harmondsworth, 1986), p. 136, calls Perkins "the high priest of the Puritans."

25. Perkins, *A Treatise of Gods Free Grace*, pp. 735–37.

26. The relevant passages of the *Christian Doctrine* dealing with regeneration occur for the most part in chapters 16–28 of the first book. Freedman, "Waiting for Samson," 43. Anthony Low, "*Samson Agonistes:* Theology, Poetry, Truth," *MQ* XIII (1979), 99; Low, *Blaze of Noon*, pp. 168–72, 200, suggested that the motions were both a reward and a confirmation of spiritual progess; see Low.

27. Wilkes, "The Interpretation of *Samson Agonistes*," p. 377. Cf. Carey, *Milton*, pp. 144–45: "Given Samson's truculence with Harapha, his dismissal of the Philistine Officer is what we should expect. When, moments later, he changes his mind, we should be unconvinced if Milton did not plainly indicate that Samson is now in receipt of premonitions from God."

28. Wittreich, *Interpreting "Samson Agonistes,"* pp. 358–59, 360. Samuel, "*Samson Agonistes* as Tragedy," in *Calm of Mind*, pp. 235–57, esp. pp. 249, 250, 252. The Dunster note is quoted by Henry John Todd, *The Poetical Works of John Milton*, 6 vols., 5th ed. (London, 1852), vol. III, p. 220.

29. For the errata as listed in the 1671 volume, see the page facing "Omissa," p. [102]. Cf. *The Poems of John Milton*, ed. John Carey and Alastair Fowler (London, 1970), p. 354n222.

30. Fish, "Spectacle and Evidence," p. 571.

31. William Empson, *Milton's God* (1961; rpt. Cambridge, 1983), p. 143. Empson neither quotes nor cites Milton to demonstrate where Milton had long been printing this; but then of course he couldn't.

32. Radzinowicz, *Toward "Samson Agonistes,"* p. 30; cf. p. 32.

33. Samuel, "*Samson Agonistes* as Tragedy," p. 245.

34. *Ibid.*, p. 257n6, points out that the use of conditional and subjunctive moods in these lines from *A Mask* signals the "distinctive Miltonic preference for the ethic of free will." Radzinowicz, *Toward "Samson Agonistes,"* p. 66, argues somewhat confusingly that the difference in Milton's theodicy between *A Mask* and *Samson Agonistes* is, first, "very great" and, then, "not so very great after all." She sees the stooping

heaven as somehow confirming rather than converting Samson's own mental activity.

35. Carey, *Milton,* p. 145. Kerrigan, *Sacred Complex,* p. 119. Christopher Hill, *The Experience of Defeat: Milton and Some Contemporaries* (London, 1984), p. 316. Cf. Wittreich, *Interpreting "Samson Agonistes,"* pp. 358–60; and Rajan, "To Which Is Added," 105, who note the difference between the "motions" in the 1671 volume.

36. For a contrary reading, see Grose, *Milton and the Sense of Tradition,* pp. 142–209. Grose maintains that Samson has managed to surmise "nothing less than than the purpose or 'reason' of the Law" (146) when he announces the "rouzing motions." In fact, Grose maintains that the motions allow Samson to announce the possession of "knowledge, wisdom, virtue" (158, 162, 177), and that the "rouzing motions" are only a "bit of outright deception, the deliberately assumed mask for a mind already made up" (168). Other critics who maintain that Samson retains his agential liberty and acts as a "Son of God" include Louis Martz, *Poet of Exile,* p. 291: "The result is a volume of austere greatness, a grandeur of self-abnegation that demonstrates in both poems, the discovery of the true inner self of the chosen son"; Hill, *Milton and the English Revolution* (London, 1977), p. 428–48; and Joan Bennett, *Reviving Liberty: Radical Christian Humanism in Milton's Great Poems* (Cambridge, Mass., 1989), pp. 119–60.

37. On the Messenger's second-hand knowledge, see Grose, *Milton and the Sense of Tradition,* p. 190; and Fish, "Spectacle and Evidence," p. 567.

38. Cf. Theodore Haak, *The Dutch Annotations Upon the Whole Bible* 2 vols. (London, 1657), vol. I, $Ss_3{}^v$: "This conclusion . . . intimateth, that this last act of Simson [sic] appertained as well to this Judge-office, as the other foregoing. As he also, especially in his death, is held to be type and figure of our Lord Jesus Christ, who conquered all his and our enemies chiefly by his death." Cf. the 1645 Puritan *Annotations Upon All the Books of the Old and New Testaments,* 2 vols. (1645; London, 1657), vol. I, $Kk_1{}^v$: "Samson was type of our Lord Christ, who humbled himself to the death, that he might save his people out of the hands of their spirituall enemies." Cf. Joseph Hall, *Contemplations Upon . . . the Old Testament,* in *The Works of Joseph Hall,* 2 vols. (London, 1628–34), vol. I, pp. 1021, 1027: "It is no marvell, if hee were thus admirably strong and victorious, whose bodily strength God meant to make a type of the spirituall power of Christ." Cf. John Gumbleden, *Christ Tempted: The Divel Conquered* (London, 1657), p. 47; Thomas Taylor, *Christs Combate and Conquest* (Cambridge, 1618), pp. 36–37, 193. See Michael F. Krouse, *Milton's Samson and the Christian Tradition* (Princeton, 1949); Wittreich, *Interpreting "Samson Agonistes,"* pp. 329–85, argues that Milton departed from the prevalent seventeenth-century tradition, presenting Samson rather as an "anti-type or a negative type of Christ."

39. Wittreich, *Interpreting "Samson Agonistes,"* p. 355, cf. 363. Fish, "Spectacle and Evidence," pp. 567, 579, 578; for Fish's reading of the post-1644 morality, see p. 576 (and above, where I discuss it briefly). Cf. A. N. Wilson, *The Life of John Milton* (Oxford, 1984), p. 238: "[Samson] is divorced from immediate consideration of whether what he does is, or is not, accordant with the will of God. In *Paradise Lost* the thrill of such moral heroism is illicit. But here, it is overtly laudable." Cf. Helen Damico, "Duality and Dramatic Vision: A Structural Analysis of *Samson Agonistes,"* in *Milton Studies* XII, ed. James D. Simmonds (Pittsburgh, 1978), pp. 91–116. John Guillory, "The Father's House: *Samson Agonistes* in Its Historical Moment," in *Re-membering Milton*, pp. 148–76, esp. p. 164, argues that the "own accord" could be read to refer to Samson's interiorization of either Calvinistic law or Freudian "will of the Father," but in the end determines that it is indeterminate. The contrary position to these may be ably represented by Louis Martz, *Poet of Exile*, p. 287: "Samson's greatness lies in his rational choice of a God-given opportunity." I have already discussed how much Samson is capable of rational choice.

40. Daniel Dyke, *Michael and the Dragon, or Christ Tempted and Sathan Foyled*, in *Two Treatises* (London, 1616), p. 219. The full sentence runs as follows: "Temptations against the light of nature, even corrupted nature, where there is no bait to entice corruption, as for a man to kil his loving and beloved parents *where there is no hope of gaine by it, no matter of displeasure to provoke, these are meerely from Sathan*" (my italics). It is somewhat ironic that Wittreich should cite this particular instance. It seems to me that Dyke suggests that some forms of killing do not come from Satan, such as where exists either the opportunity for gain, or provocative displeasure. And this is exactly the suggestion that Wittreich was attempting to avoid. Wittreich spends many pages arguing that Milton departs from the brutal tradition of Hall, *Contemplations Upon . . . the Old Testament*, in *Works* I, p. 1024: "I never read that Samson slew any but by the motion and assistance of the Spirit of God"; cf. pp. 1023, 1025, 1027, 1030. I think, though, that Milton follows the line of Hall here.

41. It will also not do to gloss over it as Samuel, "*Samson Agonistes* as Tragedy," p. 253, does by referring passingly to the "figure of the tyrant-queller." Milton's vision was not as pacific as Samuel and Wittreich would have it. For the most part, fortunately, Milton did not counsel vindictiveness, or consider the proposal of violence lightly; but there were moments in history (Israel's and England's) that Milton felt required a brutal leader of Samson's stature. See Radzinowicz, *Toward "Samson Agonistes,"* pp. 80–81, for a fuller reading of the significance of this passage.

42. Hall, *Contemplations upon . . . the New Testament* pp. 61, 153; cf. pp. 77, 145.

43. I have taken out Milton's italics and put in my own.

44. Bernard, *Most Devout and Divine Meditations,* trans. W. P. (London, 1632), p. 76. Joseph Hall, *Meditations and Vowes, Divine and Morall,* in *Works* I, p. 56.

45. Dyke, *Michael and the Dragon,* p. 237, Dyke's italics.

46. Perkins, *The Combate* in *Workes* III, p. 393: "He meanes not to oppose Scripture to Scripture, but to confute the abuse of Scripture by Scripture." Cf. Hall, *Contemplations upon . . . the New Testament,* in *Works* II, p. 36: "But what is this I see, Satan himselfe with a Bible under his arme, with a Text in his mouth?"; and Taylor, *Christs Combate,* p. 224, paraphrasing Satan: "If I had a Psalter here I could shew it thee." For my arguments on the pinnacle scene and vexed question of Jesus' alleged "divinity" and its variegated usage in the history of critical commentary on the poem, see Ashraf H. A. Rushdy, "Of *Paradise Regained:* The Interpretation of Career," in *Milton Studies* XXIV, ed. James D. Simmonds (Pittsburgh, 1988), pp. 253–75, esp. 268–71; and Rushdy, "Standing Alone on the Pinnacle: Milton in 1752," in *Milton Studies* XXVI, ed. James D. Simmonds (Pittsburgh, 1990), pp. 193–218.

47. Hall, *Contemplations upon . . . the New Testament,* in *Works* II, p. 77.

48. Fish, "Inaction and Silence," p. 43. Again, I refer the reader to my two articles cited above; also see chapter 1 on the question of self / subject.

49. Thomas Bilson, *The Survey of Christs Suffering for Mans Redemption* (London, 1604), p. 468; cf. pp. 369, 409–21, 479–82. Bilson belies his own distinction when he attributes to "astonishment" all the mental dysfunctions he had made solely the province of "amazement." Moreover, seven years later, the Authorized Version would translate the verse in Mark xiv, 33: "And he taketh with him Peter and James and John, and began to be sore amazed, and to be very heavy." Nonetheless, "amazement" as used elsewhere in Milton does mean the sort of mental dysfunction that Bilson attributes to it in the first instance. See also chapter 3 and Rushdy, "Of *Paradise Regained,*" p. 275*n13,* as well as Rushdy, "Standing Alone on the Pinnacle," pp. 193–218.

50. Shakespeare, *Hamlet,* II, ii, 533–51; my italics, in *William Shakespeare: The Complete Works,* ed. Willard Famham, gen. ed. Alfred Harbage (New York, 1969), p. 949. Hereafter all quotations from *Hamlet* will be taken from this edition. Leo Tolstoy, *What Is Art?,* trans. Almyer Maude (Indianapolis, 1960), pp. 117–18.

51. Freud, *Beyond the Pleasure Principle,* trans. James Strachey, *PFL* XI, 275–338, esp. pp. 278, 310–11, 331, 312. Norman O. Brown, *Life Against Death: The Psychoanalytical Meaning of History* (1959; rpt. Middletown, Conn., 1985), p. 112. Brown's is still the finest study of Freud's

death instinct (pp. 77–134), if not perhaps the finest study of Freud. For the application of Freudian thought generally to Milton's works, especially *Paradise Lost,* see Kerrigan, *Sacred Complex.* For the fullest reading of *Samson Agonistes* within a psychoanalytical framework—Nancy Chodorow's feminist reading of Freud, in this instance—see Jackie DiSalvo, "Intestine Thorn: Samson's Struggle with the Woman Within," in *Milton and the Idea of Woman,* ed. Julia M. Walker (Urbana, Ill., 1988), pp. 211–29. DiSalvo reads this play as a "tragedy of gender" (p. 225) and shows how Samson's "regeneration" is actually a process of "male psychogensis" (p. 218).

52. Samuel, *"Samson Agonistes* as Tragedy," p. 246, demonstrates that Samson is still egomaniacal after the motions, as evidenced in the shift in line 1436: "Our God, our Law, my Nation, or my self." Cf. Grose, *Milton and the Sense of Tradition,* p. 185.

53. Hall, *Contemplations upon . . . the New Testament,* in *Works* II, p. 279; cf. p. 1031: "our better Samson." See Jeremy Taylor, *The Life of Our Blessed Lord and Saviour JESUS CHRIST* in *The Whole Works of the Right Rev. Jeremy Taylor D.D.,* 15 vols., ed. Reginald Heber (London, 1822), vol. II, p. 236: "The nature of types is, in shadow to describe by dark lines a future substance," supposedly an echo of Ambrose's "Umbra in lege, imago in evangelio, veritas in coelo."

54. Kenneth Burke, *The Rhetoric of Religion: Studies in Logology* (1961; rpt. Berkeley and Los Angeles, 1970), p. 102.

55. It is odd that Olivier did not make much of this interplay—which seems to be a fairly prominent feature of any Freudian reading of *Hamlet*—in a production that otherwise is an almost abjectly faithful Freudian reading of *Hamlet.* But, then again, Freud himself did not point out the possibility, even though he used *Hamlet* as a regular feature of his metapsychological studies. Of the two major comments he made on the play, in the first instance he had not yet written *Beyond the Pleasure Principle* (1920), in the other he was more concerned with demonstrating how *Hamlet,* like *The Brothers Karamazov* and *Oedipus Rex* were all variations on the theme of parricide. See "Psychopathic Characters on the Stage" (composed in 1905–06, published in 1942), trans. James Strachey, *PFL* XIV, 121–27, esp. pp. 126–27; and "Dostoevesky and Parricide" (1928), trans. James Strachey, *PFL* XIV, 441–60, esp. 453–54.

56. Cf. John C. Ulreich, Jr., "'Beyond the Fifth Act': *Samson Agonistes* as Prophecy," in *Milton Studies* XVII, ed. Richard S. Ide and Joseph Wittreich (Pittsburgh, 1983), pp. 281–318; and Edward Tayler, *Milton's Poetry: Its Development in Time* (Pittsburgh, 1979), pp. 105–22, esp. 109–11, on the "proleptic form" of the play. Because of the general prophetic ambience in the air, the breach of decorum in having the Chorus describe things we know they have not seen may be excused.

57. Jameson, *The Political Unconscious: Narrative as a Socially Symbolic Act* (Ithaca, 1981), p. 144.

58. Fish, "Spectacle and Evidence," pp. 558, 585, 557, 567. Christopher Grose, *Milton and the Sense of Tradition*, p. 205, has recently defined this "radical form or type-scene within the work"—the "vestiges of narrative," as he calls it—as the mark of Milton's "mature work."

59. See Jackie DiSalvo, "Intestine Thorn," pp. 214–15, 217–19. For an extremely insightful reading of *Samson* and the absence of the mother, see Bernadette Andrea, *A Heretic in the Truth: Milton and the Construction of the Mediated Woman* (M.A. thesis, University of Calgary, 1990), chap. 4.

60. Jerome Bruner, *Actual Minds, Possible Worlds* (Cambridge, Mass., 1986), pp. 132–33. William Kerrigan, *The Sacred Complex*, p. 120.

61. Milton, *Ad Patrem*, in *John Milton: Complete Poems and Major Prose*, ed. Merritt Y. Hughes (Indianapolis, 1957), pp. 84–85.

62. On Lacan and the realm of the Symbolic, see Jacques Lacan, *Écrits: A Selection*, trans. Alan Sheridan (London, 1977), pp. 199–201, 281–91. Also, cf. Anthony Wilden, "Lacan and the Discourse of the Other," in *Jacques Lacan, Speech and Language in Psychoanalysis*, trans. and ed. Anthony Wilden (Baltimore, 1968), pp. 157–311, esp. pp. 270–84. Like all others who have an interest in Lacan, I am indebted to Margaret Homans, *Bearing the Word: Language and Female Experience in Nineteenth-Century Women's Writing* (Chicago, 1986), pp. 1–39.

63. Timothy J. Reiss, "Montaigne and the Subject of Polity," in *Literary Theory / Renaissance Texts*, pp. 115–49, esp. p. 134.

64. Barbara Lewalski, *Milton's Brief Epic: The Genre, Meaning, and Art of "Paradise Regained"* (Providence, R.I., 1966), p. 319. Kathleen Swaim, "Hercules, Antaeus, and Prometheus: A Study of the Climactic Epic Similes in *Paradise Regained*," *SEL* XVIII (1978), 137–53, esp. 146–47.

65. On the Phoenix, see Northrop Frye, "Agon and Logos: Revolution and Revelation," in *The Prison and the Pinnacle*, pp. 135–63, esp. p. 151, who sees it as an "image of divine succession"; cf. Anthony Low, "The Phoenix and the Sun in *Samson Agonistes*," in *Milton Studies* XIV, ed. James D. Simmonds (Pittsburgh, 1980), pp. 219–31.

66. Grose, *Milton and the Sense of Tradition*, p. 196. DiSalvo, "Intestine Thorn," p. 227. For a subtle reading of *Samson Agonistes* and the question of gender, see Catherine Belsey, *John Milton: Language, Gender, Power* (Oxford, 1988), pp. 53–58, and Fish, "Spectacle and Evidence," pp. 581–84. Cf. John Guillory, "The Father's House: *Samson Agonistes* in Its Historical Moment," p. 166.

In this sense of denying one facet of his parentage, his psychosexual makeup, and the spheres of self-knowledge, we might say that Samson falls into the category Bakhtin defines as belonging to "epic" worlds—that is, a world in which the "individuum" is representative of the culture in which he or she lives, and is moreover only a surface being, having no sense of domestic possibilities, no "petty private matters." See M. M. Bakhtin, *The Dialogic Imagination: Four Esssays,* trans. Caryl Emerson and Michael Holquist (Austin, 1981), p. 218.

67. Fish, *Is There a Text in This Class?: The Authority of Interpretive Communities* (Cambridge, Mass., 1980), p. 274, suggests that for some "present-day readers Christ is 'in the text' of *Samson Agonistes,* for others he is not, and before the typological interpretation of the poem was introduced and developed by Michael Krouse in 1949, he was not 'in the text' for anyone." Fish is referring, of course, to Michael Krouse, *Milton's Samson and the Christian Tradition* (Princeton, 1949). For a critique of Fish's position, see Wittreich, *Interpreting "Samson Agonistes,"* pp. 222–30.

68. Cf. Arthur Barker, "Structural and Doctrinal Pattern in Milton's Later Poems," in *Essays in English Literature from the Renaissance to the Victorian Age Presented to A.S.P. Woodhouse,* ed. Millar MacLure and F. W. Watt (Toronto, 1964), pp. 169–94; and Bennett, *Reviving Liberty,* pp. 120–60.

69. He cites David and Hezechiah as examples; one cannot say whether or not Samson fits into this category, for he is roused to disobey this law.

70. Tayler, *Milton's Poetry,* p. 106, suggests that what is now being called the "revisionist" reading of the tragedy (exemplified by Wilkes, and the one I have been promoting here) is Calvinistic. According to the tensions we discovered in Milton's assertion of liberty of will (and the role of reason in freedom of agency), the fact that Samson is directed to his final act need not be seen as Calvinistic.

71. Samuel, *"Samson Agonistes* as Tragedy," p. 254. René Girard, *Violence and the Sacred,* trans. Patrick Gregory (Baltimore, 1977), p. 136.

5. CONFRONTING THE AUTHOR: THE ART OF POLITICS

1. Fredric Jameson, "Religion and Ideology: a Political Reading of *Paradise Lost,"* in *Literature, Politics and Theory: Papers from the Essex Conference, 1976–84,* ed. Francis Barker et al. (London, 1986), pp. 35–56, esp. pp. 35, 50, 36–37. This paper was first delivered to the Essex Conference in 1980 under the title "Religion and Ideology," and first published in *1642: Literature and Power in the Seventeenth Century,* ed. Francis Barker et al. (Essex, 1981), pp. 315–36. I will be citing from the 1986 volume throughout.

2. Jameson, "Imaginary and Symbolic in Lacan: Marxism, Psycho-

analytic Criticism, and the Problem of the Subject," in *Literature and Psychoanalysis: The Question of Reading Otherwise,* ed. Shoshana Felman (Baltimore, 1982), p. 394. The essay has recently been reprinted in a revised form as "Imaginary and Symbolic in Lacan," in Jameson's *The Ideologies of Theory: Essays, 1971–1986. Volume One: Situations of Theory* (Minneapolis, 1988), pp. 75–115. The passage, as I mentioned above, is elided from the later version of the essay. I will be using both versions of the essay throughout this chapter.

3. George E. Marcus and Michael M. J. Fischer, *Anthropology as Cultural Critique: An Experimental Moment in the Human Sciences* (Chicago, 1986), p. 153. Obviously, I do not mean to intimate that anthropology is divorced from state politics. At every level of its operation, from the conditions governing field work to the institutions allowing dissemination of its findings, it is obviously regulated by state policies. I only mean to suggest that, in its mode of critique, anthropology is comparative, and in this sense, it tends to register its discoveries at the level of a state's superstructure. For an opposing point of view, and the argument that anthropology does and should operate at the level of "infrastructure," see Marvin Harris, *Cultural Materialism: The Struggle for a Science of Culture* (New York, 1980), pp. 29–114, esp. pp. 56–60. Jameson, "Religion and Ideology" p. 53. Louis Althusser, "Lenin and Philosophy," in *Lenin and Philosophy and Other Essays,* trans. Ben Brewster (New York, 1971), pp. 23–70, esp. p. 27. Marx, *A Contribution to the Critique of Hegel's Philosophy of Right: Introduction,* in *Karl Marx: Early Writings,* trans. Rodney Livingstone and Gregor Benton (New York, 1975), pp. 243–57, esp. p. 251.

4. Richard Corum, "In White Ink: *Paradise Lost* and Milton's Ideas of Women," in *Milton and the Idea of Woman,* ed. Julia M. Walker (Urbana, 1988), pp. 120–47, esp. pp. 135, 139.

5. Jameson, "Religion and Ideology," pp. 35, 50, 36–37.

6. Louis Althusser, "Preface to *Capital* Volume One," in *Lenin and Philosophy and Other Essays,* pp. 71–106, esp. p. 94; he describes it as a "break" or "rupture" on p. 93. Cf. Althusser, "Lenin Before Hegel," and "Lenin and Philosophy," both in *Lenin and Philosophy and Other Essays,* pp. 107–25, 23–70. For Jameson's comments on Althusser's distinction between the early and late Marx and its polemical place against Lukács's Hegelianism and the Frankfurt School's concept of the subject, see his "Imaginary and Symbolic in Lacan," pp. 109–10; this essay, too, is part of Jameson's working out of a conceptual system capable of articulating the "postindividualistic experience of the subject" (p. 103) and of speculating as to "the place of the subject at the other end of historical time" (p. 110).

7. Jameson, "Religion and Ideology," pp. 37–41; on "figuration" 'and religion as the "distorted anticipation of historical materialism," see p.

40. On "political allegory," see p. 37 and my footnote 20 below on Jameson's more fully developed arguments on the mode. One other way of answering Jameson's argument about the alleged "inward turn" is to refer to another tenet of Marxist literary theory—that every text is a production of social relations. See Elizabeth Fox-Genovese, "Literary Criticism and the Politics of New Historicism," in *The New Historicism,* ed. H. Aram Veeser (New York, 1989), pp. 213–24: "All fabricators of texts" write "in the name of the collectivity . . . however narrowly and self-centeredly" (p. 221).

8. Hugh Trevor-Roper, *Catholics, Anglicans, and Puritans: Seventeenth-century Essays* (1987; rpt. London, 1989), pp. 280, 277. Althusser, "Ideology and Ideological State Apparatuses (Notes Towards an Investigation)," in *Lenin and Philosophy and Other Essays,* pp. 127–86, esp. p. 171, and pp. 177–83 for the "Christian model"; I have discussed this model in chapter 1 and made some critical revisions of Althusser's "quadruple system of interpellations" to fit with Milton's model of theologico-politics (p. 181).

9. Arthur E. Barker, "Calm Regained through Passion Spent: The Conclusions of the Miltonic Effort," in *The Prison and the Pinnacle,* ed. Balachandra Rajan (Toronto, 1973), pp. 3–48, esp. p. 8; cf. pp. 10–11, 21, 35, 40. Christopher Hill, *Milton and the English Revolution* (London, 1977), pp. 244, 207–09, 336, 347, 416, 421. One exception worth noting immediately is David Quint; see his "David's Census: Milton's Politics and *Paradise Regained,*" in *Re-membering Milton: Essays on the Texts and Traditions,* ed. Mary Nyquist and Margaret W. Ferguson (London, 1987), pp. 128–47.

10. Michael Wilding, *Dragons Teeth: Literature in the English Revolu-on* (Oxford, 1987), p. 257. Andrew Milner, *John Milton and the English Revolution: A Study in the Sociology of Literature* (London, 1981), pp. 177–79. Herman Rapaport, *Milton and the Postmodern* (Lincoln, Neb., 1983), pp. 196–97. Joan S. Bennett, *Reviving Liberty: Radical Christian Humanism in Milton's Great Poems* (Cambridge, Mass., 1988), pp. 198–99, 165, 202.

11. Most of my education about seventeenth-century political thought is strongly influenced by the work of both Christopher Hill and C. B. Macpherson, especially the latter's *The Political Theory of Possessive Individualism: Hobbes to Locke* (Oxford, 1962). For Hobbes and the "possessive market society," see Macpherson, *Possessive Individualism,* pp. 53–62, and Hill, "Thomas Hobbes and the Revolution in Political Thought," in *Puritanism and Revolution: Studies in Interpretation of the English Revolution of the Seventeenth Century* (1958; rpt. Harmondsworth, 1986), pp. 267–88. For Locke and alienable labor, see Locke, *Two Treatises of Government,* ed. Peter Laslett (1960; rpt. Cambridge, 1988), pp. 287–89; and Macpherson, *Possessive Individualism,* pp. 197–262, esp. pp. 214–15. For Winstan-

ley and the economic basis of political reform, see Gerrard Winstanley, *A Watch-Word to the City of London and the Armie* (1649); and *The Law of Freedom in a Platform or True Magistracy Restored* (1652), both in *The Works of Gerrard Winstanley,* ed. George Sabine (1941; rpt. New York, 1965), pp. 315–39, 501–602; and Hill, "The Religion of Gerrard Winstanley," in *The Collected Essays of Christopher Hill,* 3 vols. (Amherst, Mass., 1985–86), vol. II, pp. 185–252; and Don M. Wolfe, "Introduction," in YP IV, pp. 20–29, 154–68. For the Levelers and suffrage, see Macpherson, *Possessive Individualism,* pp. 107–59; and Hill, *The World Turned Upside Down: Radical Ideas During the English Revolution* (1972; rpt. Harmondsworth, 1984), pp. 107–50.

12. Quint, "David's Census," pp. 138, 142, 144. Quint says that the general drift of Milton's politics consists of, first, an "inward turn to individual spirituality, [which] even as it claims to subsume politics, appears to represent a turning away from the public spirit of Milton's controversialist prose," and, second, that, even so, "the great poems of Milton's captivity continue to inscribe many of the politico-religious polemics of his earlier prose" (p. 129). I will argue that it is in the process of self-representation that we might better understand in what ways Milton's late politico-religious ideas are potentially revolutionary.

13. Teresa de Lauretis, "Eccentric Subjects: Feminist Theory and Historical Consciousness," *Feminist Studies* XVI, no. 1 (Spring 1990), 115–50, esp. p. 115.

14. Other notable instances of Milton's personalizing England include the famous passage in *Areopagitica,* in which Milton sees in his mind "a noble and puissant Nation rousing herself like a strong man after sleep, and shaking her invincible locks" (CM IV, p. 344). The most famous remark by Thomas Hobbes, *Leviathan,* ed. C. B. Macpherson (1651; rpt. Harmondsworth, 1968), pp. 227–28, on national "impersonality" is his characterization of "Leviathan" as the "One Person, of whose Acts a great Multitude, by mutuall Covenants one with another, have made themselves every one the Author."

15. E.M.W. Tillyard, *Milton* (1930; rpt. New York, 1966), p. 259. Trevor-Roper, *Catholics, Anglicans, and Puritans,* pp. 277–82.

16. On Milton's self-representation as a sort of Dadaist artist in the person of Samson and an interpretation of Samson's suicide as the "prototypical self-sacrifice of the artist," see John Guillory, "The Father's House: *Samson Agonistes* in Its Historical Moment," in *Remembering Milton,* pp. 148–76, esp. pp. 171–72. On Dadaist suicide as art and art as suicide, see A. Alvarez, *The Savage God: A Study of Suicide* (1971; rpt. New York, 1973), pp. 215–25. My interest is in Milton's representation of Jesus and Samson as "political" personae of himself. On the subtle rhetorical inversion of the ideas of the generations of "books" by "men" in *Areopagitica,*

see Christopher Kendrick, *Milton: a Study in Ideology and Form* (London, 1986), pp. 19–51, esp. p. 24.

17. Bennett, *Reviving Liberty*, p. 197. Bennett also notes that Milton mentions the pinnacle scene in *Eikonoklastes*, YP III, p. 405 (p. 226*n27*).

18. See, for example, Tillyard, *Milton*, pp. 163–71, 259, 262–63. After a quite astute examination of Milton's politics as expressed by Jesus in *Paradise Regained*, Tillyard concludes his summary: "The above is conjectural" (p. 263). Cf. Christopher Grose, *Milton and the Sense of Tradition* (New Haven, 1988), p. 141.

19. John Keats, *John Keats: Selected Poems and Letters*, ed. Douglas Bush (Boston, 1959), p. 284. The letter is dated February ¹⁸/₁₉, 1819. Samuel Taylor Coleridge, *Table Talk*, 12 May 1830, qtd. in *The Romantics on Milton: Formal Essays and Critical Asides*, ed. Joseph Anthony Wittreich, Jr. (Cleveland, 1970), p. 270. On the Romantic theorists' tendency to read Milton's works as hardly veiled allegories of his life, see M. H. Abrams, *The Mirror and the Lamp: Romantic Theory and the Critical Tradition* (New York, 1953), pp. 250–56.

20. Jameson, *The Political Unconscious: Narrative as a Socially Symbolic Act* (Ithaca, 1981), p. 80: "The operations of a political *pensée sauvage* of this kind will be found in what we will call the structure of a properly political allegory." For Jameson, this form of critical activity of exegesis of the political allegory exists at the outer boundaries of the "second phase" of critical inquiry—the study of the *ideologeme*—which is to say that it is of lesser importance, at least for a properly Marxist criticism, than the third and final phase, the study of the "ideology of form." For a more severe critique of allegorical exegesis and politically based critical practice, see Jameson, *Marxism and Form: Twentieth-Century Dialectical Theories of Literature* (Princeton, 1971), pp. 398–400. Here Jameson makes a similar remark about the allegorical possibilities within an individual life, albeit with no genuine respect for the form: "And while it may be true that such an allegorical mode is utterly lacking in any 'symbolic' freedom of expression, in any classical harmony of feature, in anything human— what is expressed here portentously in the form of a riddle is not only the nature of human life in general, but also the biographical historicity of the individual in its most natural and organically corrupted form" (p. 73).

21. Milton had earlier made such "narratological" comments about fitness of speech and fitness of character in *Tetrachordon* (CM IV, p. 93).

22. Jesus rejects Athenian wisdom in *PR* IV, 282–361. Milton affirms his love for it in *Defence of Himself* (1655), CM IX, pp. 288–89. Milton also asserts his love for Athenian knowledge in his letter to Leonard Philaras, dated 28 September, 1654 (YP IV, pp. 868–70). Samson calls Dalila a "Hyæna" in *SA* 749. Milton calls More that in *Defence of Himself* (CM IX, pp. 124–25).

23. Hill, *Milton and the English Revolution,* pp. 342–43, 345, 344, 373, 377, 384. On the question of censorship, see Hill, "Censorship and English Literature," in *The Collected Essays of Christopher Hill* I, pp. 32–71. "Historians looking only at the words on the page risk entering into an unwritten conspiracy with seventeenth-century censors" (p. 50). Stevie Davies, *Images of Kingship in "Paradise Lost": Milton's Politics and Christian Liberty* (Columbia, Mo., 1983), p. 183, also takes issue with Hill's method of allegorical explication.

24. John Dryden, *Absalom and Achitophel, A Poem* (1681), in *The Poems and Fables of John Dryden,* ed. James Kinsley (Oxford, 1962), pp. 188–216. Abraham Cowley, *Davideis, A Sacred Poem* (1656), in *The Poems of Abraham Cowley,* ed. A. R. Waller (Cambridge, 1904), p. 305. The passage occurs in the second book.

25. W. K. Wimsatt, *The Verbal Icon: Studies in the Meaning of Poetry* (1954; rpt. Lexington, 1967), pp. 3–18, esp. pp. 4, 12, on the confusion I am pointing out. I will cite from this edition and note the page numbers in the text. "The Intentional Fallacy" was first published in *The Sewanee Review* LIV (1946). They also wrote the entry for "intention" in the *Dictionary of World Literature,* ed. Joseph T. Shipley (New York, 1942), pp. 326–29. Cf. the entry by Robert W. Stallman for "intention" in the *Princeton Encyclopedia Poetry and Poetics,* ed. Alex Preminger (1965; rpt. Princeton, 1974), pp. 398–400; and Annabel Patterson, in *Critical Terms for Literary Study,* ed. Frank Lentricchia and Thomas McLaughlin (Chicago, 1990), pp. 135–46. For Gerald Graff's point about Wimsatt and Beardsley's confusion between "knowability" and "desirability," see his *Professing Literature: An Institutional History* (Chicago, 1987), pp. 202–03. For the question about axiology, see Barbara Hernnstein Smith, *Contingencies of Value: Alternative Perspectives for Critical Theory* (Cambridge, Mass., 1988).

26. Stephen Greenblatt, *Renaissance Self-Fashioning: From More to Shakespeare* (Chicago, 1980), p. 161; Greenblatt does suggest, early in the book, that "self-fashioning" has concerns with the representation of "one's Nature or intention" (p. 3). I am saying it can do one without necessarily entailing the other. Jameson, *The Political Unconscious,* pp. 180, 85. Jameson, "Imaginary and Symbolic in Lacan," p. 108. Jameson, "Religion and Ideology," (1980), pp. 55–56. Jameson, "Imaginary and Symbolic in Lacan," *The Ideologies of Theory,* p. 192n4. The footnote is unaltered from the 1977 version of the essay (in *Literature and Psychoanalysis,* pp. 340–41).

27. The other and more popular way of making this double gesture has been to invoke the idea of "text," as the 1977 Jameson quotation suggests. Made usefully ambiguous, "text" may now refer as much to the printed book as to the act of critical inquiry into it. Paul Ricoeur, "What

Is a Text? Explanation and Understanding," in *Hermeneutics and the Human Sciences*, ed. and trans. John B. Thompson (Cambridge, 1981), pp. 145–64, esp. p. 158, writes, "To read is to conjoin a new discourse to the discourse of the text." Cf. "The Model of the Text: Meaningful Action Considered as a Text," in *Hermeneutics and the Human Sciences*, pp. 197–221). The most consistent example of this critical gesture in Milton criticism is, of course, the work of Stanley Fish.

So, for Fish, for instance, the "text" of *Paradise Lost* is understood only in relation to the "text" of the reader's experience of it. One of the dangers of this argument and use of terminology is that one might just begin to forget or ignore priority of one text over another. Let's take, for example, Fish's comment on critical activity: "My fiction is liberating. It relieves me of the obligation to be right (a standard that simply drops out) and demands only that I be interesting (a standard that can be met without reference at all to an illusory objectivity)." This comment occurs in Fish's essay, "Interpreting 'Interpreting the Variorum,'" in *Is There a Text In This Class?* (Cambridge, Mass., 1980), pp. 174–80, esp. p. 180; in the end, Fish is truly more interested in the text that is "Fish"—exemplified here by the fact that he is interpreting his own prior essay—than he is in the texts comprising "Milton." That, in any case, is his theory. In practice, as M. H. Abrams, "How to Do Things with Texts," in *Doing Things with Texts: Essays in Criticism and Critical Theory*, ed. Michael Fischer (New York, 1989), pp. 269–96, correctly points out, Fish does not follow this tenet; he is more often than not "right"—and by "right" I mean that his readings of Milton have points of meaningful convergence and assent within a variety of interpretive communities of Milton scholars. See esp. Abrams, pp. 280–87: "For our prepossession is that, no matter, how interesting a critic's created text of Milton may be, it will be less interesting than the text Milton himself wrote." Abrams cites the Fish passage I've quoted above and comments: "He escapes his own theory and reads as other competent readers do, only more expertly than many of us." My comments are not meant to suggest that we, as critics, return to what, with Fish, I would agree is an illusion of objectivity. That critical inquiry involves critics' own desires, their own forms of reconstruction and own political agenda is not only undeniable, but well worth regarding as one of the very best reasons for doing criticism at all. Few have reminded us of that as much or as eloquently as Professor Fish.

28. Wayne C. Booth, *The Rhetoric of Fiction* (1961; rpt. Chicago, 1983). Roland Barthes, "The Death of the Author," in *Image-Music-Text*, trans. Stephen Heath (1968; rpt. London, 1977), pp. 142–48. Michel Foucault, "What Is an Author?" in *Language, Counter-Memory, Practice*, trans. Donald F. Bouchard (1969; rpt. Oxford, 1977), pp. 113–38. Wayne C. Booth, *Critical Understanding: The Powers and Limits of Pluralism*

(Chicago, 1979), pp. 270–71, 318–35, has developed the category of "career author" as a way of reading ambiguous texts within a framework of authorial representation, but not intention. More recently, Booth, *The Company We Keep: An Ethics of Fiction* (Berkeley and Los Angeles, 1988), pp. 254–55, has made the case for the "author as improved version of flesh-and-blood creator."

29. Paul de Man, "Autobiography as De-facement," *MLN* XCIV (1979), 919–30, esp. 921–23. On tropology as inherent to linguistic and cognitive structures, see Hayden White, *Tropics of Discourse: Essays in Cultural Criticism* (Baltimore, 1978), pp. 1–23.

30. Trevor-Roper, *Catholics, Anglicans, Puritans,* p. 280.

31. Victor Turner, *The Anthropology of Performance* (New York, 1987), p. 81.

32. I quote the final passage from the Yale translation because it more accurately reflects the Latin: "id nunc, paucioribus licet quàm putabum, perfecisse me aritror: monumentun, ut video, cujusquemodi est, non facile interiturum." The Columbia translation renders it thus: "This I now judge that I have accomplished, though more briefly than I used to count upon doing it: a memorial which, such as it is, I see will not easily perish."

33. Let me repeat, though, that I am not sure it is worthwhile discovering when a "break" occured in Milton's politics; nor am I certain that it is even a useful way of speaking about his politics. If, though, we have to speak of a "break," I would personally guess that it probably came in March 1653 when the Rump voted to use civil power to support the state church. Both the sonnets of 1652, the one to Cromwell and the other to Vane, had voiced hope that this resolution would not come to pass. After 1652, Milton did not offer any extended anti-Erastian advice again until 1659 in both *A Treatise of Civil Power* (YP VII, pp. 240–72) and *Considerations,* in which the famous reference to the "short but scandalous night" occurs (pp. 274–321). But even this evidence, suggesting 1653 as a viable date for any break, cannot account for the hints of disillusionment in the 1651 tract, although we can trace certain bits of advice about the church scattered decorously throughout *A Defence,* and certainly iterated in the *Second Defence.* See Milton, *Sonnet XVI,* "To the Lord General Cromwell" and *Sonnet XVII,* "To Sir Henry Vane the Younger," in *The Poems of John Milton,* ed. John Carey and Alastair Fowler (London, 1970), pp. 325–29.

On the critical interpretations of the "short but scandalous night" and bibliographical references to those interpretations, see Austin Woolyrich, "Introduction," in YP VII, pp. 85–87; and Hill, *Milton and the English Revolution,* pp. 165, 186, 217. Woolrych notes the various positions critics have taken toward the phrase. They include (1) Masson, who thought that the "short but scandalous night" describes the fortnight's interregnum between the dissolution of Richard's parliament and the return of the Rump; and (2) John Smart, Don Wolfe, Barbara Lewalski, and Michael Fixler, who all agree that it describes the period from 1653–1659; and (3) William Hunter, who believes it refers to the eight months of Richard's Protectorate. The fullest exploration is Don M. Wolfe, *Milton in the Puritan Revolution* (1941; rpt. New York, 1963), pp. 289–90. Hill, *Milton and the English Revolution,* p. 217, notes along with Wolfe the ambiguity of the passage. For Milton's comments about the church in *A Defence,* see CM VII, pp. 28–29, 462–63, 550–51; for his comments in the *Second Defence,* see CM VIII, pp. 2–3, 66–67, 146–47. See also Wolfe, "Introduction," in YP IV, pp. 169–77.

34. William Haller, *The Rise of Puritanism* (1938; rpt. Philadelphia, 1972), pp. 115, 296.

35. Tillyard, *Milton,* p. 163. Louis L. Martz, *The Paradise Within: Studies in Vaughan, Traherne, and Milton* (New Haven, 1964), p. 183.

36. Kenneth Burke, *The Rhetoric of Religion: Studies in Logology* (1961; rpt. Berkeley and Los Angeles, 1970), p. 197; cf. Burke, *A Grammar of Motive,* in *"A Grammar of Motives" and "A Rhetoric of Motives"* (1945; rpt. Cleveland, 1962), p. 434. Hereafter, for the rest of this section, I will be citing from *Second Defence* parenthetically (using the abbreviation *Def. 2*). All quotations will be taken from the Columbia edition. Because most of the passages that concern us here from *Paradise Regained* may be found in chapters 2 and 3 of this study, I will be referring to them by only the first line number of the pertinent passage.

37. As Donald A. Roberts mentions in his notes to the Yale edition of the *Second Defence,* Milton's dismissal of fame sits uneasily with other comments about fame that might be discovered in his works from *Lycidas* to the prose of the early 1640s; see YP IV, p. 608*n242*. On the other hand, he also notes how Milton crystalizes his thoughts here on the definition of greatness, loosely expressed elsewhere in his work; see YP IV, p. 601*n224*.

38. This entry is dated 1640–1642(?) by Ruth Mohl.

39. Other references to Rome follow much the same vein; cf. CM VII, pp. 61, 173. For Milton's comments on the "people," see CM VII, pp. 65, 363, 357. Although Milton still defined the "people" as the reasonable minority of the "better sort," and excluded anybody lower than the middle class, he nonetheless never resorts to the sort of denunciation we saw in the *Second Defence* or *Paradise Regained.*

40. Cf. Quint, "David's Census," p. 128

41. For a variety of portraits of Rome during the Renaissance, see Thomas M. Greene, *The Light in Troy: Imitation and Discovery in Renaissance Poetry* (New Haven, 1982); amd Howard Erskine-Hill, *The Au-*

gustan Idea in English Literature (London, 1983). For specific discussions of Rome in *Paradise Regained*, see Stella P. Revard, "Milton and Classical Rome: The Political Context of *Paradise Regained*," and James H. Sims, "A Greater Than Rome: The Inversion of a Virgilian Symbol from Camoës to Milton," both in *Rome in the Renaissance: The City and the Myth*, ed. P. A. Ramsey (Binghamton, N.Y., 1982), pp. 409–19, 333–44, respectively. Erskine-Hill, *Augustan Idea*, pp. 223–24, notes the ambivalence of Milton's attitude toward the Augustan establishment. He likewise points out how the spectacle of Rome might be meant to recall the triumphal coronations of 1604 and 1661.

42. *The Poetical Works of John Milton*, 6 vols., ed. Henry John Todd (London, 1801), vol. V, p. xiii. *"Paradise Regain'd." A Poem in Four Books. To Which is Added "Samson Agonistes": and Poems Upon Several Occasions*, ed. Thomas Newton (London, 1752), p. 148*n145*. Hill, *Milton and the English Revolution*, pp. 420–21, also notes the "Restoration ambience" in *Paradise Regained*.

43. John Aubrey, *Minutes of the Life of Mr John Milton*, in *The Early Lives of Milton*, ed. Helen Darbishire (London, 1932), p. 7.

44. Michel Foucault, *The Archaeology of Knowledge*, trans. A. M. Sheridan Smith (London, 1972), pp. 38, 79–87, 97. In 1969, when this book was written, Foucault was intent on placing the "subject" under several degrees of erasure; for Foucault's later statements on subjectivity, see his "The Subject and Power," in Hubert L. Dreyfus and Raul Rabinow, *Michel Foucault: Beyond Structuralism and Hermeneutics* (Chicago, 1982), pp. 208–26.

45. Althusser, *Lenin and Philosophy*, pp. 151–52. Foucault, "The Subject and Power," pp. 214–15, my italics. Cf. Jameson, "Religion and Ideology," pp. 37–41.

46. The Columbia translator renders the passage: "There is no king in the case / Where will rules and law takes not place" (CM VII, pp. 442–43). The Latin runs as follows: "Non est rex, ubi dominatur voluntas, et non lex."

47. Hobbes's fuller discussion of liberty is in "The Liberty of Subjects" (pp. 260–74), which I have discussed more fully, along with the questions raised above, in chapter 1.

48. Norbert Elias, *The History of Manners: The Civilizing Process, Volume I*, trans. Edmund Jephcott (1939; New York, 1978), pp. 136–39. Philippe Ariès, *Centuries of Childhood: A Social History of the Family*, trans. Robert Baldick (1960; New York, 1962), pp. 132–33.

49. Hobbes does consider the possibility of a mother's dominion theoretically, before negating it as a possibility, in his further examination of family situations. For the legal constraints to this possibility, see *The Lawes Resolution of Womens Rights* (London, 1632). The compilation states

that all the property a woman brings to a marriage, "all manner of moveable substance[,] is presently by conjunation the husbands, to sell, keepe or bequeath if he die: And though he bequeath them not, yet art they the Husbands Executors and not the wives which brought them to her Husband" (p. 130); cf. pp. 116, 119, 124–25. This compilation covers legal texts from "Magna Carta" to the "Quadragesima of Queene Elizabeth" (p. 405). For an examination of women's representations during the Tudor and Jacobean reigns, see Linda Woodbridge, *Women and the English Renaissance: Literature and the Nature of Womankind, 1540–1620* (Urbana, Ill., 1984), esp. p. 132. For analyses of women's legal rights during the reign of the Stuarts, see Lawrence Stone, *The Family, Sex and Marriage in England 1500–1800,* rev. ed. (Harmondsworth, 1979), pp. 109–46, esp. p. 136; and Roger Thompson, *Women in Stuart England and America: A Comparative Study* (London, 1974), p. 162.

50. As I said in chapter 1, this is Hobbes's opinion about *De Cive* also. See *The English Works of Thomas Hobbes,* ed. W. Molesworth (London, 1839–1845), vol. I, p. ix, qtd. in Macpherson, *Possessive Individualism,* p. 88.

51. Milton is discussing here the freedom granted by the gospel, but, as we saw in the last chapter, there is room in Milton's theology for granting gospel liberties to individuals in the Old Testament.

52. Macpherson, *Possessive Individualism,* pp. 89–95, esp. p. 93; cf. p. 265.

53. On Milton's ambivalent representations of the Norman yoke between *Eikonoklastes* and *A Defence,* see Hill, "The Norman Yoke," in *Puritanism and Revolution,* pp. 60–125, esp. p. *77n5.*

54. Victoria Kahn, *Rhetoric, Prudence, and Skepticism in the Renaissance* (Ithaca, 1985), p. 11. Kahn later discusses how Hobbes moves from rhetoric to logic in the course of the *Leviathan* (pp. 156–64).

55. Anthony, Earl of Shaftesbury, *Characteristics of Men, Manners, Opinions, and Times,* ed. John M. Robertson (1711; rpt. Indianapolis, 1964), p. 63.

56. Kahn, *Rhetoric, Prudence, and Skepticism,* p. 161.

57. Peter Brooks, *Reading for the Plot: Design and Intention in Narrative* (Oxford, 1984), pp. 236, 260.

58. Thomas à Kempis, *Of the Imitation of Christ,* trans. Thomas Rogers (London, 1617), pp. 233, 251.

59. Barbara K. Lewalski, *Milton's Brief Epic: The Genre, Meaning, and Art of "Paradise Regained"* (Providence, R.I., 1966), pp. 219–20.

60. Thomas Playfere, *The Whole Sermons of . . . Thomas Playfere* (London, 1623), pp. 242–43.

61. Thomas Taylor, *Christs Combate and Conquest* (Cambridge, 1618), p. 19. Lewalski, *Milton's Brief Epic,* pp. 176, 305*nn30–31,* points out that

Milton followed a lesser tradition in having the Temptation signify the regaining of Paradise. She cites Ambrose, *Expositio Evangelii secundum Lucam,* in *Patrologioe Cursus Completus,* Latin Series, ed. J. P. Migne (Parisiis, 1845), vol XV, col. 1614; and William Cowper, *The Combate of Christ with Satan,* in *The Workes of Mr. William Cowper* (London, 1623), pp. 606–07. We may add John Gumbleden, *Christ Tempted: The Divel Conquered* (London, 1657), p. 11; and the passage quoted above. David Masson, *The Life of John Milton,* 6 vols. (London, 1871–1880), vol. VI, pp. 652–53.

62. Richard Baxter, *The Saints Everlasting Rest* (London, 1649/50), p. 713.

INDEX

Absolute sovereign, 59–64, 65–72, 402–08, 409–13, 416, 418–19, 420–21, 422–24, 429–30
Adam, second, 243, 435
Adam and Eve, 146–47, 161, 179–80, 243–46, 259–60, 314; and death, 181–82, 185; and self-knowledge, 85, 89–100, 358–60; and self-representation, 101, 104–10
Adams, Thomas, 204, 225
Ad Patrem, 329–30
Agency, 28, 31, 73, 75–82, 278, 286–90, 296–98, 320
Alienation, 106–07
Allegories, 373–77: political, 335–40, 352, 357, 364, 499n20. *See also* Milton, John, self-representations of
Althusser, Louis, 9–10, 40–42, 46–47, 402: and interpellation, 31–40, 353; and Marxism, 18–30, 352
Always-already, 20–21, 32–34, 40, 47, 50, 68, 447n23
Amazement. *See* Reason, and amazement
Ames, William, 102, 199
Andrewes, Lancelot, 140, 143
Angels, 150, 154, 338: chorus of, 270–71, 302–03; as chorus in *Paradise Lost,* 157, 333; as chorus in *Paradise Regained,* 155–57, 434; as chorus in *Samson Agonistes,* 322–23, 327–28,

332–33, 337–38; perspective of, 146–49, 151–53, 155, 160–61, 226
Anxiety, 184–87, 286–87
Areopagitica, 82, 154, 236, 242, 246–47, 290–91, 411
Arianism, 80, 231
Arminianism, 7, 8, 66, 78, 82–83, 102–03, 166, 354
Ascension, 140–44, 154–55, 159, 190
Athens, Jesus' rejection of, 256, 258
Atonement, the, 109, 155
Audience, the, 228–30, 318–19, 322, 326. *See also* Reader, the
Augustine, 85, 103, 239, 263–64, 474n22: and enigma, 222–23, 224, 225, 229
Authority, 16, 65–66, 70, 178–79, 299

Bacon, Francis, 120–21, 201
Baptism, the, 75, 175: Jesus' meditation on, 148–49, 159–61, 165–67; and Satan, 205, 207, 208–09, 210–11; significance of, 151–52, 185–86
Barker, Arthur, 279–80, 354
Barthes, 119–20, 121, 376
Baxter, Richard, 145–46, 153–54, 159, 224, 247–48, 251, 259
Being, ways of, 6, 8, 47–48, 64, 65, 85–86, 359–60
Being-toward God, 83, 100, 106, 108, 109–10, 143

507

Bennett, Joan, 355, 363
Bernard, Saint, 140, 226, 314
Beza, Theodore, 102, 223
Biographical criticism, 348–49, 368–77
Booth, Wayne C., 121, 124, 376
Brooks, Peter, 162, 431
Brown, Norman O., 184, 320
Bruner, Jerome, 7–8, 328–29
Burke, Kenneth, xi, 7, 39, 100–01, 105, 110, 151, 323, 384

Cain, William, 123–24, 132
Calvin/Calvinism, 8, 102–03, 189, 474n22: and enigma, 224–26, 230–31, 238–39; and free will, 7, 80; and salvation, 187, 198–99, 455n66
Capel, Arthur, 143, 213
Capital, 19, 28–29
Capitalism, 26, 29, 30, 40, 80, 402
Carey, John, 293, 306
Cassirer, Ernst, 11–12, 158, 162, 163, 186
Centralization of government, 4, 5, 356
Choice. *See* Free will
Christian Doctrine, 74, 78, 85, 119, 182–85, 295: and the reader, 121, 154; and salvation, 101, 198
Christianity, 12, 138–39, 272, 402–03. *See also* Church, the
Christopher, Georgia, 165, 204
Chrysostom, 140, 147–48, 205–06, 209, 221–22, 261
Church, the, 202: individuals versus, 112–13, 122, 230; and state, 74, 299, 356, 381, 401–06, 410, 412–13, 421–22
Commands, 311–16, 409, 423–26
Commonplace Book, 388, 391–92
Commonwealth, xi, 59–61, 63–64, 68, 74, 117–18. *See also* State, the
Considerations, 74
Covenants, 16, 416: with absolute sovereign, 63–64, 66; compari-

sons of, 68, 406–08, 409–12, 426–28; new Christian, 179–80, 244, 340
Cowper, William, 148, 206, 239
Criticism, literary, 348–49, 479n48, 500–01n27: and New Criticism, 121, 125, 368–69, 374
Cromwell, Oliver, 117, 301–02, 356, 391–92
Crucifixion, the, 101, 414
Cultural critique, 236, 274, 280–81, 349–50
Culture, 3–6, 382, 443–44n4, 444n7: formation of, 328–29, 357–61; individuals and, x, 8–9, 10–11; Jesus' new, xi, 109–10, 161–62, 191–92, 246, 396–97; new versus old, 178, 272, 335, 343; reading and, 117–19, 128; Samson's new, 322, 327–28

De Alcantara, Peter, 140–41, 144–45
Death, 292: of Jesus, 174–75, 180–87; Samson and, 285, 305, 320, 324
Defence of the People of England, A, 75, 83–84, 363, 389, 413, 427: on church and state, 74, 356
De Lauretis, Teresa, 121–22, 128, 360
Delphic oracle, ix–xi, 11–12, 17, 84, 86, 428
Democracy, 380, 387, 388
Derrida, Jacques, 20, 119, 447–48n23, 460–61n1
Descartes, René, xiii, 54–59, 66, 82, 95, 201
Desire, 17, 46–50, 53–54, 65, 95, 102, 112, 176: divine impulse and, 298–300, 303–05; freedom from, 392, 396, 398; and subjection, 92–93, 409–12, 414; versus love, 96–98, 100, 105, 107–08, 110, 145, 362
Determinism. *See* Free will, versus necessity

Diachrony. *See* Synchrony/diachrony
Discipline, 119, 121, 123, 151
Divine impulse, Samson and, 299–305
Doctrine, 119, 121, 122–23, 151
Doctrine and Discipline of Divorce, 269
Doubt, 152, 196–97, 199–200, 205–16, 271, 273, 474n22, 476n32
Douglas, Mary, x, 5–6
Downame, John, 80, 138, 199, 213
Drama, 158–59, 324–27

Economics, 426
Eden, 106. *See also* Paradise, second
Education, 3–4, 119, 128–29, 134, 249, 260
Eikonoklastes, 363
Eliade, Mircea, x, 136, 159, 162, 186, 193–94
Engels, Friedrich, 27–29
England, 117–18, 388–93. *See also* Monarchy, English
Enigma, 214–15, 219–39, 241–42, 245, 256, 261, 273, 341
Enselfment, 59, 89
Epistemology, x, xi, 6, 11, 177
Eve. *See* Adam and Eve
Experience, 5–6, 43, 347, 436, 443–44n4

Faith, 122, 146, 149, 199–200, 227, 256, 295–96: and reason, 251, 263
Fall, the, 93–96, 99, 130–31, 153, 314: and free will, 77–78, 102; God and, 80, 103, 105; as political allegory, 243, 350–51, 358–60, 366–67
Family, 401, 414–20, 504–05n49
Ficino, Marsilio, 150, 251–52
Fideism. *See* Reason
Fish, Stanley, 105, 290–91, 300–04, 500–01n27: and the reader, 125–29, 133–34, 266–67; and Samson, 293, 309, 313, 327
"Fit audience," 239, 267

"Fit reader," 121, 126, 132, 133, 479n48
Flesh, versus spirit, 137–38, 142, 143
For Marx, 20, 22, 25
Foucalt, Michel, 17, 42, 376, 400–01, 402
Freedom. *See* Liberty
Free will: lack of, 28, 58, 82, 91, 342; and salvation, 102, 455n66; and self-knowledge, 54, 278, 290; versus necessity, 6–9, 70, 76, 101, 123, 198–99
Freud, Sigmund, 7, 43–44, 320, 493n55
Fuller, Thomas, 207–09, 219

Gender, 93, 338–39, 414, 416–17, 442–43n1, 504–05n49
German Ideology, The, 19, 28
God, 59, 122, 158, 270, 296–97, 386, 407–08, 433–34: absolute sovereign and, 409, 412–14, 422–24; and desire, 103–04, 362, 410–12; Jesus and, 175–77, 338; and Samson, 308–10, 312–14, 321, 342, 423–26; and self-knowledge, 12, 82–83, 88–90, 95, 98, 257
Goodman, Nelson, 111, 265–66
Gouge, William, 200, 210
Greenblatt, Stephen, 373–77
Grumbleden, John, 208–09, 243, 244, 247
Grundrisse, 19, 20, 29, 38

Hales, John, 245, 258
Hall, Joseph, 219, 226, 312, 314, 316, 321: faith and, 138–39, 141, 263; and Satan, 75, 206–07, 214
Hamlet, 319, 323–26, 493n55
Hegel, Georg Wilhelm Friedrich, 19, 21–22, 287–88, 360
Heidegger, Martin, 49, 185
Hill, Christopher, ix, 165, 306, 354–56, 366–67, 394

Historical change, 26, 29, 178–79
History, 111–12, 118–19, 426–27, 430, 431, 432: and lack of subject, 19–20, 25–26, 30–32
Hobbes, Thomas, 143: absolute sovereign and, 65, 423, 425; and church versus state, 402–06, 420–22; and desire, 92, 94–95; history and, 118–19, 426–28; and Milton, xiii, 112–13, 399; and the reader, 122–24, 429–30, 433; responsibility and, 66–67, 71; self-knowledge and, 72, 117–19, 436–37; state and, 360–61, 406–08, 414–20; subjection and, 37, 59–64, 71, 409–14. *See also* Narrative model, versus scientific model
Humanism, 11, 229, 259, 428

Identity, 40
Ideology, 18–19, 30–31, 33–39, 42, 122
Individual, the, 42, 380–81, 404–06, 435–36: and the family, 401, 415; importance of, 383, 386, 420–22; and the state, 394–95, 409–14; versus subject, 34–36, 44, 54, 83–84
Internal government. *See* Self-government
Internal kingdom. *See* "Paradise within"
Interpellation, 31–40, 72, 90, 91, 99, 353
Iser, Wolfgang, 121, 125, 129, 131–32

James, William, 7–8, 15, 110
Jameson, Fredric, 17, 53–54, 128, 193, 327, 373–77, 499*n20:* and Marxism, 7, 20–21; and Milton's politics, xiv, 345–48, 350–53, 432
Jesus, x–xi, 197–99, 202–04, 205–16, 219–39, 336–37, 384–87: and death, 181, 182–87, 292; kingdom of, 5, 109–10, 259–60,

265–66, 422; and meditation, 89, 136–37, 149, 159–61, 163–66; as model, 133–35, 189–90, 395–98, 432; new covenant and, 178–80, 340–41; on the pinnacle, 267–68, 269, 317; self-definition of, 188–89, 194–96, 328–31; self-knowledge and, 110, 171–78, 268, 272–74, 317; soliloquy of, 151, 162–63, 166–71, 183–84, 187–88; and son versus servant, 397, 420, 454–55*n65;* and temptations, 237–41, 243–49, 252–58, 260–63, 264, 431. *See also* 1671 volume
Judgment, 133–34, 154, 407

Kahn, Victoria, 428–29, 430
Kelley, Maurice, 74, 182
Kellogg, Robert, 155, 193
à Kempis, Thomas, 135, 219, 246–47, 432
Kerrigan, William, 280, 306, 329
Kierkegaard, Soren Aabye, 184, 185, 287
Knowledge, 55–59, 81–83, 95–96, 167, 169–70, 198–99: and culture, 4–6, 7, 10–11; and experience, 347, 436; in scientific versus narrative models, 7–8, 9, 60; and self-knowledge, 41–42, 86–87, 259–60; and Spirit, 204, 258

Lacan, Jacques, 9–10, 16, 41–54, 55–59, 65, 162–63, 186
Language, 10, 17, 47–48, 49–50, 52–53, 100, 328–29
Lanham, Richard, 15, 16, 89, 105
Lapsarian historiography, 64. *See also* Self-knowledge
Law, the, 171, 173–75, 178, 179, 187, 329, 331, 340–41, 417
Lawrence, Henry, 75, 226
Lentricchia, Frank, 3, 4, 28
Leviathan, 8–9, 119, 415, 419–20, 453–54*n57:* formation of, 117–18, 429–30. *See also* Absolute sovereign; Hobbes, Thomas

Lewalski, Barbara, 123, 234–35, 336, 434

Liberty, 6–9, 70–72, 77–79, 278–79, 331, 339, 384, 404–06: agential, 281, 306, 308–09, 317, 339–40; from desire, 410–11, 414; Jesus and, 174, 179, 185–86, 188, 454–55n65; Milton and, 73–79, 379–81, 387; reason and, 85–86, 360; and self-knowledge, 388, 395–98

Logic, 203–04, 253–57

Love, 445n10: and desire, 93, 96, 100, 410

Martz, Louis, 147, 151, 384

Marx, Karl, 20, 38, 272, 350, 352: and Hegel, 287–88, 449n34; Marxism, 7, 18–30; time and, 24, 448n25-27

Mary, and Jesus, 171–75, 218–19, 328–31

Mask, A, 216

Materialism, 6, 7, 24–25, 40, 65, 71, 111–12: historical, 18, 42, 110–12; of Hobbes, 62, 64, 123

Matriarchy. *See* Mothers

Mead, George Herbert, 15, 20

Meditation, 110–12, 146–48, 483n75: the Church and, 163–64, 469–70n69; Jesus and, 159–61, 193–94, 246–48, 258–59, 261; and meditative motion, 122, 128–29, 140–41, 154–55; and meditative theory, 135–37, 263–65; and perspective, 146–48, 153, 258; purpose and process of, 94, 142–46, 250–51, 357; and self-knowledge, 88–89, 161–63, 180

Milton, John, ix, 97, 110, 155, 191–94, 216, 299–302, 309–10, 329–31, 414–20, 434–37: agential liberty and, 73–81, 296–98, 306, 317, 331, 333, 339–43, 395–98; as anti-Erastian, 74, 355, 413; and the Church, 112–13, 122, 180, 402–06, 420–22;

and death, 183–87, 189; on divorce, 73, 227–30, 241–42, 480–81n62; doubt and, 196–97, 200–02, 209; eyesight of, 289, 385; and God, 61, 63, 84–86, 143, 215, 423–26; history and, 118, 178–79, 427–28; and the individual, 66, 290–91, 409–14, 430; and internal versus national government, 393–95, 399, 406–08, 432–33; and meditation, 163–65, 247, 252, 262–63; and the monarchy, 268, 333–35, 380–81, 383–84, 388–93; poetics of, 128–29, 133, 158–59, 166, 168, 219–20, 249–50; politics of, xi, xiii–xiv, 4–5, 83–84, 345–55, 356, 378–81, 394–95, 398–99, 502–03n33; and the reader, 117–18, 121, 122–24, 126, 128, 129–35, 150–51, 154, 241–42, 266–67, 429–30; salvation and, 101–03, 198–99; and self-knowledge, x–xi, xii–xiii, 12–13, 16, 88–91, 272, 274, 360–61, 398; self-representations of, xiii, 4–5, 349, 355–57, 361–68, 375–78, 382–83, 384–87, 394–95, 397–99, 422, 436, 498n12; theological politics of, 83–84, 278–79, 343–44; theology of, 177, 182, 336

Miner, Earl, 123, 237

Monarchy. *See* Absolute sovereign; State, the

Monarchy, English, 334, 391–92, 393–95, 402–03: and the Reformation, 6–7, 268; and the Republic, 74, 379–84, 420; and the Restoration, 4, 117–18, 268, 299, 347, 348, 354; and the Revolution, 350–51, 366–67, 397

Montrose, Louis Adrian, 277–78, 280, 326–27, 372

More, Henry, 101–02, 198, 289, 363

Mothers, 328–32, 339–40, 401, 415–17

Mountains, symbolism of, 244–45, 259–60, 481–82*n66*
Movement, 132, 135–37, 178, 260. *See also* Meditation, and meditative motion

Narrative model, 12–13, 111, 112, 166, 193, 228–29, 239, 324–27: and the reader, 125, 155, 431; and self-knowledge, 16, 40–41, 54, 90–91, 110, 150, 260; subjectivity in, 59, 98–99; versus scientific model, 7–9, 16, 32–33, 59–60, 65–70, 72–73, 83–84, 95, 110, 112–13, 123, 291, 436–37
Narrativity, 121–22, 128–29, 135, 461–62*n5*
Nations. *See* State, the
Necessity. *See* Free will, versus necessity
New Criticism. *See* Criticism, literary, and New Criticism
Newton, Thomas, 192–93, 267

Ode on the Morning of Christ's Nativity, 84, 271–72, 274
Of Reformation, xi, 241–42
Of True Religion, 74
Omniscience, 77, 80, 81
Ong, Walter J., 125, 250
Other versus self, 42, 45, 48–52, 55–56, 92, 110, 331, 445*n10*, 445*n11*: confrontation of, 162, 195, 291–92; distinguishing between, 13, 16–17, 66, 92, 97, 100

Paradise, second, 118, 432, 434–36
Paradise Lost, 66, 82, 101, 154, 159, 182, 366–67, 370–71; and the reader, 121, 126–27, 129–30; and self-knowledge, 85, 88, 90–100, 103, 358–60; and spatio-time shifts, 132, 150, 191
Paradise Regained, 119, 158–59, 182–83, 252, 271–72, 340–41, 370–71, 389–90, 394–95: and angelic perspective, 148, 150,

154, 155–57; and cultural formation, 5, 117–18, 191–94, 265–67; and Delphic oracle, x–xi, 84; meaning in, 265, 271; as narrative, 8–9, 112–13, 159; politics of, 345, 350–53, 354–55, 432–33; and the reader, 123–24, 126, 132–35, 258; and self-knowledge, xi–xiii, 83, 110–12, 136–37. *See also* 1671 volume
"Paradise within," 109, 118, 143–44, 237, 240–41, 254, 256, 257–60, 261–63, 273–74, 434
Passion. *See* Desire
Perception, 45, 58, 136, 194–96, 212–13
Perkins, William, 76–79, 102, 137–38, 209–10, 225–26, 295–96, 306
Perspective, 146–49: shifts in, 129, 131, 134–35, 150–51, 155, 157, 191. *See also* Angels, perspective of
Philosophy, 28, 60, 138–39, 197–99, 257
Politics, 6, 59–64, 243, 326–27: definitions of, 345–51; the individual and, 83–84, 189, 359–60, 399; religion as, 346
Power, 4, 5, 42, 61–62, 170, 401, 420–21, 426–27, 430–32
Predestination. *See* Free will versus necessity
Presence, 21–23, 145–46, 154–55, 272. *See also* Meditation
Preston, John, 75, 144
Prolusion VII, 357
Psychoanalysis, 42–44, 48–50, 54–56, 110–12, 188, 450–51*n40*

Radzinowicz, Mary Ann, 73, 293, 303
Ramism, 249–50
Reader, the, 121–22, 124–35, 129–35, 264–65: and angelic perspective, 126–28, 148, 154, 155–57, 159; and cultural formation, 117–24, 128, 171, 266–67; influ-

ences on, 72, 273–74, 433; and
internal kingdom, 214–15, 233–
34, 245, 257–59; and self-
knowledge, 173–74, 428–30,
435. *See also* Narrativity
Readie and Easie Way to Establish . . . , 3, 4, 378–81, 383, 390
Reading Capital, 20, 21, 22, 25, 27
Reason, 85–86, 95, 341, 360, 384,
483–84*n77:* and amazement,
317–21, 492*n49;* choice and,
81–82, 91, 99, 290; in faith,
137–40, 251
Regeneration, 292–98, 305–06,
488*n17*
Religion. *See* Christianity; Church,
the
Renaissance, 11, 121–22, 128, 236,
390
Representation, 16, 65, 67–70,
100–10, 122, 134, 140–41, 145,
287, 289, 321, 407
Reprobation, 76, 229, 231
Republic, English. *See* Monarchy,
English, and the Republic
Responsibility, 72–73, 100, 299:
and absolute sovereign, 66–68,
71, 407
Restoration, English. *See* Monarchy,
English, and the Restoration
Revisionism, 111, 188
Ritual, 274
Rome, 235–37, 256, 262, 380–81,
388–93, 395
Rowse, A. L., ix, 442*n1*

Salvation, 76, 80, 81–83, 101–03,
145, 187, 193–94, 198–99, 204,
317, 351–52, 455*n66*
Samson, 286–90, 299–305, 310–
14, 316, 318–22, 325–26, 331–
32, 397, 420, 494–95*n66:* and
meditation, 89, 161, 168; at the
pillars, 307–09, 326–27; regeneration of, 292–98, 305–06,
488*n17;* self/selfhood of, 283,
289, 313–14. *See also* 1671 volume

Samson Agonistes, xi–xiii, 5, 88,
159, 292, 323–26, 362, 423–26.
See also 1671 volume
Samuel, Irene, 293, 298–300, 321,
341–42
Satan, 108, 152, 178, 182–83, 191–
95, 272–74: and identity of Jesus, 196–97, 205–18; limitations
of, 259, 262, 265–71, 286; and
Temptation of Jesus, 176–77,
232–35, 237–41, 243–48, 252–
58
Scholes, Robert, 121, 155, 193
Science, 7–9, 18–19, 42–44, 55–
56, 444*n6*
Scientific model. *See* Narrative
model, versus scientific model
Second Defence, 4, 74, 329, 334,
363–64, 376–78: evolution of
Milton's politics and, 348, 356,
382–83, 389–90, 394–95; and
national liberty, 392, 394, 433
Self-definitions, 328–31
Self-government, 99, 118, 340–41:
achievement of, 110, 243–46,
357, 428; politics and, 144,
189–90; and the state, 360–61,
399, 407–08, 433
Self-knowledge, ix–x, 13–16, 66,
69–70, 86–90, 140, 330–32,
428, 445*n9:* and agential liberty,
46–47, 90, 278–79, 305–06;
authorial, 347, 377–78, 381;
and desire, 100–03, 105, 107,
108; family and, 343–44, 401,
414–15, 417–18; gaining of,
195–96, 257, 284–87, 289–92,
328, 431–32; and God, 57, 95,
280–81, 412; and meditation,
110–12, 122, 136, 145, 161–63;
and nations, 10–11, 117–18, 351,
357–61, 388, 393, 394–98, 407,
433; and reason, 82, 99, 150,
317, 336; and the Spirit, 84–86,
98, 110, 272–74; and subjection
and subjectivity, 9, 40–42, 47,
52–54, 71–72, 73, 90–100, 414,
420

Self-representation, 100–01, 107, 109, 110–11, 189–90, 347–48, 370–71, 372–73, 375–76, 434. *See also* Milton, John, self-representations of

Self-revelations, 168, 169–70, 186

Self/selfhood, ix–x, 13–15, 31–32, 106, 110–11, 121, 183–84: changes in, 96–97, 98–100, 108, 446n16. *See also* Other versus self; Self-knowledge

Servant versus son. *See* Subjection; Subjectivity, and son versus servant

Sexuality, 97–98

Shakespeare, 364. *See also Hamlet*

Shepheardes Calendar, The, 277–78, 326–27, 364, 372

Sibbes, Richard, 200, 225, 295

Signification, 50–52, 56, 72

Similes, use of, 335–40, 362–64, 378, 386, 414

1671 volume, 274, 277–81, 311–22, 328, 332, 335–40, 362–64, 428: Milton's politics in, 333–35, 348; Samson compared to Jesus in, 281–92, 306, 311, 315–17, 341–44; subjectivity of Milton in, 361–62, 368, 376–78

Skepticism, 199–204, 217–18, 264, 476n32

Smith, John, 204, 211–14, 217, 224–25

Society. *See* Culture; State, the

Socrates, x, 12, 86–87, 88

Sonnet XI, 229–30

Son versus servant. *See* Subjectivity, and son versus servant

Space, shifts in, 130, 132

Spenser, Edmund, 121, 128, 277–78, 364, 373–74, 378

Spinoza, xiii, 65, 82–83, 95–96

Spirit, 154

Spirit, the, 61–64, 84–86, 88, 133–35, 204, 241–43, 256–58, 264–65, 274, 283–84, 292, 296–98, 340: and the Baptism, 152, 153–54, 165, 178, 210–11;

blasphemy against, 215, 217–18, 240; and self-knowledge, 89, 98, 110, 358

State, the, 30–35, 37–38, 63, 83–84, 357–61, 401, 415–20: the individual and, 343–44, 357, 392, 393–95, 398–99, 406–08; monarchy and, 253, 408, 424–25, 426–28, 430; versus the Church, 299, 381, 401–06, 421–22. *See also* Monarchy, English

Stein, Arnold, 167, 234–35

Stierle, Karlheinz, 125–26, 129

Structure in dominance theory, 22, 26

Subject, 25–36, 44, 47–48, 54, 83–84, 129, 346, 352

Subjection, 32–35, 40, 110, 407–08, 409–12, 414, 418–20: political, 9–10, 29, 59–64, 65, 69–70, 112, 359–60, 392–93, 429–30; religious, 35–36, 404; versus subjectivity, 36–37, 41–42, 45, 47, 52–54, 60–61, 63, 65, 66, 71–73, 75, 77, 80, 83–84, 90, 91, 98–99, 274, 349, 353, 398, 436–37

Subjectivity, 8–9, 17, 31, 59, 163, 287, 288–89: of Milton, 83, 343–44, 348, 353, 355, 357, 361–62, 366, 375–78, 382; political, 18–19, 29, 71; religious, 88–89, 99–100, 419, 431; and son versus servant, 83, 85, 99, 392–93, 399, 418–20, 454n64, 454–55n65

Subject-predicate inversion, 37

Submission, 71, 84, 139

Symbols, 162, 172–73, 186, 244–45, 259–60, 481–82n66

Synchrony/diachrony, 16, 23–25, 33, 39, 44, 47, 50–52, 54, 55, 63–64, 90, 446–47n20, 450–51n40. *See also* Time/temporality

Taylor, Thomas, 214, 224, 227, 233, 244, 435

Temperance, 86–88, 96, 99, 118

Temptation, the, 75, 170, 176, 189, 196, 197, 205–16, 237–41, 246–48, 265, 267–68, 269, 483–84*n77:* and offer of the kingdoms, 234–37, 243–46, 260–63, 264, 389–90, 393, 482*n69*

Tetrachordon, The, 227–30, 266–67, 343

Text and the reader, 119–20, 125–26, 127–30, 132–35, 171, 460–61*n1,* 500–01*n27*

Thought versus action, 30, 37–38, 58, 95, 169–70, 397

Tillyard, E.M.W., 129–30, 280, 361, 384

Time/temporality, 10, 19–25, 39–40, 43–44, 60, 61, 63–64, 154–55, 177–78, 191–93, 308, 434, 448*nn2, 27:* shifts in, 130, 132, 153, 322. *See also* Synchrony/diachrony

Todorov, Tzvetan, 126, 130

Treatise of Civil Power in Ecclesiastical Causes, A, 74, 240, 299, 313, 393–94, 424–25

Trevor-Roper, Hugh, 353–54, 361, 379–80

Trinity, the, 85–86, 131

Truth, the, 241–42, 256–58, 384–85

Turner, Victor, 265–66, 274, 381–82

Tuvil, Daniel, 214, 226

Unconscious, the, 41–44, 47–50, 54

White, Hayden, 27–28, 29, 110

Wilkes, G. A., 293–94, 298

Williams, Raymond, 3, 6

Wimsatt, W. K., 368–77

Wither, George, 141, 142, 148–49

Wittreich, Joseph, 165, 293, 298, 309–11, 313, 321

Wolfe, Don, 361, 386

World-making, 265–66, 268